59843 1

720.9 FAZ

A WORLD
HISTORY OF
ARCHITECTURE

A WORLD HISTORY OF ARCHITECTURE

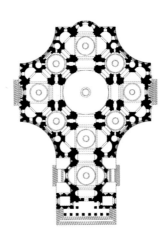

THIRD EDITION

Michael Fazio

Marian Moffett

Lawrence Wodehouse

Laurence King Publishing

LAURENCE KING

Published in 2013 by Laurence King Publishing Ltd
361–373 City Road
London EC1V 1LR
United Kingdom
Tel: +44 20 6900
Fax: +44 20 7841 6910
e-mail: enquiries@laurenceking.com
www.laurenceking.com

Copyright © 2014 The McGraw-Hill Companies, Inc.

All rights reserved. No part of this publication may be reproduced
or transmitted in any form or by any means, electronic or mechanical,
including photocopy, recording or any information storage and retrieval
system, without prior permission in writing from the publisher.

A catalogue record for this book is available from the British Library.

ISBN: 978-1-78067-111-6

Every effort has been made to contact copyright holders, but should there
be any errors or omissions, Laurence King Publishing Ltd would be pleased
to insert the appropriate acknowledgment in any subsequent printing of
this publication.

Senior Editor: Liz Faber
Designer: Allan Sommerville
Cover Designer: Jason Ribeiro
Picture Researcher: Giulia Hetherington

Printed in China

Frontispiece: Christopher Wren, St. Stephen Walbrook interior, London,
1672–87. Photo: A.F. Kersting.

Front cover: Zaha Hadid Architects, Glasgow Riverside Museum of Transport,
2011 (©James Brittain/VIEW)
Back cover, top: Basilica of Our Lady, Tongeren, Belgium (©Paul M.R.
Maeyaert); bottom: Angkor Wat, Cambodia (©Peter Adams/JAI/Corbis)

Contents

CHAPTER 11
RENAISSANCE ARCHITECTURE 287

CHAPTER 12
BAROQUE ARCHITECTURE 341

Preface

Marian Moffett, Lawrence Wodehouse, and I wrote this survey of world architecture both for students taking introductory courses and for the general reader simply interested in buildings. We have searched out the stories these buildings have to tell, considered the intentions of the people who built them, and examined the lives of those who used them. We begin with prehistory and end with the early twenty-first century. We cover the Western tradition as well as works in the Islamic world, the pre-Columbian Americas, Africa, China, Southeast Asia, Russia, and Japan.

We have written about this diverse sampling of the built environment in a straightforward but lively style that is rich with detail. The text contains extensive descriptive narrative leavened with focused critical analysis, which both allows the book to stand alone and invites lecturers to impose their studied interpretations on the material without the danger of undue ambiguity or conflict. In a world that grows smaller by the day, it presents a global perspective, and in a discipline that concerns built objects that are often beautiful as well as functional, it is copiously illustrated, intelligently designed, and consistently usable.

Because architecture is at once utilitarian and a visual art, the text and its illustrations are inseparable. This book contains over 800 photographs and line drawings, most of which have discursive captions that can be read in conjunction with the text or appreciated independently. Short illustrated essays accompany each chapter (except for chapters 7 and 16). An annotated bibliography at the end of the book provides suggestions for further reading. Also at the end of the book is a glossary that defines the key terms set in bold throughout the text.

New to this Edition

■ The page layouts have been designed for greater clarity and legibility.
■ Chapters 13 through 16 have been significantly rewritten as a group, giving them a greater cohesion and a stronger historical narrative. This significant revision also includes photographs and textual discussion of almost 50 new buildings. In addition to strengthening Chapters 13–15, these new buildings bring Chapter 16 to the present moment in architectural history.
■ There are 58 new illustrations, including the following twenty-first-century buildings:

16.25 Robert A.M. Stern, George W. Bush Center, Dallas, Texas, 2012; **16.41** Frank Gehry, 8 Spruce Street, New York City, 2011; **16.51** Zaha Hahid, MAXXI National Museum of XXI Century Arts, Rome, Italy, 1998–2010; **16.52** Zaha Hadid, BMW Central Building, Leipzig, Germany, 2005; **16.66** Renzo Piano, Modern Wing, Art Institute of Chicago, 2009; **16.68** Eric Owen Moss, Samitaur Tower, Culver City, California, 2011; **16.74** Steven Holl, Linked Hybrid, Beijing, China, 2009; **16.75** Jean Nouvel, Torre Agbar, Barcelona, Spain, 2005; **16.76** Jean Nouvel, Guthrie Theater, Minneapolis, Minnesota, 2006; **16.78** Santiago Calatrava, Liège Guillemins TGV Railway Station, Liège, Belgium, 2009; **16.80** Herzog and de Meuron, Walker Art Center, Minneapolis, Minnesota, 2005; **16.81** Herzog and de Meuron, National Stadium, Beijing, China, 2007; **16.82** Diller, Scofidio, and Renfro, High Line, New York City, 2004–09; **16.87** Thom Mayne, San Francisco Federal Building, 2005; **16.88** Thom Mayne, 41 Cooper Square, New York City, 2009.

Acknowledgments

In writing this book, we have received assistance from many sources. Our colleagues Lynn Barker, Jack Elliott, David Lewis, Daniel MacGilvray, Charles Mack, Mark Reinberger, and Julia Smyth-Pinney contributed essays. The following reviewers read portions of the manuscript at various times and made comments that assisted us in clarifying and improving the text: Jane Ostergaard, College of DuPage; Wayne (Mick) Charney, Kansas State University; Lyle Culver, Miami Dade College; Katherine Wheeler, University of Miami-Coral Gables; Eleni Bastea, University of New Mexico-Albuquerque; Phil Gruen, Washington State University-Pullman; Dane Johnson, Ferris State University; Margaret Dale Woosnam, Blinn College; Shelley Roff, University of Texas at San Antonio; Susan Wadsworth, Fitchburg State University; Kestutis Paul Zygas, Arizona State University-Tempe; Douglas Klahr, University of Texas Arlington; Brian Zugay, Texas Tech University. Six students in the School of Architecture at Mississippi State University—Yan Huang, Kai Pan, Charles Holmes, Jared Brown, Kristin Perry, and Rachel McKinley—used their exceptional talents with graphics software to produce line drawings. Thanks also to School of Architecture librarians Judy Hammett and Susan Hall for bibliographical assistance and having patience with me and with the piles of books and papers that I keep in their library.

My special thanks to Art Pomponio for his editorial guidance. At McGraw-Hill, Penina Braffman, Rhona Robbin, and Laura Wilk provided important support. At Laurence King Publishing all editorial, design, illustrating, scheduling, and production issues were expertly managed by Kara Hattersley-Smith, Liz Faber, and Simon Walsh. Allan Sommerville of blok graphic laid out this new edition with great skill, and Giulia Hetherington researched most of the new photographs.

Photographs are acknowledged in the photo credits. In addition to photographs we have taken ourselves, some were taken by our colleagues, whom we would like to thank: Gerald Anderson, Robert Craig, Mark DeKay, Jeff Elder, Jason Labutka, David Lewis, Dan MacGilvray, Rachel McCann, Allison Moffett, Kenneth Moffett, R. Bruce Moffett, Max Robinson, J. William Rudd, Brenda Sartoris, Pamela Scott, Raiford Scott, Ronald Scott, Murray Smart Jr., and Patrick Snadon.

Michael Fazio April 2012

Map 1 Central and Eastern Europe and the Middle East

Map 2 Europe and North Africa

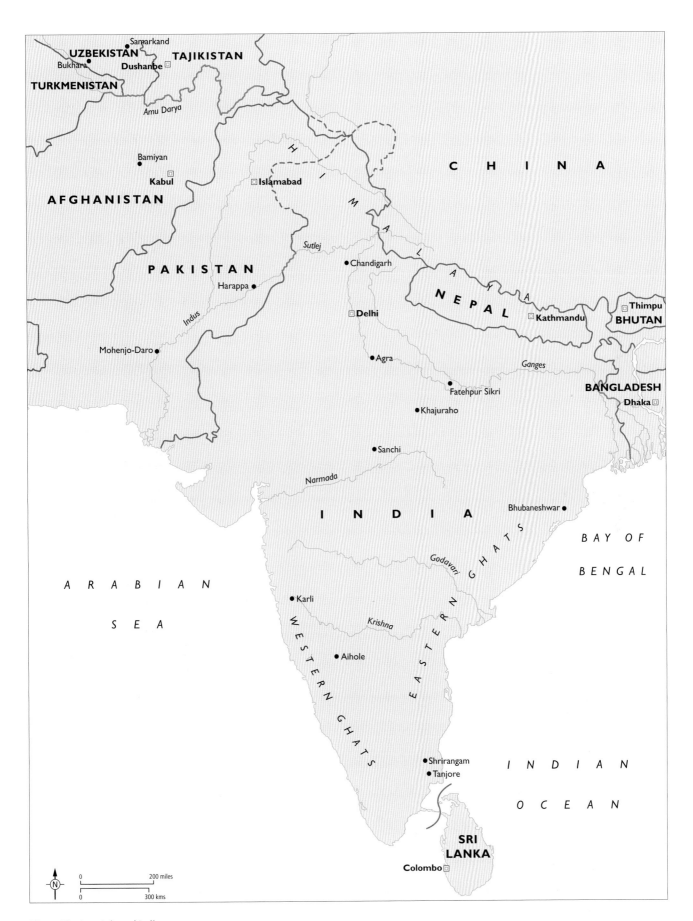

Map 3 Western Asia and India

Map 4 North America

Map 5 Central and South America

MEXICO
• Tula
Tenochtitlán
Teotihuacán
• La Venta
Mexico City
• Mitla
Monte Albán
Uxmal • • Chichén-Itzá
Palenque
Bonampak • Tikal • Belmopan
GUAT. BELIZE
Guatemala City
San Salvador Copán HONDURAS
EL Tegucigalpa
SALV. NICARAGUA
Managua
San José
COSTA RICA
PANAMA Panama City

GULF OF MEXICO

CUBA
HAITI DOM. REP.
JAMAICA PUERTO RICO

GREATER ANTILLES
LESSER ANTILLES

CARIBBEAN SEA

ATLANTIC OCEAN

Caracas
VENEZUELA
Orinoco Georgetown SURINAM
GUYANA Paramaribo
Cayenne
FRENCH GUIANA
Bogotá
COLOMBIA
Negro
Quito
ECUADOR
Marañón
Amazon
Huaca de los Reyes
at Cabalo Muerto
Chan Chan
Moche Chavín de Huantar
PERU A N D E S
Urubamba
Lima Machu Picchu
Cuzco
Saqsaywaman Lake Titicaca
La Paz
Tiwanaku BOLIVIA

B R A Z I L

BRAZILIAN HIGHLANDS
São Francisco

Brasília

PARAGUAY
Asunción

Paraná

PACIFIC OCEAN

C H I L E A N D E S

Santiago
Buenos Aires
ARGENTINA
Colorado

URUGUAY
Montevideo

ATLANTIC OCEAN

FALKLAND ISLANDS (U.K.)

N

0   400 miles

0   600 kms

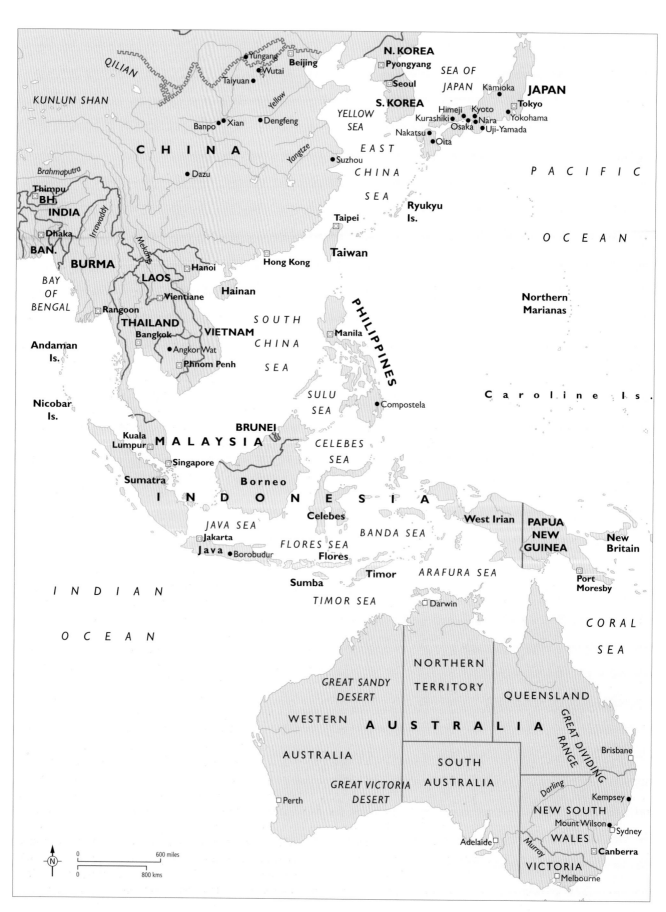

Map 6 Eastern Asia and Australia

Introduction

You, the reader, are the reason for this book. We, the authors, have drawn on our cumulative experience in teaching and writing about architectural history to convey in words and images information about some of the world's most interesting and important buildings. This book surveys Western architecture in some depth and offers an introduction to non-Western architecture in Africa, India, China, Southeast Asia, Japan, the pre-Columbian Americas, and many Islamic settings. Together the text and illustrations encourage discussion, thought, and analysis. In this introduction, we offer a guide to the effective use of this book.

Architectural history begins with buildings. In order really to see these buildings, one needs to use precise descriptive language. Hence we have tried throughout to present clear, understandable, but provocative prose, and to define basic terminology when it is first introduced. Still, if left at the level of pure information, these words produce little true insight. We have therefore written this book in a way that encourages looking, but more than that, *seeing*; and the difference between the two is considerable. Seeing requires proceeding beyond the image projected on the retina to a process of analysis and the making of critical judgments. This, in turn, calls for placing buildings in their various contexts—social, political, economic, artistic, technological, and environmental—and determining whether they fulfill their obligations to their clients, to other users, and to society at large. To do this, it is necessary to enter the mind of the architect and to suspend modern biases so that we can evaluate the work as the product of a particular time and place.

What is architecture? Certainly it is shelter, but it can be much more. The phrase "frozen music" is often used, but such a description seems to imply that architecture has only an esthetic component. The "shaping of space for human use" seems more obviously useful, but it hardly explains the fascination of the Egyptian pyramids or the symbolism of a state capitol building. The Roman architect and engineer Vitruvius, active around 40 BCE, considered the essentials of architecture to be *firmitas*, *utilitas*, and *venustas*, commonly translated as firmness, commodity, and delight. Here firmness is structural stability, commodity is the meeting of functional requirements, and delight is beauty. One can hardly disagree with the need for firmness and commodity: any building that collapses or does not provide the right kind of space for the client's purposes must be considered a failure. Delight, or beauty, however, is a more elusive term, one with standards that have changed over time. Some have argued that beauty arises naturally from the fulfillment of functional requirements. Others have seen it as an inevitable result of the logical use of building materials and structural systems. Still others have found it in applied ornamentation.

Let us consider the first two terms in Vitruvius's triad in a slightly different way by asking, why and how is architecture produced? In order to erect buildings, people must have a motive—a will to build; materials and a knowledge of how to use them—a means to build; and systems of construction—an ability to build. The will to build certainly includes responses to functional requirements, but often goes well beyond these to address spiritual, psychological, and emotional needs. For some building types, such as industrial buildings, practical concerns naturally predominate. In others, such as civic or religious buildings, meanings may be dramatically revealed through symbolic forms. To most people, for example, the interior of a religious building should elevate the human spirit, while a warehouse must only protect material goods. However, utilitarian high-rise office buildings are usually designed to reflect the corporate image that the CEO and board of directors wish to project, and homeowners commonly modify their houses both inside and out, not only to accommodate changing functional demands but also to express their own personalities and values. All architecture reflects such values, and the best of it expresses the tastes and aspirations of the entire society. More money, finer workmanship and materials, and (often) better design have typically been expended on buildings that shelter activities important to large segments of society. Thus, for many periods, religious buildings have been the principal laboratories for architectural experimentation and have been built to endure, while residential architecture and even commercial buildings have been more transitory, which explains the abundance of religious buildings in a text such as this one.

At the beginning of an architectural project, the client and architect develop a program, or statement, of projected spatial uses, sizes, qualities, and relationships. The program for an apartment building, say, would itemize the number of apartments and their sizes, the common spaces such as lobbies, the service spaces such as mechanical rooms and storage, and also include an allowance for horizontal and vertical circulation (corridors, stairs, ramps, and elevators). Because many designs can satisfy such a program, it is the architect's responsibility to develop alternatives, to select the best ideas from among them, and to present the results in the form of drawings and models from which the building can be erected.

0.1 Library of Celsus, Ephesus, Asia Minor, 114–17.
Constructed by the Romans, this is an example of post-and-lintel (column-and-beam) construction.

No matter how strong the will to build, people must also have the resources with which to build, which historically has meant local building materials. In turn, materials have strongly influenced architectural character. One of the most fascinating aspects of studying everyday buildings from the past is noticing how the simplest materials, such as wood, clay, thatch, and stone, have been employed to create architecture. If clay alone was available in abundance, people used tamped earth or made bricks. If people lived in areas that were heavily forested, they built in wood. The ancient Greeks were among the most skilled carvers of stone, but they would hardly have become so without the abundant local marble that could be chiseled with extremely fine detail.

People must also have the ability to build. That is, they must be able to assemble materials into stable systems of construction. Structural materials can be classified according to the way they accept loads: in tension or compression, or a combination of the two. When in compression, the fibers of a material are pressed together; when in tension the fibers are pulled apart. Stone, brick, and concrete are all strong in compression but not in tension. Wood is strong in both tension and compression, as is iron; but iron is also brittle. In the nineteenth and twentieth centuries, metallurgists refined iron into steel, a material to which small amounts of other metals have been added to form alloys that are highly malleable. Because it combines the compressive strength of **concrete** with the tensile strength of embedded steel, reinforced concrete is also strong in both tension and compression.

All structures respond to the vertical pull of gravity in the form of live and dead loads, and to side loads or lateral forces created by the wind and earthquakes. Live loads are the people (and/or animals) that inhabit a structure. Dead loads are the weight of the building itself and of its inanimate contents such as furniture. Wind loads are accommodated primarily by diagonal bracing, and seismic loads through flexible connections.

Only in the past 150 years has it become possible to quantify the direction and magnitude of loads and to

0.2 (below left) Arch, Kabah, Mexico, 850–900.
Built by the Maya of Central America, this is an example of corbeled construction. Note that the stones forming the triangular arch are laid in horizontal courses and slightly overlap one another as they rise.

0.3 (below) Barn, Cades Cove, Great Smoky Mountains National Park, Tennessee, 19th century.
This is an example of cantilevered construction. The second-floor loft overhangs the log cribs of the base, supported on long, wooden cantilevers extending to the sides and front-to-back across the width of the barn.

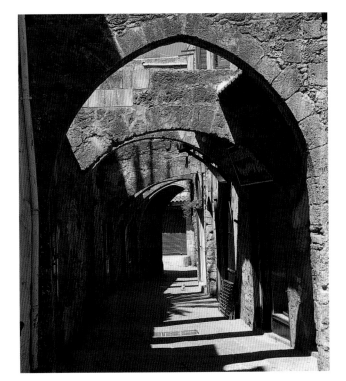

0.4 Street in Rhodes, 1100–1300.
Buildings here have been braced with arches as a result
of earthquakes. Several different arch profiles can be seen,
all constructed of wedge-shaped voussoirs.

measure the ability of specific building materials to resist
external forces, providing designers with the basis for producing mathematical models that predict structural behavior. For the vast majority of buildings considered in this
book, however, achieving a stable structure was a matter
of trial and error, based upon modifications of what had
been done in the past.

Structural systems can be classified into five categories
according to the geometric configuration of their members
and the way in which loads are resisted: (1) post and lintel (or column and beam); (2) corbel and cantilever; (3)
arch and vault; (4) truss and space frame; and (5) tensile.
Post-and-lintel systems, formed by vertical and horizontal
members, are perhaps the most common type, sometimes
known as trabeated systems (Fig. 0.1). The possible distance between **posts** is primarily determined by the spanning capability of the **beams**. Under loading, the beams
bend or deflect downward, stretching (or placing in tension) the fibers in the lower half of the member and pressing together (or placing in compression) the fibers in the
upper half. Materials such as stone tend to fail quickly if
placed in tension, so one can hardly imagine a wire made
of stone. Since materials for **lintels** should be equally
strong in tension and compression, wood, steel, and reinforced concrete are widely used.

Stone was the most durable building material available
to early societies. These civilizations found ways to overcome stone's inherent weakness in tension and so used it
to span greater distances than were possible in post-and-
lintel construction. The earliest method was through **corbeling** (Fig. 0.2). Stones were laid in horizontal courses,
with the last stone in each course projecting slightly
beyond the one below it to form a corbeled **arch**. A corbeled **dome** is made up of rings of stones (or even wood),
with each succeeding ring smaller and, therefore, projecting beyond the one below it. This same principle has been
used in **cantilever** construction, where a beam or beams
(often of wood) project beyond their supports to form an
overhang, such as an **eave** below a roof or an overhanging
second floor or **jetty** (Fig. 0.3).

Masonry arches and **vaults** (Figs. 0.4 and 0.5) are composed of wedge-shaped stones called **voussoirs** that must
be supported on a temporary framework, called **centering**, until the arch or vault is completed, at which time
the stones press tightly against one another and become
self-supporting. Such construction requires firm lateral
bracing, as an arch or vault exerts not only a downward
thrust but also a lateral thrust, which is an outward, overturning force that must be counteracted if the arch or vault
is to remain in equilibrium. While all arches behave in a

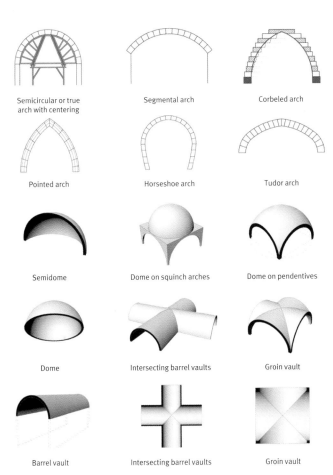

Semicircular or true arch with centering

Segmental arch

Corbeled arch

Pointed arch

Horseshoe arch

Tudor arch

Semidome

Dome on squinch arches

Dome on pendentives

Dome

Intersecting barrel vaults

Groin vault

Barrel vault

Intersecting barrel vaults

Groin vault

0.5 Arch, vault, and dome types.
Understanding masonry vaulting is crucial to understanding
most permanent construction from the time of ancient Rome
to the development of iron, steel, and reinforced concrete in
the nineteenth century.

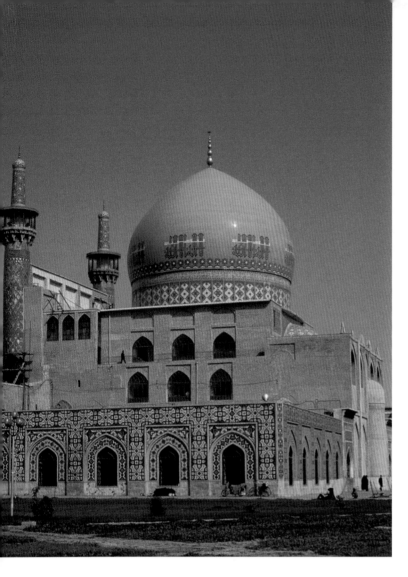

similar manner structurally, their profiles vary considerably. Semicircular (or true), segmental, **pointed**, horseshoe, and Tudor arches are among the most important historically. Domes may also vary in profile, from shallow saucer shapes to semicircular or hemispherical to steeply pitched; the steeper the arch or dome's profile, the less the lateral thrust (Fig 0.6). And domes can be supported by squinch arches or pendentives. Vaults, which are linear extensions of arches, can be intersected at right angles, producing a groin vault.

The trussing method of spanning space calls for short wooden or metal elements to be connected in triangular configurations (Fig. 0.7). The Romans developed this technique for wooden bridges, but their experiments were not continued by subsequent societies. In the medieval period, **trusses** in church roofs depended on having one member, the bottom chord, equal in length to the span being covered. Early in the nineteenth century, bridge-builders reinvented the art of constructing trusses using short members, employing first wood and then iron and steel in various triangulated configurations, many of which were patented. The Warren truss, named for its designer and composed of equilateral triangles, is probably the most common today. A truss repeated in three dimensions is known as a space frame, a twentieth-century structural development that is particularly useful for long, clear-span roofs.

Some structures are based largely on the control of tensile forces. Fabric tents with upright posts are examples of tensile structures, as are suspension bridges (Fig. 0.8). In both cases, the load is partly carried by fibers or cables woven or spun together. Builders in China and the Andes of Peru used animal or vegetable fibers such as hair, vines, and sisal to build tension structures, but these were limited

0.6 Goharshad Mosque, Mashhad, Iran, 1419.
This mosque design shows typical Islamic arch profiles and a handsome, bulbous blue-tiled dome.

0.7 Railroad bridge, Tennessee River, Knoxville, Tennessee, ca. 1906.
This bridge over the Tennessee River is composed of Warren trusses.

0.8 Seventh Street Bridge, Pittsburgh, Pennsylvania, 1925–28.
This is an example of a suspension bridge structure where vertical loads are carried primarily in tension.

in durability by the inherent weakness of the fibers and their tendency to decay. Great progress was made in the development of tensile construction in the nineteenth and twentieth centuries as engineers used iron bars or spun thin strands of steel into cables to support the world's longest bridges. Cables have also been used to suspend floors of multi-story buildings. Pneumatic structures, like balloons, have lightweight membranes supported by pressurized air, and thus are also based on tension.

The possibilities of these structural systems are vast. In addition, there are hybrid systems such as cantilevered and arched trusses. The selection of any one of them for a particular building depends on available materials, economics, spatial requirements, and the esthetic sensibilities of the architect and client.

Finally, a few words about styles and precedents. During the eighteenth and nineteenth centuries, historians developed taxonomies classifying the architectural work of various periods according to perceived common characteristics. Today, we recognize that the story is often much more complex and that the lines between the chronological classifications are blurred. The reader should take this into account when studying a chapter on, say, the "Renaissance" or the "Baroque." These are convenient terms, but they should be seen as no more than that, conveniences, and should not obscure the diversity and complexity of the historical built environment. Likewise, the buildings discussed here have been carefully chosen. In most cases, they are the so-called "canonical" buildings; that is, the ones that have been recognized by many scholars over time as best representing a time and place or the work of an individual. The canon has changed and will continue to change, particularly for buildings outside the European context and those of the more recent past. Furthermore, not only historians but also architects themselves have participated in establishing the canon. Throughout history, architects have learned from those who preceded them. The buildings that they admired, studied, and emulated became design precedents. For

instance, the exterior of McKim, Mead, and White's Boston Public Library (1887–93) (see Fig. 14.51) owes much to the principal façade of Henri Labrouste's Bibliothèque Ste.-Geneviève in Paris (1844–50) (see Figs. 14.10 and 14.11), which, in turn, was based upon the side elevation of Leon Battista Alberti's church of S. Francesco in Rimini (begun ca. 1450) (see Fig. 11.14). At S. Francesco, Alberti was inspired by the arches of the Tomb of Theodoric in nearby Ravenna (ca. 526). A similar backward trajectory can be established for the dome of the U.S. Capitol (1851–67), designed by Thomas U. Walter, who was inspired by Sir Christopher Wren's design for St. Paul's Cathedral in London (1675–1710) (see Fig. 12.47). Wren's probable precedent was François Mansart's dome of the Val-de-Grâce in Paris (see Fig. 12.37), which was in turn inspired by Michelangelo's dome for St. Peter's in Rome (see Fig. 11.42), which was itself based on Brunelleschi's dome for Florence Cathedral (see Fig. 11.3). Brunelleschi had looked for his inspiration to the ancient Roman Pantheon in Rome (see Fig. 5.21), erected about 125 CE for the Emperor Hadrian. Where Hadrian's architects got their ideas, we leave for you to discover. Throughout the ages, then, architects have been influenced by the works of their predecessors. We hope that you, our readers, whether you are concerned with history or design or both, will be equally informed and inspired by what is presented in the pages that follow.

A Word about Drawings and Images

In this book, there are many drawings as well as photographs of interior and exterior views. Architects have long relied on the convention of orthographic projections—plans, elevations, and sections—to describe buildings. A plan represents a building as seen from above once a horizontal cutting plane has been passed through it, usually just above the height of the window sills, with everything above this cutting plane removed and the lines of the plan cast onto the cutting plane (Fig. 0.9). Elements that have

0.9 Plans, elevations, and sections.
This diagram illustrates the basis of orthographic projection in plan, elevation, and section.

been cut are usually defined by the darkest lines in the drawing or are blackened in completely. Elements below the cutting plane are drawn with thinner lines, and doors may appear as arcs showing the direction of their swings. Dotted lines in a plan usually indicate ceiling elements above the cutting plane, such as vaults and **coffers**. Thus, in a single, economical drawing, a plan can indicate spatial distribution and dimensions on a particular floor and even give some idea of the structure above.

Elevations are obtained by passing a vertical cutting plane down through the ground a few feet in front of one exterior face of a building, with the image of the building then projected onto the cutting plane. Sections also result from a vertical cutting plane, but in this case one passed down inside a building with its image cast upon the plane. By convention, these cutting planes in elevation and section are placed parallel to the building's principal walls. In an elevation, the only line that is intersected by the

cutting plane is the ground line, so this line is shown as the darkest in the drawing. In a section, as in a plan, all the building elements that have been cut are usually defined by the darkest lines on the drawing or are blackened in completely, and elements beyond the cutting plane are seen in elevation and, therefore, are drawn with thinner lines. While it may take some experience to "read" orthographic drawings, they are very useful in the building process because dimensions can be scaled directly from them.

Let us see how drawings work by considering the pair of two-story houses shown in Figs. 0.10 and 0.11. They represent a common type built by early colonists in Connecticut, and both were enlarged by a one-story addition at the rear that was covered by extending the existing roof slope. The resulting form was dubbed a "saltbox" because it resembled the bulk salt containers found in nineteenth-century general stores. In Fig. 0.12, we see the plan and two elevations of another saltbox house as documented by the Historic American Buildings Survey, a national record of buildings begun in the 1930s and archived in the Library of Congress. From the plan it is easier to see the rear addition and to understand how the interior of the house was arranged. A perspective drawing,

0.10, 0.11 (left) John Graves House, Madison, Connecticut, 1675; (right) Samuel Daggett House, 1750, Connecticut.
Although these colonial houses are not identical, they share a similar form and massing around a central chimney.

0.12 Plan and front and right-side elevations of Ogden House, Fairfield, Connecticut, ca. 1700.
Fine lines on this drawing indicate dimensions taken from the building when it was measured for the Historic American Buildings Survey.

Fig. 0.13a, more closely resembles the photographs in Figs. 0.10 and 0.11, because perspective drawings show all three dimensions through foreshortening, as photography does, with elements that are farther away (the front-left and back-right corners of the house, in this case) diminishing in size. We know that in fact both front corners of the house are the same height, but in a perspective the one closer to the viewer will be taller. Because most of us readily understand perspective drawing, this drawing type provides architects with a powerful tool for communicating the appearance of buildings not yet constructed in a way that non-architects can understand. An axonometric drawing, as in Fig. 0.13b, also depicts all three dimensions, but does so without distorting these dimensions as measured along the axes of height, width, and depth. Something must be distorted to capture a three-dimensional object in two dimensions, however, and in this case it is some of the angles at which these axes intersect. At the front- and right-side elevations, some 90° angles, like those at the right front corner, have become acute angles, while others are now obtuse angles.

One of the specialized uses of drawings is to show conditions that may not be visible in the finished building. Fig. 0.13c shows a perspective view of the structure of a saltbox house, allowing us to see the heavy timber frame that is covered by the exterior siding and also to understand how the massive stone chimney fits into the core. Images of buildings, no matter how detailed, are inevitably abstractions of reality. Even photographs do not show everything "as it really is." Therefore, having multiple images, drawings as well as photographs, aids in understanding a building's structure and spatial arrangement.

0.13a (above) Perspective drawing of Ogden House.
This view is based on the dimensions of a house measured by the Historic American Buildings Survey.

0.13c (below) Analytic perspective of a saltbox house.
With the exterior siding, doors, and windows removed, one can see the heavy timber frame and masonry chimney that comprise the structure of this building.

0.13b (right) Axonometric drawing of Ogden House.
This view is based on the dimensions of a house measured by the Historic American Buildings Survey. Compare this view with the perspective drawing (Fig. 0.13a) to see how these drawing types differ from one another.

The Beginnings of Architecture

Though ancient, the structures that appear in this initial chapter are rich and varied and often sophisticated. Moreover, because they are "ancient" and always local, they are in some ways more exposed to revelation than later structures. That is, they lay bare for consideration certain fundamental principles of architecture and, arguably, certain fundamental aspects of the human condition.

In 1964, polymath architect-engineer-historian Bernard Rudofsky organized a then surprising and ultimately extremely influential exhibition, "Architecture without Architects," at the Museum of Modern Art in New York City. The exhibition created something of a sensation, appearing as it did at a time of general cultural upheaval in the United States, and the subtitle of the book accompanying the exhibition, *A Short Introduction to Non-Pedigreed Architecture*, suggests why it was so sensational or, perhaps more accurately, so iconoclastic. Illustrating, with obvious personal admiration, what he called "vernacular, anonymous, spontaneous, indigenous, rural" architecture, Rudofsky argued for a much more chronologically and geographically inclusive study of the built environment and one that did not cater exclusively to constructions for the wealthy and powerful and did not result exclusively from the efforts of what we might today call academically trained designers. The images of architectural objects that he displayed and analyzed ranged from earth mounds in China to rock-cut dwellings in Turkey, to reverse-action chimneys in Pakistan and much else in among them.

Reading Rudofsky's book and particularly the initial pages of this chapter, you will be directed away from matters of fashion and even style, in favor of "anonymous" but distinctive, even archetypal, forms, and you may come away with a deeper understanding of human responses to particularized environments, to specific local building materials, to elementary but expressively logical structural systems, and to early but nuanced social conditions. You will be able to embrace the essentials of function, space, and meaning by "beginning" with the architecture of prehistory; that is, the era before the appearance of written language.

Prehistory begins as early as 35,000 BCE and extends to about 3000 BCE in the lands of the eastern Mediterranean, and until well after 2000 BCE in parts of western Europe. On the timescale of humankind, these dates correspond to the earliest years of "modern" human evolution from cooperative hunting-and-gathering societies into agricultural civilizations with a fixed settlement area and a ruling class. In the absence of written records, archaeologists and historians must interpret the fragmentary evidence of ancient people—pottery, household implements and rubbish, burials, tombs, and building remains—found in locations scattered across Europe, Africa, and Asia. The most dramatic images from prehistoric times are the Paleolithic cave paintings in France and Spain dating back as far as 33,000 BCE. Depicting mostly animals, often in hunting scenes, they have been variously interpreted as part of religious rituals, as the hallucinogenic visions of shamans, and even as star charts. New technologies have assisted the dating of such artifacts through the use of radioactive carbon 14, thermoluminescence, and dendrochronological analysis (the study of growth rings in trees), but both the methods and the hypotheses derived from them are subject to continual revision as researchers discover new evidence and reexamine old ideas. Reconstructions based on post-holes or masonry foundations help us visualize the simple buildings erected by early societies and provide clues to the more elaborate structures that come later.

⇐ ┈┈

Ceiling of the red cows, Lascaux, Dordogne, France, 15,000–20,000 BCE.
Discovered in 1940, this cave contains some 2,000 painted images—some of abstract signs, some of humans, and some of animals, as seen here. In the absence of written records, the purpose of the paintings remains open to conjecture. Some see them as depictions of past hunting experiences or as the settings for mystical ritual experiences intended to bring hunters success. Some even argue that they depict hallucinogenic visions or are star charts. In 2008 the cave was beset by black mold and has since been closed except for brief, weekly monitoring visits by scientists.

Chronology

Beginning of prehistory	ca. 35,000 BCE
Sumerians develop a written language	3500 BCE
Construction of Stonehenge	ca. 2900–1400 BCE
Egyptian Old Kingdom	2649–2134 BCE
Construction of the pyramids at Giza	2550–2460 BCE
Construction of the Ziggurat at Ur	2100 BCE
Egyptian Middle Kingdom	2040–1640 BCE
Egyptian New Kingdom	1550–1070 BCE

PREHISTORIC SETTLEMENTS AND MEGALITH CONSTRUCTIONS

Eastern Europe

Human settlement seems to have originated at the small clan or family level, with a sufficient number of people living together to provide mutual assistance in hunting and food gathering and joint protection against enemies. Among the earliest huts to be discovered are those at sites in the central Russian Plain (today's Ukraine), dated to about 14,000 BCE. Constructed of mammoth bones and pine poles, with a lining of animal skins and a central hearth, the largest dome-shaped hut incorporated skeleton parts from nearly a hundred mammoths in its framework. Archaeologists have also found clusters of skin-covered huts dated to about 12,000 BCE between Moscow and Novgorod. The largest of these huts, measuring about thirty-nine by thirteen feet in plan, had an irregular shape formed by three interlocking cones of inclined tree branches and was open at the top to allow smoke to escape from three hearths.

Excavations of town sites suggest that larger communities were a much later development. The existence of urban settlements depends on an agricultural surplus that enables some people to assume specialized roles (priest, ruler, merchant, craftworker) not directly tied to the production of food. Two of the earliest known urban communities were Jericho, Israel (ca. 8000 BCE) and the trading town of Çatal Hüyük (6500–5700 BCE) in Anatolia, part of present-day Turkey. Jericho was a fortified settlement, with a stone wall up to twenty-seven feet thick enclosing an area of about ten acres. Its earliest dwellings consisted of circular mud huts that may have had conical roofs. The inhabitants were farmers and hunters who buried their dead below the hut floors. Although by contrast Çatal Hüyük appears to have been unfortified, the town was a dense package of dwellings without streets (Figs. 1.1a,b). Residents gained access to the dwellings across roofs, while high openings in the walls were for ventilation. Mud-brick walls and a post-and-lintel timber framework enclosed rectangular spaces that abutted the neighboring houses so that together they established a perimeter town wall. Interspersed with the houses were windowless shrines containing decorative motifs of bulls and cult statuettes of deities. These seem to indicate that the themes of prehistoric cave art—hunting and fecundity—had not been discarded by this early urban society. The settlement at Çatal Hüyük is the precursor of more sophisticated communities that developed in the fertile valleys of the Tigris and Euphrates rivers at the beginning of the fourth millennium.

Western Europe

In western Europe the transition to urban communities was slower in coming, although the shift from hunting-and-gathering societies to larger agricultural groups under

1.1a (above) Reconstruction view of buildings, Çatal Hüyük, Anatolia, ca. 6500–5700 BCE.
Notice how buildings abut one another, forming a continuous grouping broken occasionally by open courtyards. The buildings represent a mixture of dwelling houses, workshops, and shrines, all of which were accessed from the rooftops.

1.1b (below) Reconstruction of shrine room, Çatal Hüyük, Turkey, ca. 6500–5700 BCE.
The central figure on the left-hand wall represents a woman giving birth, while the horned bull skulls suggest masculine properties. Without written documentation, it is difficult to understand completely the significance of other architectural features, such as the stepped floor levels.

1.2 (below) Megalith tomb, Er-Mané, Carnac, Brittany, France, ca. 4200 BCE.
This structure presents an early example of corbeled construction, in which stones are laid without mortar in layers, with each course projecting slightly beyond the previous one, to enclose space. The same area contains other prehistoric tomb chambers and nearly 300 standing and fallen megaliths set in rows aligned to indicate the direction of sunrise at summer and winter solstices and fall and spring equinoxes.

graves for cremated or skeletal remains seems to have been not only an expression of reverence for ancestors but also a means of establishing claims to land, and megalith tombs are frequently located on prominent sites. Among the most impressive is the passage grave at Newgrange, County Meath, built about 3100 BCE on the crest of a hill overlooking the Boyne river. An earthen mound nearly 300 feet in diameter and thirty-six feet high covers the tomb, with the weight of the soil providing stability for the megaliths below. Decorated boulders surround the perimeter of the mound. (The white quartz facing is a modern reconstruction based on excavations, providing visibility from a distance.) The south-facing entry leads to a sixty-two-foot-long, upward-sloping passage covered by stone lintels terminating in a cruciform chamber covered by a beehive corbeled ceiling twenty feet high. Parts of the stonework in the passage and chamber are decorated with incised patterns, including diamond shapes and spirals, whose meanings are unknown (Figs. 1.3–1.4). The whole construction is carefully oriented so that, in the five days around the winter solstice, light from the rising sun

1.4 Entranceway, Newgrange passage grave, County Meath, Ireland, ca. 3100 BCE.
This view shows the stone façade as reconstructed by archaeologists. Note the rectangular opening that serves as a "transom light" over the portal, providing the path for sunlight on the winter solstice. Spiral designs on the stone that blocks direct entry may represent sun signs. The old stone door is visible to the right of the opening.

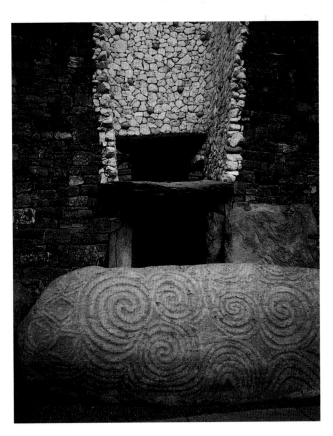

1.3 Plans and section, Newgrange passage grave, County Meath, Ireland, ca. 3100 BCE.
The cruciform chamber of this communal grave is approached through a long passage created by upright stones. The near-horizontal shaded area represents the path of early-morning sunlight on the winter solstice, which illuminates the passage and chamber floor, establishing a connection between the human and celestial worlds.

the direction of a priest-king was similar to the experience of societies on the eastern rim of the Mediterranean Sea. The significant prehistoric architectural achievements of western Europe were megalith constructions, composed of large stones or boulders (**megalith** literally means "great stone"), many of which were erected for astronomical observatories or communal tombs for the privileged classes. Before 4000 BCE, chambered tombs of dry-wall masonry (stones laid without mortar) with corbeled roofs were constructed in Spain and France. One of the earliest of the megalith tombs, dated to 4200 BCE, is at Er-Mané, Carnac, in Brittany (Fig. 1.2). As with many other chambered tombs, this one was stabilized by a covering of earth.

Ireland is particularly rich in megalith tombs, having over 500 documented sites. Constructing these communal

1.5 Stonehenge, Salisbury Plain, England, ca. 2900–1400 BCE. Perhaps the most famous monument from prehistoric times, Stonehenge exemplifies the ability of some early civilizations to organize workers and materials to create evocative ceremonial places. The heel stone stands to the upper left beyond the circle.

enters through the doorway and a **transom**-like light box, creeps along the passage, and illuminates the chamber within for about fifteen minutes (Fig. 1.4). To those fortunate enough to witness this annual event (the only time there is any light in the interior), the effect is magical and very moving. Constructing such a massive tomb (and there are two others on the same scale nearby) would have required sustained effort over many years. Available technology provided nothing harder than copper or bronze tools for shaping stone, and there were no

Heel stone
Avenue

Circle of sarcen stones

Q and R holes (locations
of bluestones)

South barrow

Trilithons

Y holes

Z holes

Aubrey holes

Ditch

h barrow

N

0   50 m

0   150 ft

1.6 Plan, Stonehenge, Salisbury Plain, England, ca. 2900–1400 BCE.
This plan includes the original earthworks. The trilithons set in a U-shape establish the axis of the avenue, which passes between perimeter stones to align with the heel stone set outside the circle. On the summer solstice, the sun rises precisely over the heel stone, when viewed from the center of the concentric circles.

wheeled vehicles or draft animals to assist with transport. Nonetheless, ancient builders made the necessary astronomical observations and organized a work force sufficient to maneuver stones weighing up to five tons.

The ability to work large stones and to observe fundamental astronomical phenomena merged in the most celebrated of megalith constructions, Stonehenge, located on Salisbury Plain in southwestern England (Figs. 1.5–1.7). At least three distinct building phases can be observed. The first phase began about 2900 BCE with excavation of two concentric circular ditches. Inside the perimeter,

fifty-six evenly spaced holes (the Aubrey holes) were dug and filled with chalk, while a northeasterly line of sight to the horizon was established from the center across a pointed upright (the heel stone) outside the ditches. About 2400 BCE eighty-two coffin-sized stones of gray-blue dolerite, weighing about two tons each, were transported from quarries in the Pressely mountains of Wales and erected in a double ring of thirty-eight pairs, with six extra stones defining the northeast approach axis. At some point, perhaps before this second phase was completed, the bluestones were removed (their sockets are the so-called Q and R holes). The third and final phase involved transporting thirty-five lintels and forty sarcen stones (a form of sandstone) weighing up to twenty tons each. These were erected in a circle of thirty uprights enclosing five **trilithons** (two uprights capped by a single lintel) arranged in a U-shape to focus on the Avenue, the axis leading northeast toward the heel stone. Knobs (**tenons**) left on the tops of the uprights fit into socket holes (**mortises**) carved into the undersides of the lintels, so that the stones lock together in a mortise-and-tenon joint when correctly positioned.

To many modern visitors, the sophisticated design and massive construction of the site has seemed beyond the capacities of prehistoric people. Thus the site has been interpreted variously as the work of giants, magicians, people imported from the Aegean, or even extraterrestrials. The truth is more prosaic but ultimately more meaningful: archaeo-astronomer Gerald Hawkins demonstrated that Stonehenge was a great observatory for determining the solstices (thus establishing the annual calendar) and

1.7 Stonehenge, Salisbury Plain, England, ca. 2900–1400 BCE.
This view from the north shows the present-day configuration of stones. Where the lintels are gone, the knobs (tenons) that held the horizontal stones in place can be seen on top of the uprights. The heel stone is the tall stone to the left.

predicting lunar and solar eclipses, knowledge that could have proved very useful in a society without almanacs. Its circular layout may well reflect a symbolic tie to the heavens, a link between human and celestial realms.

Experience gained in the construction and orientation of megalith tombs enabled early inhabitants of the British Isles to erect one of the most haunting architectural works of all time. Stonehenge represents the culmination of construction skill and scientific observation in the prehistoric era. Its builders met the challenge of moving and shaping massive stones. Bluestones from Wales were transported, largely by water, over 190 miles to the site, being dragged overland for the last leg of the journey. The larger sarcen uprights came from the Marlborough Downs, about fifteen miles from Stonehenge, and were probably dragged to the site. Modern experimentation with moving and erecting a trilithon on the scale of Stonehenge shows that erection could be accomplished with simple machines (lever and inclined plane), a sledge and greased track, wooden scaffolds, stout ropes, and about 130 people working together.

ANCIENT MESOPOTAMIA

The distinction between the prehistoric world and historic times involves the development of written language, which was achieved by about 3500 BCE by the Sumerians in the Middle Eastern land of present-day Iraq and Iran. There, in the fertile lands between the Tigris and Euphrates rivers (named Mesopotamia or "between the rivers" by the ancient Greeks), the earliest literate civilizations developed in independent urban communities called city-states. Writing first developed as a means of documenting governmental transactions and was only later employed for what might be called literary purposes, communicating the legends, glorious deeds, hopes, and fears of the people. In about 3000 BCE, perhaps as a result of contacts with Mesopotamia, another center of civilization emerged in northeast Africa, along the banks of the Nile River in Egypt. These two regions, Egypt and Mesopotamia, are considered the cradles of Western history and architecture.

Despite ongoing conflict in the Middle East, probably no culture seems more remote to the current student of architectural history than that of ancient Mesopotamia. There are strong religious images from Judeo–Christian scripture of flood stories and the Tower of Babel, both with Mesopotamian connections, but such textual images can only go so far, and Hollywood has not seen fit to dramatize the place and its people as they have Egypt and the ancient Egyptians. You can best begin, perhaps, by reading the accompanying essay for some sense of Mesopotamian culture, then consider the larger picture; that picture begins with rivers.

Mesopotamia encompasses an area about 500 miles long by no more than 300 miles wide. Its southern boundary is the Persian Gulf, the shore of which was about 130

miles farther north during the third millennium than it is today. In addition, shifts in the river channels, climatic changes, and increased salinity of formerly irrigated lands have combined to bring about profound changes in the environment since antiquity. The Tigris and Euphrates rivers flow separately into the gulf. The Euphrates originates in the mountains of eastern Turkey and meanders across the plains in its lower reaches. The more easterly Tigris rises in the same mountains, but develops into a more swiftly flowing stream because of its numerous tributaries in the Zagros mountains. As a result, the Tigris was less navigable and did not have as great a unifying effect on settlements along its banks as did the Euphrates.

The Mesopotamian cultures did great things by exploiting their rivers. They regulated them as best they could and from them they constructed elaborate irrigation canals that made possible a fertile, even Edenesque landscape. Within this landscape, they cultivated sufficiently abundant crops to permit the large-scale storage of surplus grain. This relatively stable and plentiful supply of food, in turn, permitted the growth of large urban populations and that corollary of urbanism: specialization. Mesopotamian specialists included not only priests and merchants but also artisans, artists, and architects who could make beautiful objects, express their culture's worldview, and make gestures toward the connection of humankind to the cosmos.

Sumerians, Akkadians, and Neo-Sumerians

The Sumerians are generally credited with forming the world's first civilization, which began to take shape around 4000 BCE. At this time, the people of the fertile lands of southern Mesopotamia mastered arts of agriculture and developed irrigation systems to control the waters of the Euphrates River. Their civilization, which lasted until about 2350 BCE, is known as Sumerian, and the typical form of their settlements was the city-state, a political and religious center devoted to serving gods based on natural elements. These deities included the divine triad of Anu, god of the sky; Enlil, god of the earth; and Ea, god of water; supplemented by Nannar, god of the moon; Utu, god of the sun; and Inanna, goddess of fertility. The Sumerians believed that the sky and earth were two disks that had been blown apart and that all existence was governed by the gods, who represented the unpredictable elements affecting human life. They believed that human beings were created from the alluvial silt deposits in the river valleys to serve the gods and to relieve them of toil. Because the gods benefited from human praise, they had to remain in human favor. Thus there was a balance in the creative and destructive forces of the gods and a mutual interdependence between people and gods.

Urban communities developed around religious shrines, the dwelling places of the gods and the repositories for surplus food stores, leading to the development of monumental temple complexes at the hearts of Sumerian

ESSAY
The Sumerian View of the World
by Michael Fazio

1.8 Head of a ewe in sandstone, ca. 3200 BCE, 5 ¾ inches by 5 ½ inches by 6 ¼ inches. The creator of this small, stony animal captured both its realistic "sheepness" and that enigmatic sense of the eternal to which great religious art aspires.

The Sumerians worshiped multiple gods of diverse rank and character and represented them in their art. This small object (Fig. 1.8) is the head of a ewe or female sheep carved by a Sumerian sculptor, perhaps in Uruk, more than five thousand years ago. Its current home is Louis Kahn's Kimbell Art Museum in Fort Worth, Texas (see Figs. 16.33–16.35). Lovingly made, it renders more personal and more accessible these anonymous Sumerians, who created a monumental architecture almost exclusively from mud.

We need to imagine the entire figure, its body intact, and so standing two to three feet high and having about the same length. Curators at the Kimbell interpret it as a symbol of the goddess Dittur, whose son Dumuzi was an important god of shepherding and milk (hence the sheep image), as well as the netherworld.

The ewe's head is worn, so again we need to imagine it as pristine, quite realistic and animate, and appreciate its sympathetic depiction in a society where such animals were essential to human survival. With its wide mouth, flaring nostrils, and alert ears that seem just to have heard the voice of the shepherd or shepherd god, it invites reverent touching, perhaps patting were it not so sacred. Again we can imagine the coarse warmth of its fleece and its quiet breath. We can imagine the artist working to communicate its "sheepness" and to communicate its meaning by drawing out the nature of the soft stone from which it is made.

Its home would have been a place like the White Temple (see Fig. 1.11). Here it would have been attended by priests and worshiped daily. The National Museum of Iraq in Baghdad, which was tragically ransacked during the war in 2003, contained sculpted images of such priests and other worshipful Sumerians (Fig. 1.9). These images are more formally abstract than the ewe, their upper and lower torsos wedge-shaped, like the characters of Sumerian cuneiform writing, and their most striking features are extremely prominent eyes and ritually folded, almost wringing hands, seemingly expressive of a certain anxiety. The Sumerians struggled with a host of insecurities in a land where nature, particularly the weather, vacillated wildly between benevolence and malevolence. They asked the questions we still ask. Where had they come from? How could they exercise some measure of control over their environment? What awaited them after death?

1.9 Sumerian statuette, Tell Asmar, ca. 2900–2600 BCE. Gypsum inlaid with shell and black limestone, approximately 16 in. Compare this statuette to the head of the ewe in Fig. 1.8. While the ewe is depicted realistically, the Sumerian worshiper is stylized. The same phenomenon is found in Egyptian art: lowly subjects were often represented with a high degree of realism, while images of the pharaoh or of a god were abstracted, as if this abstraction might provide some insight into the more imponderable aspects of the human condition.

1.10 Reconstruction of the Acropolis, Tepe Gawra, Sumer (Iraq), ca. 3800 BCE.
This religious structure was associated with a more complex urban society than those of prehistory. The scale of the building erected on the high point of the city reflects the importance of the society's religion and priestly class. Pilasters strengthened the mud-brick walls. The north temple stands at the upper left and measures about 25 feet by 40 feet.

side, so that a "bent axis" led from the outside into the hall and sanctuary.

Contemporary structures excavated in the nearby precinct of Eanna (dedicated to Inanna) include two groups of temples flanking a courtyard ornamented by a **mosaic** of thousands of small **terracotta** cones. The base of each cone was dipped in black, white, or red glaze, and then its apex was inserted into the clay of the wall to form a polychromatic zigzag pattern with circular elements.

In 2350 BCE, Semitic-speaking peoples based principally in the cities of Sipar and Akkad, from which they take their name Akkadian, overthrew Sumerian civilization. Surviving evidence indicates that the Akkadians were fierce, governed not only by a priestly class but also by a warrior-king. They adopted many aspects of Sumerian culture, but their centralized form of government prefigured the hegemony of Babylon some 500 years later.

The Akkadian Empire was in turn overthrown in about 2150 BCE by the Guti, a group of tribes from the mountain regions of Iran. The military influence of the Guti weakened within a century, and political allegiances reminiscent

cities. The earliest level of Eridu, the oldest city, had a small shrine with a brick altar in front of a wall **niche**, or recess, probably constructed to contain a cult statue, and altars and niches were found in all later Sumerian temples. Rebuildings of this temple at Eridu successively enlarged the relatively modest original shrine, and by about 3800 BCE the temple stood on a platform. Its **buttressed** walls enclosed a rectangular shrine room flanked by smaller side chambers. At about the same time Tepe Gawra, nearly 500 miles to the north, featured an **acropolis** with two temples, a shrine, and dwelling houses. Its major buildings formed a U-shaped open court. Their **façades** were articulated by buttressing **pilasters** (Fig. 1.10), a motif that will be seen again in early Egyptian architecture.

Most Sumerian buildings were laid up in sun-baked brick, a material easily obtained by shaping mud in molds and leaving it to dry for several weeks in the sun, but the resulting brick is not particularly resistant to weathering. As a result, much of Sumerian architecture is known only from foundations and lower sections of walls. Roofs were fabricated from lightweight wooden members or reeds that could not span great distances, so there were no large interior spaces. In both Sumerian and later Mesopotamian architecture, important buildings were given additional durability by having weather-resistant casings for the brick, and greater dignity by being raised on an artificial platform.

Such was the case at Uruk, where the so-called White Temple was built (ca. 3500–3000 BCE) on a forty-foot-high base of rubble from earlier buildings and provided with a protective coat of whitewash over its sloping walls of earth covered with sun-dried brick (Fig. 1.11). Entrance to the temple was made through a chamber in one long

1.11 View and plan of the White Temple, Uruk, Mesopotamia (Iraq), ca. 3500–3000 BCE.
Many temples in Mesopotamia were erected on raised platforms. The base of this temple was made in part with the rubble from previous buildings on the site, buttressed in a regular pattern and protected by layers of whitewash—hence the temple's name.

of the first Sumerian city-states returned in what is termed the Neo-Sumerian period (ca. 2150–2000 BCE). This period witnessed the further development of urban temple forms, particularly the temple elevated on a tiered artificial mound, or **ziggurat**. Commonly constructed of sun-dried brick bonded together with bitumen, reed matting, or rope, ziggurats were finished with a weather-resistant exterior layer of kiln-fired brick. From a rectangular base, the ziggurat rose with battered or inward-sloping walls in a series of stepped platforms, culminating in a high temple at the top. A flight of stairs set in the center of one side afforded access to the temple. (Elements so placed in the center of a symmetrical form and aligned toward a terminus are said to be axial.) Ziggurats were designed to elevate the temples to the gods so that the latter might descend from the heavens and ensure the prosperity of the community. Symbolically, the ziggurat may have also represented the mountains whence the Sumerians came. To make their gods feel at home in the lowlands of the river valley, the Sumerians and their successors in Mesopotamia may have aspired to recreate their highland dwelling place. Raising the temple well above the elevation of the valley may also have reflected a desire to protect the sacred precinct from flood waters; it certainly gave it visual prominence in the city.

Little remains of the ziggurats constructed during the brief Neo-Sumerian interlude. Once the outer casing was removed by scavengers, the earthen core of ziggurats eroded considerably. Of those lofty artificial mountains that towered over Mesopotamian cities, only the ziggurat at Ur (ca. 2100 BCE) retains some of its architectural details

(Figs. 1.12–1.13). One can still distinguish the three long stairways that converged on a tower gate at the level of the first platform. Shorter flights led to the second and third terraces, to which only the priests were allowed to ascend. These upper levels, together with the crowning temple, have been reduced to crumbled heaps, but archaeologists calculated that the original height was about seventy feet, with a base of about 200 by 150 feet.

In contrast to the grand temple complexes, the houses of the ordinary population were set in densely packed neighborhoods. Plans were roughly orthogonal, and houses were constructed around open courtyards that provided light and fresh air to all rooms (Figs. 1.14a,b). To the street, the houses presented a blank wall, thereby ensuring privacy. Courtyard houses continue to the present day to be typical of Mediterranean and Middle Eastern communities.

1.12 (below) Ziggurat at Ur, Mesopotamia (Iraq), ca. 2100 BCE.
The best preserved of the massive temple mounds that once dominated every major Mesopotamian city, this ziggurat served to elevate a temple closer to the gods. Its core is sun-dried brick, overlaid with an outer layer of kiln-fired brick and bitumen as protection against weathering.

1.13 (above) Reconstruction of the ziggurat at Ur, Mesopotamia (Iraq), ca. 2100 BCE.
This drawing shows the original details that are now lost, including recessed panels defined by pilaster strips and parapets. The population below could observe the priestly processions up the successive flights of stairs to the temple on the uppermost platform.

Labels on figure 1.14a:
- Residential area
- Ziggurat
- Fortified gate (?)
- Wall enclosing the sacred precinct
- City wall
- N
- Residential area
- 0 — 500 m
- 0 — 1500 ft

Labels on figure 1.14b:
- N
- 0 — 50 m
- 0 — 150 ft

1.14a City of Ur, Mesopotamia (Iraq), ca. 2100 BCE.
This plan shows the walled precinct with the ziggurat and
the enclosing city wall. A portion of the residential section
that has been excavated can be seen to the southeast
of the city center. Note the mazelike arrangement of the
houses, contrasting sharply with the larger open spaces
of the administrative and ceremonial center.

**1.14b Plan of the residential quarter, Ur, Mesopotamia (Iraq),
ca. 2100 BCE.**
Surviving foundations indicate houses laid out on right-angled
plans with living spaces organized around courtyards (shown
hatched), a configuration that promoted urban density while
also providing privacy and fresh air to each dwelling. Later
versions of this house type can be found in Mohenjo-Daro
(in the Indus Valley), Priene (in western Ionia), and in Islamic
cities in the Middle East and North and East Africa.

Babylonians, Hittites, and Assyrians

Beginning in 1800 BCE, the Amorite dynasty in the city-
state of Babylon dominated Mesopotamia, with the
most celebrated Babylonian king being Hammurabi
(1728–1686 BCE). In 1830 BCE, the vigorous Indo-
European Hittites overran Babylon and took over northern Mesopotamia. Farther south, the Semitic-speaking
Assyrians took control and established capitals sequentially at Calah (present-day Nimrud), Dur-Sharrukin
(Khorsabad), and Nineveh (Kuyunjik). Strongly fortified
citadels built for each capital reflect the Assyrians' relentless warring as well as the ruthless character of their kings.

Khorsabad, the royal city built by Sargon II in ca. 720
BCE, illustrates the main characteristics of Assyrian architecture and planning (Figs. 1.15a,b). Projecting through
one fortified wall of the city, the twenty-five-acre palace
occupied a plateau fifty feet above the level of the town.
Orthogonal geometry governed buildings in the palace

area, which was organized by means of a series of courts.
Rising on an axis with the ramparts was a seven-stage ziggurat, 143 feet square at the base, representing the cosmic
order of the seven planets. The palace's courts were surrounded by rectangular rooms, including the throne room
that was reached by a circuitous route, perhaps intended
to confuse or frighten visitors and to heighten the sense
of power and grandeur. Winged bulls with human heads
carved in high relief from thirteen-foot-tall stone blocks
guarded the entrances to the palace. Bone and muscle
were realistically represented, while feathers, hair, and
beard were stylized, forcefully conveying the strength of
the monarch: as man, the lord of creation; as eagle, king
of the sky; and as bull, fecundator of the herd. Other relief
carvings within the palace depicted marching armies burning, killing, and pillaging to emphasize the folly of resisting Assyrian power. Without subtlety, Sargon II had the
art and architecture of his palace communicate the overwhelming power residing in his person.

1.15a (left) **Reconstruction of the palace, Khorsabad, Assyria (Iraq), ca. 720 BCE.**
Fortified walls enclose the palace. The royal audience hall was reached through a sequence of courtyards and smaller chambers. Compare this to the axial layouts typically found in Egyptian architecture.

1.15b (right) **Plan of the palace, Khorsabad, Assyria (Iraq), ca. 720 BCE.**
The ceremonial route leading from the southeast entry to the throne room is circuitous, involving three changes in direction. The stepped ziggurat is a dwindled version of forms found in earlier cities in Mesopotamia.

Ziggurat
Temple buildings
Throne room
State court
Entrance court

0 — 250 m
0 — 750 ft

The Persians

By 539 BCE, the Persian Empire was ruled by Cyrus II. The Persians had previously overthrown the Medes, and they continued to expand outward from their capital at Susa (in present-day Iran) to conquer all of Mesopotamia, Asia Minor, and even Egypt by 525 BCE. Within a century they controlled territory from the Danube to the Indus, and from the Jaxartes to the Nile, failing to subjugate only the Greek peninsula. The greatest surviving architectural contribution of the Persians is an impressive ruin at Persepolis (Fig. 1.16), the city founded in 518 BCE by Darius as a ceremonial capital to supplement Susa, the administrative capital, and Pasargadae as centers of court life. Lacking strong artistic traditions of their own, the Persians borrowed freely from the cultures they conquered. At Persepolis,

1.16 Plan of the palace, Persepolis, Persia (Iran), ca. 518 BCE.
This great complex was created by at least three Persian monarchs as one of the capitals of the Persian Empire. Its ruins reveal architectural influences from other cultures in Mesopotamia, notably the Hittites and Assyrians, as well as the Egyptians.

Hall of 100 Columns (audience hall of Xerxes)
Stairs to terrace
Audience hall of Darius
Small Palace of Darius
Palace of Xerxes

N

0 — 100 m
0 — 300 ft

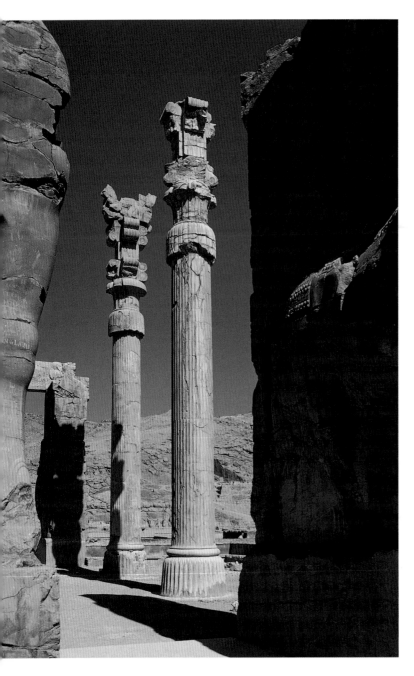

1.17 View of the ruins of the palace, Persepolis, Persia (Iran), ca. 518 BCE.
Seen here are two columns with intact capitals remaining in the audience hall of Darius. The armies of Alexander the Great sacked and burned Persepolis.

palace, able to contain 10,000 people within its 250-foot-square plan. Most of the construction was in stone. Stone **columns** supported wooden roof beams resting on the unique double-headed **capitals** carved in the form of bulls and lions (Fig. 1.17). Access to the terrace was gained via a flight of stairs flanked by relief sculptures representing delegations from twenty-three nations bringing tribute to the sovereign. These stone figures, shown engaged in the same kind of activities as real-life visitors, provided a foretaste of the pageantry and banquets waiting in the palace above.

The conquests of Alexander the Great ended Persian dominance in 331 BCE. Alexander's armies eventually reached India, where Persian craftsmen appear to have accompanied them and then remained. They helped build the capital at Pataliputra (now Patna) for Chandragupta, where the many-columned halls and animal capitals recall the palace at Persepolis. Persian architecture became one of the major influences for the early stone architecture of India.

ANCIENT EGYPT

Popular culture suffers from no shortage of ancient Egyptian images, be they from epic movies depicting Moses and the pharaohs or classic horror films where Boris Karloff, playing the mummy, wanders around menacingly, doling out ancient justice to naïve archaeologists and greedy tomb raiders. All of this is fun, as is wild speculation about the Egyptian pyramids being built by visitors from outer space using anti-gravity beams, but it threatens to obscure the real accomplishments of everyday men and women in the Nile Valley, albeit those of 5000 years ago. Like the Mesopotamians, the ancient Egyptians produced a great architecture by marshaling the forces of their entire civilization and directing those forces in the service of widely held cultural values. This architecture is much more varied than you may imagine, and it is not only largely understandable to the modern mind but also highly informative about design ideas applicable in any era.

The geography of Egypt is dominated by one great river, the Nile, which originates in the highlands of Uganda and passes through the Sudan and Ethiopia as it traverses more than 2000 miles before flowing out into the Mediterranean Sea to the north. Within the 600 lower miles of the river valley, agriculture is facilitated by the warm climate and the annual flood deposits of organic silt, which renew the fertility of the fields. On the margins of the valley in dynastic times there were marshes and open lands rich in game. (Today the desert encroaches on these areas.) Outside the rather narrow fertile band bordering the Nile, great expanses of inhospitable desert provided security from outside invasion, just as the Mediterranean served as a barrier for settlements on the Nile Delta. The culture that developed along the banks of the river was thus predominantly rural agricultural, in contrast to urban-oriented

there are echoes of Egyptian temple gates and **hypostyle halls**, Hittite audience chambers, and Mesopotamian sculpted animal motifs. The great palace, used primarily for ceremonies at the New Year and the beginning of spring, occupied a terrace 1500 by 900 feet; it contained reception courts, banquet rooms, and audience halls in a loosely organized orthogonal layout. King Xerxes's throne room, known as the Hall of a Hundred Columns and completed by Artaxerxes, was the largest roofed space in the settlements in turbulent Mesopotamia. Egyptian life was organized around the annual flooding of the river, and the cyclical rhythm of the seasons fostered a civilization that remained remarkably stable for more than 2000 years. Two centers of Egyptian civilization, with differing cultural practices, arose in prehistoric times: Lower Egypt in the broad Nile Delta, and Upper Egypt in the more narrow southern river valley. At a very early stage, Egyptians also developed writing in the form of hieroglyphs, a system using both pictorial and phonetic symbols to record information.

The history of Egypt begins in about 3000 BCE with the union of Upper and Lower Egypt by Menes, the pharaoh king of Upper Egypt, who established his capital at Memphis, near the junction of the two lands. (Please note that dates in Egyptian history, especially for individual pharaohs in the early dynasties, are still matters of scholarly debate. All dates given here should therefore be treated as approximations.) Menes, like all his successors, was both a temporal ruler and a manifestation of the falcon-headed god Horus, the god of pharaohs. When the pharaoh died, he became identified with Osiris, father of Horus and lord of the underworld, and his successor as pharaoh assumed the Horus role. Egyptian theology linked both Osiris and Horus with the sun god Ra, whose symbol in the ancient temple at Heliopolis was the phallic, cone-shaped ben-ben stone, later stylized as a pyramid. The use of pyramid shapes at the top of stone shafts (**obelisks**) or as the building form itself (as in the pyramids) was thus a visual symbol of the connection between the ruler and the sun god.

The Early Dynastic Period and Old Kingdom (First–Eighth Dynasties, ca. 2920–2134 BCE)

Egyptian history is divided into thirty dynasties, encompassing the period from Pharaoh Narmer's accession (ca. 3000 BCE) to the conquest of Egypt by Alexander the Great in 332 BCE. What we know of this early period comes largely from funerary monuments and inscriptions, where the focus is on the transition from the world of the living to that of the dead. Egyptians believed strongly in an afterlife in which the *ka*, or life-force, was reunited with the *ba*, or physical manifestation, to become an *akh*, or spirit. Elaborate rituals were performed inside tomb chambers to ensure that the transformation from life to death was successful. Preservation of the physical body (or at least a temporary forestalling of its putrefaction) after death was of great importance, as was the provision of household furnishings, surrogate servants, food, drink, and a suitable permanent chamber. The *ka* of an important person, especially the pharaoh, who was inadequately prepared for the afterlife might wander unsatisfied about the world and cause mischief for the living. It was therefore in society's interest to ensure that the pharaoh's body and spirit were well served. This goal led to the construction of enduring tombs for royalty and the development of mummification to preserve the body. Tombs, rather than temples or palaces, became the most lasting religious structures.

Mastabas, the earliest tombs, were built as eternal houses for the departed and were in all likelihood based on the design of the dwellings of the living. Ordinary houses were constructed of reed, thatch, and wood, materials wholly unsuited for a permanent residence, so the builders of mastaba tombs sought greater durability by using brick while retaining characteristic details provided by the customary bundled reeds and wooden supports. The basic mastaba (Fig. 1.18) was a blocklike structure above ground containing a small room for offerings and another chamber for the body and a statue of the deceased. Worldly goods entombed with the dead soon attracted thieves, so an early revision of mastaba design added a deep shaft under the building. The body was placed at its base, and the shaft was then filled with stone and rubble to deter would-be robbers. In the above-ground chamber, or **serdab**, a statue of the deceased would receive offerings. A later change toward increasing permanence involved using stone in the construction of the mastaba.

1.18 Drawing of the mastaba tombs.
This aerial view shows the burial chambers beneath the structures and small chambers, or serdabs, provided at ground level for offerings to the spirit of the deceased. It is thought that these tombs, constructed of sun-dried brick or stone, were based on designs of actual dwellings constructed of less durable materials.

"Hydraulic" Civilizations
by Dan MacGilvray

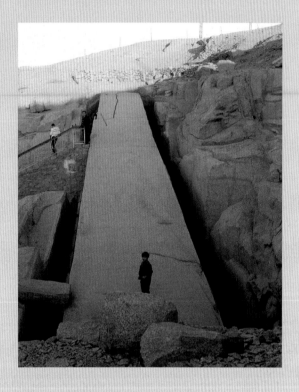

There is but little rain in Assyria. It is this which nourishes the roots of the corn; but it is irrigation from the river that ripens the crop and brings the grain to fullness: it is not as in Egypt, where the river itself rises and floods the fields: in Assyria they are watered by hand and by swinging beams. For the whole land of Babylon, like Egypt, is cut across by canals. The greatest of these is navigable: it runs . . . from the Euphrates to the Tigris . . .

. . . all the land . . . watered by the Nile in its course was Egypt, and all who dwelt lower down than the city Elephantine (Aswan) and drank of that river's water were Egyptians.

. . . there are no men, neither in the rest of Egypt, nor in the whole world, who gain from the soil with so little labour; they have not the toil of breaking up the land with the plow, nor of hoeing . . . the river rises of itself, waters the fields, and then sinks back again; thereupon each man sows his field and sends swine into it to tread down the seed, and waits for the harvest . . .

1.19 Obelisk in a quarry, Aswan, Egypt.

The Greek historian Herodotus (484–425 BCE) traveled extensively throughout the ancient world and wrote the first narrative history. He was a keen observer of culture, and these quotations define one of the essential characteristics of Mesopotamian and Egyptian civilizations: their dependence on rivers. Water is an essential ingredient of all life, and flowing water is required for the development of civilization, not only for drinking and irrigation, but also to remove the human waste that accumulates in areas of dense population. Thus, all of the early civilizations from that of the Indus to the Mayans were founded on rivers. We refer to these as "hydraulic" civilizations.

Of necessity, a hydraulic civilization is a cooperative federation, in contrast to, say, a group of squabbling city-states.

In a given watershed, strong centralized control is required for the construction of an interdependent system of canals to divert water for irrigation and drain swamps for cultivation, or dams and levees for flood control and water retention. Early hydraulic engineers learned the techniques of surveying and developed the skills to manage large-scale construction projects as they struggled to control the waters that brought both abundance and destruction. As Herodotus notes, the nation of Egypt defined itself by the Nile, and there is no doubt that the engineers of the pyramids learned to survey, to level, and to organize large work forces on the banks of the river. It has also been speculated that, because the farmers were inactive during flood times, they were available for conscription into construction work gangs for massive projects like the pyramids.

The Tigris, Euphrates, and Nile rivers also served as the primary transportation arteries for the movement of goods between the various communities that lined them. Even today, in the age of jet travel, by far the cheapest means of moving freight per ton-mile is the river barge. In medieval times it was ten times cheaper to move cargo by boat than by ox-cart. And, because of the Nile, the ancient Egyptians had no use for wheeled vehicles or even paved roads; the chariot was a foreign import that arrived late to the water-borne Egyptians, who, not surprisingly, developed sophisticated construction techniques for boats of all sizes. In tomb paintings the largest are shown laden with granite obelisks, such as that in Figure 1.19, a cargo of up to 1000 tons.

1.20 (above) The stepped pyramid, Saqqara, Egypt, ca. 2630 BCE.
As the first monumental stone construction in Egypt, this tomb set the precedent for later pyramids of the pharaohs. Its architect, Imhotep, was remembered for his genius and later revered as a deity.

1.21a (right) Plan of Djoser's funerary complex, Saqqara, Egypt, ca. 2630 BCE.
The stepped pyramid is the rectangular element in the center, dominating the Great Court, which is reached through the narrow Processional Hall at the lower left. The Egyptians provided the court's two B-shaped stone blocks so that Djoser's *ka* could continue to run the ceremonial race between them, symbolizing for eternity the governmental unity of Upper and Lower Egypt.

1.21b (below right) Section and plan of the stepped pyramid, Saqqara, Egypt, ca. 2630 BCE.
The section drawing shows the successive stages of construction, through which the original mastaba form was enlarged to become a pyramid, with the burial chamber under the center. The plan drawing shows the industry of later tomb robbers who tunneled in to recover treasure buried with Djoser.

Altar
Stone blocks
1.20 Great Court

Entrance Processional Hall Heb-Sed court Pyramid Mortuary temple

0   100 m
0   300 ft   N

0   50 m
0   150 ft   N

A   Original entrance
B   Second entrance
C   Robbers' entrance
★   Blue chambers

The First Pyramids

As the religious ritual prescribed by the priesthood evolved to enhance further the significance of the pharaoh, the mastaba was likewise enlarged, eventually producing the pyramid. At death the pharaoh accompanied the sun god on his daily journey across the sky, so he needed to be lifted skyward. The pyramid, initially an upward-stepping form like the ziggurat, whose peak caught the first rays of morning light, was the emblem of the sun god as worshiped at Heliopolis. The shape also makes symbolic reference to the annual rebirth of nature, for as floods recede, the first signs of plant life appear on small hillocks. Thus the stepped and eventually the true pyramid's form represented both daily and yearly rebirth throughout eternity.

Imhotep, architect to the Third-Dynasty pharaoh Djoser (2630–2611 BCE), is credited with designing the first pyramid, for Djoser's funerary complex at Saqqara,

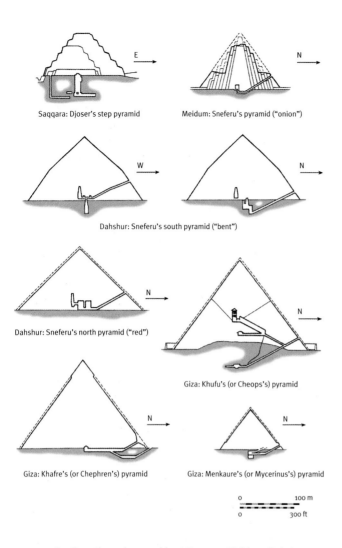

Saqqara: Djoser's step pyramid

Meidum: Sneferu's pyramid ("onion")

Dahshur: Sneferu's south pyramid ("bent")

Dahshur: Sneferu's north pyramid ("red")

Giza: Khufu's (or Cheops's) pyramid

Giza: Khafre's (or Chephren's) pyramid

Giza: Menkaure's (or Mycerinus's) pyramid

0   100 m

0   300 ft

1.22 Sections through pyramids at Saqqara, Meidum, Dahshur, and Giza, Egypt, ca. 2550–2460 BCE.
These drawings indicate the relative sizes of the major pyramids from the Third and Fourth dynasties. That of Cheops remains the largest pile of stones ever assembled, and, among the pyramids, it also has the most complex array of interior passages and chambers.

outside Memphis (Fig. 1.20). This was also Egypt's first monumental construction in stone, no small factor in its survival through 4600 years. The complex is a large rectangle in plan, covering thirty-five acres, surrounded by a wall thirty-three feet high and a mile long (Figs. 1.21a,b). There is only one entrance, a small door in the southeast corner that leads into a narrow colonnaded processional hall. At the end of the hall, one enters the main courtyard dominated by Djoser's stepped pyramid, which rises 197 feet above its 397-by-358-foot base. Begun as a mastaba, the pyramid was built up in several stages to attain its present shape, a mass rising in six steps. The exterior of the pyramid was faced with dressed limestone, while the courtyards and surrounding buildings are thought to be representations of Djoser's earthly palace in Memphis, rebuilt here to last for eternity. The appearance and typical details of the original materials are imitated in stone: reed-bundle and papyrus-stalk columns, log ceilings, even a stone hinge for an immobile stone door. North of the pyramid is the mortuary temple in which the pre-burial ritual was performed. A statue of Djoser looking outward sits in a small chamber,

with a small aperture cut in the wall in front of the statue's stone eyes being the only access to the outside world.

Djoser's complex includes areas for the practice of rituals that are not completely understood today, but that were apparently important symbols of the bond between Upper and Lower Egypt. The great court was the scene of the Heb-Sed race, run annually by the pharaoh to ensure fertility of the fields. The course consisted of four circuits of the court in each direction, clockwise for half of the kingdom and counterclockwise for the other half. Djoser had two burial chambers to symbolize his power and paternity over Upper and Lower Egypt. One chamber, located beneath the pyramid, contained his mummy in an alabaster coffin. The access passage was blocked by a stone plug six feet in diameter and weighing six tons, but this was inadequate protection against robbers, who nonetheless gained access to the tomb in antiquity. In 1928 excavators discovered the second chamber in the south side of the perimeter wall. Although it too had been plundered, the chamber originally contained the embalmed internal organs of the pharaoh, emblematic of his fertility and his protection of Lower Egypt. Grave robbers did not steal the handsome blue **faïence** wall decorations, which are now all that remains of the interior. These tiles are set into horizontal and vertical stone members to represent rush matting between wooden slats attached to larger wooden supports. On one wall is a relief carving depicting Djoser running the Heb-Sed race. Wearing the white crown of Upper Egypt, Djoser is portrayed in the manner peculiar to Egyptian art, with head, legs, and feet shown in profile and the torso shown frontally. In this one view Egyptian artists captured the essential features of the human body with great exactitude, even though the pose is not a "realistic" or natural one.

From its beginnings at Saqqara, the evolution of what we now think of as the "true" pyramid proceeds through at least three major projects before its culmination in the Fourth-Dynasty tombs at Giza, outside Cairo (Fig. 1.22). All three of these developmental pyramids were built or modified for one of the first pharaohs of the Fourth Dynasty, Sneferu (2575–2551 BCE), whose cult remained active for over 2000 years after his death. At Meidum, six miles south of Saqqara, Sneferu added an outer layer to the pyramid that may have been begun for Huni, the last pharaoh of the Third Dynasty. It began with a stepped core of seven stages, which was transformed into a true pyramid with the addition of two overbuildings. As the third and final outer casing of limestone was being installed, there is evidence that the upper portions of the work collapsed because the pyramid's stonework was insufficiently supported, given the relatively steep angle of inclination (51° 50′ 35″). Had it been completed as planned, the pyramid would have reached nearly 302 feet in height. As it stands, with its stepped core rising above the rubble, it has been given the descriptive name of an "onion" pyramid. Entrance was through a sloping corridor opening off the north side, descending below ground, and then rising a short distance vertically to the burial chamber at the center of the pyramid's base. Corbeled construction in the vault of this chamber marks the first time this technique was employed in stone by the Egyptians, although it had been used earlier in brick.

The collapse of the Meidum pyramid had an impact on another of Sneferu's pyramids under construction at the same time at Dahshur, about twenty-eight miles south of Meidum. There, a partially finished structure was transformed to create the so-called "bent" pyramid that began with a 616-foot-square base and sides inclined at 54° 27′ 44″. Observing the collapse at Meidum, the builders at Dahshur changed to a lower inclination angle of 41° 22′ when the pyramid was half-built. Eventually reaching a height of 344 feet, the bent pyramid gains added stability from its firm limestone foundation and core, large stone casing blocks that are slightly inclined to the center, and the reduced angle of inclination. These stabilizing design features were incorporated from the beginning in the third pyramid of Sneferu, the north or "red" pyramid, also at Dahshur. (The color name derives from oxidation of the limestone used for its core, exposed after stone scavengers

1.23 Pyramids, Giza, Egypt, ca. 2550–2460 BCE.
Khufu's pyramid is the farthest back, to the right of Khafre's pyramid (distinguished by the remnant of outer casing stones at its peak). In front of Khafre's pyramid is that of Menkaure, while three much smaller pyramids in the foreground belonged to queens of Menkaure.

removed the white limestone casing.) From a base 722 feet square, the north pyramid rises at a constant 43° 22′ angle to its apex 344 feet above the ground. Its profile is thus relatively low, a testimony to the conservative attitudes of its designers.

Fourth-Dynasty Pyramids at Giza

The trio of large pyramids at Giza (2550–2460 BCE) are the work of Sneferu's descendants, the Fourth-Dynasty pharaohs known as Khufu, Khafre, and Menkaure (or Cheops, Chephren, and Mycerinus in Greek transliteration) (Figs. 1.23–1.24). The largest pyramid, that of Khufu, who reigned 2551–2528 BCE, was built first and planned from the start to be a true pyramid of unprecedented proportions. The 755-by-755-foot base covers over thirteen acres; the sides rise at an angle of 51° 50′ 40″ to an apex at 481 feet. Most of the stone in the pyramid is limestone, although the large pharaoh's chamber in the center is made of granite. Nothing built in stone before or since has rivaled the Great Pyramid of Khufu for sheer size.

Khufu's pyramid is not completely solid, however. Three burial chambers are built within it, one excavated out of foundation bedrock and the other two constructed as the stone mountain was erected. Although these were once thought to represent changes made in design as work progressed, they are now interpreted as deliberate accommodations. The roughly finished lowest chamber is thought to represent the underworld. The middle chamber, the

Mastaba tombs

Pyramid of Khufu (Cheops)

Mortuary temple

Causeway to the valley temple

Pyramid of Khafre (Chephren)

Sphinx

Valley temple with causeway
to mortuary temple

Pyramid of Menkaure (Mycerinus)

Small pyramids for queens of Menkaure

1.24 **Site plan of the pyramids, Giza, Egypt, ca. 2550–2460 BCE.** Khufu's pyramid in particular has a large number of subsidiary tombs located to the west of it, including smaller pyramids and mastabas for members of the court. Khufu's pyramid has the best preserved valley temple and causeway. Note the position of the Sphinx to the north of the causeway leading to Khafre's pyramid.

so-called Queen's Chamber, probably contained an over-lifesized statue of Khufu and served as his spirit chamber, or serdab. The top, or King's Chamber, beautifully constructed of red granite, contains a granite sarcophagus in which Khufu was in fact buried. To transfer the tremendous weight of the pyramid around the ceiling of the King's Chamber, eleven pairs of granite beams were set as a gabled brace or saddle roof extending into the mass of the pyramid above the chamber. Five massive sets of horizontal granite slabs form relieving chambers stacked between the saddle roof and the flat ceiling of the crypt as a means of reducing weight and pressure from above. The corbeled gallery leading to this chamber is also a construction marvel, rising twenty-six feet in height, a splendid contrast to a four-foot-high ascending passage to which it connects.

Both the King's and Queen's chambers have pairs of small shafts angling upward through the mass of the pyramid that may have been intended for ventilation. Their particular orientation implies connection to the pole star (north side) and Orion (south side), although the precise function and symbolic meaning of these ventilation shafts remain unclear.

Next in sequence of construction (and only slightly smaller in size) is the pyramid of Khafre, a son of Khufu, who reigned 2520–2494 BCE. Khafre's pyramid is 705 feet square at the base and rises at an angle of 53° 20′ to an ultimate elevation of 471 feet. In many photographs of the Giza pyramids, this one seems the tallest of the three, but this is only because it stands on higher ground than that of Khufu. Khafre's monument is readily distinguished by the substantial fragment of the original smooth limestone

casing that survives at the apex. On the inside there is a single tomb chamber in the center of the pyramid at the base level. A passageway in the north side provides access to the room, which, like all the tomb chambers in pyramids, was pillaged in ancient times.

The smallest of the Giza trio of major pyramids belonged to Menkaure, a son of Khafre who reigned 2490–2472 BCE. Containing less than one-tenth of the amount of stone of Khufu's pyramid, Menkaure's tomb seems to have been erected hurriedly and with less care than those of his predecessors. We know that it was not finished before Menkaure died. Its dimensions—335 by 343 feet at the base, a slope of 51° 20′ 25″, and 213 feet high—maintain the general proportions established by the neighboring tombs. Menkaure's successor, Shepseskaf, the last pharaoh in the Fourth Dynasty, chose not to have a pyramid burial, and although pyramids continued to be built by later rulers, the quality and scale of the Giza trio were never exceeded.

Associated with each of the pyramids were ancillary temples that are now largely ruins. Alongside the Nile was a lower or valley temple, where the boat bearing the pharaoh's body would land to disembark its royal cargo. The valley temple may have been the place where the process of mummification took place, although the evidence is not entirely clear on this point. A causeway connected this valley temple to the upper or mortuary temple at the base of the pyramid itself. Here the corpse would receive a final ritual cleansing prior to entombment.

Of all the Giza valley temples, the lower temple of Khafre remains in the best state of preservation. Essentially square in plan, with thick limestone walls encased in red granite, its central hall is an inverted T-shape. Red granite **piers** supported a roof with a **clerestory**; the windows were set so that sunlight coming through them illuminated the twenty-three statues of the pharaoh placed around the edges of the wall. Two levels of narrow storage rooms extended into the solid wall mass. Today the temple stands without a roof or its outer stone facing beside the **Sphinx**, a man-headed lion 187 feet long and sixty-six feet high, carved in situ out of a natural rock ledge (Fig. 1.25). (It has long been presumed that the head on the Sphinx was a likeness of Khafre, but this cannot be proven. Recent speculation that the Sphinx may be significantly older than the pyramids is not generally accepted by Egyptologists.) Khafre's mortuary temple at the base of the pyramid is connected to the valley temple by a causeway running at an oblique angle to the river. The mortuary temple is rectangular in plan, with a series of axially disposed interior spaces. Its limestone structure was probably cased with a finer material, and the floor was alabaster. At the center of the temple was a large courtyard surrounded by enormous pillars, in front of which stood twelve large statues of the pharaoh.

Pyramids, especially the impressive Giza group, have long provoked two questions: How could ancient peoples, working with simple technologies, have built such enormous structures, and why would they have built them? The answer to the first question can be reasonably surmised, although this is still an area of study. Even though the Egyptians lacked metals harder than copper and made no use of the wheel for transport, they were not primitive. Their knowledge of surveying, necessary for reestablishing field boundaries after the annual flood, enabled them to lay out the pyramid's base accurately and to orient the square plan to the cardinal directions. Khufu's pyramid deviates only five and a half minutes of arc from true north; its summit is only one foot off the center of the base; and there is only an eight-inch error in the length of one side of the base. The absence of wheeled vehicles was not a serious handicap, as much of the stone transport would have been made over water or across sand, where wheels would have provided no real advantage over the boats and sledges actually used. Quarrying was accomplished with metal saws for the softer limestones or sandstones, and by repeatedly pounding balls of very hard rock (dolerite) along seams in the harder stones such as granite. The finishing of cut surfaces could be accomplished with stone hammers, chisels, axes, and sand or grindstones. By any method, quarry work was tedious, and it was probably assigned to prisoners or conscripts. Much of the limestone in the core of the Giza pyramids was quarried on-site. Finer display stone and granite was transported from more distant locations.

Construction of the pyramids was probably done by large teams of laborers during the flood season when agricultural work was impossible. The muscles of men supplied the force to haul blocks into place. Studies of ruined or incomplete pyramids have revealed that there was no single construction method used; least of all is

1.25 Khafre's pyramid and the Sphinx, Giza, Egypt, ca. 2550–2460 BCE.
Remains of the entrance to Khafre's valley temple are visible to the left.

known about the most complete monuments, the Giza trio, because their interiors cannot be inspected closely. In some cases, ramps were erected along with the rising masonry mountain to provide an inclined plane for dragging stone on sledges. It is also possible that the rising stepped core of the Giza pyramids served as a construction staircase for workers pulling and leveraging the blocks onto the upper levels, as the volume of material needed for additional ramps on these enormous buildings and the difficulty of hauling stone around corners would make inclined planes impractical. While the number of men and length of time required to see a major pyramid through to completion are still subject to debate, the Egyptians' ability to organize labor forces and quarrymen in seasonal building campaigns remains a fact and a tribute to the abilities of their engineers.

The question of why the pyramids were built has inspired both serious inquiry and speculative nonsense. Theories ranging from embodiments of standard measures (as defined in English units) to apocalyptic predictions of the end of the world have been offered to explain the dimensional configuration of Khufu's pyramid, but Egyptologists are convinced that the pyramids were first and foremost tombs for the pharaohs. Why people should devote so much effort to what we might regard as a fundamentally useless project is answerable only within the context of the Egyptian worldview. Perhaps no other society before or since has invested so much time and labor to ensure survival after death for its most important personages. Virtually all Egyptian art and architecture was very practical, intended to assist one's passage to the next world and ensure comfort and pleasant living upon arrival. While the greatest attention was lavished on the setting for the pharaoh's afterlife, all Egyptians believed in their particular view of eternal life and so all had a stake in the

1.26 (above) Reconstruction and plan of Mentuhotep's mortuary temple, Deir-el-Bahari, Egypt, ca. 2061–2010 BCE. This Middle-Kingdom temple represents an interesting synthesis of an axial temple, hypostyle hall, and burial chamber into a single composition. Its ramps and stepped terraces would be echoed in the New-Kingdom temple of Hatshepsut built about 400 years later on an adjoining site.

1.27 Plan and section of rock-cut tombs, Beni-Hasan, Egypt, ca. 2000–1900 BCE.
Even when working amorphous rock, the builders chose to replicate rectangular geometries and to carve details reflecting the wooden and plastered reed construction that doubtless characterized houses. The lower of the two plans corresponds to the section.

creation of an architecture of death and rebirth, from the modest tombs of the poor to the monumental edifices of the rulers.

The Middle Kingdom (Eleventh–Thirteenth Dynasties, ca. 2040–1640 BCE)

The first eight Egyptian dynasties gave way to a period of upheaval when local feudal lords upset the unity achieved by Menes. This era of interregional strife is designated the First Intermediate period, and it was followed by a second phase of centralized government called the Middle Kingdom. During this period, the royal capital was relocated from Memphis to Thebes, and the pharaoh's position was more that of a feudal lord over local vassals than an absolute and divine ruler in the Old-Kingdom tradition. Royal tombs were still of major architectural importance, but Middle-Kingdom tombs generally neither endured nor intimidated grave robbers.

The tomb of Mentuhotep II at Deir-el-Bahari (ca. 2061–2010 BCE) (Fig. 1.26) is an exceptional work of architectural innovation, combining temple and tomb chamber in a single composition. The complex, approached by an axial route from the Nile, had two levels of colonnaded terraces surrounding a masonry mass, long thought to have been a pyramid but more recently interpreted as a flat-roofed hall. (The building is a ruin today, so one cannot be sure of the initial design. The case for a flat-roofed hall is based on there being insufficient foundations to support even a modest pyramid.) The central **axis** continues through layers of square columns, through the flat-roofed hall, through a courtyard, and through a forest of columns until reaching Mentuhotep's actual burial vault carved in the rock cliff. The two levels of columns seen upon approach are dramatized by the contrast of their sunlit shafts with the shadowed recesses behind and anticipate Greek temples with their surrounding **colonnades**. Mentuhotep's tomb would serve as a prototype for the more elaborate adjoining funerary complex built by the New-Kingdom pharaoh Hatshepsut.

More typical of Middle-Kingdom tombs are those at Beni-Hasan, which are cut into rock cliffs and provided with sheltering **porticoes** (Fig. 1.27). Reflecting the political importance of their builders, these tombs were constructed for minor nobles and court officials, who evidently enjoyed considerable influence and wealth. Most of the architectural character was created by excavation, and the builders replicated spaces and details associated with ordinary dwellings, that is, wooden and plastered reed structures with slightly arched roofs composed of mats laid on a frame.

The New Kingdom (Eighteenth–Twentieth Dynasties, ca. 1550–1070 BCE)

The Middle Kingdom was terminated by the arrival of the Hyksos, shepherd-kings who may have come from Asia. Whatever their origins, the Hyksos were the first successful invaders of Egypt in centuries, and they ruled for about 100 years in what is known as the Second Intermediate period. They introduced metallurgy, the two-person chariot, new deities, and new weapons to Egyptian culture, but their rule produced no lasting artistic innovations. With the expulsion of the Hyksos came the New Kingdom, which was characterized by an invigorated dynastic line of pharaohs and an increasingly powerful hereditary priesthood who brought Egypt to new heights of political and cultural brilliance.

The Eighteenth Dynasty, the first of the New Kingdom, continued the Middle-Kingdom tradition of burial in rock-cut tombs, going a stage further by eliminating all

1.28 Mortuary temple of Queen Hatshepsut, Deir-el-Bahari, Egypt, ca. 1473–1458 BCE.
In its day, this great temple, with planted terraces and dignified carved colonnades framed by the cliff face, must have been a restful oasis in the dry landscape, a fitting monument to the peaceful reign of Hatshepsut, one of the rare female rulers in antiquity.

1.29 View and plan of Hatshepsut's mortuary temple, Deir-el-Bahari, Egypt, ca. 1473–1458 BCE.
To thwart thieves, New-Kingdom pharaohs arranged for their bodies to be buried in concealed tombs in the Valley of the Kings (behind these cliffs), where priests guarded against robbers. Mentuhotep's earlier tomb is seen just beyond Hatshepsut's monument.

suggestions of monumentality. It had escaped no one's notice that all the dynastic tombs had been successfully penetrated by grave robbers. The Giza pyramids were probably plundered during the First Intermediate period. To preserve the worldly remains of the pharaoh and thwart the thieves, Eighteenth-Dynasty builders relied on concealment and improved policing of the royal necropolis. New-Kingdom pharaohs were interred secretly in the desert wilderness beyond Deir-el-Bahari, a region known as the Valley of the Kings, where very modest chambers were hewn out of the cliffs, and the entrances were hidden by dirt and sand. Spiritual nourishment for the deceased was provided at increasingly elaborate separately erected funerary temples.

Among the most splendid of the Eighteenth-Dynasty temples is the funerary complex of Queen Hatshepsut (1473–1458 BCE) at Deir-el-Bahari (Fig. 1.28), notable both for its architecture and for the fact that its patron was a woman. Succession to the throne passed through the female line, but the pharaoh was almost always male. Hatshepsut was the daughter of Thutmose I, and she married her half-brother, who became Pharaoh Thutmose II. During his reign she relegated him to a subsidiary role, and after his death she ruled independently, though ostensibly as regent for Thutmose II's son by a concubine, Thutmose III. Her court favorite was a commoner, Senmut, who was also responsible (perhaps as architect) for her funerary temple. Hatshepsut was buried on the other side of the mountain range in the Valley of the Kings, so the temple complex was a mortuary chapel dedicated to the god Amun, the sun god with whom the pharaoh was associated. Ramps lead up from the valley to three broad terraces, each defined by colonnades, which also serve as retaining walls for the next level (Fig. 1.29). The overall design was doubtless inspired by the neighboring temple of Mentuhotep, although Hatshepsut's temple is considerably larger and grander. Columns in the north colonnade of the second terrace are faceted in a manner suggesting the **flutes** of later **Doric** columns (Fig. 1.30). Relief carvings and wall paintings within the sanctuary spaces and in the great hall depict Hatshepsut's divine birth as the child of Amun and the activities of her peaceful reign, including trading expeditions to Punt (perhaps the Somali coast) bearing gold, ivory, baboons, and botanical specimens. Hatshepsut herself is usually depicted as a man, sometimes as the god Osiris, wearing the apron and headdress of a pharaoh.

Today they are sand-covered and barren, but in the Eighteenth Dynasty the terraces of Hatshepsut's temple

1.30 Upper colonnade (detail), Hatshepsut's mortuary temple, Deir-el-Bahari, Egypt, ca. 1473–1458 BCE.
Behind the rectangular piers are cylindrical columns with fluting that has led to their being called proto-Doric. Certainly they are evidence of Egyptian precedent for what in Greek hands would become an aspect of the orders of architecture.

1.31 Plan of the Great Temple of Amun, Karnak, Egypt, begun ca. 1550 BCE.
This temple is celebrated more for its sheer size than for its architectural coherence. Dedicated to the sun god Amun, whose priesthood was powerful during the New Kingdom, the temple maintained a strong sense of axiality and monumental procession through all its additions.

First court
Pylon II
Hypostyle hall
Pylon III
Temple of Ptah
Pylon IV
1.33
Avenue of ram-headed sphinxes
Pylon I
Festival temple of Thutmose III
Temple of Ramesses III
Temple of Khonsu
Sacred lake
N
Festival hall of Amenophis II
0   250 m
0   750 ft

were embellished with incense trees planted in earth-filled pits to create a garden for Amun's promenades. Buried irrigation pipes supplied water to sustain the plants, and priests placed tributes to the god in the shade beneath the branches. The entire setting of the temple, from the axial-ramp approach to the termination of the processional way at a false door painted on the wall of the final rock-hewn sanctuary, is a masterly blending of architecture into a dramatic landscape including rugged cliff faces. Although Hatshepsut reigned and died peacefully, her successors did everything possible to eradicate her memory, erasing her name from inscriptions, smashing almost all of her sculptural representations, and desecrating the burial site of Senmut.

In the course of the Eighteenth Dynasty, temple complexes built to honor both gods and pharaohs became more extensive and elaborate, aided by the establishment of Amun as the main "state" god and the increased power and influence of his priesthood. Successive rulers would add new portions or renovate older temples, creating designs whose chief attribute was overbearing grandeur, not coherence or esthetic delight. The temple at Karnak,

across the Nile from Deir-el-Bahari, is an example of this process (Fig. 1.31). Begun about 1550 BCE, it was enlarged by Thutmose I, enriched by obelisks given by his daughter, Hatshepsut, and again expanded with a hypostyle jubilee festival hall constructed by Thutmose III for his own glorification. Yet another hypostyle hall, the largest of all, was built by Ramesses II.

Hypostyle halls are sizeable chambers created by rows of large columns placed closely together. The tight spacing was necessary to support the stone lintels of the roof, while the large column diameter reflected the substantial height of the stone cylinders. The net effect was a dimly lit interior without a sense of spatial expanse. Daylight admitted through slits in the stone clerestory grilles filtered through the incense smoke and the upper volume of the hypostyle columns to create a sense of mystery, the desired effect for religious ritual. The temple was the habitation of the god, who was sheltered, clothed, and fed by the priests, by now a powerful and largely hereditary group. Each day the priests performed purification rites in the sacred lake within the temple precinct, dressed the statue of the deity in rich garments, and presented it offerings at the evening ritual.

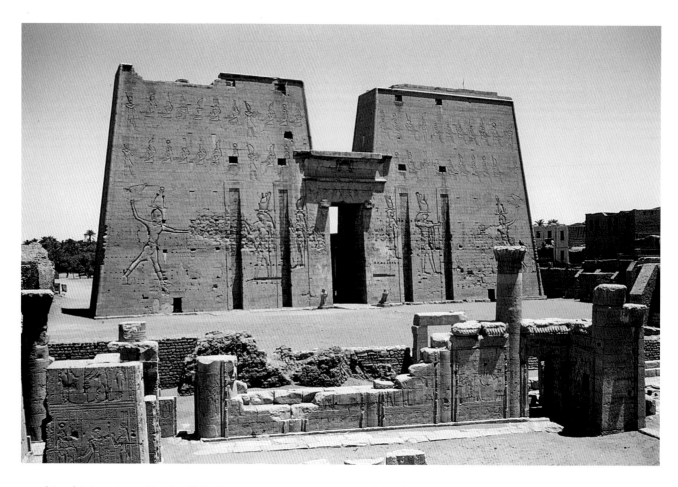

1.32 (above) Pylon gateway, Temple of Edfu, Egypt, 237–57 BCE. While this pylon dates from the Ptolomaic period after Alexander the Great conquered Egypt, it is similar in form and purpose to those at Karnak. Such a spatial threshold signified the increasing sacredness of the space beyond. The four vertical slots once held obelisks.

1.33 (below) First court, Great Temple of Amun, Karnak, Egypt, begun ca. 1550 BCE. Massive columns and colossal statues of Ramesses II define the axial path to the second pylon gate, built by Sethos I (1306–1290).

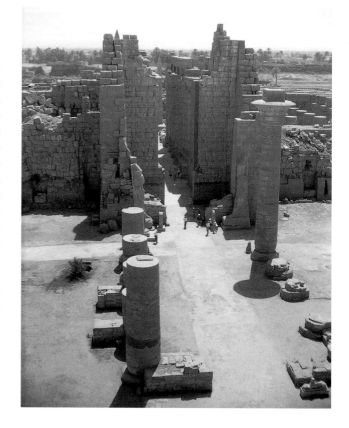

They carried small statues in processions, and placed others in the sun for rejuvenation in special festivals, such as those marking the beginning of the New Year. Monumental masonry entrance gates or **pylons** (Fig. 1.32) lined processional routes to represent the eastern mountains of Egypt through which the divine early-morning sunlight emanated. Despite their rambling plans and numerous additions, New-Kingdom temples maintained axial circulation spaces for the penetration of solar rays and the movement of priestly processions (Fig. 1.33). The pylon gates were not only symbols of the entrance through which the sun was reborn each day, but also of the gates to the underworld through which the eternal spirit must pass.

Five generations after Hatshepsut, the pharaoh Amenophis IV (1353–1335 BCE) made a major break with Egyptian religious tradition by disavowing the multitudes of deities and instituting a monotheistic religion devoted to the sun disc Aten. Changing his name to Akhenaten, which means "all is well with Aten," Amenophis abandoned the old capital at Thebes about 1350 BCE to establish a new capital 300 miles to the north at Akhetaten (the modern Tell-el-Amarna). Judging from incomplete

1.34 Plan of the central section, Akhetaten (Tell-el-Amarna), Egypt, ca. 1350 BCE.
This was the new capital city of the pharaoh Akhenaten, located away from traditional religious centers in an effort to break the power of the established Egyptian priesthood. Rites for the sun disc Aten were celebrated in temples containing large open courtyards, lit directly by the sun's beneficent rays.

Great Temple

King's House

Great Palace

Small Temple

N

0   500 m

0   1500 ft

excavations of its ruins, Akhetaten was a linear town nearly seven miles long, bounded on the west by the Nile and on the east by mountains, and lacking a consistent overall plan. Transportation was facilitated by the waterway, and a river road linked the various residential sections (Fig. 1.34). Temples had altars set in open courtyards, and there were no segregated areas for the priest class. Private houses of the wealthy were commodious, walled off from public view, with rooms grouped around open courts with tree-planted gardens. Thick mud-brick walls moderated the extremes of heat and cold. No wall surrounded the city, protection being provided by freestanding guardhouses.

CONCLUSIONS ABOUT ARCHITECTURAL IDEAS

Throughout this chapter, you have seen certain fundamental architectural ideas appear that will be consistently used during every era in every geographical location covered by this text. These ideas have to do with such issues as demarcation, orientation, sequential movement, and surface articulation. A site like Newgrange encompasses all of these, as it marks a significant spot, is aligned with cosmic events, involves a path (in this case from profane to sacred space), and includes ornament. The ziggurats and pyramid complexes exploited open terrain where the horizon was inescapable. Stepped, then true pyramids became manmade vertical foils for the natural horizontal, and in Egypt the pyramids were eventually superseded as vertical markers by the obelisk. Within both the ziggurat and pyramid environments, participants moved along an axis, toward a terminus, with architectural incidents like gateways providing a rhythm and signaling changes in spatial significance. The principles remained the same at both Middle and New Kingdom funerary complexes, where giant columns emerged as interior architectural features. While the pyramids exhibit a monolithic skin, the surfaces of ziggurats were articulated by means of brick bands and polychromatic glazes. At the funerary temple complexes of Mentuhotep and Hatshepsut, wall articulation evolved to the level of proto-columns, and columns will be the principal elements in the classical architectural language of the ancient Greeks and Romans discussed in coming chapters.

S urely then," wrote the Greek philosopher Plato in *The Republic* (360 BCE), "to him who has an eye to see, there can be no fairer spectacle than that of a man who combines the possession of moral beauty in his soul with outward beauty of form, corresponding and harmonizing with the former, because the same great pattern enters into both." Plato was expressing a commonly held view in ancient Greece: that inward conditions could be expressed through outward appearances and so that moral and ethical matters were intrinsically related to art.

A fundamental means by which the Greeks attempted to communicate this unified view of the world was through proportional relationships. This effort is illustrated by a perhaps apocryphal story involving the Greek mathematician Pythagoras. As the story goes, he was walking past a blacksmith shop as the sounds of hammer to metal came from within. Listening to the tonalities and atonalities, he posed a question: could musical harmonies somehow have a mathematical basis? In order to form an answer, he experimented with the strings of a lyre and discovered that pleasing combinations resulted when two strings with their lengths related by simple ratios, such as 1:1, 1:2, 2:3, 3:4, and 4:5, were simultaneously struck. Here, in the mind of a mathematician, was a glimpse into the very ordering of the cosmos, and it was a short step from audible musical harmonies to dimensions and their ratios or proportions in the visual world.

While we may not accept this condition as an absolute today, we can first say without doubt that beauty mattered to the ancient Greeks and that their culture reached a consensus about it; witness, for instance, the "family resemblance" of so much Greek sculpture. Second, by extending this notion to architecture, we can see that the outward beauty of a Greek building was largely derived from the dimensions of its parts and their relationships to one another. Third, we can appreciate that when proportional beauty was achieved, it yielded in the Greek mind a kind of microscopic view into the inner workings of the cosmos. Heady stuff! Fourth and finally, we can also observe that the Greeks extended such philosophical thinking to the workings of their society. If proper proportioning

applied to outer physical beauty, and it also applied to inner moral beauty, this meant that the proper behavior of a Greek citizen (a freeborn male) demanded proper proportioning (or perhaps balance is the better term) in the actions of his life. That is, the good citizen was certainly not to become one of those specialists (like a stonemason or even an architect) made possible by urbanization, but was to participate fully and proportionally in the life of the **polis**, or city-state.

And so we can go full circle. The health of the polis demanded balanced lives from its citizens; this balanced life was encoded into the very fabric of ancient Greek temples through proper mathematical proportions and, in turn, these buildings reminded citizens of their proper moral and ethical behavior. The Greek temples became great billboards communicating and reinforcing commonly held values and reflecting the culture's greatest accomplishments and highest aspirations. With this in mind, we can begin our study of Greek architecture by turning first to those Aegean civilizations that preceded classical Greece.

THE AEGEAN CULTURES

The Aegean Sea, bounded by the peninsula of Greece on the west, the mountains of Macedonia on the north, and the coast of Anatolia on the east, is studded with numerous islands. To the south is the island of Crete. By the beginning of the second millennium BCE (about the time of the Middle Kingdom in Egypt), the seafaring people of this region had learned how to exploit natural

⤎┈┈

North entrance of the palace, Knossos, Crete, ca. 1700–1380 BCE.
This section has been partially restored, including the unusual Minoan columns with bulbous capitals and downward-tapering shafts.

Chronology

Minoan civilization	ca. 3000–1380 BCE
Bronze Age in the Aegean	ca. 2000–750 BCE
Mycenaean civilization	1600–1100 BCE
Trojan War	ca. 1250 BCE
Iliad and *Odyssey* assume final form	8th century BCE
Archaic Greek period	700–500 BCE
Classical Greek period	479–323 BCE
Pericles comes to power in Athens	458 BCE
Construction of the Parthenon	448–432 BCE
Life of Plato	ca. 427–347 BCE
Conquests of Alexander the Great	333–323 BCE

resources—timber, stone, metallic ores, clay for pottery—to produce distinctive artifacts. With these, in addition to other agricultural products, they engaged in trade with Egypt and settlements along the eastern Mediterranean, where they constructed small fortified communities and agricultural villages on islands and along the coast.

An examination of Aegean artifacts suggests strong influence from Mesopotamia as well as contact with Egypt. Early Cretans worshiped nature deities associated with mountains, trees, and animals (most notably snakes), as well as flowers, including lilies and poppies. Since there are no snakes on Crete, the snake cult appears to be an imported practice, probably derived from the Sumerian water god Ea, whose attributes included creativity, wisdom, magic, and slyness. Bull-baiting was a sport of the Sumerians, and bull-jumping seems to have become a ritual game in Crete. Lions were associated with royal symbolism in both Egypt and Mesopotamia, and lion images also came to be used in fortified royal settlements on the Greek mainland. Egyptian artifacts from the Eighteenth Dynasty have been retrieved from the harbor at Kairatos, Crete, and 1300 pieces of Aegean pottery dating from 1370 to 1350 BCE have been excavated from the rubbish heaps of Akhetaten.

Historians recognize two civilizations in the Aegean during the second millennium: that of the Minoans, based on Crete, and that of the Mycenaeans, established at several sites on the mainland of Greece. They share some artistic and cultural traits, including a reliance on trade with other communities in Egypt, Mesopotamia, Asia Minor, and Cyprus. Both produced luxury goods that were traded extensively around the eastern Mediterranean—Minoan envoys bearing characteristic pottery from Crete are included in Egyptian wall paintings from the reign of Queen Hatshepsut—and Mycenaean sites were involved in the Trojan War (ca. 1250 BCE), chronicled by Homer in the *Iliad*. Both civilizations contributed to the cultural patrimony of classical Greece.

THE MINOANS

Most of what we know about the Minoan civilization comes from archaeologists, who are still making discoveries and reinterpreting older finds as a result of analysis with more sophisticated scientific tools. Not surprisingly, there is more than one theory related to the development and demise of the Minoans.

The civilization is named for Minos, which might be the name of an early king or simply the title (like pharaoh) that denoted a ruler. The later Greeks created legends associated with King Minos and his palace and **labyrinth** at Knossos, where the fearsome Minotaur, half-man and half-bull, that ate youths and maidens lived. Although numerous Minoan sites have been excavated on Crete, Knossos remains the largest and best known. Four thousand years

of Neolithic settlements lie under this Minoan site, which began in about 1900 BCE as a series of detached structures erected around a large rectangular court. When these were destroyed by a major earthquake in about 1700 BCE, the complex was rebuilt in a unified scheme on multiple levels, with ritual or ceremonial rooms, storage areas, and living accommodation connected by long corridors and staircases built around light-wells, open cores that admit sunlight to the lower levels. The courtyard continued as the primary element in the composition. Tablets inscribed in Linear A, a script that has still not been deciphered, appear in the archaeological record in about 1600 BCE. In about 1450 BCE, Knossos and all other Minoan palaces on Crete were destroyed, but Knossos alone was rebuilt. Traces of Mycenaean cultural influences, including writing in the script known as Linear B, an early form of Greek, are found in the rebuilt palace, suggesting either collusion or a forced alliance between Mycenaeans and the Cretans at Knossos. The final destruction of the site, this time by fire, came in about 1380 BCE.

Understanding the extensive ruins at Knossos is no easy task (Fig. 2.1). Sir Arthur Evans started excavations at the ceremonial center in 1900 CE. Archaeological investigation continues on the site today, and the associated town has yet to be unearthed. Evans was confident that he had found the palace of the legendary King Minos, but his chronology and efforts at reconstruction are now regarded as flawed and a recent assessment suggests that what Evans found was actually a sacred center. The function of the building may in fact have changed from a temple to a palace in its final years, but **frescoes** depicting priestesses and celebrants suggest the continuing centrality of religious practice. The charred remains of the final buildings present ambiguous evidence at best. While parts of the lower levels of the building were built in **ashlar** masonry, most of the upper floors were supported on walls built of rubble contained within squared timbers, wooden columns, and large wooden beams, the combustible portions of which were consumed in the conflagration. Evans relied on impressions of the **bases** and capitals where these touched stone to reconstruct the characteristic Minoan column, a downward-tapering shaft with a bulbous **torus** ring and **abacus** block capital (see page 34). (The columns on-site today are concrete.) On the basis of what he found, Evans also reconstructed major ceremonial rooms and several light-wells (Figs. 2.2–2.3).

Even after considerable study, however, the function of the whole complex is a matter of scholarly deliberation. Storerooms containing pottery jars for wine, oil, olives, and grain are unmistakable, but the function of other sections of the building, where several stages of construction can be detected, is still conjectural. The appearance and uses of the upper floors we cannot know, so photographs of the site today can only begin to suggest the grandeur that must have characterized the whole. When one realizes that the mainland Greeks of this period were living in far

Theater area

Stairs to
lustral basin

North entrance

p. 34

West gateway

Storage rooms

Grand stair created
by Sir Arthur Evans

Throne
Room

2.3

Lustral basin

Hall of the
Double Axes

Central Court

Bath

Queen's Megaron

Processional corridor

Upper-level plan
(much of it conjectural and
with errant reconstruction)

0   50 m
0   150 ft

Ground-level plan

2.1 Plan of the palace, Knossos, Crete, ca. 1700–1380 BCE.
The plan is organized around an open rectangular courtyard, off which major reception rooms open. As only the ground level of this three- or four-story building survived destruction, many aspects of its design are conjectural. The grand stair and associated axial sequence were an unfortunate Sir Arthur Evans creation. This portion of the palace is now being restored to its pre-Evans condition.

2.2 Restored light-well, Knossos, Crete, ca. 1700–1380 BCE.
Located on the upper story, this light-well is located directly above the Throne Room (see Fig. 2.3). The fresco shown here is a restoration.

simpler buildings, it is possible that they preserved memories of the site in the legend of King Minos, using the term "labyrinth" to describe the large, rambling, and complicated plan that is the complex at Knossos. (Although the etymology of the word "labyrinth" is uncertain, the equivalent Egyptian term was applied to an enormous mortuary temple built during the Middle Kingdom for Amenemhet III [1844–1797 BCE] at Hawara.)

So far as we know, Knossos was unfortified. The palace/temple complex sat on a hill overlooking the harbor. Nearly four acres of buildings surround a central courtyard measuring 174 by 87 feet. In the three-story western wing,

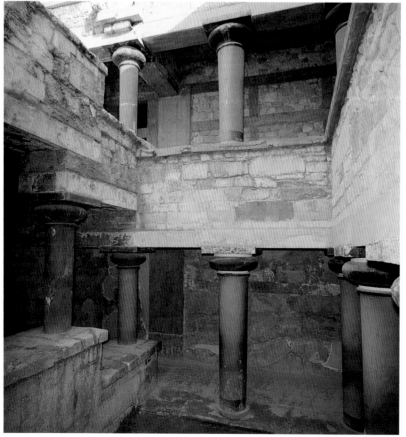

2.3 Throne Room, Knossos, Crete, ca. 1700–1380 BCE.
Named for the elaborate "throne," this room is provided with bench seating along the adjacent walls. Frescoes show griffins in lush foliage. Since a lustral basin adjoins this room, it is possible the space was used for religious ritual rather than royal audiences.

2.4 Reconstructed light-well staircase, Knossos, ca. 1700–1380 BCE.
As major ceremonial rooms were located partially underground, stairs to reach them were constructed around open shafts to bring light and fresh air to lower levels. The original wooden columns and supporting beams were destroyed in the fire that consumed the palace about 1380 BCE.

which contained ceremonial spaces, there is none of the axiality characteristic of Egyptian architecture. Instead, visitors to the palace during its final years entered through the west propylaea, or gateway, then followed a corridor lined with frescoes depicting priestesses and celebrants bearing offerings, before turning left twice to approach the courtyard from the south. On the left (west) wall near the north end of the courtyard was the entrance to the antechamber of a **lustral-basin** (depressed pool) sanctuary called the throne room because of an elaborate alabaster seat found there. On a lower level, along the southern edge of the throne room, was a lustral basin, one of several found in the complex that are thought to have been used in initiation rituals. This basin, which is only about eighteen inches deep, is concealed by a low wall and a screen of Minoan columns. Cult statues and votive offerings indicate that the site was sacred to a female deity linked to the earth and fertility. Long rows of underground storage rooms occupy the western side of this palace wing, dug into the slope of the hillside, with tall ceramic containers for olive oil, grain, and wine still in position.

Buildings on the eastern side of the courtyard have been interpreted as being residential, although some of the suites may have functioned as textile workshops and others were definitely used as storage areas. Some rooms here had views out over the valley below. The primary entrance to this section was made through a grand staircase approached from the middle side of the central court and illuminated by an open light-well. The stair led down to the Hall of the Double Axes, from which a corridor connected to the room Evans dubbed the Queen's **Megaron**, a pleasant space decorated with frescoes that include rosettes and flying dolphins. Smaller rooms behind the megaron contained a bathtub and a water closet (toilet) connected to the palace's drain system. Standards of water supply and drainage at the complex were exceptional for the time. Terracotta water pipes carried clean water through a series of settling tanks and siphons to supply baths, and sanitary sewers carried off waste water from basins and water closets, although the tub in the so-called "queen's apartments" had to be emptied by bailing.

At the northwest corner of the complex was the oldest and deepest (six feet) lustral basin, made accessible by a staircase with light-well (Fig. 2.4). Beyond this ran a series of broad steps, set into a slight rise in the ground and connected to the palace proper by a ceremonial road. This area has been labeled as a theater, although its precise use, as with so much else at Knossos, remains unclear. It seems that the large central courtyard provided the setting for theatrical ritual, including perhaps ceremonial games involving acrobatic feats by young men and women performed on running bulls. Frescoes preserved on some palace walls illustrate these amusements or rituals.

The naturalistic portrayal of the young men and women in these frescoes creates the impression that the Minoans were an energetic and cheerful people who took delight in their own beauty and that of the natural world. In contrast to the stiffness and formality of Egyptian art, frescoes and carvings at Minoan sites seem relaxed and open, emphasizing movement. Women held positions of high status, an unprecedented situation among contemporary civilizations. There is, however, a great deal that is still not clearly understood. The language(s) recorded in Minoan pictographs and on Linear A tablets remain undeciphered; the significance of the double-headed ax widely found in Minoan art is also a puzzle; and it is not known whether the appearance of Mycenaean culture in the final phase of Knossos came as a result of invasion or peaceful assimilation.

THE MYCENAEANS

The Mycenaean civilization takes its name from Mycenae, the largest but not the only citadel in a trading society that appears to have been led by warrior-kings. Mycenaean settlements located on the mainland of Greece date back to about 1600 BCE. Graves from this period preserve a large number of golden objects as well as weapons of various sorts. Heinrich Schliemann, the nineteenth-century excavator of Mycenae, found golden masks, drinking vessels, and other treasure that convinced him he had found material related to the Trojan War. In fact, his finds pre-date the era of the Homeric tales by four centuries.

Mycenae reached its period of greatness after about 1450 BCE, perhaps invigorated by contact with the more sophisticated Minoan culture. In contrast to the seemingly undefended complex at Knossos, the citadel at Mycenae was built with a strong concern for defense. The city is situated on high ground, protected by mountains on the north and south and flanked by two ravines, allowing surveillance of a wide area down to the coast (Figs. 2.5–2.7). Fortifications erected in the fourteenth century BCE were expanded in about 1300 BCE to enclose the palace compound and an earlier grave circle. These walls are eighteen to twenty-four feet thick and up to forty feet high, constructed of boulders set in position with minimal shaping and no mortar, except for the sections immediately adjacent to the gates, where the stone has been cut into large blocks. The later Greeks thought this impressively scaled masonry to be the work of giants, the Cyclopes, hence the adjective **cyclopean** to describe its construction.

Principal entrance to Mycenae was made through the Lion Gate, which was added when the citadel was enlarged (Fig. 2.8). It was positioned so that the approaching visitor had to pass along an increasingly narrow passageway parallel to the enclosing wall, allowing defenders inside the settlement ample opportunity to attack hostile forces. The gateway is of considerable artistic interest. Single upright stones support a fourteen-ton lintel across the opening, above which is a corbeled arch. The space of the arch is filled by a triangular stone with relief sculpture of two lions

2.5 Ruins of Mycenae, ca. 1600–1250 BCE.
This fabled city was strategically situated to control major transportation routes in the vicinity. The enclosing wall is composed of roughly shaped boulders. Ruins of the palace can be seen at the high point of the site.

2.6 Site plan of Mycenae, ca. 1600–1250 BCE.
This incomplete plan shows areas that have been excavated. Notice how the fortifications' walls extend to provide additional protection at the Lion Gate and the secondary gate on the north side. The palace megaron, one of the largest rooms in the city, is located at the center.

2.7 Plan of Tiryns, ca. 1300 BCE.
The palace section is located on the southern end, where two megarons can be seen, and the northern extension enclosed the lower citadel. The entrance ramp along the eastern side passed through two fortified gates and between high walls that served as fighting platforms.

with their forefeet on an altar bearing a column of the tree cult. (Mesopotamia had a tradition of venerating trees.) The lions' heads are missing; they were carved separately and attached with dowels, the holes for which are still visible. Even in its damaged state, however, the Lion Gate verifies contact by its creators with the Minoan world, for the column of the tree cult is unmistakably the same as the columns used at Knossos. To the north stands a second, smaller gate of the same age as the Lion Gate but without sculpture. There are also inconspicuous back entrances or postern gates built to provide access to a cistern and to provide outlets in case of emergency.

Beyond the Lion Gate are the remains of shaft graves where Schliemann uncovered so much golden treasure. Originally these lay outside the citadel walls, but when the fortress was enlarged the grave circle was carefully incorporated into the fortified area. The administrative and ceremonial spaces that lay beyond exist only as ruins, but

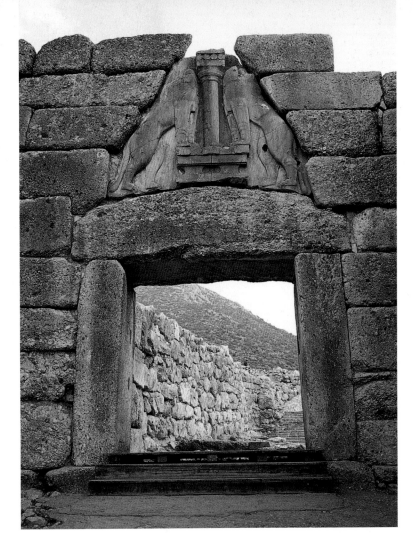

2.8 The Lion Gate, Mycenae, ca. 1300 BCE.
Notice that the carved lion figures flank a column of the tapered type seen at Knossos. The use of guardian beasts associated with royalty links Mycenae with both Hittite and Egyptian traditions.

2.9 Plan of and sections through the Treasury of Atreus, Mycenae, ca. 1330 BCE.
This corbeled tomb assumes the shape of a beehive. Its construction may be compared to the tomb at Er-Mané and the passage grave at Newgrange (see Figs. 1.2–1.3). The function of the side chamber is unknown, but it may have been used for burials.

from remaining foundations it appears that the palace at the highest elevation of the hill had many features derived from Crete, including a megaron as the major ceremonial space. Homer used this term to describe a large palace hall (hence Evans's use of the term at Knossos for the Queen's Megaron). In architectural usage, the word "megaron" is generally reserved to describe a simple rectangular space (**domos**) having solid long walls without openings and an entrance in the center of one short side, generally with an attached anteroom (**prodomos**) preceded by a court (see Fig. 2.12). It is an elementary house form still employed in Mediterranean countries, and the precursor of the classical temple. It has even been used by twentieth-century architects including Le Corbusier in his Citrohan houses (see Fig. 15.36). At Mycenae, the palace megaron is the largest room, roughly forty feet square. Bases for the four columns that supported the roof are still visible, as is the central hearth. This part of the palace was built in part on fill, supported by a retaining wall, and there is still a splendid view out over the valley from the court in front of the megaron. To the north, a smaller room with a stuccoed pool has been identified as a bathing room, which legend associates with the murder of Agamemnon on his triumphal return from Troy.

The citadel at Mycenae was surrounded by smaller settlements, perhaps comprised of extended family groups who lived in houses closely associated with the tombs of their ancestors. Nine of these tombs in circular

form (tholoi) have been found in the neighborhood of Mycenae: of these, the largest and best preserved is the **tholos**, or beehive tomb, commonly called the Treasury of Atreus (ca. 1330 BCE) (Figs. 2.9–2.11). It is a corbeled stone chamber rising forty-four feet in thirty-three horizontal courses from a circular plan forty-eight feet in diameter, with a small chamber to the right of the entrance. All the stonework, except for the stone-walled dromos, or entranceway, is covered by an earthen mound, whose

2.10 Façade and dromos of the Treasury of Atreus, Mycenae, ca. 1330 BCE.
This axial view shows the stone-walled dromos and the triangular corbeled relieving arch that diverts weight away from the massive lintel stone. Ornamentation and paint that originally decorated the exterior have disappeared.

2.11 Interior of the Treasury of Atreus, Mycenae, ca. 1330 BCE.
Although the interior space is relatively large, it is also dark, deriving its light only from the open doorway and triangular transom of the corbeled arch above it. The even courses of ashlar, or shaped, stones can be compared to the irregular cyclopean stones used elsewhere at Mycenae.

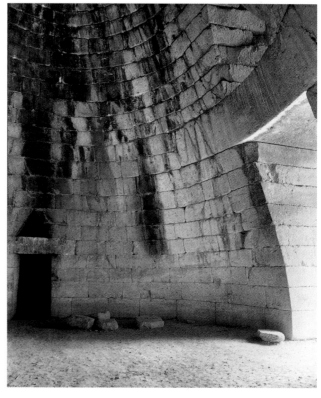

weight adds stability to the dry masonry. The corbeled construction employed here is the same technique used by prehistoric megalith builders in northern Europe and by Egyptian masons as early as the Fourth Dynasty. Originally the entrance doorway was elaborately decorated, and there is evidence that the interior was embellished with bronze plates. Whatever the tholos contained in the way of burials or goods for the afterlife disappeared long ago.

Some of the houses outside the citadel have been excavated, and their remains provide an indication of what the

Stair Domos

Terrace Prodomos

Storerooms on the west side

Corridor Court

Drain

Kitchen

House I of the Panagia Houses, Mycenae

The "Megaron" of the West House, Mycenae

The Megaron of the Palace, Mycenae

The LH IIIB Megarons, Tiryns

House at Priene

N

0   20 m

0   60 ft

2.12 Plans of the megarons at Mycenae and elsewhere.
The West House, located just outside the walls at Mycenae, combines a courtyard porch, antechamber, and megaron. The palace megarons at Mycenae and Tiryns are considerably larger, both with remains of the four column bases that supported the roof around a central hearth.

dwellings of this period were like. Near to the Treasury of Atreus are the foundations of four closely grouped residences, of which the West House provides the easiest plan to interpret, as its main floor (rather than the basement) is preserved (Fig. 2.12). Entrance was made into a court, probably open to the sky, off which there is the three-room megaron sequence of porch, **vestibule**, and domos as the major spaces of the house. Off a corridor extending along the west side are a series of small rooms and a larger terrace that was probably unroofed. Stairs at the end of the corridor led to an upper floor whose layout cannot be determined, as the house was destroyed in antiquity by fire. The roof was probably flat, and both it and the upper story were framed in wood, which accounts for the survival of only the rubble stone foundations. Except for the court area, which was paved with stone, all the floors were of clay. A large drain extends across the court and exits under the foundation of the east wall, while a lesser drain is located in the megaron's domos. The use of the small rooms off the corridor has been determined from pottery and clay tablets found in them: all were storerooms, except for the chamber directly off the court, which had both a hearth and drain and was probably the kitchen. It is surmised that the house belonged to wealthier persons engaged in the manufacture of scented oils, for which Mycenae was famous. While not all Mycenaean houses had megaron layouts, the form is commonly enough encountered for the West House to be considered a typical design.

A megaron layout on a grand scale is found in the palace at Tiryns, where the citadel sits atop a limestone ridge protected by a massive wall of cyclopean masonry that dates to the fourteenth century BCE (see Fig. 2.7). After a fire destroyed the citadel in ca. 1300 BCE, the whole was rebuilt to its present outline, including enclosure of the lower citadel with a twenty-five-foot-thick wall. An earthquake and fire in the mid-thirteenth century BCE damaged the complex, leading to the construction of the buildings whose remains are visible today. The surviving walls around the upper citadel vary from sixteen to fifty-seven feet in thickness. Like Mycenae, the citadel at Tiryns had several postern gates through which people inside could slip out unobtrusively. Corbeled galleries built into the thickness of the walls on the southeast side are handsome examples of such masonry construction. The approach to Tiryns has a more strongly defensive design than the entrance to Mycenae. An almost single-file passage beside and then between the walls made would-be attackers vulnerable well before they reached the first of two inner gates (for which the portals are gone) (Fig. 2.13). Beyond the second gate was a court bounded by porticoed chambers corbeled into the mass of the wall. These face the relatively narrow palace gate that opens into a palace court that connects on the north to a colonnaded court then to the palace megaron of porch, antechamber, and domos (see Fig. 2.12). As at Mycenae, four column bases surround the substantial central hearth, indicating the location of the roof and its opening to let out smoke. Fragments of wall paintings depicting processions of women and the hunting of boars were found in the excavations. A smaller megaron located to the east has an outer and inner court preceding the domos. Tiryns was again devastated by an earthquake in about 1200 BCE.

2.13 Inner gate at Tiryns, ca. 1300 BCE.
This view shows the imposts of one gateway. Although the portal's gates are now gone, their positions can be seen in the cyclopean masonry. Attackers who made it this far would have been at the mercy of Mycenaean soldiers above and on both sides of them.

Between 1200 and 1100 BCE, Mycenaean settlements declined, perhaps in the face of invasions by nomadic peoples from the east, the Dorians and the Ionians, pushing down into the peninsula of Greece. The invaders used mounted cavalry with iron weapons that may have enabled them to defeat the Mycenaeans, who had only bronze armory. Several centuries of cultural obscurity followed, during which the invading tribes settled down, mastered the art of writing, and assimilated certain aspects of Mycenaean culture and mythology as their own. Out of the confusion of this "dark age" rose the brilliance of Classical Greece.

GREECE: THE ARCHAIC PERIOD

During the "dark age," population on the Greek peninsula began to exceed the land's limited agricultural possibilities, where only relatively narrow strips along the coast and in the river valleys could be productively farmed. Seeking additional farmland, as well as looking for metal ores and new trading opportunities, the city-states began a program of colonization, establishing new towns around the eastern Mediterranean in Asia Minor, Sicily, southern Italy, and North Africa. These colonial settlements were laid out in an orderly fashion, generally in elongated rectangular blocks grouped around the market and temples at the center of the city. There were public facilities for recreation and entertainment, and a protective wall surrounded the whole colony.

In addition to grid-plan towns, the major contribution to architectural history made by Greek architects and builders during the Archaic period (ca. 700–500 BCE) was the temple, which originated as a home for the gods and was based on the design of the Mycenaean megaron so that its plan consists of a rear room, or **opisthodomos**, then a **naos**, or **cella**, then a front porch, or **pronaos**. Judging from small surviving clay models, the early temples were simple one-room structures, built to accommodate a statue of the deity. They had a covered portico or porch at the entrance; walls were made of mud-brick, and the sloping roof was made of thatch. In the eighth century BCE, the small Temple of Artemis at Ephesus was constructed with wooden columns surrounding the temple chamber (**peripteral columns**), giving it additional distinction and a strong sculptural quality. The Temple of Hera at Olympia (ca. 600–590 BCE) continues this same idea at a larger scale (Fig. 2.14). Here the original wooden columns were replaced with stone, perhaps to provide better support for fired-clay roof tiles that were significantly heavier than thatch. The transition to stone construction appears to have been a gradual process, doubtless influenced by Egyptian precedent and technology. Stone column **shafts** in Greek architecture are characteristically fluted (incised vertically with concave grooves) in a manner similar to Hatshepsut's mortuary temple at Deir-el-Bahari. The

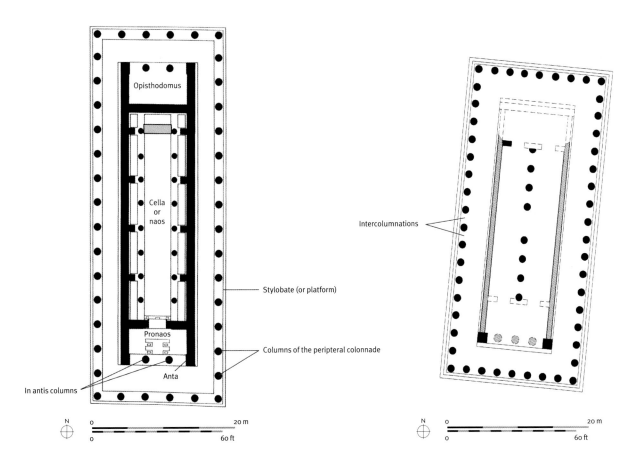

Stylobate (or platform)

Columns of the peripteral colonnade

Opisthodomus

Cella
or
naos

Pronaos

Anta

In antis columns

N

0   20 m

0   60 ft

Intercolumnations

N

0   20 m

0   60 ft

2.14 Plan of the Temple of Hera, Olympia, ca. 600–590 BCE.
The original wooden columns of this early Greek temple were
rebuilt in stone, perhaps to provide better support for heavier
roof tiles that replaced thatch.

2.15 Plan of the Temple of Hera, Paestum, ca. 550 BCE.
This temple presents one of the earliest examples of
the Doric order. It is unusual in having an odd number
of columns across the short side, placing a column in
the center where one would expect an intercolumnar
space for central, axial entry.

arrangement at the Temple of Hera includes two **in antis
columns**, or columns in the plane of the front and rear
walls and between **antae**, or wall thickenings, at the front
and rear, and peripteral columns. The Greeks also developed a highly stylized treatment for **bases**, capitals, and
the supported members, the **entablature**. In the sixteenth
century CE these assemblies were termed the **orders** of
architecture, the term by which we know them today, and
became the basis for the **classical language of architecture**. Vitruvius, the Roman architect whose first-century
BCE treatise was based in part on earlier now-lost Greek
texts, names three such orders: the Doric, the sturdiest,
was based on the proportions of a man (see Fig. 2.17); the
Ionic was lighter in character to reflect the proportions of
a woman (see Fig. 2.18); and the **Corinthian**, slenderest
of all, had a highly decorated capital to suggest the form
and proportions of a young maiden. The Doric originated
on the mainland of Greece, while the Ionic developed on
the islands of the Aegean and the coast of Asia Minor. The
Corinthian order only appeared later (see Fig. 2.31).

2.16 Plan of the Temple of Apollo Epicurius, Bassai, ca. 430 BCE.
All three of the Greek orders were used here. Doric columns formed
the external colonnade; Ionic columns were partially attached to the
cella wall; and a single Corinthian column was placed on the central
longitudinal axis. Light shone on the cult statue from an opening in
the east wall.

Doric order

Ionic order

Corinthian order

N

0   20 m

0   60 ft

2.17 The Doric order as found on the Parthenon, Athens.
The Doric's clear articulation of elements catches sunlight in
an ever-changing play of shade and shadow across the carved
surfaces. This may be one reason why it has endured even to
the present as an expressive part of Western architecture.

**2.18 The Ionic order as found on the north porch of the
Erechtheion, Athens.**
The Ionic's decorative flourishes may reflect influence from oriental
sources. Although the entablature is simpler than the Doric's, its
capitals and bases are subject to considerable artistic invention.

Each order has its own particular combination of elements. The Doric column has no base and has the simplest
capital atop the fluted shaft; its entablature consists of a
plain **architrave** and alternating **metopes** and **triglyphs**
in the **frieze**, which is crowned with a **cornice** (Fig. 2.17).
The Ionic has a base supporting its fluted column shaft
and a capital with **volutes** (scrolls). Its entablature is also
composed of an architrave and frieze. There is regional
variation in the Ionic: along the coast of Asia Minor, the
frieze is usually treated as three stepped bands of masonry,
while on the mainland of Greece the frieze often features
continuous sculpted relief (Fig. 2.18). A cornice, often
with **dentils**, concludes the order. There were also general
conventions regulating the proportions of the parts, the
overall height, and the column spacing, which the ancient
Greeks adjusted according to particular circumstances.
Italian architects of the Renaissance 2000 years later codified the practice into a set of mathematical ratios based
on the column's diameter at the base, but measurements
of surviving temples provide no evidence that the Greeks
ever reduced temple design to a single formula. The orders
of architecture were thus at once specific and flexible, not

a restriction for designers but an expressive medium that
could be adapted to specific circumstances.

The origins of the architectural orders remain obscure.
Vitruvius maintains that the orders were derived from
earlier architecture in wood, a material that we know was
once used for temples. In Doric temples, for example,
triglyphs have been seen as echoing the protective panels
applied to the ends of wooden roof beams, and metopes
the infill panels between them. In its stone incarnation,
the wooden end grain of the beams was stylized into vertical grooves, and the blank metope panel became a place
for sculpture. Recent scholarship questions this derivation,
proposing instead that the orders developed from a monumental decorative style using molded terracotta details,
with no particular reference to structural features in wood.
Even after the walls and columns were built in stone,
wooden beams continued to be used for framing the roof,
but these have not survived.

Builders of the early Doric temples made use of locally
available material, most often limestone. This imposed
structural limitations on the length of spans for lintels
and the diameter of columns needed to support the heavy

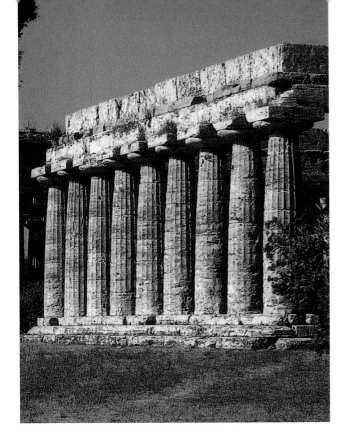

2.19 Temple of Hera at Paestum, ca. 550 BCE.
The end elevation consists of nine sturdy columns with entasis, capitals with flattened echinus profiles, and substantial abacus blocks, all supporting an entablature. Notice how shadows cast by fluting on the column shafts enhance the sense of volume.

tile roof. Ionic temples used marble, a superior stone, and thus had a more slender profile. At Paestum in southern Italy, the Temple of Hera in the former colonial city of Poseidonia is one of the most substantial of surviving Archaic temples (Figs. 2.15, 2.19). Built in about 550 BCE, it has sturdy Doric columns. The column shafts swell, then diminish, as they rise to the bulbous **echinus** molding that forms the capital. This change in column diameter is called **entasis**, and it was thought to be comparable to the muscular strength of an arm or leg, expressing visually the physical load sustained by the shaft. Each flute in the column has a precise edge, an **arris**, where the curved sections of adjacent flutes intersect, and these arrises run absolutely straight up the shaft on every column. Above the echinus is a flat square block, the abacus, which provides the transition from the cylindrical form of the column to the rectangular and linear architrave above. The logic of the Doric order is that alternate triglyphs are placed above columns, with metopes in between. This works well except at corners, where the established rhythm would make two half-metopes intersect. To avoid this problem, the final complete metope before the corner is generally elongated to allow the end triglyphs from both sides to meet at the corner. Columns near the corners may also be placed closer together—look at the rhythm of the frieze to see if this is the case. Joints between limestone blocks are easily seen at Paestum, and the limited spanning capability of the stone is reflected in the close column spacing. On the interior, the central span across the sanctuary required

additional support, so a line of columns extends through the middle of the cella. This corresponds on the exterior to the nine columns across the short side of the temple, one of few times the Greeks would plan a temple with an odd number of columns on the entrance end. An even number places the central intercolumnar space at the central longitudinal entrance axis.

GREECE: THE CLASSICAL PERIOD

During the Archaic period, the Persian Empire flourished in Mesopotamia, and Persian forces under Darius and Xerxes attacked Greek cities, both on the peninsula and around the Mediterranean. Ionian cities of Asia Minor had been under Persian domination from the middle of the sixth century. They revolted and were reconquered, and Darius attempted an invasion of the mainland, where his army was defeated in 490 BCE by the combined legions of Greek city-states at the battle of Marathon. In 480 the Persians attacked again, devastating the region around Athens and sacking the city itself, but the Greek navy scored a decisive victory over the Persian fleet near Salamis. In 479 the Persians were defeated on land and at sea, effectively ending the invasion threat to the peninsula.

A period of relative peace followed, and Athens emerged as the leading city on the mainland. To prevent further incursions by the Persians, it united with Ionian cities to form the Delian League. By 454 the League's treasury had been transferred from Delos to Athens, and a considerable portion of the money was controversially spent on rebuilding the ravaged Athenian Acropolis, which had been a military, political, and religious sanctuary since Mycenaean times (Figs. 2.20–2.21). The four buildings erected there after 479 ushered in the mature phase of Greek architecture known as the Classical period (479–323 BCE).

The Parthenon, Athens

Largest and most famous of these temples was the Parthenon (448–432 BCE), dedicated to Athena Polias, patron goddess of the city (Figs. 2.22–2.23). An earlier temple, known as the Older Parthenon, had been begun in the general euphoria that followed the victory at Marathon in 490, but was still incomplete when the Persians destroyed it in 480. The new, peripteral temple, designed by the architects Iktinos and Kallikrates and built of the finest marble from Mount Pentelikos (Pentelic marble), was erected on the same site, with enlargements, and probably made use of column **drums** and metopes carved for the older temple. It is a Doric temple, eight columns wide by seventeen deep, but it incorporates Ionic attributes, including slender column proportions, a continuous frieze around the exterior of the cella wall, and actual use of the Ionic order in the western opisthodomos (back room) that housed the Delian League treasury, where four Ionic columns support the roof. The use of eight columns across the **gable** end, unusual in the Doric, has connections to earlier Ionic temples (Fig. 2.23). Behind them at each end stand six **prostyle** columns, or columns in front of the east and west walls. Entasis, which was rather heavy-handed in the Temple of Hera at Paestum, was used subtly here to create a sense of repose. Minute adjustments in the horizontal and vertical lines of the structure enhance the perception of orthogonal geometry: the **stylobate** (the platform from which the columns rise) is actually convex upward; the columns incline imperceptibly away from the viewer; and the central axes of the columns are not vertical but lie along radii emanating from a point over 6800 feet above the ground. The columns are not the same diameter—the

2.20 The Acropolis, Athens, ca. 479 BCE, from the entrance side.
The remains of the Propylaea to the left and the tiny temple of Athena Nike in the center stand out in the foreground, with the gable end of the Parthenon visible on the right.

2.21 Site plan of the Acropolis, Athens, ca. 479 BCE.
The shaded temple plan in the center represents the foundations of an earlier temple to Athena Polias that was destroyed by the Persians. The Erechtheion's porch, with the Caryatid maidens, encroaches on these foundations, in a perpetual reminder of the destruction of the Persian War.

end ones are larger—nor are they equidistantly spaced: the corner ones are closer together. The architects made these slight variations in the column spacing and other details to avoid strict geometrical perfection and so to breathe life into their stone composition.

Sculpted figures adorned both the outside and the inside of the Parthenon. The two end **pediments** were filled with over-lifesize figures representing, on the east, the birth of Athena witnessed by the gods (Figs. 2.24a,b), and on the west, the contest between Athena and Poseidon for control of Athens. The metopes contained relief sculptures depicting struggles between Greeks and Amazons, Greeks and Trojans, gods and giants, and Lapiths (the people of Thessalonia) and centaurs (creatures combining the upper torsos of men with the bodies of horses), all commemorating the triumph of Greek civilization over barbarism. A continuous frieze ran around the outside of the cella walls behind the colonnade, portraying a sacred procession of Athenians bringing gifts to Athena, possibly as a thank offering for victory over the Persians or as a representation of the Panathenaic Festival held every four years. The procession shown on the frieze begins at the southwest corner and moves in both directions to meet again in the center of the east side, where Athena and other enthroned gods receive the offerings.

The sculptor Phidias served as artistic coordinator for the rebuilding of all monuments on the Acropolis, and he was responsible for the sculptural detail on the Parthenon, including the large cult statue of Athena housed in the

2.22 The Parthenon, Athens, 448–432 BCE.
This is how the Parthenon appears to someone leaving the Propylaea and looking southeast. As is the case with many Greek temples, the building is set so that the viewer looks up to it and sees two sides at once.

2.23 The Parthenon, Athens, 448–432 BCE, seen from the west.
The Doric order used here is elongated to an almost Ionic slenderness. Not all optical refinements are readily discernible, but note the widening of the central intercolumnation relative to the slightly closer spacing of the end columns.

Helios and chariot Demeter and Persephone Artemis Hephaistos Athena Unidentified chariot gods Hestia, Dione, and Aphrodite Selene (Moon) or Nyx (night) and chariot

Dionysius Unidentified chariot gods Hera Zeus Poseidon

2.24a East pediment sculpture from the Parthenon.
Much of the east pediment sculpture has been lost, but the scene can be fairly reliably reconstructed based on extant groupings depicting the same event, which is the birth of Athena, protectress of Athens. To her right in the drawing are Zeus, her father, and Hera, her mother. Farther to her right are Artemis, another daughter of Zeus, and Dionysius, a son of Zeus. To her left are Poseidon, brother of Zeus, Hestia, a sister of Zeus, Dione, another wife of Zeus, and perhaps Aphrodite, daughter of Zeus and Dione and so Athena's half-sister. Also to the right of Athena is Hephaistos, the god of the forge, who, during an unconventional birth process, struck Zeus's head with his hammer, causing Athena to issue forth. The horses at the pediment extremities are pulling the chariots of the sun god and the moon or night god.

2.24b East pediment sculpture from the Parthenon, detail.
This detail photograph of Dionysius, Demeter and Persephone shows part of the so-called Elgin Marbles, which are on display in the British Museum.

cella. The latter was portrayed standing, with a Nike (goddess of victory) in her right hand and a shield resting at her left. The statue had a wooden armature finished with highly valued materials. Ivory was used for all exposed parts of Athena's body; her drapery, armor, and helmet were represented in gold; and precious stones were used for her eyes and for decorating her robes and armor.

The cella of the Parthenon was one of the largest interiors built in Classical Greece. It was intended to provide a proper setting for the enormous cult statue, which was the grandest of its time. Scholars disagree as to whether the cella was completely roofed, as spanning the forty-foot width between the internal colonnades posed constructional challenges. Some speculate that the cella was open to the sky. A normally relatively dark interior would have been an appropriate location for the dramatic image of Athena, for the Parthenon was oriented so that the sun would penetrate the cella interior on the morning of Athena's birthday to shine on the great chryselephantine (gold and ivory) statue.

Time and circumstance have not been kind to the Parthenon. The statue of Athena had been broken up by the second century CE, probably for the value of its materials, and various adaptive reuses of the temple did little to preserve its best features. It became a Christian church, and then a **mosque** after the Turks occupied Greece. By 1687 it was being used for munitions storage, at which time it was bombarded by the Venetians. A direct hit caused an explosion that ripped out the cella wall and dislodged many sculptures. The victorious Venetians carried some off as trophies. Lord Elgin, the British ambassador to the Turkish Ottoman Empire from 1799 to 1803, negotiated for the remaining sculptures (Figs. 2.24a,b), which he had removed from the temple and shipped to England; his son later sold them to the British government. Known as the Elgin Marbles, they are now housed in London's British Museum, but the Greek government is eager to have them returned to a new Acropolis Museum designed by Bernard Tschumi. Industrial air pollution from the Greek capital is now the biggest threat to the surviving bits of the Parthenon. A major restoration project on the Acropolis began as early as 1975, speeded up in preparation for the 2004 Olympics, and saw Parthenon scaffolding removed in 2010.

ESSAY
Celebrating Athena's Birthday
by David Lewis

This account of the Great Panathenaic procession (Fig. 2.25) is an excerpt from the fictional journal of an aristocratic Athenian woman. It is a description of the eighth and final day of the Great Panathenaic Festival in 424 BCE celebrating the birthday of Athena.

28 Hekatombaion—the first month and our goddess Athena's birthday. The sea's wind blew warm even before the sun rose on this midsummer's day. Thousands gathered outside the city's walls. We wives and maidens dressed in purple robes and carried kannephoroi, bronze and silver trays filled with cakes, honeycombs and oak branches. Armed infantrymen, the victorious athletes, and the four men bearing the prize amphora were inside the Pompeion, while the young men who escort the 100 sacrificial cows, the equestrians and warriors on chariots, were next to the Dipylon Gate.

At the head of our procession were two maidens proudly bearing the sail-peplos of Athena, its breadth extending the whole width of the Sacred Way and facing the cavalcade, and the champion athlete with the ceremonial torch. The peplos's saffron and sea-purple linen threads glistened in the morning sun and torchlight while its silhouetted figures of Athena, Zeus, and other gods did battle with the giants. [Sail-peploi were commissioned every fourth year for the Great Panathenaic Festival and produced by professional male weavers. For the other three years, young daughters, arrephoroi, and wives of aristocratic citizens would spend months in the workshop, or arrephorion, on the Acropolis, producing a human-sized robe.]

As we walked fifteen abreast on the Sacred Way through the cramped Kerameikos, the potters, who lived there, cheered proudly as the prize amphorai filled with sacred oils passed by. These men spent the last year sculpting and painting elaborate scenes on the 1400 trophies. Even from this outer precinct we could discern the Parthenon atop the Acropolis.

Continuing downhill, we entered the Agora at the Eridanos river bridge alongside the Poikile Stoa, with its jugglers and street musicians, and the Royal Stoa. We continued diagonally through the Agora, passing the Orchestra, where athletic events took place this week. As we approached the South Stoa, we began our ascent to the Acropolis, winding around its western rock face.

At the base of the ramp, we turned to face the Acropolis. Resplendently will it embrace our procession. Delicate Athena Nike to the south perched on her own askew promontory temenos [sacred precinct] while the Propylaea meets us head on. We marched up the ramp, for all of the polis to view. We stopped at the Propylaea's blue step, allowing us to see to the north the Agora below, over our right shoulder the

same battle between the gods and giants on the Athena Nike's east pediment, and ahead glimpses of the grand Athena Promachos statue beyond the Propylaea's doors. We sift through the gateway, animals and chariots led by the peplos through the central walkway, while those of us on foot walk to the outside of the Ionic columns and through the smaller doors.

Stepping over the east threshold and between the monumental Doric columns, we entered the temenos as the sun appeared over the mountains; Athena and Pericles's glorious pentelic temples glimmered. As we marched eastward on the Sacred Way along the north face of the Parthenon, the morning sun illuminated the cella frieze. As we proceeded to the east, so did the brightly colored figures as if telling us how and where to proceed. Like the frieze, our procession broke off into two groups; the men ushering the cows, and maidens bearing the kannephoroi walked to the Great Altar, while the remainder went to the open area to the east of the Parthenon.

As the two maidens, led by the high priestess, carried the peplos into the cella, we heard "IOIOIOIOIO," cries signaling the sacrifice of the first cow.

2.25 Horsemen, Panathenaic Festival, Parthenon north frieze, Athens, 424 BCE. British Museum, London.

Other Buildings on the Acropolis

The remaining buildings on the Athenian Acropolis are disposed in a manner that at first seems almost random, yet is actually carefully planned to respond to particular qualities of the site. The Acropolis is a plateau rising abruptly above the plain of the city. From the earliest times, the route of the Panathenaic Way from the civic and commercial center (the **Agora**) to the Acropolis traversed a winding, stepped path up the western escarpment. (As most Greek temples face the east, this means the initial view one has is of the back sides of buildings.) In about 437 BCE construction began on an appropriately scaled entrance gateway, the Propylaea, designed by the architect Mnesikles. In a highly original design, Mnesikles created a dignified symmetrical entranceway amid asymmetries, accommodating a fragment of the original Mycenaean fortification wall and a gradient change through the depth of the building. His building marks the transition from the secular, or profane, world to the sacred one.

The Propylaea is essentially a Doric portico flanked by projecting wings (Figs. 2.26, 2.27). The central **intercolumniation** is wider than the rest, accommodating the processional way that passed through the axial colonnaded space into the sacred precinct of the Acropolis. This required two (rather than the usual one) unsupported triglyphs over the central space, as the architect had to take liberties with the exacting Doric. Three pairs of Ionic columns line the passageway, because the rising ground level and scale of the space dictated the choice of a more slender order. A second Doric portico terminated the Propylaea's central section. Its northern wing was a megaron, perhaps used as a picture gallery or banqueting hall, while on the south side there was a porch preceding the freestanding Temple of Athena Nike.

The overall layout of the Acropolis was designed to enhance the sense of procession as described in this chapter's essay. A visitor would first emerge from the eastern portico of the Propylaea to see the great statue of Athena Promachos close by, just left of center, balancing the majestic Parthenon, which rose farther back on the right-hand side. Even though the entrance to Greek temples is placed axially, it was the intention of the architects of the Acropolis that visitors should first view the Parthenon from below, at an angle where the west pediment and long north colonnade presented the essence of the temple's volume at a single glance. One reached the sanctuary entrance by traversing a rising pathway running the length of the Parthenon's north side, passing the exposed foundations of the old Temple of Athena Polias (destroyed by the Persians) on the left and turning south around the corner to ascend the steps into the eastern portico. Only after

2.26 Plans of the Propylaea (437 BCE) and Temple of Athena Nike (ca. 425 BCE), Athens. The Propylaea defined the entrance to the Acropolis, while the small Temple of Athena Nike stood on the forward projection, visible at an angle to those entering the Acropolis. See Fig. 2.27 for a reconstruction view of this ensemble. Evolved from earlier fortified gateways, the Propylaea had become an architectural device for marking the transition from profane to sacred space and for controlling views toward the Erectheion and Parthenon.

2.27 (opposite) **Hypothetical reconstruction of the entrance to the Acropolis, Athens.**
Compare this drawing to the photograph in Fig. 2.20. Note the wide intercolumniation in the center of the Propylaea. A large exterior statue of Athena Promachos (no longer extant) dominated the view, balancing the Parthenon on the right (read about the statue's role in the Panathenaic procession in the essay on page 51).

2.28 **View from the south of the Erechtheion, Athens, ca. 421–407 BCE.**
The entrance to Poseidon's shrine is made through the giant order Ionic portico on the left. The height of its Ionic order (see Fig. 2.18) resulted from changes in the site's terrain. This variation of the Ionic order became much admired by eighteenth-century Neo-Classical architects. To the right, the small porch displays the Caryatid maidens.

experiencing the totality of the temple exterior would the drama of the interior be unfolded.

There are two other important temples on the Acropolis. The small Temple of Athena Nike (Athena Victorious) perches on rocks that were once the site of an ancient bastion (projecting fortification) on the edge of the hilltop forward of the Propylaea. Possibly designed as early as 448 BCE by Kallikrates but not constructed until the 420s, it is a simple sanctuary that housed a wooden image of Athena holding her helmet and a pomegranate, a symbol of fertility. Four Ionic columns create a portico before the eastern entrance, and an identical set is placed at the western (rear) side, which is the elevation seen clearly from below the Acropolis. Its refined detailing and small size made it a model for garden temples in the eighteenth century.

Across from the northern side of the Parthenon stands the more complex form of the Erechtheion, begun in ca. 421 and completed in 407 BCE to the designs of an unknown architect, on the site of the Mycenaean palace that was also regarded as the location of the contest between Athena and Poseidon (Fig. 2.28). Myth has it that in a competition to decide who should be named as patron of the city, Poseidon struck his trident, or three-pronged spear, on a rock and created a spring, while Athena brought forth an olive tree. The contest was judged in favor of Athena by Kekrops, the first legendary king of Athens, whose tomb is also commemorated here. Under the temple is the Sea of Erechtheus, a saltwater spring that made the sound of the sea and had a rock bearing the mark of Poseidon's trident. The Erechtheion knits together these assorted strands of site-specific history while deferring to the dominance of the Parthenon. The Ionic was chosen as the most suitable order for a temple built on two different levels to accommodate the uneven site. The eastern

portico, distinguished by its slender Ionic columns, led to Athena's sanctuary, where an ancient wooden image of the goddess was housed, while the north porch, its stylobate ten feet lower, gave access to Poseidon's shrine through an even more elongated Ionic portico. Four Ionic columns, partially engaged in the wall, extend across the west façade to the south, where the roof of the splendid porch facing the Parthenon is supported by the six **Caryatid** maidens. Their pose is graceful, with one knee bent slightly and drapery revealing the form beneath. The base of the caryatid porch is the north foundation wall of the destroyed old Temple of Athena Polias, and the caryatids look out to the Parthenon across the ruins of the former temple, which were deliberately left exposed as an eternal reminder of the devastation wrought by the Persians. Although female figures had been used as columns (caryatids) before, the Roman architect Vitruvius explained their origins as follows:

Caryae, a state in Peloponnesus, sided with the Persian enemies against Greece [Athens]; later the Greeks, having gloriously won their freedom by victory in the war, made common cause and declared war against the people of Caryae. They took the town, killed the men, abandoned the State to desolation, and carried off their wives into slavery, without permitting them, however, to lay aside the long robes and other marks of their rank as married women, so that they might be obliged not only to march in the triumph but to appear forever after as a type of slavery, burdened with the weight of their shame and so making atonement for their State. Hence, the architects of the time designed for public buildings statues of these women, placed so as to carry a load, in order that the sin and the punishment of the people of Caryae might be known and handed down even to posterity.

We may find this punishment unjustified, given that it was the men of Caryae, not the women, who committed treachery, but it reminds us that even under Athenian democratic rule, women were no better than slaves when it came to legal and political rights.

As an example of the Ionic order, the elaborate detail of the Erechtheion has no equal in later Greek works, and the multiple complexities and scales that have been united here in a single temple are also exceptional in classical architecture. The exquisite decorative detail may well have influenced the later Corinthian order.

In all four of the Acropolis temples, one sees the architects fusing new constructions with elements from the site's history, be it the Persian Wars or the Mycenaean period. Evidence of Persian destruction was deliberately preserved in the ruins of the old Temple of Athena Polias, while historical references to the origins of the city are the very essence of the Erechtheion's design. Mycenaean fortifications were incorporated into one wall of the Propylaea, and the older Parthenon's base and architectural elements were reused for the existing building. The architects also sought to integrate the Doric architecture characteristic of Attica (the region around Athens) with Ionic elements (from Asia Minor) in an attempt to express the unity of the Delian League and Athens's ascendancy among the city-states of Greece.

When discussing the buildings of ancient Greece, it is important not only to imagine them complete, but also to remember that the Greeks never saw them as the bare stone structures we see today. Architectural and sculptural detail was generally painted in vibrant colors, perhaps with gilding, and plain walls may well have had murals. Traces of the original paint remain in protected crevices to confirm written accounts of the buildings' original appearances. If they were restored and repainted in authentic hues today, Greek temples might well appear surprising to our eyes.

GREECE: THE HELLENISTIC PERIOD

Athens's moment of architectural glory, epitomized by the buildings on the Acropolis, came to an end in 431–404 BCE with the protracted and ultimately disastrous Peloponnesian War. Rival city-states quarreled with one another, weakening themselves in the process and opening the entire peninsula to opportunistic external powers. The eventual conqueror, Philip of Macedon, came from the north and effectively annexed all of Greece in 338 BCE. The close of the Classical age in Greece is generally associated with the reign of his son, known as Alexander the Great, but the influence of Greek culture continued to spread east owing to Alexander's conquests. From 336 to 323 BCE, his armies swept through much of the civilized world, including Asia Minor, Egypt, Mesopotamia, Persia , and parts of what today are Afghanistan, Pakistan, and northern India. Alexander died at the age of thirty-three, unable to consolidate his vast territories, but his enthusiasm for Greek heritage and his adoption of oriental aspects of the Persian court accelerated the assimilation and adaptation of Greek culture far beyond the Aegean. The term "Hellenistic" is applied to the art and architecture associated with the

2.29 Temple of Apollo Epicurius, Bassai, ca. 450–425 BCE. This is one of the few Greek temples on which one can look down, perhaps a function of the site conditions, perhaps a result of greater artistic freedom in the Hellenistic period.

2.30 Floor plan (lower half) and reflected ceiling plan (upper half), tholos, Epidauros, ca. 360–330 BCE.
Parts of the beautifully detailed ceiling coffers have survived as indications of the exquisite Hellenistic detailing.

2.31 Corinthian capital, tholos, Epidauros, ca. 360–330 BCE.
Lavish Corinthian capitals like this one combined Ionic volutes with the leaves of the acanthus plant, which is still commonly found in the Mediterranean area. Only Pentelic marble or another stone with so fine a grain allows for the carving of such fine detail.

extended empire of Alexander and his successors, including the Seleucids, who ruled the area stretching from Anatolia to the Indus River, and the Ptolomies, who ruled in Egypt.

Hellenistic architecture differs from that of the Classical period by shifting away from staid traditions associated clearly with the region around Athens in favor of showier and freer interpretations as found along the western coast of Asia Minor. As the Doric order was intimately connected with the mainland of Greece, its use diminished in favor of the more ornate Ionic order, which reflected an oriental exuberance typical of the Ionian colonies. The meticulous sculptural ornamentation and coordination of column spacing required by the Doric were not part of either the Ionic or Corinthian orders, which overcame the Doric's limitations by eliminating the troublesome features. Their column flutes are jointed by flat **fillets** to simplify the carving, and the frieze runs continuously without metopes or triglyphs.

Even in the Classical period, the use of a particular order on the exterior of a building did not preclude the use of others within, as has already been seen in the Parthenon and the Propylaea. The Temple of Apollo Epicurius at Bassai (ca. 450–425 BCE) (Figs. 2.16, 2.29), designed by Iktinos, employs all three orders: the Doric for the external colonnade, the Ionic for the cella side columns (which are connected to the cella wall by extended buttress-shaped piers), and the Corinthian for the single axial column placed at the end of the cella. A statue of Apollo was set adjacent to this column so that it faced to the east through an opening in the cella wall. Among Greek temples, this one is unusual for its orientation; the main entrance faces north, rather than east. The temple at Bassai is the first known use of the Corinthian order, and also marks the first time the Ionic was used for a cella interior. These forward-looking features are counterbalanced by some seemingly

old-fashioned ones that must have been included for positive reasons, for the architect was thoroughly familiar with what was being built contemporaneously on the Athenian Acropolis. The temple's elongated plan and narrow cella have been explained as deliberate references to history (the cult of Apollo had long existed on the site, and there had been three predecessor temples here), and the earlier temples may also be the source of the spur walls connected to the Ionic columns. It has been proposed that the single Corinthian column likewise made reference to the distant past, when wooden columns were sacred symbols of the gods. The temple may thus be interpreted as a fusion of historical references with innovative design.

The Corinthian order was employed on a substantial scale in the tholos at the Sanctuary of Asklepios at Epidauros (ca. 360–330 BCE), a circular building approximately seventy-two feet in diameter, known now from its foundations and reassembled fragments preserved on the site (Fig. 2.30). Epidauros was dedicated to the god Asklepios, the son of Apollo, and both gods were venerated here in a large complex dedicated to healing through exercise, diet, and medical care. The tholos is but a small part of a site that included a stadium, gymnasia, a theater, altars, fountains and baths, temples, and accommodations for patients. Its external colonnade was composed of twenty-six Doric columns, and there were fourteen freestanding Corinthian columns in the inner circular colonnade fitted into a black-and-white rhomboidal flooring pattern. The ceiling had ornate coffers with floral decorations. An unused Corinthian capital found buried at the site shows the delicacy and grace achieved by Polykleitos, architect of the tholos (Fig. 2.31). The corner volutes, derived from Ionic models, are small, and their scroll form is complemented by the stylized curls of **acanthus**

2.32 Elevation of the Choragic Monument of Lysikrates, Athens, ca. 335 BCE.
Engaged Corinthian columns ornament this small structure. William Strickland, a nineteenth-century Greek Revival architect in America, used this monument in his design for the Tennessee State Capitol.

2.33 Reconstruction view of the Sanctuary of Asklepios, Kos, ca. 300–150 BCE.
Compare the axial, hierarchical organization of this Hellenistic shrine with the angular, non-hierarchical, Hellenic distribution of buildings on the Athenian Acropolis, as seen in Fig. 2.21. While the results are dramatically different, the means for achieving them were much the same: column files, cella walls, and strategic topographic change.

leaves that enrich the bell of the capital. How exactly this building was used is unknown. It has been suggested that its form at the upper story matches that of a shelter for a tomb (a **baldachin**) and that the circular corridors evident from the foundation remains were evocative of passages through the underworld to the tomb of Asklepios.

In a better state of preservation is the Choragic Monument of Lysikrates (ca. 335 BCE) in Athens (Fig. 2.32). This small cylindrical structure was erected to display the prize awarded to Lysikrates for the entry he sponsored in a thespian contest honoring the god Dionysos. Here the Corinthian order is used on the exterior of a building, with six columns being built into the cylinder so that they appear as half-columns. (Recall that the Erechtheion likewise had engaged columns on its western elevation. The decorative possibilities of the orders as wall articulation were exploited in Hellenistic and later Roman work.) The frieze they support illustrates the mythological story of Dionysos and the pirates of the Tyrrhenian Sea. There is no accessible interior space. Nineteenth-century American architects adapted the form of the Choragic Monument for quite varied purposes. It inspired the form of the Philadelphia Exchange and the **cupola** atop the Tennessee State Capitol in Nashville, both by William Strickland.

The introduction of multiple-building ensembles like the Sanctuary of Asklepios (ca.300–150 BCE), arranged on the sloping ground of the Aegean Island of Kos (Fig. 2.33), illustrates the change in design attitudes among Hellenistic architects. With its ascending terraces and files of columns, Kos's layout brings to mind the Egyptian mortuary complexes of Mentuhotep (see Fig. 1.26) and Queen Hatshepsut (see Fig. 1.28). At Kos, however, there is something new: a conscious definition of exterior space using **stoas** bent at right angles to become enveloping arms. Within these envelopments, temple buildings were then embedded (as at the lower-level entry), set in axial relationships with one another (as on the middle level), and treated as freestanding objects within an architectural precinct (as on the upper level). A single, central axis of

2.34 Theater, Epidauros, 350–2nd century BCE.
This shows the rows of seating. The original skene, or backdrop building, shown in the plan is no longer extant.

movement runs through the embedded portico and up consciously aligned stairs to terminate at the freestanding Temple of Asklepios on the highest ground. Some scholars have associated the hierarchical rigidity of this type of planning with the change from Classical democracy to the autocracy of Alexander's empire.

During the Hellenistic period, permanent buildings for theatrical performances were constructed in many of the outlying cities. Many of these elegant designs post-date the plays by Euripides, Sophocles, and Aristophanes that were originally presented from carts to audiences grouped on wooden benches in public open areas. Fifth-century Athenians constructed the Theater of Dionysos on the south side of the Acropolis hill, using the rising embankment to provide support for concentric seating focused on the circular **orchestra**, a flat area for dancing. Behind the orchestra was a backdrop structure, the **skene**, and the

area directly in front, the **proskenion**, was a raised platform from which actors declaimed their lines. (Note how this terminology continues to be used today: the framing arch over the stage of today's theaters is known as the proscenium, while orchestra seats are those placed directly in front of the stage.) Several doors set in the skene served as entrances and exits as needed in the drama, and actors spoke lines from the gods from the roof of the building.

Although the theater in Athens has been modified, surviving auditoria at Delphi, Dodona, Ephesus, Epidauros, Megalopolis, Pergamon, and Priene give a clear image of what Greek theaters originally looked like. The theater at Epidauros (Figs. 2.34–2.35) is exceptionally well preserved and beautifully sited in the landscape, looking out

2.35 Plan of the theater, Epidauros, 350–2nd century BCE.
Virtually every Greek city had its own theater that could accommodate a good portion of the population, as attending dramatic performances was encouraged to promote civic values.

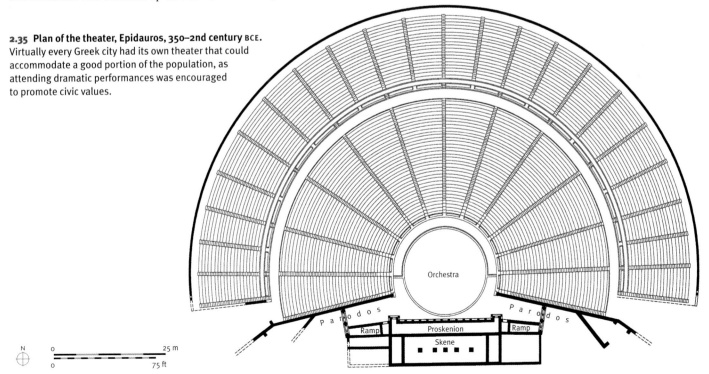

to distant hills. Tradition assigns its design to Polykleitos, architect of the tholos, but not all scholars agree with this attribution. The theater was built in two stages, the lower 5000 seats in thirty-four tiers dating from 350 BCE, with the upper twenty-one tiers being added in the second century BCE, extending the total capacity to about 14,000 seats. The ring of seats closest to the orchestra were provided with backs and used by dignitaries, while everyone else sat on continuous benches raised slightly above the row in front of them. An efficient system of radial and cross aisles provided circulation from entrances at multiple levels. Most remarkably, the acoustical design worked so well that words spoken in a normal voice from the orchestra projected intelligibly to all seats. The theater is still used for performances.

GREEK CITY PLANNING
The Athenian Agora

We have seen how the spatial experience of buildings on the Acropolis in Athens affected the placement and design of temples on the site, so that what appears in plan to be a haphazard arrangement unfolds before the visitor as a logical sequence in an ordered and balanced universe. The static poise of a colonnaded temple is enhanced by the subtle arts of the site planner, who has used surprise and a changing perspective to reveal the full drama of the architectural forms. A similar spatial approach was taken in the layout of the Athenian Agora, the civic and commercial heart of the city, which developed around the ancient track of the Panathenaic Way entering the city from the northwest and leading to the Acropolis (Fig. 2.36). Development of the public structures in the Agora began in about 600 BCE, and by the end of the Archaic period its boundaries were defined. A group of civic buildings, including temples, a shrine to Zeus, and a senate house (**bouleterion**), had been built on the western side at the base of the Agora Hill (Kolonos Agoraios). The bouleterion was an ambitious project, built on a nearly square plan to accommodate the 500 senators who comprised the elected government of Athens. A columned porch led directly to the senate chamber, with seats in rows along three sides of the rectangular space. The roof was supported on the exterior walls and four intermediate columns. Another government building was the Royal Stoa, erected on the northwest corner beside the Panathenaic Way for the city's chief religious magistrate, who was responsible for official sacrifices, administration of the city's festivals, and adjudication of priestly disputes. The Royal Stoa was a small rectangular building with a colonnade and steps along the long side facing the Agora, the first of a type that would be constructed on a larger scale for various purposes in the Classical and later eras.

After the Persian Wars, when the Acropolis was being reconstructed with its famous temples, new works were undertaken in the Agora as well. On top of the hill to the west, the Hephaisteion, a temple to Hephaistos (god of the forge) and Athena (goddess of the arts), was constructed in about 449–444 BCE. This Doric temple, still remarkably intact, was enriched with relief sculpture and an elaborate ceiling of stone coffers. A gap in the buildings at the base of the hill allowed for the extension of the eastern axis of the temple across the Agora to the Stoa of Attalos. Within the Agora, war damage to the Royal Stoa was repaired and the building slightly enlarged, while new stoas were built. The Painted Stoa (so named because it displayed paintings of Athenian military triumphs, mythical and real) had an external Doric colonnade and Ionic columns within. It was used for informal meetings as well as jury trials. The Stoic philosophers were fond of meeting there and eventually took their name from it. The Stoa of Zeus replaced the earlier shrine and was used as an informal meeting place. The first South Stoa, whose small rooms behind a double colonnade were used for commercial activities and perhaps also for dining, was constructed adjacent to the Heliaia, which was probably the main law court. A new bouleterion was constructed ca. 415–406 BCE directly behind the existing building (which was renamed the Metroon to honor Rhea, mother of the gods of Olympus, and used for city archives). Its internal arrangements are not clear from the excavations, but archaeologists believe it had a curved configuration of seats like a theater. Adjacent was a circular building, the tholos, that was used for meals served to the fifty senators who happened to be on duty. The open spaces of the Agora were used both as a racetrack and as a setting for dramatic performances and dancing.

Building in the Athenian Agora continued after the conquests of Alexander the Great. In the Hellenistic period, some Classical buildings were modified, and new ones were constructed to create a more complete sense of spatial order and closure. The dominant Temple of Hephaistos and its axial approach remained. The old Metroon was replaced by a more elaborate building serving the same functions, with an external colonnade fronting onto the open civic space. The South Stoa was rebuilt on a shifted orientation, with an additional Middle Stoa extending parallel to it on what had originally been open land. Across the Panathenaic Way, which remained unchanged, the Stoa of Attalos (Fig. 2.37) was erected at right angles to the Middle Stoa, and its southern end worked with the eastern terminus of the Middle Stoa to establish a narrow point of entry, in contrast to the openness of the Agora beyond. In the colonnaded walkways of the stoas, one had a sense of shelter while at the same time being connected to the larger open space. The stoas were thoroughly urban buildings, providing space for merchants to trade in and inviting citizens to participate in the public life of the city, a central aspect of Greek society. The concept of a colonnaded or arcaded space containing shops and facing major public open spaces will reappear in later urban designs.

Stoa of Zeus

Royal Stoa

Painted Stoa

Shrine of Aphrodite

Shrine to the Twelve Gods

Arsenal (?)

Shops

Hephaisteion

New bouleterion

2.37

Metroon (original site of the bouleterion)

Monument to the Eponymous Heroes

Stoa of Attalos

Tholos

Middle Stoa

Fountain

South Stoa

Mint

Heliaia

Panathenaic Way to the Acropolis

N

0   50 m

0   150 ft

Hellenistic Cities

Greek city planning was not always as asymmetrical and evolutionary in form as the Agora in Athens. The Greeks were perfectly capable of producing regular, orthogonal town plans and frequently employed them for colonial cities, as may be seen at Paestum (Poseidonia), which had a street pattern from the mid-seventh century BCE that produced huge, elongated, rectangular blocks (Fig. 2.38). While many cities grew organically over time, others were rebuilt, often after suffering war damage, according to the new, more regular town-planning principles. Such was the case in the fifth and fourth centuries BCE, when a number of towns were provided with grid blocks and carefully considered open spaces according to the theories of a fifth-century pupil of Pythagoras, Hippodamus of Miletus, who is often regarded as the father of city planning. This label is misapplied if taken to mean that he "invented" the grid plan, for orthogonal plans existed long before Hippodamus. More properly viewed, his contribution seems to have involved consolidating and articulating the religious, social, and commercial elements of the city center with regular blocks of houses adjusted to fit the particular circumstances of the topography. Hippodamus's birthplace, Miletus, a harbor town on the coast of Asia Minor, was in its day the leading city of Ionia. After its

2.37 Stoa of Attalos, Athens, 159–132 BCE (reconstructed 1952–56).
This building was contributed to the city by Attalos of Pergamon. In its reconstructed form, it and the Hephasteion are the only structures from antiquity remaining in the Athenian Agora. The column-file organization of the stoa form can be traced back to Egyptian complexes such as the temples of Queen Hatshepsut and Mentuhotep.

2.38 Plan of Paestum (Poseidonia), 7th century BCE.
This Greek colonial city was laid out with elongated blocks on the orthogonal pattern. Across the center was the public sector, with commercial structures, government buildings, and temples, including the Temple of Hera (identifiable by its row of central columns in the lower right). The site was submerged by the sea during the Middle Ages, but is located again on dry land today.

destruction by the Persians in 494 BCE, the city was rebuilt in the period following 479 BCE with a plan of rectangular residential blocks and an orthogonal agora. Hippodamus's design went beyond specifying the location of civic buildings, the layout of streets, and the positioning of open spaces, to encompass design of typical single-family houses for an estimated population of 15,000 to 20,000. Houses were consistently oriented with their major rooms opening to the south, and the megaron form already familiar from Mycenaean times was used again as the basic living unit of the house.

During the Hellenistic period, both architecture and city planning became more elaborate and theatrical, as can be seen in the design of Pergamon, another city in Asia

Temple of Hera   Residential blocks

2.39 Great Altar of Zeus, Pergamon, ca. 181–159 BCE.
This has now been reconstructed in the Pergamon Museum in
Berlin. This impressive shrine, originally set on a hillside above
the city, features a dramatic frieze of large sculpted figures that
contrasts with the serenity of the colonnade above.

Minor that between 282 and 133 BCE aspired to imitate
the glory that once emanated from Athens. It became the
capital of the Attalid Dynasty, whose leaders took the title
of king in part to celebrate their military victories over the
Galatians (Celtic tribes). Originating as a hilltop fortress,
Pergamon grew in terraced steps down from the summit,
with level sites for buildings supported on well-engineered
retaining walls and linked by monumental stairs. On such
a precipitous site, a grid plan was out of the question; the
road has switchbacks to minimize the slope. On the acropolis were temples, a distinguished library, the Sanctuary of
Athena, and palaces, above a banked theater carved into
the hillside that could seat 10,000 people. One of the most
celebrated buildings at Pergamon was the Great Altar (ca.
181–159 BCE), dedicated to Zeus and Athena. The high
plinth on which the altar stood became the location for
a frieze over 300 feet in length and sculpted with scenes
of battles between gods and giants, an obvious allusion to
recent battles with the Celts (Fig. 2.39). Intertwined wings,
arms, and writhing snake bodies create a dynamic composition: even the hair on the gods' heads and beards falls in
animated coils. The highly dramatic frieze contrasts with
the elegant colonnaded building above, and it also com-
plements the equally dramatic site, an architectural tour de
force that has little of the restraint and sublimated feeling
that governed the design of the Athenian Acropolis.

CONCLUSIONS ABOUT ARCHITECTURAL IDEAS

While archaeology on Minoan sites in Crete has not
yet established a satisfactory picture of Minoan design

thinking, evidence does suggest some kind of experien-
tially based planning, or perceptual thinking, as opposed
to abstract, geometric ordering, or conception thinking.
The mainland Mycenaeans invented the megaron, with its
two-spatial-unit plan of prodomos and domos. The megaron anticipated the Classical Greek temple plan, with its
three spatial units: pronaos, naos or cella, and opisthodomos. To these spaces, the later Greeks added various column configurations: in antis, prostyle and amphiprostyle,
and peripteral, using them in isolation but more often in
combination.

The impressive masonry of the Mycenaeans was succeeded by the exquisite stone craftsmanship of the ancient
Greeks, and Pentelic marble made it possible for them to
carve the fine detail required by the orders (Doric, Ionic,
and Corinthian) that form the basis of the classical language of architecture. At the core of this language lies the
ancient Greek system of arithmetic proportions. Encoded
with societal values, temples like the Parthenon were
meant to be "read," not just seen, as their sculptural programs explained the Athenian position in the world.

The approach to the Parthenon was, of course, along
a route with constantly changing orientations, culminating in an oblique view of the freestanding temple through
the column screen of the Propylaea. Such a fluid system
of movement, comparable to Minoan designs, gave way
in the Hellenistic period to geometric regularity, axiality,
and rigorously organized building ensembles and environments, and this new type of planning would be appropriated by Republican Rome. In the nineteenth century, the
classical language of ancient Greek architecture would
reappear throughout Europe in the form of the Greek
Revival, as discussed in Chapter 13.

Chapter 3

The Architecture of Ancient India and Southeast Asia

The prehistory of India is largely an account of settlements along the Indus Valley and its associated coastal plain, now part of the modern countries of Pakistan and Afghanistan, where various regional cultures flourished from ca. 3000 BCE. Its mature phase lasted about 1000 years, starting in about 2700 BCE, when Harappa (in the northeast portion of the valley) and Mohenjo-Daro (on the Indus, nearly 400 miles to the southwest) seem to have functioned as the leading cities of an extensive region. Many details about the culture remain sketchy, for there is no agreement among scholars concerning the decipherment of the Harappan script, which has over 400 characters; in any case, much of the surviving writing is found on personal seals, which hold little promise of revealing much about the civilization. The basis of the economy was agriculture, facilitated by irrigation and periodic flooding of the rivers. There was also commerce, both internal and with settlements in southern Arabia and Mesopotamia, as a result of which some external cultural influences were adopted. Literate civilization in the Indus Valley was later in developing and of shorter duration than in Mesopotamia or Egypt, but the region over which it exercised control was larger. Over 1000 Harappan sites have been identified across an area of nearly 500,000 square miles.

Archaeology reveals that Harappan settlements were laid out according to an orderly grid oriented to the cardinal directions. Orthogonal town plans are generally an indication of a high level of central governmental control, and that seems to have been the case in Harappan culture. Buildings were durable, being constructed of fired bricks of uniform size throughout the region, and houses were provided with underground drains connected to a well-planned sewer system. As the cities were built on plains beside the river, flooding seems to have been a constant menace. Mohenjo-Daro (Figs. 3.1–3.2) was repaired at least nine times after damaging floods. Cities accordingly featured a walled, terraced citadel on high ground, provided with ceremonial buildings, large public storehouses for grain, and mills that could be used in time of peril to shelter and feed the population. Rising forty feet above the plain, Mohenjo-Daro's citadel also had a great stepped

bath measuring thirty by forty feet that is thought to have served some ritual function. However, there are no clearly identified large shrines or temples like those found in Egypt or Mesopotamia. Small figurines suggest a reverence for trees and animals, a mother goddess cult, and a male god that may be the precursor of the later Hindu deity Shiva. Water and fire may have been associated with rituals that are still not understood.

In contrast to both Mesopotamia and Egypt, the Indus settlements seem to have been relatively egalitarian societies. There are neither palaces nor royal tombs, and no great temple complexes to indicate a concentration of power and wealth. Excavated residential areas of Mohenjo-Daro, the best-preserved and most extensive city, estimated to have had a population of 40,000, show tightly packed houses organized around internal courtyards that were open to the sky for light and air. The plans vary, but all houses presented virtually blank façades to the street, as external openings were set high in the perimeter walls. Rooms were small, perhaps because there was a scarcity of wood to serve as beams for second floors and roof framing. While the buildings themselves do not seem elegant in terms of architectural refinement, the clear urban layout, careful provision of a water supply through wells, and drainage and sewer systems are without parallel at the time and are marks of an efficient, highly organized society.

Reasons for the rapid decline of Harappan culture by about 1700 BCE are disputed, but natural factors (changes in river courses, failure of irrigation systems, earthquakes) and incursions by northern ethnic groups appear to have played a part. Harappan cities ceased to be inhabited, and over the next two centuries the countryside was raided by nomads from the north. In about 1500 BCE migrations by Aryan tribes from eastern Iran began, and the Aryans eventually spread over the Indian subcontinent, displacing

Kandariya Mahadeva Temple, Khajuraho, 1025–50.
This view shows the plinth and entrance terrace in the foreground. From this angle, the orderly progression of roof masses simulates a mountain range.

Chronology

Beginning of cultures in the Indus Valley	3000 BCE
Occupation of Mohenjo-Daro	2400–2000 BCE
Composition of the Vedas	1500–900 BCE
Life of Siddhartha Gautama (Buddha)	563–483 BCE
Alexander the Great in the Indus Valley	326 BCE
Construction of the Great Stupa, Sanchi	begun 250 BCE
Sculpting of the Great Buddha, Bamiyan	7th century CE
Construction of Angkor Wat	begun ca. 1120 CE

CITADEL

Great bath

Granary

**3.1 Plan of Mohenjo-Daro, Indus Valley,
ca. 2400–2000 BCE.**
The city was located on a plain beside the river,
with a higher citadel section (left) that featured
granaries and a large stepped bath. Shaded areas
represent residential quarters that have been
excavated, with one section (top center), showing
orthogonal outlines of the foundations. As the
valley was subject to flooding, storage of foodstuffs
on a high point was a sensible precaution.

**3.2 View of the remains of Mohenjo-Daro, Indus
Valley, ca. 2400–2000 BCE.**
Excavations of Mohenjo-Daro began in the 1920s,
when archaeologists uncovered remains of the
citadel and portions of the lower-lying residential
area. Bricks made to a uniform size are the major
construction materials used.

N

0   500 m
0   1500 ft

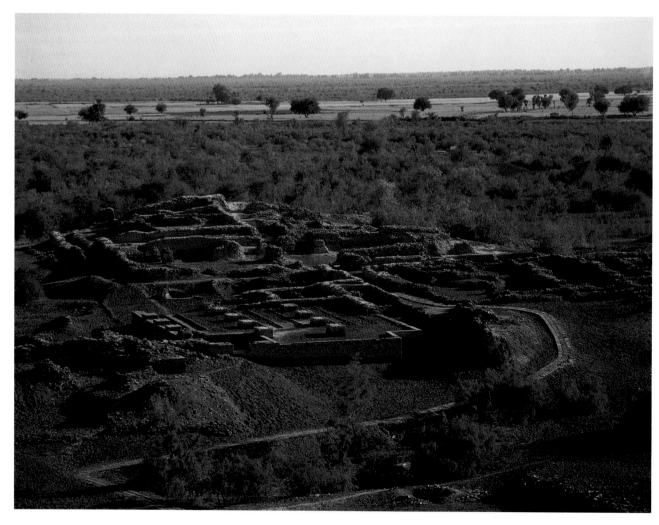

indigenous settlements. By 500 BCE their Indo-European language, the original root of many of the languages of Europe as well as Sanskrit in India, had displaced native tongues, a sign of cultural dominance. There was an ethnic factor here too: the invading Aryans were light-skinned in comparison to the darker-skinned native Indian populations. The distinction between conqueror and conquered became the earliest basis for the caste system that still operates in Indian society today.

Out of the confusion attending the migrations arose numerous small principalities. At about the time Alexander the Great was leading his army to the Indus (326 BCE), a young member of the Maurya tribe, Chandragupta, succeeded in bringing much of northern India under his command, eventually controlling most of what today is Pakistan and the eastern sections of Afghanistan as well. The empire continued to expand into southern India under his son and then grandson, Asoka (reigned 272–232 BCE), perhaps the greatest prince of the Maurya line and, as far as architecture is concerned, the first ruler of consequence. Asoka advanced the art of building in stone, bringing masons and stonecutters from Persia to construct monumental freestanding pillars, excavate caves for religious hermitages, and improve Buddhist shrines. His works have survived, and they will be considered below in the discussion of early Buddhist architecture.

A study of the ancient architecture in India and Southeast Asia is to a very large extent an examination of the development of temple architecture, for there are few structures not erected for religious purposes that have survived the passage of time. Temples were the primary buildings erected in durable materials, stone and brick, while houses and even palaces were constructed of less permanent wood, thatch, or stuccoed rubble and are therefore preserved only incidentally as, for example, in the backgrounds of scenes carved on temples. Princes, kings, and occasionally wealthy merchants were the major patrons of masonry temples, and thus architectural developments and religious preferences are closely related to political dynasties. In the period under consideration (up until about 1000 CE), the Indian subcontinent was not a unified country, although a certain level of cultural continuity was afforded by religious ties. A closer examination of Indian architecture would recognize the development of regional styles and the influences of powerful dynasties, but these will be given less emphasis here in the interests of creating a broad overview.

RELIGIONS OF INDIA

Since religious buildings assume such a prominent position in Indian architecture, it is necessary to understand the rudiments of the faiths that inspired their construction. During the sixth century BCE, the Indian subcontinent witnessed the development of three major religions that all shared a general belief in the transmigration of souls. This doctrine, which was as pervasive in India as the belief in life after death was in ancient Egypt, held that living souls passed through an endless cycle of rebirth and suffering. In somewhat differing ways, Hinduism, Buddhism, and Jainism proposed means by which people could transcend the sorrow of temporal existence.

Never the spirit was born; the spirit shall cease to be never;
Never was time it was not; End and Beginning are dreams!
Birthless and deathless and changeless remaineth the spirit
  for ever;
Death hath not touched it at all, dead though the house of
  it seems!
Who knoweth it exhaustless, self-sustained,
Immortal, indestructible,—shall such say, "I have killed
  a man, or caused to kill?"
Nay, but as when one layeth his worn-out robes away,
And, taking new ones, sayeth, "These will I wear to-day!"
So putteth by the spirit lightly its garb of flesh,
And passeth to inherit a residence afresh.

Bhagavad Gita (translated by Sir Edwin Arnold)

The common background for all three religions was a synthesis of traditional beliefs indigenous to the Indian peninsula and sacrificial cults brought by Aryans from the north. The oldest sacred writings, the Vedas, date from 1500 to 900 BCE. They contain hymns and prescribe rituals for the worship of a pantheon of gods identified with the natural elements. From an early date, there was also a cosmology that invoked the joining of male and female as a metaphor for the union of the individual with the Universal. Simple shrines gave physical expression to this idea through a **linga**, or upright stone emblematic of the male element, surrounded at the base by a **yoni**, or concentric circles representing the female principle. Observation of religious rites and sacrifices required to maintain proper relationships between people and the gods was entrusted to a group of priests or Brahmins, who came to hold considerable power within society. Ascetic cults that developed during this period promoted the view that the physical world is but a small part of a much greater cycle of birth, death, and rebirth, and they offered their followers guidance for escaping repeated reincarnations.

Partly in reaction to the dominance of the Brahmin priests and their elaborate rituals, a number of individuals sought simpler means to religious understanding and ethical living. Two lasting religious movements—Jainism, which is still practiced by about two million Indians, and Buddhism, one of the world's major religions, which is now virtually extinct in India but flourishes elsewhere— were founded by identifiable historical figures. Jainism was inspired by the life of Vardhamana, also known as Mahavira (great hero) and Jina (the victor). In 546 BCE Vardhamana found his version of the path to salvation in a complete rejection of the complex formulations of the

Brahmins. He taught that escape from the world's unhappiness was attainable only through rigorous asceticism to purify the soul and by maintaining reverence for all living creatures. His followers, mostly merchants and bankers whose livelihoods enabled them to avoid all forms of violence against animals, established Jainism (literally, religion of Jina), in which participants seek to acquire spiritual merit through charity, good works, and, whenever possible, monastic retreats. In architectural terms, Jaini temples never developed a distinctive style, borrowing elements instead from other religious groups.

In contrast, the religion founded by Siddhartha Gautama (ca. 563–ca. 483 BCE) was destined to become a major influence on architecture, not only in India, but also in Sri Lanka, China, Tibet, and southeast Asia. Born into a wealthy family, Gautama left his wife and fortune to travel as a beggar and seek an understanding of the causes of suffering. After six years of ascetic mortification and contemplation, he achieved enlightenment while sitting under the bodhi tree. Gautama's Four Noble Truths proclaimed that the world was worthless, that ignorance must be overcome, that vain craving could be renounced through yoga, and that the true path to salvation lay in the middle way between self-indulgence and self-mortification. These Truths, in conjunction with the Eight-fold Way (right views, resolve, speech, conduct, livelihood, effort, recollection, and meditation), formed the basis of his teachings, which were intended to enable his disciples to overcome worldly suffering caused by human desires and thus to achieve *nirvana* or liberation from the eternal cycle of birth and rebirth. Buddhism, the religion he inspired, took its name from the word "Buddha," the Enlightened One, the name given to Gautama after his conversion. As initially expounded, the religion required neither complex worship rituals nor a specific architectural context.

The religion of the Brahmins, which evolved into Hinduism, responded to Jainism and Buddhism by incorporating popular devotional images of gods and spirits into its rituals of worship and making these rituals relate more closely to people's daily lives. Hinduism, which remains the major religion in India today, had no single founder, and it still has no clearly defined religious hierarchy. Essential to its beliefs are acceptance of the Vedas as sacred texts, and maintenance of the caste structure, whereby society is organized immutably into four classes (priests, warriors, merchants/craftsmen, and laborers). Hindus hold that each individual accumulates the consequences of both good and bad actions through a series of lifetimes and pursues freedom from the cycle of rebirth through reverence to the gods and the elimination of passions. Of the innumerable Hindu deities, many with multiple and sharply differing aspects, there are three supreme gods: Shiva, Vishnu, and Brahma. Shiva, the great lord whose essential characteristic is procreative energy, but who can also be the great destroyer, has as his consort Devi, the mother goddess, whose alternate form includes

Kali the destroyer. Shiva's mount is the bull Nandi. Vishnu is the creator who embodies mercy and goodness, sometimes youthful romance, but who also has powers of destruction. His consort, Lakshmi, is the goddess of wealth, and his mount is the eagle Garuda. Brahma, the creator who is reborn periodically from a lotus growing in the navel of the sleeping Vishnu, has as his consort Sarasvati, patroness of learning and music.

EARLY BUDDHIST SHRINES

The Buddha had not prescribed any particular architectural setting for worship, but his disciples established shrines to give permanent form to their religion. The first shrines were created after the death of the Buddha, when his cremated remains were divided by his followers and placed in ten locations associated with his life and teaching. To mark these places, a simple mound of rubble and earth known as a **stupa** was erected over the relics, in a manner comparable to traditional **chaityas**, or village memorials, where the ashes of deceased leaders were placed in a mound, often located on the outskirts of their settlement. It was this traditional form and placement that served as the genesis of later Buddhist architecture. In time, Buddhist monks settled in the vicinity of stupas to form **viharas**, or small **monasteries** of individual cells organized around open courts. Their rituals included walking around (circumambulating) the stupa while chanting verses from scripture. A processional path, generally followed in a clockwise direction, remains central to Buddhist temple design.

The oldest surviving Buddhist stupas were enlarged with successive coverings or constructed anew during the reign of Asoka, the early Indian emperor who was converted to Buddhism. Through his contacts with Persian architecture and the Hellenistic world, Asoka brought to India builders proficient in the art of stonework, which until this time had not been used in construction. He also caused the roads leading to Buddhist shrines to be marked

3.3 Diagram illustrating the origin of the stupa.
The traditional practice of placing stones and earth over the graves of distinguished people evolved into the construction of a hemispherical form that incorporated the cosmological associations of a circle (in plan), the world mountain and dome of the heavens, and the vertical world axis.

3.4 Great Stupa, Sanchi, ca. 250 BCE–250 CE.
The elevationlike view shows a *torana* (gate), a portion of the *verdica* (fence), and, on top of the mound, the *chatra* (stylized bodhi tree), which symbolizes the tree under which the Buddha received enlightenment.

with tall columns inscribed with Buddhist teachings, known afterward as Asoka columns. These featured ornamental carving clearly modeled on Persian originals (see Fig. 1.17). Whereas the columns in Persian architecture supported a roof, in India they were freestanding elements used as commemorative markers in the landscape.

Under Asoka's patronage, the original simple stupas were enlarged and new shrines were created. All were regularized into hemispherical forms, reflecting the simplicity of the circle in plan, section, and elevation and creating a symbolic link to the cyclical nature of existence (Fig. 3.3). To provide for greater permanence, the stupas were faced with brick or stone. To indicate their sacred character, they were protected by a **verdica**, or enclosing fence, that delimited the path for circumambulation. And to mark their special association with the Buddha, they were crowned with a **harmica**, or square railing, and a **chatra**, or three-tiered umbrella form, stylized stone versions of the sacred enclosure fence and famous bodhi tree under which the Buddha received enlightenment. The triple parasol was emblematic of royalty, and its supporting stalk symbolized the axis of the world passing through the precise center of the hemispherical form of the stupa, symbol of the heavenly dome.

The monastery at Sanchi, founded by Asoka and enlarged over the next 500 years, illustrates the fundamental elements of Buddhist shrines in India. The Great Stupa, originally constructed as a mound about seventy feet in diameter, grew to become a dome that was almost 120 feet in diameter and fifty-four feet in height (Figs. 3.4–3.5).

Torana or gate

Verdica or fence

Chatra

Harmica or railing

Circumambulation path

N

0   10 m
0   30 ft

3.5 Plan of the Great Stupa, Sanchi, ca. 250 BCE–250 CE.
This plan shows the four gates and their bent-axis entry design that creates a swastika, perhaps linked to ancient sun symbols. Openings correspond to the cardinal directions. Stairs on the south side lead to the elevated circumambulation path used by priests.

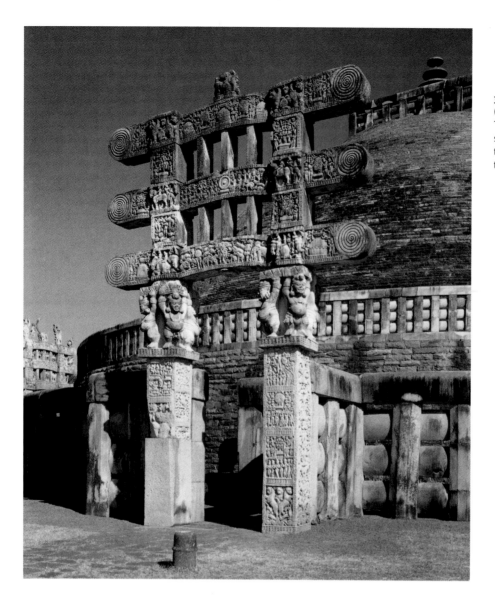

3.6 The torana (gate) and verdica (fence), Sanchi, ca. 250 BCE–250 CE. The verdica is composed of massive stones, treated in a manner analogous to wooden construction, while the toranas are richly carved.

At its top, the stupa is crowned by a chatra set inside a harmica. Its base is encircled by a two-tiered ambulatory: the upper level is reserved for priests, leaving the ground level path for pilgrim use. Enclosing the stupa is a massive stone verdica (Fig. 3.6), nine feet in height, with four carved gates at the cardinal points of the compass. The construction of this fence shows how early masons were influenced by wooden construction. Octagonal upright posts and rounded horizontal rails replicate forms already familiar in wood, reinterpreted here on a much larger scale. The elaborate **toranas**, or entrance gates, added in about 25 BCE, reflect bamboo prototypes. When built in stone, however, the size increased and it became possible, as here, to embellish the work with carved figures representing Buddhist legends, symbolism that may have been inspired by similar work on Asoka columns. The relative lack of modeling on the figures makes these gates seem more the work of woodcarvers than masonry sculptors. All four gates are set in front of the encircling fence, and they are part of a staggered, or bent-axis, approach designed to reduce distractions outside the sacred enclosure from disturbing the meditations of pilgrims circumambulating the stupa.

The shrine at Sanchi is an accumulation of buildings constructed over time, including three stupas and viharas for the monks (Fig. 3.7). In contrast to the permanent materials employed for the shrines, viharas were constructed of wood, and only their masonry foundations survive to indicate their layouts, which in many respects are an enlargement of the courtyard house already familiar from the early Indus Valley constructions and also used throughout Mediterranean civilizations. Buddhist monks lived in simple cells that were grouped around a square or rectangular open court containing community facilities, including the water supply. Sanchi also featured several enclosed chaitya halls, buildings permitting year-round devotions by enclosing a small stupa at the end of a rectangular hall. The end of the hall embracing the stupa was curved to reflect the shape contained within, and thus created an architectural form that could be erected as a freestanding structure raised on a base, or plinth, as in the so-called Temple 18 at Sanchi, or excavated from solid rock, as in the temples cut into cliffs at Ajanta, Ellora, and Karli.

Construction of these cave temples coincided with a period when the rulers of India's principalities favored Brahmin practices, and Buddhism was the religion

Temple 45 built
within a vihara

Viharas

Stupa 3 (Little Stupa)　　　　Great Stupa　　　Temple 17　　Temple 18　　Temple 40

3.7 (above) Reconstruction view of the temple complex, Sanchi.
In the center is the Great Stupa, and to the right is the so-called
Temple 40, an early chaitya hall. The rectangular plan building
at the upper left is a vihara, a residence for monks, of which only
the foundations remain.

**3.8 (below) Plan of and section through the cave temple, Karli,
ca. 100 BCE.**
Excavated in a rock cliff, this temple consists of a chaitya hall with
an ambulatory around the stupa shrine at the rear. Two freestanding
columns (one now gone) flanked the entrance, while stone and
teakwood carvings screened the opening to the cave.

primarily of wealthy merchants. Even though Buddhist
shrines were thus financed by substantial donations,
the monks increasingly sought remote sites for construction to avoid conflicts with Brahmins. Rock cliffs and
gorges provided isolated locations, and the living rock
contained durable material for masons to carve without
their having to enclose space with stone beams. At the
great cave temple of Karli (Fig. 3.8), which dates from the
first century BCE, the chaitya hall faithfully replicates the
form and details of wooden architecture that provided
its prototype, including the semicircular arched ceiling
patterned after flexible bamboo structures. Karli's dimensions, however, exceed those of wooden buildings of the
period: the hall is forty-five feet wide, a difficult span to
achieve in timber, but one that presented no problem
to the excavators. Starting from the cliff face, which was
smoothed and shaped to resemble the façade of a chaitya
hall, workers drove two tunnels 150 feet into the cliff to
establish the length of the temple, then enlarged the excavation to create a barrel-shaped ceiling with arched "ribs."
Rock on the chamber floor was cut away and columns
carved as workers completed excavating the entire interior
space. Rubble extracted from the cliff became material

Stupa

Vestibule　　　　Nave

Side aisle

0 ———————————— 20 m
0 ———————————— 60 ft

Bamiyan and the Colossal Buddha
by C. Murray Smart

3.9 Great Buddha, Bamiyan, Afghanistan, late Gandhara school, 7th century (destroyed 2001). Height 171 ft (52 m).

Traders transported Indian design and iconography east by sea to Southeast Asia and Indonesia and west through the mountain passes to Central Asia by Silk Road caravans. The main text here deals with the most spectacular examples of Indian architecture in Southeast Asia—the great works at Angkor and other sites. Equally important, however, is the great Buddhist pilgrimage complex of Bamiyan in what is today Afghanistan; it was here that the colossal image of the Buddha first appeared. Bamiyan was the western terminus of three of the trade routes that connected China, India, the Near East, and the Western world. At Bamiyan, a great monastic complex more than a mile long was carved into a sandstone cliff overlooking a fertile valley between the Hindu Kush to the east and the Koh-i-Baba mountain range to the northwest. The site was visited in the seventh century by the Chinese pilgrim Xuanzang, who described it in glowing terms. Another famous visitor, Genghis Khan, apparently found less to admire: legend has it that he massacred the entire population, turning Bamiyan into the deserted complex of today.

The monastery is terminated at each end by a colossal Buddha statue (Fig. 3.9). The figure at the eastern end, designated "Sakyamuni" by Xuanzang, is 120 feet tall; the more spectacular figure at the western end, which Xuanzang simply called "the Buddha," is 171 feet tall. It is the larger figure that is of greater importance, not only because of its size, but also because its iconography and style were replicated in small souvenir statues and exported to the home countries of visiting pilgrims. A comparison of the Bamiyan figures with those of the Dun Huang caves in China reveals that the Buddhist iconography of China was influenced directly by the figures at Bamiyan.

The two Buddhas illustrate the cosmopolitan nature of the Buddhist art at Bamiyan. They are quite different in style. In every respect except its size, the smaller figure is a typical Gandharan Buddha figure of the second or third century CE. Its construction is interesting. Only the basic armature of the body was carved; over the rough stone body and head, facial features and voluminous drapery folds were modeled in plaster made of mud and straw. The figure was finished with a coating of lime-plaster that was painted and gilded. At the time of Xuanzang's visit, the statue was completely covered with gold leaf and metal ornaments, leading him to the erroneous conclusion that it was made of metal.

As interesting as the statue are the fragments of fresco that remain. Originally, the niche in which the figure stands was completely covered with paintings symbolizing the vault of heaven. The central image of the fresco above the Buddha's head is a sun god driving a chariot drawn by horses and attended by winged angels. It could be Apollo, or Surya, the Hindu sun god, or perhaps Mithra, the Persian sun god. Two of the four flanking angels have human form and are inspired by Persian and Mediterranean prototypes; the other two are derived from Greek harpies and have birds' feet.

The drapery of the larger Buddha was modeled on ropes attached to wooden dowels driven into the stone armature. The result was an enormous replica of a late Gandharan Buddha type in which the robe was reduced to a series of lines that clung to and revealed the body form beneath. This statue is two centuries or more later in origin than the smaller figure; it probably dates from the fifth century CE. It stands in a trefoil niche that creates a double halo about the body and head; this double halo was much copied in both China and Japan.

These two figures are the first of many colossal images of the Buddha that would appear throughout the Buddhist world. Both Greece and Rome produced colossal figures that served as prototypes. And just as the colossal portrait sculptures of Roman emperors were intended to portray them as divine rulers of the world, the Bamiyan figures portray the Buddha as cosmic man, the source and substance of the universe.

Unfortunately, since this essay was written, the fundamentalist Muslim sect formerly in power in Afghanistan, the Taliban, destroyed both of these two colossal Buddha figures in 2001. Since the overthrow of the Taliban, there has been talk internationally of restoring the statues, but no plans have yet been announced.

for construction of a platform extending to the cave's entrance, a recessed, arched porch marked by paired free-standing columns supporting lion sculptures. This porch was adorned with relief carvings and (originally) painted scenes from the life of the Buddha. Inside the chaitya hall, the relatively dim light penetrating through high grilles in the windows allows the pilgrim to discern slowly the enormity of the space, measured by the stately rhythm of colonnades and dominated at the far recess by a stupa carved with the image of the Buddha. The architects of the temple at Karli achieved that elusive synthesis of space, light, and detail that characterizes the finest buildings of any era.

HINDU TEMPLES
Early Buildings

Buddhist and Hindu traditions have a long history of coexistence on the Indian subcontinent, and among followers of various sects there has been a certain commingling of beliefs as well as temple forms. Although Hinduism draws strongly on some of the most ancient indigenous beliefs, it only developed a particular architectural expression for itself later. Buddhists built the earliest surviving shrines and thereby established the model on which early Hindu architecture was based, but from the fifth century CE onward, Hinduism became the dominant religion in India. Today few Buddhist sects remain there.

As in Buddhist practice, the Hindu temple creates a link between the gods and the worshiper. However, unlike the Buddhists, who focus on the life and teachings of one leader, Hindus venerate a multitude of deities including Vishnu, a solar deity. Their temples are simultaneously dwellings of the god, places for worship, and objects of worship in themselves. Aspects of the cosmos (and thus of the gods) are incorporated into the temple by the use of specific forms, sacred geometry, careful orientation, and axial alignments. Most Hindu temple designs include forms that are symbolic of the holy mountain, the sacred cave, and the cosmic axis (Fig. 3.10). Geometry derived from a subdivided square or **mandala** is commonly used, together with a single unit that sets all proportions. Numbers associated with the gods are important in constructing and interpreting the mandala, which provides links to divine proportions, hence harmony with the cosmos. Temple complexes are usually aligned on the cardinal points, representing the four corners of the earth, with the major entrances facing east. Priests perform sacred rites at regular times for the benefit of the entire community, and private devotions may be offered at any time. Since there is no congregational worship, there is no corresponding need for a large enclosed space. Rather, the temple as a three-dimensional form in the landscape becomes a focal point for community life, much as a Christian church might serve social and artistic purposes as well as religious functions.

Some of the earliest surviving Hindu shrines are found in the rock-cut temples of Udaigiri, near Sanchi, and these show clear influence from Buddhist work. Temple 17 at Sanchi, dating from the early fifth century CE, is modeled on the rock-cut temples at Udaigiri, set on a plinth and featuring a square sanctuary preceded by a pillared porch. This two-chambered temple form is amplified and embellished in virtually all later developments. The sanctuary is typically quite small. Known as the **garbhagriha**, or womb-chamber, it contains a sacred image or element as a symbol of the god's presence. If proper rituals are not observed, the god may choose to inhabit another place, so worship involves priestly ceremonies that welcome, entertain, and honor the deity with music, food, dancing, the recital of religious texts, and the singing of hymns. The covered porch provides a transition between the outside world and the sanctuary, and on its pillars and the exterior walls of the temple the visitor can generally find sculpted panels and images that complement the image of the deity within.

Hindu gods are believed to have a particular affinity for mountains and caves. As builders became more skillful in working in stone (or occasionally brick), they gave increasingly elaborate formal expression to the vertical mound (mountain) arising over the sanctuary (cave). As an example of this process, consider the Ladkhan Temple (Fig. 3.11), built in the seventh century CE at Aihole, which preserves in its stonework the traces of a wooden village assembly hall that served as its model. The masons

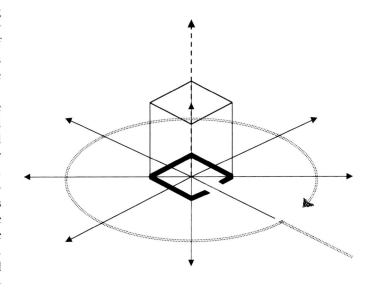

3.10 Diagram illustrating the basis for most Hindu temples. This axonometric view shows a womb-chamber (garbhagriha) that radiates energy to the cardinal and ordinal directions; a passage for circumambulation in a clockwise direction; and the sacred mountain defining a central vertical axis that towers over the garbhagriha.

3.11 Ladkhan Temple, Aihole, 7th century CE.
Notice that a columned porch precedes the pillared main hall of the temple, translating into stone architectural forms previously built in wood as village assembly halls.

3.12 Vishnu Temple, Bhitargaon, 5th century CE.
Constructed in brick, this is one of the earliest Hindu temples to have a towering mass constructed over the garbhagriha.

resolved questions of overall form and building details as a carpenter would. When translated into stone, however, the light and pliant wooden structure became overscaled and heavy.

Later Temples

Later Hindu temples rise more dramatically, as builders exploited architectural form as the basis for sculptural embellishment, sweeping masses upward in imitation of entire mountain ranges. At Bhitargaon, the brick Vishnu Temple, dating perhaps to the first half of the fifth century, presents an early example of a more prominent super-structure erected over the sanctuary (Fig. 3.12). Even in its somewhat ruined state, the temple's profile shows an unmistakable allusion to mountain forms. The passage connecting the sanctuary and the porch is unusual for incorporating **true-arch** construction. Most Indian temples are built using post-and-lintel or corbeling techniques, but this temple demonstrates that builders had knowledge of the arch even though it was seldom employed. The source of the characteristic **shikhara**, or mountain-peak roof, of mature Indian temples has been traced to lightweight thatched bamboo structures with curving sides rising from a square base. No matter how elaborate the masonry

3.13 Temple, Khajuraho, 10th century.
Dominant here is the shikhara roof commonly found over
the garbhagriha of many Hindu temples. Its towering form
creates a symbolic holy mountain over the sacred cave.

3.14 Plan of the Lingaraja Temple, Bhubaneshwar, ca. 1050–1150.
More elaborate than some, this temple plan has three separate
halls preceding the garbhagriha at the end of the processional
axis. Each hall is provided with a distinctive roof profile so that the
composition builds to the high shikhara.

temple forms became, with their exteriors covered with
carved ornament and walls adorned with sculpture, the
essence of a square sanctuary housed under the curving
shikhara roof, preceded by one or more columnar halls
or porches in axial alignment, remains the distinctive
design paradigm for the Hindu temple (Fig. 3.13). The
enormously thick masonry walls required to sustain the
towering roof amplified the womblike seclusion of the
central shrine room, enveloping the chamber within the
sacred mountain.

Two temple groups dating from the eighth to thirteenth
centuries illustrate the prolific magnificence of northern
Hindu architecture. Bhubaneshwar, in the state of Orissa,
has over a hundred temples constructed across a period of
five centuries. The plan of the celebrated Lingaraja Temple
(mid-eleventh to mid-twelfth century) is an elaboration
of the two-celled form, with three pillared halls on axis
preceding the sanctuary. From east to west, these comprise
a hall of offerings, a hall of dance, an assembly hall, and

finally the sanctuary proper (Fig. 3.14). Pyramidal roofs
over the halls resemble foothills, contrasting with the massive central shikhara over the sanctuary, whose form is
echoed on a smaller scale by the subsidiary shrines erected
inside the walled rectangular temple precinct. Within the
worshiper's field of vision, there are sculpted figures carved
with a high degree of detail as well as sensuous beauty to
enrich the wall surfaces. Unlike a number of other historic
temples, this massive shrine remains in active use.

At Khajuraho, royal city of the Chandella Dynasty,
there were at least twenty-five temples constructed over a
200-year period, with sculptural programs reflecting lavish artistic patronage as well as devotion to mystic Tantric
rites. Among the best-preserved is the Lakshmana Temple
(ca. 950) (Fig. 3.15), raised on a rectangular platform
anchored by four small shrines at the corners. The axial
approach from the east brings the visitor up several flights
of steps, whose ascent is repeated in the successively rising
roof forms over an initial open porch, a second porch, a

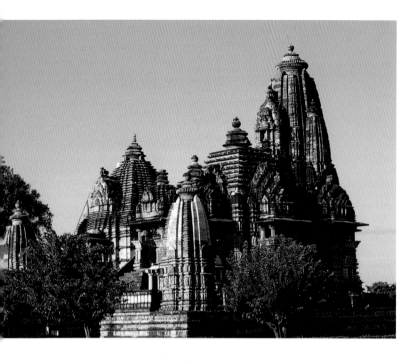

3.15 Lakshmana Temple, Khajuraho, ca. 950.
The temple stands on a platform, or plinth, a stylobate in ancient Greek architecture. Shrines at the corners reflect the main shrine at a diminished scale.

3.16 Kandariya Mahadeva Temple, Khajuraho, ca. 1025–50.
Upper levels of the roof are carved with geometric ornament, which has the effect of making the massive form seem lighter while accentuating its contours. Sculpted figures populate the lower, friezelike bands.

great pillared hall, and finally the internal sanctuary. The devotee may circumambulate the sanctuary by following an enclosed passage surrounding the shrine room. Light for the ambulatory is provided by openings placed above eye level so that the elaborate interior wall sculpture may be seen without admitting distractions from the external world. Images represented here include many animated scenes of loving couples, generally interpreted as both a literal representation of Tantric practices (which included sexual intercourse) and a symbol of the rapturous union of the human with the divine that was a goal of Hindu theology (Figs. 3.16–3.17).

All the Hindu temples considered thus far are products of dynasties that ruled primarily in the north and central sections of India. In the south, a distinctive regional style developed that featured roofs with rounded finials, walls with engaged columns or pilasters for articulation, multi-columned halls, and temple complexes that had sets of concentric walls with massive gateway entrances. As with architecture in northern India, the origin of this style can be traced to the early seventh-century rock-cut temples that generally featured a pillared hall as a prelude to a sanctuary set deep in the interior. In cave architecture, the pillared hall functioned much like a portico or porch, a transition between the outside world and the shrine. (The early temple of Ladkhan at Aihole may well have served as a model for the scheme.) The same stonecutting skills that were used to excavate cave temples were put to more sculptural use in about 650, when a remarkable set of

diminutive temples was carved out of a granite ridge at Mahabalipuram. The Dharmaraja, Bhima, and Arjuna temples seen in Figure 3.18, known as **rathas** (wheeled carts or chariots), are similar to large-scale architectural models, and each one is different. Some are obviously derived from the barrel-vaulted roofs of chaitya halls, while others are based on simple wooden shrines or elaborations of

3.17 Kandariya Mahadeva Temple, Khajuraho, ca. 1025–50.
In its lower registers, where figures are close enough to be seen by visitors, figural sculpture features prominently. Notice the figures' swaying, S-shaped postures.

3.18 Dharmaraja Ratha, Bhima Ratha, and Arjuna Ratha, Mahabalipuram, 7th century.
These three monolithic temples, cut from granite outcroppings, replicate in stone an earlier temple architecture in wood. Note the chaityalike roof on the Bhima Ratha that resembles thatch. Repetition of selected forms unites all three temples.

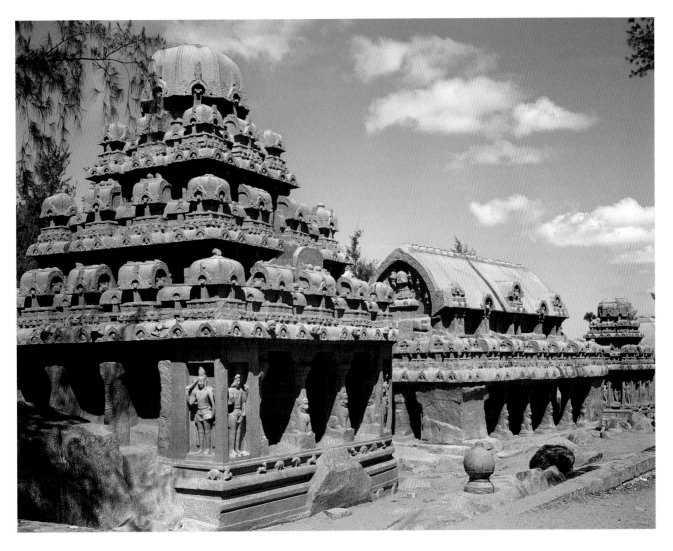

3.19 Plan of Brihadeshvara Temple, Tanjore, 11th century.
Compare this plan to that of the Lingaraja Temple at Khajuraho
to see how all elements of the temple have been greatly
increased in size. The central axis is defined by a gopura
or towering entrance gate on the east side.

Shrine of Srisubramanya

Shrine of Chandeshvara

Meeting hall

Entrance gate or gopura

Main shrine
or garbhagriha

Great hall

Nandi hall

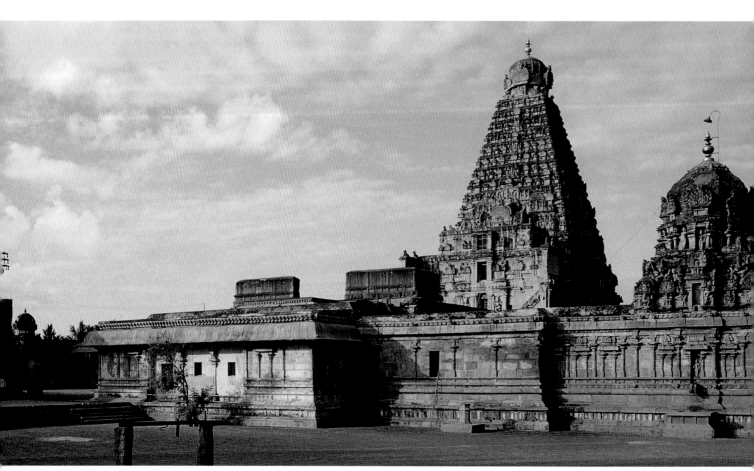

centralized designs. All are set on a raised base and make use of engaged columns or pilasters for wall articulation. Images of deities, mythological beings, and the royal family (the Pallavas) who commissioned the work are set in recesses defined by the pilasters. Multiple roofs in layers add verticality to the forms. When one realizes how much of the hard granite was cut away to create these diminutive masterpieces, it is apparent that the art of working stone had reached a high level of sophistication and taste.

What began at small scale was continued at much greater size in the eleventh-century Brihadeshvara Temple at Tanjore (Figs. 3.19–3.20). Here the builders succeeded in erecting a tower over the garbhagriha that was three times the height (200 feet) of anything else that had been attempted prior to that time. The base is substantial, an eighty-two-foot square in plan, but there is a processional space around the central shrine included in the lower story, so it is not a solid mass. Half-columns and niches define a two-story elevation rising above the base, while uncounted roof levels recede as they ascend in the towering pyramid roof, which is capped by a monolith weighing over eighty tons that forms a domelike finial. As one might expect, the temple complex is axially arranged, with a porch and two multi-columned halls preceding the shrine proper. A separate pillared shrine honoring Nandi the sacred bull is placed on axis between the temple and the great entrance gate. The enclosing wall is composed of a continuous double colonnade, and several lesser temples occupy corners of the courtyard.

Angkor Wat

Hinduism spread to other regions in Southeast Asia through the activity of Indian merchants, just as was the case with Buddhism, and the religion remains a force in those regions today. Among the numerous monuments of Hindu art outside the Indian subcontinent, one of the most impressive is the vast temple of Angkor Wat in Cambodia, which represents a fusion of Indian religion and native Khmer tradition (Fig. 3.21). Angkor Wat itself is one of the largest religious structures ever built, with a rectangular perimeter wall measuring 4275 by 4920 feet. Visitors wishing to make a complete pilgrimage according to Hindu practice would walk about thirteen miles to visit all the galleries within the complex. Begun in ca. 1120 as a temple to Vishnu, Angkor Wat was finished as the royal shrine of the Khmer Dynasty that ruled Cambodia at that time before being converted to Buddhist worship.

The Khmer civilization reached its height in the thirteenth century. At this time, the area around Angkor Wat

3.21 Plan of Angkor Wat, begun ca. 1120.
The clarity of this design is remarkable. Nested sets of galleries focus on the main shrine, the symbolic representation of Mount Mehru, home of the gods.

was the most extensive urban complex in the world, occupied by some 750,000 people. This urbanization required large quantities of food, in this case rice, which demanded vast, predictable amounts of water for its cultivation. Khmer engineers shaped an enormous artificial landscape, with its largest features being reservoirs covering as much as eight square miles. Droughts in the late fourteenth and early fifteenth centuries apparently destabilized the culture.

Early Khmer temples consisted of a tower sanctuary within a walled enclosure. The tower again represented

3.20 (opposite) Brihadeshvara Temple, Tanjore, 11th century.
Seen beyond the Shrine of Chandeshvara, the pyramidal shikhara roof over the main shrine rises from a square base, towering over 200 feet to dominate the extensive temple. Its domed top is cut from a single piece of granite in a form that resembles a Buddhist stupa.

3.22 Angkor Wat, begun ca. 1120.
This view from the east shows how the plan is translated into a three-dimensional form through the interplay of horizontal and vertical elements.

the sacred mountain, while the garbhagriha inside evoked the holy cave at the center of the cosmos. This theme was elaborated in later temples that featured multiple tower sanctuaries on a terrace. Later still, forms resembling step pyramids gave more vivid expression to the concept of the cosmic mountain. Until the construction of Angkor Wat, the most extensive interpretation of these themes in Khmer architecture came in temples that placed the tower sanctuary at the summit of a stepped pyramid, with open galleries for circumambulation extending around all four sides. Angkor takes this organization as the point of departure for an even more magnificent articulation, adding multiple towers, extended cruciform galleries, corner **pavilions**,

and elaborate entrance gates to the central tower and elevated platform (Fig. 3.22). At the heart of the composition is a 215-foot-tall central tower over the main shrine, built on a pyramid base whose corners are marked by four stepped towers that collectively are meant to symbolize Mount Mehru, the home of the gods. Two additional sets of square concentric galleries surround this core, punctuated by entrance gates in the centers of the four sides to reinforce the cardinal directions. The main axial approach passes through a square courtyard featuring artificial ponds before entering the second gallery and ascending the steep stairs to the innermost platform sanctuary. A moat nearly two-and-a-half miles in length encircles the entire site, symbolizing the oceans out of which the mountain rises.

Angkor Wat is built entirely in stone, and since it does not employ arched construction, only corbeling, there are no large interior spaces. Once laid, the stone became the domain of sculptors, who adorned walls and even roofs with ornament and shallow relief carvings. Some of the subjects are drawn from epics familiar within Hindu tradition, but these are blended with references to Khmer cosmology, and the whole serves as a mortuary shrine for Suryavarman II, the king who commissioned the work. In India, Hinduism never involved the concept of a god-king or ancestor worship, but these aspects are part of the Cambodian tradition and inform the design of Angkor Wat. Overall, the form captures the qualities both of horizontal expanse and vertical expression in a single composition. The architecture is symmetrical, balanced, and grand, the culminating expression of religious concepts begun centuries earlier in India.

CONCLUSIONS ABOUT ARCHITECTURAL IDEAS

Chapters 1 and 2 drew some attention to what were termed constituent facts, facts that seem to have relevance in multiple eras and for multiple designers, and in the current chapter a consideration of some constituent facts of architectural ordering is again worthwhile. For example, as with the architecture of Egypt and Mesopotamia, Indian and Southeast Asian architecture long made dramatic use of the vertical (Khajuraho), the horizontal and multiple horizontal datum lines (Ladkhan and Kandariya Mahadeva temples), the richness of a building's silhouette as seen against the sky (Lakshmana Temple), central plans (Sanchi), orthogonal plans (Brihadeshvara Temple and Angkor Wat), and spatial sequence (Lingaraja Temple). And certainly all of this work displays a universal concern

for proportional relationships in the careful balancing of horizontals and verticals.

Yet, we must admit that at least superficially the Indian and Cambodian results appear to be quite different. In the service of directing human energies toward a release from the cycle of existences, Hindu designers of religious structures chose to emphasize, even to exaggerate certain features and to intensify their application of certain design principles. The most obvious contrast between what we have seen previously and what appears in this chapter is the profusion within the latter of a sensual phantasma of ornamentation held within repetitive broken-frieze-like assemblies (not unlike what we will see in Chapter 9's presentation of the Gothic cathedrals in France and Chapter 10's presentation of temples in Pre-Columbian Central America). If we apply a metaphorical description, we might say that the systematic application of ornament in Indian and Southeast Asian work sometimes reaches such a level of richness, as at the Lakshmana Temple, that the building evokes the image of an exotic fruit or seed pod that has matured and burst, revealing the profundity of its inner, organic contents.

Metaphor is also useful as we look deeper, beneath the surface ornamentation to the underlying ordering principles. Consider the temple at Angkor Wat. Its plan amplifies gridded geometry to the level of tapestrylike woven-ness, such that the larger application of a systematic weft and warp is comparable to the detailed application of ornament, as if there were a single organic directive.

In the end, we can learn much about design intentions and design principles by viewing this Eastern work, both as an intrinsic part of the culture that produced it and as a universal result of human longings and aspirations and perceptions of the physical world and efforts to organize it. And this duality of viewpoint will be equally informative in the chapter that follows on the architecture of China and Japan.

Chapter 4
The Traditional Architecture of China and Japan

China is vast in size and has the largest population of any country on earth. We tend to regard it as an ancient culture because, even though historic civilization developed there slightly later than in Mesopotamia or Egypt, China holds the distinction among civilizations of having maintained the highest degree of cultural continuity across the 4000 years of its existence. China's nearly ten million square miles contain varied geographical conditions and over fifty ethnic groups, but its society has generally been defined by the Han Chinese. Unified government under strong emperors encouraged uniformity in many societal structures, including city design and building practices, and Chinese architectural traditions were remarkably stable over the centuries until the forcible intrusion of Western culture in the nineteenth century and the toppling of the last emperor in 1911.

For buildings from the period before about 2000 BCE, there is little information because so many of the sites are still occupied and thus the excavations necessary to understand early architecture have not yet been made. Archaeologists have found remains of farming and craft villages in the Yellow River Valley, most notably at Banpo, where small houses with both circular and rectangular plans have been reconstructed based on foundation remains (Fig. 4.1). The rectangular houses were sunk a half-story into the ground and had truncated, pyramidal roofs (no walls) of lightweight wooden members lashed together at the top. Earth-sheltering helped to stabilize the interior temperature in both summer and winter. Smoke from the central hearth escaped through a gap at the apex of the overriding, thatch-covered gable roof, and the sloping entranceway was protected by another gable roof. The circular huts had side walls of wattle covered inside and out by a thick layer of clay for insulation, and the same treatment was given to the truncated, conical roof, with an opening left at the peak for ventilation and covered by a gable roof, just as was the case with the rectangular houses. The doorway was recessed, and some houses seem to have had internal partitions or screens. Painted pottery remains suggest that skilled ceramists were working in these villages, and there are indications of weaving, although the

textiles themselves have long since vanished. The next millennium saw the development of larger houses that still fall within the same architectural vocabulary of timber frame, earthen plastering, and thatch.

From these humble prehistoric origins came the legendary beginning of Chinese history with the Shang Dynasty, which emerged in about 1766 BCE to dominate the Yellow River Valley and extend its control as far south as the Yangtze Kiang. Shang technology included skill in bronze casting and pictograph writing preserved on oracle bones (the shoulder blades of sheep). With the Shang begins the series of dynastic successions—Zhou, Han, Tang, Song, Yuan, Ming, and Qing, to name the major ones—that dominated Chinese history until the early twentieth century.

In China, the primary impetus for building came from the government (the imperial court and the state) rather than from religious organizations or private patrons. The most obvious manifestation of this pattern of investment is the Great Wall, begun in pieces by feudal lords, unified by the first Qin emperor in 221 BCE, and largely rebuilt and extended during the Ming Dynasty (1368–1644 CE) (see page 80). It is an astonishing piece of construction, almost 4000 miles long, ranging from the coast through varied terrain to its terminus in the Gobi Desert. Originally it was largely made with rammed earth, but during the Ming Dynasty the height of most of the wall was raised and given its present casing of brick or stone. As it exists today, the Great Wall varies from nineteen to thirty-nine feet in height, with an average width at the top of sixteen

Great Wall of China, 221 BCE–1368 CE.
Watchtowers and wall sections with battlements snake across the rugged terrain. The crenelations provide protection on the north side while on the south side (toward China) the parapet is lower and unfortified.

Chronology

Shang Dynasty	1766 BCE–1123 BCE
Han Dynasty	202 BCE–221 CE
Construction of the Great Wall	221 BCE–1368 CE
Life of Confucius	551–479 BCE
Composition of the *Kao Gong Ji*	5th century CE
Tang Dynasty	618–906 CE
Construction of the Ise Shrine	begun 690
Song Dynasty	960–1279
Composition of the *Yingzao-fashi*	1103
Yuan Dynasty	1280–1368
Ming Dynasty	1368–1644
Construction of Imperial and Forbidden cities at Beijing	15th century

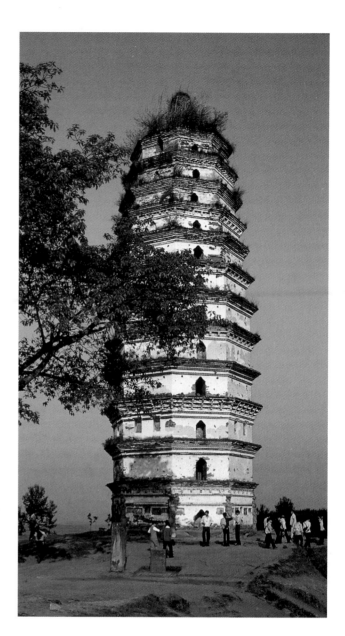

4.1 Reconstructions of Neolithic houses, Banpo, ca. 2000 BCE.
These reconstructions show rectangular and circular designs. As was the case with prehistoric houses in western Europe, these dwellings used readily available materials—wood, thatch, and earth—to provide shelter. A central hearth is also part of many houses at Banpo.

4.2 Pagoda, Dazu, Sichuan province, 12th century.
The pagoda's tiered organization is ultimately based on the chatra or stylized bodhi tree set atop Indian stupas. Its parabolic profile may also owe something to the shikhara roofs of Hindu temples.

feet. The north-facing side is capped by crenelated battlements, with watchtowers at intervals connected by a road extending along the top. In the event of attack, beacons could be used to summon reinforcements from garrison camps that were strategically located on the southern side. Only a highly organized, powerful state could command the resources required to construct and maintain an engineering work on this scale. One should not be surprised to find the Chinese achieving similarly consistent building standards in more modest projects.

Indigenous Chinese religious traditions were based on a belief in life after death, ancestor worship, and animism (a reverence for natural features such as trees, rocks, and hills, as well as cosmic elements including the sky, sun, and moon). From early times, indigenous religions had included the concept already mentioned in the chapter on Indian architecture of the complementary duality of

female and male, or *yin* and *yang*, which carries over as an artistic principle into architecture and landscape design. Chinese philosophy received its clearest articulation in the fifth century BCE through the lives and writings of two sages, Laotzu and Confucius. Laotzu's philosophy, Daoism, was mystical in approach, seeking harmony of human action and the world through the study of nature. Daoist philosophy is largely anti-rational and anti-authoritarian, as may be seen in the *I Ching*, or *Book of Changes*, an oracle text consulted in conjunction with the casting of coins to determine what part should be read for guidance in finding answers to perplexing questions. Aspects of Daoism may be found particularly in the Chinese approach to garden design, where carefully contrived views and experiences are based on the model provided by nature itself. In contrast, the philosophy expounded by Confucius relied on respect for authority as established by the state. Its innately conservative tenets have dominated Chinese social and political structures throughout history. Those in power are to act benevolently on behalf of their subjects, and ordinary people are to show proper deference to the superior wisdom and understanding of their revered leaders. Ancestor worship and respect for one's elders in the family, hallmarks of a well-ordered Confucian family, had exact parallels in the veneration that society in general owed to the reigning emperor, regarded as a virtual deity whose welfare was crucial for the stability of the state. Chinese city planning and traditional house design embodied Confucian principles in their layouts and axial alignments of buildings.

While Confucianism and Daoism are not religions in the Western sense of the term, they are philosophies that have influenced the way many people think. Buddhism would become the most widespread organized religion in China, transmitted to the country during the first or second centuries CE by merchant caravans moving along the Silk Roads across Central Asia, connecting China, Persia, and India. Architectural ideas accompanied Buddhist teachings, resulting in Chinese buildings that have roots in Indian practice. For example, the northern Indian cave temples around Gandhara, furnished with towering images of the Buddha, inspired similar cave temples with gigantic statues built in China as early as the fourth century CE. At Yungang (near Datong), over twenty large caves were cut into the steep sandstone cliffs during the fifth and sixth centuries. In their carved images and detailing, they exhibit artistic influences from India—elephants, lotus plants, scrolling vines—as well as dwindled aspects of Hellenistic art, such as acanthus leaf foliage. Modern photographs cannot do justice to the original conception of these cave façades, as their appearance has been damaged by erosion over the centuries.

More widespread than the creation of cave temples was the practice of building Buddhist temple complexes with a hall for venerating images of the Buddha and a separate **pagoda**, or tower, erected over relics symbolic of the Buddha's presence. The pagoda was inspired by the parasol-like finials atop northern Indian stupas and by multi-storied watchtowers from Chinese military construction. As a religious structure, the pagoda became a graceful multi-story building with layered roofs. Early versions can be found as carved pillars inside cave temples. The pagoda's original purpose, to house relics and sacred writings, was expanded to make the structure into a vertical marker in the landscape (Fig. 4.2). Among the earliest freestanding examples is the 130-foot-tall Songyue Pagoda at Dengfeng, built in 523, the oldest surviving brick structure in the country. This is a tapering, twelve-sided, parabolic cylinder, hollow through the center, with fifteen tiers of roofs but without means of access to the top. The parabolic shape may have been inspired by shikhara roofs on Hindu temples, and the rounded finial shows close affinity to Indian stupa designs. The Longhua Pagoda in Shanghai

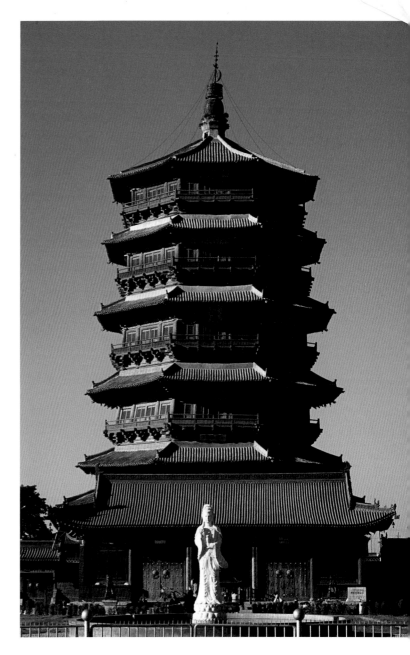

4.3 Pagoda, Fogong Monastery, Shanxi province, 1056.
Like the pagoda at Dazu, this pagoda's organization is based on the stacking up of smaller, often repetitive, elements.

(977) has a brick core and wooden perimeter galleries for viewing the landscape. The ends of the roof tiers cantilever outward and upward in a graceful fashion that was to become characteristic of Chinese roof profiles. The pagoda at the Fogong Monastery in Shanxi province (1056) is the oldest surviving pagoda constructed entirely in wood and one of the tallest wooden constructions in the world (Fig. 4.3). The 220-foot-tall octagonal building rises five levels in ten structural tiers, alternating upright posts with cantilevered roofs and balconies. On the exterior, these levels are expressed as intricately bracketed overhanging roofs and galleries that contrast with trabeated wall sections. The entire structure tapers slightly to the center, which contributes to stability and also gives the impression of greater height.

CHINESE ARCHITECTURAL PRINCIPLES

Although the earliest surviving Chinese buildings date only from the sixth century CE, there is archaeological and written evidence of older practices. Ceramic objects found in Han-Dynasty burials were cast in the form of houses or watchtowers, preserving some indication of long-vanished timber structures. Wood was the primary material of early Chinese architecture, and it was used most often in post-and-beam construction. Roof structures were based on a series of beams set in parallel tiers, augmented over time by intricate bracketing for beam–column junctions and cantilevered overhangs. A modular unit called the **jian** (with variable dimensions) was defined as the basic measure in construction (Fig. 4.4). More elaborate buildings contained additional jian, usually in odd numbers so that the distinction of a central bay was preserved, much as the even number of columns on Greek temples emphasized a space between the central pair. Since the structure was separate from the system of enclosure, Chinese buildings have a certain interior freedom in plan, as lightweight, non-load-bearing walls can be located in response to internal needs.

Except for the humblest single-jian houses, Chinese buildings tend to occur in ensembles organized around courtyards. Different functions are generally located in separate structures linked through connecting corridors or set in careful relation to common open spaces, rather than being contained under a common roof. From the exterior, there is little to distinguish buildings with different functions. Chinese architecture relies on axial arrangement, formal cues, and sequencing to establish dominance, for few buildings (aside from watchtowers and pagodas) are over one story tall.

4.4 Diagram of a typical Chinese house.
The jian serves as the basic unit for wooden construction. Houses tend to be built with separate pavilions for different functions. This diagram shows the modular basis of the house presented in Fig. 4.17.

4.5 (above) Longitudinal section through and plan of the main hall, Nanchan Monastery, Shanxi province, 782.
Among the oldest surviving buildings in China, the main hall of the temple is set on an axis in the position of greatest importance, preceded by two courtyards and level changes.

4.6 (above) Elevation of and transverse section through the main hall, Nanchan Monastery, Shanxi province, 782.
These orthographic views show details of the roof bracketing system. Note also the slight curvature given to the roof ridge and the wider spacing applied to the central intercolumniation, both of which give the structure grace and liveliness.

Chinese builders developed sophisticated systems of timber construction by the time of the Sui and Tang Dynasties, and during the Song Dynasty functionaries codified related practices in the *Yingzao-fashi*, a book of building standards. As described in this text, a timber hall such as that at the Nanchan Monastery (Figs. 4.5–4.6) was to have four parts, beginning with a raised platform, like the ancient Greek stylobate, that announced the building's importance. Columns rose from this platform to **bracket sets**, interlocking supports that both allowed the roof to overhang for protection of the wooden construction from the weather and exhibited the sophisticated Chinese joinery that transcended construction and even decoration to become art. The bracket sets began with dou or wooden blocks that sat atop the columns, not unlike a capital in Classical architecture. The dou supported pairs of gong or brackets, the first one cantilevered parallel to the hall's longitudinal axis and the second cantilevered parallel to the hall's transverse axis. This sequence could then be repeated, beginning with a second dou, with the bracket set overhanging farther each time. In some cases, ang, or downward-sloping arms, further enlivened the brackets.

The completed bracket sets supported beams and **purlins** that, in turn, supported the fourth building part: the roof and its covering of glazed tiles in a variety of colors. The ridge and the often curving hips where the roof planes intersected were covered with special tiles and embellished with animal sculptures and with curving finials, comparable to the **acroteria** on ancient Greek temples. Ornament also appeared on ceilings and around windows and on doors as paneling or lattice-work in the form of squares, diamonds, and parallelograms.

4.7 East Hall, Foguang Monastery, Shanxi province, 857.
Here the landscape has been terraced to create a higher platform for the main hall, which, as one might expect, is set on axis in the position of greatest importance.

The *Yingzao-fashi* also prescribed color schemes and the character of ornamental painting, with most remaining examples dating from the Qing Dynasty. The three Qing painting styles are *hexi, xuanzi,* and *Suzhou*. In the *hexi* style, golden dragons in various stylized postures represented the highest level of nobility. Other motifs include a chevron-like "W" pattern, phoenixes, grass, and painted elevations of bracket sets. Artists used "powder dribbling" to make raised lines that received gold leaf. Paint colors became vivid and included the well-known Chinese red, dark blue, and leaf green. *Xuanzi* painting features so-called "whirling flowers" as well as dragons and brocades and a hierarchical ordering of color from gold and jadelike blue-green down to blue, green, black, and white. *Suzhou* painting is less stylized, featuring images of houses, pavilions, garden buildings, and linear spaces as well as fruits and flowers, animals, insects, and celestial beings. Colors again descend in importance down from gold, the most prestigious.

Both Confucian and Daoist principles are evident in Chinese attention to building placement. Orientation to the cardinal directions is common, with principal buildings tending to face south to take maximum advantage of the sun and prevailing winds. Buildings of secondary importance face east or west, shielded wherever possible by generous overhangs or vegetation. The approach axis extends from south to north, and a southern courtyard ensures that the most important rooms have ample exposure to light and air. This rather predictable arrangement gives physical expression to Confucian ideals of hierarchy while also incorporating Daoist teachings regarding harmonious living with respect to natural forces. **Feng shui**, the Chinese art of adjusting the building to particular features of the individual site and its microclimate, is but a further elaboration of the Daoist principle that human actions should be in accord with the cosmos.

The earliest extant examples of wooden buildings are Buddhist temple halls on Wutai mountain in Shanxi province. The main hall of the Nanchan Monastery, dated to 782, is a relatively modest structure of three bays, about thirty-eight by thirty-two feet overall, set in a south-facing courtyard with flanking structures (see Figs. 4.5–4.6). When the hall's doors are opened, the courtyard provides a space for worshipers to view from outside the statues housed inside the hall. Monks circumambulate the altar and place offerings on the platform. The hall's central bay has extra width to emphasize its axial placement, and its roof has wide, flaring eaves, crowned by a ridge with curving, hooked ends. Essentially horizontal eave and ridge lines have been transformed into a subtle upward curve by the addition of extra eave rafters and layered bracketing, thereby creating a feeling of delicacy and lightness. The end columns are even slightly inclined to the center of the hall. The tendency to use curving rather than perfectly straight elements is part of the optical refinement found in all Chinese building. It might appropriately be compared to the use of entasis and optical corrections on Greek

4.8 East Hall, Foguang Monastery, Shanxi province, 857.
The broad eaves present an opportunity for the extensive brackets supporting the roof structure to be displayed.

temples. Similar refinements are seen at the east hall of the Foguang Monastery, constructed in 857 (Figs. 4.7–4.8). Its hillside site required terracing of the complex, so the main hall is elevated above the approaching courtyards. The front elevation is seven bays wide, with exceptionally deep overhanging eaves that cantilever over thirteen feet from the supporting column face.

Jinci, which includes the Hall of the Sacred Mother, is a temple complex at Taiyuan, erected in 1023–32 to honor ancestors in the Confucian tradition (Fig. 4.9). The site is hilly, with a running stream that encouraged the designers to integrate water features with numerous pavilions surrounding the main hall. Even within an irregular landscape, however, the idea of a processional axis is carefully maintained as a unifying idea. The visitor first passes a stage for performances, crosses a stone bridge and terrace, enters a hall for offerings, and finally crosses a four-way bridge over a square pool before encountering the Hall of the Sacred Mother (Fig. 4.10). Here the architects have supported the temple roof on an elaborate system of **transfer beams**, so that no interior columns interrupt the space for the large statues of the Sacred Mother flanked by her courtly attendants.

— Central axis

Hall of the Sacred Mother

Four-way bridge

Hall for offerings

Terrace

Stone bridge

Stage

4.9 Site plan of the Jinci temple complex, Taiyuan, Shanxi province, 1023–32.
The central axis in the center of the plan organizes the pavilions and bridge that precede the Hall of the Sacred Mother (top center). Water features are shaded on this plan.

N

0   50 m
0   150 ft

4.10 Hall of the Sacred Mother, Jinci temple complex, Taiyuan, Shanxi province, 1023–32.
Carved dragons coil around the wooden columns. The double-roof structure indicates the hall's importance.

PRINCIPLES OF CITY PLANNING

Among the earliest manuscripts to have survived in China is a treatise on city planning. Known as the *Kao Gong Ji*, or *The Artificer's Record*, it was composed in the fifth century CE as a guide for establishing a city based on Confucian teachings. According to the book, a capital city should be oriented to the cardinal directions and have a square plan roughly 4000 feet on each side. In the wall that surrounds the city, there should be three gates in each side, and roads projecting out from these establish the grid of the city's plan (Fig. 4.11). The central road on the south is the entrance for the major thoroughfare, nine cart lanes wide, which runs north to the palace complex. The palace itself is walled off from the rest of the city, preceded by an impressive courtyard and flanked by places of worship: the ancestral temple (to the east), and an altar to the earth (to the west). The city's marketplace is to the north of the palace compound. Otherwise, there are no public open spaces. Walls and a moat around the city provide protection from enemies without, while walls around the palace and residential blocks establish barriers that clarify the social hierarchy. (Unsurprisingly, the Chinese use the same word for city and wall.)

For an application of these principles, one may examine the plans of Chang'an (modern Xian), constructed in the sixth century as the capital of the mighty Tang Dynasty (Fig. 4.12). In its day it was among the richest and grandest cities in the world, with the urban area covering some thirty square miles. Its plan conforms in almost every respect with the principles articulated in the *Kao Gong Ji*: square layout, grid streets, three entrances in each side, and a 150-foot-wide tree-lined central artery leading from the

4.11 Diagram of an ancient Chinese city.
This idealized schematic plan has three gates in each of the sides of the square forming the city walls. Straight streets leading from the gates establish a regular grid that divides the city into blocks.

4.12 (right) Plan of Chang'an, 6th century.
The basic features of the ancient Chinese capital conform to the diagram in Fig. 4.11, with the major exception that the palace complex is set in the middle of the north side, terminating the north–south axis. The Confucian ideal of hierarchy is clearly embodied in this plan.

center of the south wall to the palace along the northern side of the city. The administrative center housed government offices and reinforced the north–south axis. Behind it to the north were the imperial residence of the crown prince and support spaces. An extension on the northeast side of the city contained the Daming Gong, the palace of the Tang emperors. Beyond this palace to the north was the Imperial Park, covering an area larger than that of the city proper. Within the city walls, the plan comprised 108 residential blocks, each of which had boundary walls formed by the buildings within. Market areas were provided on both the east and the west side of town.

Although much of Tang Chang'an is known only from archaeology, Beijing preserves to this day plan features that stem from the design of Chang'an (Fig. 4.13). Beijing's site has been occupied since about 2400 BCE, and it has served intermittently as a northern capital since the third and fourth centuries BCE. From 1153 to 1215 CE it was the capital of the Golden Horde, the Mongols who breached the Great Wall, overthrew the Song Dynasty, and ruled as the Yuan Dynasty. In 1368, the Ming emperors drove out the Mongols, then reestablished Beijing as their capital city in 1403. They contracted the northern boundary, slightly enlarged the area to the south, and built a new

4.13 Plan of Beijing, 15th century.
The processional axis begins on the south side at the Yung Ting Men Gate and continues for over three miles to the imperial audience hall in the center of the palace, or Forbidden City. Although no one outside of the court would walk the remaining route to the north, the axis continues through the private palaces of the emperor and empress, across Coal Hill, and finally to the Drum Tower outside the Imperial City.

Coal Hill

Shen Wu Gate (Gate of Spiritual Prowess)

Imperial Garden

Hall of Earthly Tranquillity

Hall of Mental Cultivation

Hall of Heavenly Purity

Gate of Heavenly Purity

Hall of Preserving Harmony

Hall of Middle Harmony

Taihe Dian (Hall of Supreme Harmony)

Taihe Men Gate (Gate of Supreme Harmony)

Wu Men Gate (Meridian Gate)

Moat

Duan Men Gate (Uprightness Gate)

Tian'an Men Gate (Gate of Heavenly Peace)

Tian'an Men Square

N

0   250 m

0   750 ft

4.14 Plan of the Imperial and Forbidden cities of Beijing, 15th century.
Note the alternating sequence of gates and courts through which ambassadors would pass before reaching the Hall of Supreme Harmony, where the emperor received state visitors. A moat (shaded on this plan) surrounds the walls of the Forbidden City.

set of perimeter walls, twelve-and-a-half miles in extent. A new ceremonial axis line was created to focus on Coal Hill (Prospect Hill), an artificial mound that rises above the surrounding landscape and has five pavilions for viewing the city. In 1552, to accommodate the growing population, construction on a new nine-mile-long wall to enclose the southern suburbs (the so-called Outer City) was completed. Even though much of existing Beijing is not particularly ancient by Chinese standards, almost all of it was executed in keeping with older traditions, so the city is an excellent three-dimensional realization of classical Chinese city-planning principles.

Visitors arriving in Beijing for an audience with the imperial court passed through four separate walled areas in traversing the ceremonial axis road. First came the Outer City wall, then the gates to the Inner City and the Imperial City (Fig. 4.14), before the palace, or Forbidden City, was reached. (The palace was termed "forbidden" because it was off-limits to the common people.) Moats further

augmented the feeling of separation and protection engendered by the sequence of walls to the Outer City, the Inner City, the Imperial City, and finally the Forbidden City.

The gate to the Imperial City is known as the Tian'an Men; the square directly in front of it has been greatly enlarged since imperial times to create a space for mass spectacles. Beyond it is an enclosed courtyard with trees, through which visitors pass to reach the Duan Men Gate, which leads to an elongated rectangular court. In the original scheme, there were temples in the large areas to the left and right: on the west were the Altars of Agriculture, and on the east was the temple to the imperial ancestors. (The latter has now been replaced by the People's Palace of Culture.) At the end of the court is the imposing Wu Men Gate, guarded by towers and flanking walls built over the moat that surrounds the Forbidden City. Once through its portals, visitors traverse a paved courtyard with a curved stream crossed by five bridges to reach the Taihe Men Gate, antechamber to the imperial audience hall, or Hall

4.15 Hall of Supreme Harmony, Forbidden City, Beijing, 15th century. The axial stairway with a carved central section was reserved for the emperor, whose throne raised on a dais stood at the center of the hall.

of Supreme Harmony (Taihe Dian) (Fig. 4.15). As befitted the status of the emperor, this hall is large and richly adorned, flanked by lesser structures creating a cross-axis, and elevated on a triple podium made accessible by stairs and a carved ramp over which the emperor was carried by his retinue. Although all the buildings to the north of the Hall of Supreme Harmony were private, for use by the imperial family and courtiers, the axis continues through two smaller halls used to prepare the emperor for audiences, then through gates to a walled triple-hall compound containing personal palaces of the emperor and empress before reaching the moat and northern wall of the Forbidden City. Directly behind rises Coal Hill.

There are of course many additional structures within the Forbidden City—over 9000 by one count, making it the largest ensemble of historic buildings in the country. The most skilled craftsmen and richest materials were employed in their construction, a fact that China's socialist government regards with both pride and regret, realizing that those who labored here did so "to cater for the decadent living of the ruling classes." Nevertheless, the Forbidden City has been carefully preserved as a museum.

At the point where visitors enter into the imperial presence in the Taihe Dian, they have traversed a distance of just over three miles from the Outer City gate. This whole axial approach was consciously designed to provide a suitably impressive setting for emperors who considered themselves the mightiest rulers on earth. At no point can one see the entire route or the final destination. The axis unfolds instead as a staged series of spaces, progressing logically from one to the next, and it is the cumulative experience of the sequence that gives it measured dignity and power. It may also be interpreted as a supreme expression of Confucian teachings regarding hierarchy and deference to authority.

HOUSES AND GARDENS

The emperor's halls in the Forbidden City have a great deal in common with the houses inhabited by his more humble subjects, for the ordinary house in Beijing was also constructed of wood and set within a walled compound reached by a gate from the street (Fig. 4.17). Halls serving the various needs of an extended family were organized around one or more courtyards. On axis, and in the largest hall, were living quarters for the patriarch, flanked by side halls for use as residences of his sons and their families. (A married daughter joined her husband's family.) Courtyards provided adjunct spaces for living, being used in good weather for dining or other group activities. When possible, the whole compound faced to the south, just as does the Forbidden City. Commoners' houses would, of course, have been much smaller, simpler in construction, and much more reserved in their decoration, but the architectural principles governing palace design applied to houses as well.

Traditional Chinese house design placed great emphasis on family privacy. Residential streets were typically lined by high walls fronting each house, relieved only by entrance gates, which were often identified by family crests and perhaps a touch of colorful decoration. Rarely was this entrance set on axis, for to have done so would have exposed the entire front courtyard area to public view when the gate was open. Access was more commonly to the side, facing a screen wall. In larger households, a servant would control the entrance of visitors at the gate, and a

ESSAY
Elder Brother Rock
by Robert M. Craig

4.16 Chinese garden with pavilion and Taihu rock, Suzhou, 1522–1666.

In the early twelfth century CE (Southern Song Dynasty), the scholar-poet Mi Fu (1051–1107) was appointed magistrate of the Wu Wei district of China and was invited to greet his fellow officials and their guests prior to taking up his post. He entered the official precincts but was immediately distracted by a magnificent rock that ornamented the garden. Ignoring all around him, Mi Fu bowed low in front of the great stone, paying homage to nature rather than to man, and addressed the stone respectfully as "Shixiong," or "Elder Brother Rock" (Fig. 4.16).

The (perhaps apocryphal) story of Mi Fu inspired Chinese literati, painters, poets, and garden architects, whose themes and designs universalized the central role of nature in Chinese thought. Chinese and Japanese gardens, and the architecture they contain, are marked by continuity and a commitment to tradition, rather than by the changing historic styles characteristic of the West. The Chinese term for landscape, *shan shui*, means "mountains and water," and the traditional Chinese garden, of which the best are to be found in Suzhou, is essentially a "hill and water garden." On the simplest level, this is created by the excavation of a pond and the piling up of the excavated earth to form an adjacent artificial hill. As Ji Cheng, author of the seventeenth-century treatise *Yuan Ye*, or *Craft of Gardens*, wrote: "to have mountains situated beside a pool is the finest sight in a garden . . . Never say there are no Immortals on earth." These hills and mountains often took the form of rockeries (elaborate compositions of piled-up stones creating an artificial craggy hillock), and the most renowned garden of rockeries is the so-called Lion Grove, the garden in Suzhou once owned by the family of the famed Chinese-American architect, I.M. Pei. When Pei built the Fragrant Hills Hotel in Beijing (1979–80), he incorporated such garden devices as *lou chuang*, traditional decorative windows marked by patterned grills. But it was not *lou chuang* but Elder Brother Rock that inhabited Pei's family garden in Suzhou, the Lion Grove. Many imagined they saw in the Taihu (water-washed) stones forms reminiscent of lion shapes: cubs cavorting and lion manes in profile. The Lion Grove was planned by the fourteenth-century painter Ni Tsan (Zan) and was developed and repeatedly rebuilt over the centuries of the Ming and Qing Dynasties. Retaining its traditional features, it survives today as the garden par excellence for Taihu stonework.

In his treatise on garden design, Ji Cheng noted that the Chinese had been collecting rocks since ancient times and prized especially the grotesque, eroded stones from Lake Tai. Private individuals placed Taihu rocks in their Suzhou and Wuxi gardens, and imperial emissaries sometimes transported huge rocks via the Grand Canal from southeastern China to as far north as Beijing, where they may still be seen in the imperial garden of the Forbidden City, in nearby Baihai park, and even in the nineteenth-century Summer Palace of the Qing-Dynasty empress dowager.

A Taihu rock might be sited in a garden pond not so much as an ornament as a symbolic representation of the islands of the Eastern Sea where the immortals dwelt. In Chinese mythology, it is on these islands that the gods distilled the *elixir vitae*, or "life-force," what the Chinese called *Qi*. As natural as breath itself, *Qi* is embodied in all the universe: heaven, earth, mountains, and water. The garden becomes both a representation of the cosmos and a metaphoric and quintessential embodiment of Daoist concepts of natural order. Taihu rocks were shaped by water and wind over the centuries; contorted and grotesque, they were admired for their perforations and holes, their textures and marks evidencing geologic time. The amorphous shapes, both animate and inanimate, transform inert rock to organic nature. Elder Brother Rock was an embodiment of *Qi*. The world created by Chinese garden designers was a microcosm of the cosmic universe of matter and spirit, heaven and earth, male and female, yin and yang—one becoming the other in an eternal oscillation as natural as the tides or the diurnal movement of day becoming night.

Inspired by such Daoist concepts, Frank Lloyd Wright perceived building in stone to be organic, an architecture at one with nature. He was, like Mi Fu before him, bowing in homage to Elder Brother Rock.

4.17 Plan of a typical house, Beijing, 15th century.
This extended plan shows how the independent pavilions are organized around courts. Note that the entrance from the street is off axis, thus preventing those who called at the gate from intruding on family privacy.

Pavilion of the Moon Arriving and the Breeze Coming

4.18 Plan of the garden of the Master of the Fishing Nets, Suzhou, 18th century.
The buildings are simple rectangular elements, while other features are scattered in a manner that suggests complete naturalism, as if in denial of the enormous care that has been taken in their design and placement.

servants' hall might be constructed against the street-facing wall. The precise use of any of the assorted halls comprising the house varied according to the number of occupants and their activities. The regular module of wood-frame construction used throughout permitted ready subdivision of interior spaces, for the walls, even those on the exterior, were constructed of thin wooden panels with solid and open sections. Windows were made of heavy paper that could be stored away during the summer months to encourage the free circulation of air. Broad overhanging eaves sheltered verandas that extended internal space to the exterior. In winter, however, the houses must have been both cold and drafty, for few had reliable means for being heated. Instead, people wore layers of quilted and fur-lined garments to keep warm both indoors and out. In rural areas, where brick or **adobe** was employed for construction, houses often had underfloor flues to provide heat during the cold months, but this arrangement was not suitable for buildings of timber construction.

The houses of more well-to-do or extended families

grew by the addition of courtyards of varying size. Some might be paved and others planted with a carefully selected tree. Those who could afford it might have a garden within the walled compound. In landscape design, the Confucian precepts of hierarchy and dominance gave way to Daoist principles, as the irregular and picturesque were deliberately cultivated in the quest for a relaxing setting that would foster the free exploration of thoughts and feelings in a state of meditation upon nature (Figs. 4.18–4.19). The formality that governed virtually all building design was never applied to landscape design, and the principles of yin and yang are extended to all elements. Yin encompassed not only the feminine, but also such items as the moon, night, earth, water, moisture, darkness, shadows, and plant materials that reflected these properties. Yang, by contrast, stood for items interpreted as having masculine traits: sunshine, fire, heat, brightness, solidity, and landscape materials with these properties. While some gardens, such as the famous ones in Suzhou, cover extensive tracts, even the smallest space could be made into a

4.19 Pavilion of the Moon Arriving and the Breeze Coming, the garden of the Master of the Fishing Nets, Suzhou, 18th century.
The irregular and picturesque have been carefully cultivated to create contrast, with rocks, water, and plants selected on Daoist principles.

garden by the placement of unusually shaped rocks, a tree, sand, perhaps a water feature, and a few selected plants. Garden design became an art form rooted in the imitation of the scenic values of natural forms, exploiting properties inherent in the site. In larger gardens, the experience of the visitor was carefully sequenced and controlled through attention to paving textures, viewing points, framing devices (gates) for controlling vistas, and the like. Even though the whole garden was consciously designed, the aim was to have it appear as if it had grown wholly out of nature. Designing the landscape was considered a far more intellectual exercise than architectural design, so making gardens became a suitable pursuit for poets, philosophers, and men who had risen high in the civil service. Such

wealthy and cultured individuals were responsible for the masterpiece at Suzhou.

In the eighteenth-century landscape of rural Fujian province, located in mountainous southeast China, the rural population built tulou, courtyard houses made of rammed earth. These distinctive structures were built to house multiple families brought together for their common defense. Some have square plans, some circular, with walls up to eight feet thick. Remaining examples of the circular type (Fig. 4.20) vary in size and number of stories, with the largest exceeding 200 feet in diameter and being subdivided into more than seventy rooms. Continuous porches face the courtyard, which is still used today for communal cooking and washing and agricultural processing.

4.20 Tulou houses, Hajing county, Fujian province.
Houses like these remind us that there are certain architectural constants, such as the courtyard, which have appeared repeatedly across cultures and time. They also demonstrate the never-ending inventiveness of the human mind in organizing the activities of daily life.

4.21 Plan of Horyuji temple complex, near Nara, 670–714.
Note that the composition does not follow strict symmetry, using instead a balanced asymmetry in which the verticality of the pagoda counters the lower and more massive Golden Hall. The colonnades defining the perimeter wall were added later, and they incorporate previously freestanding pavilions for bells and sacred texts.

4.22 Horyuji temple complex, near Nara, 670–714.
This bird's-eye view shows the complex roof structure and eave brackets that were based on Chinese temple designs.

JAPANESE TEMPLE ARCHITECTURE

Japan occupies an archipelago off the coast of Korea and China. It comprises four main islands and a thousand smaller ones scattered over nearly 800 miles. In prehistoric times, it was joined to the mainland by land bridges at various locations. Volcanic eruptions raised a chain of mountains, of which Mount Fuji is the most celebrated, that forms the spine of most of the islands; volcanoes and earthquakes associated with underlying plate tectonics have been and continue to be sources of disturbances and at times disasters. Although archaeologists have identified four ethnic groups among the earliest settlers in the archipelago, these have long since merged to produce a relatively homogeneous population that, like China, enjoyed lengthy governmental autonomy and minimal contact with other cultures until the mid-nineteenth century. In matters of architecture, there was early influence from China, particularly associated with the importation of Buddhism, and there are also elements in common with Korea, which functioned as an intermediary between China and Japan during the early centuries CE.

Japan's native religion is Shinto (the way of the gods), which reveres natural forces essential to agriculture through rituals and celebrations at shrines. Although the religion was already well established when its oral traditions were first recorded early in the eighth century CE, there is evidence that its myths and practices were used to help forge previously disparate farming and fishing settlements into a united people; with the rise of a powerful central government modeled on that of Tang China, the ruling priest-king styled himself as emperor and claimed direct lineal descent from the sun goddess, Amaterasu. (As part of the settlement of World War II, this claim was renounced by Japan's emperor in 1945.) But, while Shinto was the official state religion, from the sixth century CE onward it was colored by Buddhism, and in practice the two religions grew to overlap considerably in the ensuing centuries.

Buddhist Temples

The geographic spread of Japan's islands ensures that there is considerable diversity in their climates, from northern Hokkaido where snow and cold are features of long winters, to humid subtropical conditions on the southern islands. Wood has always been the primary building material, both because it was readily available and easy to work, and also because flexible wooden structures as built in Japan without significant diagonal bracing are more stable than masonry under earthquake conditions. Fire and natural deterioration have left few buildings extant from earlier than the eighth century, when the major architectural influence was that of China. Post-and-lintel building systems based on elaborately bracketed construction were used in the earliest surviving Buddhist temple complex, that of Horyuji near Nara (670–714) (Figs. 4.21–4.22).

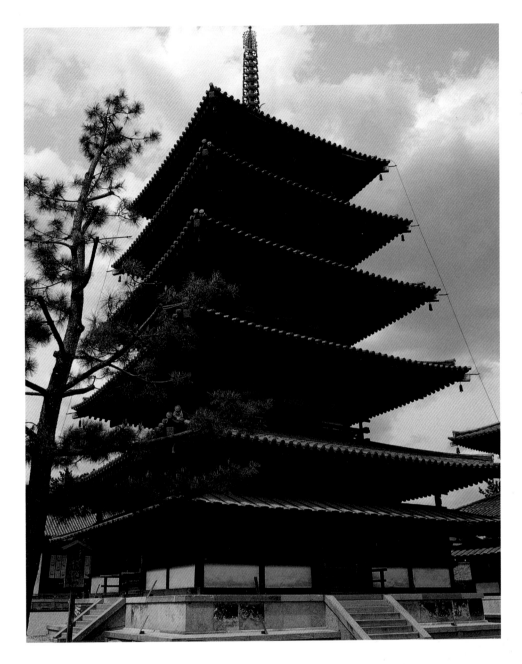

The slight upward curves of the eaves accentuate the gracefulness of the apparently hovering roof forms. A single wooden support extends from the base to the finial of the building.

The temple buildings are set within a courtyard defined by a covered perimeter corridor and made accessible through an inner gateway (chumon). Although the axiality one would expect from Chinese influence is there, the symmetry gives way to balanced asymmetry: a five-story pagoda on the left counters the so-called Golden Hall (kondo), which is larger in plan but not as tall as the pagoda. Beyond these freestanding structures is the centrally placed assembly or lecture hall (**kodo**), used for instructing monks associated with the temple. Small pavilions for housing the sutras, or sacred texts, and a bell, now incorporated into the corridor enclosure, were originally freestanding, as was the lecture hall, so the monastery as initially constructed had a simple rectangular enclosure wall. As in Chinese practice, the pagoda contained symbolic relics of the Buddha, while the Golden Hall was the repository for religious images. Horyuji's pagoda is constructed around a single wooden support that rises the full interior height of the building (Fig. 4.23), and the pagoda's gracefully flaring eaves are supported by cantilevered cloud-pattern bracket arms. There is no means for ascending to the upper levels, so the pagoda's architectural function is strictly that of a vertical element in the overall composition.

A larger-scale elaboration of this scheme may be seen at the monastery of Todaiji, begun in 760 at Nara as part of a state-encouraged program to construct Buddhist monasteries in every province of the country, with this being the major temple in the capital. The monastery included two symmetrically placed, seven-story pagodas forward of the inner courtyard enclosing the Golden or Great Buddha Hall (Daibutsuden) and kodo, all three set on axis. Smaller structures for the monks' living quarters and dining hall flanked the kodo on three sides. The vast Great Buddha Hall housed a monumental gilt bronze statue, fifty-three feet high, of Vairocana, the Buddha of the Ideal World. The hall that survives today is a reconstruction from about 1700 at only two-thirds the size of the original, yet it is still counted among the largest wooden buildings

4.24 Great South Gate, Todaiji Monastery, Nara, 1199.
The roof structure of this building reflects influences from
contemporary work in Song-Dynasty China. Eight layers of
cantilevered brackets support the projecting eave of the
lower roof, and another seven layers support the upper eave.
Bracket ends have a distinctive reverse-curve profile typical
of the Great Buddha style.

4.25 Interior of the Phoenix Hall, Uji, 1053.
This view from below shows the Buddha sitting on a lotus
flower in the lake of paradise. The sumptuous materials and
intricate details of carved and gilded figures were employed
in pious anticipation of a better world to come.

in the world. In overall design and detail, the influence of
Chinese temple design is evident. Todaiji was destroyed
in 1180 and rebuilt in a manner paralleling that of Song-
Dynasty China, which in Japan became known as the Great
Buddha style, best exemplified in the Great South Gate
completed in 1199 (Fig. 4.24). Here the eave brackets are
directly set into the supporting columns that, in turn, are
linked to each other by a succession of tie beams extending
as tenons through the centers of the posts. Inside, there is
no dropped ceiling and thus the entire roof structure is visible from below, including short rafters that radiate at the
corners to create the cantilevered overhang. Main posts rise
to the full height of the structure where, at the peak, a series
of so-called rainbow beams with frog-leg struts are stacked
to support the ridge.

Pure Land Buddhism arose during the tenth century
from an esoteric sect that sought an ideal world (the Pure
Land) through devotion to Amida Buddha, the Lord of
the Western Paradise. The movement attracted pious
and wealthy nobles, who erected halls on their estates to
house an image of Amida, and increasingly the designers
of these halls sought to capture the magnificence of paradise through elaborate and richly finished architecture.
Such was the case with the Phoenix Hall (Hoodo) of the
Byodoin, located at Uji (just south of Kyoto), constructed
in 1053 by the Fujiwara family as part of the transformation of an existing villa into a family temple. The plan and
massing of the building were inspired by the phoenix, a
mythical bird that rises from the ashes of destruction. This
was an apt image, for many believed that the year 1052

had marked the beginning of an era of spiritual decline,
when hope for escape from the cycle of birth and rebirth
was lost. Only Amida was thought to have powers sufficient to save humanity, so this period was a particularly
fruitful one for constructing Amida halls.

The Phoenix Hall's plan is symmetrical, consisting of
a central hall with open L-shaped wings stretching from
either side and a covered corridor attached to the rear like
a tail. In elevation, the roof planes and bracketing system
create the feeling of upward lift, as if to capture the sensation of flight. The central hall appears to be two stories tall
because of its double roof layers, but in fact it is a single
high space designed to provide an impressive setting for a
gilded wooden statue of Amida, over nine feet tall, seated
on a lotus throne in front of a golden mandorla frame and
under an elaborately carved wooden canopy (Fig. 4.25).
The wooden structure is painted red with golden accents,
set off by white infill panels, a color scheme that parallels
Chinese practice. The side wings rise up two stories, terminating in gable-roof pavilions and capped by turrets at the
corners of the L-shape. Viewed across the reflecting pond
onto which the hall fronts, the golden image set amid this
graceful and delicate architecture conveys the feeling of rising to that perfect paradise to which its patrons aspired.

Shinto Shrines

In contrast to the elaborate Chinese-inspired Buddhist temple designs stand the Shinto shrines, typically small in scale and modest in architectural character. The most celebrated is the Ise Shrine at Uji-Yamada, which has been precisely rebuilt at twenty-year intervals since its founding in 690 CE, thus preserving its earliest form with reasonable exactitude, although scholars concede there have been some minor changes over time. Ise actually consists of two shrines set about four miles apart: the Outer Shrine (Geku) dedicated to Toyouke, goddess of agriculture and the earth, and the Inner Shrine (Naiku) dedicated to Amaterasu, goddess of the sun (Figs. 4.26–4.28). As both the sun and the earth were necessary for agricultural prosperity, this union of opposites was in keeping with concepts of harmony and balance. The layout for each shrine is similar: four concentric sets of fences surround the shrine, each entered through a gateway (**torii**), and the buildings are symmetrically disposed to each side of a central axis. At the center is the main sanctuary, flanked by east and west treasure houses. Subsidiary buildings contain a kitchen and hall of offerings, used by the priests to prepare the daily offering of food for presentation to the deity. White stones cover the courtyard in which the shrine buildings are set, and the tranquillity and emptiness of the site are not disturbed by visitors, who remain outside the fenced enclosure. Immediately adjacent to the shrine is a cleared area,

4.26 Inner Precinct, Ise Shrine, Uji-Yamada, 690 CE–present.
In this view of the fence and treasure-house roofs, archaic forms of wooden construction are visible in all of the buildings. The shrine is part of a large complex beside the Isuzu River containing accommodation for pilgrims and priests. It is constructed anew every twenty years on adjacent rectangular sites, where the central post under the main building is retained from the previous rebuilding.

4.27 (below) Elevations and plans of Main Sanctuary, Ise Shrine, Uji-Yamada, 690 CE–present.
The simple elegance of the proportions and materials used for these buildings has come to represent the quintessence of Japanese architecture.

4.28 (below right) Main Sanctuary, Ise Shrine, Uji-Yamada, 690 CE–present.
Here you can see the chigi, or crossed-gable end rafters, and katsuogi, the short horizontal tapered wooden logs set on top of the ridge.

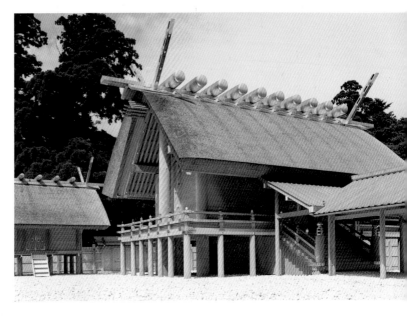

identical in size, which is the site for the next rebuilding.

Many historians see in the Ise shrine buildings the very essence of Japanese architecture. Here, building traditions were preserved and ideas were germinated that would be explored elsewhere in later periods. The architecture probably evolved from vernacular designs for granaries, utilitarian buildings that were raised on posts to protect their contents from damp and vermin. In agricultural cultures, it is not uncommon to find more care lavished on the construction of granaries than houses, for the community's survival depends on stored grain and sufficient seed to plant the fields in the following year. Raised-floor structures were also characteristic of early imperial palaces, another association that was appropriate to a shrine honoring the imperial ancestor. Ise refines this building type to a high art form, creating serene gabled-roof structures with elegant yet simple detailing.

At the Inner Precinct, the main sanctuary or shoden is raised over a central post that supports the heart of the shrine: a boat-shaped chest containing a mirror emblematic of the sun goddess and of the imperial family, who claimed descent from her. (This central post is all that remains on the site when the shrine is rebuilt on the adjacent plot of land. Covered and protected by a diminutive roof, it awaits the next cycle of construction, when it will again be the center of the sanctuary.) Only the emperor is allowed to enter the innermost shrine building. The cypress wood of which the shrine is constructed is left unpainted, although the exposed surfaces are finished with a great deal of refinement. Metal ornaments applied on the exterior reflect influence from Tang-Dynasty China. The weight of the roof rests on the shrine's exterior board walls, which over the years will settle and contract so that the posts and beams touch and thus assume a share of the structural load. Rafter extensions (**chigi**) at the gable ends recall the form of earlier bamboo structures, where rafter ends would cross after being lashed together. Horizontal tapered logs (**katsuogi**) originally set atop the ridge as weights to keep the thatch roof from blowing off in storms became decorative elements whose number signaled the importance of the building. Thus features that originated as practical reflections of construction necessities became highly refined expressions of simplicity, with enormous care being taken over even the smallest detail. This characteristic continues in most traditional Japanese architecture. Through ritual dismantling and re-creation, Ise represents continuity yet remains ever new.

JAPANESE HOUSES AND CASTLES

Houses within the capital and other Japanese cities were built of impermanent materials. As a result of frequent fires and natural decay, none has survived to the present. Contemporary scroll paintings capture images of urban life that show streets lined with one-story row houses, often

4.29 Plan of the Yoshimura House, near Osaka ca. 1620.
Minka were divided into two parts: an earth-floored section (shaded in this drawing) where animals were kept and cooking was done, and the raised-floor living area, covered in modular tatami.

with shops along the street frontage, as commerce was an important adjunct to governmental activity. The construction is simple, with wooden posts resting on foundation stones supporting a plank-covered gabled roof. Floors were of earth, although most houses may have had a raised wooden floor in at least one room. Enclosing walls were of wattle and daub or other lightweight screening, with curtains hanging over entrance doors to provide a sense of privacy. Windows facing the street were set above eye level to admit light but prohibit people from looking inside. A small garden might have been located behind the house.

Mansions of the wealthy had much in common with Chinese houses. Commonly occupying an entire city block, they were oriented to the south, with an axial main hall (shinden) facing a courtyard and flanked by side halls, although conditions particular to each site most often did not permit absolute symmetry of all parts. Perimeter walls ensured privacy from the street, and the buildings were often complemented by a pond and extensive landscaping.

4.30 Interior of a traditional house, Japan, 19th century.
This view shows sliding walls and the raised-floor section covered with tatami. Shelves and storage units hold household equipment, and furniture is minimal by Western standards.

4.31 Traditional house (minka), Japan, probably 19th century.
This minka has a thatched gable roof with a large monitor rising above the ridge to provide additional light and air for the interior. Such roofs are characteristic of minka found in Yamanashi Prefecture, to the west of Tokyo.

Traditional building techniques and materials that have long since vanished from urban locations have survived in houses in the countryside. Japan has an unusually rich array of **minka** (wooden folk houses) that collectively illustrate regional diversity as well as the pre-modern living conditions of ordinary people (Figs. 4.29–4.31). In many cases, minka sheltered animals as well as people, with barn or stabling areas connected to the living quarters. In its simplest form, the living space consisted of two areas: an earth-floor section around a central hearth, the chief source of heat and the center of food preparation, and a living section with raised wooden flooring to protect from ground damp. High roofs of thatch, bark, split bamboo, or wooden shingles were desirable to cast off rain and

handle snow (in the north), and gable peak vents permitted smoke from the hearth to escape. Minka are generally modular, and the dimensions of **tatami** (rice-straw woven floor mats roughly three by six feet) determined room proportions and sizes. Elaborations of the basic scheme introduced secondary living/dining areas, guest rooms, and sleeping rooms that could be partitioned by lightweight screens. Although minka seldom have the formal symmetry that characterizes Chinese houses, they have the same flexibility in plan. The typical Japanese house had little furniture. Floor cushions were used for seating, and mattresses for sleeping were rolled out of the way during the day, so rooms could be adapted easily to serve multiple functions. The beauty of these houses lies in their

4.32 Plan of Egret's Castle, Himeji, 1609.
This is one of the great surviving medieval castles. Its defenses include a moat (shown darkened) and massive stone foundations, but the superstructure is wood covered with thick layers of plaster.

Fortified corridor

Fortress wall

Quarters for court retainers

Residential areas

Main gate

Donjon complex

0   250 m
0   750 ft
N

4.33 View up to the donjon complex at Egret's Castle, Himeji, 1609.
Stone foundations support wooden upper stories of this castle, built on a high point in the landscape. The approach route is protected by battered stone walls and defensive positions with square openings for cannons.

simplicity, careful attention to detail, and the artistry that appears when a feature is made of the natural irregularities of the building materials. It is no wonder that Western architects as diverse as Frank Lloyd Wright and Mies van der Rohe have found inspiration in the forms and details of traditional Japanese architecture.

Japanese architecture and art often reflect qualities of composure and repose, terms that do not really describe medieval Japanese history. As the imperial family was relatively weak in the thirteenth through seventeenth centuries, feudal warlords competed for control over the country, and the incessant warfare contributed to the construction of a remarkable series of castles, twelve of which survive from the late sixteenth and seventeenth centuries. Based on earlier fortifications that are no longer extant, these castles are unusual in that they were built to accommodate and resist firearms that had been introduced by Portuguese traders in the course of the sixteenth century. The castle at Himeji (1609) is the most spectacular (Figs. 4.32–4.33). Dubbed the Egret's Castle, it shared a number of defensive features with medieval masonry castles in Europe: a strategic location on a promontory, massive foundations for the central donjon, heavily fortified gateways, and walled enclosures protected by moats. What set

Japanese castles apart from fortifications elsewhere was their reliance on timber as the primary structural material. Foundations and the lower courses of walls were stone, but the bulk of the superstructure was wood. In all cases, the wooden structure was made more fire-resistant with sand and pebbles before receiving a thick layer of plaster.

The castle at Himeji is composed of concentric layers of walls and moats, enclosing residential areas in the outer layer, quarters for court retainers in the second ring, and the donjon complex with its four towers at the center. Within this central section, a maze of passages connects the strongholds to confuse intruders. At intervals, there are overhanging galleries from which rocks or other materials could be dropped on those below. Walls are supplied with archer's slits and loopholes for firing weapons, and projecting turrets were used for surveillance. The donjon itself is framed into two massive staves that extend from basement to the roof six floors above. An internal courtyard provides light and air to rooms that would otherwise be dismal, for openings to the outside are minimal. The openings become larger in the upper stories, and there is a residential aspect to the fortress interior that is somewhat unexpected in a structure designed to resist siege. The castle's exterior presents an impressive aspect, with stacked roofs, multiple dormers, and superimposed gables. Like its European counterparts, the Egret's Castle was meant to dominate the surrounding countryside for which it served as the administrative center.

ZEN BUDDHIST ARCHITECTURE AND ITS DERIVATIVES

Zen Buddhism, which developed in China and spread to Japan in the twelfth century, gave its name to a style of Japanese architecture that was based on examples from Song-Dynasty China. The essence of Zen is enlightenment through meditation, achieved by discarding conventional modes of thought through methods that can approach the irrational. In medieval Japan, Zen grew in popularity to become the form of Buddhism most practiced by the upper classes, and as such it came to influence all aspects of cultured life, including architecture. The Jizodo of Shofukuji (1404) is the oldest dated Zen temple in Japan, and may be used to illustrate architectural features typical of the style. As with the Great Buddha style, the wooden columns are pierced by horizontal tie beams, but the roof construction differs considerably in that it uses a double or "hidden" structure that presents one pitch and profile on the interior and eave overhang, and a different, steeper one on the exterior where outer-roof supports are concealed. The gentler pitch of the eaves contributes a sense of horizontality to the building. This form of roof construction is distinctively Japanese, having no parallel in China. The layout of Zen monasteries also came to have distinctive characteristics: their bilateral symmetry and predictable placement of structures for different functions reflected in physical form the mental discipline expected of the monks.

For many later Buddhist structures, little distinction was made between sacred and secular architecture. The Katsura Imperial Villa in Kyoto provides a splendid example of a country retreat built in the Shoin style that was based on elements from older mansions of the nobility and that also embodies concepts from the Zen tradition (Fig. 4.34). Built in stages from about 1616 to 1660 by three generations of the princely Hachijonomiya family, the villa was intended for occasional occupancy as a place for reflection, relaxation, creative works, and contemplation of nature. Katsura's plan is irregular, even sprawling, but all interior spaces are governed by the tatami module (Fig. 4.35). Japanese cedar wood (*hinoki*) is employed for the structural frame, with wooden doors or white paper-covered partitions forming the exterior walls. As at the Ise Shrine, the wood is left unfinished, and it has weathered to a dark chestnut to gray color, depending on exposure to light and weather. The rather somber architecture of the villa itself is complemented by the artistic layout of

4.34 Katsura Imperial Villa, Kyoto, ca. 1616–60.
Built as a retreat for contemplation rather than as a permanent residence, this villa presents a series of spaces that can change as partitions are opened or closed, often blurring the distinction between inside and outside.

extensive gardens around a meandering lake. Sliding partitions and doors permit rooms to change dimensions and open up to the natural world in varying ways (Fig. 4.36). Exterior decks become extensions of the interior and frame views of the landscape; one serves as a platform for viewing the moon over the lake.

Nestled in the grounds are five tea houses, separate pavilions for practicing the Japanese art of the tea ceremony. Tea as a beverage originated in China, but a succession of Japanese tea masters, including Sen-no-Rikyu (1521–91), transformed informal tea-taking into a spiritual ritual symbolizing detached perfection in the Zen tradition. The ceremony involved with the making and drinking of tea, at once complex and simple, was performed in small structures that are seldom symmetrical or even regular but that were constructed expressly to incorporate the qualities of harmony, reverence, purity, and silence that are the very essence of the ritual. Tea houses are usually set, as at Katsura, in isolation from other buildings, and are approached by a path that enables the visitor to view the pavilion only at the last possible moment (Fig. 4.37). Rustic elements, such as wooden supports with the bark still attached or a wooden element of irregular shape, can be incorporated into the tea house as an extension of the natural world, for the tea ceremony aims at fusing the spiritual and the natural. Terms such as reticent, eloquent, and restrained have been used to describe these buildings. Entrance to the tea house may come through an exceptionally low door, deliberately designed so that one must

N

| 0 | | | 100 m |
| 0 | | | 300 ft |

Shokin-tei
tea house

Main gate

Geppa-ro
tea house

Entrance

4-36

Moon viewing
platform

4.34

Old Shoin

Middle palace

New palace

N

| 0 | | 25 m |
| 0 | | 75 ft |

**4.35 Plan of the Katsura
Imperial Villa, Kyoto, ca.
1616–60.**
The ordering of the pinwheel-
like plan is governed throughout
by the dimensions of tatami.
Terraces and open porches
provide opportunities to view
the landscape, and link interior
spaces with the outside world.

**4.36 Interior of the Geppa-rō
tea house, Katsura Imperial
Villa, Kyoto, ca. 1616–60.**
Sliding partitions and rice-paper
panels have been opened to
reveal views to the villa's garden.

4.37 Shokin-tei tea house, Katsura Imperial Villa, Kyoto, ca. 1616–60.
The tea house is set in a Zen-inspired landscape visually isolated from the villa itself. The tea house design emphasizes natural materials and controlled views within and without of the structure.

almost crawl to get in. Shoes are left outside; participants sit on thick tatami and drink from exquisitely shaped vessels obviously crafted by hand. Views are carefully calculated. Windows are at eye level when one is seated, and artfully selected treasures are displayed in an alcove (**tokonoma**) with a raised floor. As the tea master serves the guests, there is time to contemplate the subtle juxtapositions of texture, material, and surface that comprise the room's interior, for the designers have imparted their reverence for materials and spatial harmony, which are intended to promote reflection that will achieve inward simplicity and tranquillity of mind. The refinements of tea-house architecture encapsulate the essence of Japanese traditional design, in which architectural principles seen in the early Shinto shrines are merged with the esthetics and philosophy of Zen Buddhism.

The grounds of the Katsura Imperial Villa also include a Zen stone garden intended as both religious art and another setting for contemplation. At the renowned Kyoan-ji garden, also in Kyoto and north of Katsura, isolated, provocatively shaped rocks set in carefully manicured sand represent a serene world of mountains and seas that evoke the Buddhist universe.

CONCLUSIONS ABOUT ARCHITECTURAL IDEAS

In China, a country dominated for millennia by hierarchical social and governmental systems and one where the government carried out most of the large-scale construction, the principles of architectural ordering were codified and rigidly applied at every scale from city plans to buildings to building components. At the urban scale, Beijing and its embedded palace complex, or Forbidden City, offers the most extreme example. It was laid out according to Confucian principles adopted in the city-planning treatise called the *Kao Gong Ji* to have an intense orthogonal geometry and a primary, central, north–south axis along which the palace structures are arranged in relentless hierarchical order, culminating with the imperial audience hall. This organizational formula remained the same for Beijing's housing outside the Forbidden City, as it was based on a variable but repetitive module and laid out to have a central axis leading through courtyards to the living quarters of the family patriarch, which was flanked by the subordinate quarters of his sons and their families.

The Chinese building standards for temples were likewise codified in the *Yingzao-fashi*, which established four-part compositions of platform, columns, bracket sets, and roof, with the composition of the repetitive bracket sets specified in detail. And these specifications extended to formulaic color schemes. Chinese gardens, with their calculated irregularity, established a foil for the architecture's geometrical rigidity.

As Buddhism spread from China to Japan, Chinese Buddhist architecture did so as well. However, building ensembles such as the Horyuji temple complex exhibit a condition of stasis or equilibrium that exchanges Chinese hierarchical tension for serenity and calm. The epitome of this Japanese architectural achievement must be the Shinto Ise Shrine, where peasant buildings have been transformed to become a literally unreachable precinct fit only for the gods.

When the Japanese planned new towns like Kyoto, they employed the repetitive grid and axial thoroughfares as did the Chinese, and the traditional Japanese house was likewise modular, based on the rice-straw mat. This residential planning reached something of an apogee at Kyoto's Katsura Imperial Villa, where translucent sliding partitions enable a visitor to perceive buildings together with gardens in a unified, organic experience.

Chapter 5

The Roman World

During the first millennium BCE, while Greek civilization originated and flourished on the mainland and around the eastern Mediterranean, an enigmatic people, the Etruscans, were settling and developing their own culture in the area of north-central Italy now known as Tuscany. The origins of the Etruscans are not precisely understood; they are thought to have migrated onto the Italian peninsula from Asia Minor ca. 1200 BCE, after the collapse of Hittite power. From surviving inscriptions, art, artifacts, and architecture, it seems that the Etruscans drew on diverse roots. Greece during its early and Classical eras was a particularly strong influence, but there were other cultural connections as well. The Etruscans' language contained both Indo-European and non-Indo-European elements and was written in a script derived directly from Greek; their religion, which placed great emphasis on providing worldly goods for the afterlife, had much in common with that of Egypt. With that of the Hittites their art shares relief carvings of protective beasts at tomb entrances, and with the art of the Minoans and Mycenaeans naturalistic decorations depicting birds and dolphins. The Etruscan practice of reading omens from the entrails of animals follows that of Babylonia and Assyria, and their use of the arch and vault in monumental gateways indicates links with the architecture of Asia Minor. Even though they assimilated much from their neighbors, the Etruscans were an original people whose accomplishments left distinctive imprints on Roman civilization.

ETRUSCAN IMPRINTS

Our understanding of the Etruscans is limited by the dearth of textual records. Funerary inscriptions comprise the bulk of surviving written documentation, and although these can be deciphered with reasonable accuracy, they tell us little about the language or Etruscan society and how it functioned. Etruscan settlements appear to have been loosely organized into autonomous city-states rather like those in Mesopotamia and Greece, and the Etruscan economy was based on agriculture and international trade, especially in metals: tin was imported from Britain, silver from Spain, and iron and copper were widely available. Etruscan culture was well established by the eighth century BCE and grew in influence for the next 200 years to encompass the area from the river Po in northern Italy to the region around Pompeii, south of Rome. One of their cities, Marzabotto near Bologna, had a grid plan, with the main streets running perpendicular to one another and intersecting in the center of town (Fig. 5.1). The Romans, who would use similar plans for their military camps (**castra**), labeled the main north–south street the **cardo** and the east–west route the **decumanus**. The orthogonal plan may have owed something to colonial Greek cities, known through trade.

It seems clear that the Etruscans borrowed the orders of architecture and the temple form from Greece, modifying both to suit their own purposes. Greek temples generally had a continuous colonnade surrounding the sanctuary at the center, with entrances on both gabled ends. In contrast, Etruscan temples typically contained a tripartite, or three-part, cella oriented in only one direction, generally to the south (Fig. 5.2). The temple was set on a high podium, covered with a gable roof, and approached through a double

<----

Maison Carrée, Nîmes, France, 1–10 CE.
Located far from Rome, this is one of the best preserved temples of antiquity. Thomas Jefferson so admired it that he used it as the model for his design of the Virginia State Capitol in Richmond. The designer of the Maison Carrée employed the Corinthian order, freestanding at the front porch and attached as half columns around the cella. In ancient Roman times the temple stood within a forum.

Chronology

Height of power of the Etruscan civilization	550 BCE
The Roman Republic	509–27 BCE
Dictatorship of Julius Caesar	46–44 BCE
Reign of Caesar Augustus and beginning of the Roman Empire	27 BCE–14 CE
Vitruvius writes *De architectura*	ca. 27 BCE
Reign of Nero	54–68 CE
Reign of Vespasian	69–79
Construction of the Colosseum	completed 80
Reign of Domitian	81–96
Reign of Trajan	98–117
Reign of Hadrian	117–138
Construction of the Pantheon	ca. 125
Reign of Septimus Severus	193–211
Reign of Diocletian	284–305
Reign of Constantine	310–337

5.1 Plan of Marzabotto, ca. 2nd century BCE.
This plan shows a grid of blocks. Excavations of building foundations are shown in the same areas. The acropolis lies on the northwestern corner of the site, while the River Reno runs along the southern edge. The cardo is the Roman name for the primary north–south street and decumanus for the primary east–west street.

5.2 Drawing of an Etruscan temple, based on descriptions by Vitruvius.
Compare this plan to those of Greek temples (see Figs. 2.14–2.16). Note that the colonnades extend only across the front to create a portico, while the cella has been expanded to several chambers set the full width of the temple. The highly sculptural building of the Greeks, meant in Classical times to be viewed at an angle, has been transformed into one dominated by a central axis and meant to be seen frontally.

row of columns set at the top of a single flight of stairs. The intricate refinement of the Doric and Ionic was forsaken for a greatly simplified original order, the **Tuscan**, which had the basic characteristics of the Doric but no fluting on the column shafts or sculpture on the frieze. Intercolumnar spacing on Etruscan temples was markedly wider, the roof pitch considerably lower, and the eave overhang greater than on Greek temples, creating a broadly horizontal emphasis. Both the columns and roof structure were built of wood, while the walls were laid up with unbaked brick. More durable terracotta was employed for roofing tiles, pediment ornamentation, and sculpture.

Because of the impermanence of their materials, no Etruscan temples survive, although literary and archaeological sources provide adequate evidence of their form and terracotta elements preserve decorative features. Architectural remains are scarce, and much of what is known about residential designs has been deduced from tomb architecture and funerary urns made in the shape of miniature dwellings. Tomb excavations at Cerveteri provide clues about upper-class housing. The rooms, hollowed out of easily carved volcanic rock (tufa), are entered through a vestibule and grouped around an inner court, which suggests an **atrium**. In some tombs, the architectural features of doors, roof beams, and moldings have been reproduced, and furnishings, such as chairs, cooking utensils, and other household items, are likewise carved in stone.

At Perugia, which was the Etruscan city of Perusia, there still exists a monumental gateway (the so-called Arch of Augustus) displaying Etruscan influence, although it dates from after the fall of Perugia to the Romans in 310 BCE (Fig. 5.3). Above the double row of voussoirs, or wedge-shaped stones, forming the gateway arch is a decorative motif consisting of metopes and triglyphs similar to a Doric frieze. Circular shields fill the spaces of the metopes, and the triglyphs are actually short fluted pilasters with volutes at the top. A relieving arch flanked by Ionic pilasters is set atop the band of Doric-inspired ornament. In borrowing here from the Greeks, the Etruscans used elements of the orders with originality, if not with understanding. Later the Romans would forge a coherent and powerful architectural style of their own by employing the arch and vault for structure and using the orders largely as decoration.

The Etruscans, together with native Italian peoples, the Latins and the Sabines, inhabited the hills that rose above the marshlands on either side of the river Tiber. Etruscan builders began to drain the marshes by digging the trench that later became the Cloaca Maxima, the major sewer of ancient Rome. According to legend, the city of Rome was founded on these hills in 753 BCE by Romulus and Remus, and it was ruled from 616 to 510 BCE by members of the Etruscan royal house, the Tarquins. In about 500 BCE, the Latins overthrew the Tarquins and established the Roman Republic. The expulsion of Etruscan rulers from Rome did not signal their complete disappearance from Italy, however; other Etruscan city-states to the north continued to

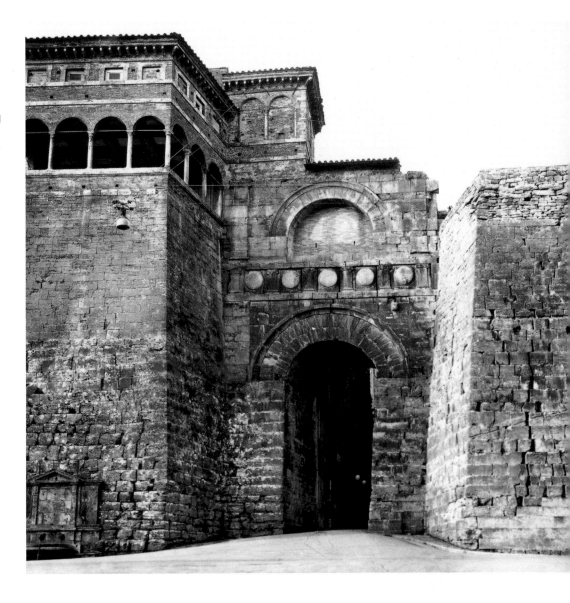

5.3 Semicircular "Arch of Augustus," Perugia, after 310 BCE. The lower portions were constructed by the Etruscans. The Romans later exploited the structural possibilities of the semicircular arch in their buildings.

thrive even as Roman authority was growing. From 396 to 88 BCE Roman forces gradually incorporated these northern settlements, but not before many aspects of their culture had merged into Roman life. Etruscan art and architecture influenced Roman work, and Etruscan customs, such as chariot racing and bloody gladiatorial contests, were also popular in Roman society.

THE ROMANS

The beginning of Roman civilization was contemporary with that of the Greeks, the Etruscans, and the later Egyptian dynasties. Unlike all of these other cultures, however, Rome continued to grow in importance as the first millennium BCE waned, reaching its apogee in the first and second centuries CE. In time Rome absorbed the Etruscans, Greeks, Egyptians, and many lesser peoples and formed an empire with a remarkably homogeneous architectural style. Roman building practices, like Roman culture, were derived from many sources, especially Etruscan and Greek, but the forms of their architecture were in many respects original.

The ancient Romans were certainly materialistic, but also very practical. Their society is often depicted in popular culture as excessively brutal, particularly regarding its fixation with the slaughter of animals and people in the Colosseum and lesser amphitheaters and its use of crucifixion as a means of capital punishment. The Romans, however, must be judged within the context of their age and locale, one when and where slave holding, the wholesale slaughter of civilians by invading armies, and savage punishment, including crucifixion, meted out by the prevailing justice systems, were common in adjacent cultures as well. As a counterpoint, the Romans were strongly devoted to family life, astute lawmakers, gifted administrators, and, most importantly for us, highly competent and innovative builders.

Their architecture changed significantly, however, as their political system changed. The city of Rome first became the seat of a republic governed by a senate with members drawn from notable families and by elected magistrates or consuls. As the Roman armies conquered more and more of Italy and beyond, the populace struggled to maintain a governmental system that could administer efficiently and that could satisfy both the landed aristocracy (patricians)

5.4 Pont du Gard, Nîmes, 20–16 BCE. The water channel (aqueduct) runs along the uppermost level, which maintains a constant incline to carry the water, through the pull of gravity, from nearby mountains into the city of Nîmes. Aqueducts ran along the contours of the land whenever possible, but when a valley had to be crossed, as here, Roman engineers used arches to span the gap. Projecting stones and inset holes were used for bracing the wooden centering, or scaffolds, needed to erect the arches, and they were left in the finished work in case repairs were ever required. This aqueduct has long been severed, so the Pont du Gard no longer carries water.

and the general class of free citizens (plebs). A crisis eventually arose in the first century BCE that resulted in the assumption of dictatorial power by the military leader Julius Caesar. Although he was assassinated, his rule ushered in the Roman Empire and a succession of emperors beginning with Augustus Caesar in 27 BCE. The breadth and complexity of the Empire demanded new construction practices capable of producing very large buildings relatively quickly and economically. It is the architecture of the Empire on which this chapter will concentrate.

We are aided (and sometimes slightly amused or bewildered) in our understanding of Roman construction during the time of the Republic by a contemporary work, *The Ten Books of Architecture*, composed in the late first century BCE by Marcus Vitruvius Pollio, commonly known as Vitruvius, who dedicated his book to Emperor Augustus. As literature, his book is not a masterpiece. Like many architects since, Vitruvius was not particularly skilled as an author, and the precise meaning of some of his writing is difficult to deduce. Based in part on Greek precursors, his text was doubtless not the only one of its kind, but it is the only intact treatise on architecture to have survived from antiquity, and as such it has been studied carefully by architects from the Renaissance to the present seeking to understand the principles of Roman architecture. Among the topics Vitruvius covers are building design, city planning, military engineering, and the design of machines, which together indicate that architects dealt with a much wider array of problems in design and construction then than they do now. His opening comments on the education of the architect are enlightening:

The architect should be equipped with knowledge of many branches of study and varied kinds of learning, for it is by his judgment that all work done by the other arts is put to the test. This knowledge is the child of practice and theory. Practice is the continuous and regular exercise of employment where manual work is done with any necessary material according to the design of a drawing. Theory, on the other hand, is the ability to demonstrate and explain the productions of dexterity on the principles of proportion. It follows, therefore, that architects who have aimed at acquiring manual skill without scholarship have never been able to reach a position of authority to correspond with their pains, while those who relied only upon theories and scholarship were obviously hunting the shadow, not the substance. But those who have a thorough knowledge of both, like men armed at all points, have sooner attained their object and carried authority with them.

BUILDING TECHNIQUES AND MATERIALS

The Romans compartmentalized their activities and were able to build large interior as well as exterior spaces to hold them. The imposing quality and size of their construction is a result of their application of engineering skills to the problems they encountered in everyday life. Roman construction exploited structural elements that acted in compression: the arch, the vault, and the dome, elements developed by earlier civilizations but used in a very limited fashion (see Fig. 0.5). In Roman hands these

5.5 Axonometric drawing of the Sanctuary of Fortuna Primigenia, Praeneste, ca. 80 BCE.
Compare this multi-level architectural ensemble to the Greek Hellenistic Sanctuary of Asklepios on the island of Kos, as seen in Fig. 2.33. The ancient Greeks had, in turn, been influenced by such Middle Kingdom Egyptian site developments as the Temple of Queen Hatshepsut, seen in Figs. 1.29 and 1.30.

elements became the basis for structural systems on a scale unimaginable with post-and-lintel construction.

A true arch consists of voussoirs set in a curved shape, often a semicircle. Building one requires a temporary timber formwork, or centering, to support the voussoirs as they are laid, for the arch will not stand on its own until all the voussoirs, including the central **keystone**, are set in place. (Contrast this true-arch construction to the technique of corbeling, where each course rests on and overhangs the preceding one (see Fig. 2.9). No centering is required, for the construction is always stable, but the form produced is not a true arch.) If the arch is continued along its longitudinal axis, it produces a vault; if an arch is rotated on its center, it produces a dome. By using arches, vaults, and domes, the Romans could enclose large areas using modestly sized stones cut carefully to shape. The space between supports, necessarily severely limited when stone lintels are used because stone in tension tends to crack over wide spans, could now be made much larger because vaulted construction carries the structural load almost completely in compression, for which stone is well suited. There is a price for this stability. The weight of the masonry in vaulted construction pushes not only downward but also outward on the supports on which it rests, and this outward thrust must be countered by dead weight. So vaulted construction requires walls or piers that are much thicker than those used in post-and-lintel buildings.

The earliest Roman vaults were built for utilitarian structures. Mention has already been made of the Cloaca Maxima, the trench begun by the Etruscans to drain the Roman marshes. By the mid-first century BCE, it was vaulted with stone, and the construction still functions as one of the main sewers of Rome. Discharging wastes into the Tiber, however, made the river water unfit for human consumption, so clean water was brought from rivers or springs in the Sabine Hills above Rome, piped in a gravity-fed system of **aqueducts** to city reservoirs, then distributed to fountains or other uses around the city. As much as possible, the water channel or aqueduct followed the contour of the land, but where it had to cross valleys, it became necessary to elevate the conduit in order to preserve the constant slope of the supply line. The Romans erected handsome arched structures for this purpose. They completed the Aqua Appia in 312 BCE and constructed three more aqueducts in the second half of the second century BCE to provide water for the growing population of Rome. They added the impressive Aqua Claudia in 38 CE to bring water from Tivoli, some forty-five miles away. This aqueduct's great masonry arches, some more than 100 feet high, extended over the countryside for much of that distance.

Perhaps the most spectacular surviving aqueduct span is the Pont du Gard (20–16 BCE) outside Nîmes in southern France (Fig. 5.4). Made of unmortared masonry (**opus quadratum**), the aqueduct strides 882 feet over the valley of the river Gard on three tiers of arches, carrying the water channel 160 feet above the level of the river. Its design is remarkably straightforward: the two lowest arch levels are identical rows of semicircular arches, sixty feet in diameter except for the span across the river, which is eighty feet. The uppermost tier has arches set on twenty-foot centers, so that a unifying rhythm ties all three levels together. Projecting stones used for support of the centering and scaffolding add surface texture, and they were retained in case repairs were ever needed. Enclosed above the highest arches is the water channel, about six feet square in cross-section, lined with mortar to prevent leaks. A roadway is carried above the lowest row of arches.

A dramatic example of Roman construction from the time of Vitruvius's childhood and one strongly influenced by Hellenistic Greek practices is the upper portion of the Sanctuary of Fortuna Primigenia (ca. 80 BCE) in Praeneste (modern-day Palestrina) near Rome (Fig. 5.5). In order to appreciate its organization, we must remember that the Hellenistic Greeks used stoas, bent and folded stoas, gateways, terraces, and stairs (see Kos, Fig. 2.33) to create architectural environments into which they inserted freestanding buildings. The Romans adopted this design strategy at Praeneste and elsewhere during the time of the Republic.

The complex is built into a steep hillside and culminates at the top with a small, circular, Corinthian temple housing the statue of Fortuna Primigenia. From the town below, ancient Roman visitors to the sanctuary would have proceeded up one of the longitudinally oriented stairs located to each side, moving, in effect, through an **opus incertum** retaining wall and toward colonnades shielding wells. At the top of these stairs, they would have turned 90 degrees left or right and moved toward the center by way of long, roofed-over ramps. At the top of the ramps and now on the centerline of the complex, they would again have moved longitudinally up a stair flanked by stoalike files of attached Ionic columns and two Ionic **hemicycles** that concealed **barrel-vaulted** compartments housing shops and acting together as a retaining wall. Atop the roof of these trabeated-arcuated shops, they would again have climbed a central, longitudinal stair flanked by more applied trabeation concealing more vaulted, retaining-wall shop compartments and ascended to a rectangular **forum** surrounded on three sides by a folded Corinthian stoa. Here they would have seen in front of them arches with applied trabeation astride another centrally located stair, this one leading up to a theater surrounded by yet another stoa, this one bent into a semicircle and serving as a final transitional experience to the circular temple. The sanctuary is in all respects a unified creation, whether seen from below along its central, longitudinal axis or experienced through time as a number of separate but related architectural incidents. While much of the original applied trabeation has been lost and the theater level has been enclosed to include flanking buildings, a visitor to Palestrina can still grasp the intended effects of this Romano-Hellenistic building ensemble.

In Nîmes itself, the so-called Temple of Diana (ca. 80 CE) uses a distinctive barrel vault of ashlar, or cut-stone, masonry to create its principal interior space (Fig. 5.6). This masonry is unusual, however, for the technique was costly and required highly skilled stonecarvers. The efficient Romans developed a more expedient building method by using a new material, hydraulic **cement**, derived from volcanic deposits first discovered around Puteoli (today's Pozzuoli) and named **pozzolana**. Vitruvius described it as "a kind of natural powder which from natural causes

5.6 "Temple of Diana," Nîmes, ca. 80 CE.
This is a fine example of barrel-vaulted masonry construction used to enclose space. Note the ribs of the vault and the use of alternating triangular and segmental arched pediments above blind windows to articulate the wall.

5.7 Ancient Roman concrete wall construction.
By the time the Emperor Hadrian built his sprawling villa (Figs. 5.41–5.42), Roman engineers had perfected the masonry-wall-construction process, using "formwork" made from two faces of stone or tiles, with the cavity between them filled with concrete. From left to right, this facing changes from uncoursed rubble masonry, to pyramid-shaped stones, to pie-shaped tiles that appear as elongated brick in the laid-up walls in Fig. 5.38.

Opus incertum   Opus reticulatum   Opus testaceum

House of Pansa

Forum Baths

Capitolium

Forum

Marine Gate

5-31

Amphitheater

Swimming pool

Palaestra

Triangular Forum   Theaters

0   250 m

0   750 ft

5.8 Plan of Pompeii, founded 6th century BCE.
This city dates back to a Greek colonial settlement, later
occupied by the Etruscans and Samnites. During the Roman
period, Pompeii was greatly enlarged to the outlines seen here.
The forum is the major civic space in the original settlement,
while recreational facilities are located in the southeast corner.

produces astonishing results." What the Romans discovered was that when pozzolana was mixed with lime, rubble, and water, the mixture reacts chemically and hardens
to a stonelike consistency, even if under water. The simple
lime mortars known to the ancients had some bonding
strength, but they were ineffective for the bridge and harbor foundations where Roman builders first exploited the
superior strength of pozzolana.

The Romans also found uses for this artificial stone
away from the water. The new material made curves and
irregular shapes much easier to achieve but the resulting
walls were generally not as handsome as ashlar stone ones,
so the Romans became adept at applying nonstructural wall
finishes such as stucco, mosaic tiles, and marble veneer.

Today, because most Roman buildings have lost their
finish surfaces, one can see the underlying construction in
a way that Roman builders never intended. Early concrete
walls were composed of rough stones surrounding a concrete core (**opus incertum**) (see Fig. 5.35), a technique
later refined to pyramidal stones (**opus reticulatum**) (Fig.
5.7 and see Fig. 5.10) with square faces and their points
embedded in the wall, which gave a more orderly exterior
appearance. In imperial times (after 37 BCE) the Romans
increasingly used triangular bricks as the concrete facing
(**opus testaceum**) (see Figs. 5.37 and 5.38), laying their
thin triangular shapes to present a smooth exterior and an
irregular inner face for maximum bonding surface with
the soupy cement mixture. (Stamps impressed on the wet
bricks in the factory have enabled archaeologists to date

many Roman structures with reasonable precision.) After
the second century CE concrete walls with stone rubble
striped by horizontal courses of brick bonding every three
or four feet (**opus listatum**) became common, the brick
courses also serving as a leveling device to keep the work
plumb and true. The strength, durability, and economy of
concrete construction gave the Romans a versatile material
for large-scale building, and by the middle of the first century CE they were using it with rapidly increasing architectural sophistication.

CITY PLANNING

City planning practices in ancient Greece and in Rome had
striking parallels. Both Athens and Rome, the cultural centers, grew without preconceived overall plans, while the
colonial cities established by each were generally provided
with orthogonal plans. Greek foundations might become
Roman settlements later, as was the case with Pompeii,
one of the best-preserved examples of a Roman provincial
town owing to its burial in the eruption of Mount Vesuvius
in 79 CE. The fabric of the city, already shaken by an earthquake in 62 CE, was engulfed by ash, lava, and mud that
preserved it until excavations begun in 1748 brought the
remains to light.

Pompeii was founded by the Greeks in the sixth century BCE, and it was briefly inhabited by the Etruscans and
Samnites before becoming a Roman city. At the time of its
destruction, it had a population of about 20,000, including great patrician families, middle-class merchants, retired
persons, and slaves. Its irregular grid plan covered about
160 acres within roughly oval town walls (Fig. 5.8). The
Roman civic center or forum was located in the southwest
quarter, near the Marine Gate entrance (Fig. 5.9). The earlier Greek center was two blocks to the east, on an acropolis

Triumphal arch

Temple of Jupiter, or Capitolium

Latrines

Vegetable market

Temple of Apollo

Basilica

Macellum (meat and fish market)

Lararium (temple for the patron gods of the city)

Temple of Vespasian

Eumachia building (guild offices and shops)

Comitium (space for elections)

City government offices

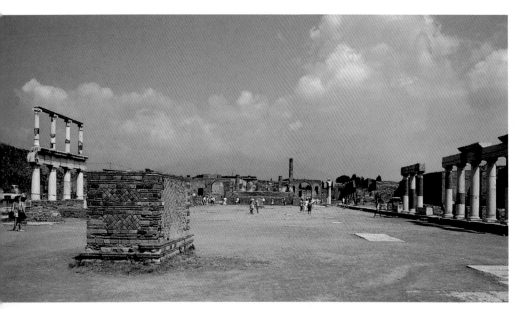

5.9 Plan of the forum, Pompeii, founded 6th century BCE.
The various buildings flanking the open space were unified with colonnades. When Vesuvius last erupted in 79 CE, the city was still being rebuilt after suffering earthquake damage in 62 CE.

5.10 The forum looking north, Pompeii, founded 6th century BCE.
Reconstructed remains of the colonnades can be seen to both sides. At the far end of the forum, the column stumps of the Capitolium rise up, and to their right is the city's triumphal arch. The square ends of opus reticulatum units appear on the face of the masonry mass in the foreground.

Cardo

Triumphal arch

Market of Sertius

Senate House

Capitolium

South baths

Library

East baths

Decumanus

Forum

Basilica

Theater

5.11 Plan of Timgad, Algeria, founded ca. 100 CE.
The original gridded layout of Timgad is generally cited as the textbook example of a Roman city because of the great regularity of its plan. It is in fact orthogonal to a degree seldom found in Roman colonial cities.

with a Doric temple and a columned portico dating from the second or third century BCE. Streets ran approximately parallel and perpendicular to the forum, their pattern being adjusted to the varying topography.

Public facilities were dispersed around the town. Within the town walls, there were three baths, a large exercise facility (the **palaestra**) with a swimming pool, covered and open-air theaters, and an **amphitheater** capable of seating the entire population. Nine temples dedicated to various gods—Greek divinities, Roman deities, deceased Roman emperors, patrons of the city, and the oriental mystery cults of Isis and Bacchus—indicate the diversity of religious beliefs in Pompeii. Cemeteries were located outside the town gates.

The forum in Pompeii was the focus of public life (Figs. 5.9, 5.10). A two-story colonnade surrounded its rectangular form, 510 by 125 feet, on three sides, the open fourth (north) side being occupied by the Capitolium, the center for state-sponsored religious observances. A **triumphal arch** marked the north entrance and prevented wheeled vehicles from intruding on the pedestrian domain. Buildings of various designs and uses flanked the forum. On the east side were the macellum, the meat and fish market; the lararium, a temple for the patron gods of the city; the eumachia building, containing guild offices and shops of the cloth workers and dyers; and the comitium, an open area where elections were held. The short southern side contained three halls used for government: offices for judges and for public works officials and the council chamber. On the west side, bordered by the road from the Marine Gate, was the large **basilica** where public assemblies for legal, commercial, and social purposes were held. It functioned much as did the stoa in the Athenian Agora,

yet the space here was enclosed and introverted. Beyond the basilica were the Temple of Apollo, which dated from the earliest period of Pompeii; the vegetable market, one of the last buildings constructed on the forum; and public latrines. Colonnades linking most of the buildings gave the forum architectural consistency (see Figs. 5.9 and 5.17). Conveying unity within such a diverse grouping of buildings constructed over three or more centuries is no insignificant accomplishment, and it indicates the high quality of Roman civic design attained even in provincial centers.

Some Roman cities began as military garrisons (castra) located in unsettled areas as a means of defense and of bringing civilization to new territories. For these, and for many colonial cities as well, the Romans had a standard plan, perhaps derived from the Etruscans and applied with consistency throughout their empire, from Britain to North Africa, Italy, and the eastern Mediterranean. It was rectangular or square, with two main roads, the cardo and the decumanus, crossing at right angles in the center of town. A wall surrounded it, and the public spaces—the forum and military headquarters—were usually located at the principal intersection in the center of town. Residential sectors were laid out in square or rectangular blocks, with land reserved for neighborhood markets and recreational facilities as the town grew. Streets could be numbered sequentially so that a stranger in town could find any given address easily. Large public buildings, such as baths and theaters, served the whole community and were located according to topography.

This standard Roman plan underlies many present-day European cities, including Florence and Bologna in Italy, Cirencester in England, and Trier in Germany. Timgad in Algeria is an original example that has not been overbuilt

5.12 View of the Forum Romanum, Rome.
This forum was largely transformed during the reign of Augustus (37 BCE–14 CE) to become a splendid civic center for Rome. Visible here (left to right) are three columns from the Temple of Vespasian, the Arch of Septimus Severus (203 CE), columns from the Temple of Saturn, and rows of column stumps from the Basilica Julia.

by a modern city, so its major features can be seen even though it is now a ruin (Fig. 5.11). Timgad was founded by the Emperor Trajan in 100 CE for veterans of the Roman legions and became a thriving regional center until it was destroyed by native tribes in the seventh century. The city walls enclosed a square, with the cardo and decumanus intersecting in the center of town. The forum is to the south, and a large theater was set just south of the forum. (Because of the theater's placement, the cardo did not continue through to the south.) Entrances into the city were framed by triumphal arches, and continuous colonnades lined the major streets to lend dignity and shelter to the

sidewalks. Timgad had a population of perhaps 15,000 within a century of its founding, and in the third century CE it began to accumulate suburban developments along the approach roads to the north, west, and south. Large baths were built north and south of the walls, and markets and temples further served the expanding population outside the walls. None of the extramural growth conformed to the grid plan of the city proper.

Trajan is also remembered for the substantial contributions he made to the urban fabric of Rome itself. Civic life in Rome focused on the Forum Romanum at the base of the Capitoline Hill in an area drained by the Cloaca

5.13 Plan of the imperial fora, Rome, with the great Forum of Trajan, 1st century CE.
Of this vast project, only the markets and Trajan's Column (located between the two library buildings) have survived.

Maxima (Fig. 5.12). Here the functions of commerce, government, law, and religion mingled, and with the growth of the city, the space became increasingly congested. From the middle of the first century BCE onward, the development expanded as new colonnaded fora were constructed adjacent to the original Forum Romanum (Fig. 5.13). Julius Caesar laid out a forum containing a temple and governmental chambers; Augustus constructed a forum at right angles to the Forum of Caesar to surround the Temple of Mars Ultor; and Vespasian built a forum around a library. The culmination of these constructions was the Forum of Trajan (ca. 100–14 CE), equal in size to all the others put together and built to the designs of Apollodorus of Damascus, who had served with distinction as a military engineer. The site was located north of the Forum of Augustus, where a ridge connecting the Capitoline and Quirinale hills was removed to provide a level area and improve access to all the fora from the north. Trajan's forum was symmetrically planned, with a monumental entranceway from the Forum of Augustus leading into the forum proper, a court 330 by 375 feet defined by double colonnades and semicircular elements (hemicycles) set on a cross-axis. Dominating the center of the court was a large equestrian statue of Trajan. Opposite the entrance was the Basilica Ulpia, a magnificent judicial building with entrances placed on its long side. Beyond the basilica was Trajan's Column, a marble shaft nearly 100 feet high set on a fifteen-foot-high base and carved with a spiraling narrative relief illustrating Trajan's victories in the Dacian Wars. Spoils from the Dacian campaign (in the region of present-day Romania) were used to finance the forum's construction. Trajan's Column, the sole surviving structure in this part of the forum, was flanked by two library buildings, one for Greek and one for Latin texts; the column's continuous frieze would have been readable from these neighboring buildings. At the terminus of the axis, in the center of a curving colonnaded courtyard, was a temple dedicated to Trajan and his wife by the later emperor Hadrian. Like those of Julius Caesar and Augustus, and like Etruscan temples, it has a deep porch with columns defining an entry space.

Needed commercial space adjacent to the forum was carved out of the Quirinale hillside behind the northeast hemicycle. Trajan's markets, a good part of which are extant, were set in a multi-story semicircle with adjoining, tiered buildings, reflecting the hemicycle of the forum below and becoming an arcaded complement to it (Figs. 5.14–5.15). The markets contained over 150 shops, offices, and a **groin-vaulted** market hall (Fig. 5.16), all of which could be reached from the forum and from streets on two higher levels. They were built of brick-faced concrete, a contrast to the marble and elaborate ornament of the forum. Durable barrel vaults provided the basic structural module both for the individual shops and for enclosed walkways between them. In the two-story market hall, piers rising from the walls between the shops to each

5.14 Axonometric drawing of Trajan's markets, Rome, 100–114 CE.
The markets are built into the hillside as a series of shops that form a semicircle and act as a retaining wall to hold back the earth in which they are embedded. At the top left, the vaulted market hall lies further up the hill.

5.15 Trajan's markets, Rome, 100–114 CE.
This view of the shops shows the great semicircle that completed one side of the principal cross-axis of the forum.

5.16 Covered market hall built by Trajan, Rome, ca. 100 CE.
Constructed in concrete, this is an early example of a groin-vaulted space with clerestory lighting and flying buttresses (one of which is visible through the near-left-end bay at the upper level). It shows the care extended by Roman builders to civic structures accommodating such mundane activities as a fruit and vegetable market.

5.17 Triumphal arch, Pompeii, before 79 CE.
Monuments such as these were the pride of the city, reflecting civic virtues and boldly marking entrances to important sites. In this case, the arch also restricted access of wheeled vehicles into the forum.

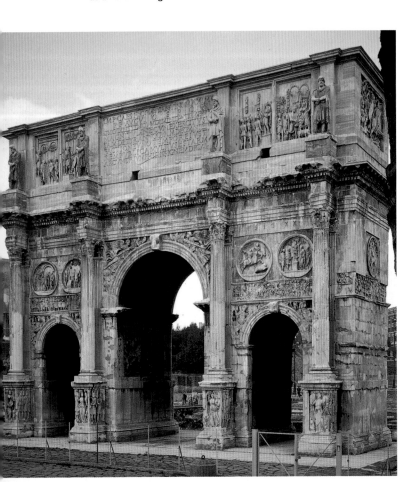

side of the central space support six groin vaults given lateral support by **flying buttresses**.

We have noted the presence of triumphal arches in both Pompeii (Fig. 5.17) and Timgad. These freestanding monuments were generally built to commemorate a military victory, and they added grandeur to the public realm by serving as reminders of civic greatness. Of surviving arches, those in Rome are the most elaborate. The Arch of Septimus Severus (203 CE) still stands in the Forum Romanum, while the larger Arch of Constantine (finished 315 CE) (Fig. 5.18) stands near the Colosseum. Both are triple-arched structures, the central arch being larger than the side arches, and the **attic** story (above the arch) is embellished with carved relief panels depicting the particular military victory for which the arch was constructed. Constantine's Arch incorporates panels from earlier monuments. As an architectural motif, the triumphal arch will have a long afterlife, being revived in **Carolingian**, Romanesque, Renaissance, and later works.

5.18 The Arch of Constantine, Rome, 315 CE.
This triple-arched form became an architectural motif adapted to later buildings. Compare the abbey gatehouse at Lorsch (see Fig. 8.4) and the west front of S. Andrea in Mantua (see Fig. 11.16) for examples of later works inspired by this design.

The Engineering Might of the Romans
by Dan MacGilvray

It now remains for us to speak of stones, or, in other words, the leading folly of the day . . . as to the mountains, nature has made those for herself, as a kind of bulwark for keeping together the bowels of the earth; as also for the purpose of curbing the violence of the rivers, of breaking the waves of the sea, and so, by opposing to them the very hardest of her materials, putting a check upon those elements which are never at rest. And yet we must hew down these mountains and carry them off . . . for no other reason than to gratify our luxurious inclinations. . . .

These very mountains are cut asunder to yield us a thousand different marbles, promontories are thrown open to the sea, and the face of nature is being everywhere reduced. . . . We now carry away the barriers that were destined for the separation of one nation from another; we construct ships for the transport of our marbles; and amid the waves . . . we convey the summits of the mountains to and fro: a thing, however, that is even less unpardonable than to . . . search amid the regions of the clouds for vessels with which to cool our draughts, and to excavate rocks, towering to the very heavens, in order that we may have the satisfaction of drinking from ice![1]

In these two paragraphs from his *Natural History*, Pliny neatly exposes both the arrogance and the capabilities of the Roman civilization. As opposed to the esthetically sensitive Greeks, the Romans were the mighty engineers of the ancient world, conquering not only all the peoples and nations of the Mediterranean, but subduing the sea itself and even the mountains that surround it.

Not since the Egyptians had architects and constructors had the routine capability of choosing building materials for their projects that came from great distances. Ancient buildings had always

reflected the local geology: the sun-dried brick walls and vaults of Babylon were built of mud scooped from the Euphrates flood plain, the gleaming white Parthenon was constructed of marble from nearby Mount Pentelikos. Even the proud Egyptians were limited to materials found within the 600-mile-long watershed of the Nile below the first cataract—limestone for the pyramids came from the Giza plateau or Tura, across the river; sandstone for the temples at Luxor and Karnak was quarried at Silsileh, a few miles conveniently upstream. Only when they required the toughest of all stones, granite, for a 100-foot obelisk or to line the pharaoh's chamber in the Great Pyramid, were the Egyptians called upon to move their stones great distances.

In contrast, Roman architects routinely constructed concrete walls and vaults using pozzolana, a natural cement mined near Naples, and the emperors adorned their temples, palaces, and baths with a polychrome profusion of thin marble veneers and graceful columns: pure white from Carrara overlooking the Lingurian Sea

5.19 Altar from Claudian period, 1st century CE. Villa Medici, Rome.

above Pisa, or the island of Proconeseus in the Sea of Marmara; *giallo antico* (antique yellow) from Tunisia; *verde antico* (green) from Greece; onion-skinned *cipolino* from the Aegean isles; purple porphyry, rose and gray granite from Egypt. Romans outdid Egyptians by pulling down the great obelisks from their temple fronts, moving them on specially constructed ships over 1500 miles across the Mediterranean, and reerecting them in the circuses, villas, and gardens of Rome (Fig. 5.19). In the process they seem to have offended not only the Egyptian gods but also Pliny, who comments on Roman "folly" and environmental arrogance.

Just as the ancient Romans indelibly marked the mountains with their quarries, Rome today still displays some of its ancient arrogance (and capabilities) as granite obelisks, marble veneers, and slender columns have been relocated to adorn public places and the temples of the Catholic Church.

---

1 Plinius Secundus, C. (the Elder Pliny), *The Natural History of Pliny, Vol. VI*, translated by John Bostock and H.T. Riley (London: Henry G. Bohn, 1862), p. 305. Pliny is referring to quartz as the material that gives the "satisfaction of drinking from ice."

TEMPLES

Discussion of the Roman fora has indicated the locations of temples, which the Romans built largely on the basis of Greek and Etruscan precedents. Generally speaking, the Romans did not build temples as isolated structures as had the Classical Greeks, but as axially approached buildings in an urban setting, like the temples of the Hellenistic period or the temples of the Etruscans. The placement of the Capitolium in the forum at Pompeii and the Temple of Mars Ultor in the Forum of Augustus in Rome was essentially the same, and the temple designs were similar. Both were raised on podiums, so that a flight of steps led up to the colonnaded portico of the cella space.

As the Capitolium and the Temple of Mars Ultor are largely destroyed, smaller Roman temples that have survived more completely provide us with a better image of temple architecture. In Rome the second-century BCE Temple of Fortuna Virilis (Fig. 5.20) superficially resembles an Ionic Greek temple. However, a closer look at the side and rear elevations reveals that the columns are engaged with the cella wall and not freestanding. Expanding the cella to the limits of the surrounding colonnade provides a larger interior space and reinforces the axiality of the whole.

Not all Roman temples were rectangular. The Greeks had built circular tholoi, and the Romans applied the circular ground plan to temples. One of the most striking is the Temple of the Sibyl (ca. 25 BCE) in Tivoli. Set on a promontory, it seems to reflect Greek precedent in both its design and siting. It is, however, distinctly Roman. The approach is axial, via a flight of stairs; the cella wall is constructed of concrete instead of marble blocks; and the ornamental frieze of the Corinthian order has Roman swags and ox skulls. Near the Temple of Fortuna Virilis in Rome is the so-called Temple of Vesta (a temple dedicated to Hercules), a circular-plan temple of the first century BCE that is similar to but slightly larger than the Tivoli example. Later modifications have changed the roof and destroyed the original entablature.

The greatest circular-plan Roman temple is the Pantheon in Rome (ca. 125 CE), considered by many to be the most influential building in Western architectural history (Fig. 5.21). Its size, the boldness of its design, and the technical accomplishment of its construction combine to make it a memorable work. Dedicated to seven planetary deities, the Pantheon was constructed in the reign of the emperor Hadrian, who is reputed to have been its architect. The entrance is an enormous portico with twenty Corinthian columns that originally supported roof trusses (their bronze covering long since removed). This portico is rather awkwardly joined to the circular cella, a space 142 feet and six inches in diameter and 142 feet high. The bottom half of the cella is a cylinder on which rests a hemispherical dome, with a circular opening or **oculus**, twenty-seven feet in diameter, at the top to let in light and air (Fig. 5.22). The contrast of the interior to the

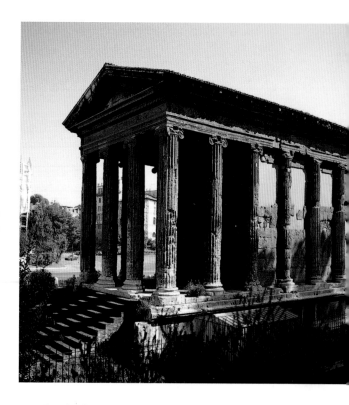

5.20 Temple of Fortuna Virilis, Rome, 2nd century BCE. An early example of a Roman temple, which uses the orders (here, the Ionic) as one might expect from the Greek example, but the building was oriented to an axis in the manner of the Etruscans.

exterior is breathtaking, even to modern senses, and it has inspired visitors ever since it was completed. Unlike other pagan temples in Rome, the Pantheon was converted to Christian use and never pillaged for its marble facings, so it remains the Roman building closest to its original state.

The cylindrical cella wall is visually divided into two stories, a ground-level Corinthian order of fluted columns and pilasters supporting an attic story with rectangular openings resembling windows set in a patterned marble wall. The lower story is varied by niches, alternately semi-circular and rectangular, set at quarter and eighth points around the circumference. Articulation in the dome is accomplished by five tiers of diminishing square coffers, designed with exaggerated perspective to enhance the sense of depth. The light pouring in from the oculus emphasizes the three-dimensionality of both the ceiling coffers and the eight niches below. For someone standing in the center of the Pantheon, the building creates the feeling that the space extends beyond the cylindrical drum and that the dome is much higher than its actual dimension.

The conceptual simplicity of the Pantheon's dome-on-drum design should not be mistaken for constructional simplicity (Fig. 5.23). What looks like trabeated construction is in fact a structure based on arches and vaults. Behind the orderly interior columns, veneers, and coffers lies a technical masterpiece, a testament to Roman skill in building with concrete. The immense structural load of the dome is distributed to concrete foundations fifteen feet thick and thirty-four feet wide through drum walls that are up to twenty feet deep. Most of the constructional

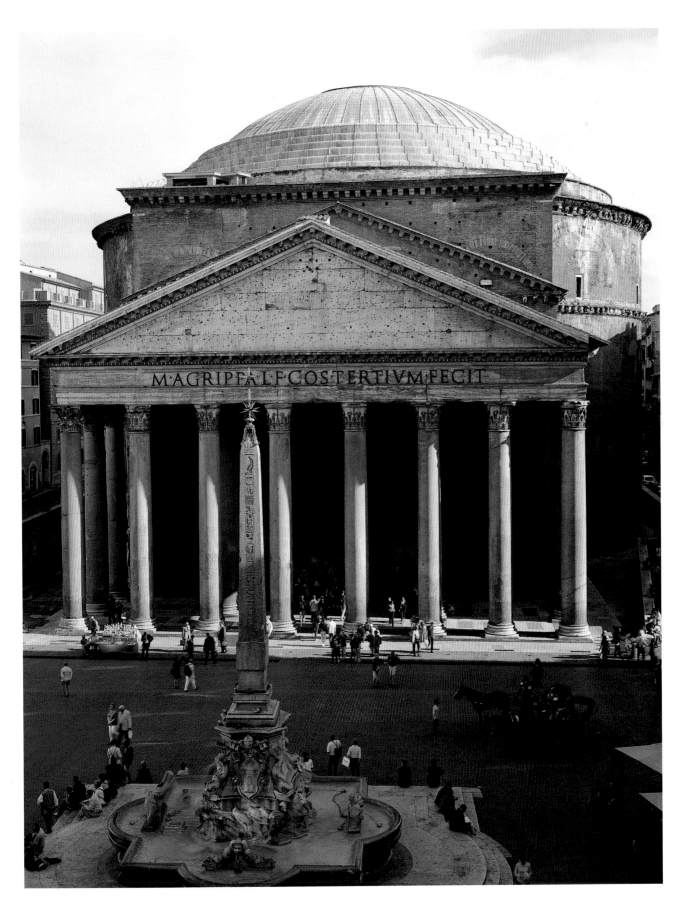

5.21 Pantheon, Rome, ca. 125 CE.
The greatest of Hadrianic architectural projects has become one of the most influential works in Western architectural history, the inspiration for virtually every subsequent domed building. The exterior is imposing, while the interior is overwhelming.

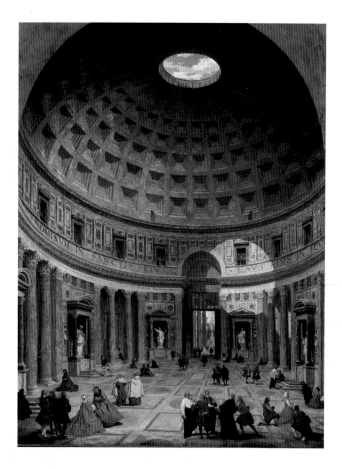

5.22 Giovanni Paolo Panini, *The Interior of the Pantheon*, ca. 1740. Oil on canvas, 4 ft 2 ½ in x 3 ft 3 in (1.28 x .99 m). National Gallery of Art, Washington, DC.
A sphere 142 feet 6 inches in diameter conceptually determines the interior volume of the great dome, which constitutes half of the sphere. Columns in the wall belie the principal structure of arches and vaults that sustain the great dome. Concrete is the primary structural material, faced with marble veneers below and left exposed in the coffering above.

Relieving arches

5.23 Axonometric section of the Pantheon, Rome, ca. 125 CE. This worm's-eye view shows part of the plan and the arched construction behind the internal marble veneers and inside the dome. Although none of this arcuated construction is visible from the interior, relieving arches can be seen on the exterior as in Fig. 5.21.

PUBLIC BUILDINGS

The Romans developed a number of public building types for specialized functions: the basilica, a large assembly hall used for law courts; the baths, a many-chambered building containing bathing and recreational facilities; and the theater, which was based on the Greek prototype but made into a freestanding structure and sometimes enlarged to become an amphitheater for spectacular entertainments. Each of these building types posed spatial and constructional challenges, and each left its imprint on subsequent architectural developments.

Basilicas

The basilica on the southwest corner of the forum at Pompeii has already been noted. Dated to ca. 100 BCE, it is the oldest known Roman basilica, though it was probably not the first. While it principally housed legal activities, it doubtless also served as a gathering place for social and commercial functions, as did the colonnades of the Greek stoas. In Greek, the word *basilica* literally means "king's hall." Rather than surrounding the exterior as in a stoa, the basilica's colonnades define the longitudinal central space. Entrance to the basilica at Pompeii was made primarily from the short side adjacent to the city governmental offices, but there were lesser entrances on both long sides. Set in a rectangular area in front of the end wall opposite the primary entrance was the tribunal seat of honor, terminating the longitudinal axis established by the colonnades. The building was covered by a wooden gabled roof.

complexity is not visible on the interior. The first two rings of coffering conceal eight great relieving arches that work with a second set, likewise hidden, to concentrate loads on the wall sections between the niches of the ground story. Even these sections are not solid, but are hollowed by chambers, accessible from the exterior, to equalize contraction of the concrete as it hardened and lessen the dead load transferred to the foundations, all this without compromising the stability of the whole. Aggregate in the concrete mix is progressively lightened, from heavy basalt in the foundations to spongelike volcanic rock (tufa) in the oculus ring.

Virtually every domed building constructed since Roman times makes reference to the Pantheon. Sometimes its influence is very obvious, as in Jefferson's design for the Library at the University of Virginia (see Fig. 13.41), and at other times the connection is less apparent, as in Brunelleschi's dome for Florence Cathedral (see Fig. 11.3). Literally hundreds of domed museums, universities, banks, churches, and railroad stations, to mention only some of the building types, may be found that are ultimately connected to this masterpiece from the time of Hadrian.

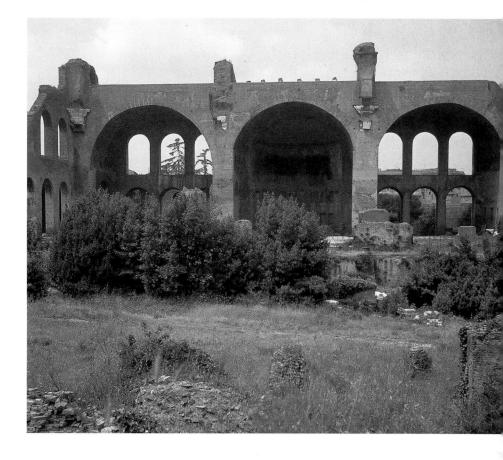

5.24 (above) **Plan of the Basilica Nova (Basilica of Maxentius and Constantine), Rome, 307–15 CE.** This large vaulted building had groin vaults flanked by barrel vaults. Illumination was provided by large clerestory windows.

5.25 (right) **Basilica Nova, Rome, 307–15 CE.** Although the groin vaults have collapsed, one set of barrel vaults remains. Astride each bay, the haunches of the groin vaults rise above the parapet. The columns that stood below them were only ornamental.

Trajan's Forum in Rome contained the more extensive Basilica Ulpia, which measured 200 by 400 feet excluding the curved end sections (**apses**). Here the entrances were placed in the building's long façades because the basilica completes one side of the forum. On the interior, double colonnades defined the long, narrow central space, and there were triple colonnades across the short sides in front of the semicircular apses. Architectural restoration drawings show the interior with second-floor galleries above the columns on both long sides and clerestory windows illuminating the central space. As at Pompeii, a gabled timber roof covered the building. Luxurious materials, financed by tribute money from Dacia, were employed in the construction: marble on floors and walls, bronze gilding suspended from the roof trusses on the coffered ceiling, and Egyptian granite for the columns. Impressive size, rich finishes, and dramatic lighting combined here to create a setting fit for the dispensation of imperial justice. Of all this magnificence only rude fragments remain, but the basilica form would become the basis for Early Christian church designs.

Not all basilicas had files of columns or were timber-roofed. The Basilica Nova (also known as the Basilica of Maxentius and Constantine) in Rome, dated 307–15 CE, had three great groin vaults over its central space, with three barrel-vaulted **bays** to each side (Figs. 5.24–5.25). Structurally, this organization allowed the semicircular barrel vaults and their support walls, all at right angles to

the principal axis of the central space, to provide lateral stability for the groin vaults. Finally, the two apses terminated longitudinal and transverse axes.

Public Baths

The interior of the Basilica Nova owed much to the greatest vaulted Roman buildings, the baths. As the name implies, Roman baths (**thermae**) were primarily hygienic facilities, but they also provided for exercise, relaxation, and informal socializing, activities more commonly associated with modern spas or health clubs than with bathrooms. The Romans actually cleaned their bodies without soap by first anointing with oil and then scraping the skin with spoonlike implements. Bathers induced perspiration in hot steam rooms (rather like Finnish saunas) and then cooled down and relaxed in a sequence of temperate and cool plunges. They might extend their time at the baths by swimming, taking walks, enjoying conversation, or reading in the baths' library.

Such an array of activities required an array of spaces: changing rooms, latrines, rooms for hot, warm, and cold bathing; exercise facilities, relaxing areas, and gardens if possible. Adequate water supplies were essential. The Romans used mineral springs when available (the city of Bath in England was one such Roman establishment) and heated the water if the supply was not naturally warm. Because bathing was a healthful diversion for the

5.26 Plan of the Baths of Diocletian, Rome, 298–306 CE.
The large bath building was set within a walled enclosure and provided with landscaped grounds used for exercising, athletic games, or restful walks.

5.27 (opposite) Remains of the Baths of Diocletian, Rome, 298–306 CE.
The central section of the frigidarium has survived and was converted into a church, S. Maria degli Angeli, by Michelangelo. Note the groin vaults and the thermal windows. The finishes remind us how grand these spaces were when intact and well kept.

Natatio (open-air swimming pool)

Frigidarium (cool baths)

Tepidarium (warm baths)

Caldarium (hot baths)

Stadium or theater seats

Changing room

Peristyle or palaestra

Gymnasium

0   250 m
0   750 ft

large urban population, the later emperors vied with one another to build ever more elaborate complexes in Rome.

The Baths of Diocletian (298–306 CE) were the largest such complex in ancient Rome, covering about fifty acres of land, and were said to have the capacity for 3000 people (Fig. 5.26). The entire complex was symmetrically designed, with the principal sequence of rooms within the bath building placed on the central axis. From the center of the southwest façade, these included the groin-vaulted hot baths (**caldarium**), domed warm baths (**tepidarium**), cruciform cool baths (**frigidarium**), and open-air swimming pool (natatio). On either side of this central suite of spaces were oval-plan changing rooms and an unroofed rectangular **peristyle** or palaestra for exercising surrounded by ancillary service rooms, the use of which cannot be completely identified. **En suite**, or adjacent, rooms on the south side may have been steam rooms leading up to the caldarium. Interiors were finished with sumptuous materials, marble veneers, and mosaics; statues were placed both inside and out; and the grounds were landscaped with trees and gardens to create a congenial environment for exercise, conversation, and relaxation. A large **exedra** in the southwest exterior wall was fitted with tiered seats for use as a theater or stadium. Rectangular rooms to either side may have contained libraries. Of this vast structure, only parts survive. In 1561, Michelangelo converted the frigidarium into the Church of S. Maria degli Angeli (Fig.

5.27), so that the interior reflects the scale and some of the splendor of the Roman original. One corner rotunda has been transformed into the Church of S. Bernardo, and a trace of the great southern exedra has been preserved in the nineteenth-century Piazza dell'Esedra near the present railroad station.

The Baths of Diocletian were exceptionally large, even by the standards of imperial times. Of ancient Rome's over 950 baths listed in a mid-fourth-century inventory, only a handful were this grand. One can appreciate the more common baths' designs by looking at buildings that remain in provincial cities, such as the Forum Baths at Pompeii (Fig. 5.28), Paris (where the Cluny Museum incorporates part of a third-century CE baths), or Leptis Magna on the North African coast, where the so-called Hunting Baths (late second or early third century CE) are exceptionally well preserved.

Theaters and Amphitheaters

Athletic competitions and dramatic performances were part of the culture of ancient Greece. The Romans, who inherited these traditions and added to them the gladiatorial combats of the Etruscans, needed theaters and stadiums in which to stage these events. Greek building practice was to carve the shape of theaters or stadiums out of hillsides, thus adapting the sloping natural setting

Men's entrance

Furnaces and cistern

Women's entrance

Shop

Shop

Shop

Shop

Shop

Stairs to inn on 2nd floor

darium

Shop

sin for cold baths

Changing

Tepidarium

Frigidarium

Caldarium

Shop

anging room

Shop

Men's entrance

Tepidarium

Shop

Service court

Portico

Shop

Shop

Gymnasium
garden

Men's entrance

N

0   20 m

0   60 ft

5.28 Forum Baths, Pompeii, ca. 80 BCE.
This is a small facility with separate but
unequal sections for men and women. A
common service area (dark shading) was
used for heating water. Shops occupy most
of the street frontage, since there was no
need for an impressive street presence.
See Fig. 5.8 for location within the city.

5.29 Perspective section through the Theater of Marcellus, Rome, 13–11 BCE.
This view shows the ramps and stairs needed to allow patrons to reach their seats. The lower two stories have survived while the upper tier was reworked during the Middle Ages and the sixteenth century. As Vitruvius recommended, the lower level was faced with the Doric order, the middle level with the Ionic order, and the upper level possibly with the Corinthian order.

to tiered seating, but the Romans chose to construct their facilities whether the terrain was favorable or not, so they developed great vaulted structures to create the slope needed for spectator viewing. An early result of this process was the Theater of Marcellus (completed 13–11 BCE) in Rome (Figs. 5.29–5.30), where a great semicircle of 11,000 seats rising in three tiers focused on a rectangular stage building that formed the backdrop for the drama. (This theater had the same capacity as the Greek theater at Epidauros.) Enough of the original construction has survived reuse, first as a medieval fortress and then as a Renaissance palace, to permit reasonable understanding of the structural ingenuity underlying the plan. Stacked radial barrel vaults accommodating ingress and egress, and ramps and stairs made of cut stone and concrete, were intersected by concentric rings of barrel vaults accommodating internal circulation. Fragmentary remains of the exterior veneer frame the arched terminations of the radial barrel vaults in the form of engaged half-columns and entablatures of the Doric and Ionic orders on the ground and second levels, respectively.

The design of theaters doubtless inspired that of amphitheaters ("amphi," meaning "both sides," so a theater on both sides), which were circular or oval in plan, with raked seating all around. The amphitheater at Pompeii, dating from about 80 BCE and the oldest surviving example, was sited so that seats at one end of the oval could be supported on rising ground (Fig. 5.31). Later amphitheaters built in southern France at Arles and Nîmes were constructed almost entirely above ground level.

5.30 Plan of the Theater of Marcellus, Rome, 13–11 BCE.
Roman theaters were based on designs already perfected by the Greeks. The difference here is that support for the seats depends not on a convenient hillside but rather on a vaulted structure of cut stone and concrete.

5.31 The amphitheater, Pompeii, ca. 80 BCE.
This oval-shaped arena was used for the gladiatorial contests of which the Romans were exceedingly fond. Part of its seating is supported on arched construction and part is built into rising ground.

Greatest of all was the Flavian Amphitheater in Rome, more commonly known as the Colosseum, completed in 80 CE (Fig. 5.32). Although the building's plan is the familiar oval and its structure is modeled on that of the Theater of Marcellus, the novel element here is size. The outside dimension of the oval measures 510 by 615 feet, encompassing seats for an estimated 50,000 people in a continuously rising tier with an additional seating band above. Except for this top level of seats, which rested on wooden supports, the entire building was masonry, a combination of cut stone and concrete resting on carefully laid foundations. Under the seating was an intricate network of structural supports, horizontal passageways, ramps, and stairs to accommodate the attending throngs. The exterior walls were clad in travertine, usually a cream-colored marble. Stacked half-columns in the Roman Doric, Ionic, and Corinthian orders combined with arches of the supporting barrel vaults to create three stories of the façade. A fourth level of Corinthian pilasters without arches completed the elevation around two upper galleries (reserved for women and slaves). Attached to this level were brackets for the poles that some historians believe to have been supports for a canvas cover (velarium) providing shade for spectators. The area under the arena floor, an oval measuring 175 by 280 feet, was a labyrinth of passageways and chambers for gladiators, beasts, and hoisting machinery to service the spectacles staged above. The Colosseum is inextricably linked with savage and cruel entertainment, including fights to the death by gladiators and the persecution of Roman Christians. During later eras the fine marble work was removed as the building became a source for ready-cut stone. It remains today as a partial ruin, but even in its crumbled condition the Colosseum testifies to Roman construction skill.

RESIDENCES

To study Roman housing, we once again return to Pompeii, for the collection of ordinary dwellings, elaborate town residences, country villas, and farmhouses preserved there provides the most complete record we have of the types of buildings in which people lived. The earliest houses have atrium plans, an indigenous Italian type in which the principal rooms of the house directly adjoin an open courtyard for access and for light and circulation of air. Such a house presents a blank wall to the street on which it fronts without setback from the sidewalk.

Urban Housing

The House of the Surgeon is the most ancient dwelling found in Pompeii, and an examination of its plan reveals the typical features of atrium houses (Fig. 5.33). It is an irregular quadrilateral because it exactly fills the plot of land on which it was built. On the street side it has three

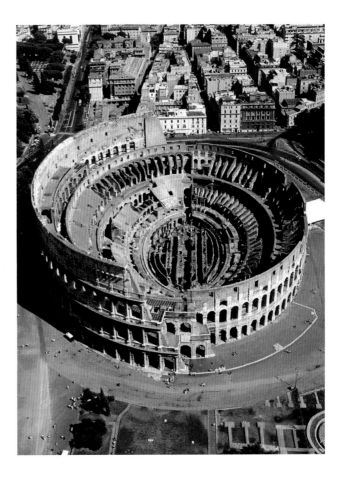

5.32 The Colosseum (Flavian Amphitheater), Rome, completed 80 CE.
Grandest of all the Roman arenas, the Colosseum was once entirely clad in travertine, some of which remains in the form of applied orders, as seen here on the left side of the image. From bottom to top, these are Doric, Ionic, and Corinthian attached columns and a crowning level of Corinthian pilasters. On the right side of the arena these have been lost, exposing the structural piers and arches. Tiers of seating on the inside worked their way down to the chambers beneath the former floor.

doors, two of which provide access to shops, one connected to the dwelling and the other forming part of a self-contained environment with living quarters upstairs. The center doorway, dignified by two entrance steps, was the principal entry to the house, and its location defines the axis of symmetry for the house proper. Passing through a vestibule, a visitor would next encounter the atrium, where a roof provided covering and shade except for a relatively small central area that was left open to the sky. Water running off the roof would fall in a basin (**impluvium**) in the center of the atrium. On either side of the atrium were chambers generally used as bedrooms; straight ahead on axis was the main reception room (**tablinum**), flanked by a dining room (**triclinium**). Beyond was a portico that opened onto the rear walled garden. Service spaces, including chambers for servants and the kitchen, were set in the wing beside the dining room. All the internal spaces depended on the unroofed atrium or the garden for light, as the exterior walls were without openings. Only the tablinum, the most distinguished room in the house, had direct access to both sources (and thus to the cooling breezes that would pass through); most of the remaining rooms must have been rather dim, even during the day.

The atrium plan had formal dignity and practicality too. The owner could rent the frontage shop with second-floor living quarters to a tradesman or artisan and use the shop connected to the interior of the house as his own place of business. The functioning of either shop was independent of domestic activity, which was in turn isolated from street noise. The scale was ample. The private quarters in the House of the Surgeon covered about 5500 square feet, including the garden. Nevertheless, in the second century BCE wealthier citizens were constructing expanded atrium houses. These newer houses might have more than one atrium, and the garden was greatly enlarged and surrounded by a colonnade to become a peristyle (Figs. 5.35–5.36).

The House of Pansa at Pompeii is an example of the atrium-peristyle house that has been dated to the mid-second century BCE (Fig. 5.34). It occupies virtually one entire city block (approximately 27,000 square feet, over half an acre) and thus might have had windows on any of its four sides, but it has none, relying instead on an atrium, peristyle court, and a large walled garden for light and air. The entrance establishes an axial disposition of spaces similar to that at the House of the Surgeon. The small rooms around the atrium were used as bedrooms, with the dining rooms set adjacent to the peristyle. Beyond the peristyle, the axis passes through another reception room and portico to the walled garden, which occupied about a third of the site. Such a large house was uncommon in Pompeii. Examples of three smaller houses can be seen along the side street of the House of Pansa, where they were created out of the main house in a later remodeling. Lacking an atrium or internal court, these houses had windows for light and air, but they opened to the street, thus sharing the dust, noise, and smells of the public way. The two remaining sides of the House of Pansa contained shops. One can see the masonry mass surrounding the oven of a bakery on the plan.

Inward-looking houses such as those at Pompeii present a virtual wall to the street, an effect completely unlike the residential districts of American cities but not so dissimilar to the modern towns in Mediterranean countries. The streets in Pompeii were usually narrow, ranging from under eight to just over twenty-two feet. Major streets had raised walks on either side, and raised stepping stones at intersections enabled pedestrians to cross the street without sinking into the muck that often filled the roadway (Fig. 5.37). These crossing stones also permitted wheeled carts to pass, carefully, and thus controlled traffic speed. The walls in most sections of town were covered with graffiti. Election slogans, public notices, advertisements for commercial establishments and public entertainments,

5.33 Plan of the House of the Surgeon, Pompeii, 2nd century BCE. This plan is organized around a central open space or atrium that admitted fresh air and light to surrounding rooms. A portico or porch at the rear opened into a small garden. Positioned between these two elements was the tablinum or main reception room.

5.34 Plan of the House of Pansa, Pompeii, 2nd century BCE. This house is so extensive that it occupies virtually an entire block and includes a spacious walled garden at the rear. Fresco paintings decorated its walls and mosaic tiles many of its floors.

5.35 Atrium of the House of Venus in the Shell, Pompeii, 2nd century BCE.
The roof has been restored to give an idea of the original space and light quality. Water running off the roof collected in the impluvium at the center of the atrium. Fresco painting can be seen at the left. The opening in the center led to the garden peristyle. Notice the opus incertum stonework facing of the walls.

5.36 Peristyle of the House of Venus in the Shell, Pompeii, 2nd century BCE.
The house takes its name from a fresco found on the peristyle wall (to the left, not visible in the photograph). Fragments of other wall frescoes are evident to the rear. The dining room opened on the garden.

and obscene remarks have all been found in the excavations of the city. On streets where tradesmen had shops, the walls sometimes contained murals illustrating the particular trade or product available within. Shop fronts opened directly to the street for the display of goods and were secured at night by wooden roller shutters.

Interior finishes in the houses at Pompeii have proven almost as interesting as the architecture. Art historians have identified four styles of wall paintings at Pompeii. One of these, in which imaginary scenes were painted as viewed from high or low vantage points, anticipates the elaborate Baroque creations that were used in the seventeenth

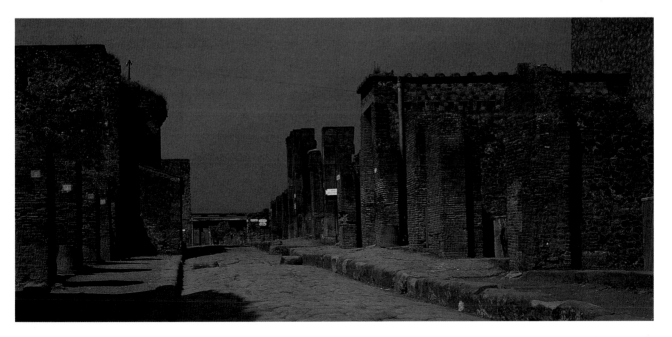

5.37 Street in Pompeii, 2nd century BCE.
Shop fronts predominated along the street, with the entrances to houses being rather modest openings. Carts could pass between the raised stepping stones and sidewalks. Notice the opus testaceum stonework facing of the walls here and in Fig. 5.38.

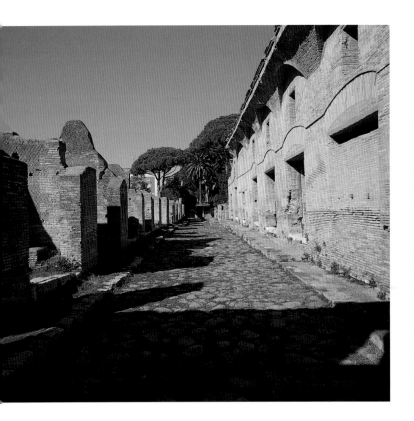

5.38 Insula (tenement building), Ostia, 2nd century CE.
Much of the urban population in Rome lived in accommodation similar to this building. Cooking facilities for all units were located on the roof to minimize odors and the danger of fire, and water had to be carried from the public supply.

century to expand optically the physical boundaries of walls and ceilings.

Stone and brick were the primary materials used in the construction of houses, although a surprising amount of timber was also employed, particularly for roof beams. In less affluent situations, walls were often provided by a wooden structural frame filled with rubble or brick, rather like the **half-timbering** construction of medieval Europe. Dwellings were originally one story, but as a city grew and urban land became more valuable, construction inevitably became multi-story, and older houses were converted to apartments. By the time of Pompeii's destruction, in fact, many of the atrium-peristyle houses had been divided into multi-family dwellings, as the wealthier citizens had moved to more spacious residences on estates outside the city.

For city residents, the dominant housing type after the fire that destroyed much of Rome in 64 CE came to be the apartment block or **insula**. An inventory made in the fourth century of buildings in Rome counted 46,000 insulae, while there were fewer than 1800 single-family houses. The best surviving insulae are found in the port city of Ostia (Fig. 5.38). These apartment buildings, ranging up to six floors in height, occupied substantial plots of land and were designed around central courtyards. Shops or commercial ventures were located on the ground-floor street frontages. Unlike the atrium houses, however, the upper-floor walls of insulae had windows opening to the street, so that rooms could draw on both the courtyard and street for light and air.

Rural Villas and Urban Palaces

Residences outside cities were called **villas**, and at Pompeii, a fine example is preserved just beyond the city wall. Known as the Villa of the Mysteries (Fig. 5.39) because of the wall paintings in one room that relate to the mystical cult of Bacchus, it grew gradually over a period of 300 years from a simple house to a complex of sixty rooms. Elements from atrium houses remain in its plan, including the preference for axial symmetry, but the ordering of rooms differs. The entrance led into the peristyle, followed by the atrium and finally the tablinum, while extensive terraced gardens surrounded the villa on the three non-entrance sides. Based upon the original inward-focused house, the architectural developments at the Villa of the Mysteries seem to suggest a building in which the exterior elevations and their connection with the surrounding countryside were becoming more important.

The ruins of the Palace of Domitian, built to the design of the architect Rabirius for the emperor Domitian (finished in 92 CE) on the Palatine Hill (Fig. 5.40), suggest the complexity of elements incorporated into an imperial residence. The northwestern section contained a suite of official

5.39 Plan of the Villa of the Mysteries, Pompeii, ca. 120–80 BCE.
This plan resulted from some 300 years of development and enlargement. The germ of the plan is still the atrium/peristyle combination seen in urban residences, but the house also opens out to the landscape through numerous porticoes.

Domus Flavia, or official reception rooms

Domus Augustana, or private appartments

Basilica

Lararium

Audience hall

Peristyle

Guest rooms

Vestibule

Guest rooms

Peristyle

Peristyle

Peristyle

Triclinium

Fountains

Library

Library

Peristyle

Walled garden

N

0   50 m

0   150 ft

rooms, arranged along cross-axes, with a grand audience hall, peristyle with fountain, and a large vaulted triclinium with an exedra at the end to mark the emperor's seat. The more private residence section to the southeast was also organized cross-axially, and its more intimately scaled rooms on two levels present a virtuoso display of architectural ingenuity, incorporating varied room shapes, colonnaded gardens with fountains, and ornamental sculpture.

Interest in exploring such complex arrangements continued at the imperial villa erected by the emperor Hadrian outside Tivoli (Figs. 5.41–5.42). Constructed between 117 and 138 CE, it is a vast, sprawling accumulation of geometrically controlled building groups sited to follow the topography and linked to one another by a shifting set of axes and cross-axes. Passionate about architecture and widely traveled, Hadrian may have intended his villa to evoke architectural forms from all parts of the world, but there are no Disneyland-like copies of foreign buildings. Rather, it is the sheer variety of interior volumes

and exterior vistas, as if the designers were experimenting with imaginative and untried forms, that make this a treasury of sequential spatial experiences without precedent.

The most recent scholarship on the villa has stripped away sometimes fanciful names traditionally associated with features found here in preference for descriptive terms, as the old names (given here in parentheses) were assigned by romantically inclined amateurs and not Hadrian himself. An enclosed garden around a rectangular fish pond forms the East–West Terrace (the Poikele), the largest single element in the villa. Below the western end of the terrace are tiers of rooms where as many as 700 villa staff and servants were housed out of sight but close at hand.

To the east was the Island Enclosure (Maritime Theater), a circular, enclosed colonnaded area surrounded by a moat that provided a retreat for meditation or intimate meetings. Water is also the central feature of the Scenic Canal (Canopus), a long colonnaded pool that was lined with statuary and focused at its southern end on a

5.41 Plan of Hadrian's Villa, Tivoli, 117–38 CE.
It is hard to convey in a single drawing the complexity of this sprawling collection of buildings, which covers twice as much area as the city of Pompeii. Hadrian's architects exploited the structural possibilities of concrete to build unprecedented forms and compositions around water features.

Nymphaeum

Entrance pavilion

Library Court

Water Court

Palace

Pool

Large baths

Grand Triclinium

Scenic Canal

Island Enclosure

Terrace

Small baths

Triclinium

East–West terrace

N

0   200 m

0   600 ft

grand triclinium (the Serapeum), or banqueting hall, that became a grotto.

To the north of the Island Enclosure was the residential area, which included parts of an earlier family villa on the site, grouped around a rectangular court. Of greater interest from the standpoint of design sophistication is the Water Court (Piazza d'Oro or Golden Court), built on the northeast edge of the villa. The central axis of the composition was defined by an octagonal domed entrance pavilion that sat opposite the celebrated reverse-curve **Nymphaeum** or water pavilion.

CONCLUSIONS ABOUT ARCHITECTURAL IDEAS

The Romans were the first ancient people to build large interior spaces. They did so by mastering the art of masonry vaulting, using brick and stone throughout the Empire and concrete within the Italian peninsula, where the raw ingredient pozzolana was available. In the end, it is impossible to understand the arrangement of spaces at such sites as the

Palace of Domitian or Hadrian's Villa without understanding the structural principles at work. In fact, from ancient Roman times to the second half of the twentieth century, it will be the supporting of the ceiling, most commonly with masonry vaulting, on which architects will lavish the most time and expense.

While the work of the Republic was largely trabeated and benefited from the planning experiments carried out by the Hellenistic Greeks, the architectural work of the Empire utilized elements of the classical language, particularly the orders, primarily as an exterior and interior veneer or as screens, giving elegance and proportion to the huge piles of compressive masonry that did most of the real work of spatial enclosure. The Colosseum, with its intersecting stacks of radial and concentric barrel vaults that provide access tunnels and support the seating and with its superimposed Doric-Ionic-Corinthian orders around the outer perimeter wall, provides a famous example, as does the Pantheon, with its system of relieving arches and its coffered dome, still the standard by which domed spaces are measured.

A complex such as the Forum of Trajan illustrates the continuity of Hellenistic planning for official or corporate

5.42 Aerial view, Hadrian's Villa, Tivoli, 117–38 CE.
The orientation of this photograph is an inversion of the
site plan seen in Fig. 5.41, so that north is more or less to
the right. The basin of the East–West Terrace can be seen
at the upper right, with the circular Island Enclosure below
it. The baths and Scenic Canal extend to the left. Part of the
irregularity of the layout can be attributed to the designers
accommodating various terrain features.

spaces and the introduction of vaults for utilitarian ones.
Within the forum, stoalike files of columns are folded and
bent to capture exterior spaces that become the precincts
for a temple, a triumphal column, and an equestrian
statue, and the intervening basilica is also completely trabeated. The Markets of Trajan that hold back the earth to
the northeast employ barrel vaults throughout and groin
vaults with flying buttresses in the great hall, while the classical language is largely absent. Much the same can be said
of the public baths and the Basilica of Constantine, where

their ruined state allows us to appreciate their arcuated and
domed construction, without the veneer of frescoes, mosaics, and applied orders that have largely fallen away.

Like the builders of Egypt, Mesopotamia, and Greece,
the Romans built houses around interior courts, either
the paved atrium or gardenlike peristyle. However, their
most distinctive housing type was the tenement or insula,
with its lower-story shops facing the street. While Rome
itself grew over time in an often haphazard way, it was not
considered the ideal. When given the opportunity to plan
new towns, the Romans employed grid layouts into which
they inserted public spaces, temples, baths, theaters, and
amphitheaters, as at Timgad (see Fig. 5.11).

In Western Europe, all of this Roman architecture
would lie fallow for centuries after the fall of the Empire,
only to be reborn in the fifteenth century as a result of
investigations and experiments, first made by Italians,
then by others through Europe and England, as will be discussed in Chapter 11.

Chapter 6

Early Christian and Byzantine Architecture

Christianity, the religion developed by followers of Jesus of Nazareth, began as a reforming sect of Judaism whose members regarded Jesus as the promised messiah. Over three centuries after Jesus's death, the religion developed into an organized Church with a hierarchy of bishops and clergy. The earliest expression of its beliefs is found in the Nicene Creed (325 CE with later revisions), still used by the Eastern Orthodox Church, the Roman Catholic Church, and some Protestant denominations:

I believe in one God the Father Almighty, Maker of heaven and earth, and of all things visible and invisible; and in one Lord Jesus Christ, the only-begotten Son of God, begotten of His Father before all worlds; God of God, Light of Light; Very God of Very God; Begotten, not made; Being of one substance with the Father, by whom all things were made; Who for us men, and for our salvation, came down from heaven; And was incarnate by the Holy Ghost of the Virgin Mary, and was made man; And was crucified also for us under Pontius Pilate. He suffered death and was buried; And on the third day He rose again according to the Scriptures; And ascended into heaven; And sitteth on the right hand of the Father. And He shall come again with glory to judge both the quick and the dead; Whose kingdom shall have no end. And I believe in the Holy Ghost; The Lord and Giver of Life; Who proceedeth from the Father and the Son; Who with the Father and Son together is worshiped and glorified; Who spake by the prophets. And I believe in one Holy Catholic and Apostolic Church. I acknowledge one Baptism for the remission of sins. And I look for the Resurrection of the dead; And the Life of the world to come.

In the context of the late Roman Empire, Christianity was one of a number of religions troublesome to governmental authorities because its followers refused to acknowledge the state-sponsored deities, so the early history of Christianity is one of underground meetings and official persecution. Not until the emperor Constantine proclaimed toleration for all religions of the Roman Empire in the Edict of Milan in 313 did Christians have authority to construct buildings for public worship. Prior to that time services were held in private homes, where common

domestic rooms, most often the triclinium (dining room), sufficed for worship. Christians developed congregational worship with a liturgy that focused on the celebration of the Eucharist (also known as communion), symbolic of the Last Supper of Jesus with his disciples and by extension of his sacrifice for humanity. One table was used for the Eucharist and another for offerings, with participants in the service sitting on the remaining furnishings or standing.

As the liturgy became more elaborate and the congregation grew, larger and more extensive sets of rooms were needed. In many cities Christians established community houses with a hall for worship, a **baptistery**, and rooms for the distribution of alms to the needy. They also organized separate cemeteries to distance their burials from those of other religions. Christians disapproved of cremation, and if suitable land for a graveyard was not available, the community developed underground cemeteries, generally begun in abandoned quarries, which became known as catacombs. Portions of the catacombs in Rome are among the oldest surviving Christian spaces, providing a glimpse of early religious decorative art.

Christian architecture after 313 derived in large measure from Roman precedent, and Early Christian and Byzantine buildings continue certain aspects of Classical antiquity. When, for reasons of security, Constantine relocated his capital from Rome to the town of Byzantium (on the western shore of the Bosporus Strait) and renamed it Constantinople (modern Istanbul), he began the bifurcation of the Empire, with modern-day Greece and Turkey at the heart of the eastern portion and Italy in the western part. At the same time, stylistic developments in this period contributed to later buildings in the medieval

S. Marco interior, Venice, rebuilt 1063–89.
This late Byzantine church, modeled on Justinian's Church of the Holy Apostles in Constantinople, is finished inside with elaborate mosaic figures on a golden background.

Chronology

Reign of Caesar Augustus	27 BCE–14 CE
Life of Jesus	ca. 8–4 BCE–29 CE
Reign of Constantine	310–337
Constantine legalizes Christianity	313
Construction of Old St. Peter's	318–22
Founding of Constantinople	324
End of the Roman Empire in the West	476
Reign of the Emperor Justinian	527–65
Construction of Hagia Sophia	532–37
Fall of Constantinople to the Ottomans	1453

6.1a (above) Plans of Old St. Peter's, Rome, 318–22; S. Apollinare in Classe, Ravenna, 532–49; and S. Apollinare Nuovo, Ravenna, ca. 490.
The fundamental elements of basilican church plans are evident here: a longitudinal axis leads from the entrance (through an atrium and/or narthex) through the nave to the terminating apse, where the altar is located. High (clerestory) windows illuminate the nave. Triumphal-arch-like elements appear at both the entry into the atrium and that from the nave to the altar area, symbolizing the entry into more sacred territory.

6.1b (left) Plan of the Church of the Nativity, Bethlehem, ca. 333.
This innovative building combines the form of a double-aisle basilica with an atrium forecourt and an octagonal rotunda over the traditional site of Jesus's birth. The design thus accommodates the functions of worship while providing circulation space required for pilgrims visiting the holy site.

period, thus creating a transition between the classical past and the medieval era in western Europe.

EARLY CHRISTIAN BASILICAS

In giving official sanction to Christianity, Constantine became the sponsor of some of its early church-building efforts, most of which were based on the Roman basilica. Pagan associations rendered Roman temples unsuitable models for Christian worship, but the connotations of assembly hall and court of justice pertaining to basilicas suited the new religion much better. Basilicas could accommodate large crowds, an important consideration for a religion attracting increasing numbers of converts, and their layout created processional space that was part of worship services. With relatively minor modifications, the Roman basilica form was adapted to Christian ritual.

The altar was placed in the apse where the magistrate's seat had formerly been, entrances were set in the opposite short wall, and an atrium set in front of the entrances accommodated gatherings before services and enabled the unbaptized to hear but not participate in the Mass. The longitudinal arrangement of atrium, nave, and apse formed an impressive axis for processions that terminated at the altar (Figs. 6.1a,b).

Constantine gave the Lateran Palace in Rome to the early church to serve as a residence for the bishop, and one of the earliest basilicas was built adjacent to the palace in about 313. Much rebuilt and extended, it stands today as St. John Lateran and is still the cathedral of Rome. (**Cathedral** is the designation given to a church that contains the seat or cathedra of a bishop. While cathedrals are often larger or more elaborate than ordinary churches, this is not necessarily the case, nor is every large church a cathedral.) The original building had paired **aisles** on either side of a lofty nave, which was concluded by an apse containing the cathedra and seats for the priests. Clerestory windows high in the nave wall illuminated the central space, while smaller windows in the outermost aisle and above the first aisle colonnade provided light for the ancillary spaces. Open wooden trusses spanned the nave and aisles, supported on brick-faced concrete walls and marble columns salvaged from earlier Roman buildings.

A more formulaic example of an Early Christian basilica is found at Ravenna in the church of S. Apollinare Nuovo, constructed about 500 as the palace church for the Ostrogoth King Theoderic and given its present name centuries later (Figs. 6.1a, 6.2, and 6.3). Constructed of brick with single aisles flanking the nave, the church interior focuses on the semicircular apse (not the original). The walls above the nave **arcade** are finished with mosaics arranged in three horizontal layers. The lowest tier depicts stately processions of female saints (north side) and male martyrs (south side) advancing toward the altar. (This mosaic tier was installed in the ninth century, replacing original work whose subject we do not know.) Between the clerestory windows are single figures that may represent Old Testament prophets and New Testament evangelists and apostles. In the highest sections of the nave wall are scenes representing the Passion story (south side) and the miracles of Christ (north side). This elaborate interior decoration not only communicated Christian teachings to a largely illiterate public, but also symbolized the richness

6.2 S. Apollinare Nuovo, Ravenna, ca. 490.
The tall nave of this early basilica has changed relatively little since its construction, preserving the very plain brick exterior that was common in many Early Christian churches. The vaulted arcade across the front is a sixteenth-century addition.

6.3 S. Apollinare Nuovo interior, Ravenna, ca. 490.
Grained marble columns define the aisles and nave. The nave walls are finished with mosaics and above them light enters through clerestory windows.

of the kingdom of God to which the soul could aspire. The sober exterior brickwork gives little indication of the shimmering golden mosaic work contained within.

MARTYRIA, BAPTISTERIES, AND MAUSOLEA

Basilicas were not the only religious buildings erected by early Christians. Among the structures raised to serve Christian purposes were **martyria**, buildings erected as memorials to commemorate saints or sites of special importance to the Christian faith. Celebrated martyria might attract large crowds for services and thus need to function as churches, but major importance was always attached to the tomb or shrine around which they were built. Old St. Peter's in Rome (318–22), predecessor of the present Basilica of St. Peter, began as a martyrium marking the tomb of St. Peter and seems to have been used for several centuries as a place of burial for other Christians as well (Figs. 6.1a, 6.4). Its basilican plan has double aisles on each side of the nave and a transverse element or **transept** projecting beyond the side walls and extending across the nave in front of the apse. Placed at the junction of transept and apse was the tomb of St. Peter, surrounded by a railing and marked by a canopy rising on twisted spiral columns that reputedly came from the Temple of Solomon in Jerusalem. The transept spaces accommodated those coming to venerate the shrine, while the enormous nave (300 by 64 feet) and aisles functioned as a covered cemetery with space for burials and commemorative funeral

6.4 Section perspective of Old St. Peter's, Rome, ca. 318–22.
This building began as a martyrium, a cemetery developed around the grave of the apostle Peter. Notice how the lower aisle roofs permit direct light to enter the nave through high clerestory windows.

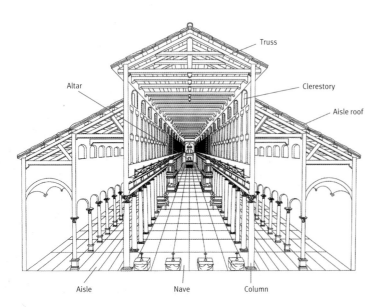

meals. During the procession-dominated services, the nave accommodated only the clergy, with the laity relegated to the aisles. A spacious atrium preceded the martyrium, and the whole scheme provided the model for a number of churches built later, both in Rome and elsewhere.

A similar program influenced the design of the Church of the Nativity in Bethlehem, constructed under the patronage of Constantine in about 333 over the grotto that tradition identified as the birthplace of Jesus (Fig. 6.1b). As at St. Peter's, this building was a basilica preceded by an atrium, but rather than transepts and an apse, the Church of the Nativity had an octagon at the head of the nave. A passage around the octagon allowed pilgrims to circulate and view the grotto below through an opening in the floor, and there may also have been stairs going down to the actual level of the shrine. The junction of a basilica with an octagon shows Early Christian willingness to explore new forms in the course of seeking appropriate and functional religious buildings.

Baptism is an important Christian rite, and in the Early Christian period special buildings were often erected for this sacrament alone. Most were centrally planned around the baptismal pool, for at the time baptism was by complete immersion, and baptistery plans were frequently octagonal to encode the number eight, which symbolized regeneration or the Resurrection, since Jesus was said to have risen from the dead on the eighth day after his entry into Jerusalem. The Baptistery of the Orthodox in Ravenna (ca. 458) is a domed octagonal volume surrounding the octagonal marble font (Fig. 6.5). The central scene in the ceiling mosaic depicts Christ's baptism in the river Jordan, encircled by the twelve apostles and an outer ring illustrating altars in semicircular niches and empty thrones (Fig. 6.6). As was the case with S. Apollinare Nuovo, the plain brick exterior, articulated primarily by eight arched windows and corbeled arches with pilaster strips, gives no hint of the sumptuous finishes inside.

Mausolea, buildings erected to contain the tombs of important people, were also in the repertory of Early Christian architecture. Following Roman practice, these were often centrally planned, and they served as models for later domed churches. In Rome the mausoleum of Constantine's daughter Constantia was built around 350 as a circular monument with a cross-section paralleling that of the basilica, having lower aisle spaces flanking the higher nave lit by clerestory windows (Figs. 6.7, 6.8). In Constantia's mausoleum, now known as the church of S. Costanza, the basilican cross-section was rotated about the center axis to create a circular building, rather than being extended longitudinally to form a basilica. Originally the resulting dome with encircling **ambulatory** focused the visitor's attention on the sarcophagus placed in the center. Twelve paired sets of columns support the drum wall from which the dome rises, lit by twelve clerestory windows. The aisle vaults are finished with mosaic, and the columns are of polished marble.

6.5 Baptistery of the Orthodox, Ravenna, ca. 458.
This view shows the brickwork embellished primarily by pilaster strips and shallow arches near the eaves. These decorative elements are known as Lombard bands because they were developed by the highly renowned Lombard masons.

6.6 (top right) Baptistery of the Orthodox, ceiling mosaic, Ravenna, ca. 458.
Directly over the baptismal font in the center of the building is an image of the baptism of Jesus by John the Baptist. The dove of the Holy Spirit hovers above Jesus, while an old man, a personification of the River Jordan, stands in the water on the right side.

6.7 (below) Plan of S. Costanza, Rome, ca. 350.
This plan shows the original narthex and the stairs descending to the crypt. Paired columns support the drum and dome.

6.8 (right) S. Costanza interior, Rome, ca. 350.
Erected as a mausoleum for the Emperor Constantine's daughter, this central-plan building was converted into a church. A section through it resembles that of a basilica, but rather than being extended longitudinally, the section is rotated about the central vertical axis to generate a central-plan building.

Stairs to the crypt

Narthex

6.8

0   50 m
0   150 ft

ESSAY
Eusebius and Constantine
by Lynn K. Barker

A round 315, a visiting bishop rose to address the congregation gathered for the rededication of the new cathedral in the Levantine city of Tyre. He turned and both dedicated and addressed his "Festival oration on the building of churches" to his friend, the inspiration behind the cathedral's construction and its bishop, Paulinus. The speaker was Eusebius (Fig. 6.9), himself bishop of the nearby coastal see of Caesarea. He was famous both as the "father of Church history" and as Constantine's biographer and eulogist.

The adage "history is written by the winners" is nowhere more strikingly illustrated than in the generation of Eusebius and his contemporary, Lactantius, whose work *On the Deaths of the Persecutors* recounts the grisly deaths, divinely sanctioned as retribution, of the church's enemies at the turn of the fourth century. In his own *Historia Ecclesiastica*, Eusebius describes with eyewitness authority the sufferings of Palestinian martyrs under Galerius and Maximinius.

When Eusebius came to describe the world that he thought had been transformed by Constantine's practice of toleration of all religions, he thought of no better way to depict the new order than by inserting, at the beginning of Book X of his *Historia Ecclesiastica*, a full transcription of his address that day in Tyre.

Soon after peace came building:

6.9 Anon, Eusebius of Caesarea, engraving.

"The next state was the spectacle prayed and longed for by us all—dedication festivals in the cities and consecrations of the newly built places of worship, convocations of bishops . . . unification . . . harmony . . . There came together bone to bone and joint to joint."

The fine new basilica at Tyre was the inspiration of the bishop, standing second only to Christ. Eusebius eulogizes his friend Constantine as "a new

Bezalel" (Exod. 35:30); the "Solomon . . . of a new and far nobler Jerusalem;" "a new Zerubbabel," restoring the Temple to a "glory far greater than the old."

For all its spendor, however, this earthly building pales beside the more sublime truths of the archetypes behind it. The soul is a building, whose fall into sin Eusebius likens to the destruction of church properties at pagan hands. The "divine spiritual edifice in our souls" (what we call the image of God) fell to the battering rams of sin, "till not one stone of virtue was left." The work of Christ was directed to rebuilding the human soul. But while the bishop rebuilds his material church more splendidly than before, the true building project is God's work in history: raising up the edifice of the universal Church, in which God sets the people themselves as "living, securely-laid, and unshakeable stones." Even what Augustine of Hippo would one day call the city of man is a building, composed of most men in the world—"bad builders of bad buildings."

Modern historians have caught Eusebius out in promoting his vision of unity in harmony at the expense of a messier reality called historical truth; Constantine's Church was neither unified nor harmonious. Little wonder, then, that Eusebius's vision of God's edifice would nourish the architects—actual and metaphorical —of a Christian empire for a millennium to come.

BYZANTINE BASILICAS AND DOMED BASILICAS

The division between the Early Christian and Byzantine eras is generally made at the reign of Justinian (527–65), who, as emperor based in Constantinople, put an end to factional disputes, reasserted imperial influence in portions of North Africa and Italy that had fallen to heretical rulers, and engaged in a vigorous program of church-building. People living at the time probably did not perceive the change. As historians look back on the period, however, Justinian's reign serves as a convenient marker to differentiate increasingly separate developments in western and eastern sections of what had been the Roman Empire. Work tied by patronage or tradition to Constantinople is termed Byzantine. One characteristic of much Byzantine architecture is a clear preference for domes on both basilican and centrally planned churches. Like the Romans, the Byzantines saw the dome as symbolic of the heavenly sphere, complementary to the earthly realm of floor and walls below.

Early Christian traditions were not entirely discarded, however. Basilicas were the most common church plan

6.10 S. Apollinare in Classe, Ravenna, ca. 532–49.
Many Byzantine buildings continued the tradition of sober exteriors and rich interiors already seen in Early Christian times. The tall volume of the basilica and its lower narthex porch read clearly. The campanile rises to the rear.

constructed in the sixth century, although none of the examples built in Constantinople survives. We turn instead to the church of S. Apollinare in Classe near Ravenna, constructed under Justinian's patronage from 532 to 549, for an example of a wooden-roofed basilica without transepts (Figs. 6.1a, 6.10–6.11). Its splendid apse mosaics are the glory of the interior, where St. Apollinaris, the first bishop of Ravenna, guards a flock of twelve sheep (representing the disciples by number and the people of Ravenna by extension) grazing in a lush meadow. Overhead is a golden cross with the image of Christ in the center, set in a starry blue sky, and figures of four early bishops of Ravenna are installed between the windows. Rich marble columns form the nave arcade, with portraits of saints set in **roundel** frames above the arches. In character and design the church is similar to the earlier S. Apollinare Nuovo, but its scale is considerably larger. In the century after its construction, the apse floor was raised to permit access to the crypt tomb of Apollinaris.

The innovative domes seen in Justinian's churches are notable contributions to architectural history. In Constantinople, two domed basilicas rose simultaneously and survive as models for the type. The smaller, S. Irene (begun in 532 and remodeled in 564), has a rectangular plan divided into nave and aisles with a projecting semicircular apse (Fig. 6.12). (The church seen today is largely a rebuilding after an earthquake in 740.) Two domes cover the nave, and their thrust is countered by massive rectangular piers, pierced by openings, and effectively

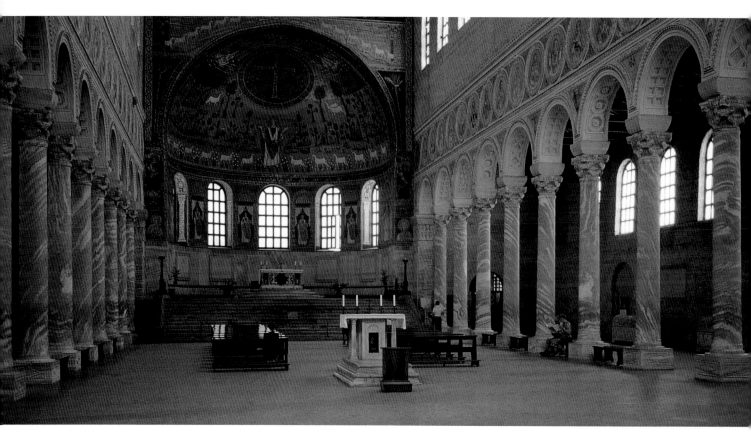

6.11 S. Apollinare in Classe interior, Ravenna, 532–49.
Windows glazed in thin sheets of alabaster reduced the intense Italian sun and provided soft light suitable for appreciating mosaic work and marbled columns. Note the absence of seating: congregations stood or knelt during services at this period.

6.12 S. Irene interior, Constantinople, 532–64.
Lower sections of one pendentive supporting the dome are visible. Galleries (seen to the left) erected over the aisles braced the structure and were used by women during services. One needs to imagine the mosaics that were intended for this almost bare interior.

strengthened by barrel-vaulted **galleries** over the aisles. The outlines of the aisle vaults articulate the exterior side walls, where tiers of arched windows admit light to the aisles and galleries. More windows are placed at the base of the dome and around the apse. S. Irene thus represents a new interpretation of the basilica, combining the liturgical logic of the longitudinal plan with the centralizing or heavenly qualities of domed construction. This same idea, on a much larger scale, was carried out at a contemporary church in Constantinople: Hagia Sophia, the Church of the Holy Wisdom.

Hagia Sophia (532–37) is one of the great buildings of the world and is without question the masterpiece of Byzantine architecture (Figs. 6.13, 6.14–6.16). We know the names and backgrounds of its architects, Anthemius of Tralles and Isidorus of Miletus. Both were mathematicians and scientists skilled in mechanics, geometry, and engineering. These talents were all needed to design and supervise the construction of the exceptionally large Hagia Sophia. In plan it is a basilica with a central dome, complemented by pairs of semidomes at the front and rear. This configuration is at once linear, with a dominant longitudinal axis, and centralized, with a dome on piers at its core. Its 107-foot-diameter central dome, supported on pendentives, rises 180 feet above the floor and is flanked by two lower **semidomes** of the same diameter, a clear span of nearly 250 feet. In the description of the

Aisle with gallery above

Nave (or naos)

6.16

Hagia Sophia, Constantinople

6.14

6.13 Plans of Hagia Sophia, Constantinople, 532–37; S. Vitale, Ravenna, 538–48; SS. Sergius and Bacchus, 527–36; and S. Marco, Venice, 1063–89. These Byzantine churches are grouped to allow comparisons of scale.

6.18

6.20

Apse

see p.132

6.19

6.17

S. Vitale, Ravenna

SS. Sergius and Bacchus, Constantinople

S. Marco, Venice

0   50 m

0   150 ft

church written by Justinian's court historian, Procopius of Caesarea, the dome was seen to hover over the interior.

> *[It] seems not to rest upon solid masonry, but to cover the space with its golden dome suspended from Heaven. All these details, fitted together with incredible skill in mid-air and floating off from each other and resting only on the parts next to them, produce a single and most extraordinary harmony in the work, and yet do not permit the spectator to linger much over the study of any one of them, but each detail attracts the eye and draws it on irresistibly to itself.*

Aisles with galleries above range on either side, while a colonnaded atrium (no longer extant) and groin-vaulted double **narthex** precede the church proper.

The structural problems posed by such an audacious design were many, yet the necessary supports do not intrude on the internal space, creating the feeling that the dome floats effortlessly above the billowing interior

volumes. Nothing could be farther from the actual case. While the brick used does constitute a relatively light construction material and the vaults are amazingly thin to minimize both thrust and weight, the size of the building means that the gravity forces are large. The forty windows at the base of the dome are set between buttresses that stabilize the junction of dome and **pendentives**. From this point the load is transferred to four great stone piers, which are further buttressed by being extended above the gallery vaults to join in great barrel vaults along the sides of the church (Fig 6.14). The semidomes, which appear to brace the narthex and apse ends, probably contribute little to the structure's integrity, however satisfying they are visually. The masonry mass of the four piers is more obvious on the outside than internally. Anthemius and Isidorus's structural daring overstepped the physical limits of their materials, and the first great dome collapsed in 558. It was reconstructed with a steeper pitch and ribbed construction in 563, but the western half of the rebuilt dome fell again in

6.14 (above left) **Hagia Sophia, Constantinople, 532–37 and later.**
This audacious building contains the greatest dome of its age, only slightly smaller than that of the Pantheon. This exterior view shows buttresses around the base of the dome added after earthquake damage. Four minarets were added when the church was converted into a mosque.

6.15 (above) **Axonometric section through Hagia Sophia, Constantinople, 532–37 and later.**
This view shows the massive arches that support the great dome. The dome is built of brick, which accounts for its relative thinness, and pendentives transform the square bay defined by the piers into a circle from which the dome springs.

6.16 (left) **Hagia Sophia interior, Constantinople, 532–37 and later.**
This view of the central space shows the multiple levels of windows that illuminate the interior. Windows set between the dome's ribs create the illusion that the dome floats unsupported. Hagia Sophia's architects intended to create a building that would rival the Pantheon, and their work has both inspired and challenged later builders who sought to emulate its space and structural daring.

989. Following repairs, the eastern half collapsed in 1346; the replacement dome is the one on the building today.

Structural problems aside, the effect of the arches, vaults, exedrae, semidomes, and domes is ethereal. Light pours in from windows at many levels, playing over surfaces enriched by polished marbles and mosaic. From a position at the center of the nave, the repetition of curved forms reflects the great dome overhead and creates a pervasive harmony that is constantly varied. From the aisles and galleries, the view into the nave is dramatic, providing a partial perspective of the interconnecting layered spaces surrounding the interior volume. In the church ritual for which Hagia Sophia was built, the major space was reserved for two groups, the ecclesiastics and the retinue of the emperor. The clergy claimed the sanctuary space before the apse, while the imperial court occupied the region at the narthex, or entry, end. The meeting of patriarch and emperor and celebration of the Mass under the great dome marked a high point of the religious ritual. Ordinary people were relegated to the aisles and galleries, women on one side and men on the other, where they could observe the impressive ceremonial processions and symbolic joining of Church and state in this magnificent setting.

CENTRALLY PLANNED BYZANTINE CHURCHES

Roman temples such as the Pantheon and Early Christian baptisteries and mausolea had featured centralized plans. Not surprisingly, these precedents combined well with the Byzantine fondness for dome-building and contributed to the development of the most characteristic Byzantine churches, which had circular or **Greek-cross plans**. Justinian's churches again provide the dominant models for later centuries.

SS. Sergius and Bacchus (527–36) in Constantinople and S. Vitale (538–48) in Ravenna illustrate two variations on the theme of central plans. SS. Sergius and Bacchus (Figs. 6.13, 6.17) is essentially a domed octagon surrounded by aisles and galleries encased in a square, whereas S. Vitale's octagonal dome is echoed by octagonal galleries and aisles. The strong centralizing tendencies of both churches are countered somewhat by apsidal projections opposite the narthex side, and the interior space is more fluid than that seen in Early Christian S. Costanza, where a similar organizational idea is carried out in circular form. In SS. Sergius and Bacchus, the eight piers supporting the dome are interspersed with pairs of columns, set alternately beneath curving and straight arches, so that the domed area penetrates the surrounding corner spaces. The sixteen-sided "pumpkin vault" dome reflects the configuration below in alternate straight- and curved-profile sections above its rather low drum.

Although the dome at S. Vitale (Figs. 6.13, 6.18–6.19) is smaller, the church design is more sophisticated, with a

6.17 SS. Sergius and Bacchus interior, Constantinople, 527–36.
This central-plan church features a "pumpkin vault" in its dome, a form that had been used in Roman times and that reappears in the Baroque era.

higher drum and greater internal cohesiveness than at SS. Sergius and Bacchus. Clerestory windows illuminate the nave directly, and between the piers of the octagon all the niches are semicircular, carving into aisles and galleries to borrow additional light from windows in the exterior wall. Semidomes over each of the niches complement the dome that rises over the nave. The proportions of the exterior are equally fine. Red-tile roofs in direct volumetric expression of the internal space cap simple arched windows set in brick walls articulated by pilasters. SS. Sergius and Bacchus has lost most of its original interior mosaic, but S. Vitale displays the beautiful products of imperial workshops in both marble and mosaic. Carved capitals complete richly veined marble column shafts, **book-matched** marbles face the lower wall surfaces, and both geometric and figural mosaics complete arch soffits, upper walls, apse, and floors. Mosaic donor panels set on the sides of the apse portray Justinian and his court across from the empress Theodora and her attendants. The apse semidome shows Christ flanked by angels, with St. Vitalis to Christ's right and Bishop Ecclesius to the left. The bishop holds a model of the church, and Christ passes a crown to

6.18 S. Vitale, Ravenna, 538–48.
Another of the exceptional churches built under imperial
patronage, S. Vitale is based in plan on an octagon. Using
local Ostrogoth technology, its dome is constructed of
hollow clay pots to create strength while minimizing weight.

6.19 S. Vitale interior, Ravenna, 538–48.
This view looking toward the apse shows the rich array
of book-matched marbles and mosaic work.

St. Vitalis. The splendor of Byzantium glows throughout
this handsome church.

For the Justinian prototype of centralized churches
on a Greek-cross plan, we must rely on fragmentary evidence provided by the now-vanished Church of the Holy
Apostles in Constantinople. Erected by Constantine as his
own mausoleum and rebuilt by Justinian from 536 to 550,
it was demolished in 1469 to provide the site for a mosque.
A standing church built on the model of Justinian's Church
of the Holy Apostles is S. Marco in Venice, begun in 830
and rebuilt in 1063–89 (page 132 and Figs. 6.20–6.21).
Hemispherical internal domes cover each arm of the
Greek-cross plan, and a central one crowns the **crossing**.
All are set on pendentives, with barrel vaults connecting
the large pierced piers that sustain the downward thrust
of the domes. Windows at the base of some domes illuminate the upper regions of the church and allow light
to sparkle across the gold-ground mosaics of the interior.
While the basic design concept for S. Marco stems from
Byzantium, much there reflects other architectural traditions. For example, the present exterior portal hoods date
from the fifteenth century, and the external dome profiles, raised on a timber framework above the masonry
work, reflect the shape of Eastern domes. Nevertheless, S.
Marco is substantially Byzantine. It became the model for
Romanesque churches in the south of France shortly after
its completion.

In addition to the domed Greek-cross plan used at
S. Marco, Byzantine churches built in the centuries after
Justinian also followed two other general plan types, the
cross-in-square and a single dome placed on a longitudinal base. The cross-in-square or **quincunx** plan has nine
bays, with the central one domed, and diminutive domes
over the corner bays. All other sections are barrel-vaulted. In
cross-domed plans, the arms of the Greek cross are reduced
and covered with barrel vaults that surround the crossing
dome. Aisles and galleries enclose the church on three sides,
and three apses complete the fourth side. Many of these
churches were erected on a rather modest scale, so the vaulting did not pose undue constructional complications.

We can see both these plan types at the monastery of
Hosios Lukas, located at Phocis northwest of Athens, where
two churches were built adjacent to the shrine erected over
the tomb of St. Luke, a local hermit who died in 953 (not
to be confused with the evangelist of the same name). The
smaller of the churches, designed on a cross-in-square
plan with three apses, was dedicated in about 1000 to the
Theotokos, the Greek term for the Mother of God (Fig.
6.22). Built of squared stones surrounded by brick, the
Theotokos church has a central dome raised on a drum.
Groin vaults rather than domes were built over the corner
bays, perhaps because the scale is so small: the central
dome is eleven feet in diameter. Although the interior today
is devoid of fresco, mosaic, or marble facing, it was probably once richly finished to accord with the carved screen
separating the nave from the chancel that is still in place.

6.20 S. Marco, Venice, rebuilt 1063–89.
With a Greek-cross plan based on Justinian's Church of
the Holy Apostles in Constantinople, S. Marco has five
domes, of which the central one is highest. The west
front and raised external dome roofs were added later.

**6.21 Longitudinal section through S. Marco,
Venice, rebuilt 1063–89.**
This view shows the original dome profile and
the taller shells erected in the fifteenth century
to dramatize the exterior effect. Note particularly
the turrets atop the domes, which resemble the
characteristic onion domes of Russian churches.

6.22 **Plan of monastery churches, Hosios Lukas, ca. 980–1025.**
There are two churches shown here, the Theotokos (*above*) and
the Katholikon (*below*). The Theotokos church is a quincunx design,
while the Katholikon has a single large dome buttressed by galleries.

6.23 **Interior of the Katholikon, Monastery of Hosios Lukas, 1020.**
This interior space repeats at a greatly reduced scale some of the
dramatic lighting and rich interior of Hagia Sophia (see Fig. 6.16).
Frescoes in the dome replace the original mosaic work that fell
during an earthquake in 1593.

The larger Katholikon was constructed in the following twenty years immediately to the south of the Theotokos church, thereby sharing proximity to the saint's shrine and allowing pilgrims to circulate on all sides of the tomb. Its plan is in some respects similar to S. Irene in Constantinople, with a large dome set over the nave, braced on three sides by a second level gallery. **Squinches** transform the square central bay into an octagon that supports a drum and dome thirty feet in diameter (Fig. 6.23). The interior was sumptuously finished, with marble facing on the walls and mosaics on the vaults and dome. The dome mosaics, destroyed in an earthquake in 1593, were replaced by frescoes of the original subjects. On the apse semidome, in a field of gold mosaic, is a majestic Mary holding the infant Christ.

CHURCHES IN RUSSIA

Many of the features of later Byzantine architecture are reflected in Russian church designs, for that country's architecture is inextricably identified with the legacy of Byzantium. In the period under consideration here, roughly from 990 to 1725, Russia included what today are the independent states of Belarus, Georgia, and the Ukraine. Much of the territory west of the Urals is rolling countryside, covered with extensive grasslands, vast forests, lakes, and marshes. Its rivers were the first tracks through the wilderness, and by the ninth century Viking explorers had settled along water routes requiring minimal portages to travel from the Baltic to the Black Sea, where they traded with the Byzantines. Aside from the rivers, the Urals, and the Carpathian mountains, there are few natural boundaries, so the area has long been open to nomadic incursions. Russian history begins with the legendary Rurik, a Viking who was invited to Novgorod in about 856 to bring order to the scattered trading settlements along the trade route to Constantinople. Although Rurik's descendants ruled the country until the sixteenth century, the history of Russia was severely interrupted for the period from 1239 to the fifteenth century, when the region was effectively a surrogate state of the Mongol khans of Central Asia. For a variety of historical reasons, Russia became isolated from western Europe, so the chronologies and stylistic periods defined for France, Italy, England, or Germany do not apply here. Byzantine work influenced church architecture in Russia for centuries after the fall of Constantinople in 1453. Difficulties in maintaining contact with Church authorities in Constantinople and growing differences within the Russian Church led to the proclamation in 1443 of a Russian Orthodox Church, having its own primate or metropolitan independent of the patriarch in Constantinople.

Masonry construction records only part of the story of Russian architecture. Until the twentieth century, wood was the dominant building material in Russia. It was readily available, easily worked, and its insulating qualities

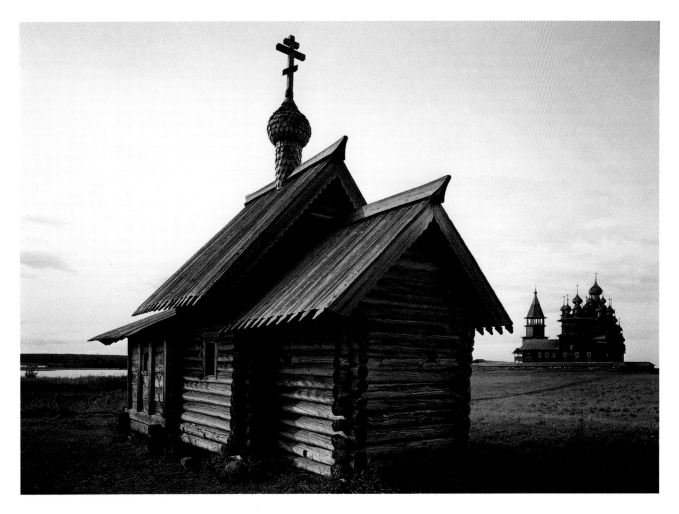

6.24 Church of the Raising of Lazarus, Muromansky monastery, now at Kizhi, ca. 1391.
Reputedly the oldest wooden church surviving in Russia, it has three different roof pitches and two different forms of wall construction. The diminutive dome on a stalk marks it as a church rather than a simple log house. (Church of the Transfiguration in the background; see Fig. 6.29.)

were superior to masonry for comfort during the long winter. Horizontal log construction, employing notched corner joints similar to those seen in American log cabins, was used for houses, fortifications, and churches. (A major difference between Russian, indeed European, log construction and that usually seen in the United States is the sturdiness of the former and the relative impermanence of the latter. European log buildings were meant to last for centuries, whereas most American examples were hastily erected then abandoned as soon as something better could be built.) Foreign visitors remarked repeatedly on the fact that Russian cities seemed to be composed entirely of wooden buildings. Wood of course is subject to both decay and fire, and these destructive forces have greatly reduced the number of old buildings available for study.

Both legend and physical evidence suggest that the oldest surviving Russian wooden building is the small Church of the Raising of Lazarus (ca. 1391) from the Muromansky monastery, now relocated to the open-air museum at Kizhi (Figs. 6.24–6.25). It is a simple, three-celled structure, composed of a vestibule, nave, and chancel, each covered

by its own gable roof and each roof having a slightly different pitch. The oldest sections are the nave and chancel, constructed in horizontal log work, while the vestibule has wooden planks inserted into upright wooden members. A small shingle-covered dome on a stalklike drum rises over the nave. Aside from the dome and the slight outward flare to the upper wall sections, there is little about this building that is different from what might be built for a house, but from these humble beginnings, far more elaborate designs would develop. Larger churches with higher gable roofs were built to stand out more prominently in the countryside, and their floor levels were raised a story off the ground to keep the entrance above winter snow levels. Covered access stairs and enclosing galleries were added to provide a protected place for those who may have traveled considerable distances to attend services.

These elements may be seen in the Church of the Nativity of the Virgin (1593), originally in the village of Peredki and now preserved at Novgorod (Fig. 6.27). The church has a Greek-cross plan, with an octagonal tower over the crossing that is capped by a tent roof (**shatyor**) to create a strong vertical landmark. Logs in diminishing lengths are well suited to support such a roof, and shatyor roofs became common not only for churches but also for fortress towers (Fig. 6.28). The church also has a great external gallery that wraps around three sides of the building, supported on stacked cantilevers (**pomochi**) extending from the wall underneath. One gets a clear idea of the depth of winter snow from the height of this

6.25 Elevation and plan of the Church of the Raising of Lazarus, Kizhi, ca. 1391.
The three sections are an entrance porch, nave, and sanctuary.

0   5 m
0   15 ft

6.24

6.26 Plan of and longitudinal section through the Church of the Transfiguration, Kizhi, 1714.
While the external effect is spectacular, the interior is not particularly exceptional and the iconostasis cuts abruptly into the nave. The same three-part division in plan seen in the small Lazarus church is repeated here.

0   20 m
0   60 ft

6.29

6.27 (above) Church of the Nativity of the Virgin, Peredki, now at Novgorod, 1593.
This building is clearly more elaborate than the Lazarus church, having a Greek-cross plan and a shatyor roof over the crossing to increase the sense of verticality.

6.28 (above) Diagram of the construction of a shatyor roof.
Logs of diminishing length are laid in an octagonal plan to create a tentlike shatyor roof. The weatherproof cap is made of long wooden boards with angled terminations to cast water away from the building.

6.29 Church of the Transfiguration, Kizhi, 1714.
This masterpiece church of 22 domes rises from a Greek-cross plan. Aspen used for shingles on the domes and bochki (reverse-curve gables) weathers to a silver gray that gleams like polished metal. To the left is the companion Church of the Intercession, built for use in winter and provided with a stove.

gallery! Russian builders understood the properties of different woods and how to use them effectively. Larch logs that resist rot well are used for the lowest log rounds, while pine is the usual material for the upper sections. Wall logs are cut away on the bottom edge to match the rounded profile of the log below, thus ensuring a tight joint and providing no place for water to collect. Birch bark is used for flashing where roofs intersect walls. Aspen wood was employed for shingles because it weathers to a smooth silvery color. Shingles were split or rived along the grain and then cut to create an interesting pattern and texture when installed. Boards used for the roof have pointed ends to encourage water to drip quickly at the edges. Roof pitches on the towers change near the base to cast run-off clear of the supporting walls. Not everything is so strictly functional, however, for there is also poetry. Folk symbols

that date to pre-Christian times are seen in the sun signs on barge boards (decorative trim at the gable ends), and a carved bird may grace the ridge to bring good fortune.

Both practical concerns and symbolic elements are turned to stunning advantage in the masterpiece Church of the Transfiguration (1714) at Kizhi (Fig. 6.29), the only survivor of what were at least three churches with multiple domes constructed under the patronage of Peter the Great. Its plan is based on a Greek cross with the crossing transformed into an octagon (Fig. 6.26). What at Peredki was treated as a tent roof here becomes the entire external composition, a central tower that steps back in two stages with reverse-curve gables (**bochki**) and domes (Fig. 6.30). The church in fact has twenty-two domes on slender drums, creating a pyramidal composition. Counting from the top, there is a large single dome at the summit, four domes on the middle stage of the octagon, and eight on the lower octagonal story. Two more sets of four domes each are stacked at the bochki gables over the arms of the Greek cross, and the lowest single dome is placed over the sanctuary. This church continues the tradition begun nearly 700 years earlier at St. Sophia in Kiev: an elaborately domed exterior and an interior of smaller compartmentalized

6.30 Church of the Transfiguration detail, Kizhi.
This view shows the elaborate shingle work and framing of bochki. Note the stepped shapes of shingle ends, cut not only for decorative effect but also to promote water run-off and minimize capillary attraction.

spaces not necessarily reflected in the overall massing. At Kizhi, there is a suspended ceiling across the octagonal tower, so the interior does not share the soaring volume suggested by the tower of domes. Furthermore, the internal space division in plan is not what one might expect from the outside. The vestibule wraps around the Greek cross, obscuring the actual shape of the nave, and the **iconostasis** projects into the center of the octagon, resulting in an irregular shape for the congregation. Kizhi is dramatic in the expansive northern landscape. On the inside, it is the icons that capture one's attention rather than the volume of the space.

The widespread destruction and economic upheaval that accompanied the invasion by the Mongols or Tartars in 1238–40 brought an end to the dominance of Kiev as a center of Russian government. Russian cities paid annual tribute to the khans of the Golden Horde, leaving little for investment in major buildings at home, so there was a corresponding decline in construction skills. Over the

course of the fourteenth and fifteenth centuries, Moscow gradually established itself as the leading Russian city and became the seat of the metropolitan of the Russian Orthodox Church. Church and state combined efforts to overthrow the domination of the khans. Moscow's central fortress, the Kremlin, was gradually reconstructed in stone from the original wood, and new churches were erected there under patronage of the princes of Moscow, who now styled themselves as tsars (from the Latin *caesar*).

Motifs from wooden architecture found their way into masonry building, particularly the tent roof already seen in the church from Peredki, which came to be used for votive churches (as opposed to churches needing to accommodate a congregation) built in Moscow during the sixteenth century. The most famous of these is Moscow's Cathedral of the Intercession on the Moat, more usually known as St. Basil the Blessed (1555–60) (Fig. 6.31), erected on Red Square just outside the Kremlin walls to commemorate Ivan IV's victory over the Horde at the battle of Kazan in 1552. The architects were Barma and Posnik, who came from Pskov. Their design is fundamentally a central sanctuary surrounded by four large octagonal chapels and four smaller chapels that are square in plan. Eight of the chapels are dedicated to saints whose days coincided with key dates in the siege of Kazan, and the ninth is dedicated to the Entry into Jerusalem, so in some respects this building is really nine chapels sharing a common foundation. The central sanctuary is covered by a tall shatyor roof, while the eight subsidiary chapels receive individual vertical expression as domed towers. It is a tribute to the architects that this diverse array of elements, including also the covered entrance galleries and stairs, reads not as a random collection of parts but as a complex, intriguing whole, interesting from whatever angle it is approached. A close look at the exterior reveals decorative elements including layers of semicircular and triangular gables, pilasters, and diamond-shaped motifs, along with the expected onion domes, which are actually seventeenth-century replacements for helmet domes of the original design. These replacement roofs are a riot of glazed tiles in faceted, zigzag, spiraling, and striped designs that contribute additional color to the already elaborate red-brick and white-stone trim of the exterior. Interior space is highly compartmentalized. Since the volume under each tower is open to the chapel below, processing through the church is like traveling along a passage connecting a series of discrete chambers, each the size of a domestic room in plan but having an enormously tall ceiling.

St. Basil's is a reasonable place to conclude this consideration of the Byzantine architecture of Russia. Even though its construction coincides chronologically with buildings of the late Renaissance in Italy, St. Basil's is still rooted in traditions begun a millennium earlier in the eastern empire centered in Constantinople. Byzantium's lasting impact would continue in Russia as foreign architects came to build Baroque churches during the seventeenth

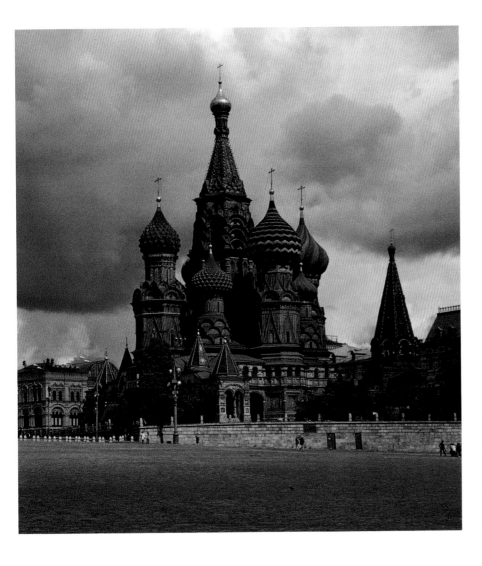

6.31 St. Basil the Blessed, Moscow, 1555–60.
The architects, Barma and Posnik, utilized forms from wooden churches to create an extraordinary design in masonry. The riot of forms and colors on the exterior is more memorable than the interior, which is extremely compartmentalized.

and eighteenth centuries. Under Peter the Great, who avidly sought to end Russia's cultural isolation and overcome its perceived backward ways, secular Russian architecture came to resemble contemporary European architectural movements more than honoring its own historical past.

CONCLUSIONS ABOUT ARCHITECTURAL IDEAS

Early Christian and Byzantine architecture affords an opportunity for the didactic comparison of longitudinal versus central planning. Driven by the liturgical importance of the processional, designers of western (what became Roman Catholic) churches most frequently based their layouts on the ancient Roman basilica, with its long, tall, clerestory-lit hall flanked by lower, narrower aisles and terminated by an apse. They sometimes projected twin wings, or transepts, from the chancel area, producing a Latin-cross plan: one with three short arms and one longer arm in the form of the nave and aisles. These Early Christian designers also commonly used central, often circular plans for smaller martyria, baptisteries, and mausolea.

In the Byzantine east, what we know today as Greek Orthodox churches took on central plans that emphasized

not the processional but the Mass. The simplest of these plan types was the quincunx or nine-part grid with perimeter bearing walls and a columned core. The most complex was the great, unique Hagia Sophia, with its interlocking system of piers, walls, vaults, domes, and buttresses.

Both longitudinal and central schemes solved myriad liturgical, esthetic, and constructional problems. The Early Christian basilican plans allowed for a separation of the uninitiated from the initiated and from the clergy and frequently promoted the viewing of relics. The Byzantine central plans took on numerous forms, from octagons to Greek crosses (four equal arms) to the complex merging of a powerful longitudinal axis with a central nave or naos at Hagia Sophia. In both east and west, but particularly in the east, light interacting with faceted mosaic surfaces yielded overtly spiritual environments epitomized by Hagia Sophia's, one of almost palpable luminosity that still moves visitors today and must have stunned those who experienced it in the sixth century.

As an exotic coda, the churches of Russia offer regional interpretations of Byzantine models, many of them built of masonry but some constructed of plentifully available wood. They are so distinctive that the image of such a structure as St. Basil's in Moscow has remained a consistent popular image even through the anti-religious period of the U.S.S.R.

Chapter 7
Islamic Architecture

As we have seen, the Early Christians went through an extensive process to develop architectural forms suitable for and expressive of their religion. Followers of the religion founded by the prophet Mohammed experienced a similar evolutionary process, but one that led to quite different results as they created buildings to serve and symbolize Islam.

Islam originated in Arabia. In 610 the angel Gabriel is said to have appeared to Mohammed in Mecca and over time expounded the revelation of God, or Allah ('Al-lah' meaning 'the God'). These revelations were collected into a holy book, the Qur'an (or Koran), which expressed in Arabic the message of Islam, a word signifying submission to the will of Allah. Each Muslim accepted five basic truths or duties: to believe in the oneness of God, and that Mohammed was the messenger of God; to pray five times daily; to fast from sunrise to sunset during the month of Ramadan; to give alms to the poor; and to make at least one pilgrimage to the holy city of Mecca, wealth and health permitting.

Conversion of the tribes to Islam was accompanied by an intense awakening of Arab fervor; the courage and fighting skill of Arabic tribes, previously exploited by the Sassanian and Byzantine empires, was turned against these masters in a fury of rapid conquests, frequently aided by local contempt for the corruption associated with Byzantine rule. By 661 Islamic armies had swept through what is today Iran, Iraq, Israel, Syria, and Egypt, and they then moved across the North African coast to enter Spain in 711. From Spain they pushed northward into France, where forces led by Charles Martel stopped their European expansion in 732 at the battle of Tours. Islamic settlers remained in central and southern Spain until 1492, however, and their armies continued to batter the southern borders of the Byzantine Empire until, under the Ottoman Turks, they finally conquered Constantinople in 1453. Through trade, Islamic dynasties made contact with China and India, where their religion would eventually take root, and strong Islamic influence made a leap as far east as modern-day Malaysia and Indonesia. With military conquest came economic, social, and cultural dominance as Islamic customs and the Arabic language replaced

surviving practices in the old Roman Empire. Islamic policy toward conquered populations was generally one of accommodation. Islamic rule was often preferred by the natives of occupied lands to that of harsh Byzantine governors, and the multicultural society the invaders fostered provided a model of respectful interaction that the modern world might do well to rediscover. The heady mix of learned men from Islamic and Jewish traditions, sometimes joined by Christian theologians, contributed to a highly productive era in the arts and sciences from the ninth through sixteenth centuries.

Today, Muslims represent a majority of the population in the Middle East, North Africa, parts of Central and South Asia, the Malaysian peninsula, and the Indonesian archipelago, but sizeable minorities also live in Europe and the United States. Islamic worship requires prayer five times a day, and this prayer is practiced at four levels of participation: 1) the individual or small group, 2) the neighborhood congregation, 3) the entire populace of a small city, and 4) the whole Muslim world. Discrete structures are built for the first three levels of worship. For daily prayer (except on Fridays), small numbers of worshipers use the modestly sized **masjid**, containing a prayer niche, but no facilities for preaching. For universal corporate worship, a Muslim town requires an idgab, a very large, unroofed open space with a long prayer wall on one side. The residents of a neighborhood attend the most well-known Islamic religious structure: the congregational or Friday mosque, where the principal or weekly service is held, hence its naming for a day of the week. It is in the covered prayer hall of such a Friday mosque that mass prayer takes

Chronology

Qibla iwan of the Friday mosque, Isfahan, 12th century.
What began in the ninth century as a columnar hall mosque was transformed over time into a more elaborate plan, culminating with a large four-iwan courtyard. Note the iwan's muqarnas vaults.

7.1 Muslims at prayer in the Mosque of the Prophet, Mecca.
This dramatic photograph illustrates a consistent patterning of highly ordered worshipers at prayer, the repeated orthogonal structural bays, and polychromatic masonry. All the worshipers are facing the prayer wall.

place. Worshipers assemble in tightly packed ranks and files, placing themselves as close as possible to the prayer wall, which explains the square or wide-rectangle shapes of such halls as opposed to the long, narrow plans of Christian churches or the central plans of Byzantine ones. Prayer is directional, oriented toward Mecca, and requires that worshipers, after ritual purification, proceed through a series of bowings, prostrations, and recitations from the Qur'an (Fig. 7.1).

Islam prescribes that ornamentation be **aniconic**, meaning symbolic or suggestive rather than literally representational. This ornament is sometimes executed in stone, but more frequently in glazed brick or tile, gypsum stucco, glass, or even wood. The exterior envelopes of Islamic religious buildings are treated like a skin that can receive universally applied decoration. The ordering of this decoration, though apparently complex, is typically controlled by primary and secondary grids and makes extensive use of repetition, symmetry, and patterning. This ordering can be subdivided according to four design strategies: 1) the repetition of an architectural element like an arch, 2) geometric manipulations like rotated and interlocking polygons, 3) organic growth in the form of plantlike foliation, and 4) calligraphy. Architectural elements can be two- or three-dimensional and appear most commonly as window

or door openings. Geometric motifs allow for almost endless creativity and include the ribbing of vaults. Two- and three-dimensional organic compositions can be highly stylized or approach naturalism, and as they become linear and seemingly endless produce a so-called arabesque, or intricate pattern of interlaced lines. Calligraphy is the most important of the four strategies because it records the word of Allah. It can be flowing, or cursive, as well as angular. Some ornamental conditions exploit light, such as glass or translucent screens that filter illumination, and **muqarnas** vaults that both reflect and refract it.

EARLY SHRINES

For their earliest buildings, the largely nomadic Islamic Arabs assimilated techniques and forms from the civilizations they encountered. Syrian and Christian influences are clear in one of the most prominent early shrines, the Dome of the Rock (687–91) in Jerusalem (Figs. 7.2–7.4). Its location on Mount Moriah was sacred to the Jews, both as the site on which Abraham had offered his son Isaac as a sacrifice to the Lord and as the location of Solomon's Temple. Muslims honored it for Abraham's presence, but also venerated it as the place from which Mohammed ascended in his night journey to paradise. At the center of the Dome of the Rock is a rock, under which lies a small cave with a single opening. The shrine is carefully positioned around this rock, the domed central portion enclosing the rock and a concentric aisle permitting circumambulation. The building's form was probably

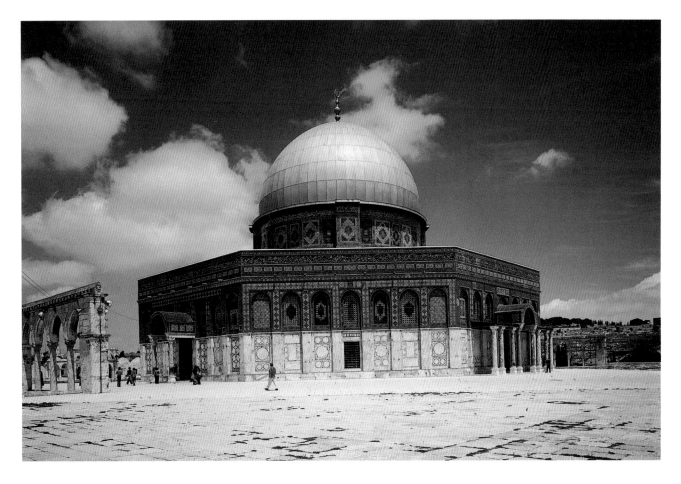

7.2 Dome of the Rock, Jerusalem, 687–91.
One of the earliest Islamic shrines, this octagonal domed
building has a double ambulatory surrounding the rock from
which Mohammed ascended on his journey to paradise.

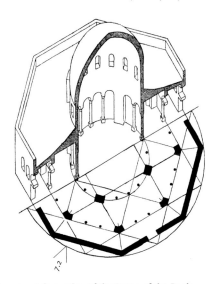

**7.3 Axonometric section of the Dome of the Rock,
Jerusalem, 687–91.**
This section shows the sophisticated geometry involved
in the Dome of the Rock's design, a characteristic shared
by a number of fourth- and fifth-century Syrian churches.

7.4 The Dome of the Rock interior, Jerusalem, 687–91.
This celebration of a holy site through the erection of a dome,
in this case over a rock above a cave and by Jews and Muslims
in Jerusalem, can be compared to the building of the dome
of St. Peter's by Christians in Rome (see Chapter 11) over the
spot where the apostle Peter is believed to have been buried.

7.5 Muslims circumambulating the Ka'ba during the Haj, Mecca.
The idea of pilgrimage is one shared by Christians and Muslims. In this scene in Mecca, throngs of pilgrims surround the Ka'ba. In Chapter 8, you will find Romanesque churches along the pilgrimage roads in France and Spain that lead to the city of Compostela and the highly venerated tomb of the apostle James, son of Zebedee.

derived from Christian precedent. Constantine's Church of the Holy Sepulcher in Jerusalem had featured a similar rotunda, and there were, of course, many centrally planned domed churches throughout the Byzantine world. Unlike most Byzantine domes, however, the structure here is of wood. (There is evidence that early Christian shrines also had wooden domes, although none has survived to the present day.) The dome of the Jerusalem sanctuary, sixty-seven feet in diameter, is constructed of a double shell, each shell having thirty-two converging wooden **ribs**, and the whole rests on a cornice atop a masonry drum. The inner ribs are plastered and adorned with painted and gilded designs (fourteenth-century reconstructions), while the exterior is sheathed with boards and finished with lead and gold leaf.

The general scheme employed at the Dome of the Rock, that of a central shrine around which the faithful could circulate, was used earlier at Mecca in rebuilding the Ka'ba, the goal of Islamic pilgrimage (Fig. 7.5). This cloth-draped cubical shrine contains the Black Stone, believed to have been given to Abraham by the angel Gabriel. The stone was venerated in pre-Muslim times. Mohammed destroyed the idols placed around it, and his successors cleared neighboring buildings in order to provide clear circulation space around the stone. At the Haj, or annual

pilgrimage, the devout process seven times around the Ka'ba, following the sets of concentric rings set in the pavement encircling the shrine.

CONCEPTION OF THE MOSQUE

The building type most closely associated with Islam is the mosque, the primary place of worship, which evolved from several sources. These included the House of the Prophet at Medina (ca. 622), Christian churches, and perhaps the audience halls of Persian kings.

Beside Mohammed's house stood a square enclosure, with small chambers set in the southeast corner for his living quarters (Fig. 7.6). The remainder of the space was a partially open central court. Although constructed originally for domestic purposes, it also served as a gathering

7.6 Reconstruction of the House of the Prophet, Medina, ca. 622.
This building became a prototype for the mosque. Followers of Mohammed assembled in the open courtyard to hear sermons and participate in group prayer, functions that had to be accommodated into mosque design.

7.7 Plan of the Great Mosque, Damascus, 706–15.
This plan shows the columned prayer halls preceded by an open court or sahn.

place for his followers to hear sermons and prayers, and after Mohammed's death its form was imitated in simple worship facilities built in other settlements.

The Great Mosque at Damascus (706–15, with later rebuildings) is the oldest extant mosque and illustrates a process through which the form developed (Fig. 7.7). The site is an ancient one on which had stood a Roman temple dedicated to Jupiter and a fourth-century Christian church dedicated to St. John the Baptist. For a time after the Islamic conquest of the city in 635, both Christians and Muslims worshiped on the site, but in 706 the church was pulled down and an impressive mosque, based in part on tripartite aisle-and-nave basilican church plans, was constructed under the caliphate of al-Walid I. The mosque's outline was determined by the shape of the Roman shrine that was entered through a gateway in the center of the shorter, east side. Four towers, or **minarets**, provided elevated platforms at the corners of the site from which a caller (muezzin) could summon the faithful to prayer. The general design of these towers may have been based on earlier fortification towers or lighthouses, but, with their incorporation at Damascus, minarets became standard features of subsequent Friday mosques. Just as belltowers or raised domes do for churches, minarets serve to identify the mosque in the landscape. Much later, particularly important mosques were sometimes given multiple minarets, but one generally sufficed.

Over half of the inner space is given over to an open arcaded court, or **sahn**, containing a domed fountain pavilion for ritual ablutions and an octagonal pavilion originally used for the public treasury. The covered prayer hall, or **haram**, extends along the entire long south wall. Two parallel rows of columns divide this hall longitudinally into thirds, near the center of which the arcades are

interrupted by a broad transverse element similar to a nave, with a wooden dome over its central bay. This element develops in later designs into the **maqsura**, a special processional area reserved for the retinue of the caliph, thereby justifying its dome as a special architectural accent. The south wall being the prayer wall, or **qibla**, there are three niches, or **mihrabs**, set into it to indicate the direction of Mecca. A raised pulpit, or **minbar** (not indicated on the plan), from which Qur'anic readings, sermons, or official proclamations and addresses are given, is located to the right of the central mihrab.

REGIONAL VARIATIONS IN MOSQUE DESIGN

Because mosques have been built throughout so much of the world, it will not be possible to represent their full diversity in this short chapter. The discussion that follows concentrates on 1) columnar or hypostyle mosques favored in Arabia, North Africa, and Spain, 2) **iwan** mosques popular in Iran and Central Asia, which consist of a rectangular court flanked by large, often vaulted spaces, or iwans, and 3) large, centrally organized, domed-space mosques found in Turkey.

Columned Hall or Hypostyle Mosques

The Great Mosque of al-Mutawakkil at Samarra, Iraq (848/49–52) has both a columned hall and a single, extraordinary minaret. Enormous in size, the mosque consists of a rectangular burned-brick-wall enclosure more than 800 feet by more than 500 feet, with attached semicircular towers. To the north along the enclosure's

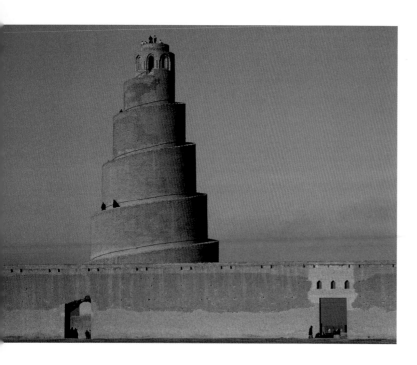

7.8 The Great Mosque of al-Mutawakkil, Samarra, 848/849–52.
This prominent minaret in the form of a tall spiral has a lineage traceable as far back as the Mesopotamian ziggurats. Note how the long, horizontal outer wall serves as a foil for the minaret's rich, strongly vertical silhouette.

central, longitudinal axis rises the brick minaret (Fig. 7.8), its spiral form associated by some with the ziggurats of ancient Mesopotamia. Inside the mosque's walls, a forest of square columns once surrounded a rectangular sahn, with the qibla adjacent to the deepest accumulation of column bays, altogether a highly ordered, even profound composition.

The Great Mosque begun in around 785 in Córdoba, Spain (Fig. 7.9), evolved to have a much more complex columnar hall form than that at Samarra. In the first construction period, the mosque occupied a nearly square plan, half comprising the sahn and the other half the haram, which contained ten rows of eleven columns to create an eleven-aisled sanctuary. In the haram, superimposed arches connect the columns, the lower arch being horseshoe-shaped and the upper one not quite semicircular (Fig. 7.10). The effect of this work is light and delicate, and although both the tiered arcades of the Damascus mosque and the stacked arches of Roman aqueducts have been suggested as the inspiration for the superimposed arches, their treatment here is entirely original. Both arch levels are polychrome, composed of white stone voussoirs set alternately against red brick ones.

Beginning in 833, this mosque was enlarged three times. In the first renovation campaign (833–48), the prayer hall was extended to the southwest by the addition of eight new bays that maintained the alignment and

rhythm of the original mosque but necessitated reconstruction of the qibla and mihrab. In 951, the sahn was extended to the northeast and a new minaret erected. The haram was again expanded to the southwest beginning in 962, when another twelve bays were added along with a new qibla and mihrab. The new mihrab was a richly ornamented niche, given prominence on the interior by a virtual forest of lobed and cusped arches, covered by a dome formed by boldly interlacing arches (Figs. 7.11, 7.12), flanked by smaller domes also composed of interlaced arches in the bays to either side. So far as we know, these exceptional domes are an original invention here, and they are the possible inspiration for similar domes built in the Italian Baroque by Guarino Guarini (see Fig. 12.25). The final extension of the mosque took place in 987–88 along the southeastern side, adding another eight aisles running the full length of the existing haram, and enlarging the sahn as well to create the largest mosque in Spain. In the sixteenth century, after the Moors were expelled from Spain, the cathedral of Córdoba (Fig. 7.13) was inserted inside the mosque, disrupting the colonnaded expanse of the haram but perhaps inadvertently preserving a good portion of the Islamic fabric through the mosque's conversion to a place of Christian worship.

7.9 Plan of the Great Mosque, Córdoba, 785 and 833–988.
This mosque, like the Great Mosque of Damascus, has columned prayer halls preceded by open courts or sahns.

7.10 The Great Mosque interior, Córdoba, 833–988.
This view of the prayer hall shows the horseshoe-shaped polychrome stacked arches that dominate the interior. Eventually 610 columns defined the immense space.

7.11 The Great Mosque vault above the maqsura, Córdoba, 833–988.
Note the use of lobed arches, polychromy, and the interlaced-arch structure of the dome.

7.12 The Great Mosque vault above the mihrab bay, Córdoba, 833–988.
This vault also employs interlaced arches in its construction.

7.13 The Great Mosque from the minaret, Córdoba, 833–988.
Parallel rows of ridge-and-valley roofs cover the prayer hall, and the foreground trees are growing in the sahn. One regrets the intrusion of a later Christian church in this splendid Islamic building.

7.14 Plan of the Bibi Khanum Mosque, Samarkand, begun 1399.
Compare this modular mosque plan with the equally regimented ranks and files of Muslim worshipers in Fig. 7.1 and remember that they are called to prayer five times daily. This rigorous prayer regime is mirrored in the rigorous planning of the mosque.

7.15a Plan of the Friday mosque, Isfahan, 8th–17th centuries.
This mosque is interesting for its early incorporation of substantial domes within a multi-columned prayer hall. In its final form, the mosque evolved into a four-iwan type, having a large central courtyard bisected by cross-axes established by the iwans.

7.15b (below) Plan of and section looking southeast through Masjid-i-Shah, Isfahan, 1611–ca. 1630.
The mosque sits at the top of the public square. Entrance to it is centered in the arcades defining the square, but the axis turns to bring the mosque into alignment with Mecca. Madrasas, or theological schools, are located beside the mosque.

Iwan Mosques

To the east, in Central Asian lands now part of Iran, Uzbekistan, Turkmenistan, and Afghanistan, mosque designs developed initially from multi-columned halls. The Bibi Khanum Mosque at Samarkand, Uzbekistan, begun in 1399 by the military and political leader Timur, who founded a dynasty at the end of the fourteenth century, presents the essentials of the multi-columned iwan mosque form. Its constituent element, the iwan, is a vaulted or domed volume, walled on three sides and open on the other. At Samarkand, the plan (Fig. 7.14) is comparable to that at Samarra, with a sahn inside ranks of columns forming four L-shaped halls, all bounded by a rectangular perimeter wall. Here, however, an entry portal, with stumps of flanking minarets remaining, opens into one short side of the sahn, and iwans appear at the center of the other three sides, becoming porchlike extensions of the central open space. The iwan facing the entry and terminating its axis is the qibla iwan and is domed and flanked by additional minarets.

7.16 (right) Masjid-i-Shah, Isfahan, 1611–ca. 1630.
In order to respect the direction of Mecca, the mosque is turned forty-five degrees to the axis of the public square (left side of the photograph) laid out by Shah Abbas.

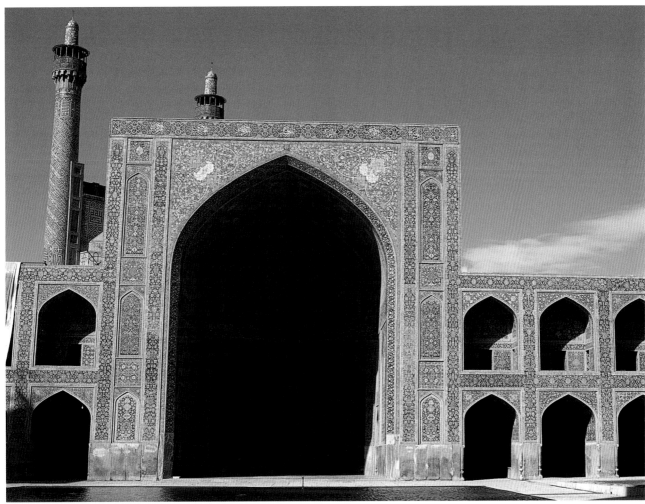

7.17 Iwan, Masjid-i-Shah, Isfahan, 1611–ca. 1630.
Two-story arcades flank the central arch, which is finished with elaborate tile decoration and a muqarnas vault. In the background is the rear of the entrance iwan on the public square.

The earliest mosque about which we have reliable archaeological information is the Friday mosque in Isfahan (Fig. 7.15a), begun in the eighth century, finally achieving a form not unlike that at Samarkand and reworked repeatedly until the seventeenth century. The original form seems to have been a rectangular multi-columned hall covered with a wooden roof, with a large sahn at its core. In 1086–87 a domed chamber was introduced at the southwest end of the existing building, probably to serve as a maqsura. It differed significantly in scale from the domes already seen as part of the maqsuras at Damascus and Córdoba: rather than covering one bay of the columnar hall, the southern dome covered twenty bays. In 1088, a slightly smaller dome was added in an axial line to the north. It is not clear what function it served initially, for it was outside the building at the time of its construction but was soon incorporated into arcades.

At some later date, Isfahan's Friday mosque was modified again to include four iwans, one set in the center of each side of the sahn. Their boldly scaled arched openings provided builders with an opportunity to exercise their skills in geometric ornamentation, including the application of glazed tiles in shades of blue, turquoise, white, and yellow, and stalactitelike muqarnas vaults, the ornamental treatment of curved wall surfaces with corbeled concave elements that has the overall effect of dissolving the

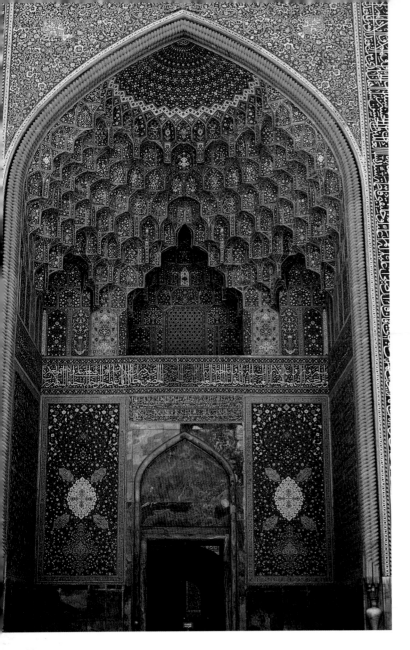

7.18 Masjid-i-Shah, entrance to prayer hall, Isfahan, 1611–ca. 1630.
This view shows the elaborate blue-glazed tilework and muqarnas vault. Sometimes compared to a honeycomb, these cellular vaults are formed by corbeling.

the plan. From the entranceway, one can see the iwan constructed in front of the qibla, but the circulation path leads first laterally to either side of the initial iwan, then toward the sahn, thereby accomplishing the axial shift with finesse. Apart from the transitional elements at the entrance, symmetry governs the entire design. A still pool at the center of the sahn reflects the blue-background glazed tilework covering the four iwans and the great dome of the haram. Among the decorative elements portrayed in the tiles are peacocks, reflecting the builders' willingness in this case to depict animals in art rather than confining ornament to recursive geometric elements and calligraphy. The domed prayer hall is augmented by rooms on either side, also covered by a succession of small domes, that served as a winter mosque, and it is further complemented by two religious schools (**madrasas**), thus continuing an established tradition of incorporating education with worship. (The study of law and religion are inseparable aspects of Islamic higher education.)

Islam came to India in successive waves of military invasions in the eleventh through thirteenth centuries, challenging the established religions of Hinduism and Buddhism with its fundamentally different religious perspective. India's cavelike temples with interiors used only by priests and covered inside and out with intricately wrought sculpted figures were totally alien to the Islamic idea of the mosque with accessible open courtyards, spacious prayer halls, and scrupulous avoidance of the human figure in representational art. Hindu and Buddhist temples were replaced with mosques initially based on multi-columned hall designs. Beginning with the ascendancy of the Mughal Dynasty (mid-sixteenth to eighteenth centuries),

material presence of the wall into facets that seem to hover in space. The mosque is also renowned for its intricate brickwork patterns in the domes.

During the reign of Shah Abbas I, the core of Isfahan was greatly expanded, as a whole new market area was developed at some distance from the older settlement around the Friday mosque. Included in the new construction was a congregational mosque, the Masjid-i-Shah (1611–ca. 1630), built to designs of Badi' al-Zaman Tuni and Ali Akbar al-Isfahani (Figs. 7.15b, 7.16–7.18). Entrance into it is made through the center of the southern side of the market, so as to provide a monumental portal to the public area and match the gateway to the **bazaar** at the opposite end of the square, but the mosque itself is turned forty-five degrees so as to be correctly aligned with Mecca. The skill with which the designers accommodated the change in axis is one of the most admired aspects of

7.19 Plan of the Friday mosque, Fatehpur Sikri, ca. 1568–71.
The monumental gate is on the southern side of the mosque, preceded by a wide stairway, while the haram is set to the west.

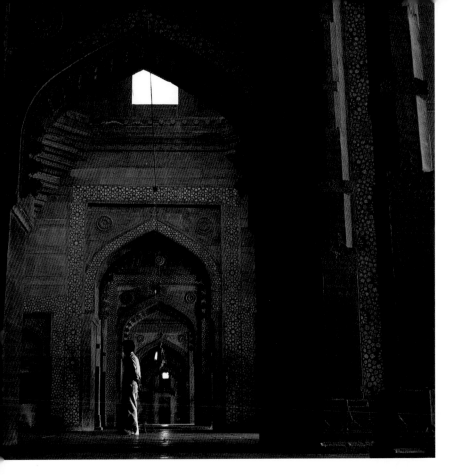

7.20 Friday mosque interior, Fatehpur Sikri, ca. 1568–71.
This view shows the distinctive detail developed by Akbar's architects as they fused Islamic forms (the pointed arch, for example) with elements from Hindu and Buddhist traditions already well established in India.

7.21 Friday mosque gateway, Fatehpur Sikri, ca. 1568–71.
As Akbar's city was set on a plateau above the surrounding terrain, a monumental flight of steps is required to gain entrance to the mosque from the southern side. It serves as a plinth for an impressive arched gateway.

however, one sees a distinctly Indo-Islamic style come into being, spurred on in large measure by the arrival of foreign craftsmen from Central Asia. Some of these individuals were descendants of Indian craftsmen taken captive by the Mongol conqueror Timur in 1398. Their return in the sixteenth century brought skilled builders familiar with the Islamic architecture of Persia to India, and the resulting works done for the Mughal rulers are some of the most magnificent to be found in the Islamic world.

Jalil al-Din Akbar, the third Mughal emperor, who ruled 1556–1605, was responsible for constructing an entirely new capital at Fatehpur Sikri (1569–ca. 1580), a site abandoned after his death and preserved now as a national monument in India. The monumental palace buildings are all that remain, but sixteenth-century accounts describe it as a city larger than London at the same period, which explains in part the grand scale employed for its Friday mosque (ca. 1568–71) (Figs. 7.19–7.21). Constructed in red sandstone, the mosque has an immense sahn, 312 by 387 feet, entered from the south through a monumental gate enlarged in 1596. From the palace, entrance was made through the Emperor's Gate, placing it on axis with the haram on the western side. Behind the western iwan is the major dome of the haram, flanked by two smaller domes, setting a pattern for Indian mosques that would often be repeated. In its architecture, the building reflects arched and domed forms familiar from examples in Iran, but some of the detail also borrows elements from the Hindu and Buddhist architecture of India, a blend that contributes a distinctive quality to Islamic buildings on the subcontinent. The mosque's sahn contains the exquisitely detailed marble tomb of Salim Chishti (d. 1572), a holy man who had predicted that the childless Akbar would have three

7.22 Shezade Mosque, Istanbul, 1545–48.
Sinan's first major mosque, this building is notable
for its clearly articulated geometry of squares.
One square comprises the sahn, while the second
defines the domed haram. Minarets are incorporated
into the corners where the squares join.

sons. Fatehpur Sikri was built in celebration of the birth
of Akbar's son Jahangir in 1569, and the east–west axis
through the Friday mosque aligns with Chishti's hermitage,
which was already on the site.

Multi-domed Mosques

In Asiatic Turkey, or Anatolia, the spread of Islam came at
the expense of the Byzantine Empire, which was gradually
reduced in size until the fall of Constantinople in 1453
brought an end to a civilization over 1000 years old. The
victors were the Ottoman Turks, led by Sultan Mehmet II,
who thus completed the Islamic conquest of the Balkans.
Hagia Sophia, the most impressive church in the eastern
Mediterranean, was converted into the city's congregational mosque; minarets were eventually added. Ottoman
architects, who already had experience in building domed
structures set on cubical masses, received new inspiration
from the city's great Byzantine churches, which now stood
before them as models, and in succeeding centuries they
constructed a number of mosques that in structure and
architectural detail rank with the best religious buildings
that Byzantium produced.

  Among these one must count the works of Koca Sinan
(ca. 1490–1588), a distinguished engineer and architect

**7.23 Longitudinal section and plan of Shezade Mosque,
Istanbul, 1545–48.**
These drawings show how Sinan took Hagia Sophia's theme
of the central dome with flanking semidomes and expanded
it into a completely centralized design. The square plan of
the sahn matches the square enclosed space of the haram.

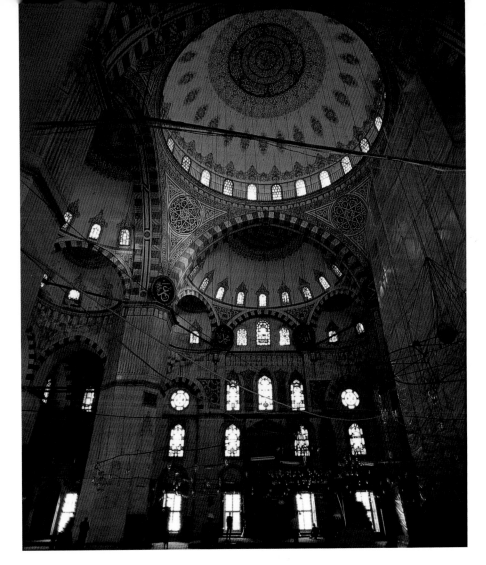

7.24 Shezade Mosque interior, Istanbul, 1545–48.
This view shows the piers supporting the great dome and the flanking semidomes.

who has been compared with his Italian contemporary Michelangelo. Born to a peasant family of non-Muslim background, Sinan was recruited for governmental service as a youth and trained in the corps of Janissaries, elite infantry units of the Ottoman army composed of non-Muslims abducted as children and forced to convert to Islam. After participating in military campaigns in Austria, Greece, and Mesopotamia, he served as court architect in Constantinople for fifty years, during which time he designed and supervised construction of a large number of projects, including waterworks, bridges, fortifications, and buildings. Sinan's career coincided with the reigns of generous sultans, and he was undoubtedly fortunate to have the vast Ottoman building corps of skilled workmen at his command. Without both liberal patrons to finance them and capable assistants to carry them out, major projects could not have been realized, no matter how brilliantly designed.

Sinan's first major architectural commission in Constantinople was the Shezade mosque complex (1545–48), commissioned by Sultan Süleyman in memory of his son, who had died as a young man. Constructed on the site of Justinian's Church of the Holy Apostles, the mosque is composed of two joined squares (Figs. 7.22–7.24). One square contains the sahn, which has a central fountain and is surrounded by domed bays behind arcades. The second square is the enclosed haram, where the central dome is complemented by four semidomes set at the sides,

with smaller domes and semidomes filling the remaining spaces. The elegantly symmetrical geometry of the plan is matched by the balanced volumes of the interior space and the exterior massing, punctuated by paired minarets at the corners where the two squares adjoin. Sinan has handled the great piers and necessary buttressing so as to minimize the apparent bulk of the masonry. As a result, window openings are larger and the volumetric massing on the exterior presents a harmonious composition of successive layering of domes and semidomes. Associated with the mosque are the tomb of Shezade Mehmet, a madrasa, a hospice for the infirm, a school, and a **caravanserai** (accommodation and markets for foreign merchants who sold at wholesale prices), reminders that even in a well-established city, mosques provided space for both civic and sacred functions. It was Ottoman practice to provide separate buildings dedicated to different particular needs.

A similar quality marks Sinan's celebrated mosque of Süleyman the Magnificent (1550–57), within a vast complex, or **Külliye**, containing the mosque and cemetery at the center, with four madrasas, a primary school, a medical school, a caravanserai, a hospital, a community kitchen to feed the poor, a hospice, public baths, and even a house for Sinan (Figs. 7.25–7.26). It was sited on the sloping side of a hill fronting on the Golden Horn (harbor of Constantinople), and Sinan located the complex so as to exploit the dramatic possibilities of the terrain, which

7.25 (above) Mosque of Süleyman the Magnificent, Istanbul, 1550–57.
Constructed as the centerpiece of a larger complex of schools, shops, and community facilities, the mass of this mosque is balanced by the slender vertical accents of its four minarets.

7.26 (below) Site plan of the Külliye of Süleyman the Magnificent, Istanbul, 1550–57.
The site plan provides concrete evidence of the Islamic integration of church and state, with combined facilities for worship, education, medical care, and social services.

7.27 Selimiye Mosque, Edirne, 1568–75.
Generally held to be Sinan's masterpiece, this mosque is essentially a single dome supported on eight great piers and braced by external buttresses. The minarets are exceptionally tall and provided with internal spiraling staircases of considerable geometric complexity.

7.28 Plan of and section through the Selimiye Mosque complex, Edirne, 1568–75.
Sinan attempted here to equal the dome of Hagia Sophia and exceed its integration of interior space.

required that the layout be asymmetrical. Marked by four slender minarets, the mosque dominates the ensemble of buildings. Its plan is familiar: an arcaded sahn, a domed haram, and a walled cemetery set on a linear axis. The haram is a variant of that at Hagia Sophia, having a central dome flanked by two semidomes, but here the aisles, also domed, are so configured as to allow the entire building to exist within a square. Spatially, the interior functions as a single volume, with aisles and nave available for prayer. (There is no second-level gallery as at Hagia Sophia.) The whole presents a more consistent articulation, both inside and out, than was achieved in the Byzantine building. Buttressing elements, arches, vaults, and domes work together structurally and visually to create a satisfying architectural composition. The octagonal mausoleum of Süleyman (d. 1566), placed in the center of the cemetery behind the qibla wall, has a plan inspired by the Dome of the Rock, although this is not evident from the exterior treatment.

Sinan's final major work was the Selimiye Mosque in Edirne, built in 1568–75 for Selim II, successor to Süleyman (Figs. 7.27–7.28). The complex contains the usual madrasas and commercial buildings (whose revenues helped to offset the running costs of the mosque and its related educational and charitable facilities), but it is the domed haram that commands particular attention. Sinan boasted that here he had built a dome both wider and taller than Hagia Sophia, which is not quite the case, but his method of conceiving the space transcends that of the Byzantine original. There are no semidomes. The dome is set directly on eight piers, six freestanding and two engaged in the qibla wall. Arches connecting these piers support the dome, which rises above ranks of windows pierced in the exterior wall. Buttressing necessary to brace the dome's lateral thrust is placed within the walls and seen more clearly on the exterior. One must marvel not only at the daring of the dome but also at the slenderness of the four minarets that mark the corners of the haram.

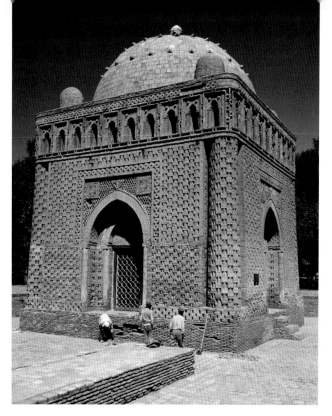

7.29 Tomb of Ismail the Samanid, Bukhara, ca. 900.
In places where constant, bright sunlight is the norm, architects of various cultures have used cast shadows to great advantage. Here smooth wall surfaces have disappeared in favor of advancing and receding masonry units that create a rich patterning of light and dark.

Squinch arch above

7.30 Section and plan of the Tomb of Ismail the Samanid, Bukhara, ca. 900. Note how the reentrant, or notched-out, corners are filled with circular columns that decorate the joining of the tomb's faces. The arched openings in each façade are splayed so that the arches become wider as they advance outward. The same device was frequently used in the medieval churches of Europe.

Of exceptional height (232 feet), they are grooved to accentuate their verticality. Inside two of them are separate staircases leading to each of the three balconies, a complex exercise in spiraling geometry and a structural challenge that Sinan boasted proudly that he had met successfully.

TOMBS

It is common for a mosque to include the tomb of a founder or holy man. Freestanding monumental tombs, usually with domes, also became popular by the tenth century. The Tomb of Ismail the Samanid in Bukhara, Uzbekistan, dates from ca. 900 or even earlier. A cubelike mass with inset cylindrical corners houses a single domed chamber supported by four squinch arches and ringed by an upper-level ambulatory (Figs. 7.29–7.30). Most distinctive is its highly textured brickwork laid in forceful geometric patterns that contrast solids and voids.

Returning to Samarkand, location of the previously discussed Bibi Khanum Mosque, we find the Gur-i-Amir, built as the resting place of Timur's grandson, who died in battle. It consists of a Greek-cross-plan interior space, with its four arms crowned by **muqarnas** vaults inside an octagonal mass that is surmounted by a tall cylindrical drum on squinch arches and tall, bulbous dome (Fig. 7.31). The interior ornamentation is lavish, including hexagonal alabaster panels, jasper, and even painted, molded paper.

With the construction in Delhi of the tomb of Humayun, father of Jalil al-Din Akbar, the idea of the

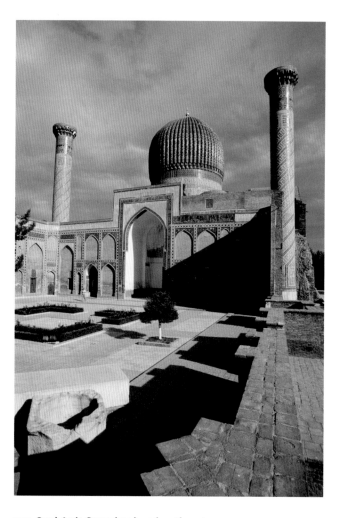

7.31 Gur-i-Amir, Samarkand, early 15th century.
The bulbous dome, a dome that grows wider above its drum before curving inward, is a distinctive Muslim device and one comparable in profile to the Muslim horseshoe arches seen in Fig. 7.10.

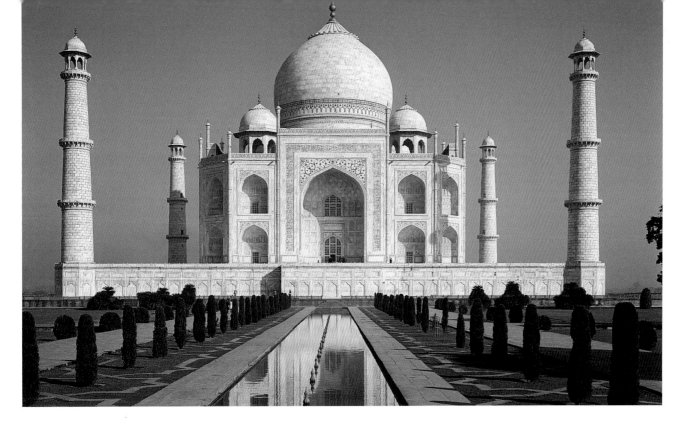

7.32 Taj Mahal, Agra, 1631–47.
This tomb is one of the world's most famous buildings. Its serenity derives in part from its sheer elegance and its placement in a totally designed landscape of plants, water, and paving.

domed-chamber tomb arrived in India. The most famous of these domed tombs is the Taj Mahal in Agra (1631–47) (Figs. 7.32–7.33). Its builder was Jahangir's son, Shah Jahan, who ruled from 1628 to 1658 and is remembered as a prolific Mughal patron of building. Aided by a well-trained group of architects attached to his court, Shah Jahan promoted a style that included an emphasis on bilateral symmetry, the use of cusped arches, and white marble or stucco facing instead of red sandstone for exterior finishes.

Because of its great size, elegant massing, refinement of detail and ornamentation, and general countenance of serenity, the Taj Mahal is unquestionably one of Islam's and indeed the world's most celebrated buildings. It was built as a tomb for Shah Jahan's beloved wife, Mumtaz Mahal, by a trio of architects: Ahmad Lahawri, along with 'Abd al-Karim Ma'mur Khan and Makramat Khan, all three assisted by craftsmen from Persia, Central Asia, and India. The site adjoins the Jumna River to the north, and the tomb is placed next to it, rather than being in the center of the layout as was Humayun's. Entrance is made from the south, through a main gateway set on axis with the tomb. In between the two lies a square garden, with canals dividing the square into quadrants defining the central and cross-axes. Flowering trees, cypresses, and blooming plants originally grew in the garden areas as symbols of rebirth and immortality. The tomb itself is symmetrical, crowned with a large bulbous dome raised on a drum and graced by smaller octagonal pavilions with domical roofs set at the corners. Highly polished and inlaid marble adorns the exterior, so that the building glistens in the sun. The whole structure is raised on a square platform, the corners of which are marked by minarets. Flanking the

7.33 Site plan of the Taj Mahal, Agra, 1631–47.
In this orthogonal scheme, the tomb (top) is set in a larger landscape of square courts divided into quadrants by watercourses, creating a nested hierarchy of axes and cross-axes that allude to the garden of paradise.

Roof terrace for
sleeping in summer

Screens
covering
projecting
windows
overlooking
street

Internal screens
to protect
family privacy

Interior courtyard

Earth-sheltered room

7.34 (left) Axonometric section through a traditional house, Baghdad.
This house incorporates many characteristics of Islamic urban dwellings in hot, dry climates. Under the courtyard floor is an earth-sheltered room that provides cooling air during the day. Screened rooftop areas are used for sleeping in hot weather. Grilled windows at upper levels can be opened for air circulation while preserving privacy.

7.35 (below) Plan of the Maidan-i-Shah (public square) and related developments, Isfahan, 1590–1602.
Shah Abbas had an ambitious new city center laid out around the Maidan-i-Shah, a twenty-acre urban square. The Masjid-i-Shah (Shah's Mosque) was built at the south end to draw the faithful from the older Friday mosque.

tomb are symmetrically placed red sandstone buildings, to the west a mosque and to the east a guest house, whose color contrasts deliberately with the shimmering white marble. Against a verdant foreground of plant material, accentuated by reflecting water channels, the Taj Mahal seems ethereal, its proportion and detail so finely wrought as to capture the beautiful memory of the woman whose untimely death prompted its construction.

HOUSES AND URBAN PATTERNS

Across the broad geographic area that comprises the Islamic world, there is obviously considerable diversity in climate, traditional house forms, and construction materials, making it impossible to propose a single definition for an Islamic house. From the Qur'an and related texts comprising traditions and laws, however, there developed certain principles governing both private and public life that also regulated aspects of house forms and city planning. Islam recognizes the fundamental right of privacy for the family within its own house, hence in many places houses present plain exterior walls to the street. In hot, arid climates, residences tend to be designed around courtyards that preserve privacy and also modify the microclimate advantageously (Fig. 7.34). Doorways of houses on opposite sides of the street must be located so that one cannot look from one dwelling into the other when both doors are open, and ground-level windows are set so high that those passing by cannot look in. Windows above the ground floor may be larger, but they may not be placed so as to overlook courtyards or rooftop areas of other houses and thus invade the privacy of those occupying them. These upper-floor windows may project beyond the plane of the wall, and they are frequently provided with elaborately carved screens to restrict the view from the outside. Within the family, women and children are segregated from men and visitors, so the family living area (haram: note that the same word describes a mosque's prayer hall; in both cases they are spaces "set apart") is separated from reception facilities provided for male guests, and from

Friday mosque
(see pp.160–62)

Old city

Government buildings   Caravanserai

Covered bazaar connecti
to old city (see Fig. 7.36)

Palaces of
Nobles

Entrance to the Qaysariya
or shah's bazaar

Maidan-i-Shah

Sheikh Lutfullah Mosqu

Ali Kapu Gate

Masjid-i-Shah or Sh
mosque (see pp.16

Grand avenue

Ziya

N

0   500 m

0   1500 ft

7.36 View of the bazaar at Isfahan.
The bazaar is composed of a street linking merchants' stalls and small shops, interspersed with baths, workshops, and theological schools. Vaults over the street provide relief from the intense sun, while skylights admit necessary daylight and fresh air.

the entrance to the house one cannot see directly into living areas. Privacy and seclusion are often achieved by the use of separate doors and carved screens or grilles, which admit light and air while also allowing those behind to look out without being seen.

Islam has a lengthy urban tradition, and aspects of the Prophet's teachings were applied to the problems inherent in establishing rights when living in larger communities. Pre-modern Islamic society made no distinction between the sacred and secular realms. In many traditional settlements located from North Africa to the Middle East, the essential features of an urban area were a Friday mosque large enough to serve the community and surrounding settlements, a governor who exercised control over the territory, and a bazaar or market with covered stalls for the city and surrounding countryside. The Friday mosque and the bazaar were inseparable. Market stalls were grouped by trade or type of merchandise, with those of highest status (perfume, books) located closest to the mosque entrance, and those associated with noise or noxious odors (coppersmiths, leatherworkers) farthest away. Interspersed with the public areas might be fountains, cafés, caravanserais, public baths, and madrasas. This whole public area was the domain of men, and its plan tended to be irregular, built up over time. The city's neighborhoods or residential quarters began as homogeneous groupings of families affiliated by a common trade or religious and ethnic connections. At one time, many quarters had a gate or door that could be used to close off the area

when desired. Within the neighborhood, families shared a mosque, fountains, public baths, communal ovens, and shops. The distinctive organization of residential quarters helps to explain why the street plans of traditional Islamic cities such as Tunis or Isfahan have few through roads, on which are found the major public places and markets; a limited number of secondary streets; and hundreds of cul-de-sacs, along which most houses stand. The street pattern resembles a maze with many dead ends, far more than in the grid layouts more common in Europe.

The Iranian city of Isfahan provides perhaps the most handsome example of the application of Islamic principles of city planning, although one must admit from the start that its royal quarter and new section as laid out by Shah Abbas I (1587–1629) are not typical of the growth by accretion associated with traditional Islamic urbanism (Fig. 7.35). In the older part of town, around the Friday mosque, one finds the traditional network of streets and cul-de-sacs. The historic trade route extending south toward the Ziyanda River grew into a linear covered bazaar (Fig. 7.36) of small shops that meandered past entrances to other facilities that lay behind the merchants' stalls: caravanserais, madrasas, mosques, baths, fountains, and craft workshops. Shah Abbas, determined to bring greater glory to his capital city, undertook redevelopment of the public square established just outside the traditional area and defined it as a formal rectangular square, the Maidan-i-Shah, lined with shops and punctuated by major monuments: two mosques, the Ali Kapu gate (the imperial porch, which served as a viewing stand), and the entrance to the Qaysariya, the shah's bazaar. The center of the open space was normally available for small vendors to sell their wares in, but it could also be cleared and used for military or athletic events, the two-story arcades around the edges providing a good base for observation.

The Shah's contributions to this grand urban scheme included construction of a complex of governmental buildings on the western side of the square behind the Ali Kapu gate. Directly opposite the gate was the imposing entrance to the small Sheikh Lutfullah Mosque (1602), which has a bent-axis entry around two sides of the square haram to bring the faithful into the mosque on the axis aligned with Mecca. The Masjid-i-Shah, or Shah's mosque (see pages 160–62), occupies the short southern end of the square, set opposite the grand entrance to the shah's bazaar on the northern side. This formally conceived space comes as a surprise after the more organic city core, but its layout is not out of character, for it displays at a large scale what many of the older buildings, including the Friday mosque, had become over a longer period of time: spaces with biaxial symmetry and uniform perimeter articulation, whether in arcades or colonnades. Shah Abbas's ambition was to link the Maidan-i-Shah, by means of a grand new avenue lined with palaces of nobles, to the river and a new bridge, making accessible gardens and the commercially important Armenian settlement beyond, but not all of his program came to fruition.

THE PALACE AND THE GARDEN

Some of the formal concepts that characterized the planning of Isfahan are also seen in the fortress-palace of the Alhambra, a royal citadel erected above the city of Granada (Fig. 7.37). Built in the thirteenth and fourteenth centuries, the Alhambra was the work of the Nasrid Dynasty, which governed the dwindling Islamic territories of southern Spain until expulsion in 1492 by Ferdinand and Isabella, the monarchs who also financed Columbus's expedition to the Indies in the same year. Some parts of the Alhambra are now ruined, and the center of its site on a ridge overlooking the city is crowded by the later palace of Charles V. The red-brick exterior wall bristles with towers capped by crenelated battlements. It originally enclosed an entire palace city, including common dwelling houses, craft workshops, the royal mint, several mosques, public baths, and a military garrison, in addition to seven palace buildings. Archaeological work on the surviving buildings is ongoing as historians try to understand the site's construction history.

Of the surviving palace chambers, the two most impressive are grouped around rectangular courts: one known as the Patio of Arrayanes or Myrtle Trees, which provided access to the Hall of the Ambassadors; and the other called the Patio of Leones or Lions, so named for the fountain at its center. The Patio of Myrtle Trees has a central rectangular pool fed by gently overflowing fountain basins at opposite ends (Fig. 7.38). Arcaded galleries are set across the short sides, and rows of myrtles parallel to the pool on the long sides are reflected in its smooth surface. At the north end is the Comares Tower, which contained the square-plan Hall of the Ambassadors, thirty-six feet on a side, with a soaring sixty-foot height (Fig. 7.39). This was the throne room of the sultan, and its domed ceiling, composed of over 8000 wooden sections, captures the effect of thousands of stars in the seven levels of heaven as described by Islamic theology.

7.37 Plan of the Alhambra, Granada, 13th–14th centuries.
This plan shows what were originally two separate palaces. In the center are the Patio of Myrtle Trees and the associated Hall of the Ambassadors, constructed on the foundations of a military tower. To the right is the Patio of Lions.

Comares Tower with Hall of the Ambassadors

Sala del Mexuar (original Throne Room)

Myrtles

Pool

Patio of Arrayanes or Myrtle Trees

Hall of the Two Sisters

Patio of Leones or Lions

Hall of the Abencerrajes

N

0   25 m

0   75 ft

7.38 Patio of Myrtle Trees, Alhambra, Granada, 13th–14th centuries. This view shows the reflecting pool and the Comares Tower in the background. The delicacy and grace of late Islamic architecture in Spain is evident in the arcade.

7.39 Ceiling and upper wall, Hall of the Ambassadors, Alhambra, Granada, 13th–14th centuries. Thousands of small wooden pieces are suspended from the roof timbers to transform this ceiling into the seven layers of heaven surrounding a small dome at the center representing the heavenly throne. Pierced grilles filter sunlight.

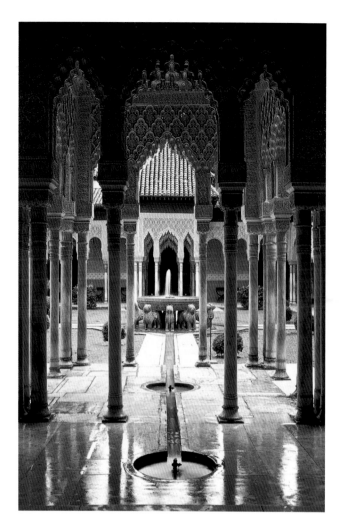

7.40 Patio of Lions. Alhambra, Granada, 13th–14th centuries.
This view shows the central fountain and the water channels
dividing the court into four quadrants. In the background is
the roof of the Hall of the Two Sisters (see Fig. 5.41).

In contrast to its simple exteriors, the Alhambra's interiors are enriched by a profusion of decorative detail that
covers all surfaces, conveying splendor, ineffable lightness,
and the ethereal quality of a dream world. Marbles, colored ceramic tiles, and carved and gilded wood or stucco
screens create changing patterns of shadow as light reflects
on water and polished surfaces, or flickers through pierced
walls and ceilings. Pattern and texture abound in both geometric arabesques and stylized plant forms embellished
with flowing Arabic inscriptions; arches are lobed and
cusped; windows have elaborate grilles; and ceilings feature stalactites of carved wood or plaster. Behind the ornament, the underlying rubble masonry construction is not
of the highest quality—it was the effect of magnificence
that was desired rather than its actual substance. Even
without its interior furnishings and original courtyard
plantings, however, the Alhambra's sumptuous character
can still be appreciated today.

By 1492, when the Moors were expelled from Spain,
many aspects of Islamic architecture had long since found
their way into buildings in western Europe. During the
medieval period, interactions among learned men from
Islamic, Hebraic, and Christian traditions had generally
been amicable, undermined primarily by intolerance for
non-Christian religions on the part of the Catholic Church.
Elements that became important features in Western architecture, among them **polychromy**, the pointed arch, and
domes with interlacing ribs, originated in mosque designs,
and the gracious elegance of palaces integrating landscape
and architecture, such as the Alhambra, were unmatched
in northern Europe.

CONCLUSIONS ABOUT ARCHITECTURAL IDEAS

While the basic forms of Islamic architecture, including
those of the mosque—the building type emphasized in this
chapter—can seem bewilderingly unfamiliar to Western
eyes, they are actually remarkably limited but extremely
versatile. As evidence of this condition, consider the abam-
bars, or urban cisterns, found in Iran. Their function is, of
course, simply to store water in a cool, fresh condition, and
they must be easily and regularly cleaned. At the heart of
the abambar is the storage reservoir, which is covered with
a dome, a quintessential element of Iranian mosques. The
ventilation device for this reservoir is a minaretlike wind-
catcher that directs air down to the storage level. Entry into
the reservoir is made by way of a stair that descends to an
iwanlike porch, sometimes including muqarna vaults.

The Patio of Lions (Fig. 7.40) includes arcades resting on slender columns, and is divided into four parts by
shallow watercourses emanating from the lion fountain
at the center. As with the Tomb of Humayun and the Taj
Mahal, this layout is thought to symbolize the Qur'anic
vision of paradise—a garden below which four rivers flow
with water, wine, honey, and milk—and the courtyard
was originally planted. Square pavilions on the short sides
project into the court and have clustered columns supporting intricately carved arcades. There has been considerable
scholarly discussion about the dates and origins of the
fountain's twelve lions, which as figurative representations
of animals would seem to have no place in Islamic art. The
basin is clearly Islamic, as attested by its fourteenth-century
inscription, but it does not match the animals in style. It
has been speculated that the lions originated in a Jewish
palace formerly on the hilltop, where they may have replicated the animals supporting the great bronze basin that
was found in the courtyard of the Temple of Solomon.
Opening off the long sides of their court are two chambers,
each of which is a jewel of ornamental vaulting. To the
south, the Hall of the Abencerrajes is covered with a splendid muqarnas vault in the shape of an eight-pointed star.
The northern room, the Sala de las Dos Hermanas (Hall of
the Two Sisters), has an octagonal drum supporting what
appears to be a star-shaped muqarnas vault that is actually
suspended from wooden trusses (Fig. 7.41).

Altogether, the abambar can be interpreted as a domed iwan mosque disassembled and its constituent parts reassembled as a utilitarian structure. This repetitive use of certain architectural, as well as ornamental, forms has, in fact, been a principal theme in this chapter.

When initially faced with the production of religious structures, Islamic designers assimilated and reinterpreted the buildings left around them by the ancient Romans, Sassanians, and others. They derived their conception of the mosque from the form of Mohammed's own house in Medina. Based upon his teachings, they quickly established the sahn (court), haram (prayer hall), qibla (prayer wall), and mihrab (prayer niche) as essential elements. After an initial period of experimentation and depending on the location, they settled on several, regional, mosque-design variations. The columnar or hypostyle mosque, most popular in Arabia and across North Africa, includes numerous ranks and files of columns surrounding a court, with a prayer hall at one end. The iwan mosque, preferred in Iran and farther east, includes a court, possibly with surrounding columns, expanded on three sides by vaulted or domical porches, with one of these porches lying opposite the entry. The domed, central-plan mosques of Turkey begin with a court surrounded by domed bays

7.41 Hall of the Two Sisters, Alhambra, Granada, 13th–14th centuries.
The Muslim fascination with patterning takes on three-dimensional form in muqarnas vaults like this one. While much more elaborate than the results produced by civilizations such as the Mycenaeans (see Figs. 2.8 and 2.9), the vault in the Hall of the Two Sisters still relies on the elementary structural device of corbeling.

and conclude with a domed worship space surrounded by more domed bays. Large Islamic tombs also frequently have central plans, sometimes expanded by porchlike arms.

Gardens for enjoyment as well as the evocation of paradise were sometimes integrated with funerary architecture and with palaces, which is exemplified nowhere better than at the Alhambra, where landscaped courts with water features reflect highly ornamented wall surfaces. Islamic ornamentation is generally prolific, over not only exterior walls but interior ones as well and even across ceilings, where it is integrated with exposed structural elements. Ranging from puzzlelike fields of geometric figures to plant-inspired arabesques to organic or angular calligraphy, this abstracted ornamentation reached a level of invention and sophistication arguably unexcelled by any designers and craftsmen at any other time and in any other place.

Chapter 8

Early Medieval and Romanesque Architecture

While Byzantine and Islamic cultures were flourishing in eastern Europe and around the southern rim of the Mediterranean, those portions of western Europe that had been part of the Roman Empire entered a sustained period of decline. From the first centuries of the Christian era, outposts of the Empire had been repeatedly besieged by waves of nomadic peoples migrating from Central Asia. These tribes, called barbarians by the civilized Romans, eventually overran the frontiers established by Rome and occupied the city of Rome itself by 476. Many place names across Europe preserve the memory of these nomadic tribes. The Franks settled in what eventually became France. The Burgundians in east-central France and the Lombards in northern Italy gave their names to Burgundy and Lombardy, respectively. The Goths and the Visigoths were memorialized in the architectural style called Gothic, and the behavior of the Vandals, who went everywhere and often wreaked havoc, is remembered in the word "vandalism." Gradually the nomads settled down, became converts to Christianity, and attempted to continue Roman governmental traditions, which they greatly admired although they lacked the necessary administrative expertise. The period in western European history extending from the decline of Roman authority until the beginning of the Renaissance (approximately 400 to 1400) is known as the medieval period or the Middle Ages, because historians saw it as a middle era separating antiquity from modern times.

Roman culture was based on city life and depended on a strong central government. In the chaos that accompanied the barbarian invasions, the basic skills required to maintain governmental authority, such as literacy, virtually disappeared. Urban settlements and the money economy that sustained them were replaced by small agricultural units organized by local strongmen, who lived in fortified dwellings and controlled the surrounding land by force of arms. Peasants tilled the land in exchange for meager sustenance and the physical protection afforded them by the strongman's military might. Over the centuries this arrangement of mutual service and protection developed into the feudal system, embracing all levels of society from peasant to king in an intricate social, political, and economic order.

Because feudalism meant a geo-politically fragmented Europe, architectural styles were necessarily regional and even local in character. But this fragmentation did not mean universal architectural parochialism. The popes resided in Rome (with part of the fourteenth century spent in Avignon, France), and the papacy controlled or at least strongly influenced a considerable portion of central Italy. Widespread monastic communities thrived and frequently became centers for architectural innovations, as well as agriculture, education, and religion. From its capital in Constantinople, the Byzantine Court ruled over an ebbing and flowing empire that stretched as far west as Ravenna and exercised influence even more widely through political alliances and dynastic marriages. For Islam, it was a time of geographical expansion, as cultural influences as well as armies from the Middle East swept across Africa and up into Spain, and Islamic incursions constantly threatened Byzantium. In a countercurrent, European Crusaders eventually carved out Christian kingdoms in the Holy Land and so established and maintained transportation routes from west to east. In Italy and southern France, ancient Roman classicism remained highly visible in the form of abandoned and often reoccupied buildings and sites. Most importantly for architectural development, throughout Europe and beginning modestly, even crudely, there arose an almost universal impetus toward fireproof, masonry-vaulted construction for churches and monasteries. Eventually, migrating medieval stonemasons, one of the few groups of individuals within the feudal system allowed to move about fairly freely, made the Middle Ages a period of extensive and extraordinary building construction.

Chronology

Reign of Caesar Augustus	27 BCE–14 CE
End of Roman Empire in the West	476
Defeat of Islamic forces at Tours by Charles Martel	732
Reign of Charlemagne	768–814
Construction of the Palatine Chapel at Aachen	792–805
Charlemagne crowned Holy Roman Emperor	800
Development of the plan of St. Gall	817
Rise of Santiago de Compostela as a pilgrimage site	ca. 900
Founding of the monastery at Cluny	910
Battle of Hastings	1066
Construction of Durham Cathedral	1093–1113

Interior of the nave, Ste. Madeleine, Vézelay, France.
This barrel-vaulted nave is divided into bays by transverse arches constructed of polychromatic masonry. Each arch springs from two colonettes attached to the nave wall. Between the colonettes are arched openings connecting the nave to the side aisles.

CAROLINGIAN ARCHITECTURE

Outside the Italian peninsula and the Mediterranean coast, where Early Christian traditions were maintained in a number of masonry basilicas and baptisteries, very little architecture in western Europe has survived from the period 400–800. Caught in the chaos created by barbarian invasions, most of northern Europe experienced several centuries of unsettled life, during which the stability needed to allow the design and construction of durable buildings was lacking. From the many strongmen who were leaders in the developing feudal system emerged one whose strength and military might enabled him to dominate his rivals. Known as Charles the Great, or Charlemagne, he was the grandson of Charles Martel, the Frank who had led assembled forces to victory over the Islamic army at the battle of Tours in France in 732. During his reign (768–814), Charlemagne unified a large portion of present-day France, the Low Countries, and Germany through a series of successful military campaigns. Charlemagne's influence extended even to Rome where, on Christmas Day in the year 800, Pope Leo III crowned him Holy Roman Emperor. This illiterate descendant of barbarian chieftains had become the spiritual heir of the Roman Empire, the temporal equivalent of the pope.

The Revival of Masonry Construction

Charlemagne aspired to a renaissance of Roman achievements, including the excellence Rome had exhibited in government, literature, and the arts. He summoned the greatest minds to his court, established schools for the training of governmental administrators, had his scribes assemble and copy ancient manuscripts, and encouraged architecture by donating lands and money for the construction of churches and monasteries. The resulting buildings, termed Carolingian (from *Carolus*, the Latin name for Charles), are in many cases based on the Early Christian and Byzantine buildings Charlemagne visited during his travels in Italy. Such was the case with the palace complex built at Aachen (Fig. 8.1). The overall plan is modeled on the Lateran Palace in Rome, with the chapel derived from S. Vitale at Ravenna and the audience hall being a Roman basilica. In keeping with Roman tradition, the whole complex was laid out on a square grid. What survives today is the buildings (or foundations) that were constructed in stone, but there were doubtless wooden buildings that contained living accommodation. Much as Charlemagne and his architects admired Roman buildings, they lacked the construction skills necessary to duplicate them and did not have access to the pozzolana from which the Romans made concrete, so in comparison to their Roman prototypes Carolingian buildings may seem somewhat unrefined. We should not judge these works too severely, however, for Charlemagne was effectively reviving monumental masonry construction in a region that had not built in this way for about half a millennium.

The Palatine Chapel at Aachen (792–805) was designed by Odo of Metz and probably built by Lombard masons using stone salvaged from nearby Roman structures (Figs. 8.2–8.3). A sixteen-sided aisle with a gallery overhead surrounded its central domed octagon. The construction, including barrel- and groin-vaults and an octagonal **cloister vault** in the dome, reflects late Roman practice rather than the Byzantine techniques employed at S. Vitale, and its plan simplifies the complex geometry of the Ravenna building. The main entrance is dominated by a **westwerk**, that is, the western façade including the entrance vestibule, rooms at one or more levels above, and one or more towers. The addition of a westwerk to churches is one of the Carolingian contributions to the Western architectural

8.1 Plan of Charlemagne's palace, Aachen, 792–814.
The sixteen-sided building is the Palatine Chapel, connected by a passageway to a basilican audience hall. Note that the chapel was preceded by a forecourt or atrium. From a loggia at the second level of the chapel, Charlemagne could address an audience assembled there. Only the chapel remains from this ambitious complex.

8.2 Palatine Chapel interior, Aachen, 792–805.
S. Vitale at Ravenna served as a model for this building, but the chapel also
contains original features. The second level was used by Charlemagne and
his court to observe services without interfering with those celebrating holy
offices. This view includes the choir section added in the Gothic period.

8.3 Palatine Chapel, Aachen, 792–805.
The Carolingian building in the center has been modified by the addition of a higher roof over the dome and a Gothic choir and chapels to the left and in the foreground and the westwerk tower to the right. Only the lower wall sections of the central part are authentic from the time of Charlemagne.

8.4 Abbey gatehouse, Lorsch, ca. 800.
Influences from Roman architecture can be seen in the overall form, derived from the triumphal arch, and the arch-and-column motif used on the ground level.

tradition. Early Christian churches featured freestanding **campaniles**, or **belfries**, if they had towers at all, but during the Carolingian period towers were often incorporated as integral components of the church.

The interior of the Palatine Chapel has a heavy effect, particularly the eight great piers that support the dome, but the proportions of the arched openings at the ground and gallery levels are well chosen. Polychrome masonry is used in the semicircular arches of the main floor, while sixteen polished marble columns from the Palace of the Exarchs in Ravenna were hauled over the Alps to be reused in the arcade of the gallery. Locally cast bronze balustrades at the gallery level and mosaics in the dome contributed to the richness of the interior. Charlemagne's throne was set on the gallery level on axis with the altar. As the first domed building north of the Alps since the decline of the Roman

Empire, the Palatine Chapel is comparable in scale, if not in elegance, to S. Vitale, and it reflects Charlemagne's intense desire to revive classical ideals in architecture.

Of the abbey at Lorsch, which was endowed by Charlemagne, only a small freestanding gatehouse now remains (Fig. 8.4). Its architectural precedents can be found in Roman triumphal arches, such as the Arch of Constantine in Rome (see Fig. 5.18), and also at Old St. Peter's in Rome, where a triple-arched pavilion marked the entrance to the atrium. Arches supported with Corinthian columns articulate the gatehouse at Lorsch, and triangular frames in a decorative pattern derived from late Roman sarcophagi surround the second-floor windows. One could never confuse the gatehouse with an actual Roman building, however, for it features such non-classical elements as a steeply pitched roof and decorative red and white tiling. The roof pitch was dictated by the potential snow loads of the northern European climate, while the tiled designs seem to have been devised by local masons, perhaps influenced by Islamic polychromy or Roman opus reticulatum.

Another small building surviving from Carolingian times is the oratory at Germigny-des-Prés (806–10), which was built for Theodulf, Bishop of Orleans, Abbot of Fleury, and close advisor to Charlemagne (Figs. 8.5–8.7). Conceived as a private chapel for quiet reflection and prayer, the oratory was designed with a Greek-cross plan and a square central tower. (Compare this plan to that of a Byzantine cross-in-square scheme as shown in Fig. 6.22.) Horseshoe arches are found in both plan and elevation.

8.6 (below) Plan of the Oratory, Germigny-des-Prés, 806–10.
This plan, comparable to the Byzantine quincunx, reflects connections between the Carolingian court and Constantinople.

8.5 (above) Oratory, Germigny-des-Prés, 806–10.
This small, centrally planned building combines elements from Byzantium (the central plan and an apse mosaic) with horseshoe arches found in Islamic work in Spain and the semicircular arch of Roman work.

8.7 (below) Interior of the Oratory, Germigny-des-Prés, 806–10.
This view of the crossing and apse shows that the horseshoe shape is used both in elevation and plan.

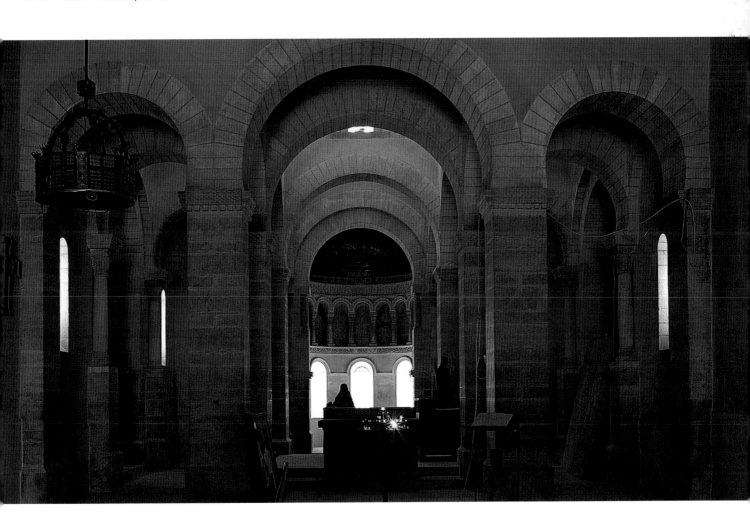

Together with the centralized plan, these suggest influence from Mozarabic churches (those in which art and architecture was produced by Christians under Islamic rule) in Muslim-dominated Spain. This assumption is made more plausible by the fact that Theodulf was from Septimania, the area between present-day France and Spain along the Mediterranean coast. Rather surprisingly, the oratory also has a magnificent mosaic depicting the Ark of the Covenant in the eastern apse, the technique and style of which both indicate artistic contributions from Byzantium. In these few surviving Carolingian buildings, one can thus trace elements from Roman, Early Christian, Byzantine, Islamic, and northern European civilizations, combined in what must be seen as the beginnings of an architecture unique to western Europe.

Monasteries

Charlemagne's unifying work did not long survive him. In 843, on the death of his son and heir, Louis the Pious, the Carolingian Empire was divided among Charlemagne's three grandsons. Governmental power in western Europe gradually reverted to the hands of local or regional lords. The one cohesive social institution that transcended regional groups was the Church, which organized medieval Europe into ecclesiastical dioceses, each administered by a bishop. The seat of episcopal authority was frequently a town that had been a Roman provincial center, and there was much of Roman governmental structure preserved in the organization of the Church.

Complementary to the town-based diocesan units were the largely rural monasteries that grew and flourished widely during the medieval period. Charlemagne had encouraged their establishment as a matter of practical policy for the settlement of conquered territories, in addition to their spiritual and educational contributions. Few institutions had as extensive an impact on the architecture of the medieval period as monasticism. Indeed, it would be difficult to discuss almost any aspect of medieval history and culture without considering the role played by monks of the various orders. Medieval society was divided broadly into three classes: those who fought (the land-owning lords and knights); those who labored (the peasants); and those who prayed (the priests and monks). The work of each was considered essential to the well-being of all. Prayers of the monks were particularly necessary, it was thought, to provide a never-ending flow of praise to propitiate a God who was justifiably wrathful about humanity's errant ways. Medieval Christians considered their heavenly Lord to be as susceptible to flattery as his earthly counterpart.

The concept of monasticism, the withdrawal from the corruption of everyday life in order to contemplate things spiritual, originated in fourth-century Egypt, where Christian hermits led solitary lives in the desert wilderness. At about the same time, the idea developed that groups of monks might live together communally, and both the hermitic and communal forms of monasticism spread rapidly from Egypt to the edges of the Christian world. Irish monks were active from 432 until 793, when Viking raiders destroyed their settlements. Communal forms of monasticism became the dominant models for the organization of Western monasticism, while hermits continued to be common in the Eastern Church. In most cases, twelve monks and an abbot were sufficient to found a monastery, and the monks often selected remote sites for building. Their major requirement was a reliable water supply. During the Middle Ages, new monastic foundations eventually numbered in the thousands. Monastery schools brought learning to every part of Europe, and monastic building and farming enterprises preserved and advanced the best in architecture, the arts, and agriculture. Medieval civilization throughout western Europe was achieved in no small measure through the work of the monks.

Charlemagne's interest in centralizing and standardizing administration extended to religious institutions. After examining several models of monastic organization, he required that all monasteries within his realm should follow the Rule of St. Benedict, a flexible but rather specific set of regulations formulated by Benedict of Nursia in around 535 for monks living communally under the direction of an abbot. (St. Benedict's precepts relating to the organization and management of a monastery were called a "Rule" because they regulated the lives of those who followed them.) The monastic life of prayer, contemplation, and mental and manual work, marked by poverty, chastity, and obedience, was intended to emulate the example of Christ. In 817 abbots from leading Carolingian monasteries held a conference to resolve differences in interpretation of the Benedictine Rule. Out of its discussions came a document detailing a model layout for a Benedictine **abbey**. We know of this drawing through a copy sent to the abbot of the monastery of St. Gall, where the plan remained in the abbey's library until rediscovered in the eighteenth century (Fig. 8.8). Known now as the Plan of St. Gall, this manuscript is the oldest surviving architectural drawing from the medieval period, and from it modern scholars Walter Horn and Ernest Born have deduced much about monastic life and building practices in the Carolingian age.

The Plan of St. Gall clearly sets forth the major components of a self-sufficient religious community. The largest building was the church, a double-ended basilica in plan, with a western hemicycle flanked by twin cylindrical towers. Inside the masonry-walled and timber truss-roofed church was the worship space for the monks. Altars were located throughout the nave, transepts, and apse, as medieval religious practice, which placed growing importance on the veneration of relics, required multiple altars to honor individual saints. On the south side of the church was the **cloister**, 100 feet square, surrounded by a covered, arcaded walk connecting the major buildings on its sides: the **chapter house**, workroom, and warming room below

Garden for medicinal plants

Physician's house

Kitchen and baths for medical units

House for bloodletting

Sacristy

Library

Abbot's house

Reception for visiting monks

External school

Distinguished guest house

Caretaker's lodge

Kitchen for guest house

Probably quarters for retinue of distinguished guests

Infirmary

Novitiate

Kitchen and bath

Orchard and cemetery

Kitchen garden

Geese

Fowlkeeper's lodge

Gardener's house

Chickens

Chapel

Chapel

Dormitory

Latrines

Barn

Bath

Refectory

Craft workshops

Church

Cloister

Bakery

Mill

Brew house

Wine press

Kitchen

Malt kiln

Cooper

Granary

Parlor

Wine and beer storage

Hostel

Bulls

Stable

Bake and brew house for pilgrims

Sheep

Goats

Cows

Barns and stables for animals

Servants

Pigs

Horses

N

8.8 Plan of St. Gall, ca. 817.
This drawing sets forth the major elements of a Benedictine monastery, establishing a model that would be used for the next 400 or more years as the basis for monastic design.

8.9 Cutaway axonometric view showing the cloister, St. Gall, ca. 817.
Visible around the cloister are the monks' beds in the dormitory to the east (right), the tables in the refectory to the south (bottom), and the casks of wine or beer in the room to the west (left), with the south side of the church in the background.

the dormitory on the east; the refectory (dining hall) on the south; and the cellar or storeroom on the west (Fig. 8.9). A stairway connected the dormitory with the south transept since the monks arose at 2 a.m. for Matins, returning to sleep until Lauds at daybreak. Six more services—Prime, Terce, Sext, None, Vespers, and Compline—completed the daily cycle.

By counting the beds drawn on the plan, Horn and Born have concluded that the monastery was designed for approximately 110 monks. Service buildings were grouped outside the cloister and staffed by an additional 130 to 150 workmen and servants necessary to provide for the monastery's sustenance. A bake and brew house, artisan craft workshops, and a complete working farm, with pens or barns for goats, geese, pigs, horses, and cows, are indicated on the plan to the south and west of the cloister, although their actual arrangement on the land would doubtless have been adjusted to the location of fields and pasture. They are grouped here to have all the buildings fit on the parchment. To the east of the church, the plan indicates a miniature double cloister to house the novitiate and the infirmary, together with a house for two physicians, a medicinal herb garden, and the cemetery. On the north side of the church was the abbot's house, connected to the transept by a passage. As the administrator and spiritual leader of the monastery, the abbot was responsible for the management of the monastery's life, and as its representative to the outside world he was charged with public relations and with providing hospitality for distinguished guests. Adjacent to the abbot's house were the external school, required by Charlemagne's decree to provide education for young men

not intending to become monks, and the guesthouse and stables for high-ranking visitors. The more common sort of traveler would be cared for by the almoner at the cloister gate to the south of the church entrance.

Through its clear ordering of the practical requirements for a monastic community, the Plan of St. Gall encapsulates the high quality of functional planning achieved by Carolingian architects. While no monastery ever built followed the Plan of St. Gall precisely, its general disposition of monastic buildings was employed in Benedictine abbeys throughout the medieval period.

VIKING ARCHITECTURE

The Vikings, also known as Danes or Norsemen, both terrorized western Europe and served as intrepid explorers and traders, maintaining contacts with places as remote as Constantinople. (Recall that one of their number, Rurik, was invited in 856 to become the founder of the ruling family in Russia, and that Leif Ericsson led an expedition that reached the North American continent in about 1003.) In Britain, they harried the Anglo-Saxon kingdoms, occupying the whole of East Anglia and land as far north as York, which became a Viking city. The Danes extracted annual payments (the danegeld) from territories under their control, while also profiting from organized piracy on the cities of Europe. When shallow-draft, swift Viking ships sailed or rowed up the navigable rivers along which medieval settlements clustered, the burning, looting, and massacre visited on these communities only added to the instability of the time.

The artistic legacy of the Vikings is best seen in smaller objects, including jewelry, ceremonial and household objects, and military regalia, which are adorned with intricate interlaced ornament based on stylized plant and animal forms (hence its name, the Animal Style), an artistic tradition that has links to the fierce Scythians who came from the steppes of Central Asia. Interlace ornament finds its way into Romanesque architectural decoration.

Scandinavia itself remained outside the Christian sphere until the middle of the eleventh century, when Anglo-Saxon missionaries who returned with Viking raiders from England succeeded in converting the vigorous pagans of Norway. The missionaries brought knowledge of Anglo-Saxon church architecture with them, so the simple plans of parish churches in Britain, themselves based on Early Christian precedent, became the models for equally small Norwegian churches. The combination of these simple plans with native building traditions created a unique and distinctive architecture, the **stave** church, or narrow-board church.

The church at Urnes, Norway, the oldest extant stave church, dates from about 1125–40, and its design illustrates the type (Figs. 8.10, 8.11a, 8.12). The staves are upright poles, usually pine trees from which the bark has

8.10 Stave church, Urnes, Norway, ca. 1125–40.
Building volumes reflect plain elements: the tall nave with lower aisles, the rear choir, and apse extension each have a separate expression.

been removed, that form the basic structure for the building. They are supported on four crossed horizontal sills forming a rectangular chassis. The chassis is raised off the ground by large flat stones at the intersections of the sill planks because excavated foundations would have been subject to heaving as the ground froze and thawed. These corner stones also protect the timber structure by isolating it from ground moisture. Low exterior walls, made of vertical boarding anchored by rounded corner posts, rest on an outer chassis sill supported on the short cantilevered ends

of the main chassis, while the upper wall, braced above head height by one or more clamping beams that encircle the staves, follows the vertical line of the stave frame up to the roof rafters. A cupola completes the roof ridge visually, although it has no connection to the interior space. The major structural elements, the staves, are kept dry by shorter exterior boards that are renewed from time to time as required. Urnes and other stave churches are very dark inside, for the original design had no windows, depending instead for light and ventilation on small circular openings (wind-eyes) located high in the walls. Scandinavia and Anglo-Saxon Britain are the major places where one finds wooden buildings constructed of upright staves rather than horizontal logs. It is interesting to note that the stave church at Greensted was associated with a Viking settlement.

Stave

Wooden
sill plates

Carved portal
(see Fig. 8.12)

8.10

Turret

Wind-eye

Gallery

8.11a (left) Plan (north to the top) of section through the stave church, Urnes, Norway, ca. 1125–40.
The foundation of the building is a rectangular grid of wooden sill plates laid on foundation stones resting on the ground. On this chassis rest the ends of upright poles or staves that form the vertical structure of the church. The tower shown in Fig. 8.10 is not included in the section.

8.11b (bottom left) Plan of and section through the stave church, Borgund, Norway, ca. 1150.
Like Urnes, the Borgund church relies on small openings, or wind-eyes, high in the wall to admit light and air, and to relieve wind pressure against the sides of the structure.

8.12 (below) Carved portal from an earlier church at Urnes, ca. 1015.
This portal is now preserved on the north wall of the present church. The intertwined snakes and dragons represent the end of the world according to the Norse legend of Ragnarok. Christian missionaries substituted this local imagery for the Last Judgment as a way of making Christian teaching more accessible.

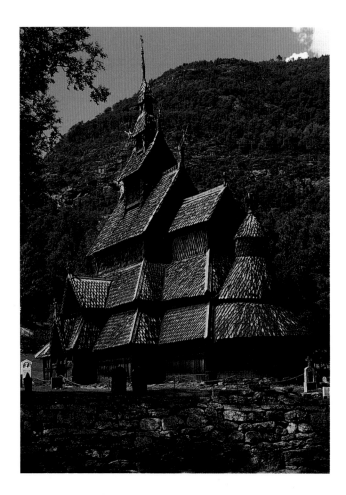

8.13 Stave church, Borgund, Norway, ca. 1150.
While this church looks considerably more elaborate than
that at Urnes, it is fundamentally the same in structure,
but with additional roof turrets and an external gallery
at the base.

Cupola

Roof truss

Horizontal arch

Diagonal bracing

Clamping beams

Stave

Sill

8.14 Diagram showing the construction of a stave church.
The church illustrated here comes from Gol, one of
a number of stave churches that were restored in the
twentieth century according to features seen in the
church at Borgund.

Urnes also possesses a remarkable carved portal, now
located on the north wall of the church, which probably
belonged to a previous church of about 1015 built on the
same site (Fig. 8.12). Bands of boldly undercut figures,
carved from single planks of wood, represent four-legged
beasts and serpentlike animals intertwined in intricate
patterns with a scrolling vine. The similarity of this work
to Animal Style ornament is immediately apparent. What
is less clear at first glance is why such carving should be
found as ornament around a church doorway. Although
no documents provide absolute proof, scholars believe
that these figures represent a carry-over from the pagan
past applied to the fresh purposes of the Christian faith.
In Norse mythology, the end of the world was to come
when snakes and dragons, representing the forces of evil,
were locked in mortal combat. Known as Ragnarok, this
struggle was the Norse equivalent of the Christian Last
Judgment, which became established as a subject for sculpture on the doorways of churches in other parts of Europe.
The best explanation for the snakes and dragons on stave
churches seems to be that in Norway, as elsewhere, early

missionaries found it convenient to adapt established traditions to the causes of the Christian Church.

Stave churches were widely constructed in the sparsely
populated and isolated valley communities along the
fjords of Norway. As late as the nineteenth century, 322
such buildings could be documented through remains
or textual references, but today only thirty-two survive.
The church at Borgund, dated to about 1150, probably
represents the most authentic mature stave church, and
aspects of its form and detail have served as models for
the restoration of other stave churches that were not so
fortunate in preserving their original character across the
centuries (Figs. 8.11b, 8.13–8.14). Borgund began much as
Urnes did, but in the thirteenth century it was embellished
with an external gallery and elaborate turret that give it
a more complex profile. Crosses and dragons were placed
on the ends of the roof gables to protect the church
from the powers of darkness as pagan forces, though
banished by Christianity to remote areas, still remained a
potential menace to be countered by these prominently
displayed symbols.

EARLY ROMANESQUE ARCHITECTURE

The monastery of St. Martin at Canigou (1001–26) in southwestern France survives as an example of the process by which monasticism spread, and its buildings illustrate architectural accomplishments of the early Romanesque period (Figs. 8.15–8.16). Its patron, the Count of Cerdagne, landlord of this mountainous territory in the Pyrenees, endowed the monastery on a rocky outcrop to expiate his sins. Although it never housed more than about thirty monks, its place in the history of architecture is assured because it has survived, with the aid of an entirely sympathetic twentieth-century restoration, as one of the earliest completely vaulted Romanesque churches. In plan the church is a basilica without transepts but with semicircular apses terminating the aisles and nave. The barrel vaults of the nave and aisles rest on ten supports—eight stubby columns and two grouped piers—and the solid exterior walls (Fig. 8.17). The only natural light enters through small windows at the east and west ends, resulting in a very dark interior. On the exterior, the entire monastery forms a harmonious composition. A square-plan tower abuts the side of the church, guarding the entrance to the abbey, while the cloister and its related buildings form an irregular quadrangle on the limited building site rather than the neat square indicated on the Plan of St. Gall. The stone construction is simple, articulated primarily by semicircular arches used over windows and also set as surface relief in horizontal bands. The stepped crenelations atop the tower recall Islamic fortifications found in neighboring Spain.

St. Martin at Canigou exemplifies the early Romanesque style. As the name implies, Romanesque buildings have a certain affinity with Roman architecture, primarily because they tend to employ the semicircular or Roman arch. Beyond this simple generalization (which itself is not always true), it is difficult to characterize Romanesque buildings with great precision. The style flourished from around 1000 to 1250. Romanesque buildings tend to be massive and heavy. The construction problem that Romanesque builders set for themselves, that of efficiently supporting a ceiling made entirely of small stones, posed a real challenge and encouraged varied approaches according to the materials available, the experience of the builder, and the ambitions of the patron. It is perhaps easiest to understand the Romanesque as a great series of experiments directed toward enclosing and illuminating interior space, using incombustible masonry construction to reduce the chances of fire and thus protect the valuable relics held in churches.

Most Romanesque buildings rely on the mass of continuous walls to sustain the weight of the vaulting overhead. Medieval builders could not make structural calculations as we can today. (Indeed, the systematic study of materials and structural theory was not sufficiently advanced to be applied to ordinary buildings until about 1850.) Trial

8.15 St. Martin at Canigou, monastery, 1001–26.
Founded as a pious act by the Count of Cerdagne, this monastery sits on a mountainous site that is difficult to reach even today. The presence of a freely running spring made habitation possible here, and a small monastic community continues to occupy the buildings.

and error based on previous projects formed the basis of building practice. Yet within the span of 150 years the structural experiments of hundreds of Romanesque builders led to the refined masonry techniques that made Gothic architecture possible. It was a long process, however, for the semicircular arch is not a particularly efficient structural element. The Romans had employed it extensively for its esthetic qualities and ease of construction (the

ower ————

arrel vault ——

Aisle ——

Nave ——

ower church ——

Cloister ——

8.15

8.17

0   10 m

0   30 ft

8.16 Cutaway axonometric view of the church and cloister, St. Martin at Canigou, 1001–26.
The church has two levels, both vaulted. Romanesque architects had to rediscover building techniques used by the Romans, and here one gets a sense of their struggle to produce durable and fireproof construction.

arch scaffolding or centering is relatively uncomplicated to build), qualities that doubtless recommended it to Romanesque architects as well, even though the outward, overturning thrust it generated caused problems, which were commonly resolved by building massive supporting walls. Since openings could weaken the supporting wall, Romanesque builders used windows very sparingly to avoid challenging the structure's integrity. The semicircular arch, the barrel vault, and the groin vault (two barrel vaults intersecting at right angles—see Fig. 0.5) also imposed geometric constraints. Square or rectangular bays could be handled easily, while irregular or circular sections posed esthetic and structural difficulties.

8.17 St. Martin at Canigou interior, 1001–26.
Windows are minimal, for every opening cut into the wall weakened the structure. Since the monks knew the services by heart, dim light levels inside the church were not a problem.

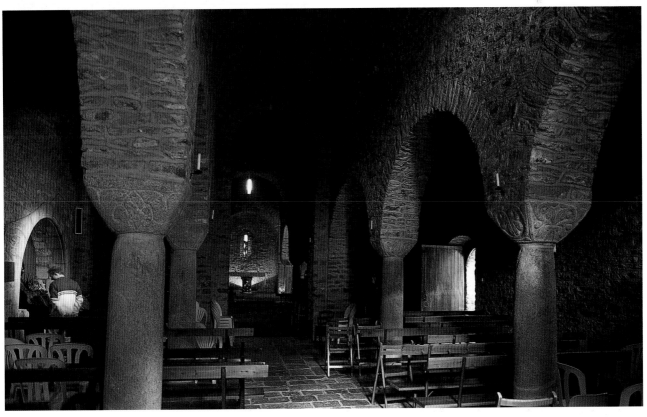

ROMANESQUE ARCHITECTURE OF THE HOLY ROMAN EMPIRE

The middle portion of Charlemagne's empire, corresponding roughly to modern Germany and northern Italy, eventually came under the control of the vigorous House of Saxony, whose three successive heads each named Otto gained the title of Holy Roman Emperor in the course of their capable leadership. Their rule, termed Ottonian, extended from 936 to 1002, but its effects lasted nearly a century longer.

Ottonian architecture is in many respects an extension of Carolingian traditions: it is the German expression of Romanesque. An outstanding example is the Ottonian church of St. Michael at Hildesheim (1010–33), which is a double-ended basilica with entrances along the side aisles as in many original Roman basilicas (Fig. 8.18). Its two apses also recall the general church layout indicated on the Plan of St. Gall. On the interior (Fig. 8.19), the eastern apse contains the altar, and the western apse contains a raised platform for seating the emperor and his court. Illumination is provided by clerestories, simple punched openings in the unarticulated nave wall, while the supporting nave arcade has a subtle A-B-B-A rhythm established by piers alternating with two columns. Polychrome arches, boldly carved column capitals suggestive of Italian examples, and an elaborately painted wooden ceiling enrich the interior.

Slightly later than St. Michael at Hildesheim is the spacious imperial cathedral at Speyer, built about 1030 and revised in three successive building campaigns until 1082 (Figs. 8.18, 8.20–8.21). It is a massive and majestic construction, extending over 425 feet from the thick walls of its imposing westwerk to the semicircular apse flanked by a pair of square-plan towers. The nave is wide, long, and tall, framed by semicircular arches surrounding each wall bay. Covered at first by a flat wooden ceiling, the nave received groin vaults set over paired bays and separated by **transverse arch** bands in the course of building activity from 1082 to 1137. At 107 feet above the floor, these vaults rank as the highest built in the Romanesque period and approach the accomplishments of Roman construction. The piers become compound assemblies of projecting pilasters and colonettes between sometimes-recessed arched openings. Interior decoration is restrained, even severe, with the variegated warm yellow-to-pink hues of the stone enlivening the surfaces of walls and piers. Influences from Lombardy are seen in the cubiform capitals of the crypt and the Lombard bands (corbel arch tables and pilaster strips) of the exterior wall.

In the southern regions of the Holy Roman Empire, the classical heritage of Rome heavily influenced Romanesque architecture. Italian cities developed their own versions of Romanesque architecture, retaining a strong reliance on the classical past with little influence from northern Europe. In general, the Early Christian basilica remained the standard

Speyer Cathedral

St. Philibert, Tournus

Chapel for relics below

Ambulatory

Transverse barrel vaults above

St. Michael, Hildesheim

8.18 **Plans of Speyer Cathedral, ca. 1030–82; St. Philibert, Tournus, ca. 950–1120; and St. Michael, Hildesheim, 1010–33.** Speyer Cathedral was one of the most ambitious Romanesque buildings of its time, with groin vaults on a scale with major Roman baths. St. Philibert is notable for its radiating chapels off an ambulatory and transverse barrel vaults in the nave. St. Michael is an interesting example of a double-ended basilica with wooden roofing.

8.19 (left) **St. Michael interior, Hildesheim, 1010–33.**
The square module that governs much of the plan is defined by the piers and the bay under the eastern tower, outlined by bold polychrome arches.

8.20 (below left) **Speyer Cathedral east end, ca. 1030–82.**
Speyer is distinguished by its large scale and multiple towers. The two seen here are set at the junction of choir and transepts, and they are taller than the dome over the crossing. Note the use of Lombard bands.

8.21 (below) **Speyer Cathedral nave, interior looking east, ca. 1030–82.**
The groin vaults were erected in 1082–1137, making this one of the highest vaulted churches of its time.

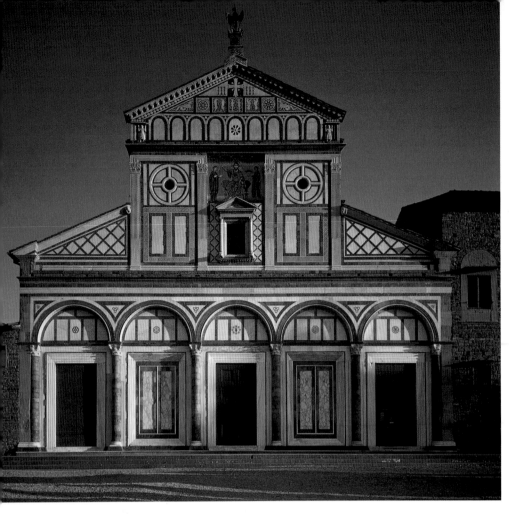

8.22 S. Miniato al Monte west front, Florence, 1062–90.
This façade would not have seemed strange to the ancient Romans, for it continues the use of marble veneers in geometric patterns combined with arch-and-column motifs familiar from the classical past.

8.23 (below) Plans of S. Ambrogio, Milan, ca. 1080–1140; S. Miniato al Monte, Florence, 1062–90; and Pisa Cathedral, 1063.
S. Miniato preserves the plan of simple Early Christian basilicas. S. Ambrogio includes an atrium and two separate campaniles, while the cathedral at Pisa has a cruciform plan, with transepts that are treated as smaller basilicas. Pisa's oval crossing dome provided the impetus for Florence to attempt an even more ambitious dome for its cathedral.

S. Ambrogio, Milan

S. Miniato al Monte, Florence

Pisa Cathedral

church form, seldom having a westwerk or attached towers as in Ottonian or Carolingian architecture. The church of S. Miniato al Monte in Florence (1062–90 and later) is typical (Figs. 8.22–8.24). A single pair of aisles flanks the transeptless nave, which is terminated by a simple semicircular apse. Alternate bays of the nave are grouped by diaphragm arches (where a wall is built to create a level, horizontal top), above which wooden trusses support the roof. Its façade is articulated on the ground level by five arches supported by Corinthian half-columns, with Corinthian pilasters and a gable defining the roof of the nave. Geometric patterns set in marble veneers enliven the essentially flat wall plane, and the entire elevation clearly follows the profile of the basilican space behind it.

The freestanding cathedral at Pisa (begun in 1063 and finished 1089–1272) is more elaborate, although still close to Early Christian tradition (Figs. 8.23, 8.25). In plan the cruciform basilica has double aisles and galleries flanking the nave, and single aisles and galleries flanking the transepts. At the crossing, an oval dome is raised on squinches and shallow pendentives, recalling the centralized church plans of Byzantium, while wooden trusses roof the remainder of the church. The exterior is articulated with marble arcades, stacked row on row across the western façade and continuing around the church. The interior is marked by polychromy, in this case alternate courses of dark and light marble set in horizontal bands, and there are Byzantine mosaics in the apse. The cathedral is complemented by two adjacent structures, a circular

8.24 S. Miniato al Monte interior, Florence, 1062–90 and later.
During the Romanesque period Italian churches frequently had wooden roofs like this one. Like the façade, the interior walls depend for their effect on a veneer of polychromatic marble that allows for the creation of complex geometric patterning.

8.25 Pisa Cathedral west front, 1063; 1089–1272.
Marble arches and columns march around the building, which is further enriched with alternating bands of dark- and light-colored marble. The campanile is better known as the Leaning Tower of Pisa, a building that has never been vertical because of difficult foundation conditions.

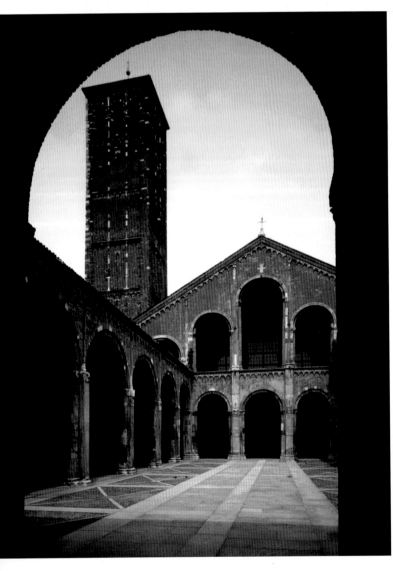

8.26 (left) S. Ambrogio interior, Milan, ca. 1080–1140.
The wide bays of this church have groin vaults to which brick ribs have been added along the line of the arris. Note that the use of corbeled arches continues on the interior.

8.27 (below left) S. Ambrogio west front, Milan, ca. 1080–1140.
The façade and atrium are ornamented with the rows of corbeled arches known as Lombard bands. Lombard work may be seen in Romanesque buildings found in many parts of Europe, as Lombard masons traveled and built widely. Notice also the attenuated colonnettes.

baptistery and a cylindrical campanile, the famous Leaning Tower of Pisa, now over thirteen feet out of plumb.

In the northern Italian region known as Lombardy, the outstanding Romanesque building is the abbey church of S. Ambrogio in Milan (Figs. 8.23, 8.26–8.27). The dates of this important monument are still a matter of scholarly debate. Research indicates that work on the present brick structure began in around 1080, and the nave was begun after 1128. The **rib vaults** of the nave were probably built in about 1140. In plan S. Ambrogio continues Early Christian practice. An arcaded atrium precedes the church proper, and a semicircular apse and smaller semicircular chapels at the ends of the groin-vaulted aisles terminate the transeptless basilica. Galleries over the aisles help buttress the thrust of the nave vaults, but they preclude the possibility of clerestory lighting.

PILGRIMAGE ROAD CHURCHES

In addition to monasticism, the medieval period was marked by another important religious institution: pilgrimage. To atone for sins, seek a cure, or assure salvation, medieval men and women traveled as pilgrims to shrines containing the relics of saints. All churches established since Carolingian times were required to possess relics for each altar, providing local, regional, or international opportunities for pilgrimages. Jerusalem and Rome were the most celebrated centers, but they were also the most expensive and hazardous for northern Europeans to visit.

Around the year 900 a new center for pilgrimage arose to rival the popularity of Rome and Jerusalem, the shrine of the apostle James (Iago in Spanish), located at Compostela in northwestern Spain. With considerable assistance from the Church, Compostela became the goal for thousands of pilgrims as stories of miracles wrought by St. James encouraged people from all parts of Europe to visit his tomb and pray for his assistance. Gradually an entire network of roads and hospices developed to support the growing tide of pilgrims traveling to Compostela. Monasteries, the traditional centers of hospitality for travelers, found the increasing numbers of visitors disruptive to their prescribed cycle of services. The monks accommodated these pilgrims by modifying the basilican church plan to include an ambulatory, like that found at

Transept

Nave   Aisle

Chapels

Ambulatory

8.29

front
's

Choir

Crossing

St. Sernin, Toulouse

8.33   8.32

St. Foy,
Conques

St. James, Compostela

0   50 m
0   150 ft

8.28 (above) **Plans of St. Sernin, Toulouse, ca. 1077–1119; St. Foy, Conques, ca. 1050–1130; and St. James, Compostela, ca. 1075–1211.** All three of these churches are located along the pilgrimage routes to Santiago de Compostela, and they share common traits, including aisles linking to an ambulatory and so providing a continuous path for pilgrims to access relics in the chapels.

8.29 St. Sernin interior, Toulouse, ca. 1077–1119. The colonnettes, or attenuated columns attached to the nave piers, rise to support the transverse arches. The resulting ensemble is extremely dramatic when seen in perspective.

Transverse arch

Quadrant vault

Colonnette

Gallery

Groin vault

Nave

Aisles

8.30 Worm's-eye axonometric view of St. Sernin, Toulouse. The paired aisle vaults work together with the gallery vaults over the inmost aisle to brace the thrust from the high barrel vaults with transverse arches in the nave and choir.

St. Philibert at Tournus (see Fig. 8.18), which worked as an extension of the aisles to provide a continuous passageway around the entire church. At the east end, radiating chapels opened off the ambulatory, and there were sometimes additional chapels located on the east side of the transepts for use by monks who were also ordained clergy. These chapel altars could also be visited by pilgrims without interrupting monastic services being sung in the **choir**.

Churches built in response to the pilgrimage are common on the major roads to Compostela. Five of the largest are so similar in plan, scale, and architectural detail that they illustrate strikingly the transmission of artistic ideas up and down the roads. The oldest of the five was St. Martin at Tours (now destroyed), where a rebuilding of the apse as early as 918 introduced the scheme of radiating chapels and ambulatory attached to a large nave and spacious transepts. By the middle of the eleventh century, this theme had been picked up by the churches of St. Martial at Limoges (now also demolished), St. Foy at Conques, St. Sernin at Toulouse, and St. James at Compostela, producing a series of buildings with an unmistakable family resemblance (Fig. 8.28).

8.31 (above) St. Foy, Conques, ca. 1050–1130.
Set in a remote mountain valley, this is the smallest of the great pilgrimage road churches. Site restrictions limited the length of the building.

8.32 (right) St. Foy crossing, Conques, ca. 1050–1130.
This view shows the gallery over the aisle and the squinches supporting the crossing lantern. Placement of the altar at the crossing is modern; the medieval altar was set in the choir.

The church of St. Sernin at Toulouse clearly illustrates the group (Fig. 8.29). St. Sernin remains a major monument of the Romanesque even though its west front was never finished and its crossing tower was greatly enlarged in the Gothic period. Begun in about 1077, the choir was consecrated in 1096, and the transepts and nave were probably complete, except for the vaulting, by 1119. In plan the church has paired aisles on each side of the nave, four chapels on the east of the large transept, and five radiating chapels around the apse. At nearly 360 feet it is a long building, with a width of nave and aisles totaling about 100 feet, spaciousness that may have been inspired by Old St. Peter's in Rome. The barrel vaults, with transverse arches supported by colonnettes, or columns conceptually captive in the wall, rise about sixty-five feet and are braced by second-floor galleries over the inner pair of aisles (Fig. 8.30). This organization gives the church a triangular cross-section, but precludes the insertion of clerestory windows to light the nave directly. Windows at the east end and light from the windows in the crossing tower provide relative brilliance near the altar in contrast to the dim light of the nave. The exterior arrangement of chapels, ambulatory, and choir rising to the great crossing tower is harmoniously composed, and the ensemble is enhanced by its construction materials, red brick trimmed with stone.

St. Foy at Conques in a remote region of central France is the smallest of the pilgrimage-road churches examined here (Figs. 8.31–8.32). In plan it has only a single pair of aisles and galleries flanking the nave, but its structural scheme is identical to that at St. Sernin. Over the crossing is an octagonal **lantern** built on a squinch, a series of corbeled arches that makes the transition from a square bay to an octagon. (Pendentives as seen at Hagia Sophia do the same thing in a different geometric configuration, but the squinch is more commonly found in Western buildings.) St. Foy preserves on its **tympanum** (the semicircular panel created under the arch of a doorway) a magnificent sculpture (ca. 1140) of the Last Judgment (Figs. 8.33–8.34), including visions of heaven and hell. Christ the judge sits at the center, the largest figure because he is the most important. On his right (the viewer's left) is a line of people

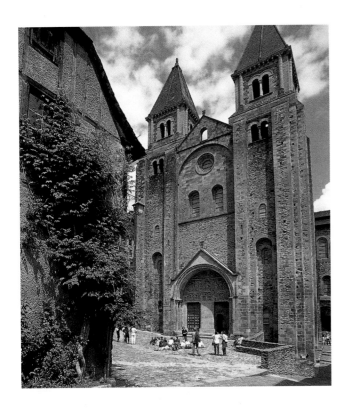

8.33 (left) St. Foy west front, Conques, ca. 1050–1130.
This view shows the large tympanum depicting the Last
Judgment set over the doors. Church authorities used
sculptures such as this one to communicate Christian
teachings to a largely illiterate public.

8.34 (below) St. Foy tympanum, Conques, ca. 1140.
Here we see Christ as the large central figure. Heaven
is depicted at the lower left, while the varied torments
of hell occupy the corresponding position on the right.
Persons awaiting judgment line up on Christ's right hand.

appearing at Judgment Day, led by Mary, St. Peter (carrying
the key), and Church personages escorting Charlemagne
and his family, who are remembered because they gave
money to build earlier churches on the site. Under Christ's
feet is the weighing of souls, and on the lintel at the left is
the serenity of heaven, where the architecture, fittingly, is
Romanesque. On the right lintel is a more active scene of
hell, entered through the mouth of the monster Leviathan.
Presiding over various punishments is the devil, identifiable by his spiked hairstyle and assisted by reptilian
minions. Close observation reveals that the Seven Deadly
Sins, among other transgressions, are rewarded by appropriate punishments, graphically illustrating the concept
that Dante would use centuries later in the *Divine Comedy*.
Those entering the church could not fail to understand
the connection between their actions and their fates in the

world hereafter. This tympanum, like most Romanesque
sculpture, had a strong didactic purpose in addition to its
decorative role.

At Compostela, the church of St. James still functions
as a major pilgrim shrine. It was planned with a full complement of nine towers: one at the crossing, pairs at the
entrances (west front, south and north transepts), and two
more flanking the intersection of nave and transepts (see
Fig. 8.28). At the east end is an axial chapel with a door
to the plaza outside that is opened on jubilee years (those
years when St. James's Day, July 25, falls on a Sunday or
other years as declared by the Church) so that the faithful may enter directly from the east. All three of these
churches—St. Sernin, St. Foy, and St. James—reflect the
religious devotion that for centuries has motivated pilgrims
to travel great distances in search of the holy.

THE ORDER OF CLUNY

In 910, Duke William of Aquitaine, desiring to atone for his less than saintly life and seek divine favor, endowed a monastery on his lands at Cluny, where there was a Gallo-Roman villa or farm. Through an unusual provision in its charter, the new monastery was exempted from the jurisdiction of the local bishop and made directly responsible to the pope. Twelve monks, led by Abbot Berno, came to Cluny seeking a stricter observance of the Benedictine Rule, and their monastery prospered. The exemplary life of its monks attracted more converts and bequests; its position in Burgundy on the route from Paris to Rome and its virtual independence from local religious authorities allowed it to grow into an influential organization, with 1450 abbeys and priories all over Europe; and the exceptional leadership and longevity of its early abbots brought distinction to the Congregation and Order of Cluny. By 1088, the church and monastic complex (known as Cluny II), built after the original villa had been outgrown, had also become too small, and a new church (known to historians as Cluny III) was begun to accommodate the ever-increasing number of monks.

The church of Cluny III (Figs. 8.35–8.37) had the features of mature Romanesque architecture, for it was appropriate to the monastery's importance that its major church should be the largest and most splendid in Christendom. Based on the basilican plan, the church was enriched by a double set of transepts and further augmented by a series of radiating chapels around the apse and eastern walls of the transepts. The nave, 100 feet high and 496 feet long, was large enough to accommodate impressive processions and was flanked by two aisles on each side, the innermost

pair of which continued around the choir as an ambulatory, linking the five radiating chapels of the east end. On the exterior, each of the plan elements was clearly expressed as an individual volume, but all were beautifully integrated into a coherent whole. Towers provided vertical emphasis: a pair at the western entrance, one over each arm of the major transept, the highest tower at the intersection of the major transept and nave, and a shorter tower over the crossing of the minor transept. Viewed from the east, the church appeared as a triangular mass, with roofs ascending from the chapels to the ambulatory, the apse semidome, the minor crossing tower, and finally the major crossing tower. Inside, the effect was even more wonderful, for the sanctuary was filled with light from the many windows in the chapels and clerestories. Images of how this may have appeared come largely from the research of Kenneth John Conant, since the actual church of Cluny III was dismantled for its stone after the French Revolution. Only the south arm of the major transept remains (Fig. 8.38).

Considered from the standpoint of structure, Cluny III shows the great progress made in building art since the completion of St. Martin at Canigou. The paired aisles, which stepped down in height, buttressed the high vaults of the nave. The vault itself was not a continuous barrel vault as at St. Sernin, but a broken barrel vault, banded with transverse arches in each bay for visual articulation and structural reinforcement. Whether by accident or deduction, the monks who served as the architects of Cluny III, the musician Gunzo and the mathematician Hézelon, found that vaults constructed on the profile of a pointed arch exert less outward thrust than the Roman arch, and they exploited this discovery in the vaulting of

8.35 Reconstruction view of the monastery of Cluny III, seen from the east, 11th century.
This was the largest church in western Christendom at the time of its construction. In the foreground to the left stand the infirmary and the abbot's palace.

8.36 (left) Plan of the monastery of Cluny III, 11th century.
Remains of the atrium and east end of the church of Cluny III can be seen to the right of the much larger new church. The site plan follows the standards set forth in the plan of St. Gall.

8.37 (below) Transverse section through the nave of the church of Cluny III, 11th century.
This view looking east shows how the paired aisles worked to brace the nave vaults. Note the use of broken or pointed arches in the profiling of the vaults.

8.39 (left) Cluny III capital from the choir, 11th century.
This column detail depicts one of the tones of the musical scale shown as a figure playing an instrument similar to a lute. The monks of Cluny were great patrons of the arts, as they believed beautiful surroundings, including lovely music, helped the mind to contemplate spiritual values.

8.38 (left) Cluny III south transept, 11th century.
This is all that remains of the once-grand monastic church.

ESSAY
The Mystic Mill from Vézelay
by Marian Moffett

8.40 Ste. Madeleine south aisle capital, the "Mystic Mill," Vézelay, France, 1120–38.

Romanesque artists undertook the task of adapting their work to fit architectural frames. Doorways and columns became the domain of sculptors, while wall surfaces were taken over by mural painters. The artists worked not only to ornament architecture but also to make church buildings a visual extension of Christian teachings by using images that could be understood by the largely illiterate population. Within the limitations imposed by functional parts of the building, these artists created memorable scenes that illustrate principles of medieval theology.

One particularly fine example of their efforts is the Mystic Mill capital from the nave of the abbey church at Vézelay (Fig. 8.40). Its subject, the grinding of grain to produce flour, depicts a common activity in the Middle Ages, a necessary first step in the production of bread. Grain as harvested from the fields cannot be consumed by people until the hard outer coating (the bran) is broken and the nutritious kernel inside is pulverized, actions accomplished by milling either in hand querns or between the large millstones of a water-powered mill.

For medieval pilgrims, this scene depicts a theological allegory, for this is no ordinary mill, and the figures operating it are not local people. The man pouring the grain on the left is Moses, and the figure bagging the flour is the apostle Paul, while the mill itself

represents Christ. Note the cross-shaped brace of the mill's toothed wheel. The two figures, one from the Old Testament and one from the New, are brought together by Christ. The scene thus represents the transformation of promises and prophecies of the Old Testament (the grain) into the teachings and blessings of the New Testament (the flour) through the action of Jesus Christ (the mill). Reconciliation of the Old and New Testaments was a key concern of medieval theologians, and in this one image the artist has captured this abstruse concept through analogy to a process familiar to all. By extension, flour from the mill represents communion bread, the body of Christ. The transformation of grain into flour also implied the conversion of the Jews to Christianity, an event medieval people believed prefigured the Second Coming of Christ.

This scene also embodies a yet deeper meaning that would have been understood by the more learned monks. Just as the bran protects the nutrients of the wheat kernel, the true meaning of scripture is concealed from unbelievers. Through the study of biblical texts and guidance from sacred commentaries, symbolized by the figures of Moses and Paul, those seeking a fuller insight into religious truths could eventually crack the outer shell of appearance and gain spiritual nourishment from the truths revealed only to those who attained the highest levels of religious learning. While not all the capitals at Vézelay are this rich in meaning, they remind us that medieval art existed for more reasons than to delight the eye. Art worked with architecture to advance Christian teachings.

the nave and aisles. Even so, a portion of the nave vault collapsed in 1125, but it was repaired before the general dedication of the church on October 25, 1130. Light for the nave was provided directly by rather small clerestory windows located just under the vaulting, since the great loads sustained by the walls severely restricted the possibilities for larger openings.

The great vaulted spaces of the church created excellent acoustics for the exceptionally beautiful and elaborate services sung by the monks. The rich splendor of the heavenly kingdom was further reflected in the artistic embellishments, particularly sculpture, lavished on the building. Some of this sculpture survived post-revolutionary destruction, although in considerably damaged condition (Fig. 8.39). To assess the artistic impact of Cluny, therefore, it is necessary to see the better-preserved work at its affiliated foundations, for where the religious influence of

Cluny traveled, so did its policy of artistic patronage. At Ste. Madeleine, Vézelay, the abbey was enlarged during a period of Cluniac reform, and the church nave preserves its stately Romanesque dignity (Fig. 8.41). (The choir was rebuilt during the Gothic period.) Polychrome, transverse, semicircular arches divide the nave vault into bays, each of which is groin-vaulted. Splendid sculptural work on column capitals and the narthex portals remains. Nave capitals depict a range of subjects, from Old Testament events to the lives of the saints and allegories illustrating teachings of the Church. The tympanum over the door from the narthex to the nave (dated 1120–32) represents the descent of the Holy Spirit at Pentecost, in which Christ sends the apostles to the corners of the earth to preach, teach, and heal the sick (Fig. 8.42). The sculptor here has bordered the central scene with signs of the zodiac, illustrations of the months of the year shown through

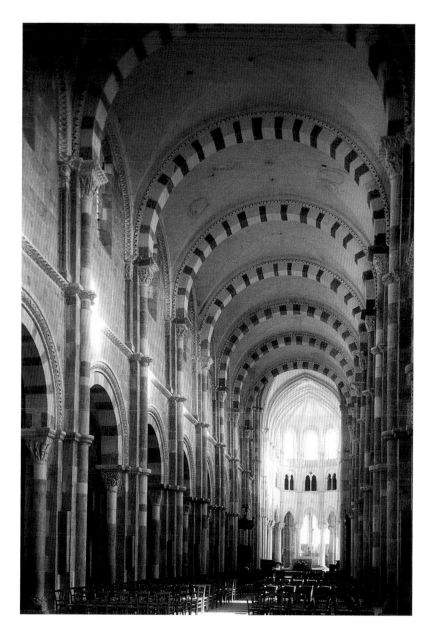

8.41 (left) Ste. Madeleine nave, Vézelay, 1120–38.
The nave was constructed while the abbey was part of the Cluniac order. Even though the building does not resemble Cluny architecturally, the tradition of creating a handsomely embellished environment for worship continues here.

8.42 Ste. Madeleine narthex portal, Vézelay, 1120–38.
The portal shows the descent of the Holy Spirit at Pentecost. The apostles look startled, reflecting the surprise at encountering the risen Christ. Faces on many of them were damaged during the turmoil of the French Revolution.

8.43 (above) **St. Lazare, Last Judgment, west-front tympanum, Autun, 1120–32.**
The subject is the same as that at Conques, although the placement of particular scenes is different. This work was signed by its sculptor, Gislebertus, in the band under the feet of Christ.

8.44 St. Lazare capital (formerly in the choir), Autun, 1120–32.
This work shows the Flight into Egypt, with Mary and Jesus riding a donkey led by Joseph. Note the nimbus or halo behind the heads of Mary and Jesus. Romanesque sculpture often exaggerates the sizes of heads and hands, as these are the most expressive parts of the body.

agricultural labors, and imaginative depictions of diverse peoples of the world, including Scythians with collapsible, elephant-sized ears, Ethiopians with pig snouts, and pygmies with ladders. As a totality, the tympanum expresses the assertion that Christ and his teachings are present at all times, in all places, to all people.

There is a more austere tympanum at the nearby Cluniac church of St. Lazare at Autun (Fig. 8.43). Here the subject is the Last Judgment, replete with hideous demons and risen souls summoned to the final reckoning. An impassive and enormous figure of Christ occupies the center of the panel, with heaven on his right and the weighing of souls on his left, next to the miseries of hell. (Notice that, as at Conques, the devil's agent in the weighing of souls cheats by placing his hand in the balance pan!) The interior of the church repeats many of the architectural features of Cluny III at a reduced scale, while the beautifully carved capitals of the nave and choir present a range of biblical stories, including a Nativity cycle (Fig. 8.44), as well as fanciful beasts and foliage.

AQUITAINE AND PROVENCE

As one would expect from a period when the means of communication were limited and political control was dispersed, a number of regional variants of the Romanesque developed in France. All share the common heritage of Romanesque influences, but they differ according to the materials, culture, and artistic interests of the individual locales. The major portion of France south of the Loire comprised Aquitaine, an important region that was successively independent, allied with the king of France, and a possession of the king of England. Seat of a flourishing culture, its architecture was perhaps the most open to varied influences from other parts of Europe, especially from eastern Christendom. Aquitaine has a series of some seventy churches with domes, an atypical feature in Western medieval architecture. That they reflect Byzantine influence is strongly implied by their use of pendentives, a characteristically Eastern device.

The church of St. Front at Périgueux, built largely after 1120, provides an interesting parallel with S. Marco in Venice (Fig. 8.45). S. Marco, itself modeled on the Greek-cross plan of the now-vanished Church of the Holy Apostles in Constantinople, was rebuilt after a fire, with the work being completed about 1089. Nearly thirty years later, the existing church of St. Front at Périgueux was greatly enlarged into a Greek-cross plan remarkably similar to S. Marco. Five domes on pendentives rise from massive pierced piers to cover the arms and crossing of the church. The stonecutting, or **stereotomy**, is exquisite. At Périgueux, the work lacks both the typical Byzantine mosaic decoration inside and the exterior profile of later Byzantine domes (Fig. 8.46). Instead the detailing is based on classical architecture, including closely spaced classical columns on the lantern turrets above the conical roofs over each dome.

S. Marco, Venice

St. Front, Périgueux

St. Pierre, Angoulême

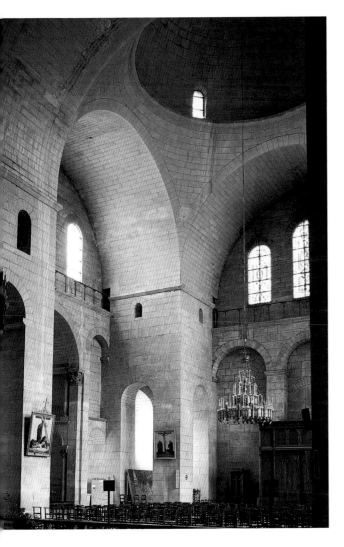

8.45 (above) Plan of S. Marco, Venice, 1063–89; St. Front, Périgueux, ca. 1120; and St. Pierre, Angoulême, 1105–28.
St. Front's design seems derived from that of S. Marco in Venice, while the cathedral at Angouléme has domes on the scale of those at Périgueux.

8.46 St. Front interior, Périgueux, ca. 1120
In the south of France, it is unexpected to find a centrally planned church having domes on pendentives. (Compare this interior to that of S. Marco on page 132).

Périgueux is somewhat exceptional even among the unusual churches of Aquitaine. The other domed churches there, such as the cathedral of St. Pierre at Angoulême (1105–28 and later), are aisleless basilicas with domes replacing the customary vaulting in the nave (Figs. 8.45, 8.47). Major structural loads in each bay are concentrated by pendentives to four piers set in the wall, allowing a reasonable area to be opened for windows, thereby providing direct illumination to the nave. The sequence of pointed arches framing each bay provides a stately processional space. On the west front is an inaccurately restored sculpture depicting a vision of the Second Coming of Christ.

The region of Provence, along the Mediterranean coast close to Italy, remained most faithful to the classical architecture of ancient Rome. Provence had been a major Roman colony, and well-preserved Roman buildings still exist at Nîmes and other cities. Not surprisingly, therefore, Romanesque architecture there exhibits strong Roman influence in its composition, proportions, and details. The Cluniac priory church of St. Gilles-du-Gard (ca. 1140–70)

8.47 Cathedral of St. Pierre interior, Angoulême, 1105–28.
This view shows the nave with domes on pendentives. Note the pointed arch used to define each bay. The domes permit direct light into this aisleless church.

8.48 St. Gilles-du-Gard west front portals, ca. 1140–70.
The sculpture has a Classical character, and the overall design recalls a triple-arched Roman triumphal arch.

8.49 St. Trophîme west front, Arles, ca. 1140–70.
As with St. Gilles, this church façade is based on a triumphal arch and the sculpture recalls Roman models. Provence was relatively close to Italy, and it had a substantial store of authentic Roman works.

(Fig. 8.48) has a triple-arched west façade based on the model of a Roman triumphal arch. Accurately proportioned Corinthian columns, some of which were actually recycled from Roman buildings, are incorporated in the work. Aside from the façade, little remains of the original church, which was an important regional center of pilgrimage. The contemporary façade of the former cathedral of St. Trophîme at Arles also recalls Roman construction in its dignified setting of sculpture in classical surroundings (Fig. 8.49).

CISTERCIAN MONASTERIES

The eleventh century witnessed the establishment of several new monastic groups, including the Order of Cîteaux, known as the Cistercians. Like the Cluniacs, the Cistercians originated in Burgundy, but in terms of artistic and religious development they were in many respects the antithesis of Cluny. The Cistercians were founded in 1098 by a group of twenty-two monks from Molesme who desired to follow a stricter observance of the Benedictine Rule, and their name came from that of their first monastery, at Cîteaux, in a wooded swamp donated by the Viscount of Beaune. The first years were difficult, but the new monastery gained an important convert in 1112, when a young nobleman named Bernard joined the order. His religious

zeal and organizational skill shaped the Cistercians into a uniform, highly regulated ascetic community. (Other members of his family also eventually joined the order, and their financial contributions doubtless helped as well.) In 1115 Bernard founded the third daughter house at Clairvaux, from which he was to continue to act as the guiding spiritual force for all Cistercian houses until his death in 1153.

In time the Cistercians rivaled the Cluniacs in influence. Although their affiliated monasteries totaled only about half the number of Cluniac houses, they spread throughout western Christendom. The Cistercian Order required a great measure of conformity from its dependent monasteries, and this uniformity extended to architecture. As was appropriate to the austere life laid out for their monks and following principles laid down by Bernard, Cistercian abbeys were of the simplest possible construction consistent with durable masonry building. In sharp contrast to the Cluniacs, the Cistercians initially did not allow luxurious features like towers, stained-glass windows, or paved floors. They shunned expensive materials and discouraged sculptural ornament. Cistercian monasteries had straightforward, orderly plans based on a square module, devoid of the elaborate articulation of many Cluniac designs. Thus the Cistercians produced an international set of buildings with unmistakable common features.

Church

8.52

Cloister

Fountain

8.53

Night stair to dormitory on
second floor, over chapter
room and workroom

Chapter room

Workroom, or scriptorium

Guest house

Refectory

Forge

N

0   50 m
0   150 ft

8.50 Plan of the abbey, Fontenay, 1139–47.
This Cistercian plan recalls the Plan of St. Gall,
with church, dormitory, and refectory defining
three sides of the cloister. The original refectory is
missing. On the south side is the forge, a utilitarian
building equipped with water-powered machinery
that could full cloth, forge iron, or accomplish other
heavy tasks. The monastery's vegetable garden was
located immediately to the east.

8.51 West front, Abbey Church, Fontenay, 1139–47.
Compared to the embellished buildings of Cluny, this
Cistercian church seems rather severe, observing the
artistic strictures established by St. Bernard, under
whose direction this monastery was founded.

Cistercian houses were founded at least twenty miles from any existing settlement, preferably at the end of a narrow valley that had a reliable water supply. While the monks did not shun their obligation to extend hospitality to visitors, they did not locate their buildings so as to encourage pilgrim traffic. Persons able to endow monasteries through gifts of land soon learned that even the most unpromising sites became productive in the hands of the Cistercians, and the example of their superior agricultural management spread to surrounding areas. Whatever long-term spiritual benefits attended the initial donation were generally compounded by very tangible increases in rents and revenues. In the early years the monks provided for all their own needs, supplying their vegetarian diet from garden plots adjacent to the monastery, but soon the care of crops and animals required more time than monks could spare from their religious duties, so lay brothers assumed most of the manual labor, leaving the monks to prayer and the copying of manuscripts. As with many medieval monastic movements, success spoiled the Cistercians. They became wealthy and relaxed the rigors of their religious observances, behaving more like other monastic groups, and when religious institutions came under attack in the post-medieval period, Cistercian abbeys were particularly targeted for their luxury. While their original ideals remained intact, however, they were a powerful religious and architectural presence, contributing much to the spread of learning, progressive agricultural practices, and sound building techniques across western Europe.

The abbey of Fontenay in Burgundy is today among the best preserved of early Cistercian monasteries. Built from 1139 to 1147, with some portions reconstructed in the thirteenth and sixteenth centuries, it is a clear illustration of Bernard of Clairvaux's architectural ideals. The monastery is closely modeled on the layout of the Plan of St. Gall, having a modular unit established by the square bay of the church aisle (Fig. 8.50). Two of these units determine the width of the nave; four, the area of the crossing; and one for each of the four chapels on the east wall of the transept. The module continues as the standard unit for the cloister walk, and it is repeated in the chapter house, workroom, and forge building. (The non-modular refectory is a sixteenth-century structure.)

The same simplicity distinguishes the three-dimensional reality of the buildings (Fig. 8.51). The nave, modest in height, is covered by a broken banded barrel vault, while the aisles have transverse broken barrel vaults over each bay (Fig. 8.52). Light for the church comes from windows in the aisles and at the east and west end walls, as there are no clerestories. The church floor is of compacted earth, with only the raised choir section being paved in stone. The harmonious proportions relieve the utter plainness of the construction. The cloister walk, with its semicircular arcading, reflects sunlight softly and creates an appropriately human scale (Fig. 8.53).

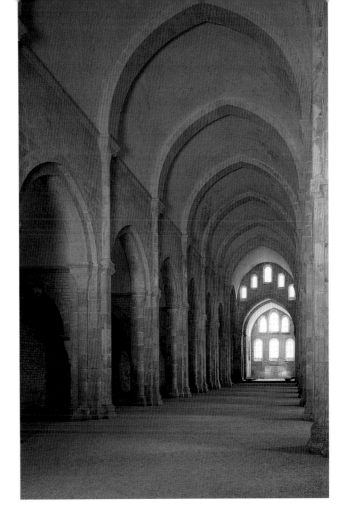

8.52 Fontenay Church interior looking west, 1139–47.
Note the pointed transverse arches and the absence of clerestory windows. The church is not tall, and its architectural detail is austere.

8.53 Cloister walk, Fontenay, 1139–47.
The cloister connected major monastic buildings and served as a covered passage for meditation or exercise. In good weather, monks sat on the ledges under arches to read. Modular proportions and restrained architectural detail create a sense of repose.

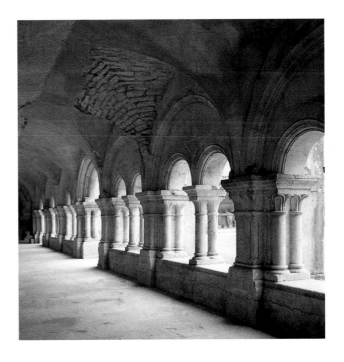

The Cistercians built well. Their standardized designs did much to spread sound building practices and the progressive Romanesque style preferred by Bernard across most of Europe. After Bernard's death, many Cistercian houses expanded and built more elaborate structures than those at Fontenay. Choirs in particular were enlarged, as in the plan of Cîteaux, where the original square-ended chapels were replaced with a radial layout, producing a design copied later at many daughter houses. Although minor regional variants are reflected in Cistercian work, monasteries as distant from one another as Fossanova in Italy, Sénanque in Provence, Poblet in Spain, Maulbronn in Germany, and Fountains in England all share the fundamentally straightforward and unadorned character of Cistercian architecture, the first international style of the medieval period.

NORMAN ARCHITECTURE

We have already noted how the Vikings in Norway became converts to Christianity and built stave churches there. Other Vikings became permanent residents outside of Scandinavia: in 911 a group led by Rollo was granted territory in western France in exchange for a cessation of its raids on settlements within the Frankish kingdom. The settlers became known as Normans, their land as Normandy, and their ruler as the duke of Normandy. Within the span of a century they developed into capable builders in stone, and, like Charlemagne, they encouraged the construction of monasteries.

In 1068 work began on the abbey church of St. Etienne at Caen, also known as the Abbaye-aux-Hommes (1068–1120), founded by William, Duke of Normandy, to expiate his consanguineous marriage (Fig. 8.54). Initially the church had a long nave with two western towers. Aisles flanked the wooden-roofed nave, and groin vaults supported the galleries above. Between 1115 and 1120 the wooden roof was removed, and the upper stage of the nave wall was rebuilt to incorporate ribs of sexpartite vaulting constructed across the nave. These vaults, encompassing two bays of the nave for each unit, engage existing major and minor supports in the alternate grouped and single wall shafts so as to continue the line of the vaulting rib down to the floor.

Duke William is remembered in history for more than his endowment of St. Etienne. In 1066 he led an army of Normans across the Channel, defeated the assembled Anglo-Saxon forces at the battle of Hastings, and extended Norman rule to England. Henceforth he was known as William the Conqueror, and his military triumph was to have lasting consequences for English history and architecture. Compared with contemporary Norman work, Britain's Anglo-Saxon buildings were small and poorly built. William reorganized the English Church and began a major campaign of church- and castle-building. He

8.54 St. Etienne west front, Caen, 1068–1120.
The façade of this church is austere, with a straightforward ordering of doorways, windows, and wall buttresses. The more florid upper stages of the towers are later additions.

encouraged monasteries, and great cathedrals arose at Canterbury, Durham, Lincoln, Winchester, Gloucester, Norwich, Ely, and other sites.

At Durham, the cathedral of St. Cuthbert (Fig. 8.55) was constructed from 1093 to 1133 under the leadership of Norman bishops as a replacement for an earlier monastic church containing the relics of St. Cuthbert. It remains one of the best-preserved major Norman churches in England, interesting for its impressive massing and early use of rib vaulting and creation of striking geometric

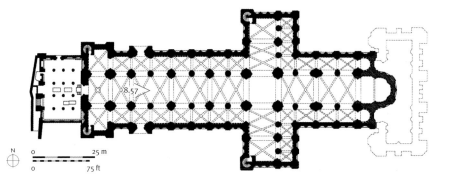

8.55 **Plan of and section through the cathedral of St. Cuthbert, Durham, 1093–1133.**
The original semicircular apse was rebuilt in the thirteenth century as a transept with nine altars to house St. Cuthbert's shrine. The builders reduced the height of the gallery over the aisle to leave room for a clerestory window tucked between the folds of the rib vaulting. Compare this section to that of St. Sernin, which uses a similar technique.

patterns on its piers, arches, and ribs. Two west-front towers and a square crossing tower announce the cathedral's presence on the hilltop above the river Wear. The original plan was an aisled basilica with transepts, with the choir terminating in a semicircular apse and the aisles concluded by chapels. (The apse was rebuilt to its present transept

8.56 **Nave vaults, St. Cuthbert, Durham, 1093–1133.**
Here Norman builders used septpartite, or seven-part, vaults between pointed, transverse arches. Notice how the ribs spring from the corbels above the triforium.

design in the Gothic period.) Evidence suggests that only the choir was initially planned for vaulting, but eventually vaulting was undertaken throughout the church. In the choir aisle vaults, built in about 1096, the ribs were built integrally with the vault cells. When rib vaults were begun over the nave, in about 1128–33, masons used the ribs as a framework from which to construct vault infill that was significantly thinner than corresponding work in the choir, indicating that they understood rib vaulting's constructional advantages (Fig. 8.56).

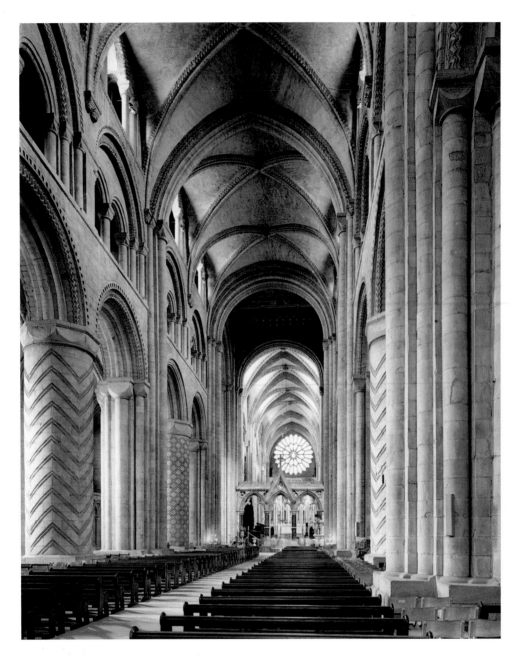

8.57 Nave looking east, St. Cuthbert, Durham, 1093–1133. The nave features compound piers alternating with magnificently bold cylindrical columns, each having an incised design. The continuous ridge line produces spatial unity among the vault bays.

Durham's high vaults lack the vertical continuity from **diagonal** ribs to wall shaft that characterize the interior of St. Etienne at Caen. Although the nave and choir are composed of double bays comprised of compound piers alternating with distinctive cylindrical columns (Fig. 8.57), the vaults are septpartite, and their diagonal ribs spring from corbeled heads high on the gallery wall rather than connecting with wall shafts. Pointed, transverse arches define the double bays by connecting compound piers across the nave. The heavy quality of construction is increased by the relative absence of figural ornament. Striking geometric designs of chevrons, spirals, and diaper patterns are incised on the cylindrical columns, almost like the abstractions of Viking interlace work, while the arch moldings in the **Galilee** Chapel attached to the western end of the cathedral in about 1170–75 have zigzag patterning.

Vaulting strategies that Norman builders explored at Caen and Durham led to structural changes that are associated with the Gothic style. By finding ways to exploit the constructional advantages of rib vaults and the structural efficiency of pointed arches, masons reduced the material (and thus the weight and cost) required to vault a building. The square bays and diagonal groin vaults from Roman times were transformed into rectangular bays having continuity of line from wall shaft to vaulting rib. Uninterrupted walls that were so important to structural stability in early Romanesque vaulted buildings were abandoned in favor of a skeletal system with loads concentrated at particular points, and a new esthetic of spaciousness and light came into being in the style we term Gothic.

CONCLUSIONS ABOUT ARCHITECTURAL IDEAS

Charlemagne's ninth-century attempt to associate himself with the ancient Roman Empire produced a false spring of classical revivalism. While his scribes aggressively assembled and copied ancient manuscripts, thereby assuring their preservation until the present day, Charlemagne was unable to reconstitute the classical way of thinking, and Carolingian builders were equally unable to recapture the essence of classical architecture. Charlemagne drew upon what he had seen in Italy, particularly the church of S. Vitale in Ravenna, and the knowledge of Lombard builders whom he enticed to come north, and fused the accumulated models and technologies with Germanic building traditions. This fusion produced his Palatine Chapel at Aachen and, speaking a related architectural language, the Oratory at Germigny-des-Prés, which sits atop a nine-part, or quincunx, plan that came from Anatolian Byzantium. Charlemagne used monasteries as instruments of settlement and control of the countryside. The document known as the Plan of St. Gall illustrates that his planners conceived a universal monastic ideal that could be adapted to local conditions, as, for instance, was the case at Cluny.

Anglo-Saxon and Viking builders exploited wood in the form of logs and staves. Inventiveness reached apogees of ornamentation and vertical ascent in Norway with richly energetic woodcarving and telescoping building masses covered by multiple, steep gables. But it was massive, fireproof, stone masonry that most appealed to Romanesque builders, and they gradually explored structural capabilities and visual effects inherent in round-arch-penetrated, mostly stone bearing walls supporting barrel vaults and sometimes groin vaults and even domes.

Designers for Ottonian rulers who followed Charlemagne in the northern reaches of the Holy Roman Empire loved multiple towers, including the Carolingian westwerk tower, and built in local, often polychromatic stone. Lombard masons contributed such features as corbel-arch tables, or Lombard bands. Nave walls in churches eventually took on three-dimensionality in the form of advancing layers of pilasters and colonnettes, the latter appearing as columns conceptually captive in the wall, and sometimes-receding layers of round-arched openings. The great, fully vaulted nave of Cluny in Burgundy spoke much the same architectural language, as do the remaining, related churches along the pilgrimage roads to Santiago de Compostela. Rigorous in their planning as a result of repetitive bays of barrel and groin vaults in naves and aisles and repetitive, projecting chapels (as at Cluny), such buildings as St. Sernin and St. Foy include transverse nave arches that continue visually down to the floor in the form of colonnettes between which recessed arches open up at the nave and gallery levels. In Aquitaine in southwest France, vaults gave way to repetitive domed bays, producing interiors where the French skill in stonecutting, or stereotomy, produced a zenith of spatial lucidity.

Builders in Normandy on the northern French coast exported their regional style across the channel to England by following the armies of William the Conqueror. While England's Durham Cathedral was eventually fully vaulted, perhaps its most distinctive characteristic is the intensity of its carved-stone textures, from chevron-incised piers to zigzag patterning on arches and vault ribs. Ribs also appeared early in Lombardy in northern Italy. At the brick church of S. Ambrogio, Lombard construction signatures, such as the repetitive corbeled arches named for them, also appear, as do mutant classical orders and uncomfortably attenuated external colonnettes.

In central Italy, the heavy northern Romanesque style never pushed aside the classical tradition, meaning the maintenance of basilican plans and the appearance of few attached towers. The availability of marble in various colors encouraged the subdivision of façades according to geometric patterning; the use of repetitive, polychromatic, horizontal banding; and the repetitive stacking up of carefully carved quasi-classical motifs. Classical reinterpretations also continued unabated along the southern French coast in Provence, where many ancient monuments remained intact to serve as models.

While the subsequent, more extravagantly vertical and dramatically lit Gothic architecture of the Île de France around Paris, covered in the next chapter, emerged from Romanesque stock, this extraordinary change does not in any way suggest that heavier, darker Romanesque work was inferior or immature. Rather, Romanesque builders north of Italy and southern France unashamedly exploited the weighty, shadowy massiveness of stone masonry and reveled in this exploitation.

Chapter 9
Gothic Architecture

As we consider the Gothic, the final phase of medieval architecture, we are faced with defining the style. The term "Gothic" was first applied in the seventeenth century to denote designs not based on precedent from classical antiquity, and the label was applied with derision. By the nineteenth century, pejorative connotations had largely been overcome, but historians have struggled since to clarify what exactly constitutes the Gothic style. The most obvious definition involves key elements employed in many Gothic buildings—the pointed arch and the rib vault—although, as we have seen, these were also found in some Romanesque work. There are, however, elements original to Gothic buildings, including flying buttresses, windows with tracery, and piers composed of colonnettes or shafts bundled around a core, that serve as hallmarks of the style (Fig. 9.1).

Another common definition relies on the way these elements were brought together in the structure of large-scale churches and cathedrals, particularly those built in the region around Paris during the period from 1140 to 1220. Unlike Romanesque buildings, in which a continuous mass of wall is necessary to sustain the load, the Gothic structure is a skeletal system that transfers overhead loads down to the ground at discrete points, thereby freeing large expanses of wall to be opened for windows. Secular buildings seldom have this wall section, however, so a purely structural concept is insufficient by itself to define the Gothic. One can define Gothic buildings by their spatial characteristics, which tend to emphasize the vertical, consist of articulated but unified cells of space, and have a sense of openness afforded by the construction system. Lastly the style can be seen as a reflection of the historical era and religious imagery of the period in which it arose, connected both to the growth of urban society and to theological analogies to Old Testament tabernacles and temples and concepts of the New Jerusalem. We need to keep all these definitional perspectives in mind as we seek to understand Gothic architecture.

Let us look more closely at the key elements associated with Gothic structure—pointed arches, rib vaults, and flying buttresses. Pointed arches are better approximations of catenary curves that represent the line of compressive force acting in any arch, and thus they exert less outward or overturning thrust. They also present considerable design flexibility, as one can vary to some extent the angle of the arch. By contrast, the dimensions of a semicircular arch are established by the width of the span. Pointed arches are probably a contribution from Islamic architecture, having been used in Syria and North Africa before their earliest application in northern Europe. They were used in a number of major Romanesque buildings, including the great church of Cluny III and St. Pierre Cathedral at Angoulême. Rib vaults can also be found in late Romanesque architecture, those constructed at St. Etienne at Caen and Durham Cathedral being generally thought to be among the earliest examples. Ribbing a groin vault had the virtue of visually "tidying up" the sometimes awkward arris created at the fold of the groin vault, but builders soon discovered that there were constructional advantages to be gained from laying up the ribs first, then using them as in-situ scaffold for erecting the thinner web sections of the vault. Builders also found they could lighten the webbing, thereby reducing the material weight of groin vaults. As the dead load on the vaulting was created primarily by the weight of the stone, reducing this weight not only economized on materials but also eventually facilitated greater building heights. The third element, the flying buttress, was probably first used at Sens Cathedral in about 1160, but it can be seen in embryonic form in the quadrant vaults over galleries of the pilgrimage road churches. Since Gothic construction concentrates loads at piers rather than distributing it continuously along the wall, the need for reinforcement at specific points is great. Gothic architects soon developed external buttressing, set at right angles to the wall and connected to it at strategic junctions by arches, which appear to "fly" or leap as they reach out to strengthen the upper sections of the skeletal frame. (Gothic openness can be achieved

Chronology

Battle of Hastings	1066
Beginning of the crusades	1096
Construction of the choir at St. Denis	1140–44
Construction of Notre-Dame Cathedral, Paris	1163–ca. 1250
Construction of St. Etienne Cathedral, Bourges	1195–1250
Construction of Salisbury Cathedral	1220–58
Notebooks of Villard de Honnecourt	ca. 1225–50
Collapse of the choir vaults at Beauvais Cathedral	1284
Completion of Milan Cathedral	1572

Notre-Dame Cathedral interior, Chartres, 1194–1230.
Chartres has an exceptionally wide nave because of the dimensions of the earlier Romanesque basilica.

Pinnacle

Buttress flyer

Roof over aisle

Buttress pier

Aisle window

Aisle

Diagonal vaulting rib

Vaulting web

Transverse arch — Clerestory

Tracery window

Wall shaft — Triforium

Arcade

Pier

9.1 Section perspective showing the Gothic structure of a major church.
Arrows indicate how dead loads from the vaults are transferred to the piers of the arcade and, through the lower flyer, to the buttress piers outside the building. The upper flyer helps to resist lateral or side loads caused by the wind blowing against the building.

without flying buttresses, particularly in smaller structures where wall buttresses suffice to handle the structural loads. In Italy, builders developed alternate structural solutions to obviate the need for flying buttresses, as we shall see.)

Gothic architecture is more than a collection of structural techniques, however, for it embraces an integrated esthetic system. The flexibility of the pointed arch allowed irregular areas to be vaulted while maintaining a common ceiling height. Elements of the church plans that in Romanesque had been expressed as separate volumes (nave, aisle, chapel) could be combined into a unified, ordered composition, thanks to the geometric freedom offered by the combination of rib vaults and pointed arches. Gothic builders learned to integrate vaulting ribs with wall shafts, thus visually anchoring the floating overhead canopy to the ground. With the reinforcement provided by external buttresses, entire wall sections could be devoted to windows, particularly in the clerestory, where increased window height and width contributed to a diaphanous interior effect. Window **tracery**, the decorative intersecting stonework in the upper sections of windows, was introduced and became increasingly slender, evolving from plate tracery (punched openings in a solid field) to bar tracery (thin lines of cut stone set in geometric patterns). As the Gothic style developed, one can sense the desire to reduce solid building mass and to enhance

the quality of space and light, for both metaphysical and practical reasons, thus stimulating technical and artistic innovations.

EARLY GOTHIC
The Abbey Church of St. Denis

The Gothic style originated in northern France, in the region around Paris known as the Île-de-France. This area had relatively little Romanesque building, so perhaps it was more open to developments from other places. It also was the home of one of the period's most energetic, informed, and innovative patrons of the arts, Abbot Suger, who rose from humble origins to become one of the most powerful Church figures of his age. Suger's parents had donated him to the abbey of St. Denis when he was three years old, and he was raised in the monastery school to become a monk. Among his young companions in the school was the future King Louis VII of France. Suger's diplomatic and administrative skills were soon noticed, and he rose rapidly in the Church hierarchy. In 1122, at the age of thirty-six, he was elected abbot of St. Denis.

Located about six miles north of Paris, St. Denis was the French royal monastery. It was the burial place of Denis, the first bishop of Paris, who was martyred by the Romans in the third century and later designated the patron saint of France. The kings of France were buried at the abbey, and the royal banner, the Oriflamme, was kept there between military campaigns. For all its prestige, the abbey was overcrowded and somewhat decayed when Suger became abbot. The existing building, consecrated in 775, was a Carolingian basilica that had received an enlarged eastern chapel in 832. Suger wanted to rebuild the church for the greater glory of God and France, but first he had to set the abbey's financial affairs in order and respond to criticism from Bernard of Clairvaux by reforming the religious practices of its monks. While he worked toward these goals, Suger developed images of what he wished the new church to be. He studied biblical descriptions of the Temple of Solomon, a design specified by God; he examined writings attributed (incorrectly) to St. Denis, in which there was much discussion of the mystical and metaphysical properties of visually manifested spiritual images, especially phenomena associated with light; and he inquired of travelers from Constantinople for descriptions of Hagia Sophia (see Fig. 6.16), widely regarded as the most splendid church building in Christendom, which Suger was determined to exceed.

By 1137 Suger was ready to build. To enlarge the church he constructed a new west front and narthex forward of the existing structure, probably to the designs of a Norman architect capable of translating Suger's ideas into reality (Fig. 9.2). This work, consecrated in 1140, incorporated both the twin-towered west façade of Norman churches and the tradition of sculptured portals developed in the south of France. The three doorways had carved tympana and jamb

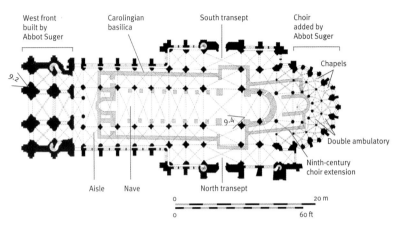

9.2 (left) St. Denis, west front, 1137–40.
Generally recognized as the first Gothic building,
this church has lost its northern tower.

9.3a (above) Plan of St. Denis, 1137–40.
This plan shows in hatched outline the basilica of 775
enlarged in 832. Suger built his new west front well forward
of the existing building and had the choir positioned to
incorporate foundations of the older building.

statues, while the articulation of windows, including a circular or rose window, went beyond the linear façade compositions of Normandy. On the interior, rib vaults in the narthex sprang from grouped piers, thus exploiting the potential for continuity of line.

So enthusiastic was the reception for this new work that construction began almost at once on an enlargement of the east end (Fig. 9.3a). Less than four years later (1144) the new choir was dedicated in elaborate ceremonies involving distinguished churchmen and royalty. Suger's preoccupation with colored light is clearly manifested in the seven shallow radiating chapels of the choir, each with two large stained-glass windows (Fig 9.4). The irregular bays of this complex plan are consistently covered by rib vaults rising to a uniform crown height, while slender buttresses, set in the angles between the chapels, reinforce the upper wall. The ensemble creates an airy, luminous, rich interior that glows like jewels, precisely the effect desired by Suger: "a circular string of chapels, by virtue of which the whole church would shine with the wonderful and uninterrupted light of most sacred windows, pervading the interior beauty."

9.3b Plans of Notre-Dame, Laon, 1155–ca. 1205, and Notre-Dame, Paris, 1163–ca. 1250.
Notice that Laon has a pronounced cruciform plan, whereas Paris has transepts that scarcely project beyond the line of the buttress piers. The initial design for Paris had no radiating chapels off its double ambulatory, but chapels (shown here) were subsequently inserted between all the buttress piers.

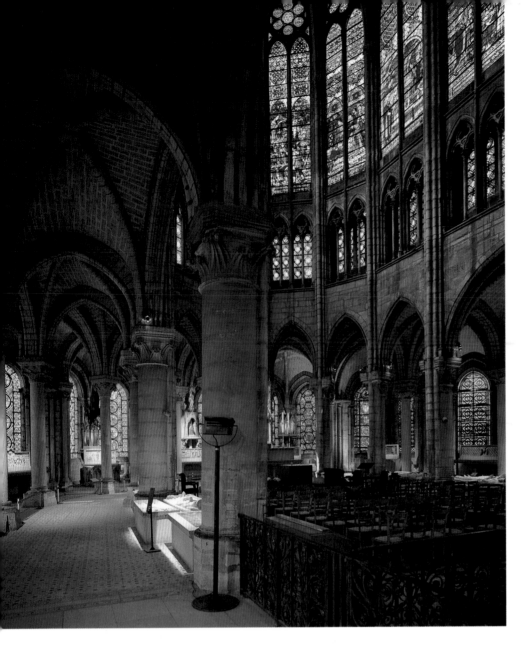

9.4 Abbey Church ambulatory and choir, St. Denis, 1140–44 and later. The ambulatory (left) dates from Suger's abbacy, while the triforium and clerestory are a century later, constructed anew when the nave of the church was completed. The skeletal nature of Gothic construction facilitated the installation of large windows in the shallow chapels surrounding the apse, creating the wondrous luminosity desired by Suger.

Planned next for construction was a nave to link the new narthex and choir, but Suger did not live to see the completion of his ambitious dream. Louis VII departed for the Second Crusade in 1147, leaving Suger in charge as regent of France, with neither time nor money for building. He died shortly after Louis returned from the Holy Land in 1151. The present nave at St. Denis was completed nearly a century later, when the upper stories of Suger's choir were rebuilt to match the height of the new nave vaults.

The wondrous quality of light and space created by the new choir at St. Denis was not lost on the Church authorities and lay people who visited the abbey. Within two decades of its dedication, Gothic churches were under construction at several sites in the Île-de-France, both for monasteries and increasingly for cathedral churches in the growing towns. The style seemed to flourish particularly within the orbit of the king of France's political influence. In regions such as the south of France, where royal control was weak and religious interest in the theology of divine manifestations was not strong, the mature Romanesque style continued to be used for at least a century after the Gothic had been developed.

Early Gothic Cathedrals

Gothic architecture also coincided with an increase in the veneration of the Virgin Mary. As a mother who had suffered great sorrow, she had enormous popular appeal and became an important intercessor figure, standing before Christ the judge and pleading for leniency for erring humanity. Many of the great cathedrals were dedicated to her—she is "Notre Dame" in French, "Our Lady" in English—and sculpture and stained glass featured her far more often than was the case in Romanesque work. One index of this change is the way in which the Last Judgment was depicted on west-front portals. In Gothic work the scene is more lifelike, appealing to the viewer's empathetic identification with theological verities rather than impressing with abstractly conceptual representations of the same spiritual issues.

Two early Gothic cathedrals in northern France are of particular interest. The cathedral of Notre-Dame at Laon was begun in about 1155 to replace an older structure that had become too small for the needs of the prosperous town and the growing cathedral school (Figs. 9.3b,

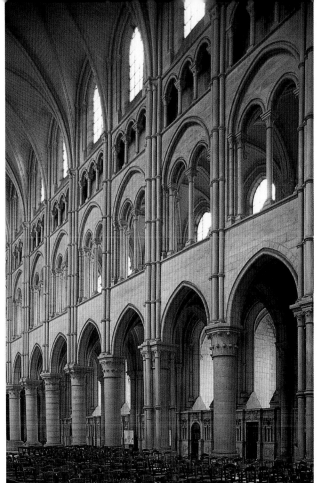

9.5 Notre-Dame Cathedral west front, Laon, 1155–ca. 1205.
This façade has a greater feeling of depth and openness than was seen at St. Denis. Deep hoods protect the entrance portals, and the upper stages of the twin towers change to octagonal plans.

9.6 Notre-Dame Cathedral nave, Laon, 1155–ca. 1205.
The nave has a four-story elevation: aisle arcade, gallery, triforium (corresponding to the section where the roof over the aisle abuts the exterior wall), and clerestory. Bundled wall shafts correspond to ribs of the sexpartite vaults overhead.

9.5–9.6). The choir and transepts were finished within twenty years, and the nave, west front, and crossing tower were completed by about 1205. To provide more space for the cathedral's canons, the original semicircular Gothic apse was replaced early in the thirteenth century by the present elongated choir with its rectangular east end. The flying buttresses may not be original to the church, because the galleries and their roofs over the aisles stabilize the vaults. Some scholars believe they were added in the thirteenth century to provide additional bracing against lateral wind forces.

At Laon one can see how cautious architects and builders were in experimenting with new Gothic techniques. In its pre-1205 state, Laon retained elements from Romanesque works, including the long nave, **sexpartite rib vaults**, lantern crossing tower, galleries, semicircular apse, and western towers that could be found in Norman churches. The critical difference on the interior is the incorporation of the pointed arch into the profile of the diagonal ribs of the sexpartite vaults. Ribs from the vaults and moldings around the clerestory windows continue as clustered wall shafts to the capitals of cylindrical piers in the nave arcade, thus emphasizing verticality. The three-dimensional, sculptural quality of the west front, built in 1190–1205, also departs from Romanesque precedent, for even Caen or the most ambitious of Cluniac churches were never conceived this

boldly. Protective porch hoods over the three portals project from the plane of the façade, creating a sense of depth that is repeated in the arched windows flanking the rose window in the story above. The western towers begin on square plans and are transformed into octagons in the upper stages. Stone oxen peer down from the towers' heights, silent tributes to the patient animals that hauled the construction materials up to the ridge on which the cathedral sits. In the early thirteenth century, Villard de Honnecourt, whose sketchbook has survived to modern times, drew the towers of Laon and noted, "I have traveled in many lands, but in no place have I seen such a tower as the one at Laon." Even with its later modifications, Laon stands as the purest example of the Early Gothic.

In about 1150–55, the bishop of Paris began construction on the new cathedral of Notre-Dame to replace a sixth-century basilica, clearing a site on the Île de la Cité and laying substantial foundations for the church (Fig. 9.3b). Work began on the choir, progressing to the nave by 1178–1200. The west front was completed between 1200 and 1250. During the course of construction, however, modifications were made to the fabric of the church, so that what one sees today is an altered version of the original twelfth-century design. Notre-Dame is a tall church, 110 feet from the floor to the crown of its vaults, and the direct light admitted into the nave by the original

9.7 Notre-Dame Cathedral south side, Paris, 1163–ca. 1250.
Note the large transept rose window. Thanks to Victor Hugo's *The Hunchback of Notre-Dame* (1831), this building was restored after decades of neglect. It is important both as an early Gothic monument and as a nineteenth-century example of historic preservation.

clerestories proved insufficient for the height of the space. To bring in more light, the clerestories all around the cathedral were enlarged in about 1225, flying buttresses were added to the choir to stabilize the great hemicycle, and the original nave buttresses were rebuilt (Fig. 9.7). The transepts with their enormous rose windows are another addition. The north transept was built from 1246 to 1257 to the designs of Jean de Chelles, and the south transept was constructed in 1258–61 by Jean de Chelles and Pierre de Montreuil. In the course of the late thirteenth century, chapels were inserted between all the buttresses around the choir and nave. Finally, in the nineteenth century, Eugène Emmanuel Viollet-le-Duc restored the cathedral, rebuilding all the flying buttresses, returning the bays at the crossing to their original design, and repairing the sculpture on the exterior (Fig. 9.8).

Despite all these modifications, the Early Gothic qualities of Notre-Dame in Paris are remarkably well preserved on the interior (Figs. 9.9–9.10). Although less pure than Laon, the cathedral remains an important monument of the period. Its original plan was innovative and ambitious. A long church, completely surrounded by a double ambulatory, it was the first Gothic building to exceed the height (but not the length) of Cluny III.

The west front, a splendid study in proportions, has a solid, almost military quality, in contrast to the more open

Rebuilt design | Original design | Rebuilt design | Original design

Exterior   Interior

9.8 Exterior and interior nave elevations of Notre-Dame Cathedral, Paris, 1150–55–ca. 1250.
This view shows the original form (right side of each drawing), which included a roundel opening in the triforium. When flying buttresses were added in about 1175–80, the clerestory was enlarged.

character of Laon (Fig. 9.11). At Paris it is the strength of the wall that commands attention. Triple portals are surmounted by the horizontal Gallery of Kings, representing twenty-eight kings of the Old Testament. A radiant rose window, flanked by paired lancet windows, forms a halo backdrop for a sculpture of the Virgin and Child with two angels. Below the twin towers is a second arcaded horizontal gallery that lightens the upper wall while completing the basically square configuration of the lower façade. This elevation rewards close study, for the more one looks, the more visually delightful detail one finds. From a distance the basically symmetrical disposition of features within the overall composition is obvious, while the slight irregularities in individual elements become noticeable (and endearing) upon examination. None of the three portals is the same size or shape, and the great towers are unequal in width. The sculptural programs of the three portals extend Christian teachings to those who could not read, just as Romanesque work did. On climbing the stairs to the upper levels, one gets an intimate view of the individually designed **crockets** projecting from the stones at the corners of the towers and of the fanciful sculpture (generally of the nineteenth century) perched high up on the parapets.

9.11 Notre-Dame Cathedral west front, Paris, ca. 1250. What seems at first glance to be an obvious symmetrical composition turns out on closer examination to be not entirely so. These small variations and details make this a highly individual building.

9.9 Notre-Dame Cathedral nave and choir, Paris, 1163–ca. 1250. Compare this photograph with the drawings in Fig. 9.8 to see the revised interior elevation built when the clerestory windows were enlarged. Later Gothic cathedrals featured much larger windows.

9.10 Notre-Dame Cathedral nave vaults, Paris, 1163–ca. 1250. These are sexpartite vaults constructed over two bays. Notice how there is continuity of line from the vaulting ribs to the wall shafts, giving the interior a vertical sweep.

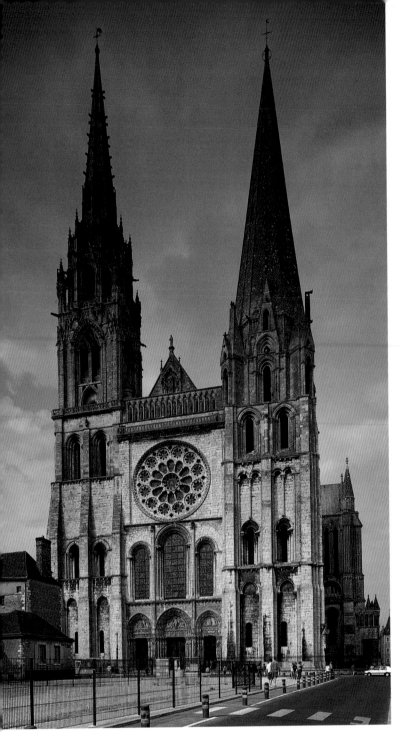

9.12 Notre-Dame Cathedral west front, Chartres, 1194–1230.
The triple doorways, lancet windows, and tower bases were built ca. 1150 as a new façade for a predecessor church. The horizontal string course just below the rose window marks the seam between Romanesque and Gothic work. The north tower was finished in 1513.

interior elevations to three divisions: the nave arcade, the **triforium** passage, and the clerestory windows. In the process, the clerestory windows increased markedly in size, and vaulting shifted from sexpartite (over two bays) to **quadripartite** (over one bay).

Chartres Cathedral has an even more complicated chronology than the cathedral of Paris. The site had long been a place of veneration for the Virgin Mary, and the cathedral treasure contained, among other valuable relics, a tunic believed to have been worn by Mary. Chartres became a center of pilgrimage, and from 1020 to 1037 a Romanesque basilica with three deep radiating chapels was constructed to replace an earlier church destroyed by fire. By the twelfth century, this church had itself been enlarged, and a fire in 1134 had damaged the westwerk. Work began that same year to build a new west front and narthex in much the same manner that Abbot Suger was to extend St. Denis. Sculptors from the workshops at St. Denis came to Chartres in 1145–50 to carve the three portals of the new west façade, and the three lancet windows overhead were filled with stained glass depicting themes pioneered at Suger's church: the infancy of Christ, the Passion story, and the Tree of Jesse or the genealogy of Christ.

On the night of June 10, 1194, fire again struck the cathedral and town, destroying the wooden-roofed basilica and eighty percent of the city. Even though the new west front survived without major damage, the people of Chartres interpreted the fire as a sign of divine displeasure. Sensing the general feeling of hopelessness, the visiting bishop of Pisa called a town meeting, during which the sacred tunic was carried out, miraculously unharmed, from the ruins of the crypt. The mood quickly changed from sorrow to jubilation as the townspeople decided that the fire was a sign that Mary desired a larger church. Building funds were raised with remarkable speed and construction commenced. The Gothic cathedral at Chartres was built in the span of twenty-six years, from 1194 to 1220, and the sculpted north and south transept porches were finished between 1224 and 1250. However, the north tower on the west front was completed only in 1513, giving the west front at last a balanced asymmetry of form and style.

In rebuilding the cathedral, the master masons reused the foundations and crypt and incorporated the surviving west front. On the exterior one can still see the seam where the new work was joined to the old, a horizontal string course immediately below the western rose (which itself is slightly off center). The Romanesque apse was transformed into a Gothic choir by the insertion of four shallow chapels between the three existing deep chapels of the crypt, thus creating seven shallow chapels with a double ambulatory

HIGH GOTHIC

The incorporation of flying buttresses at Notre-Dame in Paris integrated the three major structural components of Gothic, and redundant features from the Romanesque could be deleted from subsequent Gothic building. The period of tentative exploration was over, and the mature or High Gothic that followed saw the erection of churches with increasingly refined artistic and structural features.

Chartres and Bourges

The first monument of the High Gothic was the cathedral of Notre-Dame at Chartres, where flying buttresses were planned from the start so that the galleries were unnecessary (Figs. 9.12, 9.13, and 9.15). This simplified the

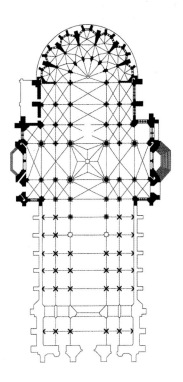

9.13 Plans of Chartres Cathedral, 1194–1230, and Bourges Cathedral, 1195–1250.
These buildings, begun within two years of one another, show different approaches to Gothic design. Chartres continues the tradition of pronounced transepts seen at Laon, while Bourges has a double ambulatory rather like Paris.

9.14 Projected plan of Beauvais Cathedral, ca. 1225–1573.
Built in discontinuous campaigns, the choir, transepts, and one bay of the nave (shown here in black) were all that was completed. After the nave vaults collapsed in 1284, pairs of additional piers were inserted in each of the three choir bays to create sexpartite vaults.

9.15 Elevations and sections of Laon Cathedral nave and Chartres Cathedral nave.
These have been drawn to the same scale. Notice the changes from Early to High Gothic, as well as the greatly increased width and height of the arcade and clerestory at Chartres. Neither drawing includes the wooden roof trusses.

on the main level. The builders also added a transept to the original Romanesque basilica plan and, after construction was underway, decided to include three sculpted portals on each transept arm, giving Chartres a total of nine entrances.

The completed cathedral glows inside with a wonderful luminosity, in part because the clerestory window height has increased to equal the height of the arcade, while clerestory width has expanded to consume virtually all of the wall area between the wall shafts. Compare the interior nave elevations of Laon and Chartres (Fig. 9.15) to appreciate how substantially the proportions of window to wall

have changed in the shift from Early to High Gothic work. Note also the development at Chartres of plate tracery in the rose windows above the paired lancets of the clerestory. At Chartres, visible structural elements, including the vaulting ribs and wall shafts in particular, are slender and deeply undercut so that they appear to float free of the surfaces to which they are connected. Alternate nave piers have cylindrical and octagonal cores, with wall shafts that are either faceted or cylindrical, respectively. Even the buttresses, particularly the flyers around the choir, have a sense of lightness. Of all Gothic cathedrals, Chartres alone

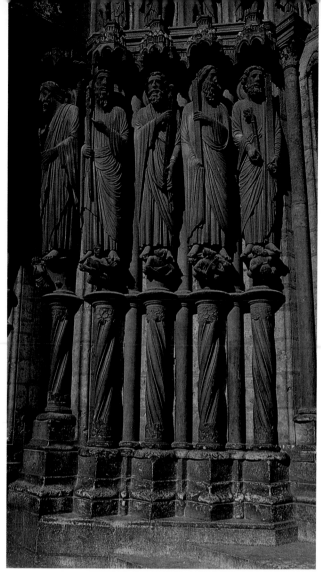

9.16 Jamb figures from the central portal of Chartres Cathedral, west front, ca. 1150.
These elongated crowned figures, representing Jewish kings and queens from the Old Testament, have timeless staring faces and stylized drapery suggesting Byzantine influence. They are probably the work of the sculptors from St. Denis, who came to work at Chartres when Suger's west front was completed.

9.17 Jamb figures at Chartres Cathedral south porch, ca. 1250.
The transept sculptures demonstrate the increasing naturalism of later Gothic work. These apostles inhabit bodies that are closer to actual human proportions, and their poses are more animated. From left to right are Saints Matthew, Thomas, Philip, Andrew, and Peter.

has preserved about two-thirds of its original stained glass. Bold figures of the holy family and the saints dominate the high clerestory windows, while more intricately detailed illustrations of biblical stories and saints' legends predominate in the windows of the aisles and ambulatory. Old Testament subjects are shown in the glass of the north transept, balanced by New Testament themes in the south-transept rose and lancet windows. On the west front, the twelfth-century lancets relating the genealogy and life of Christ were retained from the pre-Gothic church. Suger's ideal of pervasive interior beauty is nowhere more evident than at Chartres.

The west-front doorways, known as the Royal Portals because of the crowned figures in the jambs, provide a splendid image of the theology of salvation as it was visualized in 1150 (Fig. 9.16). The influence of Suger's façade at St. Denis can be seen in the stately, elongated jamb figures, while the tympana subjects reflect the teachings of the School of Chartres, a prominent medieval center of

learning associated with the cathedral. The portals carved a century later on the north and south transepts provide a measure of increased naturalism that occurred in Gothic sculpture (Fig. 9.17). Some of the subjects shown are repeated from the Royal Portals, but their treatment is far more lifelike.

The cathedral of St. Etienne at Bourges (1195–1250) presents a conceptual contrast to Chartres (Figs. 9.13, 9.18–9.20). Its plan shares features with Notre-Dame in Paris. Double aisles flank the nave and continue in uninterrupted arcs around the choir and sexpartite vaults are used in the nave and choir. A glance at the interior, however, indicates immediately that Bourges is no copy of Paris, but an original adaptation of High Gothic vocabulary. The paired aisles increase in height to help brace the high vaults of the nave and choir, recalling the triangular cross-section of Cluny III, with the addition here of flying buttresses that follow the slope of the roofs. At Bourges, choir and nave vaults spring from alternating major and

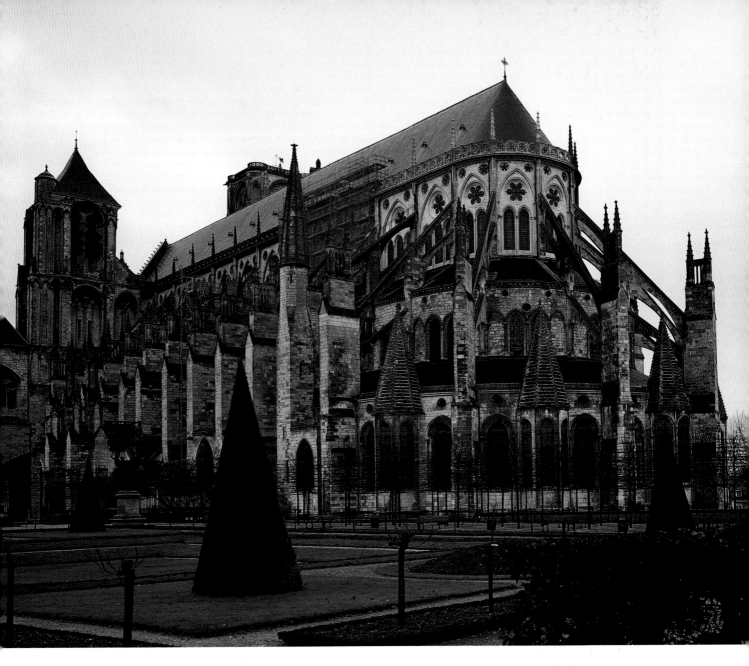

9.18 Bourges Cathedral from the east, 1195–1250.
This view shows the buttresses that provide bracing for the
high vaults. Notice how much smaller the clerestory windows
are than those at Chartres.

minor piers set on a square module plan. The spatial effect
is one of breadth and expansiveness, but the layered aisle
vaults and roofs preclude clerestory windows as tall as
those of Chartres, although here too they fill virtually the
entire wall area between wall shafts. On the west front, the
five major interior volumes are reflected in five portals,
completed in about 1285.

Robert Mark, an engineer who has researched the
structural behavior of historic buildings, documented
the structural logic of Bourges, which achieves a comparable interior height and area to Chartres, yet requires
significantly less stone. Despite its cost-effectiveness (for
stone was a major expense in building construction), the
double-aisle design of Bourges was seldom used thereafter,
while the more costly and inherently less stable model of
Chartres was adopted for the tallest cathedrals—Reims,
Amiens, and Beauvais (Fig. 9.14)—of the Gothic era. One

**9.19 Section through Bourges
Cathedral, 1195–1250.**
This view shows how the inner
and outer aisles function with
the buttresses to brace the
high vaults of nave and choir.

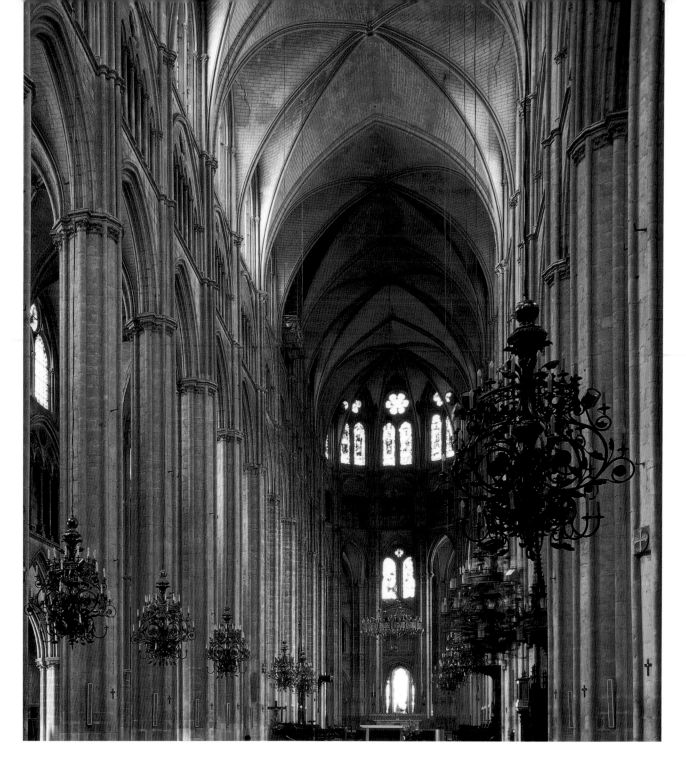

9.20 Bourges Cathedral nave, 1195–1250.
Because of the distinctive cross-section (see Fig. 9.19), Bourges Cathedral has not only relatively small clerestory windows in the nave but also exceptionally tall nave piers. Note also the use of sexpartite vaulting that replaced original quadripartite vaulting.

suspects that building patrons, in northern France at least, preferred the dramatic luminosity afforded by the tall clerestory windows of the single-aisle design more than structural efficiency, since Gothic was not primarily an expression of technique but an architectural embodiment of religious and cultural ideals. Cathedrals built on the model of Bourges are found in Spain and Italy, where bright skies prevail. The Cathedral of Milan, a late Gothic building, uses a cross-section similar to Bourges Cathedral to attain a nave vault height equivalent to that of Beauvais.

The Sainte-Chapelle

Even as the great French cathedrals were being built, there were also smaller Gothic projects under way. One particularly lovely example is the Sainte-Chapelle (1243–48), added by Louis IX to the royal palace in Paris as a repository for relics he had acquired from Constantinople, including the Crown of Thorns and a piece of the True Cross (Figs. 9.21–9.23). The relics cost twice as much as the building. The Sainte-Chapelle has two levels, a ground-floor chapel for use by the household servants and an upper chapel, surrounded by stained-glass windows with bar tracery in the new **rayonnant** style, for use by the royal family. This upper chapel is filled with jewel-like color by walls diminished to slender piers set between great expanses of largely original stained glass. Wall buttresses are linked together

9.21 Upper chapel interior, Sainte-Chapelle, Paris, 1243–48.
In great expanses of stained glass, most of it original, these
windows illustrate stories from both the Old and New Testaments
in chronological sequence from the entrance door to the apse.

9.22 Sainte-Chapelle, Paris, 1243–48.
Built as a palace chapel by King Louis IX to house relics he had acquired from Constantinople, this small jewel of High Gothic design is a virtual glass-walled structure, with stone cross-sections reduced to a minimum. The relatively small scale and internal metal tie-rods make flying buttresses unnecessary.

9.23 Transverse section through Sainte-Chapelle, Paris, 1243–48.
The low-ceilinged room below is the chapel for household servants, while the spacious upper chapel was the domain of the royal family.

horizontally by iron tie-rods that encircle the building concealed in the masonry, passing across the windows as part of the framework supporting the glass. As a miniature statement of the dematerialization of masonry walls and the wondrous properties of colored light sought by Abbot Suger, the Sainte-Chapelle has no equal.

ENGLISH GOTHIC

Although the Gothic style originated in France, it spread to other parts of Europe, particularly England, Germany, and Italy, and became the predominant style of northern Europe until the fifteenth century. English builders soon formed their own Gothic esthetic, and within a century had created Gothic churches that differed considerably from those built in France.

Nineteenth-century historians who first studied the Gothic buildings of England categorized the work in three overlapping phases, which are still useful for describing the progressive development of English medieval architecture (Fig. 9.24). **Early English**, built from 1175 to

1265, corresponds roughly to High Gothic work in France. Vaulting is straightforward, usually quadripartite, and windows have lancet-shaped heads. The **Decorated** period, extending from about 1250 until about 1370, uses vaulting elaborated with extra ribs, called **tierceron** and **lierne**, or decorative, ribs (meaning those that neither rise from a pier colonnette nor are ridge ribs), and window tracery worked into **trefoil** (three-part) or **quatrefoil** (four-part) cusped shapes, intersecting lines, or flowing curvilinear shapes. The final phase, the **Perpendicular**, is the most distinctly English. In fashion from about 1330 until 1540, it is distinguished by panel tracery and vaulting in elaborate conical fan shapes. Despite their visual magnificence, **fan vaults** (see Fig. 9.36) represent no structural advance; in fact, they are best suited to smaller churches where great heights and spans are not required. It is not possible to examine English cathedrals in strict chronological order, as portions of all three medieval periods are represented in the fabric of many of them. Discussions here will present the buildings as a whole.

Early English

Canterbury Cathedral was rebuilt in a Gothic style after the Norman church, begun in 1070, was devastated by fire in 1174 (Figs. 9.26a, 9.27). Leading master masons of England and France were summoned to give their advice about rebuilding the ruined site, and William of Sens was

Early English   Decorated   Perpendicular

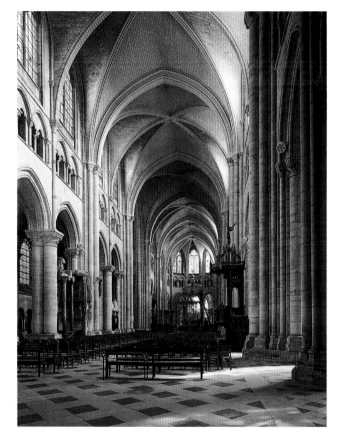

9.25 Sens Cathedral choir, ca. 1135–1180.
Sens was a French Early Gothic cathedral that served as the model for Canterbury Cathedral. Compare this image to the choir of Canterbury (see Fig. 9.27).

9.24 (above) Examples of English Gothic window tracery.
As many English churches were built over extended periods, variations in window tracery provide one clue to the construction sequence.

1179, leaving his assistant, William the Englishman, to complete the work.

The choir at Canterbury was designed to house England's most popular shrine, that of St. Thomas à Becket, Archbishop of Canterbury and advisor to King Henry II, who in 1170 was murdered in the northwest transept by four of Henry's knights. Pilgrims from all over Europe soon flocked to Canterbury to partake of the miracles performed at the tomb of St. Thomas, and the monks, enriched by pilgrims' offerings, needed suitable accommodation both for the steady stream of visitors and their own services. (Recall that the destination of Chaucer's pilgrims was Canterbury.) As was the case in earlier pilgrimage churches, a satisfactory arrangement involved an aisle and ambulatory, which linked the site of Thomas's martyrdom with his shrine in the Trinity Chapel.

Canterbury's somewhat rambling plan can be explained by the reuse of the Norman crypt and the pilgrim traffic to Becket's shrine. The Norman church had both east and west transepts and two apsidal chapels set at angles to the main axis rather than radiating from it. Beyond these spaces to the east, William the Englishman built the Trinity Chapel and its single axial chapel, the Corona, which terminates the church on the east. A second, smaller transept was constructed to the west of the choir; and the wider, majestic nave was built early in the Perpendicular period, 1377–1405, possibly to the designs of Thomas of Hoo. The crowning element in the cathedral is the 235-foot-high crossing tower named Bell Harry after the bell hung there, which was erected in the mature Perpendicular period (1491–98) to the designs of John Wastell. The fan vaults of the tower are forerunners of those Wastell would erect later at King's College Chapel in Cambridge.

selected to direct the work. He convinced the monks to demolish the remaining sections of the choir because the fire's heat had damaged the stonework beyond repair, but he confidently retained the fine Norman crypt and aisle walls. Between 1175 and 1184 the choir was rebuilt to a Gothic design based on the French cathedral of Sens (Fig. 9.25). During this time, William was severely injured in a fall from the scaffolding, and he returned to France in

Apsidal chapels set at an angle

East transepts

West transepts

Norman church

Corona Chapel

Trinity Chapel with Shrine of St. Thomas à Becket

Choir, built ca. 1175–84

Crossing tower or Bell Harry, built 1491–98

Site of St. Thomas à Becket's murder

Nave, built 1377–1405

Gothic church

N

0   50 m
0   150 ft

9.26a (left) **Plans of Canterbury Cathedral, 1175–84.**
These plans show the Norman church (*left*) and its Gothic replacement (*right*), which used much of the foundations from the earlier church. Canterbury incorporates the shrine of St. Thomas à Becket, who was murdered here in 1170.

9.26b (below) **Plans of Salisbury Cathedral, 1220–58; King's College Chapel, Cambridge, 1446–1515; and Lincoln Cathedral, 1192–1280.**
Both Salisbury and Lincoln have plans that reflect Cistercian rectangular chapels and double transepts inspired by Cluny III. The rectangular plan of King's College Chapel was designed for preaching.

Cloister

Chapter house

Salisbury Cathedral

King's College Chapel, Cambridge

West Front

Tierceron, or intermediate rib

Nave

Greater transept

Cloister

Chapter house

Angel Choir

Lierne rib

Choir

Eastern (lesser) transept

Lincoln Cathedral

0   50 m
0   150 ft

9.27 (left) **Canterbury Cathedral choir, 1175–84.**
The choir was built to the designs of William of Sens and William the Englishman. Although many features superficially resemble Sens Cathedral, there are characteristic English elements here, most notably the darker Purbeck marble trim that is used to emphasize horizontal lines.

ESSAY
A Wool Church
by Marian Moffett

Across Europe are legions of parish churches that originated in the medieval period—England alone has about 8000 surviving examples that collectively constitute a national treasure. More than the great abbeys and cathedrals that attract the attention of scholars (and tourists), these modest churches give us an indication of how medieval architecture was experienced by ordinary people of the time.

Parish churches were built in an era when all Christians in a given community worshiped in the same church and regular attendance (not to mention compulsory financial support in the form of tithes) was the norm. When the local economy was strong, well-to-do individuals tended to invest in building churches as a means both of ensuring divine favor and displaying their wealth, which in the late medieval period in England came largely from trade in wool and woolen cloth. St. Agnes's at Cawston in Norfolk (Fig. 9.28) is known as a "wool church" because its fifteenth-century nave and western tower were largely financed by Michael de la Pole, Earl of Suffolk, whose fortune derived from the wool trade. (The fourteenth-century chancel from an earlier church was retained.) St. Agnes's size is clearly in excess of what was required by Cawston's medieval population, so we must understand the building as a demonstration of the earl's piety and pride. His family crest is carved above the entrance. Stone imported from France was used for the tower and nave arcade, rather than the cheaper local knapped flint. As is common in English parish churches, the nave and aisles were covered by timber roofs rather than vaulting. Even here, however, the earl's munificence is evident: Cawston's nave has a

9.28 Interior of the church of St. Agnes at Cawston, Norfolk, 14th–15th century.

spectacular hammerbeam roof, adorned with standing angels at the ends of the beams, with three more angels hovering on outstretched wings above each clerestory window.

Not all the medieval work on the interior survives. When Henry VIII broke with the Church in Rome, he set in motion more than a century of religious unrest, during which English churches were stripped of images—altars, sculpture, paintings, and stained glass—that were regarded as being "popish." Traces of a mural over the

chancel arch remind us that these walls were originally painted, and remnants of stained glass now set in the south-aisle windows hint at what colored splendor once filled the windows. The wooden screen separating nave and chancel originally supported a gallery on which stood the rood, sculptures of the crucified Christ flanked by Mary and St. John. Its lowest tier still retains sixteen panels painted with figures of the saints, including St. Simon, who most anachronistically is wearing eyeglasses. It's a naïve yet touching detail, like the dragons and wild men carved in unexpected places, reminding us of the fundamental humanity of the artists who created these churches.

Salisbury Cathedral presents the rare example of an English Gothic cathedral built almost entirely in a homogeneous style, Early English (Figs. 9.26b, 9.29–9.30). It was begun in 1220 on an entirely new site, the cathedral and town having been relocated from Old Sarum to be near more reliable water sources. Construction of the majority of the church progressed with remarkable rapidity and was completed by 1258, leaving only the soaring crossing tower and spire to be built from 1334 to 1380. Salisbury incorporates features from monastic plans, including the double transepts of Cluny III and the square east end of the Cistercians, in a long, orthogonal building that is unmistakably English. On the interior, quadripartite vaults rise from three-story nave elevations, yet the continuous vertical line exploited by the French has been replaced by a horizontal emphasis created by a string course under the triforium and another under the clerestory windows. Even the ribs of the vaults do not extend down the wall but

spring instead from wall corbels at the base of the clerestory. Surfaces are articulated by shafts and trim in black Purbeck marble, an English stone that is not actually marble but takes a highly polished finish. The exterior receives the same horizontal emphasis as the interior. Flying buttresses do not have a strong vertical character, and the walls are coursed in horizontal bands that extend across the west front. With all this horizontality, the 404-foot tower and spire provide the necessary vertical counterpoint, and their great weight has noticeably deformed the piers at the crossing. The cloisters (completed 1284) are fine examples of early Decorated tracery, and off the east range one finds a lovely octagonal chapter house (begun 1263). Salisbury,

9.29 Salisbury Cathedral, 1220–58; tower 1334–80.
A cathedral built almost entirely in Early English Gothic. Note the lancet windows of the west front and clerestory and the horizontal lines that carry across the exterior.

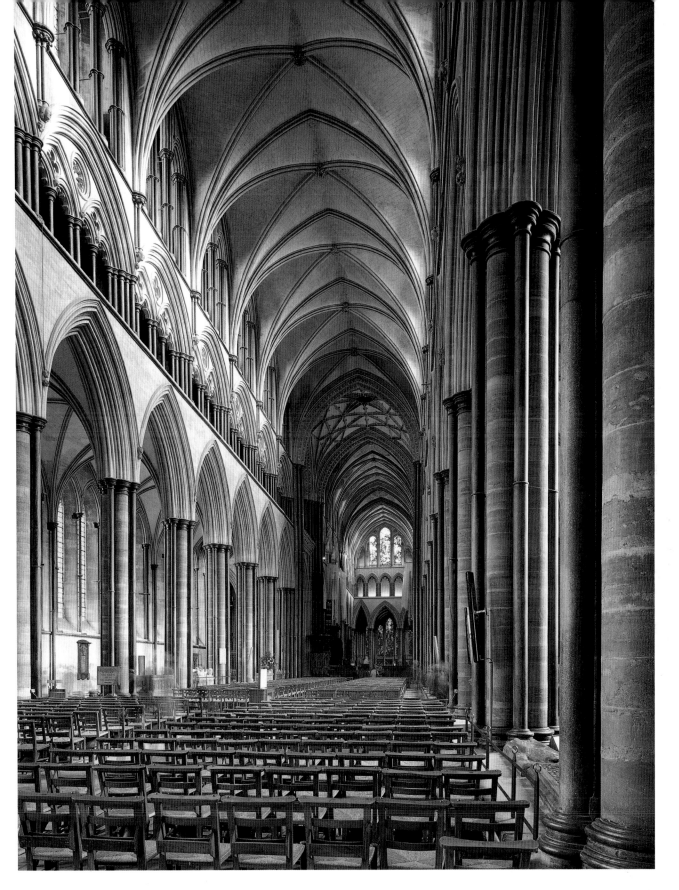

9.30 Salisbury Cathedral nave, 1220–58.
This view shows how horizontality prevails on the interior as well as the exterior. Notice how vaulting ribs do not extend as wall ribs down grouped piers, but spring instead from corbels set between the clerestory windows. Horizontal string courses along the triforium direct the eye down the length of the nave.

like many English cathedrals, was both an abbey and a cathedral. Accommodation was accordingly needed for the brothers to meet daily to hear a chapter from the Rule of St. Benedict read and elaborated; hence the polygonal chapter house. In Romanesque monasteries, this was generally a square or rectangular room off the cloister, but in English cathedrals it becomes an occasion for elegance in vaulting an octagonal space of considerable size.

9.31 Lincoln Cathedral choir vaults, 1192–1280.
Lincoln provides a wonderful sampler of vaulting. The transepts are sexpartite, while the nave features tierceron and lierne vaults of the Decorated period. Most unusual of all are the choir vaults, known as "crazy" vaults because their rib pattern is asymmetrical.

9.32 (left) Lincoln Cathedral, Angel Choir, 1192–1280.
The Angel Choir is the easternmost extension of the church, concluded with an enormous wall of stained glass.

Decorated and Perpendicular

At Lincoln Cathedral, a more complicated building history has resulted in a splendid combination of English Gothic periods (Figs. 9.26b, 9.31–9.32). The Norman church, damaged by an earthquake in 1185, survives today only in the lower portions of the west front. Rebuilding work, started in 1192, continued harmoniously through 1280. Construction began with the choir and eastern (lesser) transept, followed by the western (greater) transept, chapter house, nave, and west-front upper portions. The retrochoir (meaning "behind the choir" and here known as the Angel Choir) was begun in 1256. Concluded by an enormous eastern window, it was finished in 1280.

Lincoln offers several novel architectural features. Most obvious on the interior are the varied vaulting systems, including the tierceron vaults of the nave that link with an ornamented ridge rib. The "crazy" vaults of the choir are an asymmetrical experiment showing an original and

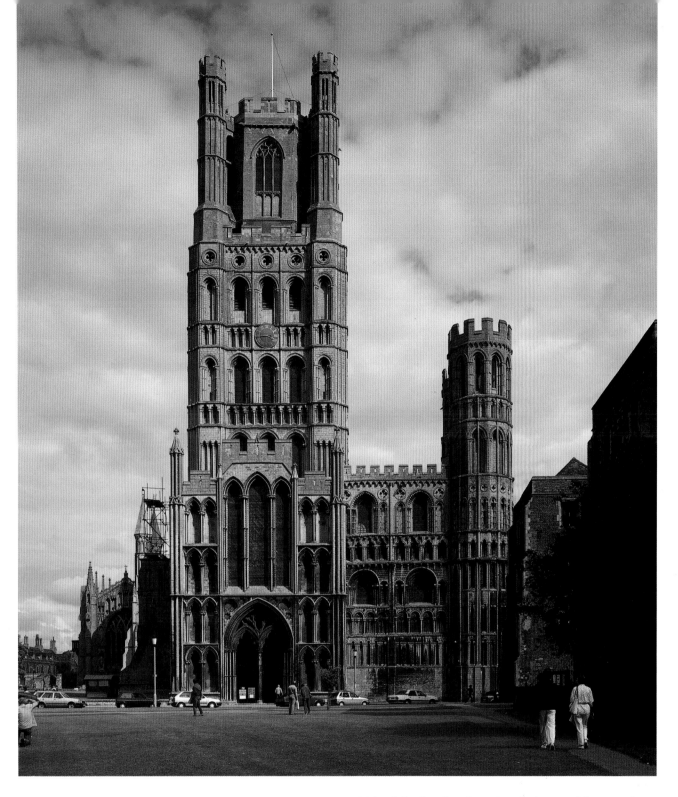

9.33 Ely Cathedral west front, begun 1081; lantern built 1322–36.
Most of the façade dates from the Norman period. The west front
was originally symmetrical: a tower to balance the one on the right
side no longer exists.

free interpretation of established Gothic conventions.
Throughout the cathedral, but above all in the Angel
Choir, there is a wealth of elaborate trim in the form of
Purbeck marble shafts, stiff-leaf capitals, and the sculpted
angels that give the retrochoir its name. The Angel Choir
clerestories and east-end window have tracery of the
Decorated period. On the west front, a broad screen wall
extends from the Norman work to increase the apparent

width of the façade, obscuring the bases of the west-front
towers, which define the actual width of the church.
Finally, the ten-sided chapter house with its bold flying
buttresses is a departure from the usual octagonal form.

Ely Cathedral illustrates another aspect of medieval
architecture in England, large-scale construction in timber (Figs. 9.33–9.34). Norman work predominates in
the nave, which is covered by a timber roof; on the west
front, a late Norman project designed with transepts but
never finished; and in the transepts east of the nave. The
original Norman choir was enlarged (1230–50) by an
eastern extension of six additional bays, based on the Early
English nave of Lincoln. The collapse of Ely's Norman
crossing tower in 1322 provoked the most extraordinary

9.34 Ely Cathedral lantern, 1322–36.
Notice how the octagon is turned 22.5 degrees to the axis of the nave. Wooden ceilings are treated on the interior as if they were stone vaults. The painted wooden ceiling of the Norman nave extends to the left side.

Principal rafter

Hammerbeam

Hammer brace

9.35 Hammerbeam truss, Westminster Hall, London, 1394–1402.
A hammerbeam is a short, horizontal member attached to the foot of a principal rafter. Notice how the wooden assembly comes to rest on the masonry wall, with the hammerbeam partially supported by the hammer brace.

construction. The church foundations were judged insufficient to support a masonry reconstruction, so the tower was replaced by a lantern in wood, the design of which also increased the light and usable space at the crossing. The designer of this masterpiece of medieval engineering was William Hurley, the King's Carpenter. He used eight giant oak posts—sixty-three feet long, forty inches thick, and thirty-two inches wide—for the vertical members of the octagonal tower, which has a diameter of sixty-nine feet. These are supported on **hammerbeams** (see Fig. 9.35) tied to the masonry crossing piers. The octagon itself is set at 22.5 degrees to the axis of the nave, providing a spatial contrast at the crossing. Most of the vaulting of the octagon is wood made to look like stone; the actual structural members are visible only if one climbs into the lantern via the access stair.

Ely's exceptional crossing tower is not the only example of English monumental timber construction. A number of late medieval hammerbeam roofs survive, the grandest being Westminster Hall in London (now incorporated into the Houses of Parliament, a nineteenth-century building). The hall itself dates back to the early 1100s, when it was constructed as an aisled space for royal banquets. By the late Middle Ages, a covering not requiring intermediate supports was desired, so in 1394–1402 the hall was roofed, using hammerbeams that are supported on the older walls (Fig. 9.35). Hammerbeam construction is actually a series of successive short cantilevers that enable builders to roof a span wider than the length of available timbers. The craftsmanship behind the hammerbeam roofs, with their interlocking pegged joints and elegantly carved finials and angels, is a testimonial to the technical skills and artistry of medieval carpenters.

As an example of Late Gothic masonry construction in England, the chapel at King's College, Cambridge, deserves attention for its exceptional fan vaults designed by John Wastell (Figs. 9.26b, 9.36). Begun in 1446 with donations by Henry VI and completed by 1515 with contributions from Henry VIII, the chapel was designed for use in an era when the sermon had become an important aspect of worship services; it was built with a simpler plan and smaller area to reduce reverberation so that speech could be better understood. Medieval monastic chant is enhanced by long reverberation times, but the spoken word is virtually

9.36 King's College Chapel interior, Cambridge, 1446–1515.
The fan vaults make this glass box a masterpiece of late
medieval architecture. As in the Sainte-Chapelle, the walls have
been reduced to glass screens set in a skeletal stone frame.

9.37 St. George Church nave and aisle, Nördlingen, 1427–ca. 1500.
This is a hall church, where the nave and aisle vaults are virtually
the same height. Gray stone ribs form intricate geometric patterns
on the plastered surface of the vaults.

incomprehensible in the same space. Medieval churches
still in use for church services employ electronic amplifi-
cation systems that help cancel out reverberation. King's
College Chapel is basically rectangular in plan, with
Perpendicular tracery in the large windows and majestic
fan vaults overhead. The ornate organ loft atop the choir
screen divides the space into two parts, one for townspeople and the other for students. The chapel is contemporary
with the High Renaissance in Italy, and the woodwork of
the choir screen contains classical detail in what is otherwise a late medieval building.

GERMAN, CZECH, AND ITALIAN GOTHIC

Hall Churches

Just as the Romanesque developed regional variants as
it responded to local traditions and preferences, so too
did the Gothic. German builders initially used French

cathedrals as models, occasionally importing master
masons, but they were soon creating their own versions
of the Gothic style. Particularly characteristic of German
Gothic is the **hall church**, a type where the vaults of both
the nave and aisles are essentially the same height. This
is the design used at St. George in Nördlingen (1427–ca.
1500), a church without transepts but that has aisles on
either side of the six bays of the nave that continue up the
five bays of the choir to a chapel at the eastern polygonal
end (Figs. 9.37–9.38). A massive tower on axis anchors
the western front. On the interior, the structure is clearly
expressed: gray stone cylindrical columns with attached
shaft moldings support a vaulted ceiling where ribs
describe intricate patterns. Aisle windows, set between the
buttress piers, are treated as punched openings, but they
are tall and without colored glass, so they provide ample
illumination. Mies van der Rohe, the twentieth-century
German-American architect who advocated "skin-and-
bones" buildings in glass and steel, found much to admire
in such German Gothic hall churches.

9.38 St. George Church vaults, Nördlingen, 1427–ca. 1500. This view shows the pattern created by the ribs.

St. Barbara at Kutná Hora in the Czech Republic is an extraordinary example of Late Gothic with a complex history and form. The town's economy was fueled by silver mines and the king of Bohemia's royal mint. Construction began in 1388 on the model of a French Gothic cathedral with eight radiating chapels, perhaps designed by Johann Parler, but work stopped in about 1400 and was not resumed until 1481, after the turmoil of the Hussite Wars had subsided. In 1489, Matej Rejsek completed the choir more or less according to the original design. A new master, the royal architect Benedikt Ried, assumed direction of the work in 1512, and in building the nave, he departed from the basilican scheme by building the nave piers as freestanding elements to support the vault of a hall

church, with well-lit galleries over the side aisles. Intricate net vaulting in the choir was joined in the nave by flowing ribs that emerge near the piers to swirl into six-petal forms (Fig. 9.39). Whereas the vaulting ribs at Nördlingen were defined within each bay, the pattern on the thin shell vault here exists almost independently of a bay structure and creates an extraordinary sense of weightlessness.

Italian Gothic Variations

Italian designers modified the Gothic style to fit local conditions, and the differences one observes from northern European versions of the style should be understood as adaptations that demonstrate the flexibility of the Gothic

9.39 St. Barbara Church nave vaults, Kutná Hora, 1388–1512.
The supporting piers rise as unbraced shafts above the inner aisles to vaults that match the height of the nave. Large gallery windows flood the interior with light, illuminating the flowerlike ribs that flow gracefully across the vaulting shell.

to accommodate varying interpretations. Given Italy's bright skies, large windows were not necessary to provide illumination inside buildings. Italian Romanesque builders were proficient in **domical vault** construction that reduced lateral thrust and thus required less in the way of buttressing. Cultural esthetics predisposed Italians to prefer internal tie-rods instead of visible external buttressing, so flying buttresses appear only rarely. (Tension ties also make sense in earthquake-prone areas.) Many of the religious orders desired churches that maintained a sense of openness and visibility, qualities that could be achieved using the Gothic.

Gothic architecture first came to Italy with Cistercian monks, who had slipped easily into the style after absorbing the architectural sensibilities of Bernard of Clairvaux. Other monastic orders, particularly the mendicant Dominicans and Franciscans who came to minister to growing urban populations, also tended to build in Gothic. Among the earliest of their buildings was the great Dominican church of S. Maria Novella in Florence (1279–ca. 1310), built to a plan that would seem familiar to a Cistercian (Fig. 9.40a). The nave consists of nearly square bays and a square crossing and chancel. Four square chapels opening off the transept give the church structural clarity. Plain wall surfaces contrast with polychrome stonework outlining arches of the arcade, transverse nave arches, and vaulting ribs in the nave and aisles (Fig. 9.41). By constructing ribbed domical vaults in the nave, the builders minimized lateral thrust to the point where support from the high aisle vaults and buttresses concealed under the aisle roofs was sufficient to brace the structure. A connection to the classical orders is evident in the half-columns engaged in the slender piers of the arcade. Aisle windows

9.40a (top) **Plan of S. Maria Novella, Florence, 1279–ca. 1310.**
There is a Cistercian-like simplicity to this plan, which was built for the Dominican Order. Its ribbed domical vaults are braced by buttresses concealed under aisle roofs, thereby avoiding the need for flying buttresses.

9.40b (above) **Plan of Milan Cathedral, 1387–ca. 1572.**
This is the largest Gothic church in Italy, and its structure is based on the cross-section of Bourges Cathedral, where pairs of aisles help to brace the high nave vaults. Master builders from France, Germany, and Italy were consulted concerning its design and construction.

9.41 S. Maria Novella interior, Florence, 1279–ca. 1310.
This view shows the polychrome ribs of the vaults. Notice the small roundels in the clerestory.

**9.42 Milan Cathedral buttresses and pinnacles,
1387–ca. 1572; 19th century.**
The west front blends classical and Gothic motifs.
Flying buttresses were added in the nineteenth
century as the exterior was completed.

are small, and the clerestory consists of modest circular
openings punched near the top of each bay. A large triple
window in the chancel wall provides the strongest direct
light. The internal effect is open and clear, well suited to a
church for preaching to a congregation. We will encounter
S. Maria Novella again in the Renaissance chapter, when
its façade is completed.

At Todi, the Franciscans built S. Fortunato (1292–early
1400s) to a hall church design. Here the highest point
(crown) of the vaults is uniform across the church, unlike
the billowing ceiling compartments created by domical
vaults and transverse arches in S. Maria Novella. Without
lower aisles to counter the vaulting thrust, the builders here
constructed braces from the exterior wall to the nave piers
in order to stabilize the building. As at S. Maria Novella, the
nave bays are essentially square. Slender half-column shafts
on the piers align with graceful vaulting ribs, giving a sense
of considerable spaciousness to the interior. On both sides
of the nave, chapels for use by the brothers are set between
transverse buttressing walls. Tall windows above the chapels light the interior, complemented by illumination from
five windows in the polygonal choir.

Italy's largest and most ambitious Gothic church is
Milan Cathedral, begun in 1387 and not finished until
1858, although it was essentially complete by 1572. Its plan
features a broad nave with double aisles, an aisled transept, and a polygonal apse with ambulatory (Fig. 9.40b).

The aisle bays are square in plan, while the nave bays are
rectangular. The structure follows the model of Bourges
Cathedral, where the aisles rise in a roughly triangular section to brace the nave vault, and the height of the nave, at
157 feet, is virtually equal to that of Beauvais Cathedral.
Remarkably, it was constructed without flying buttresses,
the ones on the cathedral today having been added in the
nineteenth century.

Less than two years after construction began, decisions
of the master builder Simone da Orsenigo were being sec-
ond-guessed by consultants engaged by the client. Italian
master builders, artists, and mathematicians gave opinions
regarding theory, design, and technology, and building
experts from France and Germany were summoned to give
their views as well. Because some of the debate that ensued
was transcribed (albeit by persons who did not fully understand what was being discussed) and these written records
still exist, documents relating to Milan Cathedral provide
an extraordinary insight into the variety of Late Gothic
theory and practice, and the contrasting approaches to art
and science. Opinions held by these experienced builders
and theoreticians reflect differences in regional traditions
and esthetics: the Italians favored broad proportions, the
French argued for the particular vaulting techniques that
they employed, and the Germans advocated soaring verticality. Consultations continued for more than a decade as
the work was assigned first to one and then another master.
In the end, proportions advocated by the Italian mathematician Gabrielle Stornoloco were used: the cathedral's section, based on an equilateral triangle, establishes the height
of the nave at three times the height of the outermost aisle
and one-and-a-half times the height of the inner aisle.
Italian masons, accustomed to building within the load

9.43a (left) The notebook of Villard de Honnecourt, ca. 1225–50.
Villard collected drawings from various places, intending to pass his work on to others. This page shows methods for obtaining the solution to geometric problems, important skills for medieval builders.

9.43b (center) The notebook of Villard de Honnecourt, ca. 1225–50.
This sketch combines wrestling men with the scheme for a Cistercian church and the plans for the choir at Reims Cathedral. Villard's drawings are the earliest record we have of a medieval builder's graphic representation of buildings.

9.43c (right) The notebook of Villard de Honnecourt, ca. 1225–50.
Here Villard drew two Cistercian church choirs. Some scholars think that he was involved in rebuilding the choirs of Cistercian churches to more elaborate designs. Notice that these plans show wall thickness and vaulting ribs.

requirements of domical vaults, used them in the aisles and in a modified form in the nave, reinforcing the vaults with strong iron tie-rods. This approach was foreign to the French and German masters, but it worked.

The resulting building is unlike most other Italian Gothic churches, lacking a sense of spatial openness because of the bulk and close spacing of its piers. The volume is enormous, and as the small clerestory windows are filled with stained glass, even in full Italian sunshine little light enters the nave. Windows in the choir provide brilliance, however, drawing the visitor to the liturgical center of the church. Much of the exterior is post-medieval, but the work was carried out to the very end within the Gothic esthetic (Fig. 9.42). The exterior of Milan Cathedral is a veritable forest of carved marble and spiky pinnacles from the vantage point of the roof level, which is accessible.

MEDIEVAL CONSTRUCTION

Milan Cathedral is exceptional in having preserved documents relating to its design and construction. For most of the great medieval building campaigns, the absence of written or graphic material limits our ability to make definitive statements about the nature of medieval architectural practice or construction procedures. Nevertheless, historians have analyzed the materials that are available—a few sketchbooks, isolated drawings and preserved tracing floors, works accounts, monastic chronicles, and the evidence provided by the buildings themselves—to piece together some understanding of building in the medieval world.

A building designer in the Middle Ages was usually called a master builder, the title of architect not being used until late in the period. The master builder's training would have included the acquisition of language and mathematical skills in a grammar school run by the local priest or monastery, followed by apprenticeship in one of the building trades (carpentry or masonry) at about age thirteen. The apprentice would be taught all aspects of the craft, including theoretical matters and practical applications, especially the construction of arches and vaults using centering. After three to seven years thus spent under the direction of a master craftsman, the apprentice would be certified as a journeyman, a worker qualified to hire himself out for a daily wage. For several years, he would work on different building sites, traveling about and keeping a sketchbook while gaining practical experience. To advance to the level of master he would be required to present a masterpiece—either an actual building or a finely executed model—to the masters of his craft guild, who would evaluate his fitness to direct journeymen and teach apprentices. Only the most capable and experienced master craftsmen would acquire the title of master builder.

A collection of drawings made by Villard de Honnecourt, who was active ca. 1225–50, constitutes the earliest surviving documentation from the medieval period (Figs. 9.43a,b,c). His notebook includes a wide range of observations and sketches: geometry problems and their solutions; timber roof trusses; sculpture and carved ornament; nature sketches; church plans; sketches of details from cathedrals at Laon, Chartres, and Reims; machines and devices; and such esoteric information as how to tame a lion. Other than what is contained in his notebook, little is known of Villard or his works. He claims to have traveled from the Low Countries to Hungary and back, and some historians surmise that he may have been employed by the Cistercians, perhaps in rebuilding **chancels** in the more elaborate Gothic style employed after the death of Bernard of Chairvaux. Others believe that he was merely a collector of drawings with a particular interest in details. From an inscription on the opening pages of the book, it is obvious that Villard intended his collection to be used by others. He identifies geometry as the basis of drawing, claims to present advice on masonry and carpentry, and asks that readers remember him and pray for his soul. His drawings show the earliest known representations of interior and exterior elevations (for Reims Cathedral) and also contain architectural plans with wall thicknesses specified, unlike the single-line walls marked on the Plan of St. Gall. Whatever his role in the building trades, Villard's drawings show that architectural ideas traveled as workers moved from site to site and also through the exchange of sketches and notations.

Geometry was indeed the theoretical core of medieval architecture. Following Roman practice, the master established basic building dimensions by a module and derived all other measurements from this standard through the manipulation of compass and straightedge. (Medieval people used Roman numerals that were uncongenial for all but the simplest arithmetical calculations.) The "secrets" of the masons were primarily principles of plane and solid geometry and knowledge of how to use triangles, squares, pentagons, and other figures to generate proportional lines, most of which have dimensions represented by irrational numbers. Just as beauty in medieval chant was defined by proper relationships in the intervals between musical tones, so beauty in architecture was assured if the proportions of major elements and minor details were in geometric harmony.

Building a church of any size required money to pay skilled craftsmen. Masters and their workshops moved around according to the availability of construction funds, so it is sometimes possible to trace specific crews from project to project. The idea that churches were built either by monks or by volunteer laymen is a misconception. The overall size of the church and its major features would be determined by the master builder in consultation with church officials, and then professional quarrymen, masons, carpenters, sculptors, glaziers, and tilers would be employed to execute the work. Depending on the wealth of the client, a major cathedral could be built in as little as thirty years, as was the case at Chartres, or construction could drag on in discontinuous campaigns stretching over centuries.

MEDIEVAL HOUSES AND CASTLES

Our consideration of Romanesque and Gothic architecture has necessarily concentrated on the design of religious buildings, primarily because the Church commanded the best design talent and greatest financial resources. Medieval buildings remaining for study are from 400 to 1100 years old now, and only the best-constructed architecture can be expected to last that long. In the Middle Ages, churches formed the main group of buildings erected with great care, so inevitably they comprise the bulk of medieval architectural history.

Housing

Enough secular structures survive from the Middle Ages to give a general idea of the buildings in which ordinary people lived, and archaeological investigation is providing more information all the time. Rural houses of peasant families were simple, providing minimal shelter for

9.44 Reconstruction view of an early medieval longhouse, Bremerhaven, Germany.
Entrances set on opposite sides of the long walls divide the building into two parts, one with a hearth for cooking and warmth, and the other with stalls for animals.

9.45 A medieval manor house.
The hall was the main living space, provided with a central hearth for warmth. Meals would be taken here in common with household servants and retainers.

9.46 Brace heavy timber frames (half-timbering) used in medieval construction.
Notice the slight cantilevers or jetties that extend the floor space on the upper levels. Along narrow medieval streets, these overhangs would reduce available light.

cooking and sleeping. These buildings used local materials, mostly earth, wood, and thatch, and basic construction techniques, as they were probably built by the families that inhabited them. The combined house-barn or longhouse is a type that was widely used throughout the medieval period (Fig. 9.44). It was built on a rectangular plan entered through doorways placed opposite one another on the long sides, thus providing cross-ventilation and dividing the building into two sections. One end focused on an open hearth, around which the family gathered, and sometimes there was a second chamber partitioned off for sleeping or storage. The remaining section housed livestock, whose body heat helped warm the interior. As the building lacked a chimney, smoke would filter into the high volume overhead, where it could exit through gaps left in the gable ends without igniting the thatch of the roof. Peter Brueghel the Elder depicts just such a house in the background of *The Birdnester*, painted in 1568, which indicates that these rural structures were even then common sights in the countryside.

Land-owning families who were several steps further up the social ladder might inhabit a house (without animals) divided into a hall and solar, a private room on an upper floor. The hall was the major gathering and entertaining space (Fig. 9.45), warmed by a fire or central hearth, and the solar was a more private space reserved for the family. By the late Middle Ages, these basic rooms were usually improved by the addition of a buttery (for storage of drinks and other foods to be kept cool), a pantry (for storage of dry foodstuffs), and a passage screening circulation space to these storage rooms and the kitchen, which was a separate structure. The solar might move to an upper story and have its own stair for greater privacy. Since the nobleman fed his guests and retinue of servants in the hall, meals were important occasions for displaying hospitality and wealth. (It is ironic that the hall in modern houses has dwindled to an entryway or connecting passage, when once it was the major living space.)

Houses built in towns were more compact, often including several floors to conserve available land. The structure would again be wood, the roof would be thatch, and the entire building would accordingly be very combustible. Devastating fires are frequent events in the chronicles of medieval cities. Larger towns eventually regulated building by insisting on masonry construction and tile or slate roofs to reduce the spread of fire. Nevertheless, some wooden dwellings survive in England and on the European continent to illustrate half-timber construction (Fig. 9.46). Buildings so designated have a heavy timber frame, exposed on the exterior, which is completed by non-structural wattle and daub, plaster, brick, or other infill. Whether of masonry or timber, town houses would typically have a shop on the

9.47 Medieval house, Cluny, 12th century.
This townhouse is typical of many medieval urban residences, combining workshop or commercial space on the ground floor with the owner's living quarters on the floor above.

9.48 Tower houses, S. Gimignano, 13th–14th centuries.
In many northern Italian towns medieval families constructed towers on masonry houses out of a sense of competition or perhaps for defense. In S. Gimignano, they were apparently also used to hang lengths of dyed cloth.

ground floor and the dwelling apartments on the floors above (Fig. 9.47). The kitchen would be on the ground floor separated by a small light court from the rear of the shop to keep its odors and fire hazards away from the main part of the house. Italian cities tended to have houses built in brick or stone, with tile roofs, and a number of Italian towns preserve substantial numbers of medieval masonry houses. S. Gimignano is particularly notable for the towers that survive on some houses (Fig. 9.48). While tower houses elsewhere may well have been constructed for defense, their likely function here was drying lengths of fabric away from sunlight, a necessary process to fix the local yellow dye.

Castles

Fortified residences or castles were homes of the nobility, although they probably offered little more in the way of creature comforts than the homes of the more modest folk. Castles were constructed for defense, guarding strategic roads or rivers, and they also served as administrative centers for the surrounding territory. The earliest such

fortifications were wooden, and only post-holes survive for archaeologists to base their conjectural restorations on. More easily visible are the earthworks that accompanied the early wooden castles, **motte and bailey** (mound and yard) being the most common form for these (Fig. 9.49). For a better command of the surrounding countryside, castles were constructed atop a mound (the motte), based whenever possible on an existing hillock and enlarged by fill from a ditch, or **moat**, dug around the base. Between the ditch and the motte was an open area (the bailey) that provided room for the more temporary accommodation of castle retainers—servants, craftsmen, soldiers, horses, and the like. Enclosures of wooden palings, similar to the palisades erected in American frontier forts in the eighteenth and nineteenth centuries, were built around the bailey, and a watchtower might protect the sole gateway. Hundreds of motte-and-bailey sites are detectable today, the outlines of their mounds and surrounding ditches still visible in aerial photographs.

The pace of castle construction in England increased markedly after the Norman invasion of 1066. William the

9.49 Plan and section through a motte-and-bailey castle, Castle Acre, Norfolk, 12th century.
The castle buildings are long gone, but the earthworks survive to show the motte or mound and the moat that surrounded the bailey or courtyard associated with the mound.

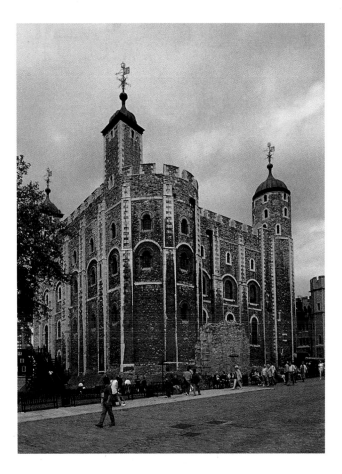

9.50 (above) The White Tower (Tower of London), London, 1078–80.
Its three floors are vaulted to make them fireproof, and the roof served as a fighting platform. A Norman chapel occupies the rounded section on the third level.

9.51 Plan of the Tower of London, 1078–80.
This view shows the ancillary walls and moat constructed since William's day. When first built, the Tower sat just inside the Roman wall around London.

Conqueror may have brought pre-cut wooden timbers on his ships to build a castle on the coast at Hastings, for his fortification there was completed in the very short timespan of two weeks. The Bayeux Tapestry depicts peasants digging the ditch and piling dirt for the motte. (The site of the castle at Hastings has since been partly claimed by the sea.) When William came to London, however, he desired something more permanent to signify his jurisdiction over the most important city in the country, and he was granted a site on the eastern edge of the Roman wall surrounding the City of London, where he constructed the White Tower (Figs. 9.50–9.51), now better known as the Tower of London (1078–80). It is a three-story masonry **keep**, or stronghold, basically rectangular in plan, with a semicircular projection reflecting the apse of a chapel constructed within at the third level. In the years since its construction, turret roofs of the corner towers have changed its profile, and layers of enclosing walls and ancillary buildings have been added around William's castle, but the massive strength of the original Norman keep remains.

9.52 (above) Carcassonne, built 800–1300.
Carcassonne is a medieval French city with fortifications dating back to the seventh century. These early fortifications were extensively repaired and provided with a second set of walls from 1248 to 1290.

9.53 (right) Plan of Carcassonne, built 800–1300.
This plan shows the fortified *cité* (*lower right*) and the grid-plan bastide that was established in 1248 across the river Aude. When the second set of walls was planned for the *cité*, the hilltop became essentially a military camp.

Bastide (new town)

Marketplace

Aude River

Castle

0 — 500 m
0 — 1500 ft

Double fortification walls   *Cité* (old city)

MEDIEVAL CITIES

There is an obvious connection between medieval castles and cities, for both relied on well-built fortifications to withstand attack, and they are frequently found together. Most medieval cities were provided with a solidly constructed wall with lockable gates that in ordinary times enabled the municipality to collect taxes from merchants entering the city. As the innumerable armed struggles characteristic of the Middle Ages usually had the capture of towns as their objective, the town walls served important defensive purposes as well. Fortunately for cities, medieval warfare was seldom a sustained event with large armies, and weapons before the introduction of gunpowder and metal cannonballs in about 1400 were rather primitive: battering rams, catapults, siege ladders or towers, and bows and arrows. Fire and pestilence could also be used for strategic advantage. A well-built fortification, punctuated by towers, provided defenders with a platform from which to return catapult and arrow fire and to dump stones or boiling liquids on persons trying to undermine or scale the wall. The most common form of attack was the siege, in which attackers tried to cut off supplies to the town and thereby force the inhabitants into surrender.

Experience gained over time suggested that the most defensible wall was one protected by projecting towers of cylindrical rather than rectangular shape, equipped with archer slits that would allow defenders to shoot almost parallel to the section of wall between towers. Moats or ditches provided useful protection, and a double set of walls made attack that much more difficult. Most of these innovations can be seen at Carcassonne, a strategic site that had been fortified successively by the Gallo-Romans, the Visigoths, and local counts before Louis IX of France gained control of it in 1248 (Figs. 9.52–9.53). Louis's intention was to make the city an impregnable stronghold as he sought to bring the south of France under royal control. In addition to repairing and strengthening existing work in the old fortified town (the *cité*), he constructed a second ring of towers and walls (Fig. 9.54). The resulting fortifications were so formidable that the city was never seriously attacked thereafter. Carcassonne's strategic importance waned with the medieval period, but when

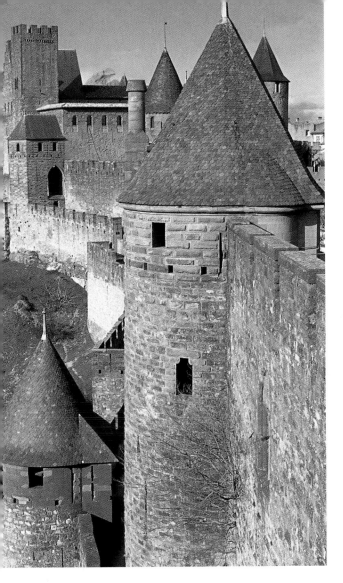

9.54 Carcassonne walls, 1248–90.
Notice the square holes left near the tops of towers
for the construction of timber hourds, projecting
galleries that could be quickly erected for defense.

9.55 Plans of four bastide towns, southern France, 1220–1375.
Note the tendency to provide a square arcaded marketplace
at the center of town. In most cases, the church is set away
from the square, where commerce was most important.

there was a proposal to pull the crumbling walls down in
the nineteenth century, preservationists intervened and
restored the battlements and tower roofs to the condition
seen today. It is one of relatively few French cities to have
its medieval defenses intact.

To encourage commerce and trade without overcrowd-
ing the *cité*, which had essentially become a military garrison, Louis IX developed a new town in the valley below
Carcassonne. Its regular grid plan organized around a central marketplace contrasts sharply with the irregular layout
of the hilltop city, which like many medieval towns grew
without regulation or advance planning. This lower town
is in fact one of about 500 new-town foundations known
as **bastides** that were made in the south of France in the
period between 1220 and about 1370. The motive behind
establishing new cities was primarily economic: the bitter
campaign against the Albigensian heresy had devastated
the countryside, and as several parties—the kings of France
and England, along with local counts—had claims to the
territory, they sought to encourage settlement through
the granting of freedoms and economic privileges associated with town residence. Not all bastides were built to
the same plan, but many share certain characteristics: an
orthogonal street layout, a central market square (often
surrounded by arcaded buildings) and town hall, and uniform lot sizes for houses. The church is usually relegated to
a side location. Monpazier, founded by Edward I in 1284,
is often cited as the "typical" bastide, but its actual layout
is not so regular as the idealized plan would suggest. The
plans of Revel, Mirande, and Villefranche-de-Rouergue
illustrate some of the variations found in bastide layouts
(Fig. 9.55). While the architecture of bastide towns is usually not extraordinary, the clarity conferred by the plan creates a unifying harmony that makes many bastides small
gems of urban design (Fig. 9.56).

A similar colonizing intent in central Europe resulted
in the founding of hundreds of regularly planned towns
under German influence in Poland, Slovakia, and
Hungary. Trade was the prime objective, because the
founder collected sales taxes from commerce, so the cities encouraged settlement with charters based on the Law

Revel   Mirande   Villefranche-de-Rouergue   Monpazier

9.56 Monpazier market square, ca. 1300.
The architecture here, as in many bastides, is not exceptional, but the clear urban pattern and use of arcades around the square gives these cities a strong sense of urbanism.

of Magdeburg that guaranteed citizens freedoms of the market. One particularly handsome example of a deliberate foundation under Magdeburg customs may be seen in Kraków, the historic capital of Poland, where an old castle and related settlement pre-dated the new foundation created with the granting of a Great Charter in 1257 (Figs. 9.57–9.58). An area immediately north of the existing town was laid out around a major market square, 600 feet on a side, with uniform building plots marked on the surrounding square blocks. The only exceptions to the grid were two existing churches, which remained where they were. In time, a substantial cloth hall, large and small weigh houses, market stalls, and the city hall were built in the market square. Fortifications added in the fourteenth century linked the town and castle. Although few medieval houses survive, the original street layout and plot divisions continue to govern the fabric of the historic core.

Italian towns and cities experienced a slightly different situation during the medieval period. There, the commercial activity on which all urban life depends never completely ceased in the period following the decline of Rome, although urban services, most notably the public water supply, tended to fall below standards established under Roman jurisdiction. Medieval Italian communes participated vigorously in the revival of long-distance trade that characterized the later Middle Ages. Larger city-republics functioned as independent states, controlling smaller communities in the region and squabbling with other city-states for rights to border areas. At Siena, a medieval town formed by combining three separate ridgetop settlements and citizens celebrated the merger by building a new urban center on a marshy field (campo) where the ridges joined

9.57 Plan of Kraków, Poland, generated by the Great Charter of 1257.
The orderly town plan (shown hatched) includes a large market square. Building lots were laid out to maximize frontage on important streets and around the square.

(Figs. 9.59–9.60). The town hall or Palazzo Pubblico (1298) dominates the bowl-shaped open area, which is an irregular fan-shaped **piazza**. Even though it has no regular geometry, the Campo was deliberately shaped and governed by municipal regulations that required façades of

9.58 (above) Kraków market square, showing
St. Mary's Church (*left*) and the Cloth Hall.
Textile merchants were very important. Their trading
hall had stalls on the ground floor and rooms for the
cloth guild upstairs.

9.59 (left) Palazzo Pubblico, Siena, 1298.
The slender brick belltower, one of the tallest in all
Italy, serves as a vertical marker for the town hall.

Palazzo Pubblico

N   0 ————————— 100 m
     0 ————————— 300 ft

9.60 (above) Plan of the Campo, Siena, 1298.
The fan-shaped piazza slopes down to the Palazzo
Pubblico, set at the lowest part of the site. While this is
often not the best location for a prominent building, the
citizens of Siena made sure that all buildings fronting on
the Campo were compatible with the town hall.

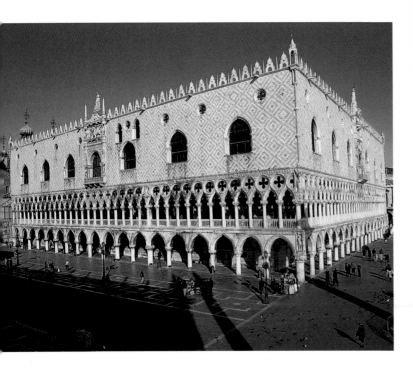

9.61 Doge's Palace, Venice, 1309–1424.
This is a splendid example of the Gothic style adapted
in Venice. Mixed with exotic influences from the East,
the Gothic in Venetian hands becomes a lacy filigree
to adorn buildings adjacent to the water.

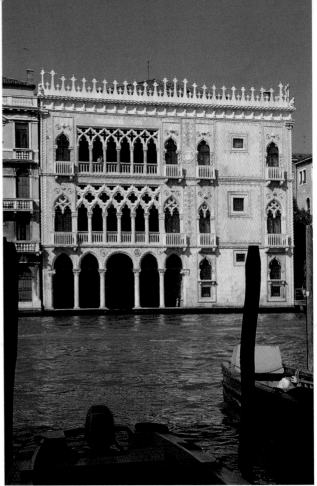

9.62 Ca' d'Oro, Venice, begun 1421.
This is an exceptionally fine merchant's house facing onto the
Grand Canal. Its name, House of Gold, came from the gilding
that was once applied to the exterior detail. Even without the
gold, its lacelike arch tracery and marble walls shimmer in the
light reflected off the Grand Canal.

surrounding structures to harmonize with the town hall.
The Palazzo Pubblico is nominally Gothic in style, but
elements of the style have been used more for surface
articulation than for structure. Crenelations and **machi-
colations** atop the building and its slender belltower are
likewise ornaments in the modern style rather than serious
attempts at fortification.

In Venice, a maritime republic that dominated trade
between Europe and the Byzantine Empire, a decorative variant of the Gothic developed in which northern
European features were blended with exotic influences
from the East. The result is an airy, delicate architecture
animated by the shimmering light reflected by the city's
canals. The Doge's Palace is perhaps the most famous
example of Venetian Gothic (Fig. 9.61). A blocky structure
with an open courtyard, it has a solid exterior wall resting
on two stories of open arcades. Pink and white diaper patterns enliven and lighten the visual impact of solid wall,
so that it does not appear to overload the delicate filigree
of the arcades below. The Ca' d'Oro illustrates Venetian
Gothic applied to the traditional merchant's house, with
its central section of large arcaded windows that open onto
the **grand salon**, the major living space that extends the
full depth of the house (Fig. 9.62).

In general, however, the Gothic was strongly identified
with northern Europe and never attained great significance
in Italy. By the fifteenth century a new artistic movement,
based on the ideals of classical antiquity, was developing
in the urban centers in the north of the country. In the following centuries this new style, the Renaissance, would
spread to the rest of Europe. In isolated communities,
however, medieval building traditions continued with

little change until the nineteenth century, and medieval
house forms are reflected in the earliest American architecture, particularly in New England and Virginia. There
is even an American church built in 1682, St. Luke's in
Isle of Wight County, Virginia, that is considered part of
the Gothic survival. In the nineteenth century, the Gothic
Revival originated with reform-minded Victorians as a second flowering of medieval art and architecture.

CONCLUSIONS ABOUT
ARCHITECTURAL IDEAS

It is useful to speak of the Gothic architecture conceived
in the Île-de-France as a "system" in which pointed arches,
ribbed vaults, and flying buttresses, their effects enhanced
by stained glass, were made to interact structurally and
esthetically. Obsessed with what he believed to be the mystical quality of light, Abbot Suger at St. Denis near Paris
called upon his builders to erect a sunlight-filled masonry-
defined space for the new choir of his church. Their experiments set in motion an inquiry into the nature of stone as
a medium for erecting a framework of slender vertical supports, arching lateral stabilizers, and thin-webbed, ribbed
ceilings as an alternative to the thick, continuous walls and

heavy barrel and groin vaults of the Romanesque. Within the development of Western architecture, there has been no more dramatic change in the conception of form and space.

Experiments proceeded along various lines. At Notre-Dame Cathedral in Paris, masons erected six-part nave vaults atop walls rising in four stories: nave arcade, gallery, triforium, and clerestory. At not-too-distant Notre-Dame Cathedral in Chartres, builders changed to four-part nave vaults and a three-story elevation of arcade, triforium, and a much taller clerestory. It was this larger-windowed system that carried the day in northern France. Proving that decisions were being made on the basis of appearance as much as, if not more than, structural logic, St. Etienne Cathedral in Bourges received a triangular cross-section that was more efficient, therefore more economically built, than either Paris's or Chartres's, but its model was largely ignored. French churchmen continued to push builders toward the construction of ever-wider, ever-taller vaults until the collapse of the choir at Beauvais defined the limits of thirteenth-century masonry technology. The much smaller Sainte-Chapelle in Paris—its upper level akin to a cathedral shorn of all but its nave core—became a jewel box of stained-glass-tinted light admitted through virtually floor-to-ceiling windows with rayonnant tracery.

In fog-shrouded England, builders never considered light to be the essence of their chauvinistic interpretation of the Gothic. Here, churches have typically been categorized as Early English, Decorated, and Perpendicular. While most English cathedrals are agglomerations from more than one of these periods, Salisbury presents itself as pure Early English. Orthogonal in plan, including the choir, as was the English (by way of Cistercian) preference, it has four-part ribbed vaults, though the ribs do not extend visually down to the floor in the form of colonnettes, as in the French system, meaning a much lessened sense of verticality. Dominant instead are receding layers of arched openings at the nave, triforium, and low-clerestory levels that feature a rich patterning of severely molded arches springing from their own colonnettes. Traceable as far back as the nave at Durham, this English fascination for textured surfaces is also vividly displayed on Salisbury's west façade.

No cathedral in the Decorated style is nearly so pure as Salisbury. This style represented an extension of French rayonnant taste, and is characterized by ornamental richness and the appearance of new rib types. Lincoln Cathedral includes Decorated tracery in its Angel Choir and tierceron, or secondary, ribs in the nave that produce "crazy" vaults, so called for their asymmetry. King's College Chapel at Cambridge exemplifies the Perpendicular style, somewhat confusingly named, as it is really characterized by strong verticals, as seen in the mullions of the chapel's lateral windows. In the ceiling, the ribs become filigree defining fan vaults, making the ceiling texture as insistent as that of the side walls.

While the German Gothic produced some monuments dependent on French models, German masons, especially those in Bohemia, emancipated themselves from French inclinations by pushing ribs to ornamental extremes. They made them flow and swirl in organic, florid compositions, something like stone icing piped on the vault web with a giant pastry tube. In extreme examples, ribs detach themselves from the web, and "fly," in apparent defiance of structural logic.

The Gothic remained something of an interloper in sun-drenched, classically disposed Italy. The Cistercians brought the style south, but no structural innovations were made there. Producing Milan Cathedral's spiky countenance involved almost endless consultations about proportioning systems rather than the esthetics of light or the techniques of stone masonry, a far cry from Abbot Suger's initial intentions.

During the Middle Ages, building experts were stonemasons, and the most skilled of these men became masters capable of supervising and coordinating the construction of cathedrals. In addition to their expertise in the physical laying of stone and their empirical knowledge gained through experience, they possessed certain "secrets," which turned out to be geometric manipulations needed to determine proper dimensions and shapes.

Smaller medieval buildings, including residences, were often constructed using half-timbering, or heavy-timber framing, infilled with masonry. The results were extremely impressive and required great carpentry skills to accomplish them, but the manner of building was not a very efficient one. Some houses, especially urban examples, were constructed of stone and given Romanesque and Gothic features. In the case of S. Gimignano in Italy, houses sprouted tall towers that could be used as strongholds, or as indicators of family prestige, or for drying long lengths of fabric.

Medieval castles, in a time before gunpowder-charged cannons, were constructed of heavy masonry. British versions included a keep, or stronghold, in a central tower; then a surrounding yard; then the perimeter walls, often fortified with towers of their own; and finally a moat. These castles developed in isolation or as part of cities that grew around or adjacent to them. Medieval city plans were either modular and orthogonal like the bastide, or planned new town, at Carcassonne, or organic, like Carcassonne's old town, with its double layer of towered, masonry walls. In such cities, open spaces were typically located adjacent to castles, churches, and city halls, with the most active being the central marketplace, where a municipal fountain could provide public water.

While aberrant in its substitution of canals for streets and its extremely eclectic building styles as a result of far-ranging international trade, Venice provides a fitting conclusion to this overview of the Gothic style. Gothic buildings in Venice have an exotic quality, and, likewise, the local Renaissance style, discussed in Chapter 11, exhibits a sensuality and suppleness unique to the Veneto, or Venetian region.

Chapter 10

Indigenous Architecture in the Americas and Africa

The widely accepted "out-of-Africa" hypothesis proposes that the human species arose in the African continent 150,000 to 200,000 years ago, and then between 60,000 and 120,000 years ago began a series of migrations that spread across the globe. Scientists continue to debate the paths and timing of Homo sapiens' migration into North, Central, and South America. Many associate the timing with the last Ice Age some 12,000 years ago, when the low ocean level produced a land bridge from Asia to what we know today as Alaska. A more nuanced view suggests that migrants first traveled by boat from island to island, then perhaps by both land and sea. Geneticists have examined the DNA of Native Americans in the western hemisphere and concluded that their ancestors arrived 15,000 to 17,000 years ago and moved along two routes. One group traveled down the Pacific coastline of North America and eventually reached the southern tip of South America, while the other group moved along the land bridge and perhaps through a breach in the Canadian glacier and into the heartland of North America.

These are the peoples who fashioned the architecture discussed in this chapter, from the tents of nomadic Moroccans to the portable teepees of the Great Plains, from the rock-cut churches and stone fortresses of Ethiopia to the precise stonework of the Inca in Peru, as seen in the photograph opposite.

NORTH AMERICA

As in Europe and Asia, indigenous architecture in North America responded to complex social, economic, political, and environmental forces. However, its salient characteristics were a directness of construction and an honest use of materials. To some extent, such directness and honesty were inevitable, as most native cultures did not build road systems or construct large ships, and, while there was extensive trade between different peoples, it mostly involved smaller objects. This meant, with a few notable exceptions, that construction materials were drawn from local sources. Yet a feeling remains among many that the indigenous cultures of the Americas maintained a

connectedness to place, a reverence for nature, and a noble forthrightness in their building that has been all but lost in today's society. Figure 10.1 shows the geographical distribution of the North American tribes.

Tribes of the Great Plains and the Great Lakes

Tribes like the Lakota Sioux, hunting bison on horseback and led by their famous chief Sitting Bull in his eagle-feather headdress, have come to represent the Native American in the modern imagination. At their peak, some sixty million bison roamed the Great Plains, and Plains tribes based their cultures on these huge but skittish animals, using their meat for food, their hides for clothing and housing, and their bones for tools. In the seventeenth century, the Spanish introduced horses into New Mexico. Native Americans quickly recognized their value, and horses soon became available on the Great Plains, where they made it possible for nomadic peoples to accumulate wealth, carrying large quantities of valuable possessions with them in the form of food, housing, clothing, and other amenities. With this rise in the standard of living came a dramatic growth in population. These conditions,

Chronology

Earthen pyramids built in Peru	ca. 3000 BCE
Rise of the Olmecs	1300 BCE
Castillo built at Chavín de Huántar	900 BCE
Occupation of Teotihuacan and the Classic period in Pre-Columbian Mexico	200–1000 CE
Maya culture in Central America	ca. 300–1450
Chimor Empire begun at Chan Chan	ca. 1000
Occupation of Mesa Verde	1100–1275
Occupation begins at Poverty Point site in Louisiana	1200
Construction of fortress complex of the Great Zimbabwe	1200–1300 CE
Building of Great Mosque in Djenne	1200–1300 CE
Construction of St. George's Church, Lalibela	1200–1300 CE
Founding of Tenochtitlán	1325
Construction of the palace at Gedi	1400s and later
Founding of the Inca Empire	1438
First voyage of Christopher Columbus	1492
Spanish conquest of the Aztecs	1519
Spanish conquest of the Inca	1532
Construction of Bobo-Dioulasso Mosque	late 19th century

Machu Picchu, Peru, ca. 1450.
One could hardly imagine a more dramatic site. However, its exact function—ritual center, military outpost, or something else—remains unclear.

Arctic
Eastern Aleut
Central Aleut
Western Aleut
Trans-Arctic Eskimo

Subarctic
Eastern Aleut
Central Aleut
Western Aleut
Trans-Arctic Eskimo

Plains
Crow
Hidatsa
Mandan
Omaha
Arapaho
Blackfeet
Cheyenne
Kiowa-Apache
Pawnee
Comanche

Northeast / Great Lakes
Chippewa
Kickapoo
Micmac
Naskapi
Penobscot
Iroquois
Winnebago

Southeast
Creek
Natchez
Cherokee

Northwest Coast
Haida
Chinook
Quinault
Tillamook

Plateau
Nez Perce
Kutenai
Umatilla
Yakima

California / Great Basin
Yurok
Hupa
Tolowa
Karok
Pomo
Maidu
Miwok
Wintu

Southwest
Navajo
Papago
Pima

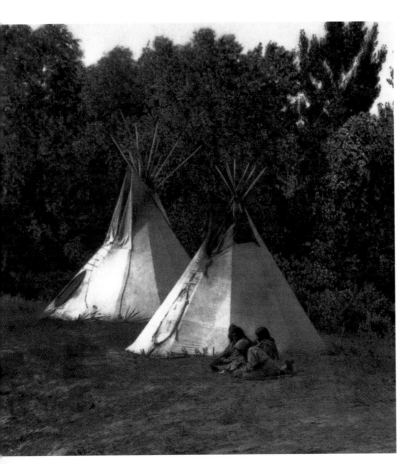

10.1 Distribution of Native American tribes.

10.2 A Great Plains teepee.
A response to both numbing cold and blazing heat, the teepee was also portable. It has become one of the most vivid images in movies depicting the conflict between indigenous American people and European and American settlers.

in turn, increased warfare between tribes over the best grazing lands.

Because tribes moved about frequently, or at least had separate summer and winter dwellings, their architecture was necessarily temporary, rapidly constructed, mobile, and reusable. The best known of such nomadic structures is the teepee, a conical skeleton of poles covered with bison hides (Fig. 10.2). It was preferred by such tribes as the Arapaho, Blackfeet, Cheyenne, Comanche, and Crow, all names made familiar to moviegoers during the heyday of so-called "westerns." Most often depicted in this medium only as savage obstructionists bent on thwarting white settlement, these Plains-dwellers were in fact able designers who developed the teepee as a flexible solution to the contradictory problems of raging winds, numbing cold, internal fires and smoke, and blazing heat. Accordingly, the teepee had its vertical axis tilted and its plan distorted to an egg shape in order to combat prevailing winter winds, while its covering could be opened up

10.3 A Midwest wigwam.
This domical structure is covered with mats. The mats overlap like shingles to prevent the entry of moisture.

for hot-weather ventilation. This covering also provided a mural surface for painted images, which typically depicted sacred symbols and the significant events of inter-tribal warfare. The teepee achieved its great size, requiring a covering of thirty or more bison hides, only after the horse became available to drag it on a travois of two poles joined by a frame.

Other tribes produced temporary buildings in different forms and using different materials. The Kiowa-Apache of the northwestern Plains constructed the wikiup as well as the teepee. To build it, they bent saplings into arch-shaped profiles, collectively forming a domical skeleton that they covered with smaller saplings and finally thatch. Tribes of the southern Plains assembled their similar grass houses by bending saplings like ribs over a ring of wooden posts, then covering the saplings with overlapping bundles of thatch.

Various Plains tribes, including the Mandan and Hidatsa, built earth lodges. They began by constructing a post-and-lintel rhombus of logs; next they leaned poles against it in a conical configuration; finally they covered the poles with earth to produce a cone- or dome-like enclosure. The Mandan and Hidatsa founded agricultural towns along rivers in Missouri, making some of them into market centers. Nomadic groups from the north and west brought exotic and precious items like dentalium, a type of mollusk shell, to trade for the local surplus of maize.

Tribes of the Northeast

In the northeast, hunting tribes such as the Penobscot, Micmac, and Naskapi constructed their versions of the teepee and covered them with bark. Various others, including the Great Lakes Chippewa, moved the teepee cone along a horizontal axis to form an extended version that was used as a multi-family dwelling.

Similar to the teepee and wikiup was the wigwam (Fig. 10.3), which was made by bending enough saplings into arch-shaped cross-sections to form a vault- or dome-like volume, then covering it with mats or bark. In the northeast, various Algonquin tribes, including the Chippewa, Kickapoo, and Winnebago, favored the wigwam. When the first English settlers arrived to found the Massachusetts Bay Colony, they also lived in wigwams until they could erect larger structures like the ones they were accustomed to in England.

In what is today upstate New York, tribes of the Iroquois Confederation erected longhouses, vaultlike wigwams extended along their primary axes, sometimes to a length of more than 300 feet. The Iroquois used these large buildings as community halls for holding religious rituals. They practiced agriculture, growing maize, beans, and squash, and trapped animals for their pelts. They established a fur trade with Europeans in the early seventeenth century, competing with and eventually dominating their Algonquin neighbors. By the late eighteenth century, the English and the French were themselves competing for furs, and the Iroquois threw in their lot with the English. Though the Iroquois attempted to remain neutral during the Revolutionary War, they soon found themselves fighting a losing battle with the settlers and retreated to reservations, as would many other Native Americans as the new arrivals spread across the continent.

Tribes of the Mississippi River Basin

Tribes of the Ohio River Valley and the southeast were distinguished by their construction of earth mounds. The Adena culture (ca. 800 BCE–400 CE), in what is today Ohio, is admired for its earthwork depictions of animals. Perhaps the best known of these, the so-called Serpent Mound,

ESSAY
The Birthplace of the Choctaws
By Jack D. Elliott

10.4 Nanih Waiya mound, rural Mississippi, ca. 100 CE.

The reality of things, it appears, cannot be fully understood in terms of the world and its time; for the things are circumfused by an ambience of mystery that can be understood only in terms of the myth.
Eric Voegelin

The landscape is suffused with symbolism. Even for information-obsessed moderns who fancy themselves to be detached and objective observers, it still has evocative associations. Like most peoples, early Native Americans lived in landscapes replete with mythological symbols. In particular, mounds, relic landscape features built by earlier settlers who were forgotten by their successors, often took on mythical associations.

Nanih Waiya (Choctaw—"bending hill") is an earthen mound that stands in rural central Mississippi (Fig. 10.4). Today it is approximately twenty-five feet high and covers about seven-tenths of an acre at its base. Early accounts indicate that the site also once possessed a smaller burial mound and a

surrounding earthen breastwork. These features have been destroyed as the result of agricultural practices during the nineteenth and twentieth centuries. Recent research conducted by Ken Carleton, archaeologist for the Choctaw tribe in Mississippi, suggests that the mound dates to the Middle Woodland period, that is, about 2000 years ago, almost certainly pre-dating by centuries the emergence of the Choctaw tribe.

The mysterious mound came to be regarded by the historic Choctaw tribe as sacred through linkage to their origin myths; it was the "ishki chito," "the great mother." Two basic themes are to be found. According to the more prevalent story, the Great Spirit created the first Choctaws in the interior of the mound, whence they crawled forth wet and moist through a cave or hole into the daylight and lay out in the sun to dry. During the early nineteenth century there was a "large and deep" hole in the top of the mound. The Choctaws' regard for the great mother mound was such that if they were hunting in the vicinity, they would bring a portion of their kill and throw it into the hole, feeding their mother, as they saw it.

The second story was the migration legend, in which the ancestors of the Choctaws moved from the west led by prophets, who envisioned a land with fertile soil and abundant game, carrying a pole. They traveled eastward, and at the end of each day they camped and planted the end of the pole in the ground so that it stood vertically. In the morning they would find that the pole had tilted, and their journey would resume in the direction in which it had tilted. The journey continued for months until one evening they arrived at Nanih Waiya and planted the pole; the next morning they found it still standing erect. This was interpreted as an oracle indicating that they had arrived at their new home.

We often smile today at the mythologies of the past; the details, for the most part, are not factually true. Yet there is more to our appreciation of these stories than whether they contain strict historical fact or not; the linkage between mythic story and place makes us see places as we might not otherwise see them. They evoke in us a sense of wonder at things that we have all too often lost in a world where the mystery of Being is often ignored.

meanders some 600 feet in an oscillating curve. The Adena people also constructed conical mounds, some more than sixty feet tall, covering log structures used for burials or as depositories for cremated remains. A full explanation of the motivations that so inspired these ancient builders has not yet been developed; some mounds were obviously effigies and some were funerary, others apparently defined ritual spaces, and others still may have been built to provide relief from periodic flooding.

Tribes throughout the Mississippi Basin found abundant wildlife and other natural resources around them and cultivated maize, beans, and squash like their neighbors to the northeast. They also established long-distance trade routes. Excavations in Cahokia, Illinois have unearthed copper objects from the Great Lakes, mica from the southern Appalachians, and seashell ornaments from the Atlantic coast. In around 1000 CE, Cahokia was the largest city north of Mexico, covering five square miles and having a population of some 30,000 inhabitants. Among Cahokia's platform mounds is the so-called Monk's Mound, built entirely of earth, which is half the size of the enormous Pyramid of the Sun (see Fig. 10.15) at Teotihuacán near modern-day Mexico City. This pyramidal structure is situated at the head of a great plaza and large posts in the ground nearby probably once facilitated astronomical observations.

Development of the vast Poverty Point site, in what is today northeast Louisiana, is believed to have begun in about 1200 BCE. Some have argued that it was a regional trading center established by the Olmecs of eastern Mexico. Poverty Point consists of concentric semicircular, ridge-like mounds enclosing a plaza 1800 feet across. In order to shape such a landscape, the amount of earth that had to be moved was prodigious. Light wooden houses, long since gone, once stood atop the ridges. Mound-building was still being practiced by the Natchez tribe on nearby sites in the early eighteenth century when the phenomenon was observed and commented on by French explorers.

To the east, Native Americans also constructed mounds, such as those in Moundville, Alabama (Fig. 10.5), which are situated on a high bluff above the Black Warrior River. On a site covering 300 acres, there are twenty mounds, most with their ramps still visible, surrounding a large plaza. Dwellings once ringed the mound complex and were protected by a wooden palisade. Atop the mounds stood timber-frame structures with walls covered in plaster on lath formed of smaller limbs and twigs and with roofs covered in bark.

At Moundville, a museum was opened in the 1930s that allowed visitors to look at skeletal remains in an excavated burial site. While this display seemed reasonable at the time, the modern view is that such exhibitions, made without the permission of associated parties, represent inappropriate intrusions upon the most personal kind of human settings. Consequently the excavation has now

10.5 Earth mound, Moundville, Alabama, 1200–1500.
This earth mound at Moundville in west-central Alabama was constructed as a base for a temple or residence of an important person. Unlike the pyramids in Mexico, it was never encased in a stone veneer.

been sealed off from public view. Likewise, museums throughout the country have returned for reinterment Native American remains removed unilaterally by archaeologists in years past.

While mound-building has received the most attention, more modest Native American constructions in the southeast are equally interesting. The Creeks of Alabama and Mississippi erected buildings with mud-over-timber-frame walls, which they arranged around square courts, as well as octagonal townhouses and, as communal centers, buildings on round or polygonal plans with conical roofs. They sealed their walls using a whitewash made of ground oyster shells and covered their roofs with a variety of materials including thatch and bark. Farther south, the lower Creeks built the chickee, a raised platform protected by an openwork wood frame supporting a thatched gable or **hipped roof**.

Arctic and Subarctic Tribes

The Aleuts of the Aleutian Islands in Alaska favored whale meat for food, but made use of the entire animal, from its intestines to its bladder and tongue. They hunted whales in boats called baidarkas, constructed, appropriately, with whalebone frames. These boats seated as many as forty men, though a typical hunting party usually had only ten or so. They also plied the waters in kayaks in search of smaller game such as sea lions, seals, and porpoises. On land, they used sleds, but still had no dogs as late as 1000 CE. The Aleuts called their semi-subterranean sod-covered house a barabara, and entered it through a roof hatch. Underground buildings took advantage of soil mass to moderate temperatures. In the Arctic, the Canadian Inuit (Eskimos) also lived in subterranean houses, which they built of stone, wood, and almost any other available material. Traditionally, Inuits have hunted sea mammals and caribou, living in villages in winter and then separating and moving inland in the summer. To this day, they

10.6 Inuit iglu.
While the iglu is shaped like a dome, it is actually made of spiraling courses, with the bed of each block sloping inward. The blocks are cut from packed snow, meaning ice crystals rather than solid ice, so that trapped air provides insulation.

10.7 Bird's-eye view of a northwestern shed house.
Shed houses could be quite large, with eaves rising to twenty feet and main rooms stretching up to 100 feet across. The production of individual planks by splitting and finishing them with an adze was a technological challenge in a culture that had no power-drive saws.

continue to construct the well-known iglu (Fig. 10.6), a structure made of snow blocks. They cant blocks inward to create a stable domical profile, but rather than laying them in courses, spiral them upward. They enter the completed iglu through a small barrel-vaulted porch.

The teepee form was adaptable even for the subarctic region. Here, tribes built the tupik, a teepeelike structure that they covered with animal skins. During the summer months, Arctic Inuit constructed a tupik that appears at first glance to have been a type of extended teepee, but was actually a tent made of poles covered with skins that mimicked the form of their winter iglu, even to the inclusion of a tunnel-like entry.

Tribes of the Northwest and Northern California

Native American cultural patterns were similar along the Pacific coast from Alaska to Baja California. Diet was diverse, including plentiful fish and sea mammals and a variety of indigenous plants. The Quinault tribe of Washington state is famous for its potlatches, enormous feasts celebrating a child's coming of age, a death and subsequent memorialization, or the annual salmon run.

Along the northwest Pacific coast, the Quinault, as well as the Chinook and Tillamook, built **shed houses** (Fig. 10.7), log frames sheathed in cedar planks and covered with single-sloping or gable roofs. Such constructions were long on a locally abundant building material but short on technology, using inefficient structural cross-sections such as circular beams and joists and simple fasteners such as

cedar-bark ties. Farther north, tribes such as the Haida built **plank houses** and also erected **totem poles**, carving them with images of stylized animals. Some scholars argue that such carving could have been done with bone and shell tools; others see it as a later development dependent on the appearance of metal. The tribes of the northwest also applied similar painted images to the exterior walls of their chiefs' houses.

The Nez Perce, famous for their hospitality to the Lewis and Clark expedition in 1805, wintered in small villages along the Columbia river in carefully chosen, sheltered locations. They lived off salmon, root vegetables, and bulbs, which they preserved by drying them on racks or in earthen ovens. They then stored the processed items in baskets lined with salmon skins, and finally placed them in specially designed storage houses or stone- or bark-lined pits. They also hunted game and, having horses, bison as well. The Nez Perce and Yakima occupied **pit houses** (Fig. 10.8), timber frames set above three to four-foot-deep pits and covered with pine needles, reed or grass mats, and earth. They erected these timber frames in a configuration akin to conventional post-and-lintel and hipped-roof framing.

Northern California is a land of rugged topography and dense forests. The preservable carbohydrate that Native Americans here favored was flour made from acorns and buckeyes, and their preeminent craft was basketry. The Yurok, Karok, Hupa, and Tolowa tribes built gable-roofed frames above pits but covered them with planks from locally available redwoods. In central California, the Maidu and Miwok tribes constructed oval and octagonal

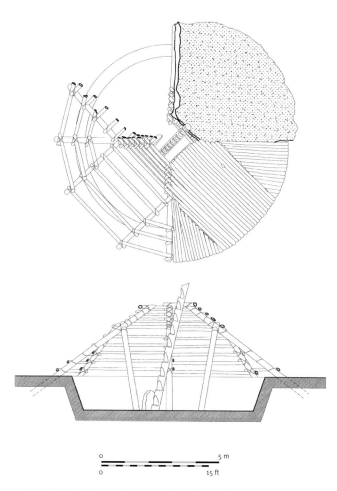

10.8 Overhead view and cross-section of a northwestern pit house.
Such domestic environments took advantage of the insulating qualities of surrounding rather than covering earth. While rarely seen in Europe, the entry from above was not uncommon in North America.

have vanished"; and the Ancestral Pueblo, long called the Anasazi, which has often been translated as "Ancient Ones." By 300 BCE the Mogollan culture of central Arizona and southwestern New Mexico had established villages atop mesas, or steep-walled plateaus. They built pit houses enclosed by timber frames covered with brush and earth and entered down a ramp or ladder. Along the Gila and Salt rivers, the Hohokam people developed sophisticated systems of irrigation and built castlelike structures with adobe walls as much as five feet thick.

The Ancestral Pueblo began their culture in what is today Utah, then gradually migrated into southwestern Colorado, eastern Arizona, and western New Mexico. They developed a distinctive form of black-and-white pottery, as well as methods for conserving and managing precious water for irrigation. Their building of compact, permanent settlements reached a zenith in 1100–1300 near the Four Corners region at Mesa Verde and Chaco Canyon, and consisted respectively of extensive alcove dwellings beneath protective mesas (Fig. 10.9) and agricultural and trading townships.

Ancestral Pueblo architecture began as pit houses entered from above, with excavated floors covered with timbers and then earth. In around 700 the Ancestral Pueblo modified their construction practices, erecting their houses for use during the summer months at ground level, using sandstone masonry for walls and adobe over small timbers for roofs. They combined these houses in a party-wall fashion, arranged them around irregular plazas, and continued to provide entry into them only from above. In around 1000, they began to transform their remaining

pit houses using radiating poles set atop polygonal frames. Over the poles, they layered sticks, then grass or tule mats, and finally a coating of earth.

Tribes of the Southwest

In the southwest, members of the Pima and Papago tribes lived in **ki** or **ramada** depending on the season. A ki began as a shallow pit surrounded by a low wall made from the excavated spoil. This walled pit was then roofed with a domical structure made by covering sapling frames with brush, then mud. Working together, the two systems lessened the effects of both heat and cold. Both tribes made a warm-weather ramada by planting upright posts in the ground to support a brush-covered roof. Family groups lived in rancherías, communities of farmsteads located near water sources.

Unique conditions in the southwest also led to a permanent indigenous architecture. Three cultures contributed: the Mogollan—named for the Mogollan mountains in southwestern New Mexico; the Hohokam—their name taken from a Pima word meaning "those who

10.9 Mesa Verde, southwest Colorado, 1100–1275.
The Mesa Verde site was chosen for habitation for practical reasons rather than for its dramatic landscape: it offered protection from winter winds out of the north and security against potential invaders.

10.10 Pueblo Bonito, Chaco Canyon, New Mexico, 900–1120.
This view gives a sense of the expanse of the site. Its semicircular arrangements of terraces, now in ruin, responded to the path and inclination of the sun. A disadvantage of this kind of tiered arrangement was that it created a high percentage of unlit interior rooms.

pit houses into sunken, circular **kivas**, sacred and social spaces that celebrated their clan-oriented society. Each kiva contained a **sipapu**, or ceremonial opening, to the world below. Around a kiva, the Ancestral Pueblo distributed several suites of living spaces. As their population increased, they added second and third stories to their already-dense housing complexes, called **pueblos**, probably relegating the largely unlit lower-level rooms to use for food storage. The vast Ancestral Pueblo alcove dwelling or Cliff Palace at Mesa Verde contains some 200 rooms and twenty-three kivas. While Mesa Verde's stone masonry is today much admired for its intricate workmanship, it was originally covered with adobe plaster to protect it from the elements.

The Ancestral Pueblo developed numerous settlements, typically in compact, naturally sheltered locations like Mesa Verde, which enabled them to combat invaders, mitigate the effects of harsh climate, and orient structures to important celestial events. For example, at Fajda Butte in Chaco Canyon, during solstices and equinoxes, upright stones still allow the passage of thin bands of light between them that frame a spiral petroglyph. Atop the mesas at Mesa Verde, they developed terraced gardens like those of the Incas and constructed reservoirs for agricultural- and drinking-water retention.

At Pueblo Bonito in Chaco Canyon, the Ancestral Pueblo built an intricate irrigation system that included

dams, ditches, and flood gates. They erected a great five-story, tiered, semicircular megastructure with some 800 rooms and at least thirty-seven kivas facing the arc of the sun as it traversed the southern sky; only ruins remain today (Fig. 10.10). They built walls from bonded wythes of stone set in thin beds of clay mortar and applied a veneer of coursed ashlar covered with adobe plaster. As at their other sites, they arranged for entry into rooms only from above via ladders. They also developed an extensive system of roads, many of them still apparent in aerial photography. Based upon the exotic artifacts found here, such as seashells and parrot feathers, it seems clear that Pueblo Bonita was the major trading center in the Ancestral Pueblo southwest.

The Ancestral Pueblo culture declined rapidly after 1300 for reasons that are not yet adequately understood. The most likely cause was an extended drought resulting from changing weather patterns. Their descendants, including the Zuni, the Hopi, and the Navajo, still dominate in the region. The Navajo nation, in what is today northeastern Arizona and northwestern New Mexico, represents the largest tribe in the United States, some quarter of a million strong, and occupies some nine million acres of reservation land. Traditionally, the Navajo lived in hogans (Fig. 10.11), which consisted of various configurations of log frames covered with earth. Some of these log frames were conical; some began as post-and-lintel squares against which smaller logs were then leaned; and some had notched log walls and corbeled log roofs. The Navajo are particularly noted for their silverwork and their blankets. They also made sand paintings by sprinkling colored sand and maize meal over flat surfaces.

10.11 A southwestern hogan.
To build a hogan, a log frame was covered with earth, producing a living environment compatible with climatic extremes. Wood provided the structural integrity, while the earth covering provided the insulation.

MEXICO AND CENTRAL AMERICA

The following discussion of Pre-Columbian Mexico and Central America covers multiple cultures and sites, from the Olmecs at La Venta to the Aztecs at Tenochtitlán.

The Olmecs of the Eastern Mexican Coast

Men and women migrated east across the Bering Straits more than 30,000 years ago. They settled all along the way, traveling down through North, Central, and South America. The earliest evidence (ca. 1500 BCE) of a sophisticated culture in Mexico comes from the Gulf Coast in the northern portion of the state of Tabasco and southern portion of the state of Vera Cruz. This was the land of the Olmecs, best known for their jaguar motifs and great bodyless stone heads (Fig. 10.12) with seemingly oriental features. Olmec sculptors carved these heads from six- to eight-foot-tall basalt blocks weighing up to thirty tons that had to be imported from quarries located in the Tuxtla mountains some distance away. They are probably depictions of real rulers, but this has not been proven.

While knowledge of the Olmecs is limited, their position as progenitors of Mesoamerican culture in Mexico and Central America is well established. They invented a calendar, a numbering system, and hieroglyphic writing, and made astronomical observations. They began the worship of the region's principal gods. They invented the ball court that became a widespread device for public rituals. They established a hierarchical society with a nobility and perhaps kings. Finally, the Olmecs created the first Mesoamerican artistic style that united an ethnic group, and they may have created an empire of city-states.

10.12 Olmec stone head, before 900 BCE.
This artifact, relocated from its original site, displays the distinctive Olmec facial features and ceremonial headdress.

The most impressive Olmec ceremonial center is La Venta (Fig. 10.13), where the oldest known earthen pyramid in Mexico, almost 100 feet tall, served as one terminus for an axis defined by an orthogonal arrangement of earthen platforms surrounding a ceremonial plaza lined with basalt columns. The basic elements of this composition would be repeated again and again throughout the region.

Teotihuacán in the Valley of Mexico

During the Classic period of Pre-Columbian Mexican culture (ca. 200 BCE–900 CE), a vast, planned urban development was created at Teotihuacán (Fig. 10.14), meaning "place of the gods," in the Valley of Mexico, by a people whose name we do not know. It arose northwest of the Olmec sites subsequent to the Olmec decline, covers some thirteen square miles, and once served a population as large as 200,000 people. In the city's ritual center, designers laid out a great north–south causeway, terminated on the north by the stepped Pyramid of the Moon. Alongside the causeway, they placed a series of earthen terraces with battered walls faced with stone veneer; a great stepped pyramid—the Pyramid of the Sun (Fig. 10.15); and walled enclosures, some sunken and some defined by trabeated construction covered with low-relief sculpture.

The horizontal plane dominates here, perhaps inspired by the sprawl of the valley floor. This horizontality is celebrated by means of two distinctive ordering devices. The battered walls of the terraces and pyramids display the **talud** and **tablero** motifs that would be repeated with many variations throughout Mesoamerica. The talud is a sloping plane and the tablero a frieze of random stones framed by plain moldings (see Fig. 10.15).

Exquisitely carved columns in the so-called Palace of the Quetzalbutterfly, located on the west side of the

10.13 Diagram of La Venta, Tabasco, Mexico, 1100–400 BCE.
The conical earth mound and stepped pyramid stand at the opposite ends of an axis defined by earthen platforms and walled enclosures. Such a sequential organization of space and mass can be compared to Egyptian pyramid complexes and Mesopotamian ziggurats and their compounds.

Pyramid of
the Moon

Plaza of
the Moon

Palace of the
Quetzalbutterfly

Causeway, or Avenue of the Dead

10.15

Pyramid of the Sun

To the Palace
of Ateltelco

Great
Compound

Citadel

N

0   500 m

0   1500 ft

10.14 Plan of Teotihuacán, Valley of Mexico, Mexico, ca. 200 BCE–900 CE. As at La Venta, the principal forms are pyramids and platforms, here stretched out beside a long causeway.

10.15 Pyramid of the Sun, Teotihuacán, begun ca. 100 BCE. Made of earth with a stone-veneer covering, the Pyramid of the Sun has a profile of ascending, sloping taluds. The platforms in the foreground, which once supported temples, have more complex talud–tablero arrangements. The variations on a basic theme offered by these companion motifs provide unity among diversity at the many Pre-Columbian sites in Mexico and Central America. Various talud–tablero combinations appear as pyramid tiers, building walls, and even roofs.

10.16 Plan of the Palace of Ateltelco, Teotihuacán, ca. 200 BCE–900 CE.
This pattern of interlocking orthogonal geometries attests to the sophisticated design ideas of the people of Teotihuacán. Notable are the cross-axial organization, the column screens, and the resulting rich sequence of spaces.

plaza and in front of the Temple of the Moon, document the appreciation among Teotihuacán's inhabitants of the hard-edged quality of stone. The plan of the Palace of Ateltelco (Fig. 10.16), located well west of the causeway and just north of the so-called Citadel, demonstrates—in its complex geometry of interlocking squares, its many level changes, its proportioning systems, and its layering of columns, piers, and walls—a sophisticated understanding of geometric ordering and spatial sequence.

The Zapotecs and Mixtecs at Monte Albán, Oaxaca

In Oaxaca, south of the Central Plateau of Mexico, the Zapotecs also rose in prominence after the decline of the Olmecs. They transformed their local culture into a territorial one, with the populace scattered throughout the Oaxaca Valley. At Monte Albán (600 BCE–1000 CE), they organized their great ritual center quite differently from that at Teotihuacán. By leveling the top of a mountain some 1300 feet above sea level, they developed an earthen platform on which they built a series of stepped pyramids as bases for their temples (Fig. 10.17).

The Zapotecs arranged these pyramids around the perimeter of their site, creating a great plaza, 1000 feet long and almost 500 feet wide, and, within this plaza, they placed two additional pyramids, making them built objects inside a larger built environment; such ideas can be compared conceptually to those of Hellenistic Greece in the fourth to second centuries BCE. Equally spatial is the ball court at the southwest corner of the site. This form type appeared throughout Mesoamerica where its misleadingly serene composition of talud-and-tablero-like battered walls and platforms provided a setting for ritual games played with a small resilient ball, games in which the consequence of losing was death (Fig. 10.18).

The Zapotecs built their pyramids using talud–tablero motifs but emphasized wide stairs often bracketed by sloping cheekwalls. Their interpretation of the talud–tablero was strongly linear, with corbeled layers configured as if

10.17 (above) Monte Albán, Oaxaca, Mexico, 600 BCE–1000 CE.
Unlike Teotihuacán's axial organization, Monte Albán's is spatial and centrally planned. Platforms once capped by temples define a plaza in which the Zapotecs placed two structures, one certainly an observatory that was canted in plan to align it with significant stars or planets.

10.18 (right) Ball court, Copán, Honduras, before 800.
This ball court, like that at Monte Albán, has sloping talud walls resembling modern stadium seating. However, these slopes were a part of the play field, with onlookers standing on the platforms above.

overlapping and turned down at their extremities. Atop their pyramids, the Zapotecs placed temples with notable plan configurations. Each temple was one or two spaces deep (like an ancient Greek cella and porch) with frontal columns in antis or prostyle. Particularly interesting is the sunken court at the southern end of the site, which is comparable in its plan to the Palace of Ateltelco. A square with four smaller, overlapping squares at its corners, it was approached by means of a wide stair, then through a portico with a double file of square columns. Such an exploitation of ranks and files of columns was rare in Pre-Columbian America, but would appear again among the Toltecs in both northern Mexico and Central America. Excavations at Monte Albán have unearthed the tombs of the Zapotec nobility and the largest cache of jewelry found in North America.

The Mixtecs followed the Zapotecs in Oaxaca (ca. 800). Their sacred city of Mitla includes the Palace of the Columns. Here the tablero motif took on a much more intricate character than any seen before. A plain talud serves as the base from which rise tiers of tablero elements framed by corbeled bands. The tablero is formed of inlaid panels of geometric ornamentation in both orthogonal and diagonal patterns (Fig. 10.19).

The Maya

East of Oaxaca, in what today is Guatemala, Honduras, the Mexican state of Chiapas, and the Yucatán Peninsula, another great Pre-Columbian culture developed, that of the Maya. At its height, the Maya civilization included some fifty independent states and more cities than anywhere else in the Pre-Columbian Americas. The Maya developed irrigation systems and cultivated a wide variety of crops, particularly maize, which they made into tortilla-like pancakes. Maya society was rigidly stratified, with peasant farmers at the base and the priest class, merchants, and warriors above. At the top was a hereditary king, who was both a civil ruler and a priest.

The Maya were unique in the Americas in developing a system of writing, recording their history and ritual practices on paper. While their libraries were destroyed by the Spanish, many of their hieroglyphic texts survive, carved in stone, modeled in stucco, and painted on pottery or in murals. Their glyphs, long a subject of intense study, have only recently been deciphered. They include signs that represent both individual sounds and whole words. Unfortunately, because the only extant texts are displayed on public architecture, they represent the official government interpretation of events and do not allow for alternative points of view. Still, they offer rich insights into such matters as the Maya concept of time and their worldview.

The Maya saw their world as made up of three distinct regions: the starry realm of the heavens above, the middle realm of the earth, and the dark nether realm below. Building on concepts developed by the Olmecs, and

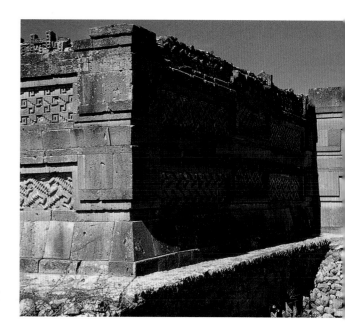

10.19 Talud–tablero wall, Mitla, Oaxaca, Mexico, ca. 800. The contrast between the geometric ornament here at Mitla and the organic Maya ornament farther south (see Fig. 10.26) is striking. Perhaps it has to do with the differing contexts in Oaxaca and the Yucatán.

perhaps the Teotihuacános, the Maya created a worldview in which religious rituals codified a shared reality. Some of these rituals involved the introduction of trancelike states, including as a principal device the act of bloodletting— particularly from the tongue and penis, which in their most exalted form, the Maya believed, allowed their kings to make contact with the other regions. Their creation myths included sacred twins, who played a sacred ballgame, died through decapitation, were resurrected, and eventually outwitted the gods. Within this mythic structure, the Maya ball court was a place of confrontation and communication. While ballgames could be played among friends in an ordinary setting, in their most elevated form they symbolized the twins' life-and-death battle. From this myth, the Maya arrived at beliefs in triumph over death through ritual, victory over enemies through outwitting them, and resurrection and rebirth through sacrifice.

The Maya developed a complex set of interlocking calendars, which were of extreme importance because they believed that history was cyclical. Their solar calendar included 365 days broken down into eighteen months of twenty days each, with five residual days, and it was the most accurate anywhere in the ancient world. A separate religious calendar had 260 days, and the two calendars coincided every fifty-two years. This interval was viewed as a birth–death–rebirth cycle and was celebrated with lavish rituals. The rebirth was accompanied by the igniting of a ritual flame and by the reconstruction of significant temples and pyramids.

Maya astronomers meticulously plotted celestial movements, including those of the planet Venus, and predicted events such as lunar eclipses. They developed a bar-and-dot system with which they could carry out mathematical calculations and either invented zero or inherited its use

10.20 Plan of Tikal, Guatemala, 600 BCE–ca. 900 CE.
This site contains thousands of structures and stone monuments,
with the most extensively excavated areas located around
the North Acropolis at the junction of the three causeways.
Archaeologists must uncover such ruins advisedly, as they then
become vulnerable to the effects of wind, sun, and rain, and must
somehow be protected from the encroaching jungle vegetation.

from the Olmecs—only the Sumerians and Hindus did so
elsewhere. After 800 CE, some catastrophic event or combination of them led to the complete collapse of Maya civilization. Scholars have reached no definitive conclusions
about how the Maya downfall came to pass, but recent
theories suggest that a shift in weather patterns leading
to prolonged drought and subsequent famine may have
played a key role in the disaster.

Tikal

Perhaps the most impressive Maya city is Tikal, set within
the lowland jungles of the department of El Petén in
Guatemala. The city was not only a ceremonial site, but
also a true urban center with a permanent population
of some 45,000 inhabitants. The site plan (Fig. 10.20)

is organized by means of causeways laid out in a rough
triangle and linking major building complexes. At the
southeast corner of this triangle stands the so-called
North Acropolis, a closely packed cluster of pyramids
facing a great plaza to the south. This plaza is defined on
its eastern and western extremities by large pyramids and
bristles with **stelae**, upright slabs with inscriptions. The
units of pyramid composition are again the talud and
tablero. Talud elements, in the form of sloping embank-
ments, define platforms. Atop these platforms sit stepped
pyramids formed of largely unarticulated sloping talud
and equally plain vertical tablero motifs relieved only by
horizontal returns and recessed panels, both of which cast
sharply defined shadows (Fig. 10.21). Tikal's pyramids are
its most distinctive built forms with their steep but plain
tablero and talud walls and surmounting temples (Fig.

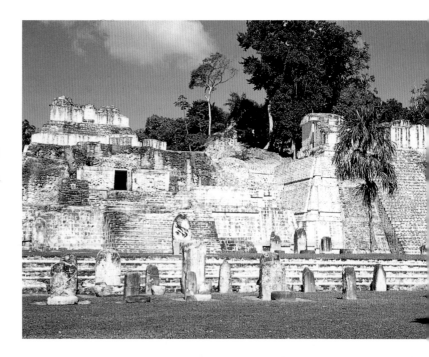

10.21 North Acropolis, Tikal, ca. 700.
The portion of the city seen here includes the great plaza in the foreground, with stelae and the pyramid bases of the North Acropolis beyond. The Maya used temples and their bases to shape outdoor spaces intended for ritual spectacle.

10.22 (below) Pyramid, Tikal, ca. 650.
Most striking about Tikal's pyramids is their verticality. However, they were once part of a densely developed urban fabric rather than being isolated towers amid a dense jungle canopy as they are today.

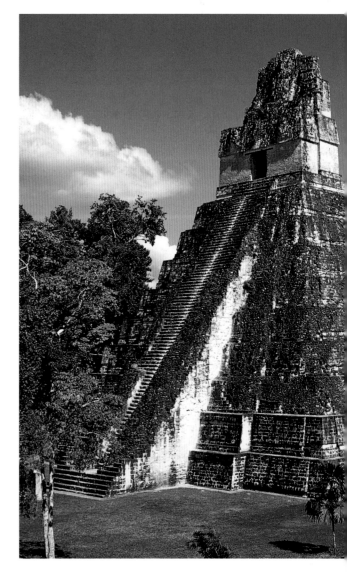

10.22). Atop the taludlike roofs sprout flamboyant, richly carved roof combs, repetitive taludlike elements that rest on the temples' corbel vaults. Steep stairs rise up one side of each pyramid and lead to the temple doorways. The original stucco reliefs have now almost completely vanished. Inside, modest spaces were created by the Maya's use of the corbeled vault, a structural device not seen at Teotihuacán or in Oaxaca. The complete ensemble of pyramids is extraordinary for its verticality, all the more so when the multiple pyramids are viewed as an urban unit; today they rise like great stalagmites from the jungle floor in so dramatic a fashion that George Lucas chose an aerial view of them to represent a moon of the rebel planet in the first *Star Wars* movie. Together with ball courts, a rain-storage reservoir, and the low-rise market structures, also composed using talud and tablero elements, the ritual pyramids at Tikal define a series of linked acropolises, open markets, and plazas.

Mural paintings have been discovered at Tikal in which artists drew black lines over a red-painted background. The most famous Maya murals are those at the modest site on the Usamacinta River, dubbed Bonampak (Maya for "painted walls") by archaeologists. Here the images are unusual for their realistic depiction of scenes from everyday life.

Copán and Palenque

Copán lies southeast of Tikal and was famous for its periodic gathering of astronomical experts. The ceremonial center is roughly rectangular, with a great plaza to the north and acropolis to the south and the ball court seen in Figure 10.18 between them. Perhaps its most distinctive features are the many stelae: in this case, vertical, carved

10.23 Stelae, Copán, Honduras, 600–800.
Upright stone objects have appeared in cultures around the world, the most obvious type in the West being the tombstone or grave-marker. The Maya erected them for various purposes, including the commemoration of significant events.

10.24 (top) Temple of the Inscriptions, Palenque, Chiapas, Mexico, completed by 683.
This stepped pyramid is embedded in the mountain behind it. A vaulted stair descends from the temple to the tomb chamber at the level of the pyramid's first stage.

10.25 (above) Tomb chamber, Temple of the Inscriptions, Palenque, completed by 683.
Stone lintels complement the corbel vault in this space. The incised images on the sarcophagus lid depict King Pacal descending the trunk of the world-tree to the otherworld from which he was to arise like the hero twins.

monoliths, conceptually not unlike Aluit totem poles (Fig. 10.23). The style of carving has been characterized as "baroque" and "oriental" because of its organic complexity, but was perhaps derived from the lush jungle environment in which it was created. The Maya called these stelae "tree-stones" and carved them with images of kings, so that plazas filled with them both recounted the sequence of rulers and symbolized the tropical forest.

At Palenque in Chiapas, similar elements appear but with distinctive adaptations: earthen platforms; stepped pyramids, sometimes with wide stairs; and temples, often with elongated plans. The Temple of the Inscriptions is unusual for having within it a tomb built contemporaneously with the pyramid and reached by a series of subterranean passages that were long ago sealed off. The burial chamber is twenty-three feet long, twenty-three feet high, and about twelve feet wide. Within it resides a huge sarcophagus carved from a single block of stone and covered with a richly ornamented slab. A skeleton draped with jade jewelry was found inside (Figs. 10.24–10.25). Many façades and some interior walls of Palenque's temples were once covered with stucco, ornately modeled in low relief and painted, and their roofs are crowned by lattice-like roof combs.

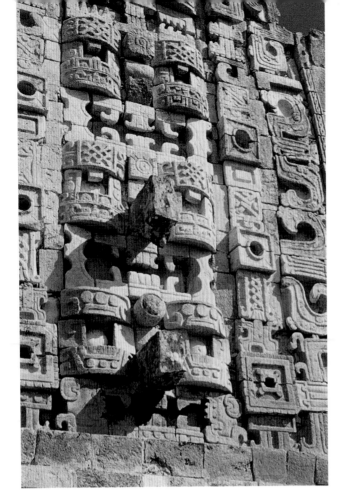

10.26 Nunnery masks, Uxmal, Yucatán, Mexico, ca. 900.
Here, the ornament is both highly geometric and highly organic, the latter reflecting the Puuc style developed in northwest Yucatán. While the individual stones are modular, the images, dominated by the nose piece of the rain god Chac, are boldly sculpted.

10.27 Governor's Palace, Uxmal, ca. 900.
This building has a three-part composition, with a dominant central mass separated from smaller masses to each side by a setback, or recessed strip. This composition is comparable to the schemes developed by celebrated sixteenth-century Italian architect Andrea Palladio for his villas.

Uxmal and Chichén-Itzá

At Uxmal in the Puuc region, the Maya laid out their ceremonial center as objects on raised platforms, several of them taking the form of quadrangles, freely distributed in space. The geometric ornamentation here is reminiscent of Mixtec work, while the contrasting organic ornament reaches its highest level of elaboration in the interlocking masks of the rain god Chac (Fig. 10.26).

Two of Uxmal's most distinctive buildings are the so-called Governor's Palace and Nunnery (Figs. 10.27–10.28). The Governor's Palace is a single, elongated rectangle in plan, some 328 feet long, while the Nunnery consists of four smaller such rectangles defining a quadrangle. The Governor's Palace is divided into three parts by inset bays with corbeled vaults, making for a five-part composition. On the interior, some twenty rooms of various sizes are covered with corbeled vaults. At their lower levels, both buildings display large areas of mural wall surface and windows with recessed frames. In the frieze above, sculptors at the Governor's Palace combined orthogonal and diagonal geometries with multiple Chac masks. At the Nunnery, stunted columns appear on the north side, supporting a frieze similar to that at the Governor's Palace. Around the perimeter and inside the quadrangle, the frieze is alternately aggressively geometric and organic, with Chac-mask compositions above some openings and projecting dramatically at corners.

10.28 Nunnery, Uxmal, ca. 900.
The ornamentation of this tablero can be compared to the frieze of the classical Greek or Roman temple. Here, however, the effect is created not by large panels but by many small geometric units that interlock.

10.29 The Caracol, or "Observatory,"
Chichén-Itzá, Yucatán, Mexico, after 900.
This unusual structure displays not only the
Maya-inspired masks for the rain god Chac,
but also depictions of the plumed serpent
brought south by Toltec invaders.

Chichén-Itzá, in Yucatán at the delta of the Usumacinta and Grijalva rivers, is a Maya site that combines native elements of the Putún culture with those of Toltec raiders. The Putún, who were merchant seafarers in control of the ocean trade routes around Yucatán, were called Itzá in that area. In around 900 they conquered new lands, including Chichén, hence the name of the Chichén-Itzá site. By the eleventh or twelfth century, the city was controlled by the Toltecs.

The most notable buildings here are the so-called Caracol (Fig. 10.29), Castillo, and the Temple of the Warriors. Located to the south of the central section of the city and, some have argued, used as an astronomical observatory, the Caracol, meaning "snail," is unusual in Maya

10.30 Temple-palace, Tula, Valley of Mexico, Mexico, after 900.
In its ruined state, this building at Tula makes clear the Toltecs' dramatic use of the column, their square stumps seen in the foreground. As much symbols of militancy as structural elements, the ranks and files capture the warlike nature of the culture that created them.

architecture for its circular-plan tower. It is ornamented with Maya masks of Chac but also with elements brought here by the Toltecs: images of the plumed serpent and heads of Toltec warriors. Inside the Caracol's central cylinder, a series of openings made possible specific observations of the planets and the stars. The Castillo, or Temple of Kulkulkán, is equally distinctive, a pyramid with stairways leading up each of its four sides. This configuration is explained by its location inside a colonnaded plaza; it is an architectural object placed within an urban space, making Chichén-Itzá comparable in its spatial conception to Monte Albán. The Castillo's form may also have cosmological symbolism, as each stair has ninety-one risers, making a total of 364 in all. If one adds the base on which the pyramid sits, the total becomes 365, or the number of days in the Maya year. Furthermore, a plumed serpent at the base casts a shadow across the stair at an equinox or solstice. Standing east of the Castillo and overlooking the plaza is the Temple of the Warriors, which bears a striking resemblance to the pyramid complex at Tula, both in its planning and execution. Here, finely carved ranks and files of columns flank two sides of the pyramid, as densely placed as the columns in an Egyptian hypostyle hall. The carving includes eagles and jaguars devouring human hearts, plumed serpents, and Toltec warriors.

The Toltecs in the Valley of Mexico

In around 900, the warlike Toltecs from the north of Mexico settled in the Valley of Mexico, at a time when the culture of Teotihuacán was in decline, and eventually continued south to interact with the Maya. From among the Toltecs sprang the myth of Quetzalcóatl, the plumed serpent, who, they believed, set out on a journey to the east, promising one day to return. Subsequently, this prophecy would have profound implications for the Aztecs.

The greatest Toltec city was Tula (Fig. 10.30) in the state of Hidalgo. Its ritual center includes the remains of a multi-columned palace and a pyramid supporting huge carved male warrior figures, once inside a temple but now exposed. The most striking features of the complex are the two- and three-deep files of stuccoed columns that define one end of the ceremonial plaza and continue around the west and south façades of the palace. Ranks and files of columns are repeated inside the palace, where three great rooms, once roofed except for central openings, stand side by side.

On the north side of the pyramid, portions of talud and tablero motifs remain. On its other three sides, its taludlike stepped layers have only individual projecting stones as shadow-casting ornamentation. In this Toltec interpretation of the decorative form, a plain talud supports a two-tiered tablero, its upper levels stepped back, that serves as a frieze displaying images of coyotes, jaguars, eagles devouring human hearts, and effigies of gods. On both flanks and the rear, a so-called serpent wall once enclosed the pyramid and was crowned by seashell-shaped symbols of Quetzalcóatl.

The Aztecs at Tenochtitlán

The sun-worshiping Aztecs arrived in the Valley of Mexico in the thirteenth century and proceeded to assemble a large military and economic empire. Legend held that their capital and chief ceremonial center of Tenochtitlán (Fig. 10.31), the remains of which lie beneath modern-day Mexico City, had been identified to the Aztecs through the sighting of an eagle grasping a snake while perched on a prickly pear or tenochtli. By the time of the Spanish conquest in 1519, Tenochtitlán had a population of some 200,000 people and some eighty ritual-related structures, and the Aztec Empire extended from northern Mexico as far south as present-day Guatemala and El Salvador.

Tenochtitlán was established on a series of small islands. The Aztecs filled in earth among them to produce a unified setting that, ironically, dazzled their Spanish conquerors. They constructed four long causeways that divided the city into quadrants, each with its own neighborhoods, shrines, and administration buildings. In the center, they laid out a great ceremonial center and built the by-now-requisite platforms, pyramids, ball courts, and temples, including the central ritual complex, or Templo Mayor, once again using the talud and tablero as their basic ordering forms. A centerpiece of this architectural ensemble was the skull rack displaying the heads of sacrificial victims.

The Aztecs imagined Tenochtitlán to be at the center of the world and the city itself to be the cosmos in miniature, with its causeways oriented to the cardinal points. They believed the causeways' central intersection to be the point through which a vertical axis ran upward through thirteen levels and downward through nine more and believed souls, once released from their physical bodies, made a quest for eternal peace, beginning at the lowest level and assisted by magic charms interred with their physical remains. The Aztecs further believed that their empire and the cosmos depended on one another for existence and that the Aztec state was obliged to express this reciprocal relationship through ritual, including the practice of human sacrifice, most often by cutting out the hearts of their victims using obsidian knives.

The Templo Mayor included two subsidiary temples, one dedicated to the rain, water, and agriculture god Tlaloc and the other to Huitzilopochtli, the god of the sun, war, conquest, tribute, and dominion (Fig. 10.32). The Aztecs' religion required that they perform human sacrifices to Huitzilopochtli, their patron deity, in order to ensure that the sun rose each day and that they remained in the god's favor. The religious demands for human sacrifice were reinforced by military, political, and economic factors. The Aztecs fought wars not only to control territory but also to exact tribute. Once conquered, however, tribes constantly sought to disengage themselves from the empire, and tensions were understandably exacerbated by the Aztecs' never-ending demands for more sacrificial captives. Additionally, long-distance trade made luxury goods available to the Aztec elite, who then had to rely on military conquest and expansion both to maintain access to these goods and to obtain wealth through tribute. Thus, Aztec religious practice reinforced the expansionist materialism of a warrior state.

Temple of Quetzalcóatl

Causeway

Ball court

Temple of the Sun

Causeway

Causeway

Temple of Tlaloc

Temple of Huitzilopochtli

Palace of Moctezuma

N

0   250 m

0   750 ft

10.31 Plan of Tenochtitlán, location of present-day Mexico City, Mexico, after 900.
Focused on the skull rack at its center, this orthogonal layout makes use of the same platform and pyramid types seen centuries earlier at nearby Teotihuacán. What set this city apart and what first amazed Spanish explorers was its dramatic location at the center of a lake. The lake has long since disappeared, as have the remains of Tenochtitlán beneath the modern-day city.

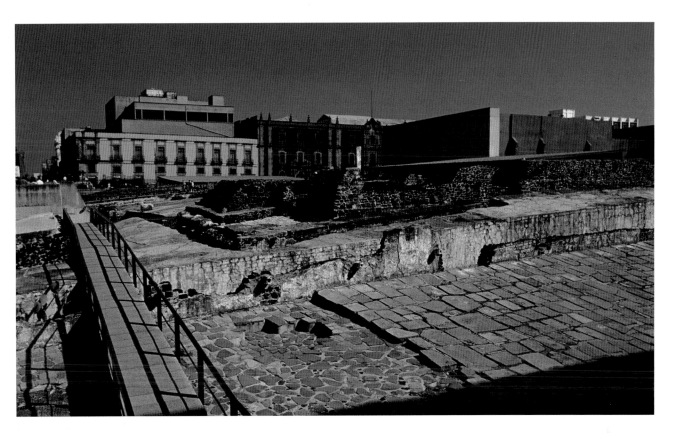

10.32 Excavated ruins of the Templo Mayor, Tenochtitlán, Mexico City, Mexico, after 900.
The ceremonial center of Tenochtitlán lies beneath modern-day Mexico City, so that only rarely are its excavated remains made visible. Likewise, it has been impossible to excavate more than a fraction of the city's ritual burial sites, so that information about Aztec sacrificial practices must come from other locations.

When the conquistador Hernán Cortés appeared with his small army, some of the Aztecs may have believed him to be the god Quetzalcóatl returned from a mythical journey, which, in turn, may have caused their king Moctezuma to act indecisively in the face of the Spanish threat. Whatever the case, allied with other tribes eager to end Aztec domination, in possession of more advanced weapons, and unwittingly assisted by the devastating spread of European diseases among the native population, the Spanish were able to conquer the vast Aztec Empire relatively quickly, decisively altering the course of Mesoamerican history.

SOUTH AMERICA: THE ANDEAN WORLD

The Andes mountain chain runs the length of South America's Pacific coastline. It is in this region, particularly in what is now Peru and Bolivia, that a number of advanced Pre-Columbian civilizations flourished. Several "commodities" stand out as critical determinants of architectural development in the Andes: earth, stone, and water. As for earth and stone, these were basic construction materials: adobe for building walls near the coast and rubble and ashlar stone for laying up walls in the mountains. Water was manipulated everywhere and on an enormous scale for agricultural irrigation and occasionally and much more modestly, but extremely dramatically, for ritual purposes. Other factors such as altitude and weather, specifically drenching rains and parching droughts resulting from the appearance and disappearance of El Niño ocean currents, played important roles, too. Altitude, stemming from the precipitous rise of the Andes from the Pacific Ocean to a spine of peaks over 20,000 feet, greatly influenced the culture of Andean civilization. The highland peoples to the east and the river-valley cultures nearer to the coast were confronted with very different environments and, therefore, presented with various options for food production, principally systematic agriculture, fishing, and animal husbandry. As for the weather, fluctuations in El Niño events could lead to dramatic shifts in meteorological conditions, sometimes lasting longer than a year.

Remains of agricultural canals, lakes, and terraces, as well as ritual settings and urban developments, built by the Pre-Columbian peoples of South America's Pacific coast and highlands are so vast that they now represent the largest archeological "site" in the western hemisphere. Caral, near the modern city of Lima, Peru, is the oldest known, large-scale, urban ceremonial complex, perhaps the oldest major settlement, in the Americas. Covering some 165 acres, it includes earthen pyramids built almost 5000 years ago (at a time when Old Kingdom Egyptians were only building mastabas), and between the time of Caral's occupation and the rise of the Inca in the fifteenth century, numerous cultures and hundreds of cities and ritual centers were occupied, developed, and abandoned. The discussion that follows can only introduce a few of the sites of greatest architectural interest.

Early Cities on the North Coast of Peru

More than 1500 years after Caral's development, Sechín Alto, located on the Sechín branch of the Casma Valley, rose to become what was then the largest architectural complex in the Americas (Fig. 10.33). The ceremonial center's U-shaped plan consists of a granite-veneered stepped pyramid, 300 feet on its long sides, facing a sunken court flanked by low buildings and establishing an axis uniting a series of terraces. This was a precocious design, and its U-shaped planning pattern would be much emulated in later South American architecture.

Further to the north and contemporary with Sechín Alto, the ceremonial center of **Huaca** de los Reyes at Caballo Muerto displays the same U-shaped plan, but with a much greater degree of building articulation and with U-shaped structures repeated at various scales (Fig. 10.34). Here, a principal axis extending out over descending terraces is countered by cross-axes terminated by flanking

files of rooms, some fronted by in antis columns. In addition, there are a sunken court, embedded stairways, and colonnades with double and triple ranks of square columns. As construction began here ca. 1500 BCE, Middle Kingdom Egyptians were building the similarly organized Temple of Queen Hatshepsut.

Early Development in the Northern Peruvian Andes

About 900 BCE, as Sechín Alto and Huaca de los Reyes were in decline, a new location rose to prominence as a cult center in the north-central highlands. Here, at Chavín de Huántar, coastal organizational principles were united with the skillful working and laying of stone, including monumental incised panels and freestanding sculpture. The site lies at almost 10,000 feet in the Andes but in a dramatic valley at the confluence of two rivers such that surrounding mountains still tower above it. The largest construction is the castillo, or castle, built in two stages

10.33 Plan of Sechín Alto, Peru, 1800–900 BCE.
This large-scale development combines design strategies employed in Mexico at both Teotihuacán and Monte Albán. Like the former, its strong central axis has both architectural and cosmic significance. And like the latter, its enclosing of space with repetitive building elements creates a sacred precinct.

10.34 Reconstructed plan of Huaca de los Reyes, Peru, 1800–900 BCE.
As at Sechín Alto (Fig. 10.33), repetitive forms heighten the ritual significance of this large ceremonial site. Often juxtaposed, U-shaped buildings define axes, and cascading platforms work their way down to sunken courts once used for religious spectacles.

10.35 Eastern façade of the New Temple, Chavín de Huántar, Peru, after 900 BCE.
The Inca are widely celebrated for their ability to carve stone. However, pre-Inca sites like this one show that skilled stonemasons had been at work in Peru for centuries before the Inca assembled their vast empire.

and faced with polished sandstone, limestone, and granite, with its U-shaped plan enveloping a sunken, circular court (Fig. 10.35). Evidence suggests that designers manipulated river water here for ritual purposes, possibly even creating dramatic sound effects by rushing it unseen through channels left within the stone construction. A larger labyrinth of corridors in the castillo connects to a chamber holding the Lanzón, a carved effigy of the principal god. The religious experience in this provocative physical and acoustical environment was apparently enhanced by the ingesting of hallucinogenic substances.

On the north coast of Peru, the Moche culture thrived from the first to the eighth centuries CE. Moche craftsmen fashioned exquisite metalwork, particularly in hammered gold, and the Moche power structure became the first in Peru to bring coastal populations into a regional development, which included the Moche River Valley and the parallel Chicama Valley. At the coastal capital of Cerro Blanco, located just south of the Moche River's entry into the Pacific Ocean, workers built two great, adobe-brick structures (Fig. 10.36) by 100 CE: the Huaca del Sol (Pyramid of the Sun), 1130 feet by 525 feet on its sides and 130 feet tall, and the smaller Huaca de la Luna (Pyramid of the Moon), both

10.36 Huaca del Sol, Peru, before 100 CE.
Temple mounds, of which this is a very large South American example, appeared all the way from what is today the state of Missouri to Bolivia. This one measures more than 1100 feet on a side, making it much larger than the largest Egyptian pyramid, that of Khufu or Cheops (see Fig. 1.24).

10.37 Gateway of the Sun, Tiwanaku, Bolivia, after 200 CE.
Of all pre-Inca stonework, this monolithic gateway must be the most impressive. The incised frieze includes an effigy of the weather and sky god Thunupa standing atop a stepped platform.

now much deteriorated due to erosion. What were actually irregularly shaped, stepped adobe platforms now face one another across only the remains of residences and workshops. Moche artisans depicted one local deity, known as the decapitator, as an anthropomorphic spider with a fanged mouth. The prominent image of another fanged god, this one half human, was frequently shown holding a ceremonial crescent-shaped knife, suggesting that the platforms were at times the setting for human sacrifice. Rather than being practiced continuously, as among the Aztecs, these sacrifices may have taken place only during El Niño years, when the Moche sought divine intervention to end the destructive rains. By 600 CE, such a rain event and the floods it triggered so ravaged the irrigation system of the Cerro Blanco site that occupants began to abandon it.

The Nazca on the Peruvian South Coast

At the same time the Moche occupied Cerro Blanco, the Nazca to the south were renowned for their ceramics and textiles, their engineering of underground conduits and reservoirs, and their construction of enormous glyphs laid out across the hillsides above the Pacific. By removing the upper desert strata of rusted metallic particles, Nazca glyph-makers exposed the lighter-colored sediment beneath. Some giant glyphs depict humans, llamas, and even a monkey and a spider. On flat terrain, the glyph's lines appear to have been used as ritual pathways, with lines running for distances greater than ten miles and defining such geometric forms as triangles, trapezoids, zigzags, and spirals.

An Empire in the Western Bolivian Highlands

Southeast of the Nazca region, inland from the coast, near Lake Titicaca, at more than 13,000 feet above sea level are the northern Bolivian highlands. Here, the city

of Tiwanaku thrived for some 800 years, with occupancy beginning by 200 CE. The city had a population of at least 20,000, possibly as many as 40,000, and an economy based on llama and alpaca herding and agriculture. It was not an isolated urban settlement but one among many centers united by a road system that helped consolidate the region into South America's first, and longest lasting, empire. Tiwanaku's ceremonial-center monuments are most impressive for their exquisitely hewn, monumentally scaled, ashlar sandstone and feldspar masonry that anticipates the celebrated stonework of the later Inca. The city's largest structure is the Akapana temple, a sandstone-faced, stepped pyramid with an earthen core, some 650 feet on a side, with a sunken court atop it. As at Chavín de Huántar, water was probably manipulated here as a part of religious rituals. There are also numerous stelae, one 24 feet tall, and gateways, including the Gateway of the Sun (Fig. 10.37), made from a single stone block and ornamented with an incised frieze and projecting image of a deity.

The Chimor Kingdom

While Tiwanaku was part of an impressive regional development, the Chimor Kingdom was even larger, exceeding in size all South American empires except that of the Inca. It eventually combined coastal and Andean cultures and was governed from the Pacific-coast capital city of Chan Chan founded about 1000 CE. The city's most distinctive architectural features are ciudadelas, or large palace compounds (Fig. 10.38), roughly rectangular in plan and most often divided into three sequential precincts: a large, northern entry court with smaller adjacent courts, U-shaped audiencias, or offices, and files of small storage rooms; a burial platform adjacent to family living quarters and more multipurpose rooms; and a smaller area reserved for a well and probably quarters for servants. Throughout the remainder of the city, with its orthogonal streets, lie the remains of neighborhoods with cane-walled residences, two large plazas, cemeteries, sunken gardens, reservoirs, and ceremonial mounds.

The Inca

The Chimor Empire and others in the Andean world were eventually conquered by the Inca, and no culture in the Pre-Columbian Americas occupied an environment more dramatic than theirs. A militaristic and intensely socially stratified people, they organized the precipitous terrain of the Andes by terracing the rugged mountainsides and by providing sophisticated irrigation systems for agriculture. The Incas eventually controlled an area stretching some 2500 miles throughout much of modern-day Colombia, Ecuador, Peru, and Bolivia; their greatest era of empire-building was 1438–1532, only a short time before the appearance of Francisco Pizarro and the beginning of the Spanish conquest.

10.38 Aerial view of Chan Chan, Peru, after 1000 CE.
This Moche Valley city covered almost 5000 acres and
housed a population estimated by some at 250,000. The wall
construction is adobe brick, which was frequently carved in
high relief, covered with plaster, and then painted.

While they had no written language, they kept numerical records using knotted cords. Their knowledge of medicine and surgery was highly developed, and included the
practice of cutting circular openings in human skulls,
perhaps to relieve internal pressure. They domesticated
the alpaca and llama, and grew a wide variety of crops,
from maize to sweet potatoes and tomatoes to peanuts,
and even cotton from which they wove cloth. They built

extensive road systems and suspension bridges, and formidable stone fortresses. No other contemporary culture in
the western hemisphere was so skilled at fashioning and
laying cyclopean stone masonry.

The Incas located their capital at Cuzco, between the
Huatanay and Tullumayo rivers. While the construction there does not exceed one story in height, the site
is impressive for the rigor of its linear stone buildings
grouped around quadrangles and for the great fortress of
Saqsaywaman, where enormous stone blocks were exquisitely set without the use of mortar (Fig. 10.39). Among
the city's temples is the Corichanca, which has a radial
organization determined by forty-one celestial sight lines
extended into space by means of freestanding pillars.

10.39 Cyclopean masonry, Cuzco, Peru, ca. 1500.
In Inca stonework, each stone was dressed, then
placed adjacent to its neighbors without the use
of mortar. Masons then marked the outline of the
new stone on those already in place, removed it,
and pounded out a new profile to receive it. This
process was repeated again and again until a tight
fit was achieved.

Perhaps even more impressive is the dramatic royal estate developed at Machu Picchu by the Inca ruler Pachacuti (see page 250), which is located at a height of 7600 feet in the Andes. The site includes 200 or so houses that could have sheltered only about 1000 persons, in a climate that can only be described as inhospitable other than in the summer months. Here, the Incas transformed a saddle of land into a cohesive ensemble of agricultural terraces, distinctive house types, meeting halls, and carefully defined plazas. The houses are notable for their stone construction, sometimes battered walls, tall end-wall gables, trapezoidal openings, and distinctive plans, many of which have three closed sides and only a pier or piers on one long side. Their light wooden roof framing and covering of thatch have long since disappeared, leaving their isolated, tall gables to form the dramatic Machu Picchu skyline.

Pizarro, who had come to the New World as early as 1510, returned in 1530 with only 180 troops. Arriving in Peru, he found the Inca Empire recovering from civil war and two brothers, sons of the previous Inca emperor, vying for power. Pizarro captured one brother just after he had ordered the murder of his sibling. The Inca political system was so hierarchical that he was able to take complete control and ransack the culture. It was a sad end to an unfortunate period of Spanish-led cultural destabilization.

AFRICA

Before we begin our exploration of the indigenous architecture of Africa, first some comments about African buildings and sites found elsewhere in this book. The ancient Romans occupied North Africa, and their city of Timgad (see Fig. 5.11) in Algeria is discussed in Chapter 5. Islamic invaders subsequently spread across North Africa, and Islamic influence percolated south and west into the African continent. Two Islamic mosques are discussed below because their construction methods are singularly African; other mosques, as well as a discussion of mosque planning, appear in Chapter 7. Various European powers colonized Africa from the late fifteenth through the twentieth centuries and generally brought their architecture with them. While this widespread work is not covered, one example of modern African architecture appears in Chapter 16 (see Fig. 16.38).

Second, a recognition that what follows is unfortunately brief, given that the African continent includes several dozen countries with widely varying climatic conditions, vegetation, and building materials, and that many of them have radically different cultures. In addition, Africans continue to suffer from more than their share of war, famine, and disease, and partly because of these problems, a comprehensive, in-depth history of African architecture has yet to be written.

Third, an explanation of this section's organization. There are three broad, geographical regions on the African continent: 1) the North Atlantic and Mediterranean coasts (including the coast of Egypt); 2) the Sahara Desert; and 3) the sub-Sahara. While the first two are represented here, the vast majority of the examples are drawn from the third: the sub-Sahara. This means that building types, rather than region or tribe as used above for the Americas, offer the most logical categories for organization, specifically: 1) portable fabric structures, 2) permanent dwellings, 3) urbanization and fortification, 4) palaces, and 5) churches and mosques. In all instances, sites are located according to modern country names, but peoples are identified according to traditional tribal names.

Portable Fabric Structures

For the seminomadic people of the western Sahara, the tent is the only practical means of shelter, as it can be folded up and moved about on the back of a camel. In southern Morocco, herdsmen maintain both sheep and goats in a desert environment that includes plenty of scrub brush as well as occasional luxurious oases. Atop grass-mat flooring, families erect two poles, running longitudinally and forming a triangle, and stretch over them a pieced-together trapezoidal cloth, its wider side to the front and woven from animal hair, and lash it down using guy ropes attached to pegs driven in the ground (Fig. 10.40). They make the tent-cloth by sewing together woven strips running the full width of the piece, the width of each strip determined by the size of their loom. They insert short poles at the front and rear of their tent to lift the edges of the cloth, providing for access and ventilation, and they add skirts at both sides for closure. These tents are only tall enough for sitting or kneeling and sleeping inside.

Larger tents used by desert nomads farther east are supported by pairs of upright wooden poles spanned by a third horizontal pole and so forming a wicketlike frame. Using one of these frames in the center and one to each side, the nomadic builders raise up their tent structures to the height of conventional rooms.

In sub-Saharan, largely forested, central Zaire, the Kuba tribe uses mats of split palms tied to closely spaced reeds to enclose their gable-roofed houses (Fig. 10.41). They frame up walls using light poles and infill them with a lattice of smaller sticks, then attach the horizontal mat strips that they weave into elaborate geometric patterns. The Fulani people of Burkina Faso use woven mats to cover their sapling-frame domical structures, which can be compared to the Native American wigwams of the Midwest (see Fig. 10.3).

Permanent Dwellings

Structures like those of the Fulani present only one example in the dizzying variety of small, round- and square-plan dwelling types developed in the sub-Saharan region. These may have (or have had) walls of upright poles or bamboo, sapling lattice (or wattle) covered with clay (or

10.40 (above left) Two-pole tent of nomadic Moroccans.
Compare these portable fabric structures with the Great Plains teepee developed by Native North Americans (Fig. 10.2). In both cases, nomadic people brought their dwellings to needed resources rather than bringing the resources to fixed habitations.

10.41 (above) Gable-roofed Kuba house made of mats of split palms, Zaire.
Pervious, or permeable, surfaces like the palm mats seen here are ideal for enclosing space in southern African Zaire's hot and sunny climate. They allow both light and air to filter through them while they maintain privacy for occupants.

10.42 (left) Conical adobe structure, Musgum, Chad.
On no other continent has the potential of adobe, or soil with clay content, been more thoroughly investigated as a construction material than in Africa. Among its assets are a receptivity to carving and sculpting as well as paint.

daub), or of rubble stone or adobe or a combination of the two, with conical (often concave- or convex-profile) thatched roofs, or they may have no upright walls at all, but pointed-arch or triangular cross-sections and be built of adobe, sometimes dramatically textured (Fig. 10.42), or sapling frames covered with coarse grass.

Among these dwelling types are the cylindrical, adobe tower houses of the Botammariba tribe in northeast Togo, which have recently been added to the United Nations' list of World Heritage Sites (Fig. 10.43). In adjacent Benin, coastal fishing tribes build pole-frame houses on rectangular plans and cover them with thatched hipped or gabled roofs. They raise these houses above the water on multiple stilts that also form the vertical framework for submerged fish-farming pens. While these houses are raised in the air,

African dwellings elsewhere consist of subterranean dugouts and even artificially enlarged caves.

The rectilinear houses in such places as Cameroon may have, via the Atlantic slave trade, influenced the development of architecture in the southeastern United States. The Tikar tribe of Cameroon still builds square- or rectangular- or sometimes round-plan houses on stone bases, with walls of vertical bamboo or bundled palm fronds chinked using mud and with tall, slender, wooden posts supporting gabled or hipped, thatched roofs and porches (Fig. 10.44). Some remaining slave dwellings in the Caribbean and the cotton plantations of Mississippi and Louisiana have similar forms and the interconnections are still being studied.

The Ashanti (or Asante) people in Ghana have long built houses that display a common African residential layout: a square or rectangular courtyard surrounded by four, wide, shallow, gable-roofed rooms (Fig. 10.45—plan and section). In their larger houses, they combine several of these courtyard-and-four-room units. They use adobe for walls on which they develop low-relief ornamentation in the form of stylized animals and geometric motifs.

In the nineteenth century, the militant Zulu tribe in what is today northeastern South Africa constructed domical structures (Fig. 10.46). After digging a circular trench, they inserted saplings or bundles of saplings into it and bent them into concentric arches, one set leaning back from the front door and another leaning forward from the rear. On top of this frame, they sometimes overlaid a similar set of concentric arched saplings increasing in arch size from left to right and right to left until meeting at the top, the four arching semidomes together forming a single lattice. If necessary for stability, they erected post-and-beam frames of sapling poles inside the dome and attached the two systems. Atop their domes, they placed concentric grass mats, overlapping them from bottom to top like shingles, and tied them down with circumferential grass ropes. Zulu descendants continue to build some similar structures, but changing economic and social conditions have greatly diminished the number of such traditional buildings.

Urbanization and Fortification

As an urban vessel for their complex, polygamous, cattle-herding social organization, the Zulus arranged their circular dwellings to form circular villages. At the center and surrounded by a palisade, they laid out a parade ground for military maneuvers, which also served as an open pasture for the king's cattle. Outside the palisade, they distributed the individual houses, several structures deep, with their own cattle pens. And around the houses, they raised

10.43 (top left) **Adobe tower house of the Botammariba tribe, Koutammakou, Togo.**
In the United States, significant historical buildings are listed on the National Register of Historic Places. The most significant of these become National Historic Landmarks. On the scale of the entire planet, the United Nations identifies World Heritage sites like this one.

10.44 (above left) **Thatch-roofed Tikar home, Bali, Cameroon.**
The canny builders of these houses combined construction materials and methods to very good effect: stone at the bottom for the moisture-resistant sill, bamboo or palm fronds and a mud sealant for the protective walls, and thatch sloped to shed water for the roof.

10.45 (left) **Plan and section of Asante home, Ghana.**
Within the pages of this book are found many examples of courtyard houses built by multiple cultures at multiple times. Notice here that access to the courtyard is made along its edges rather than toward its center, a non-axial and therefore less formal and hierarchical arrangement.

10.46 Dome-shaped Zulu homes, northeastern South Africa.
These constructions look more like giant pumpkins than conventional buildings. While the historical Zulus are best known for their fierceness as warriors, today's Zulus clearly exhibit an extreme design sensitivity in fashioning such supple habitations.

up a second, taller palisade. Some of these tribal developments were huge, a mile or so in diameter, and accommodated several thousand inhabitants.

Members of the Fali tribe in northern Cameroon still lay out similar settlements. Beginning with generally cylindrical structures, having adobe walls and thatched roofs, they form walled compounds that include kitchens, sleeping quarters, and granaries. In some cases, they link these compounds together to form a larger, roughly circular farm enclosure in which there are granaries and pens for the head of the family's livestock (Fig. 10.47). In the complex, spatially-based cosmic symbolism of the Fali, the granaries

are the most important buildings. Historian of urbanism Enrico Guidoni says that "as places where edible seeds are stored, they represent the ark that descended from the sky in the mystic age and contained, among other things, all the vegetable species." Granaries like those of the Fali are so essential to village life that attention has invariably been lavished on their design and construction. Bernard Rudofsky celebrated such structures in areas as widely separated as Ivory Coast and Libya. In the former, miniature silos with thatched roofs are made of clay, some cylindrical, some cook-pot shaped with a curving bottom, both types raised on stubby, clay legs that serve to avoid dampness and lend an anthropomorphic character to these inanimate objects. In the case of the example in Figure 10.48,

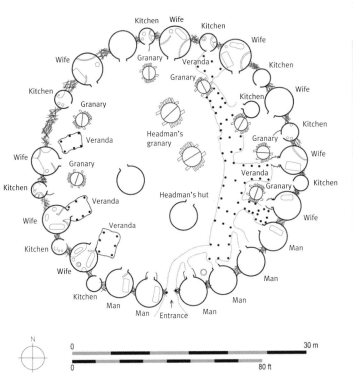

10.47 Plan of Fali tribe compound, Cameroon.
The expression "circling the wagons" is a familiar one in American westerns, and it suggests forming a circle for purpose of security. Here the Fali tribespeople have applied the same strategy to a permanent settlement.

10.48 Cylindrical granary, Yenegandougou, Ivory Coast.
It would be difficult to imagine a more direct and personal way of marking a building than with handprints. Likewise, there could be a no more classic composition than this one, with its bottom, middle, and top comparable to the base, shaft, and capital of the classical column.

10.49 Qasr (storage fortress), Kabao, Libya.
The extension of horizontal wooden members through adobe
walls, as in this multi-story structure, is a device that has been
widely used in arid climates. For instance, similar Spanish
Colonial construction remains in the American Southwest
and farther south in Africa at Djenne in Mali (see Fig. 10.56).

whitewash handprints provide exuberant, personalized
ornamentation. In Kabao, Libya, individual family storehouses have been agglomerated as storage fortresses, or
qasr. With walls made of rubble stone and adobe and an
inner structure of wood that frequently penetrates to the
outside to support balconies, they have been constructed
over time as places of security for crops but also for families in times of danger (Fig. 10.49).

No African settlements are more provocative than
those of the Dogon people, who live in the upper Niger
River region of Mali, and none have more impressive art or
more elaborate myths to explain a state of being. Because
of their density and the absence of wheeled vehicles and,
therefore, the need for any kind of grid or even short,
straight streets, and because they are often raised up amid
the detritus of fallen rocks beneath cliff faces, Dogon villages have a shockingly chaotic appearance to modern
Western eyes (Fig. 10.50). Seen from the air, they look to
be, Rudofsky wrote, no more than "debris." These villages
and their structures are, in fact, laid out not according to
principles of geometric regularity or caste hierarchy but
according to a common cosmological view. A diagram of
a Dogon village derived by anthropologist Marcel Griaule
from his interviews with tribal elders is anthropomorphic,
based upon a reclining male figure. Among other things,
this diagram situates the meeting house at the head, altars

at the feet, and male and female symbols (vertical phallic
shaft and circular stone with a cavity) at the positions of the
genitalia. The Dogon meeting house, or toguna, is usually
rectangular, but sometimes round, is freestanding, oriented
to the cardinal points, open on one side, and raised up on
wooden uprights or stones, and the uprights are sometimes
embellished with fetish images (Fig. 10.51).

Dogon houses are intended not only to serve the functional needs of the family but also to induce fertility. They
have cruciform plans, with large central rooms surrounded
by four stubby projections. The central room accommodates sleeping and weaving, with a kitchen in the projection to the rear and storerooms to either side, and a porch
at the entry. Like the village, the dwelling plan has anthropomorphic connotations, representing a female figure on
her back prepared for sexual intercourse, with the door
opening from the porch to the central room symbolizing
genitalia. These houses rise up two stories but with very
low ceilings. Their adobe walls are covered with thatched
roofs shaped like slightly deformed cones.

It cannot be surprising that the inventive Dogon minds
have created a fantastic, fanciful, and potent art. Dramatically
painted figures of serpents, hyenas, and crocodiles appear to
emerge from adobe walls. In an arid land, water spirits, or
nommo, are sculpted in clay, wood, and iron, with raised
arms producing elongated figural proportions. Decorations
carved into wooden granary shutters connect owners to the
totemic altars, or binus, of their kinship groups.

We have already examined Moroccan tents. In their
country's southern valleys and Atlas Mountains, Moroccans
have also built compact, fortified towns with both circular-
concentric and orthogonal layouts. These towns include a
repetitive building type, the kasbah (Fig. 10.52), a fortified

10.50 (above) Dogon cliff village, Bandiagara Escarpment, Mali.
The complexity of this low-rise but dense urban settlement seems disorienting from the air and to the untrained eye. However, the Dogon navigate its unpaved, winding paths as deftly as Venetians travel through their no-less-irregular city of canals and paved pedestrian walkways and piazzas.

10.51 (right) South side of a toguna, from the Dogon village of Madougou, Mali.
Dogon craftsmen are highly skilled in working with wood, as can be seen in the carved wood posts at the base of this toguna. The carvings represent Dogon fertility beliefs.

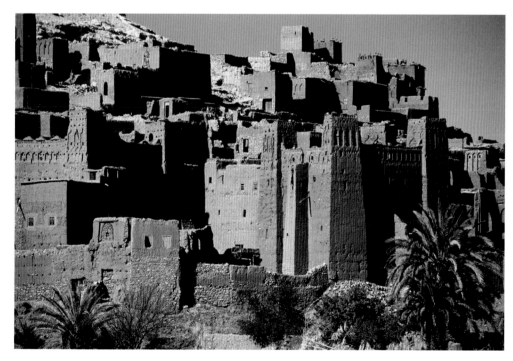

10.52 Kasbah, Ait-Benhaddun, Morocco.
For some movie watchers, the word kasbah evokes images from films steeped in intrigue. In reality, a kasbah is no different from a fortified castle in medieval Europe.

10.53 **Plan of Gedi, Kenya, 15th century and after.**
Another courtyard house, this time part of a palace complex. One of the giants of twentieth-century architecture, Ludwig Mies van der Rohe (see Chapter 15), spent considerable time exploring the design potential afforded by this residential type.

10.54 **Outer and inner walls of the main audience room, palace, Gedi, Kenya.**
This view of the main audience hall gives an impression of the scale of the Gedi complex. While the architectural forms may appear European, the palace pre-dates Portuguese incursions in the sixteenth century.

multi-family house with a square plan anchored at its corners by square, projecting, battered towers. These dwellings are constructed of stone, brick, and adobe and sometimes rise up to ten or more stories. The upper reaches of the tower walls are ornamented with unframed windows and repetitive smaller openings and recesses—frequently involving corbeling, and are sometimes capped with crenelations, all of which produce a distinctive silhouette and a dramatic pattern of light and shadow in the brilliant desert sunlight.

No African fortress complex has been more celebrated than the Great Zimbabwe (for which the country is named), a cluster of stone structures laid up in coursed granite without mortar, with a fortified, terraced acropolis on an adjacent hill, all covering some 1800 acres. More ruins, including cattle pens, lie between the two sites. The perimeter wall of the main compound, more than ten feet thick and thirty feet high, runs along a circumference of more than 800 feet, with a smaller secondary compound inside it, anchored by the solid-stone so-called "elliptical tower," its base more than seventeen feet in diameter. Inside this secondary compound lie the remains of housing units: circular-plan structures surrounding central sunken courts that were entered by way of tunnels. Activity on the site dates back as far as 1000 CE, with most of the construction carried out in the thirteenth and fourteenth centuries at a time when the population may have reached

40,000 inhabitants. The Great Zimbabwe was gradually abandoned in the fifteenth century. Also impressive are the fortresses in the Gondar region of Ethiopia, begun during the thirteenth-century reign of King Facilidas. (Gondar's rock-cut churches are discussed below.) Most notable in this group is the walled city of Fasil Ghebbi, built in the sixteenth century.

In Kenya on the Indian Ocean, a cosmopolitan population arose by the mid-thirteenth century as a result of extensive regional trade. The indigenous Swahili tribe, influenced by the spread of Islam, built cities along the coast and, in the case of Gedi, a few miles inland. This city flourished for some 200 years, went into decline, and was abandoned by the seventeenth century. Excavations have revealed a development covering almost fifty acres, with a palace and a mosque and courtyard houses. The one-story houses began as a wide, shallow principal room behind a street-front court, with secondary, more private rooms to the rear and to each side. Eventually, the builders added an inner court for cooking and enclosures for commercial use along the street (Fig. 10.53). A kind of annular arrangement of such courtyard houses can still be seen in Marrakech, Morocco.

Palaces

The palace at Gedi, probably dating to the fifteenth century and later, is a larger version of the city's houses, with an entrance court opening off the town square and an audience court for public receptions, as well as other courts elsewhere, all adjacent to rectangular rooms. Like the houses of the wealthy, this palace was constructed of stone and, even in its ruined state, still displays sophisticated moldings, arches, and other finely worked features (Fig. 10.54). The audience court was also richly detailed

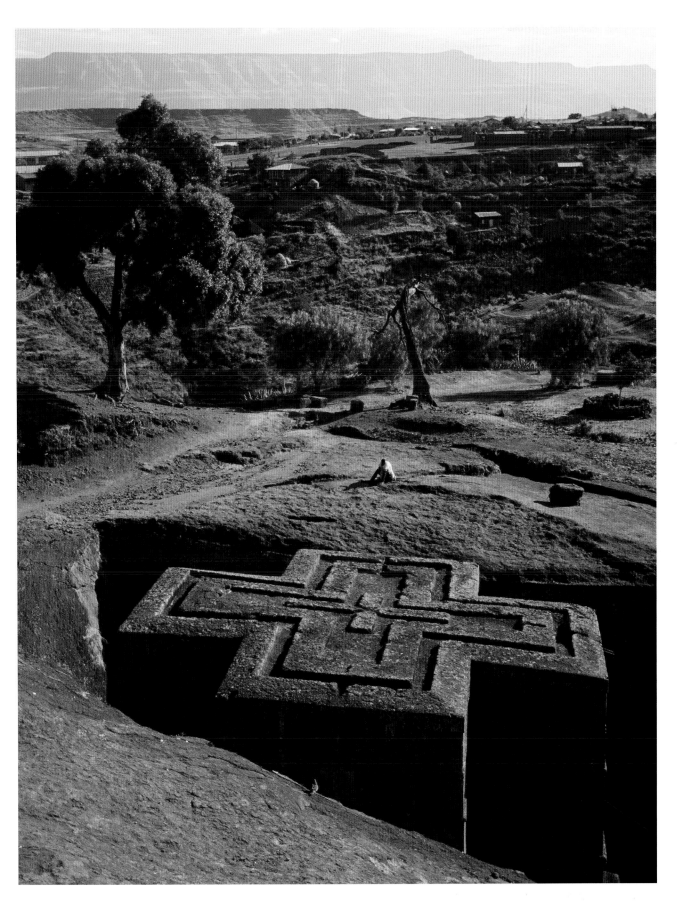

10.55 View from above St. George's Church, Lalibela, Ethiopia, 13th century.
It is unusual to find architectural space, like the interior of this church, carved out of live rock rather than enclosed by quarried stones. Other celebrated examples are the cave temples of India and the city of Petra in Jordan.

10.56 Great Mosque, Djenne, Mali, 1906–07.
While adobe construction has been prominent in this chapter, nowhere has it been exploited to greater dramatic effect than in this mosque. Some controversy continues regarding possible French contributions to this building's design and construction.

and included pegs for hanging ornamental carpets. In Uganda, at the headwaters of the Nile in what was then the Kingdom of Buganda, the palace of the chiefs, or kabakas, was constructed in 1882 and transformed into a royal tomb in 1884. It sits on a hilltop, is circular in plan, and is constructed of wood and wattle and daub and covered with a thatched roof. The royal palaces of the Abomey in Benin, now converted to museums, contain celebrated bas reliefs dating from as early as ca. 1700.

Churches and Mosques

Ancient Egyptian architecture influenced building styles to the south in Ethiopia and the Sudanese desert, resulting in the construction of temples, pyramids, and obelisks, including the giant shaft and the ruins of the palace at Aksum, both in place by the early fourth century. Christianity made its way into Ethiopia in the early years of the Church and was well established there by this time. Among the architectural results are a remarkable series of freestanding churches, each carved from a single mass of live rock. Constructed (or excavated) in the thirteenth century by the craftsmen of King Lalibela, they include St. George's Church, which has a cruciform plan extruded to form a cruciform mass (Fig. 10.55).

Mosques of distinctly African character can be found in Mali and Burkina Faso. The Great Mosque in Djenne, Mali is the third on the site and dates to 1906–07 in a city that was founded in the third century BCE. Oral histories and surface archaeology suggest that the second structure, dating from the thirteenth century, was constructed of adobe, and was almost 200 feet long and more than 100 feet wide and surrounded by a moat; its outer walls were apparently articulated with a relentless file of picketlike towers and sloping buttresses. The present Great Mosque (Fig. 10.56) is also constructed of adobe, with buttressing pickets, pinnacled towers, and prominently projecting, horizontal, wooden members that cast dramatic shadows and so are comparable to Spanish Colonial work in the American Southwest. The same type of handmade clay construction extends to the houses of Djenne and to those in Timbuktu, located to the northeast, and to those in other towns of Mali, Niger, Ivory Coast, and Burkina Faso. In the latter, the Bobo-Dioulasso Mosque (Fig. 10.57), which probably dates from the late nineteenth century, can only be described as fantastic, with its "ancestral pillars" shaped like attenuated pyramids and sprouting spiky, wooden projections and mottled with white and terracotta-colored pigments.

10.57 Mosque, Bobo-Dioulasso, Burkina Faso, late 19th century.
One might expect such an architectural phantasm to occur only within the "mysterious" continent of Africa. However, Dutch architects in Amsterdam in the early twentieth century produced brick-and-wood apartment buildings that display kindred forms.

CONCLUSIONS ABOUT ARCHITECTURAL IDEAS

In North America, indigenous peoples produced a wide variety of portable, or at least temporary, architecture. Where conditions allowed, or even demanded, they also produced impressive permanent structures: "frozen" ones in the far north; sandstone and adobe pueblos in the arid southwest; and monumental earthworks in the Ohio and Lower Mississippi valleys and the Southeast, especially in the form of pyramids and pyramidlike structures that dominated ceremonial centers here as well as throughout the remainder of the Americas from Mexico to Bolivia.

Sophisticated architectural ordering systems imposed on large complexes appeared very early on in both the Gulf Coast of Mexico and in Peru. In the former, during the second millennium BCE, the Olmecs at La Venta built an earth mound that terminated an axis defined by flanking plaza-defining buildings. The Teotihuacános in the Valley of Mexico, who adopted Olmec devices, articulated the faces of their stepped platforms and pyramids with sloping talud and friezelike tablero elements. The axially organized city of Teotihuacán stands in stark contrast to spatially organized Monte Albán in Oaxaca, where stepped platforms, once crowned with temples, define a central space in which other platforms reside, including one canted at an angle, presumably for the purpose of celestial alignment.

The Maya of the Yucatán Peninsula and Central American lowlands developed astronomy to its ancient American apogee, including their invention of a highly accurate calendar. In their cities of Tikal, Copán, and Palenque, amid dense jungle foliage, they built tall pyramids and low-slung ball courts as part of large ceremonial centers or acropolises, constructed corbel-vaulted temples, and sculpted stelae in the form of tree-stones that celebrated the reigns of their kings. Their wall articulation using the talud and tablero explored variations on themes set forth earlier in the Valley of Mexico.

At the Yucatán city of Chichén Itzá, the Toltecs from the north merged their aggressive architectural style with the sometimes geometric, sometimes organic, even ornate stone assemblies preferred by the Maya. The most distinctive features of Toltec religious buildings in their capital city of Tula in Hidalgo are ranks and files of columns, which are seen as well in the hypostyle hall-like Temple of the Warriors at Chichén-Itzá.

Back in the Valley of Mexico by the thirteenth century, the Aztecs used the by now familiar stepped pyramids and platforms, plazas, and talud–tablero combinations to create the ceremonial center of their orthogonally planned capital of Tenochtitlán. The sophistication of their ordering systems reflects a design continuity in Mexico and Central America that dates back more than 2000 years to the Olmecs.

In South America the scope of development was comparable to that in Mexico and Central America. In the Andean world, ceremonial centers with stepped pyramids were impressive, but no more so than the vast irrigation systems and sprawling giant glyphs laid out on Peru's south-coast hillsides and plains. At such Peruvian sites as Sechín Alto and Huaca de los Reyes, pyramids dominated U-shaped complexes organized by means of axes and cross-axes and carefully defined plazas. Stone masonry was already well developed at these ceremonial centers by the first millennium BCE, but became even more so at the Bolivian city of Tiwanaku, and yet more so again among the Inca, with their highland buildings, fortifications, and agricultural terraces. Despite the effects of erosion, the two great adobe-brick pyramids built by the Moche at Cerro Blanco are still impressive, as are the remaining "footprints" of palace compounds occupied by the Chimor kings at Chan Chan.

In the end, Pre-Columbian architecture and planning, from southern North America, through Mexico and Central America, and into South America can be seen as all of one piece, with certain design themes pursued across millennia and cross-culturally. In North America, where periodic or continual migrations were common, a diversity of architectural forms and construction methods were largely a response to building-material availability and the demands of climate. None of these constructions is a more elegant result of such constraints than the Great Plains teepee. Limited wood for frames and plentiful buffalo hides for coverings inspired a lightweight, conical structure that could be adjusted to accommodate both extreme heat and extreme cold.

The collapse of indigenous cultures in Mexico and farther south began with internal strife and environmental pressures, then was rapidly accelerated by the Spanish importation of Old World diseases, the overpowering effect of European weaponry, and blatant Spanish greed. In North America, the pattern was similar but took place over a much longer period of time, until virtually all Native American tribes had been forced onto reservations. Despite their mistreatment, the indigenous peoples of North America have not disappeared, be they the Mississippi Choctaw tribe; the Navajo descendants of the Ancestral Pueblo of the Southwest; or the Maya and Inca descendants who still populate Central America and Peru respectively. Vivid evidence of this continuum can be seen at the National Museum of the American Indian on the Mall in Washington, D.C. (with satellites in Maryland and New York City), where the "diversity of cultures and the continuity of cultural knowledge among indigenous peoples" is celebrated.

Reaching meaningful conclusions about indigenous architecture in Africa is difficult. Artificially configured and governed during the colonial period, then left largely adrift after the exit of European colonial powers, the vast African continent now offers up equal parts of beauty and mystery and of conflict and tragedy. Where its architecture has been closely studied, the work has most often been done by anthropologists and not architectural historians and so is probably most familiar to the public through the pages of such publications as *National Geographic Magazine,* and while African art became extremely influential in Europe and America in the early twentieth century, African architecture has not achieved such prominence, a condition exacerbated by the sheer difficulty and sometimes outright danger involved in visiting many of the important monuments and sites. In addition, the intuitive, highly symbolic, natural-world connectedness of so many African structures and landscapes (while appropriately compared to many Native American constructions) has made them seem remote and even incomprehensible to those conditioned by Western architectural traditions.

As among Pre-Columbian Americans, African tribespeople have erected and continue to erect many types of portable structures using a wide variety of local materials. Available materials have also been the principal form-determining agents for their more permanent buildings, with some form of adobe being the most common medium for everything from modest shelters to the largest, most exotic mosques. African builders have also worked stone when they have found it available, producing sprawling complexes like the Great Zimbabwe and the fantastic, monolithic, rock-cut churches of Ethiopia.

In the end, the study and appreciation of African architecture must be viewed as a work in progress. Those who find fascination in the diversity of the built environment can only hope that all Africans will, sooner rather than later, achieve a state of peace and prosperity and that this, in turn, will make it possible for the rest of the world to appreciate better their rich building traditions.

Chapter 11
Renaissance Architecture

European mariners began their voyages of exploration first to Africa and then to the Americas in the fifteenth century, a time when architecture in Europe was undergoing a dramatic change from the Gothic of the late Middle Ages to that of the Renaissance. Chapter 9 on the Gothic period contained little discussion of buildings in Italy. Here, Romanesque churches were never completely purged of their classical elements, and monumental Gothic religious architecture never became completely at home in the one-time center of the Roman Empire, where vestiges of a grand classical past loomed about portentously.

Still, the fabric of most Italian cities, particularly that of the everyday residential buildings, was woven in the eleventh through fourteenth centuries. In such inland centers as Florence, these buildings were rather plain: heavy masonry blocks punctured by arched openings and sometimes provided with shady **loggias** or porches. Likewise, medieval governmental buildings anchored the civic cores of cities and caused to form around them the open spaces or piazzas that to this day speak the very language of urbanism. It was within this well-established medieval context that Renaissance architects would make their radical proposals.

While both France and England were unified monarchies by the end of the Middle Ages, Italy remained an assemblage of fractious but vigorous city-states and fiefdoms. Trade flourished as a result of Italy's position between western Europe and Byzantium in the east, which was then the trade hub for products coming out of the Orient. Aggressive merchants exported luxury goods and organized textile industries. Civic life in the principal Italian city-states became dominated by families whose wealth arose not from the traditional source of inherited landholdings but from new mercantile profits. The economic stimulus prompted by the boom in trade led to urban and cultural revival in the leading Italian city-states.

Nowhere was this change more dramatic than in Florence, the city regarded as the birthplace of the Renaissance. Here the newly wealthy wool merchants and powerful bankers, including members of the Medici family, sought prestige and status through their patronage of

arts and letters, and local artists and architects were up to the task. The spirit of their revolutionary painting, sculpture, and architecture arose from the new Renaissance worldview of humanism (and its accompanying condition of secularization), which celebrated rationality and individuality and mankind's ability to make and act upon empirical observations of the physical world. Humanist scholars and artists recovered Classical Greek and Roman texts, including Vitruvius's *De architectura*, and aspired to create a modern world rivaling that of the ancients. Within their new intellectual construct, it was not only permissible, but even desirable, to achieve fame, meaning that, unlike the largely anonymous designers of the Middle Ages, Renaissance architects became celebrated as personalities such that their identities and even details of their personal lives have come all the way down to us today.

These architects, absorbing the writings of the Greek philosopher Plato, set out to create an architecture of mathematical perfection. In pursuit of this goal, they turned to whole-number ratios, such as 1:1, 1:2, 2:3, and 3:4, taken from the musical consonances discovered by the Greek mathematician Pythagoras, and concluded that the innate harmony of these ratios would be impressed upon anyone experiencing spaces determined by them. Humanists were further convinced that God's cosmic order

Chronology

Filippo Brunelleschi, Pazzi Chapel, S. Croce, Florence, 1430–33.
Brunelleschi chose as his precedent for this façade the Roman triumphal arch. Here, rather than massive, as in ancient examples, it appears somewhat brittle. The shed roof above and the drum with conical roof and cupola were not part of Brunelleschi's design.

could be expressed on earth through such mathematical proportions, which were inevitably related to the mensuration of the human body.

Renaissance architects maintained the interest in geometry that had so strongly influenced medieval architecture. Rather than using the complex, geometric transformations of medieval master masons, they held in particular reverence such "ideal" forms as the square and circle. In this context, the central-plan church came to represent the most perfect form, absolute, immutable, echoing celestial harmony. Artists made drawings of the human figure inscribed within a "perfect" geometric context and, thereby, "proved" that human proportions reflected divine ratios. Of these drawings, the most famous is the *Vitruvian Man* (Fig. 11.1) found in the notebooks of Leonardo da Vinci, which, like the other examples of its type, illustrates the precedent established by Vitruvius in his third book. Vitruvius wrote:

> *For if a man be placed flat on his back, with his hands and feet extended, and a pair of compasses centered at his navel, the fingers and toes of his two hands and feet will touch the circumference of a circle described therefrom. And, just as the human body yields a circular outline, so too a square figure may be found from it. For if we measure*

> *the distance from the soles of the feet to the top of the head, and then apply that measure to the outstretched arms, the breadth will be found to be the same as the height, as in the case of plane surfaces which are perfectly square.*

FILIPPO BRUNELLESCHI

From the beginning of the fifteenth century to 1494, when French armies overran the city, Florence flourished as the center of the early Renaissance, and the figure who ushered in this profoundly creative period for architecture was Filippo Brunelleschi (1377–1446). The son of a notary, Brunelleschi was trained as a goldsmith. In 1400 he entered the competition to design a new set of bronze doors for the baptistery of Florence Cathedral. His main competitor, and the man who won, was Lorenzo Ghiberti (1378–1455). Discouraged by his loss, Brunelleschi set off for Rome with his friend, the sculptor Donatello (1386–1466), and his subsequent career as an architect owed much to the extended visit he paid to the Eternal City and the observations he made there.

During his stay in Rome, and perhaps as a means to record more accurately what he saw, Brunelleschi codified the principles of geometrically accurate linear perspective, making possible the exact representation of a three-dimensional object on a two-dimensional surface. Various artists in Italy had struggled with the question of how best to depict spatial relationships in their paintings, but their solutions fell short of the precision achieved by Brunelleschi. In making careful drawings of such repetitive elements as the arches of aqueducts, he realized that parallel horizontal lines converge at a point on the horizon and that elements of like size diminish proportionally into the distance. His development of this new system of spatial representation had a profound effect on art, architecture, and civic design during and after the Renaissance.

Brunelleschi must have assisted his friend, the painter Masaccio (1401–1428), in the application of linear perspective to a fresco painting, *The Trinity* (1427–28) at S. Maria Novella in Florence (Fig. 11.2). It depicts God the Father standing on a large sarcophagus supporting the crucified Christ. Below are Mary and St. John with two kneeling donors. The holy figures are framed by modified Ionic columns supporting an arch that creates a coffered, barrel-vaulted chapel, accurately projected according to the rules of perspective. Masaccio, it would seem, was illustrating Brunelleschi's momentous discovery.

11.1 Leonardo da Vinci, *Vitruvian Man*, ca. 1485.
Probably no image has been more frequently used than this one to convey the spirit of the Renaissance. Here, Leonardo has drawn the so-called *Vitruvian Man* to illustrate the era's belief that the human body was proportioned according to divine ratios.

Florence Cathedral

By 1407 Brunelleschi was again living in Florence. In that year the directors of the cathedral works consulted distinguished engineers and architects from France, Spain, England, and Germany for advice on the cathedral's dome. The cathedral was begun in 1292 to the designs of Arnolfo di Cambio and continued by Francesco Talenti. It was always intended to have a dome exceeding the Romanesque cathedral of Pisa in size. Arnolfo and Talenti produced a building with some obvious Gothic characteristics such as pointed arches and ribbed vaults atop piers. Their work proceeded to the level of the octagonal drum, from which a dome reaching nearly 150 feet on the diagonal was to spring, but without anyone having a firm idea about how to achieve such a huge span. The outward thrust of such a dome, built using conventional techniques, without internal tension members, and unbraced by extensive buttresses, would have burst the drum. In addition, the scale of centering required to support the masonry while construction was in progress vastly exceeded anything attempted in the medieval period. This was the situation that Brunelleschi inherited when the works directors eventually turned to him (Fig. 11.3).

Brunelleschi drew upon his knowledge of ancient Roman construction as well as lingering Gothic traditions to produce an innovative synthesis (Fig. 11.4). In order to reduce the outward thrust, he employed a Gothic pointed-arch cross-section instead of a semicircular one. In order to reduce the dead load, he created a double shell of radial and concentric ribs, a strategy traceable both to ancient monuments such as the Pantheon and to Florentine medieval work such as the nearby cathedral baptistery. In order to reduce the amount of temporary construction, he devised portable centering that supported concentric courses of masonry until they were completed as stable compression rings, and he used this rising masonry to support scaffolding that in turn supported more centering.

The cleverness of Brunelleschi's system of ribs is worthy of more detailed description. He devised as his principal structural members sandstone ribs rising from each of the eight corners of the octagonal drum. At the springing of the dome, they have a cross-section of eleven by seven feet, and they taper upward to an apex ring beneath the cupola. Between each of these corner ribs, Brunelleschi placed a pair of intermediate ribs, making a total of twenty-four vertical ribs. To hold the inner and outer shells apart, he inserted five horizontal rings of sandstone, connected by tin-plated iron clamps: he had observed such imbedded metal fastenings in the ruins of Roman construction. Finally, near the base of the dome, he placed twenty-four chestnut timbers, each one foot square and twenty-three feet long, banded together with straps and bolts into a continuous wooden tension ring that resists the outward thrust of the dome. However, according to modern structural analysis, the action of this ring is negligible.

11.2 Masaccio, *The Trinity*, S. Maria Novella, Florence, 1427–28. Brunelleschi first demonstrated his invention of mechanical perspective by displaying his painted view of the Florence Cathedral baptistery. He obviously showed the artist Masaccio his method, and Masaccio used it to create this illusion of a coffered barrel vault housing the crucified Christ.

Double-shell dome

Drum

Exedra dome

Other Florentine Buildings

Work on the cathedral dome continued throughout Brunelleschi's lifetime; the cupola was completed after his death. Concurrently, he was able to build several smaller projects in which the ideals of Roman architecture could be expressed more directly than in the cathedral dome. In these commissions, which had fewer troublesome technical problems, Brunelleschi was able to express outwardly his empathy for ancient Rome. The earliest, the Ospedale degli Innocenti or Foundling Hospital, is often considered the first building of the Renaissance. Designed in 1419 and built from 1421 to 1444, it continues the link with classical tradition that had been maintained in Florence through such proto-Renaissance buildings as the Romanesque S. Miniato al Monte and the cathedral's baptistery. The Foundling Hospital has a continuous arcade, carried on Corinthian columns across its main façade and around an internal courtyard that is comparable to the ground-floor

11.3 (above) Filippo Brunelleschi, Florence Cathedral transverse section, 1292 and later.
The pointed-arch profile of the Florence Cathedral dome reveals its medieval inspiration. However, internal construction techniques such as a double shell resulted from Brunelleschi's close observation of ancient Roman building methods.

11.4 Filippo Brunelleschi, Florence Cathedral, 1292 and later.
The body of Florence Cathedral was designed by Arnolfo di Cambio and Francesco Talenti, but the dome was only completed by Brunelleschi in the fifteenth century. The campanile, or belltower, was begun by the painter Giotto in the fourteenth century.

11.5 (left) Filippo Brunelleschi and Michelangelo Buonarroti, plan of S. Lorenzo, begun 1421.
The church of San Lorenzo is part of a larger monastic complex that includes chapels and the Laurentian Library by Michelangelo (see Fig. 11.36). The major spaces are organized around a square cloister that corresponds to the modular regularity of Brunelleschi's church plan.

11.6 (below) Filippo Brunelleschi, S. Lorenzo interior, Florence, begun 1421.
The nave and aisle configuration of S. Lorenzo is no different than that of Romanesque and Gothic churches in Florence. Brunelleschi simply substituted classical elements for medieval ones: Corinthian columns and an arcade as at the Foundling Hospital. His design innovation is the modular regularity in plan, visible here in the floor pattern.

arcading in marble veneer that adorns both S. Miniato and the baptistery; these Romanesque elements were ultimately based on Roman architecture. At the hospital, the arcading is three-dimensional, creating a loggia with domed vaults in each bay. Semicircular arches span the width of the loggia, from the freestanding columns with abaci to corbeled brackets on the opposite wall.

A similar columnar arcade is found in the aisles of the Latin-cross church of S. Lorenzo (Figs. 11.5–11.6), begun in 1421. Here, Brunelleschi defined each bay with arches that spring from columns of the nave arcade to pilasters set between side-aisle chapels. This configuration achieves a more balanced effect than the wall corbels at the hospital, yet Brunelleschi found an even more satisfactory resolution in his design for the church of S. Spirito (Fig. 11.7), begun as late as 1445, where he attached half-columns to

11.7 (left) Filippo Brunelleschi, Plan of S. Spirito, Florence, begun 1445.
Brunelleschi perfected his system of modular planning at S. Spirito. Perhaps he intended for the building's exterior perimeter to have a continuous series of projecting semicircular chapels. If so, these proved objectionable to his patrons as the walls were infilled to be externally flat.

11.8 Filippo Brunelleschi, plan and elevation reconstruction of the Pazzi Chapel, Florence, 1430–33. Here is one possible reconstruction of Brunelleschi's dome. If it is accurate, it displays on the exterior the perfect circular form on which the plan was based.

11.9 (above) Filippo Brunelleschi, Pazzi Chapel interior, Florence, 1430–33.
As with the Florence Cathedral dome, Brunelleschi looked here to local traditions for design motifs, in this case the gray pietra serena stone used for the framing elements: pilasters, entablatures, and arches. New is the classical language and the geometry based upon squares, half-squares, semicircles, and circles—comparable to the squares and circles bounding Leonardo's *Vitruvian Man*.

the wall in place of the pilasters he had used at S. Lorenzo. This may seem an undue emphasis on Brunelleschi's part on admittedly minor architectural details, but such attention to each element and to the relationship of all elements to one another characterizes the proper manipulation of the classical language of architecture.

In both S. Lorenzo and S. Spirito, Brunelleschi sought to accommodate the traditional practical requirements of his clients within a unifying system of mathematical proportions. At both churches, the square bay of the aisles defines a module that is repeated throughout. At S. Spirito, four modules form a double bay of the nave, and this larger square is repeated four times down the nave and then once for each transept, the crossing, and the choir. Equally carefully proportioned Roman elements such as the semicircular arch, Corinthian columns, and coffering impart a classical monumentality to the interiors of both churches.

Brunelleschi made prominent use of simple numerical ratios in three of his smaller commissions. For the church of S. Lorenzo, he erected the Old Sacristy (1421–28) in a corner of the south transept. The floor, walls, and pendentives are contained in a cube, capped by a hemispherical dome with an oculus. Pilasters, an entablature, and arches of gray **pietra serena**, a local stone much favored for architectural detail, are set against the white plaster of the walls, giving a linear definition to the interior. The thinness of the pilaster strips as they turn the corner and the isolated, undersized brackets "supporting" the entablature

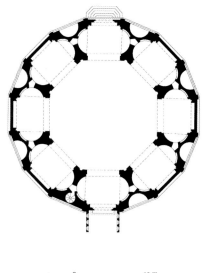

11.10 Filippo Brunelleschi, Plan of S. Maria degli Angel Florence, 1434–37.
Brunelleschi had observed the circular temples of antiquity. His proposal for a pure, central plan was the first of the Renaissance, but it was a theme that would be explored by almost every Renaissance designer thereafter.

have been pointed to as signs of Brunelleschi's "uncertainty" in manipulating the still-new classical language.

Slightly larger than the Old Sacristy is the Pazzi Chapel (1430–33), erected off the major cloister at the monastery of S. Croce. While it is not certain what Brunelleschi intended the façade (page 286 and Fig. 11.8) to be like above the Corinthian columns that support a series of square panels flanking a central arch, the interior is entirely his (Fig. 11.9). The space is a carefully conceived but occasionally awkward essay based on numerical ratios, the classical language, and local building practices. The plan is generated by placing the circle of a dome above a square divided into three bays, and expanded one barrel-vaulted bay to each side and one domed square bay in depth. All these bays are defined by Corinthian pilasters supporting a continuous entablature with arches above, and all are delineated in gray pietra serena against white plaster.

Renaissance architects considered the central plan to be an ideal type. Brunelleschi's design for S. Maria degli Angeli (1434–37) was the first such structure of the fifteenth century (Fig. 11.10). While it was left unfinished at Brunelleschi's death and subsequently badly reconstructed and altered in the 1930s, engravings probably based upon the original drawings survive to indicate Brunelleschi's intentions. The church's plan and massing were to be Roman, with a domed octagon expanded by eight lozenge-shaped chapels. Piers composed of clustered pilasters provided support for the dome, and the overall spatial effect would have suggested that the chapels were carved from the solid exterior wall. Had the dome been constructed, its monolithic single shell would have been true to Roman prototypes.

MICHELOZZO BARTOLOMEO AND THE PALAZZO MEDICI

Michelozzo Bartolomeo (1396–1472), a student of Brunelleschi, worked not only in Florence but also in other northern Italian cities. Although not so celebrated a designer as his teacher, Michelozzo was a capable architect and was awarded several commissions by those archetypal Renaissance patrons, the Medici. Most noteworthy of these was the Palazzo Medici (Fig. 11.11) in Florence, begun in 1444 after an earlier design by Brunelleschi was rejected as being too ostentatious. The client, Cosimo de' Medici, did not want to arouse feelings of envy among other important families in the city. Michelozzo's design reflects his

11.11 (above) Michelozzo Bartolomeo, Palazzo Medici, Florence, begun 1444.
The palazzo form of this urban house built by the Medici family can be added to the temple, stoa, and basilica as fundamental form types that have been repeated and reinterpreted down to the present day. The Medici intended its fortified quality to afford them protection in a Florence accustomed to political intrigue.

11.12 Michelozzo Bartolomeo, Plan of the Palazzo Medici, Florence, begun 1444.
The fortified quality of the exterior walls belies the delicate openness of the arcaded cortile or courtyard. It is as though Michelozzo had taken the external arcade used by his friend Brunelleschi at the Foundling Hospital and made it an internal element reflecting humanist preoccupations.

awareness of traditional Florentine domestic buildings and his admiration for Brunelleschi's Foundling Hospital arcade and its traditional Florentine courtyard plan. The **palazzo**'s square plan includes such a central courtyard, or cortile, serving as a circulation core for perimeter rooms that open to one another en suite, that is, without a continuous corridor (Fig. 11.12). Michelozzo made use of **rustication**, stone blocks with deeply recessed chamfered joints. He arranged the street elevation in three tiers of graduated textures, beginning with rock-faced stone at the street level and concluding with smooth ashlar at the third level below a ten-foot-high crowning cornice with **modillions**, **egg-and-dart moldings**, and a dentil course, the first such cornice since ancient Roman times. The cornice projects out eight feet from the building, supported by acanthus-leaf modillions or large brackets, and it combines with the string course between the floor levels to create a strong horizontal emphasis, even though the façade is eighty-three feet high.

The ground floor originally had three open arches along the street, the central one giving access to the courtyard and rooms serving the Medici banking business. From the courtyard a staircase led to the major family rooms on the second floor, or **piano nobile**. Deep shadows in the courtyard make the palazzo's core cool and quiet, and the upper-level galleries provide access to and shade for the individual rooms. Typical Romanesque windows with circular heads are used throughout. While without radical innovations, the Palazzo Medici reflects Michelozzo's connection to Renaissance circles through its symmetry, inclusion of classical elements, and careful use of mathematical proportions.

LEON BATTISTA ALBERTI

In contrast to the pragmatic and technically skilled Brunelleschi, Leon Battista Alberti (1404–1472) was a classical theorist who saw architecture as a way to address societal order. The Renaissance architect, in Alberti's mind, was to be a universalist, an intellectual, a man of genius, and a consort of those in positions of power and authority. In his autobiography (written in the third person), he offered this description of himself:

> [He was] assiduous in science, and skilled in dealing with arms, horse, and musical instruments; as well as the pursuit of letters and the fine arts, he was devoted to the knowledge of the most strange and difficult things. His genius was so versatile that you might almost judge all the fine arts to be his. He played ball, hurled the javelin, ran, leapt, wrestled, and above all delighted in the steep ascent of mountains. He could leap over the shoulders of men and had almost no equal among those hurling the lance. . . . He was considered an expert among the leading musicians.

Alberti was not being immodest: an accomplished scholar from an exiled Florentine family, he became one of the most influential thinkers of his time. His education at the universities of Padua and Bologna included mathematics, music, Greek, Latin, philosophy, and Roman law.

On completing these studies, Alberti entered the Papal Chancery in Rome as secretary to the chancellor. Living in Rome provided him with many opportunities to meet artists visiting the monuments of antiquity, and his travels gave him the chance to observe the works of artists in many cities throughout northern Italy. Because Alberti searched the writings of Plato, Aristotle, Plutarch, and Pliny the Elder for references to the arts and carefully studied the collections of antique sculpture that were being assembled by patrons of the arts, his writings reveal a mixture of scholarly research and informed observations.

Writings

The manuscript of Alberti's *Della pittura*, or *On Painting*, completed in 1435, documents Brunelleschi's theories of perspective. It was dedicated to the five young artists of Florence whom Alberti most admired and who came closest to creating a personal style that reflected the art of ancient Rome. We now regard these five—Brunelleschi, the sculptor Ghiberti, the painter Masaccio, and the sculptors Donatello and Luca della Robbia (1399–1482)—as among the founders of the Renaissance.

Alberti's interest in architecture was probably first aroused when he came across the already well-known manuscript *De architectura libri decem*, Vitruvius's *The Ten Books on Architecture*. While there may have been many such treatises, it is the only one to have survived. Vitruvius was a mediocre writer at best, and owing to the uncertainty of his language, his text is often ambiguous; nevertheless, as an authentic book from Roman times, the work was greatly respected by Renaissance architects. In response to the obscurities in Vitruvius's text, in order to discuss principles of Roman buildings designed after the time of Vitruvius, and in order to argue that architects should be highly educated humanists, like himself, Alberti began writing his own treatise, modeled on the antique text and, like it, organized into ten books or chapters. He worked on his book, which he titled *De re aedificatoria*, or *On Building*, from the early 1440s until his death, completing a first version by 1452, which was circulated in manuscript form. The text as we know it was published posthumously in Florence in 1485. As the first architectural treatise of the Renaissance, it is important for cataloging the features and proportions of the orders of antiquity and establishing a theory of harmonious proportions to be observed in buildings. Alberti adapted proportioning systems expounded by Vitruvius because he believed that they should unify plans, elevations, and sections of a building. For example, church plans could be centralized, using a circle, hexagon, octagon, decagon, dodecagon, or based on a square, such as a square-and-a-half, square-and-a-third, or double square. Whatever the plan selected, the three-dimensional realization was to be derived from it. Furthermore, to assume their proper symbolic role in the cityscape, churches needed to be centrally located, isolated from other structures so that they could be seen from all sides, and raised above ground level on a plinth or base.

Although Alberti was concerned with the theoretical and esthetic implications of proportional systems, he was equally attentive to the practical aspects of architecture and city planning. Vitruvius had written of public health considerations in the siting of towns, and Alberti extended this approach to include other factors such as the purity of the water supply and the distribution of land uses. He suggested that arrangements should respond to both convenience and hygiene. He recommended that facilities for noxious trades, such as dyeworks and slaughterhouses, be positioned away from residential districts, and he studied the location of recreational facilities and the dimensioning of streets and open spaces with respect to the heights of buildings. He proposed individual house plans with consideration for the needs and ordinary uses of the inhabitants. As kitchens are noisy, he proposed that they should be away from quiet parts of the house and yet near enough to the dining room. Bedrooms should face east toward the rising sun, and the parents' rooms should be near the children's quarters. Old people should have rooms without drafts, and guests should have rooms near the entrance to enable them and their friends to enter and leave without disturbing the whole household. A country house could be more elaborate in design than a town house, where restrained ornamentation could add to the unity of the streetscape. He even described the quality of basic building materials in a manner not too different from the style used in modern specifications. Sand, he said, should be clean and free of impurities, lime should be well slaked, and timber should be straight, well seasoned, and free of knots and checks.

The Palazzo Rucellai, Florence

Some of this advice is reflected in Alberti's design for the façade of the Palazzo Rucellai in Florence (1446–51) (Fig. 11.13). To organize it, he applied **superimposed** Doric and Corinthian orders to demarcate the individual floors; this was the first use of the classical orders on a Renaissance domestic building. He raised the order of the ground floor on a high plinth scored into diamond shapes in imitation of Roman opus reticulatum, where diamond-shaped masonry units were used as formwork for concrete walls. Here, however, the subdivision serves only as a surface texture reflective of antique practices.

Churches in Rimini, Florence, and Mantua

Alberti's four other major commissions were ecclesiastical. Sigismondo Malatesta was his client for the modernization

11.13 Leon Battista Alberti, Palazzo Rucellai, Florence, 1446–51. Alberti's palazzo proposal owes more to ancient models than to Michelozzo's Palazzo Medici. Superimposed orders like those used at the Colosseum articulate the three floors, and diamond shapes at the base of the first floor mimic Roman opus-reticulatum masonry.

of the thirteenth-century church of S. Francesco in Rimini (Fig. 11.14), begun in 1450 but never completed. Malatesta was a consummate Renaissance despot as defined by the Florentine political theorist Machiavelli in his influential treatise *The Prince*. Alberti's wrapping of the existing medieval building with new walls is so thoroughly classical that the building is known to this day as the Tempio (Temple) Malatestiano.

Malatesta wished the structure to serve as a tomb for himself and his wife and for the scholars of his humanist court. For the sepulchers of the scholars, Alberti chose to subdivide the building's flanks using heavy round arches modeled on those of the Tomb of Theodoric (ca. 526) in nearby Ravenna. This composition inspired a series of subsequent buildings including McKim, Mead, and White's late-nineteenth-century Boston Public Library (see Fig. 14.51). At the front façade of S. Francesco, Alberti superimposed a temple front over a triumphal-arch form, like the ancient Roman Arch of Augustus a few blocks

11.14 Leon Battista Alberti, S. Francesco, Rimini, begun 1450. Alberti never saw this church completed, but he certainly visited the site, modeling the façade on the nearby ancient Roman Arch of Augustus. Arches along the right side wall house sepulchers for humanist scholars.

11.15 Leon Battista Alberti, S. Maria Novella, Florence, ca. 1456–70. Alberti's façade composition for this church became a prototype much reinterpreted by other Renaissance designers. Its two-story central bays capped by a pedimented temple-form conceal the gable-roofed nave of a basilican cross-section, and the flanking scrolls mask the shed roofs over the aisles.

away, and proposed to place the tombs of Malatesta and his wife in the blind-arched portals flanking the central entry. Alberti's on-site assistant, Matteo de' Pasti, updated the Gothic interior of the church but never constructed the huge Pantheon-like dome that Alberti envisioned.

The task of adapting classical details to the façade of a church with a basilican cross-section was a compositional problem for Renaissance architects. Alberti's work on S. Maria Novella in Florence (ca. 1456–70) produced the first completed design for a church façade in the Renaissance, but in some respects it is an extension of eleventh-century Florentine traditions with its geometric panels of white and green marble (Fig. 11.15). Alberti was obliged to preserve some Gothic aspects of the existing church, particularly the pointed arches of the lower level and the central rose window above. Rudolf Wittkower's analysis of Alberti's façade emphasizes the predominance of the square as a unit of composition. As at S. Francesco, Alberti attempted to unify the façade by linking lower aisle roofs to the pedimented higher nave with flanking scrolls, a solution that was much repeated throughout the Renaissance.

Farther north, in Mantua, Alberti worked for the Gonzaga family. Here he gave the church of S. Andrea (1472–94) an entrance portico based, like S. Francesco, on a temple front and triumphal arch, and he intended to extend this treatment to the east and west transepts (Fig. 11.16). The temple portion's order of Corinthian pilasters stands on pedestals; this order reappears on the interior, supporting the great barrel vault of the nave. A shorter Corinthian order supports the arch of the central portal and an entablature that disappears beneath the temple-front pilasters; it also reappears on the interior in the jambs of the barrel-vaulted chapels.

The church's plan (Fig. 11.17) is that of the ancient Roman Basilica of Constantine, with the transverse barrel vaults of the chapels and their bearing walls resisting the lateral thrust of the longitudinal barrel vault of the nave. It would serve as the pattern for many subsequent churches. The assemblage of classical elements on the interior presents the first Renaissance vision rivaling the monumentality of the interior spaces of such ancient Roman monuments as the basilicas and baths. Unfortunately, Alberti did not live to walk through his creation, as he died early in the construction process. (S. Andrea's choir and transepts cannot be positively attributed to Alberti. Its dome was added by Filippo Juvarra in the eighteenth century.)

S. Sebastiano (begun 1460), which stands not far away, was designed as a Greek cross with a hexastyle pilastered temple front. The central interior space is spanned by a groin vault, not a dome as one might expect; the stubby arms of the Greek cross are barrel-vaulted. In its present incomplete state, the church does not clearly reflect its designer's intentions, but it does illustrate Alberti's interest in the centrally planned church.

11.16 Leon Battista Alberti, S. Andrea, Mantua, 1472–94.
Here Alberti built upon his experience in Rimini to produce a confident synthesis of the temple and triumphal-arch forms. The two are effectively interlaced by the entablature that disappears behind the Corinthian pilasters of the temple front.

11.17 (below) Leon Battista Alberti, Plan of and longitudinal section through S. Andrea, Mantua, 1472–94.
In contrast to Brunelleschi's S. Spirito and S. Lorenzo, S. Andrea has no internal files of nave columns. Rather, this church is based upon the Basilica of Constantine, itself derivative of the Roman baths. The chapel walls provide the buttressing necessary to resist the lateral thrust of the monumental barrel vault.

The Ideal City

Alberti's vision of the centrally planned temple was also represented in Perugino's fresco *Giving of the Keys to St. Peter* (1481–82), Raphael's painting *The Marriage of the Virgin* (1504), and the *cassone* panels (the sides of a wooden chest) in the Palazzo Ducale in Urbino. Each of these artworks depicts the Albertian ideal of the temple of God in the center of a geometrically planned city. Alberti's design for S. Sebastiano, as well as his theoretical writings, emphasized the ideal-city form, in which a centrally planned church is set in a broad piazza in the middle of the town. The horizontal cornices of the buildings along the approach streets converge as lines of perspective at the focal point, the church. This ideal was less often realized by architects than painters, who were not restrained by the physical dimensions of actual cities and the costs associated with demolition and new construction. Renaissance planning contrasts with medieval practice, where the church commonly formed part of the piazza's edge, if there was a sizable open space at all. Ideal-city schemes drawn by various Renaissance architects often extended the centralized concept to include radial streets and a polygonal town wall with arrowhead-shaped bastions at

Pius's Resolutions
by Charles R. Mack

11.18 Bernardo Rossellino, Cathedral (left) and Palazzo Piccolomini (right), Piazza Pio II, Pienza, 1459–64.

Although respect for the visible presence of the ancient past was not universal during the Italian Renaissance's first century, there is abundant evidence for a renewed interest in the remains of classical Italy and for a desire to record and preserve its monuments. This preservationist impetus is nicely seen in the actions of Pope Pius II (ruled 1458–64, the humanist Aeneas Silvius Piccolomini). It is true, of course, that Pope Pius did have marble transported from the Colosseum to rebuild the steps leading up to St. Peter's and despoiled the Portico of Octavia for columns to be used in the new Benediction Loggia that he ordered built across the front of the same basilica. But Pius also issued a papal bull (probably the first official document in the history of the historic preservation movement) on April 28, 1462 forbidding the destruction of antiquities in the Roman region. That the document accorded the pope the privilege of violating his own injunction is interesting and demonstrates two aspects of the Early Renaissance's attitude toward its antique heritage. It prohibited the unrestricted dismantling of Roman ruins by the lower classes, but it allowed the utilization of the surviving remnants of ancient glory in new campaigns of officially sponsored construction. The melding of the remains of pagan antiquity into the fabric of a reconstituted Christian Rome was typical of the age's attitude toward the past.

Curiously, the same Pope Pius, while still a cardinal in 1456, could criticize the title of Flavio Biondo's *Rome Restored* by complaining: "Even if all the forces of Europe were to unite, they could not restore Rome to its early form, for towns also have their end; the fallen ones cannot rise any more than the old can grow young." Perhaps the future pope was just expressing a momentary fatalism inherited from some ancient Etruscan forebear or was simply imitating the cyclical view of history found in the writings of Roman philosophers during the reign of Caesar Augustus (31 BCE–14 CE). In any case, the concept of rebirth was very much on the mind of the confident new pope Pius II only a few years later. It formed a conscious part of his plans for the refurbishing of the Vatican and was very much evident when he set about reforming his very own rustic birthplace of Corsignano, renamed Pienza in his honor (Fig. 11.18). Pius must have recollected his earlier comments concerning the futility of attempting a Roman restoration when he visited his hometown in February of 1459. There he found both the companions of his youth and the community itself "bowed down with old age," but, instead of accepting the inevitable, that towns like people "also have their end," he determined upon a truly Renaissance course of action that led to an extensive reconstruction of the town, incorporating much of the classicizing vision he must have held for Papal Rome. Pienza exists today as the very model of the integrating spirit of Pope Pius's generation, a generation that adapted the vocabulary of ancient art and architecture to new, post-medieval circumstances.

11.19 Palazzo Ducale cortile arcade, Urbino, 1450–ca. 1480s.
The clifflike façade of the palace conceals this serene three-story arcade around the cortile. Its informed manipulation of the classical language includes pilasters above arcaded columns.

11.20 Plan of the Palazzo Ducale, Urbino, 1450–ca. 1480s.
The irregularity of this plan reflects the need to fit it onto a precipitous but dramatic site. Once inside, one finds light, airy rooms that made it an island of Renaissance culture in a sea of medievalism.

the vertices. Such fortifications are also a departure from the towers and turrets of medieval city walls. Changes in military technology, most notably the introduction of metal cannonballs and gunpowder after 1400, rendered high city walls vulnerable, as a well-aimed shot could shatter the masonry. Renaissance town walls became low and earth-sheltered, to absorb the impact of projectiles, and complex outerworks of ditches and moats set in the cleared area beyond the wall impeded an attacking army's advance. Cannons pivoted on the bastions could direct their fire over a range of more than 180 degrees, even firing in enfilade, or parallel to the town walls, if necessary.

THE SPREAD OF THE RENAISSANCE
Urbino

Not far from Sigismondo Malatesta's Rimini is Urbino, situated in hilly terrain about twenty miles from the east coast of Italy. Here the humanist and condottiere Federigo

da Montefeltro held court, governing an area of about 3600 square miles that included 400 villages. Federigo was a loyal commander who served the dukes of Naples and Milan and three popes and raised an army for Florence in 1448. His military accomplishments were balanced by his patronage of liberal learning. Humanists resided at his court, and dozens of scribes were employed to hand-copy ancient manuscripts.

Dalmatian-born architect Luciano Laurana expanded Federigo's Palazzo Ducale (1450–ca. 1480s) (Figs. 11.19–11.20) in 1464–72. Architect-engineer Francesco di Giorgio followed Laurana and continued the work until some time in the 1480s. The palace surrounds di Giorgio's **cortile** of ca. 1475 but is slightly more rambling in plan than a typical Florentine merchant's residence; its rooms are light, airy, and carefully proportioned. The walls of Federigo's small study are covered with exquisite varie-gated wood **intarsia** or inlay executed by Baccio Pontelli to designs by Botticelli. Cupboards apparently with doors ajar exhibit their contents. A spinet, a squirrel, and a basket of fruit on the ledge of a colonnaded opening are all rendered in varied types of wood on the two-dimensional surface. Even the distant landscape is shown beyond the simulated open window. Such a unified illusionistic extension of space beyond the actual walls of a room illustrates the complete assimilation of perspectival space in fifteenth-century art and anticipates the trompe-l'oeil effects of sixteenth-century design. In Urbino, what began as a fortress overlooking the Valbona River became a monument to humanist optimism. It celebrates man's ability to observe, to reason, to act effectively in the physical world, and to create civilized society.

Milan

For almost thirty years before being sacked in 1499 by the forces of Louis XII of France, Milan was a focal point of the Renaissance, attracting both Leonardo da Vinci (1452– 1519) and Donato Bramante (1444–1514) in the early 1480s. Renaissance influence had come early to Milan when the local duke, Francesco Sforza, gave Cosimo de' Medici a palace for a branch of the Medici bank, which was vital to Florentine trade links with the north. Michelozzo's alterations to the two-story palace, which became the Banco Mediceo in the 1460s, paid homage to the applied brick-and-terracotta decorative traditions of Milan. The bank's elaborate central entrance, while composed of nominally classical elements, approaches northern Gothic flamboyance. On the piano-nobile level, Gothic cusped and pointed arches are set between classical roundels.

LEONARDO DA VINCI

Leonardo prepared sketchbooks illustrating his inventions, observations, experiments, and discoveries in order to demonstrate his potential to prospective clients. Pages from these sketchbooks, which have been widely dispersed over the centuries, include anatomical drawings; studies of geological formations, air currents, and water movements; proposals for architecture and city planning; and a host of drawings, sketches, and studies related to his paintings and sculptures. Other drawings illustrate his inventiveness with such diverse devices as canal locks; underwater craft; parachutes; helicopters; wing attachments for flying; and tanks, guns, cannons, and other instruments of war. Leonardo's experiments and research brought him close to understanding blood circulation in the human body, to verifying that the earth was more than 5000 years old (as was believed at the time), and to proposals for magnifying glasses to observe the moon, all discoveries that would later be made independently by other men. In his sketchbooks, Leonardo noted various designs for centrally planned churches (Fig. 11.21).

S. Maria della Consolazione at Todi (begun in 1508) (Fig. 11.22) is so similar to some of Leonardo's sketches

11.21 Leonardo da Vinci, Sketches for centralized churches, ca. 1490. The central-plan church interested Renaissance designers more than any other architectural problem. Even Leonardo carried out investigations, possibly as a result of his contact with Bramante.

that its master mason, Cola da Caprarola, must have been influenced by them, perhaps through Bramante's works. The church at Todi is square in plan, with one semicircular and three polygonal apses. Projected into three dimensions, the square generates a cube, while the apses are capped by semidomes. Above the major interior space rises a dome set on a drum and pendentives.

At the Sforza court in Milan Leonardo designed costumes and masques for the marriage and entertainment of Ludovico and his wife Beatrice d'Este; he proposed a two-level city with pedestrian and vehicular separation; and, when the 1485 plague in Milan killed 5000 people, he suggested building ten satellite towns, each of 30,000 people, to reduce the likelihood of subsequent outbreaks. Between 1487 and 1490, he and Bramante worked on designs for the central crossing of Milan Cathedral; these were never built. The 1499 attack on Milan by French forces brought down the Sforza family, and Leonardo briefly sought employment as a military engineer to the infamous Cesare Borgia. Leonardo later returned to Milan to work for the French military governor, Charles d'Amboise, eventually becoming a painter and engineer for King Louis XII. In 1516 he moved to France under the patronage of Francis I and lived in comfort near Amboise until his death in 1519.

11.22 Cola da Caprarola and Donato Bramante (?), S. Maria della Consolazione, Todi, begun 1508.
Various architects, including Bramante, have been associated with the design of this church. Compare its design to the central-church plans by Leonardo in Fig. 11.21.

11.23 Donato Bramante, Plan of and longitudinal section through S. Maria delle Grazie, Milan, 1492–97.
Here Bramante grafted a central-plan crossing onto an existing medieval nave. The union is awkward. The problem was more satisfactorily solved by Andrea Palladio in the Venetian church of Il Rendentore.

DONATO BRAMANTE

In Milan from 1482 to 1499 Leonardo was a close associate of Donato Bramante, and he undoubtedly influenced two of the younger architect's commissions that emphasized the concept of central planning. The first was an addition to the wide Milanese church of S. Maria delle Grazie (Fig. 11.23), a medieval building consisting of a nave, aisles, and chapels. Between 1492 and 1497 Bramante added the centralized crossing, capped by a dome sixty-five feet in diameter and completed on either side by transept apses and a choir with apse. Although in harmony with the spirit of Leonardo's sketches of centrally planned churches and consistent with the spirit of Renaissance detail on the interior, Bramante's design is behind the times, its decorative exterior details falling into the Milanese tradition of brick-and-terracotta appliqué. The church's major interior feature, the hemispherical dome, is not even expressed on the exterior.

A far more original design is Bramante's earlier church, S. Maria presso S. Satiro (1482–92), a rebuilding project that included part of the old ninth-century church and campanile of S. Satiro (Fig. 11.24). Bramante's design for the interior included a barrel-vaulted nave and transepts that intersect at a central crossing with a coffered dome on pendentives concluded by an oculus. An existing street restricted the site east of the crossing, preventing Bramante from adding a conventional choir. While the wall behind the altar is almost flush with the east wall of the transepts, Bramante created there a low relief that, when viewed on axis, has the convincing appearance of a barrel-vaulted choir (Fig. 11.25). Using the illusionistic potential of linear perspective, he simulated the space he wished to build in actuality, creating in the process what must be the ultimate use of this device in fifteenth-century architecture. Bramante's reworking of the quincunx plan of the ninth-century chapel, and his addition of an octagonal sacristy similar to Brunelleschi's sacristy at S. Spirito in Florence, both anticipated his more ambitious central-plan proposals in Rome, culminating with his designs for a new St. Peter's basilica.

11.24 (right and below right) Donato Bramante, Plan of and longitudinal section through S. Maria presso S. Satiro, Milan, 1482–92.
The oddity of this plan, with its stunted nave, resulted from site conditions that prohibited Bramante from building a spacious chancel. His solution was to have painted on the slightly telescoping chancel walls a perspective image of a barrel vault.

Ninth-c[ ] chapel

Bramante's new nave

11.25

Bramante's octagonal sacristy

Illusionistic choir

N

0   25 m
0   75 ft

11.25 Donato Bramante, S. Maria presso S. Satiro interior, Milan, 1482–92.
Here is the visual effect of Bramante's clever illusionistic manipulation of the shallow chancel wall. The effect works perfectly, of course, only for someone standing along the center line of the nave.

The Tempietto, Rome

Leaving Milan after its sack by the French in 1499, Bramante moved on to Rome where, like Brunelleschi and Alberti before him, he was able to study the ancient monuments first-hand; the effect on his design thinking was profound. In 1502 he was provided with an ideal opportunity to create a cerebral synthesis of humanist worldliness and Christian piety. The clients were conveniently remote: King Ferdinand and Queen Isabella of Spain, most famous for their support of the voyages of Christopher Columbus. The program called for the erection of a monument atop the spot where St. Peter was believed to have been martyred and adjacent to the recently completed church of S. Pietro in Montorio.

11.26 (above) Donato Bramante, Plan of the Tempietto, Rome, begun 1502. Bramante planned for his interpretation of the circular temple to be placed in this ideal environment. As was so often the case with such grand Renaissance plans, it was never fully realized.

11.27 Donato Bramante, Tempietto, Rome, begun 1502. Bramante placed the principal door opposite the altar. However, the only absolutely logical way geometrically to enter the circular plan would have been in the center and from below.

Bramante's site plan (Fig. 11.26), though never realized in this form, is critical to an understanding of his complete vision. It called for the creation of a circular cloister, a perfect hermetic architectural environment, and the insertion into it of a circular temple. Bramante designed his building to embody both the Platonic preference for ideal form and Christian reverence for tradition, in this case reverence for the circular martyria of the early church. His command of form and detail approaches perfection.

Known as the Tempietto (Fig. 11.27) the completed building is a two-story cylinder capped by a hemispherical dome and surrounded by a one-story Doric colonnade with entablature and balustrade. The metope panels of the frieze display symbols connecting the current authority of the pope to the grandeur of antiquity, specifically keys, chalice, and paton (or plate for the eucharist), incense boat, and tabernacle—all symbols of St. Peter—and liturgical instruments of the Mass. Only the doorway is awkward in its random positioning within one of the sixteen repetitive column bays, its uniqueness celebrated only by a modest set of steps.

St. Peter's, Rome

In 1505 Michelangelo was at work on a tomb for Pope Julius II. Because such a huge monument would not fit readily into the old and crumbling basilica, now almost 1200 years old, the pope hired Bramante to help him explore his options. They first considered a centrally planned addition for the tomb at the western end of the existing church, similar to Bramante's addition to the church of S. Maria delle Grazie in Milan.

This was not the first Renaissance attempt to modify or add to St. Peter's. Pope Nicholas V had instructed Alberti to report on the condition of the building. Not surprisingly Alberti found the walls out of plumb and the aging fabric in such a dilapidated state that he considered repairs inadvisable. Nicholas accepted this recommendation and in 1451 appointed Bernardo Rossellino to design an apse as the first stage of an anticipated new St. Peter's. The deaths of Nicholas in 1455 and of Rossellino in 1464 terminated this project, even though Rossellino's choir was eventually built.

After this tentative beginning, the project to rebuild St. Peter's languished for another fifty years. Eventually Julius II decided that a completely new church was the only suitable accommodation for the tomb he envisioned for himself, and Bramante created an appropriately bold Greek-cross design in 1505 (Fig. 11.28). A medal cast in 1506 depicts Bramante's scheme, which represented a building on the scale of the Baths of Diocletian capped by a dome comparable to that of the Pantheon. This combination was carefully considered by Bramante. A drawing of the church in his notebooks shows it surrounded by gardens and a colonnade; on the reverse of the sheet is his drawing of the baths. Rather than merely continuing patterns of antiquity, Bramante was attempting to outdo Roman builders

11.28 Donato Bramante, Plan of St. Peter's, Rome, 1505.
The delicacy of the plan, almost like embroidery, foreshadows the problems Michelangelo would face when he replaced Bramante as architect at St. Peter's. The central piers proved to be insufficient to support the projected dome.

by proposing a domed structure more ambitious than any ancient edifice. The structural concept of a dome and drum supported on pendentives and semicircular arches actually had more in common with Byzantine work, which had itself developed from Roman models, than with any authentic Roman construction. Bramante's audacious design exceeded his structural understanding, however, for the piers he proposed would undoubtedly have been inadequate for the great loads imposed by the dome.

The cornerstone of this vast project was laid on April 18, 1506, as a labor force of 2500 began the foundations for the crossing piers. Bramante died in 1514, when they were scarcely above ground level. By the time the church was completed nearly 150 years later, almost every major architect of the sixteenth and seventeenth centuries had been engaged here at one time or another. Thus, the rebuilding of St. Peter's embraces work of several periods, from the High Renaissance to the Baroque.

High Renaissance buildings were generally more Roman and three-dimensional in spatial conception than the less massive Early Renaissance ones. Architects such as Bramante had reconciled the theoretical positions of Vitruvius, Alberti, and Leonardo with the realities of Roman construction practices and had developed the confidence to design buildings suitable to the requirements of their own age, while at the same time maintaining the spirit of antiquity. They handled matters of proportion, the manipulation of space, and correct detailing skillfully and subtly, so that in the span of less than a century the explorations of Brunelleschi had matured into the calm, self-assured style of the High Renaissance.

The Belvedere Court and the House of Raphael, Rome

Pope Julius II also directed Bramante to organize the land north of the basilica into a great palace. Bramante inherited a modest irregular palace contiguous with Old St. Peter's and, some 900 feet away, a fortresslike **belvedere** used as a summer residence. Intent upon the creation of a complex rivaling the imperial villas of antiquity, he masked the irregularity of the existing structures by adding new façades: the one to the south eventually made

into a semicircular theater, and the one to the north organized around a central hemicycle (Fig. 11.29). His strategy for connecting them produced the first great landscaped urban space of the Renaissance and involved the first use of monumental stairs since ancient times. It looked back, as was by now expected, to various inspirations from antiquity, including the villas described by Pliny the Younger. In order to tame the irregular topography, Bramante took inspiration from the Roman Sanctuary of Fortuna Primigenia at Praeneste (now Palestrina; see Fig. 5.5) near Rome, specifically its use of stairs and ramps as

VERO DISSEGNO DELI STVPENDI EDEFITII GIARDINI BOSCHI FONTANE ET COSE MARAVEGLIOSE DI BELVEDERE IN ROMA

11.29 (left) Donato Bramante, Belvedere Court, Rome, begun 1505, engraving.
This great outdoor space adjacent to St. Peter's was intended by Pope Julius II to recreate the grandeur of ancient Rome. One can imagine him and Bramante walking through the ruins on the Palatine planning to recapture the site's former glory.

11.30 (right) Donato Bramante, Transverse section through the Belvedere Court, Rome, begun 1505.
This view (looking from left to right in Fig. 11.29) makes clear Bramante's use of the Roman Hellenistic Sanctuary of Fortuna Primigenia at Praeneste (now Palestrina) as one of his models. It also demonstrates the continuing Renaissance fascination with a single viewpoint — the station point, or position of the observer, in mechanical perspective.

a means of organizing space within a view based upon a contrived perspective vista (Fig. 11.30). For the flanking east and west walls, he chose as his model the Colosseum, in effect turned inside out, articulating the three stories at the lower, south end of the site with first Doric, then Ionic, then Corinthian pilasters defining bays for arcades and windows, and articulating the one-story section to the north with arcaded openings flanked by Corinthian pilasters. The stairs, ramps, and punctured east and west walls provided vantage points for spectacles staged in the lower court. Many changes have been made to Bramante's scheme in the final built version, most notably Pope Sixtus V's insertion of a library that cuts across the court, eradicating the ramps and stairs and subdividing the space.

Bramante also built a house for himself in Rome (ca. 1512) (Fig. 11.31). It was purchased by the artist Raphael (1483–1520) after he had been summoned to Rome to decorate the papal apartments, and so became known as the House of Raphael; unfortunately, it has long since been demolished. Like many urban dwellings and following the model of the ancient Roman insula, it had shops at the street level, treated by Bramante as the rusticated base for pairs of engaged Doric columns articulating the piano nobile above. It was a distinct innovation in palace design because it produced a more three-dimensional façade, especially when compared with the flat modeling of the orders on Early Renaissance buildings such as the Rucellai Palace. It became one of the most influential models for façade designs in Western architecture, particularly in England and France in the eighteenth century.

THE LATE RENAISSANCE AND MANNERISM

While the architects of the Early and High Renaissance saw the buildings of antiquity as models to be emulated, those of the Late Renaissance, often called Mannerists, sought to achieve a more personal artistic expression through the imaginative and individualistic manipulation of the classical language. Mannerism began in the 1520s and has sometimes been associated with the political destabiliztion surrounding the Sack of Rome by the army of Charles V, emperor of the Holy Roman Empire. While the High Renaissance designers were disciplined and resolute and attempted to produce integrated, harmonious buildings, Mannerists favored disharmony, discord, imbalance, tension, distortion, and unresolved conflicts. However, the difference in the two periods was not quite so simple.

The term "Mannerism" was derived from the Italian word *maniera*, which, in the sixteenth century, connoted virtuosity, refinement, and grace, but, by the seventeenth century, had come to mean self-indulgence, self-consciousness, and superficial artifice. Both definitions can reasonably be applied to Mannerist work, depending upon the talent of the practitioner and the attitude of the viewer.

Among the more inventive Mannerists were Raphael, Giorgio Vasari (1511–74), and Giulio Romano (ca. 1499–1546). The genius of Michelangelo Buonarroti (1475–1564), whose career was contemporary with these men and whose designs share some qualities with theirs, transcended any stylistic label. Likewise, Andrea Palladio (1508–80), at work during the same period, was inspired at one point by Giulio Romano but looked back more to the models of Bramante. In the end, Palladio produced a body of work that arguably has been the most written about in all of Western architecture.

11.31 Donato Bramante, Elevation of the House of Raphael, Rome, ca. 1512.
This modest building has been as influential a prototype as any created by a Renaissance architect. Its rusticated, arcaded ground floor and columned piano nobile with entablature would reappear at various scales in France and England and eventually in America. Its own model was the ancient Roman insula or apartment house.

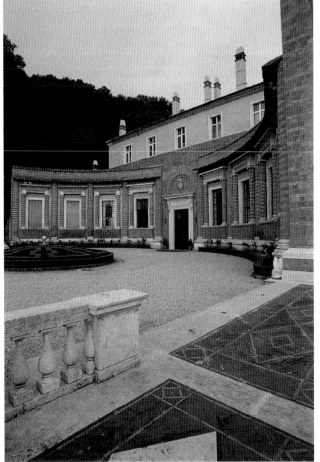

The Villa Madama, Rome

A good place to begin is the Villa Madama, designed by Raphael for Cardinal Giulio de' Medici, who was later Pope Clement VII; intriguingly it was left half-completed (Figs. 11.32–11.33). The villa was to become a characteristic building type for Renaissance architects. In contrast to the urban dwelling or palace, it was a country retreat, ostensibly inspired by the Roman **villa rustica** or estate farm. The villa's essential architectural attribute was a loggia or open elevated porch, from which visitors could view carefully designed gardens and perhaps enjoy a distant vista. The wealthy owner of a villa would come there to escape the city's summer heat, to rest and relax, and to stroll about and talk with friends. At the Villa Madama, the building was set into the hillside on a south-facing slope of the

11.32 Raphael, Villa Madama rotunda, Rome, begun ca. 1516.
As constructed, this villa represents only half of Raphael's plan. If completed, the central feature would have been an open rotunda, modeled perhaps on the Island Enclosure at Hadrian's Villa; but it was left incomplete as a semicircle.

11.33 Raphael, Plan of and longitudinal section through the Villa Madama, Rome, begun ca. 1516.
The plan shows constructed and unconstructed portions of the villa. The section along the principal axis shows, left to right, the half-completed cortile, the short passage to a domed bay of the loggia, the loggia, and the parterres atop their arched terrace. Raphael and Giulio Romano painted the vaulted bays of the loggia with grotesques based on the wall paintings in the recently discovered Palatine wing of Nero's Golden House.

Monte Mario, beyond the walls of Rome, with a view over the city and the Tiber. The hillside, terraced into a number of levels, had formal gardens with fountains spouting and pouring water from level to level. Had its buildings been finished, the villa would have had a circular cortile with a design based, like the Belvedere Courtyard, on the superimposed orders of the Colosseum, off which loggias, a theater, and an overlook would have radiated. Only half the work was completed, however. Its major space consists of a loggia opening onto a **parterre**, inspired in part by the three partially extant groin-vaulted bays of the Basilica of Constantine, except that the middle space here is covered by a dome on pendentives. Pavements are set in mosaic tiles, and walls and ceilings are covered with frescoed festoons containing mythological, religious, and Medicean symbolism inspired by the excavations, then being directed by Raphael, going on at Nero's Golden House. Most of the paintings were completed after Raphael's death by his two

major assistants, Giovanni da Udine, who rediscovered the lost technique of Roman stucco, and Giulio Romano.

The building and its grounds posit new conditions and problems for sixteenth-century designers. Movement through the site offers choices and potential moments of indecision. The various areas—cortile, garden theater, and parterres—offer abrupt and dramatic contrasts. At the Villa Madama, the classical language reached a new level of sophistication, particularly in the frescoed loggia, but also documented the change from the self-assured countenance of the High Renaissance to the anxiety and ambiguity of Mannerism.

The Uffizi, Florence

Giorgio Vasari's design for the Uffizi in Florence (Fig. 11.34), begun in 1560, illustrates the Mannerist attitude toward urban design. The building, an office annex for the

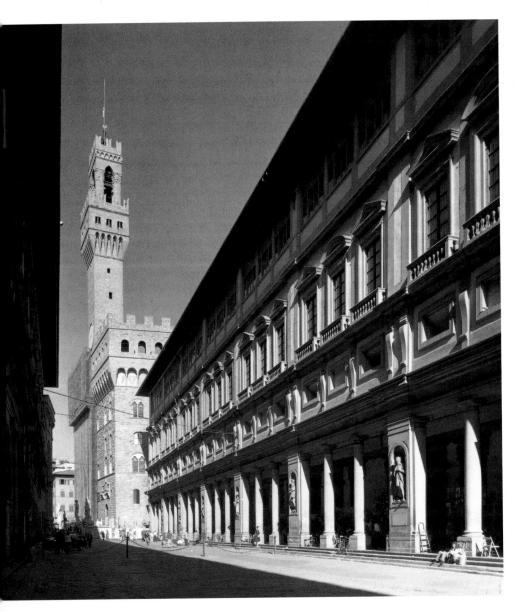

11.34 Giorgio Vasari, Uffizi, Florence, begun 1560.
Vasari so composed his Uffizi complex that it framed this view of the medieval Palazzo Vecchio. Such urbanistic interaction of existing and new construction was a significant contribution of Manneristic planning.

Palazzo Vecchio, consists of a long, narrow cortile flanked on its two long sides by multi-floor wings to which Vasari applied crisply modeled window surrounds and broken **belt courses** that move aggressively forward and back. One end of the cortile terminates at the River Arno with a series of three openings, the center one wider and arched, and the opposite open end discharges into Piazza della Signoria, with the tower of the Palazzo Vecchio standing off-center. While the river end of the cortile confronts a road and the spatial corridor of the Arno, a view in through the central arched opening captures the perspective diminution of the Uffizi cornices together with the Palazzo Vecchio's tower. Rather than creating a static, hermetic urban ensemble as Bramante had chosen to do with the Tempietto, Vasari created an open-ended interactive one in which he dexterously combined old and new and stressed the dynamics of motion and change over time.

The Palazzo del Tè, Mantua

Unlike many artists of the High Renaissance working in Rome, Giulio Romano was actually born there, so his understanding of the buildings of antiquity came from his personal, intimate experience of the city rather than from study undertaken for professional reasons. Therefore, it is not surprising that, as one of the creators of Mannerism, Romano chose to represent the ruined condition of ancient monuments as his contribution to sixteenth-century architecture. This can be seen in one of his early paintings, *The Stoning of St. Stephen* (1523), in which Roman ruins in the background provide the setting. Giulio's architectural works feature the willful and amusing misuse of classical elements. In his own house at Mantua (1544), he built a Pantheon Salon, with an image of Julius Caesar, his namesake, carved over the fireplace.

His most important building is the Palazzo del Tè (1525–34), designed for Federigo Gonzaga as a honeymoon villa on an island at the edge of Mantua. The Gonzaga family were horse-breeders, supplying steeds to the courts of Europe, and they were also extensively involved in political intrigue and military alliances. The palace was originally conceived as an enormous stable complex. It consists of a large square cortile, enclosed on all four sides by a series of rooms arranged en suite, with central entrances on the north and east sides. A loggia on the west side leads into a garden, at the end of which is a semicircular colonnade. The garden is laid out in geometric flowerbeds, and a moat used for staging miniature naval battles was dug adjacent to the villa, which is linked to the garden by a bridge. The loggia is barrel-vaulted and supported on alternate paired and single columns, while the north entrance has rusticated columns, deliberately made to appear unfinished. These columns support lintels with keystones, above which is an octagonally coffered ceiling as in the Basilica of Constantine. In the courtyard, heavy Doric columns support parts of the architrave and frieze with triglyphs dropped down out of place as if part of an ancient Roman ruin (Fig. 11.35). Together with the unframed niches and windows, pediments lacking a bottom cornice, and heavy rustication, these features create extreme contrasts and a sense of ambiguity and tension.

The illusion of imbalance and the perverse use of classicism continue on the interior. The wall and ceiling surfaces of the rooms around the courtyard are filled with frescoes by Giulio Romano and his assistants, with

11.35 Guilio Romano, Palazzo del Tè cortile, Mantua, 1525–34.
It is unclear whether the effect was intended to shock or amuse, but Giulio Romano designed some of the stones of the entablature to be displaced downward as if part of a ruin.

additional enrichment provided by inlaid doors and mantels of oriental jasper, gold, and marble. Cracked brick lintels painted on the wall surfaces above doors create an uncomfortable feeling in visitors passing beneath them. Above the cracked lintels in the Sala dei Giganti is painted a scene of great destruction, with the weight of collapsing columns crushing the limbs and bodies of giant figures, one going cross-eyed as his head becomes trapped between two falling boulders. Walls merge into billowing clouds painted on the ceiling, the center of which carries a representation of a colonnaded drum supporting a hemispherical dome. Horses painted in the Sala dei Cavalli stand on cornices more than half the height of this large chamber, and behind them are landscapes seen through painted window surrounds between the pilasters and architectural detailing.

The Palazzo del Tè was never finished, yet it remains a masterpiece of the Late Renaissance, designed by a sophisticated architect as a play on the conventions of revived classicism. Only those who shared Romano's understanding of Roman architecture could fully appreciate his accomplishment.

MICHELANGELO

Michelangelo Buonarroti, widely regarded as one of the greatest geniuses of Western art, made important contributions to the fields of sculpture, painting, and architecture during the course of his long and productive life. The second son of a minor governmental official in Florence, he was apprenticed at the age of thirteen to the painter Domenico del Ghirlandaio, despite his father's reluctance to have his son become an artist. His training in sculpture began a year or so later when Michelangelo was invited to join the workshop sponsored by Lorenzo de' Medici as part of the Medici effort to revive the sculptural arts of antiquity. Until the death of Lorenzo in 1492, Michelangelo lived in the Medici Palace as a member of the household, gaining a humanist education from the eminent scholars, writers, and poets who gathered there under Lorenzo's patronage.

S. Lorenzo, Florence

Under Pope Leo X, the younger son of Lorenzo de' Medici and successor to Pope Julius II, Michelangelo embarked on the first of three architectural commissions for the monastery of S. Lorenzo, Florence, in 1515. His design for the façade of the basilican church was a screen consisting of two equally developed stories divided by an attic, forming a backdrop for relief panels and sculptures set in niches. Nothing had come of this design by the time Leo died in 1521, and the church exists today without a façade, but Michelangelo's proposals established a second tradition in façade architecture, providing an alternative to Alberti's S. Maria Novella type.

Before the façade design was abandoned, the Medici asked Michelangelo to design a funerary chapel adjacent to the north transept for the burial of Lorenzo de' Medici and four of the lesser Medici (see Fig. 11.5). This New Sacristy, or Medici Chapel, was to complement Brunelleschi's Old Sacristy located off the north transept.

Michelangelo paid homage to Brunelleschi by employing a similar form, a hemispherical dome on pendentives, over the cubical main space, and using some of the same materials: white stucco walls trimmed with gray pietra serena. The tombs themselves are marble. The number of statues and Michelangelo's placement of them underwent a series of changes; his sketches show that he considered a central mausoleum, but he finally placed two sarcophagi on either side of the chapel. Each supports symbolic but unfinished sculptures of the Times of Day, with seated figures of the dukes Lorenzo and Giuliano placed above in niches set into the wall. The large symbolic figures of Day and Night, on Giuliano's tomb, and Dawn and Dusk, on Lorenzo's, recline precariously on top of the sarcophagi, their very weight seeming to cause them to slide off the curved lids. The ghoulish mask on Night suggests nightmares. These sculptures are in the lowest of three levels within the chapel, where a profusion of architectural elements—heavy blank tabernacles above the doors, tapering blank windows, and even pilasters without capitals—vie with one another. Above are **lunettes**, punctuated with tapering windows; and surmounting the whole ensemble is a coffered dome with oculus, capped by a cupola.

Pope Leo X's illegitimate cousin, elected to the papacy as Clement VII, wished to house the Medici library for use by scholars within the cloister of S. Lorenzo, the family parish church, perhaps to emphasize that the Medici were no longer mere merchants but members of intellectual and ecclesiastical society. Michelangelo therefore began work on the so-called Laurentian Library in 1524 (Figs. 11.5, 11.36). It was built above existing monastic quarters on the east range of the cloister, with an entrance from the upper level of the cloisters. Michelangelo wanted to use a skylight over the vestibule, but the pope believed that this would leak, so clerestory windows were incorporated into the west wall overlooking the cloister instead. Thus the vestibule (Fig. 11.37) is shocking in its verticality, almost half as tall again as it is wide. Blank tapering windows, framed in pietra serena, surround the interior of the vestibule; these are separated by paired columns set into the wall. The normally illogical recessing of columns into a wall would seem to be a Mannerist invention, yet the column positions are actually necessitated by the location of the existing walls of the building beneath the library. The walls between columns are like a taut skin stretched between the vertical supports. Michelangelo further emphasized the seeming instability of the whole by having the columns appear to be supported on **consoles**, so that weight seems to be carried on rather weak elements, and one cannot determine visually whether the columns or

11.36 (right) Michelangelo Buonarroti, **Plan of and longitudinal section through the Laurentian Library, Florence, begun 1524.** One should not forget that the sculptural drama of Michelangelo's entry vestibule is only a prelude to the principal space: the reading room for Greek and Latin texts. Here he abandoned his preferred tension and dynamics in favor of a modular serenity befitting the space's function.

Reading room

11.37

0   20 m

0   60 ft

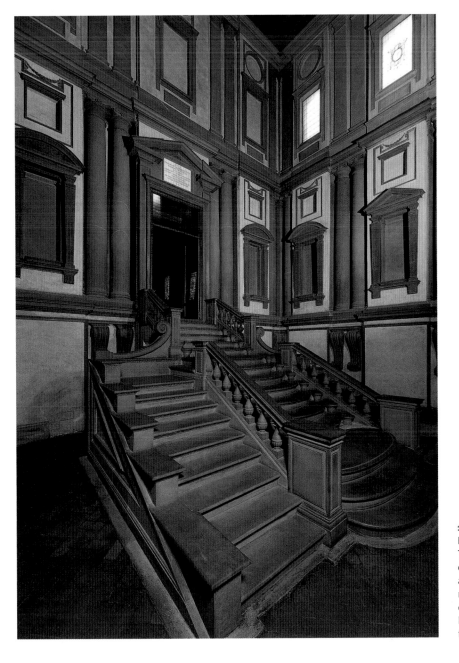

11.37 Michelangelo Buonarroti, **Laurentian Library vestibule, Florence, begun 1524.** The vestibule stairs appear to cascade downward from the reading room doorway as though its treads and risers were once molten. The impacted columns astride this doorway create in architecture the same kind of tension expressed in the reclining figures at Michelangelo's Medici Chapel.

walls support the roof. The sense of ambiguity is increased further by the apparently unorthodox forms of the tabernacle windows, and all of the architectural elements have been compressed together, creating a sense of tension and constrained energy.

The tour de force of this restless space is the huge staircase leading up to the reading room. Michelangelo's original sketches for the library show the stair as divided flights placed against the wall. By 1558–59, when the present stair was designed, his proposal had grown into a piece of dynamic sculpture that appears to pour forth from the upper level like lava and compress the limited floor space of the vestibule. As it descends, the stair divides into three flights, the outer ones having no handrails. On the central flight, the convex treads vary in width, making the whole arrangement somewhat disquieting. By contrast the library's reading room is serene, quiet, and restful, entirely appropriate for research and study. In the manner of monastic libraries, it is a long room lit by evenly spaced windows set between pilasters in the side walls. Thus reading desks, arranged perpendicular to the side walls, were amply illuminated by natural light.

The Campidoglio, Rome

In 1534, with both the Medici Chapel and the Laurentian Library still incomplete, Michelangelo left Florence for Rome, where he remained until his death in 1564. Only seven years before, in 1527, Rome had been sacked by Charles V. One of Michelangelo's first architectural commissions there came from the local government authority, which decided to reestablish the grandeur of Rome by developing the Campidoglio, the ancient seat of government on the Capitoline Hill occupied since the twelfth century by a communal palace. Shortly thereafter Pope Paul III had transferred the great equestrian bronze of Marcus Aurelius specifically for use as the centerpiece of the site. Thus Michelangelo was required to provide a setting for the statue and to bring order to an irregular hilltop already encumbered by two crumbling medieval buildings set at an acute angle to one another. Despite these conditions, it was in one sense a Renaissance architect's ideal commission, for it offered the opportunity to build a monumental civic plaza for a major city. Michelangelo produced a brilliant response to this awkward commission. He planned a trapezoidal piazza to regularize the difficult geometry established by the existing buildings, and intended to inset an oval paving pattern that would focus attention on the equestrian statue in the center (Fig. 11.38). Precedent for this general disposition of elements can be found in Rossellino's plan for the cathedral piazza at Pienza (1459–64; see page 298), although the scale and coherence of Michelangelo's design are much greater.

Axiality and symmetry govern all parts of the Capitoline

Piazza

0 ————— 50 m
0 ————— 150 ft

Palace of the Senators

Capitoline Museum

Statue of Marcus Aurelius

Palace of the Conservators

S. Maria in Aracoeli

11.38 Plan of the Campidoglio, Rome, 15 This plan is based upon a nineteenth-century engraving by Paul Le Tarouilly, bu with Michelangelo's design (since execute for the central oval superimposed.

11.39 Michelangelo Buonarroti, Campidoglio, Rome, begun 1537. Engraving by Le Tarouilly.
Le Tarouilly's view is deceptive. The absolute regularity gives no hint of the previous disorder of this formerly rutted hill with its hulks of medieval buildings disposed in an asymmetrical and non-orthogonal configuration. Michelangelo's genius was to unify the unrelated parts.

Hill work. Michelangelo gave the medieval Palace of the Senators (Fig. 11.39), remodeled in ca. 1547 and later, a central campanile, a renovated façade, and a grand divided external staircase. He designed a new façade for the colonnaded Palace of the Conservators, with a giant order of Corinthian pilasters extending over two stories, and projected an identical structure, the Palazzo Nuovo (now the Capitoline Museum), for the opposite side of the piazza. On the narrow side of the trapezoidal plan, Michelangelo extended the central axis with a magnificent ramp-stair to link the hilltop with the city below. Work on the Capitoline Hill was incomplete when Michelangelo died, but his designs were carefully followed in subsequent centuries, down to the installation of the paving pattern in 1928.

The Palazzo Farnese, Rome

In 1546 Pope Paul III employed Michelangelo to continue construction of the Palazzo Farnese (Fig. 11.40), his family residence, begun in 1517 by Antonio da Sangallo the Younger. At the main façade, Michelangelo added the cornice and the central window with coat of arms at the

11.40 Antonio da Sangallo the Younger and Michelangelo Buonarroti, Palazzo Farnese, Rome, 1517–46.
This joint effort became the model for a variety of urban monuments in the late nineteenth and early twentieth centuries. Unlike the Florentine interpretation of this type, this palazzo has rustication only in the form of quoins at the corners and at the entry and has classically inspired window surrounds.

piano-nobile level. In the courtyard, he added the two upper floors, compressing the pilasters, attached columns, and windows in a manner not unlike the entry vestibule at the Laurentian Library. As an expression of the social position and wealth of the newly rich Farnese family, the palace commands the piazza on which it fronts, lending an impassive dignity to the space.

St. Peter's, Rome

Pope Paul III had been in office five years before the Vatican had amassed adequate funds to resume the building of St. Peter's, begun in 1506 by Bramante. Plans had been submitted by Raphael, Giuliano da Sangallo, and Baldassare Peruzzi, but the Sack of Rome by the army of Charles V in 1527 had emptied the Vatican coffers and prevented much actual construction from being carried out. Antonio da Sangallo the Younger spent the amount required to build a small church in making a model to illustrate the ungainly agglomeration of underscaled classical orders he proposed for the north and south

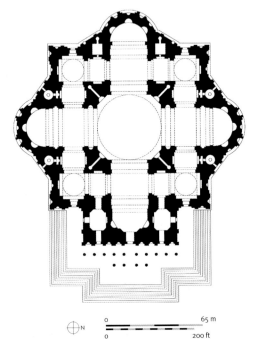

0   65 m
0   200 ft

11.41 Michelangelo Buonarroti, Plan of St. Peter's, Rome, begun 1546.
A comparison of this plan to Bramante's (see Fig. 11.28) reveals that the column screens have disappeared, the central piers have been enlarged, and an entry portico developed. If completed in this form, it would have represented the culmination of centrally planned church explorations during the Renaissance.

transept ambulatories. Even though these admitted only indirect light into the great central space, the southern transept was completed according to his designs in 1546, the year in which he died. Michelangelo's appointment as architect-in-charge provoked Vasari to write that Paul III was indeed fortunate that God had ordained that Michelangelo should live during his pontificate, saying: "How great are thy merits elevated by his art." Michelangelo, who considered himself primarily a sculptor, agreed to the assignment as a pious act for the glorification of God, and he accepted no more than a minimum living wage for his architectural work on St. Peter's. He quickly saw the faults of Sangallo's unimaginative scheme and razed the exterior walls of the transept ambulatories, in part because they encroached on the Vatican Palace and would have necessitated the destruction of several buildings had they been completed around the church. They would also have provided dark internal passageways

in which, Michelangelo said sarcastically, vagrants could hide and attack pilgrims. Michelangelo made a small clay model of the church, from which a wooden model was then constructed; the design restored Bramante's initial conception of a Greek-cross plan, but in a reduced and simplified version (Fig. 11.41), and increased the size of Bramante's under-structured central piers, the foundations of which were already in the ground. Michelangelo corresponded with his nephew in Florence to learn the dimensions of Brunelleschi's cathedral dome there, a design he admired and wished to emulate. "I am going to make its sister bigger, yes, but not more beautiful," he wrote.

Although construction on the dome of St. Peter's was not begun in his lifetime, Michelangelo endowed its design with internal and external unity (Fig. 11.42). Brunelleschi's dome for the Florence Cathedral has a tall Gothic profile; Michelangelo chose instead a hemispherical form. He also increased the number of stone ribs expressed on the outside of the dome from eight to sixteen in order to eliminate the faceted octagonal massing of the Florence Cathedral dome. Had the dome been built as planned by Michelangelo, the outward thrust of the ribs would have been enormous, and it is doubtful whether a masonry drum could have withstood the accumulated forces. Giacomo della Porta, who constructed the dome after

11.42 Michelangelo Buonarroti, St. Peter's, Rome, begun 1546.
It takes a view such as this one to get a sense of the centrally planned massing intended by Bramante and Michelangelo. The dominant feature here is the great dome, which, at ground level, is no longer the case today as a result of the extension of the nave by Carlo Maderno.

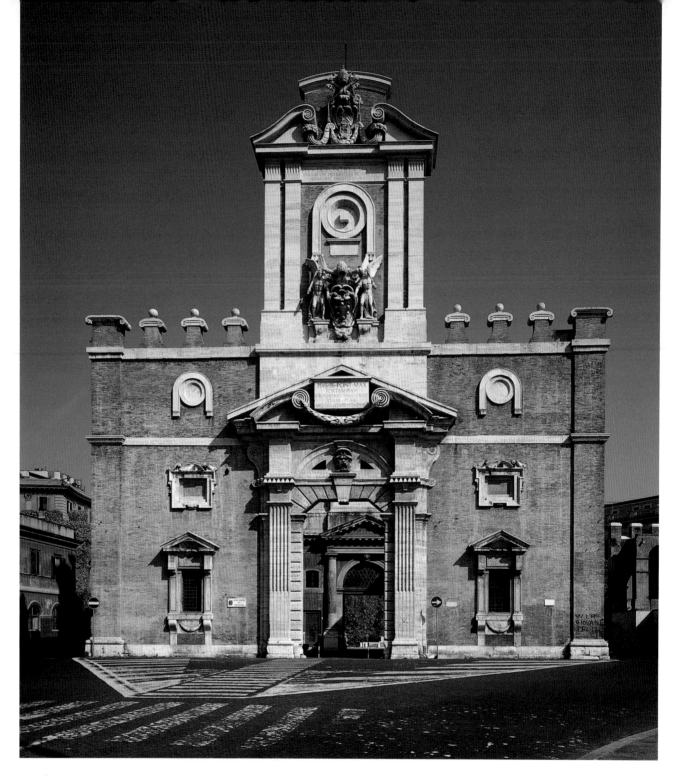

11.43 Michelangelo Buonarroti, Porta Pia, Rome, 1561–65.
This gateway still welcomes people approaching the city from the east. When first constructed, its unorthodox elements, ambiguous structural systems, and discordant textures must have shocked anyone seeing it for the first time.

Michelangelo's death, employed a slightly taller profile in order to decrease the lateral thrust and used the lantern cupola to force the weight of the dome downward to the drum. He used columns, attached visually to the drum by a broken entablature, to act as buttresses that further force the loads downward to the arches and four great piers of the central crossing. Even so, tension chains were subsequently incorporated into the brickwork of this double-shelled dome, which is only five feet smaller in diameter than that of the Pantheon. The triangulated massing of the whole project rises to a height of 452 feet, enough to have strong visual presence had Michelangelo's façade been built as planned. Eventually, however, St. Peter's was completed early in the seventeenth century with a nave and entrance façade designed by Carlo Maderno (see Figs. 12.4–12.5) that diminished the effect of the dome.

Porta Pia, Rome

In his later work Michelangelo anticipated the Baroque in several ways, as in his design of the Porta Pia (Fig. 11.43), a city gate built at the end of the Via Pia. Rather than a defensive gateway within a fortified city wall, it was and is a scenic backdrop terminating a vista. Stone architectural elements, many of them unusual, are isolated against a plane of brick: a broken pediment stuffed with an over-sized swag and plaque, oddly draped-over roundels, and volute-topped crenelations. Michelangelo emphasized the central passageway by packing within it an array of redundant structural elements—arch, rusticated arch, and broken pediment above deeply grooved pilasters with **mutules** in their capitals; the concatenation of architectural details recalls Renaissance stage-set designs. Begun in 1561, the Porta Pia was almost complete, unlike so many of Michelangelo's other architectural commissions, at the time of his death.

Sforza Chapel, Rome

Michelangelo's most adventurous project spatially is the Sforza Chapel at S. Maria Maggiore in Rome (Fig. 11.44), built for the same family that had employed Leonardo da Vinci in Milan. Like the Laurentian Library, it is both dynamic and ambiguous. The chapel combines central and longitudinal planning and emphasizes not orthogonal but diagonal directionality, defined by four columns attached to rotated piers and supporting a groin vault that can be described as "billowing." The curving wall segments that cradle the lateral altars are the boundaries of an incomplete circle with the vaults above them equally incomplete and sail-like. The principal altar opposite the entrance, as at the Pazzi Chapel, resides in a subsidiary square. The Sforza Chapel offered a source of inspiration for a host of spatial experiments by designers for at least the next 150 years.

ANDREA PALLADIO

Andrea Palladio was born Andrea di Pietro della Gondola in 1508 and was trained as a stonemason. When he was about thirty, he was employed on a building site, where his talents attracted the attention of the humanist Count Giangiorgio Trissino. Trissino became his mentor, renaming him Palladio after a character in his epic poem *Italy Freed from the Goths*, and providing him with a humanist education. Along with several study trips to Rome, this gave Palladio an education in architecture. In particular, by measuring the buildings of ancient Rome, he collected accurate information on classical proportions, which he later used in designing his own buildings.

Palladio's profound influence on the development of Western architecture can be attributed to both his writings and his buildings. In 1570 he published his *I quattro libri dell'architettura* or *The Four Books of Architecture* (Fig. 11.45), in which he illustrated and discussed his own work as well as that of antiquity. Palladio wrote about the orders of architecture, domestic architecture, public buildings, town planning, and temples, "without which," he said, "no civilization is possible." Although he could measure and illustrate actual Roman temples, theaters, bridges,

11.44 Michelangelo Buonarroti, Plan of and longitudinal section through the Sforza Chapel, S. Maria Maggiore, Rome, 1564.
There was no more revolutionary Renaissance building than this one. Its column and vault configuration and resulting spatial dynamics and spatial interpenetrations inspired designers throughout Europe for more than a century afterward. While stone obviously cannot billow, this word does express the feeling that Michelangelo captured. The vault appears to be held down by the columns rather than resting heavily upon them.

triumphal arches, and baths, Palladio had to speculate about the design of Roman houses, so he included ideal versions of his own buildings—often at odds with these designs as built—to demonstrate antique ideals. Numerals printed on the plans give the widths and lengths of rooms, and sections and the text sometimes have indications of heights. Making reference to his buildings and their dimensions, he published the Renaissance's most coherent system of proportions. He began with modules based on wall thicknesses, then determined all of his rooms' dimensions using ratios derived from the musical consonances, and arranged these rooms according to modulated grids. Here, as in all his architectural designs, he was concerned with practical convenience as an essential component of good design; firmness, commodity, and delight were to him the basic tenets of all architecture. Eventually many architects, beginning with Inigo Jones in England in the seventeenth century, used Palladio's publication as a

11.45 Frontispiece to the second book of Isaac Ware's English edition (1738) of Palladio's *I quattro libri dell' architettura*. While various garbled editions of Palladio's book had appeared in England from the mid-seventeenth century, this was the most reliable and the first one approved of by the Neo-Palladians.

11.46 Andrea Palladio, Basilica, Vicenza, 1549. The roof is a nineteenth-century addition. Palladio's two levels of arches conceal the medieval vaults of the old basilica or town hall.

guidebook and made close observation of his buildings their primary objective during travels through Italy.

Buildings in Vicenza

Palladio's first public commission was a new skin for the medieval market and council hall, or basilica, at Vicenza; he added a two-story arcade of Doric and Ionic columns (Fig. 11.46). He submitted proposals for the project in 1546 at the request of the civic authorities, who accepted them with modifications in 1549. Construction was based on Roman brick groin-vaulting techniques, but the dominant element of the design is the repeated unit of three openings, the central one arched, supported on pairs of small columns, set off with a larger half-column between each bay. The end bays are smaller to give the appearance of strength to the corners, which have double columns. Although Bramante was the first Renaissance architect to use an arch flanked by square-headed openings, the unit is sometimes known as a **Serliana** because it was first illustrated in Sebastiano Serlio's publications. In using the Serliana here, Palladio was undoubtedly most directly influenced by the use of the motif at Jacopo Sansovino's Library of S. Marco (1537–53) in nearby Venice (see Fig. 11.57).

Some of Palladio's palazzo designs in Vicenza reflect his Roman experiences. The Palazzo Valmarana, for

instance, includes the giant order used by Michelangelo at the Campidoglio. More original is his Palazzo Chiericati (1550–52), which was erected on a very shallow site with a long frontage onto a public open space (Fig. 11.47). Palladio treated the building like a Roman palace, two stories high, fronting onto a forum, with a ground-level Roman Doric colonnade intended to link with other colonnades (never constructed) on buildings around the remaining sides of the square. Like those of many Palladian houses, the palace's façade is divided into three parts, the central section being a pavilion or projecting bay accentuated by clustered columns that create an impression of strength. The second floor is composed in the Ionic order, with loggias flanking the main salon. Thus, by projecting the salon over the public colonnade below, Palladio gained additional space for the largest room in the house. The palace is open and airy. Because of the restricted site, the long axes of its entrance hall and the majority of its rooms run parallel to the street, rather than being perpendicular to it.

Villa Designs in the Veneto

Rather than his urban houses, it was Palladio's villa designs that gained him such a wide following among later architects. Unlike most Renaissance villas, his

11.47 Andrea Palladio, Palazzo Chiericati, Vicenza, 1550–52.
Palladio intended for the first-floor Doric colonnade to be continued around a forumlike piazza. The openness of the façade is surprising, particularly the cagelike corner spaces on the second floor.

country estates were generally working farms owned by the younger sons of Venetian nobles. Their lands were located on the mainland north of Venice, the Veneto, to which capital generated by maritime commerce had been redirected as Venetian trading opportunities diminished. Although isolated from sophisticated Venetian society, these gentleman farmers maintained an elegant and cultured life in appropriately grand houses. Two of Palladio's early clients were Daniele Barbaro, a scholarly author and editor of a published version of Vitruvius, and his brother Marcantonio. Palladio designed the Villa Barbaro at Maser for them (1557–58) (Fig. 11.48). As with all his villas, the scheme is symmetrical, the central living block balanced by end pavilions connected by flanking arcades. The building is sited on a slight rise, so although it is strongly

horizontal, it affords a view out into the landscape. The elegance of the composition belies the building's practicality. Following ancient Roman practices, Palladio combined the many functions of a large farm into a single structure, including storage for hay and equipment, provision for livestock, and spaces for threshing grain.

Inside the Villa Barbaro, the rooms are gracefully proportioned, well lit, and ingeniously ornamented with perspective frescoes by Paolo Veronese (ca. 1528–1588). Through the skillful application of pigment, walls merge into barrel-vaulted ceilings. In one room, balustraded balconies appear to support spiraled columns, behind which are painted openings where the mistress of the house can be seen emerging with a page boy, a domestic servant, a lapdog, and a parrot. Shadow projections increase the sense of depth in a series of rooms where actual architraves and pedimented doorways may be confused with those painted on flat wall surfaces. Huntsmen and children appear in open doorways, and sculptures stand in niches flanked by columns, all conjured into existence by the painter's brush. Landscapes lead the eye beyond columns

11.48 Andrea Palladio, Villa Barbaro, Maser, 1557–58.
Palladio's combining of living and agricultural functions into a single, extended structure enabled him to make farm buildings monumental. He was the first Renaissance architect to use the temple front extensively on domestic buildings.

and pilasters in the dining room into imaginary vistas inspired by scenes from antiquity.

With the Villa Barbaro, Palladio made a significant contribution to the development of residential design that continues to influence the architecture of our own time, even though he had no idea that he was being innovative: this was the application of the columns and pediment of a temple front to a house. He had interpreted Vitruvius as saying that Greek temples had evolved from houses, an observation that may refer to the similarity of the megaron and the cella of a temple. Having no knowledge of the megaron, Palladio assumed Vitruvius's remark to mean that Greek houses looked like Greek temples, which he knew to have columns and a pediment. Therefore, in using these elements on the façade of a house, Palladio believed that he was following Greek precedent, when in fact he was breaking new ground.

Palladio designed the Villa Foscari at Malcontenta (1559–60), located on the Brenta Canal outside Venice, on a single axis, with the intention that side courts would mask the end elevations, but the courts were never built (Figs. 11.49–11.50). Dog-leg stairs lead to a portico on axis at the piano-nobile level, and the entrance from the portico opens into a vaulted cruciform space extending

the full depth of the building. One of the barrel vaults in the arms of the cross is expressed on the rusticated garden front. There is a consistent proportioning system used throughout the house, all rooms having ratios of 1:1, 2:3, 1:2, or 3:4. In plan the building's measurements of length to width conform to the Golden Section ratio of 5:8, while the height is the same as the width.

By far the most famous residence by Palladio is the Villa Americo-Capra, also known as the Villa Rotonda, located just outside Vicenza (1566–70) (Figs. 11.51–11.52). The client for this villa was a retired churchman, who used the house for elaborate entertainments as well as for agricultural processing. The Villa Rotonda is square in plan, with, as the name implies, a central two-story rotunda. According to Palladio, "there are loggias made on all four fronts" so that "it enjoys from every part most beautiful views, some of which are limited, some extended, and others which terminate with the horizon." Internally the central domed space radiates out to the four porticoes and to the elegantly proportioned rooms in the corners. It is a simple yet powerful scheme, one that would be copied many times.

Palladio started from the same plan in his project for the Villa Trissino at Meledo (Fig. 11.53), an ambitious scheme of which only a tiny end fragment was ever built. To the basic cube of the house, he added quadrant-shaped colonnades on either side of one porticoed entrance, widening it out to define a rectangular forecourt. Such colonnades would become a popular feature in gigantic Neo-Palladian country houses in England and in the smaller American Georgian houses of the eighteenth century. Comments

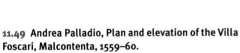

11.49 Andrea Palladio, Plan and elevation of the Villa Foscari, Malcontenta, 1559–60.
Compare this elevation to the adjacent perspective view. The prominent roof disappears through foreshortening, while the portico becomes more dominant.

11.50 Andrea Palladio, Villa Foscari, Malcontenta, 1559–60.
This perspective view reveals Palladio's genius for creating monumentally without relying on great size. He relied instead on large mural wall surfaces and careful proportioning and avoided scale-diminishing elements like handrails.

11.51 (above) Andrea Palladio, Villa Americo-Capra (Villa Rotonda), Vicenza, 1566–70.
Careful study of the bricks in the stairs has revealed significant changes since the villa's construction. Arched openings at the center of these stairs once allowed carts to carry grain into the basement.

11.52 (right) Andrea Palladio, Plan and elevation/section of the Villa Americo-Capra (Villa Rotonda), Vicenza, 1566–70.
These orthographic views show how Palladio illustrated his work with woodcuts in *I quattro libri*. He included the whole-number proportions of his rooms in the plan.

11.53 Andrea Palladio, Plan and elevation of the Villa Trissino, Meledo, begun 1567.
While never completed, this villa design anticipated the sprawling Neo-Palladian compositions of early eighteenth-century England. The quadrant-shaped connectors between the central block and wings were to become a popular motif in eighteenth-century America.

11.54 Andrea Palladio, S. Giorgio Maggiore, Venice, begun 1565.
Three scales of orders and three sizes of pediments give this façade clarity and richness. Palladio's use of overlapping temple forms would be much copied in America. Thermal windows are visible above the roof of the aisle.

made by the architect about the villa indicate that the ground floor was to be given over to domestic services, while the dependencies were to shelter farm activities.

Churches in Venice

Palladio's most significant church is S. Giorgio Maggiore in Venice (Fig. 11.54), which has a façade design derived from his earlier S. Francesca della Vigne, also in Venice. Both churches offered a new solution to the Renaissance problem of placing a classical façade in front of a basilican cross-section. Palladio combined two temple fronts: a tall one, consisting of four Corinthian columns on pedestals that support a pediment at the end of the nave, superimposed over a wide one, with smaller Corinthian pilasters, that matches the sloping aisle roofs. Vitruvius had discussed a double arrangement of gables, and the idea of using double pediments on one façade was further legitimized by the example of the Pantheon, where an attic level with cornice stands between the portico and the rotunda. At S. Giorgio, the Corinthian columns and pilasters on the front carry through to the interior arcading between nave and aisles, providing an Albertian unity in this ecclesiastical building. Palladio looked to the Roman thermae for a precedent in handling the interior. Barrel vaults are illuminated by the semicircular clerestory, or thermal, windows found in such baths as those of Diocletian, and the whole is painted white to reflect light and emphasize the church's volumetric clarity.

11.55 Andrea Palladio and Vincenzo Scamozzi, Teatro Olimpico interior, Vicenza, 1579–80.
This stage set by Scamozzi was not intended to be permanent. It represents the kind of ideal cityscape imagined by many Renaissance town planners. The buildings' façades are configured so as to create a false perspective. Not only do the cornices and belt courses converge in reality, but so also do the floor and ceiling planes.

The Teatro Olimpico

One of Palladio's last works was the Teatro Olimpico in Vicenza (1579–80), inspired by Roman theaters with a proscenium like the Theater of Marcellus, but roofed here with a ceiling painted to depict the sky. Steeply banked rows of seats are arranged in a semicircle facing the stage; to this day, the original stage set, designed by Vincenzo Scamozzi (1552–1616), remains as the scenery for all productions in the theater. Scamozzi's set shows an urban piazza, from which three streets extend back into the distance, their apparent length exaggerated by the false perspective of a sloped floor plane and artificially diminishing building heights (Fig. 11.55). When the actors leave the stage, they appear to recede along the street, even though their own height does not diminish according to the perspective of the set.

The continuing influence of Palladio on Western architecture is in no small measure due to the logical planning, careful proportioning, and conceptual clarity that characterize his designs. Indeed, the principles Palladio advocated have been found applicable to a variety of circumstances. Both his writings and buildings demonstrate the achievements of this stonemason turned architect who declared, "Vitruvius is my master, Rome is my mistress, and architecture is my life."

PALLADIO'S VENICE

Palladio's Venice, located in Italy but with commercial connections to Constantinople and farther east, developed its own exotic form of Gothicism, which it overlaid with selected Renaissance ideas. Although Venice ultimately contained a considerable amount of Renaissance architecture, the style developed as a variant relying on local traditions, climate, and disposition. The Palazzo Vendramin -Calergi (1500–10) of Mauro Coducci (ca. 1440–1504) has Corinthian pilasters, columns, and cornices framing large round-headed windows that are also decorated with classical detailing. These windows catch the breezes coming off the lagoon and cool the loggia and central hall that replaced the cortile found in Florentine palaces. Martino Lombardo employed perspective relief panels, executed

Procuratorie Vecchie   Campanile   S. Marco

Procuratorie Nuove

6.20

Library

Doge's Palace

11.57

11.58

La Zecca or the mint

11.56 Plan of the Piazza S. Marco, Venice, 1487–90.
The space between the Procuratorie Vecchie and Procuratorie Nuove, both housing offices for city officials, was gradually hollowed out to produce the piazza's present form. While Venice has many smaller piazzas, this one symbolized the power of one of the West's greatest trading cities in the tenth through the eighteenth centuries.

11.57 Jacopo Sansovino and Vincenzo Scamozzi, Library of S. Marco, Venice, begun 1537, completed 1583–88.
The library's façade can be read as three layers: the arched openings, the columns and entablatures, and the lavish ornamentation. The resulting scenographic effect appealed to the sensual nature of sixteenth-century Venetians.

by Tullio Lombardo, at the ground level of the Scuola di S. Marco (1487–90). The scenes depict lions, the animal identified with St. Mark, peering out from an implied barrel-vaulted space behind the plane of the façade.

Perhaps most vivid in the mind of anyone who has visited this dowager-queen city of the Adriatic is the Piazza S. Marco (Fig. 11.56). Located at the point where the Grand Canal empties into the lagoon, it is one of the great civic spaces in Western urban design and offers a cross-section of Venetian architectural developments in the fourteenth to sixteenth centuries. The piazza is L-shaped with a wide shaft of space extending from the water between the Doge's Palace and the Library of S. Marco to the campanile, around which it pivots to form a long trapezoid, which, though it evolved over a long period of time, appears as a perfect spatial response to the exotic cathedral of S. Marco that faces it.

The Doge's Palace (see Fig. 9.61) and S. Marco (see Figs. 6.20–6.21) have been discussed earlier. The campanile collapsed in the nineteenth century and was rebuilt. The loggetta at its base and the adjacent library (begun 1537, completed 1583–88) (Fig. 11.57) were the creations of Jacopo Sansovino (1486–1570) and Vincenzo Scamozzi. Sansovino was a friend of the Venetian painter Titian, whose nudes and landscapes have a supple, luxurious, and slightly mysterious character. The library has the appearance of a Titian interpreted in stone. Its bays are defined by attached Doric and Ionic columns with open Serliana between them. The composition is capped by a balustrade and a deep frieze filled with a fecund array of swags, **putti**, and masks. The effect, often described as scenographic, is one of sensuality and vividly contrasts with the relative brittleness of Renaissance monuments in Florence and the gravity of those in Rome. Adjacent to the library and facing the lagoon is Sansovino's La Zecca, or mint building (begun 1536) (Fig. 11.58). Its complete rustication obviously reflects the influence of Giulio Romano, and its related massiveness is ideally suited to its function as a great vault. The third story is a later addition, meaning that the original building-façade composition corresponded to Bramante's House of Raphael.

11.58 Jacopo Sansovino, La Zecca, Venice, begun 1536.
Heavy rustication conveys a sense of security in the building where Venetians minted their coins. Its massive, highly textured walls are particularly impressive when seen across the Venetian lagoon. The Library of S. Marco stands to its right.

11.59 Michele Sanmichele, Palazzo Grimani, Venice, begun ca. 1556.
Venetian palazzi like this one became models for cast-iron façades applied to wood and masonry commercial buildings in nineteenth-century America. The repetitive columns, elaborate windows, and detailed cornices were ideal for mass production.

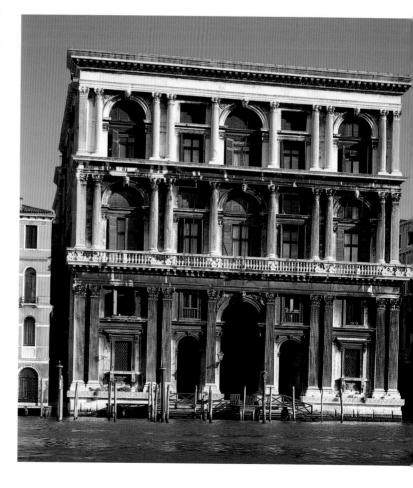

The sculptural quality of these public buildings also carried over into Venetian palazzi. The Palazzo Grimani (begun ca. 1556) (Fig. 11.59) by Michele Sanmichele (1484–1559) has robust attached columns, in this case of the Corinthian order, and a heavy overhanging cornice.

GARDEN DESIGN

The history of landscape architecture is in some respects more difficult to reconstruct accurately than the history of architecture, because without continual maintenance and replanting, the living materials that constitute the designer's work decay more rapidly and change and vanish more completely than do most buildings. We know that the sacred enclosures and sanctuary precincts of Egypt, Mesopotamia, the Aegean, and Rome were landscaped, although the appearance of these gardens is known now only from reliefs, descriptions, or other representations of them. Better preserved are many Islamic works, such as the Alhambra, where the garden embodied the idea of paradise. The medieval gardens illustrated in manuscripts and described in literature tended to be functional, laid out in orderly beds and contained within a wall or hedge. Many of these were purposeful plantings for culinary or medicinal herbs, as in the plan of St. Gall.

During the Renaissance the garden as an extension of architecture became important once again, with designs that originated as free adaptations of antique landscapes. Roman terraced gardens, for example, influenced both Bramante's design for the Belvedere Court (see Figs. 11.29–11.30) and Raphael's designs for the Villa Madama (see Figs. 11.32–11.33). At the Villa Madama, geometric perimeters of miniature box hedges encircled colorful planting beds, and the taller backdrop of trees defined the limits of the garden. During the Renaissance, however, landscape architecture was raised to the level of a major art, providing a stage setting for the enactment of the splendor of the aristocracy and princes of the Church. Pope Julius III, who commissioned the Villa Giulia just outside Rome, made use of its loggias and courts for theatrical performances and leisurely promenading. Late Renaissance gardens were elaborate, using water, sculpture, and foliage in an architectural manner. A number also provided a foretaste of Baroque urban planning.

Renaissance gardens began modestly, as at the Medici Villa (1458–61) in Fiesole, north of Florence (Fig. 11.60). Designed by Michelozzo and intended as a retreat for the Medici family and their humanist associates, it includes two levels of parterres, a lemon garden, and an occasional fountain, whose quietly flowing waters once provided an environment for scholarly contemplation.

Larger and more dramatic is the Villa Lante at Bagnaia near Viterbo (begun 1566) (Fig. 11.61), probably designed by Vignola, which uses perspective as an organizing agent. While the gardens were originally entered from below,

11.60 Michelozzo di Bartolomeo, Plan of and section through the Medici Villa, Fiesole, 1458–61.
Florentine gardens of the Early Renaissance were quite small compared to the Roman gardens of the next century and the French gardens that appeared around seventeenth-century châteaux. Here the villa's loggia opens out onto a parterre, with another parterre one level below. The back side of the villa looks out over a smaller lemon garden.

N   0 _____ 50 m
         0 _____ 150 ft

11.61 Giacomo Barozzi da Vignola, Plan of and section through the Villa Lante, Bagnaia, begun 1566. The Villa Lante's typically Roman organization includes stairs and water features and a parterre at the lowest level. The central axis in the form of an allée is defined by boscos or dense groves of trees.

N

0   50 m
0   150 ft

11.62 Pirro Ligorio, gardens of the Villa d'Este, Tivoli, ca. 1565–72. Most striking in the fully developed gardens are the myriad water features. In this view a waterfall stands behind fishponds.

the mature vegetation now makes the most dramatic view one from above, where a square upper parterre is extended down the sloping site through a shaft of space or **allée** defined by a **bosco**, a dense planting of trees. The allée is reinforced by twin casinos that act almost like sighting mechanisms for the perspective view; stairs and ramps occupy the space between them. Water features appear at the various levels, beginning with the Fountain of the Deluge at the top. Water then disappears and reappears at intervals down the central axis, sometimes as fountains, sometimes as a cascade, and finally as four placid pools in the center of the parterre on the lowest level.

The first major Mannerist garden was built at the Villa d'Este in Tivoli (Fig. 11.62) outside Rome, to the designs of Pirro Ligorio (ca. 1510–83). His client, Ippolito II Cardinal d'Este, owned a site that included both a north-facing slope and a large reliable water supply. Anyone visiting the gardens today during the hot summer months is struck by the marvelous microclimate—cool by virtue of shady trees and water everywhere. As designed by Ligorio, however, the gardens were intended as a setting for the Este family's sculpture collection, with plantings mostly in the form of

11.63 Château, Francis I wing, Blois, 1515–24.
The medieval-Renaissance style of Francis I resulted from the king's contacts with new architectural developments in Italy while on a military campaign. Though a hybrid, the château was much admired as a source for early twentieth-century residential designs in America.

low shrubs and hedges. Furthermore, while visitors enter today through the villa on the garden's high ground, the original entrance was from below. This lower access meant that the entire site could be taken in at a single glance rather than being experienced as a series of episodes along channels of large-scale greenery, as it is today.

Ligorio took as his principal theme the god Hercules, to whom the d'Este family traced their lineage mythologically. Hercules's strength and the magnitude of his labors were represented metaphorically by the efforts required in modeling the site, constructing aqueducts, and digging tunnels up to 3200 feet long. Ligorio's plan emphasized orthogonal and diagonal cross-axes above; large rectangular fishponds and parterres below, with every manner and scale of water feature; architectural environments from an artificial cave to a huge water organ to a model of ancient Rome; and myriad pieces of sculpture, much of which now resides in the Capitoline Museum in Rome and elsewhere.

THE RENAISSANCE IN FRANCE

The extension of artistic developments from Renaissance Italy to France was hastened in part by French military interventions in the peninsula. In 1494 the armies of King Charles VIII invaded Italy in pursuit of his claims to the kingdom of Naples; in 1498 Louis XII attacked Milan,

toppling the Sforza family from power (precipitating Bramante's departure for Rome); and Francis I campaigned in Italy until 1525, when his defeat at Pavia brought a halt to French pretensions in the region of Milan. Although these military excursions ultimately resulted in no permanent expansion of French territory, the reverse flow of Italian artistic ideas was to have lasting consequences for architecture in France. By the end of the fifteenth century, France was changing from a feudal society into a strong centralized state headed by the king. Unlike urban-centered Italy, where merchant princes eclipsed the landed nobility and commissioned works from the great Renaissance artists, the court was the dominant force in French society, and the king led the way in supporting design in the Italian style. As Milan was the center of French contacts in Italy, the early Renaissance buildings there, including the Certosa at Pavia, were the best known and most generally admired structures, perhaps because their combination of highly ornamented surfaces and classical details was not far removed from the Late Gothic

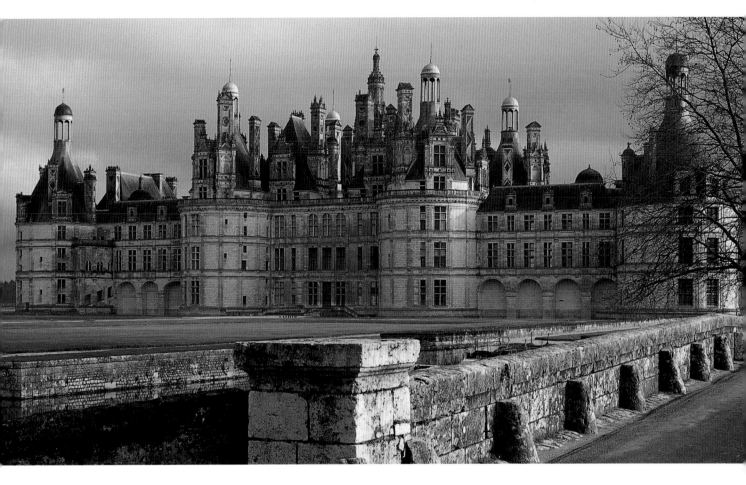

11.64 Domenico da Cortona, Château, Chambord, 1519–47. Chambord appears as a Renaissance trunk with medieval branches sprouting above it. The outbreak of steep roofs, dormers, and chimneys reflects an accommodation of the classical language to the northern climate.

style with which the French were most familiar. From the last years of the fifteenth century, the French transported Italian art back to their own country, invited Italian artists and architects north to undertake commissions, and sent French artists to Italy to train in Renaissance workshops.

Châteaux in the Loire Valley

The cultural center of France in the early sixteenth century was not Paris, but the valley of the Loire, where the king and his nobles maintained elaborate **châteaux** or castles for leisure, entertaining, and attending to the pleasures of the hunt. Within these châteaux are found some of the earliest French architectural manifestations of the Renaissance style. Blois in particular illustrates the transition from the Middle Ages to the Renaissance through the successive stages in its construction. The château was begun in the thirteenth century with the erection of a large medieval hall and associated rooms. Between 1498 and 1504, Louis XII added an east wing, incorporating an

entrance gate to what would ultimately be a large courtyard. The construction, in red brick with light-colored stone trim at corners, doorways, and window surrounds, reflects the continuity of medieval traditions. Above the entranceway there is an equestrian statue of Louis set into a large niche with double-cusped pointed arches and other Gothic detailing in stone. Windows align one above the other, culminating in elaborate Gothic **dormers** in the steeply pitched roof; these dormers read as a series of vertical elements, even though string courses and the cornice establish horizontal lines. Between 1515 and 1524, Francis I embarked on extensive building operations at Blois, adding a north wing to the medieval hall to form the north side of the court, with the opposite side facing over the town. Francis demolished an old tower and upon its foundations built the famous open spiraling stair (Fig. 11.63). It features decorative carving of wreaths, porcupines, and salamanders, emblems of the royal family. Windows on the courtyard façade are regularly arranged, although once again their vertical emphasis clashes with horizontal elements. All rooms are placed en suite, an arrangement the French long preferred. On the town façade, the Francis I wing is like a cliff face, with two loggias and an open third story with freestanding columns, modeled on papal palaces at the Vatican and at Pienza. Its mixture of classical columns and details also includes Gothic motifs.

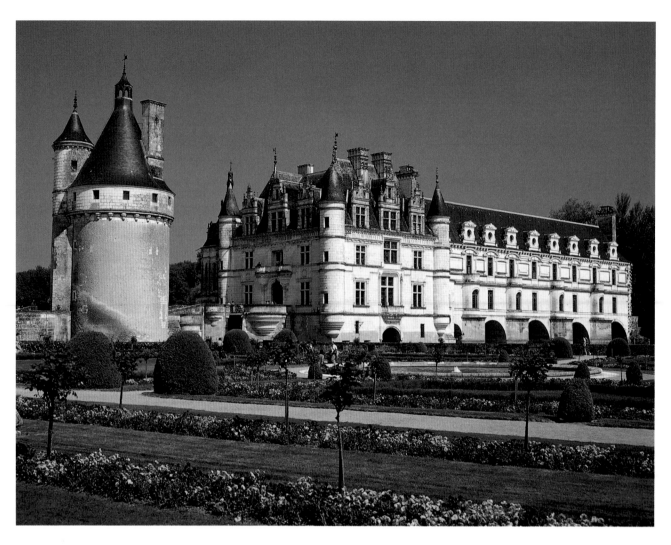

11.65 Philibert de l'Orme, Jean Bullant, and others, Château, Chenonceau, begun 1515.
There is no more picturesque château than this one. To the rear of the main block, the bridge was first added by Philibert de l'Orme. It then became a base for the grand dining hall designed by Jean Bullant.

In contrast to this town-based château, the château of Chambord (1519–47) was built in the countryside in the style of a fortified castle within a bailey or outer wall, thus neatly overlaying Renaissance symmetry and detailing on a fundamentally medieval building type (Fig. 11.64). Its Italian architect, Domenico da Cortona, employed simple cylindrical towers, which were to have been surrounded by open loggias; the latter were never built, however, since shade from intense sunlight was not as necessary in France as in Italy. The keep, or defensible core of the castle, has a suite of rooms in each corner, divided by a cruciform circulation pattern and a double staircase undoubtedly influenced by a sketch of Leonardo's. People ascending one set of risers in the double-helix staircase can do so without seeing people descending the other. A great lantern above the staircase is one of a whole cluster of cones, chimneys, and dormers on the roof, presenting an almost medieval profile against the sky. Surrounding this abundance of vertical roof features is a terrace from which the ladies of the court could view the progress of the hunt in the wooded

countryside beyond the château. The contrast between the ordered clarity of the walls and the wild exuberance of the rooftops reflects the partial assimilation of Renaissance architectural ideas into a firmly established medieval building tradition.

Not all the Loire châteaux were built for the king. Chenonceau (Fig. 11.65) is an example of a château constructed by a wealthy courtier and financier, Thomas Bohier. Begun in 1515, Chenonceau has a regularized plan, with all the major rooms opening off a central corridor, and a straight-run stair that illustrates Renaissance influence in its design, even as its moat, turreted corners, and chapel with rib vaults, pointed arches, and buttresses reflect medieval practices.

Sebastiano Serlio and Philibert de l'Orme

A second phase of Renaissance development in France began around 1540 with the arrival of Sebastiano Serlio (1475–1554), an Italian architect who came north at the invitation of the king, and the return of Philibert de l'Orme (ca. 1510–70), a Frenchman who trained in Rome and settled in Paris to practice as an architect and engineer. Both men brought knowledge of High Renaissance work in Rome, especially that of Bramante, and their writings did much to explain Renaissance design principles and modify building practices in France. Little of Serlio's architecture

11.66 Pierre Lescot and Jacques Lemercier, Louvre, Paris, begun 1546.
A small portion of Pierre Lescot's sixteenth-century Louvre is still visible to the left. In the center, on Jacques Lemercier's seventeenth-century Pavilion de l'Horloge, the orders are used extensively but in a distinctively French manner of pairs surmounted by pavilion roofs. Lemercier's additions continue to the right.

survives, aside from the exteriors of the château of Ancy-le-Franc, a mediocre square-plan building with a central courtyard. The design, with its corner pavilions, Doric pilasters, and rustication, is almost entirely north Italian in derivation, but the high pitched roof is typically French.

Of greater importance than his buildings were Serlio's writings on architecture, published in several installments from 1537 to 1551 and gathered together in 1584 as *Tutte l'opere d'architettura et prospettiva*, known today as *The Five Books of Architecture*. The first architectural treatises not composed in Latin, these books contained woodcut illustrations, and the text addressed the ordinary builder more than the architectural scholar. Book One explains geometry; Book Two covers the construction of perspective drawings; and Book Three illustrates antique Roman buildings and the High Renaissance works of Bramante and Raphael. Book Four outlines the five orders of architecture (Doric, Ionic, Corinthian, Tuscan, and **Composite**), illustrates arched rusticated door and window surrounds appropriate for each order, and includes notes on construction materials. Book Five features centralized church designs. Three more volumes containing many of Serlio's own designs complete the opus.

Philibert de l'Orme's writings were also practical in nature. His first volume, published in 1561, was *Nouvelles inventions pour bien bastir et petits frais* (*New Inventions for Building Well and Economically*). It considers the construction of vaults and roofs from an engineering standpoint.

His major work, *Architecture*, was published in 1567. While it draws some content from the earlier treatises by Vitruvius and Alberti, it relies extensively on de l'Orme's personal experiences in building to offer architects guidance grounded in both theory and practice.

Of the many projects on which de l'Orme worked, only a few remain. One of the most celebrated is the addition he made to the château at Chenonceau, a bridge over the River Cher composed of five arches of varying span (see Fig. 11.65). The building atop the bridge was added later by Jean Bullant.

The Louvre and the Place Royale

After 1526, when the French capital became fixed in Paris, Francis I decided to update the medieval Louvre Palace, beginning with the removal of the cylindrical keep in the center of the square courtyard. Some years later, he decided to rebuild one wing of the enclosed court, with the possibility of extending the design around all four sides of the palace. Serlio proposed a design incorporating a series of courtyards, but the commission for rebuilding the Louvre wing went instead to the French architect Pierre Lescot (ca. 1500–78). Lescot's design (Fig. 11.66) dates from 1546, and while it is more correct in its use of the classical orders than most French buildings of the same period, it could never be confused with Italian work. Lescot's façade emphasizes verticality rather than the horizontal line characteristic of the Italian Renaissance, even though it has cornice lines between floors. The courtyard façade is three stories high including the attic and is composed of Corinthian and Composite half-columns and pilasters, with elongated windows and pavilions at the extremities and in the center. The architecture is complemented by sculpture executed by Jean Goujon, one of the most talented artists of the period. It is possible that Lescot's façade was derived from Serlio's

11.67 Place Royale (Place des Vosges), Paris, 1605–12.
Around the Place Royale lie regularized residential
façades, all connected by a continuous ground-level
arcade. The taller pavilions were constructed by Henry
IV, who promoted the project.

**11.68 Bird's-eye view of the Place Royale (Place des
Vosges), Paris, 1605–12.**
The French *place* is a paved residential square. It focuses
inward, in contrast to the subsequent Baroque spaces
linked by axial boulevards.

courtyard plan for the Louvre, although it seems that both
miscalculated the interior implications of the courtyard's
proportions. The great height of the building in relation
to the width of the courtyard was such that, had the three
additional façades been built to form the intended courtyard, the palace rooms would have received little direct
sunlight. As events progressed, however, a later designer,
Jacques Lemercier (1585–1654), enlarged the courtyard
in 1624 to 400 feet square, more than four times the size
proposed by either Serlio or Lescot.

For the last four decades of the sixteenth century,
France was tormented by civil strife, the so-called Wars of
Religion, which had economic and social causes as well
as religious ones. Order was not restored until the arrival
in 1594 of King Henry IV, whose policies brought an end
to domestic and foreign turmoil. During the relative tranquillity of his reign, France implemented Italian ideas of
town planning that were to have an impact on later architecture in both Britain and colonial America. In an effort
to unify the aristocracy and rebuild Paris, which was still
largely medieval, Henry IV sanctioned the construction of
a number of residential squares, bounded by row houses
with uniform façades. The Place Royale—now Place des
Vosges—(Figs. 11.67–11.68) was the first of these urban
squares used exclusively for residential purposes; it was
laid out from 1605 to 1612. In addition to lending the
enterprise his title, Henry supported the project by constructing two pavilions, one each in the center of both
the north and south sides of the square. Thirty-eight plots
surrounding the 460-foot-square court were then leased

on condition that the row houses to be constructed there
conformed to the overall design scheme: each house was
to be four bays wide and three stories high, not including the dormered attic story, built of brick with stone
trim and roofed with slate. The royal pavilions featured
more elaborate details and higher rooflines than adjacent
structures, although they shared the continuous ground-
level arcade that linked the buildings, a feature derived
from Renaissance squares in Italy, such as the Piazza
S. Annunziata in Florence onto which Brunelleschi's
Foundling Hospital fronts. Originally the central open
space of the Place Royale was unplanted and its sand
surface used for festivals and tournaments. An equestrian
statue of the king later served as the focal monument in
the center. The houses proved to be too small for the aristocrats whom Henry wished to attract to Paris, however,
so the first residents of the Place Royale were minor nobility and wealthy Parisian merchants instead.

11.69 Robert Smythson, Wollaton Hall, Nottinghamshire, 1580–88.
While Robert Smythson was well aware of the work of the Italian Renaissance, including that of Andrea Palladio, his design decisions reflect a concern for the local context, most obviously in the provision of many windows, a response to the often overcast English climate.

THE RENAISSANCE IN ENGLAND

As was the case in France, Gothic architecture continued to be the predominant building style in England long after the Renaissance had originated and matured in Italy. Perpendicular Gothic, a particularly English variant, enjoyed favor well into the sixteenth century. The earliest expression of the Renaissance in Britain is found in sculpture and the decorative arts. In about 1511, King Henry VIII brought Pietro Torrigiani (1472–1528) and other artists directly from Italy to work on a number of royal commissions, the most important of which was a tomb for Henry's parents, Henry VII and his queen, in the Late Gothic chapel at Westminster Abbey in London. Cardinal Wolsey employed Italian sculptors, including Giovanni da Maiano, to make ten glazed terracotta roundels containing busts of Roman emperors. These roundels, which followed antique models and were thoroughly Renaissance in spirit, were ultimately incorporated into the gateways of the Cardinal's medieval castellated palace at Hampton Court, begun in 1515. After Wolsey's fall from royal favor, Henry VIII confiscated the palace and enlarged Hampton

Court to more than twice its original size. He added courts, galleries, a chapel, and a hall, but the building remained more medieval than Renaissance, including the hall with its splendid hammerbeam truss roof of 1531–36.

Another essentially Gothic building of the same era is King's College Chapel, Cambridge (see Fig. 9.36), begun in 1446 and completed in 1515. Inside, however, the wooden choir screen is a piece of early Renaissance design. It was erected in 1533–35, as a gift from Henry VIII, to separate collegians from townspeople and to support the organ. The artist is unknown, but his work represents the first truly Renaissance design in Britain, exhibiting a wide range of classical details with only a few pendants suggesting Gothic influence.

Henry broke with the Church of Rome in 1534, and numerous Italian artists of the Roman Catholic faith left Britain soon thereafter. Thus, the full flowering of the Renaissance in Britain was delayed until the beginning of the seventeenth century. This does not mean that Italian ideals ceased to influence Britain, but that the direct inspiration from Italian artists resident in Britain stopped, while indirect influence continued to come from Italy via the Low Countries and France. The treatises of Scamozzi, Vignola, and Serlio were translated into English from the Dutch, not directly from the Italian, and numerous Dutch architectural books were exported to England. These illustrated strapwork, low-relief designs based on studded leather straps, that was arranged in geometrical and sometimes interlaced patterns. The strapwork decoration

11.70 (above) Robert Smythson, Ground-floor plan
of Wollaton Hall, Nottinghamshire, 1580–88.
This plan had its origins among the English castles of
the Middle Ages. In the center is the Great Hall, and at
the corners are the square-plan rooms that evolved from
fortified towers.

11.71 (right) Robert Smythson, Great Hall, Wollaton Hall,
Nottinghamshire, 1580–88.
Renaissance influence is apparent in the Doric frieze of
the wood paneling. The hall is dominated by medieval
hammerbeam trusses that support the roof.

11.72 Robert Smythson, Hardwick Hall, Derbyshire, 1590–97.
"Hardwick Hall more window than wall" went the popular refrain
of the time. Above the many windows, the filigreelike gables reflect
Dutch influence itself based on so-called strapwork—leatherwork
derived from Italian Renaissance ornament in plaster.

published by Flemish and Dutch architects, such as Hans Vredman de Vries, found its way into the works of the English architect Robert Smythson (1536–1614).

Elizabethan Country Houses

Renaissance influence from Italy came into Britain via Flanders during the reign of Queen Elizabeth I. Her own architectural commissions were insignificant, but her courtiers and governmental officials built on a lavish scale for the Queen and her traveling entourage. Wollaton Hall in Nottinghamshire (1580–88) is an example of a great house built during the Elizabethan era (Figs. 11.69–11.70). Designed by Robert Smythson for the sheriff of Nottingham, the house draws on numerous sources. The building's symmetrical square plan with corner pavilions is taken from Serlio; in the center of the scheme, the Great Hall with ancillary accommodation is medieval; and the **long gallery** for the lodging of courtiers comes from France. Although Wollaton Hall is built of masonry, the huge expanse of windows is comparable to the fenestration found in timber construction. Renaissance pilasters and cornices punctuate the elevations, while the **parapets** are inspired by de Vries, and the upper clerestory levels of the Great Hall (Fig. 11.71) protrude above the roofline like a medieval keep with pepper-pot corner turrets.

Another great Elizabethan mansion, in all probability designed by Smythson, is Hardwick Hall in Derbyshire

(1590–97) (Fig. 11.72). It shares many of Wollaton's characteristics in plan and elevation, but of greater importance here is the symmetrical arrangement of the main hall and its contiguous exterior colonnades, which reflect contemporary Italian design. Moreover, its plan appears as a Wollaton ripped open, less concerned with defense and more interested in light and warmth from the sun. Like all these grand and pretentious late sixteenth-century country residences, Hardwick helped advertise the wealth and social standing of its owner, the extremely wealthy Elizabeth of Shrewsbury, known as Bess of Hardwick. Her initials, E.S., are displayed in the house's decorative crowning balustrade.

Inigo Jones

It is amazing how heterogeneous this second phase of the English Renaissance appears when compared to what was initiated under Henry VIII or what was to come during the reign of Elizabeth's successor, James VI of Scotland, who became James I of England. Inigo Jones (1573–1652), an architect of profound significance in English architecture,

11.73 Inigo Jones, Queen's House from the front, Greenwich, begun 1616.
The change in appearance from Hardwick Hall to the Queen's House is stunning. Its design reflects Inigo Jones's close study of Palladio's work while traveling in Italy.

11.74 Inigo Jones, Plan of the Queen's House, Greenwich, 1616.
The Queen's House plan reflects the same Renaissance rigor as the façades. Its two wings are connected by a bridge that once spanned a road passing through the site.

emerged during the reign of James I. Jones was born seven years before the death of Palladio, and his first building, the Queen's House at Greenwich, introduced Palladian ideals to England. With the appearance of Jones, English classical-revival architecture immediately mirrored that of late sixteenth-century Italy.

Unlike earlier English architects, Jones acquired his knowledge of Italian architecture first-hand. He was in Italy as early as 1601. Two years later he traveled to Denmark, and he made a second trip to Italy during 1613–14 in the entourage of the earl of Arundel. In his baggage

11.75 Inigo Jones, Banqueting House, Whitehall, London, 1619–22.
Notable here is the English emphasis on the surface texture of the stone façade. It was a fixation of English designers at least as far back as the construction of Durham Cathedral, where many of the piers were carved with chevron patterns that defied their circular geometry.

Jones carried a copy of Palladio's *Four Books of Architecture*, which he annotated generously. He met Scamozzi and visited Vicenza, where Palladio's works profoundly influenced him. Upon returning to England, he designed stage sets for the court in which he was able to experiment with Renaissance forms.

His first building commission, the Queen's House (Fig. 11.73), begun in 1616 but still being extended in 1661, was situated astride the road from Deptford to Woolwich, which divided the building in two. A bridge spanned the road at the second-floor level and acted as a **porte-cochère**, or covered drive-through for vehicles, leading to the entrance in the center of the building (Fig. 11.74). From the rather modest doorway, one is led directly into a room with the proportions of a cube. Access to the second floor is gained by a circular stair without a **newel**, or central post, a daring structural accomplishment in its day. A **balcony** across the cube room connects second-floor rooms, including the queen's bedroom, with the bridge. The garden façade of the house is based on Palladio's Palazzo Chiericati (see Fig. 11.47) at Vicenza; but, whereas the Palladian building has a two-story colonnade interrupted in the center of the second floor by a ballroom, the garden front of the Queen's House is a fenestrated wall with a central recessed loggia, well protected from the cool winds of Greenwich. Solid and void have been reversed in the exteriors of the two buildings.

Jones's most famous structure, the Banqueting House (1619–22) at Whitehall in London (Fig. 11.75), was built to replace an earlier building that had burned down. Its design, part of a much larger vision for an enormous Whitehall Palace complex, is an anglicized version of a Vitruvian basilica as interpreted by Palladio. The main interior space consists of a double-cube room with continuous balcony. In Jones's first project, he expressed this volumetric arrangement on the exterior as a two-story composition with a pedimented central pavilion at the principal façade. Jones eventually modified this elevation, articulating it in three parts according to the example of Palladio and omitting the pediment. He placed half-columns on the central three-bay pavilion to provide a contrast in depth with the flat pilasters of the two bays on either side. He arranged the windows to have alternate segmental and triangular pediments along the piano nobile, distinguishing it from the heavily rusticated masonry of the base, where he employed flat lintels. He masked the roofline with a balustrade.

When Jones proposed a new design for the whole of Whitehall Palace in 1638, the Banqueting House was to be incorporated into half of one side of the central court. The enormous palace, based on Palladio's and Scamozzi's interpretations of a large Roman domus, here expanded to a gargantuan scale, would have replaced an area of rambling medieval structures. Although Jones's palace design was never built, the Banqueting House stood tall and monumental in its surroundings of earlier, domestically scaled medieval buildings, and its basic features were adapted in subsequent centuries for the ranks of overscaled governmental buildings that form its present-day context.

On a site approximately halfway between the Banqueting House and the City of London to the east, the fourth Earl of Bedford employed Jones in 1630 to design a speculative development, called Covent Garden, in the grounds of Bedford House. Jones collaborated with Isaac de Caux in this work, the first of several English residential squares based on the designs for the French king Henry IV's Place Royale in Paris. As in its French predecessor, the houses facing Covent Garden had continuous ground-level arcades, masking their individual entrances but providing a covered passageway around two sides of the square (Fig. 11.76). Five streets entered the square, which had Bedford House to its south and, to the west, the first completely new London church erected since the Reformation. Although rebuilt after a fire in 1795, the church of St. Paul (1631–35) (Fig. 11.77) still resembles Jones's original design, a simple box with a Tuscan-order portico, false door and altar at the east end, and the actual entrance at the west. The open space of the square soon became the site of a flourishing market, a use that continues to this day in permanent cast-iron halls constructed during the nineteenth century.

St. Paul's Cathedral in London was in poor repair at the beginning of the seventeenth century, and Jones was

11.76 Inigo Jones, Bird's-eye view of Covent Garden, London, 1658.
With residential units built up into large blocks, this scheme focused on a church (labeled "chapell"), making it the first such composition in Renaissance England. The purpose of the project was to turn the Earl of Bedford's agricultural land into a cash-producing real-estate development.

commissioned to restore it. He added a Corinthian portico to the west front, incorporating large scrolls to mask the aisle roofs, but the whole church was badly damaged in the fire of 1666, and both church and portico were demolished to make way for the later design of Christopher Wren. Wren's works belong to the seventeenth century and will be considered with those of other Baroque designers in Chapter 12.

11.77 Inigo Jones, St. Paul's, Covent Garden, London, 1631–35. Referring to its use of the rustic Tuscan order, Jones called his church the "handsomest barn in England." It was rebuilt after a fire in 1795.

CONCLUSIONS ABOUT ARCHITECTURAL IDEAS

Central to the fifteenth-century Renaissance reconception of architecture was the return to the classical language, which had a vocabulary of elements based on the orders, and a set of rules, or a syntax, establishing their proper arrangement and mutual relationships. With this vocabulary and within this syntax, structure, in the form of free-standing or applied columns and beams, was routinely and logically displayed. And within the new Renaissance way of design thinking, the mind of the designer was equally apparent, so much so that his personality could, and even should, show through in his finished work. Also within this new design system, each architectural element was both clearly discernible and subordinate to the whole. This condition can be observed in the Tempietto in Rome (see Figs. 11.26–11.27), which makes manifest the rebirth of purified classicism. The Tempietto is serene and measured, with its every element derived from antiquity, literally or by analogy, and systematically disposed. Additionally, its central plan represents the Renaissance ideal, even without the perfect circular environment planned for it by Donato Bramante.

Filippo Brunelleschi set this new architecture in motion by traveling to Rome in search of the design and construction knowledge he believed to be embedded in the city's antique monuments, and legions of designers from across Europe would eventually follow him. His Florence Cathedral dome, made possible by his new understanding of ancient technologies, still had a Gothic pointed-arch profile. His Pazzi Chapel exhibits elements of the classical language both inside and out, but with some tentative and awkward moments. His associate Michelozzo arrived at a new form-type, the palazzo, by creating outwardly imposing domestic quarters for the rich and powerful, but apprehensive, Medici family. His friend Masaccio exploited Brunelleschi's invention of mechanical perspective by painting the *Trinity* fresco inside the Church of S. Maria Novella. Its juxtaposition of biblical figures with contemporary ones within an illusionistic, classicized-but-modern architectural space celebrated the reestablishment of the classical tradition, the piety as well as the status of the donors, and the new Renaissance way of seeing the world.

Leon Battista Alberti approached classicism not through practice but through theory. Expanding Brunelleschi's vision, he aspired, as evidenced by the vast, coffered, barrel-vaulted nave of S. Andrea in Mantua, to recreate the scale and splendor of the ancient Roman world, an idea appropriated by Bramante once he came to Rome to work for the papacy and closely studied the ruins there himself. We can imagine him in the company of Pope Julius II, wandering through the decrepit fabric of old St. Peter's and the adjacent scattered constructions of the Vatican, and imagining the return of the city to its former imperial grandeur.

While his centralized plan for new St. Peter's was structurally unsound, his vision—placing the Pantheon's dome atop a vaulted square equivalent in scale to the ancient Roman baths—was profound enough to satisfy even Michelangelo, who took over the project on Bramante's death. Striking out north from St. Peter's and the Vatican, Bramante created the Belvedere Court, an exterior space,

rivaling in scale the Colosseum on which its inner stacked orders were based.

Bramante's self-confident, High Renaissance production was short-lived, as political, as well as artistic, turmoil brought on the insecurities and accompanying ambiguities of Mannerism. With the artistic accomplishments of antiquity now matched and even superseded, many sixteenth-century Italian architects grew impatient with the restraints placed on them by the perceived rigidity of High Renaissance esthetic thinking and so flouted the rules of classical ordering, some would say to troubling excess. At the Sforza Chapel, Michelangelo transcended compositional mischief and created a wholly new kind of plan and vaulting type that yielded a dynamic spatiality, one that pointed toward the Baroque style (presented in the next chapter) that would accompany the Catholic Counter-Reformation. One sixteenth-century architect, Andrea Palladio, never yielded to the extremes of Mannerism, and in his body of work in the Veneto, particularly his villas, created a set of form-models that would be perhaps the most influential in all of Western architecture.

Palladio's buildings made a profound impression on the Englishman Inigo Jones, who came south (a copy of Palladio's *I quattro libri* in hand), made close observations of Palladian buildings, then carried Palladio's ideas in a pure form back to England, where they eventually superseded the raucous medieval-Renaissance hybrids that had arisen during the Elizabethan and Jacobean periods. Likewise, Renaissance architectural thinking was carried back to France when French armies returned home from their Italian incursions at the end of the fifteenth century. Here, like the initial Renaissance work in England, the early-sixteenth-century châteaux of the Loire Valley display Renaissance forms applied superficially and with little appreciation of underlying ordering principles. The results, while impure, are somehow both chaste and exuberant and reflect the optimism of a nation, long in a state of almost constant turmoil, enjoying a period of prosperity and influence. This condition encouraged French architects to visit Italy and Italian architects, like Sebastian Serlio, to move to France. Urban architecture of the period, most notably the Parisian Louvre Palace, demonstrates that French designers were searching for ways to make the newly imported Renaissance classicism their own, but without abandoning the spirit of the extraordinary Gothic architecture that was still highly regarded in the Île-de-France. The mature products of their investigations, what some have termed French Baroque classicism, are discussed in the next chapter.

Chapter 12
Baroque Architecture

Just as the bankers and merchants of Florence supported Early Renaissance artists and architects, so the Catholic Church was the primary patron of art and architecture around Rome in both the seventeenth and eighteenth centuries, and the works it commissioned gave rise to a new style, the Baroque.

By the end of the Renaissance, the Church had great temporal power, but its moral foundations had deteriorated. The office of cardinal was sold openly; high and low Church officials maintained mistresses and sought sinecures for their sons, who were euphemistically called "nephews"; and donations from the pious were spent on projects wholly lacking in spiritual purpose. The popes lived grandly, treating the Church's treasury as personal funds. To finance both sacred and secular projects, the Church instituted questionable fundraising practices, such as the sale of pardons and indulgences to save the payer or a relative from a stipulated number of days in Purgatory.

THE REFORMATION AND COUNTER-REFORMATION

As might be expected, the corruption of the Church brought about calls for religious reform, some as early as the thirteenth century. The most dramatic and influential reaction came from the monk Martin Luther of the monastery at Wittenberg, Germany. In 1517 he nailed his ninety-five theses or propositions to the door of All Saints' Church, in the opening salvo of what would become known as the Protestant Reformation. Until this time the Church had always overcome challenges from deviants within its ranks, usually by declaring them heretics and destroying them by force. This time, however, the discontent was too widespread for inquisitional methods to work, although they were tried.

The Church's more reasoned response was the Catholic Counter-Reformation, a program that involved both reform within the Church and a sustained campaign to win people back to the beliefs of Catholicism. The Council of Trent convened in 1545 and decreed that art was an essential tool for spreading the prestige and teachings of the Church. All the arts were deployed in this public-

relations effort, and the artistic style that developed to restate traditional Catholic teachings became known as the Baroque. The results were openly propagandistic, overtly emotional, and long on sensory appeal. Based on an elaboration of classical forms, already made highly individualistic by artists and architects in the early sixteenth century, the Baroque was a didactic, theatrical, dynamic, and dramatic style. Later critics have faulted its exaggerated gestures, excessive ornamentation, and unconcealed emotionalism. In context, however, Baroque ecclesiastical work should be seen as aiming to involve people directly with religious ideals. In general, Baroque architecture is characterized by spatial complexity and drama created by light from undisclosed sources. Its effects were achieved through the dynamic play of concave against convex curves; a preference for axial and centralized spaces that found particular expression in the ellipse or oval, at once axial and centralized; and the imaginative integration of painting, sculpture, and architecture to create illusions and dissolve physical boundaries.

Il Gesù, Rome

Among the new institutions of the reformed Catholic Church was the militant Order of the Society of Jesus, established by Ignatius Loyola in 1534 and commonly known as the Jesuits. Serving as missionaries and educators, particularly in remote areas, the Jesuits reached China by 1550 and accompanied Spanish conquistadors to the Americas. Their headquarters were in Rome, however, and it is fitting that one of the earliest Baroque architectural

---

Johann Balthasar Neumann, Würzburg Residenz Stair Hall, 1720.
Tiepolo's painted ceiling looks down on this stair, which seems to float inside a great room of its own. The level of ornament and drama befits men in uniform and women in court dresses.

Chronology

Martin Luther presents his 95 theses	1517
Catholic Church establishes the Society of Jesus	1534
Council of Trent and the beginning of the Counter-Reformation	1545
Jesuits build Il Gesù	1568–76
Papacy of Pope Sixtus V	1585–90
English Civil War	1625–49
Bernini works at St. Peter's	1629–80
Reign of Louis XIV in France	1661–1715
Peace of Westphalia and introduction of Renaissance influence into Germany	1648
Great Fire of London	1666

designs, Il Gesù (Figs. 12.1–12.2), was their principal church, begun in 1568 to plans by Giacomo Vignola and completed in 1576 by Giacomo della Porta, who designed the façade as built and the dome.

Il Gesù resembles Alberti's S. Andrea at Mantua in plan, having transverse-barrel-vaulted chapels (in place of aisles with columns) flanking a longitudinal-barrel-vaulted nave. However, Vignola's motives for using such a plan were quite different from Alberti's. Alberti had sought to recreate ancient Roman grandeur and monumentality. By

12.1 Giacomo Vignola and Giacomo della Porta, Il Gesù, Rome, 1568–76.
Innumerable church designs were based on this one, the mother church of the Jesuit order. The three-dimensionality and accumulation of detail in the central bay suggest a new kind of façade composition.

12.2 Giacomo Vignola and Giacomo della Porta, Plan of and section through Il Gesù, Rome, 1568–76.
The stunted nave announces that this is a preaching church of the Counter-Reformation. The use of piers and lateral chapels provided an alternative to the column-and-side-aisle plan inherited by Brunelleschi from the Middle Ages.

suppressing the transepts and shortening the nave, Vignola produced clear sightlines and acoustics that allowed for preaching to be heard clearly. The Gesù design was also forward-looking in its strong axial emphasis and in the three-dimensionality of elements on its west front. The composition of this façade is traceable to Alberti's S. Maria Novella in Florence, but with classical orders replacing the traditional Florentine subdivision based on geometric shapes. At Il Gesù, pairs of pilasters step out from forward-projecting planes until, on either side of the entrance, engaged columns support a triangular pediment, which in turn is framed by a segmental pediment supported by flanking pilasters. The original interior design was absolutely plain; the interior seen in the church today reflects a later decorative campaign that began in the late seventeenth century. Looking up at the nave ceiling, one is never sure where the architecture stops and the sculpture begins, or where the sculpture terminates and the fresco of the *Adoration of the Name of Jesus,* which was painted between 1675 and 1679 by Giovanni Battista Gaulli, begins. Clouds, draperies, and human bodies float in space, and one is swept up by this vision of heaven.

POPE SIXTUS V AND THE REPLANNING OF ROME

Within a decade of the completion of Il Gesù, early Baroque influences could be seen in the modifications made to the urban pattern of Rome. Pope Sixtus V (1585–90) began radical changes, and his design program both guided the city's development for the next hundred years or more and influenced urban design throughout Europe and eventually in America.

Sixtus V was not the first pope to be concerned about the neglected physical appearance of Rome. His work can be seen as a vigorous elaboration and extension of initiatives taken in the 1450s by Nicholas V (1448–55), the first Renaissance pope to gain full control over the city following the long period of unrest when the popes resided instead in Avignon, France. Nicholas had undertaken fundamental repairs to ancient structures, such as the city walls, bridges, aqueducts, and roads on which Romans still relied, and he also had certain monuments modified to meet current needs, such as the conversion of Hadrian's Mausoleum into the Castel Sant'Angelo, a fortress for the papal court. Pope Sixtus IV (1471–84) had restored old churches and commissioned the building of others, and had attempted to improve circulation within the chaotic and densely populated medieval quarter by straightening the streets that led to the Ponte Sant'Angelo, the bridge over the Tiber that connected the bulk of Rome with St. Peter's. Julius II (1503–13) continued Sixtus IV's projects, as discussed in the last chapter in connection with Julius's patronage of Bramante and Michelangelo. In addition to those notable works around the Vatican and St. Peter's, Julius directed his energies toward civic improvements, including the creation of three straight streets (Strada Leonina, Strada del Corso, and Strada del Babuino) radiating like spokes from the Porta del Popolo, the northern city gate. One of Julius's successors, Paul III (1534–50), commissioned Michelangelo's redesign of the Capitoline Hill. Pius IV (1559–65) laid out a straight avenue, the Strada Pia (1561–62), for which Michelangelo designed the Porta Pia (see Fig. 11.43) as the terminating portal.

These interventions in Rome were accelerated and intensified during the five years and four months of the pontificate of Sixtus V. Public works were undertaken, including the building of twenty-seven new fountains and the provision of a reliable water supply through the repair of ancient aqueducts and the construction of a new one, and law and order were restored to the city. The wool and silk industries were revived, further increasing employment opportunities. Had Sixtus lived another year, the Colosseum might have been refurbished into a wool-spinning establishment!

The people who most benefited from the changes wrought by Sixtus were pilgrims coming to see the major Christian shrines. Recognizing that these religious visitors were important to the city's economy, Sixtus planned to link Rome's seven Early Christian basilicas with direct processional routes, punctuated by vertical elements and fountains to mark major points along the way (Fig. 12.3). This was a much larger realization of ideas first developed in sixteenth-century gardens, such as the Boboli Gardens in Florence. Given the irregular topography of the city, it would be no easy task to superimpose a paper plan of straight roads on the terrain. The reworking of the city proposed by Sixtus was so convincing, however, that nearly all architects, planners, and civic authorities who have continued the work in the following centuries have done so in accordance with his scheme.

Sixtus began with the construction of a new street, the Strada Felice, which extended from S. Maria Maggiore to S. Croce in Gerusalemme in one direction and in the other direction to SS. Trinità dei Monti on the Esquiline Hill. The initial intention was to continue this street on to the Porta del Popolo, the major entry point for those arriving from the north, but the intervening hills prevented this idea being realized. As a related project, the Piazza del Popolo was later redesigned (see pages 354–55) to provide an appropriate entranceway for pilgrims. After passing through the gate, visitors entered a space that focused on a central obelisk. Radiating from this center were the three straight streets added by Julius II, which provided direct access to major districts of the city. From the Piazza del Popolo, the

left radial street, the Strada del Babuino, led to a fountain at the base of the Esquiline Hill on which sits the church of the Trinità dei Monti. Sixtus dedicated the church in 1585, and a stair linking the church and the fountain below was built over a century later (see pages 354–55).

St. Peter's

The most important Christian monument in Rome was the Basilica of St. Peter, located across the Tiber from the older parts of the city. During Sixtus's reign, work was resumed on the construction of the dome after twenty-five years of relative inaction following the death of Michelangelo. Sixtus also turned his attention to the route linking St. Peter's to the rest of Rome. Pilgrims crossed the Tiber on the Ponte Sant'Angelo, at the end of which was the massive Castel Sant'Angelo. The route to St. Peter's continued to the west, but the direct link projected by Sixtus did not become a reality until the 1930s, when the Fascist

12.3 Sixtus V's plan for Rome, 1585–90.
With S. Maria Maggiore at the center, Pope Sixtus V developed axial connections to the city's seven principal churches. With this plan, the Renaissance concept of static, self-contained spaces gave way to the Baroque concept of dynamic axial connections between important urban points.

dictator Benito Mussolini pushed through the Via della Concilazione to provide a majestic axial approach to the great church. From a distance one can clearly see the dome of St. Peter's rising above the nave and wide façade, although Michelangelo's dome, designed for a naveless church, gradually recedes from view as one comes closer to the building.

In the center of what is now the Piazza of St. Peter's is Sixtus's contribution to the shaping of the space in the front of the basilica, the eighty-three-foot-tall Vatican Obelisk, which was installed there in 1586. Technical direction for this monumental feat of engineering was provided by Domenico Fontana, who later wrote a book describing and illustrating the entire process. The Vatican Obelisk was the largest intact specimen of the dozen Egyptian obelisks moved to Rome during the empire. How the ancient Romans maneuvered these monoliths into place is unknown, but the presence of several broken ones indicates that their methods were not always successful. Fontana's task was to lower the 681,221-pound obelisk from its position in the former Circus of Nero and move it about 260 yards to its new location in the Piazza of St. Peter's, all without damaging the shaft or its carvings. His solution to the problem involved encasing the obelisk in a protective timber framework, transferring it to a horizontal position by means of ropes and pulleys, which were controlled by the coordinated action of men and horses working thirty-eight windlasses, and then moving it over rollers to the new site. An elevation drop of approximately thirty feet between the old and new sites facilitated the horizontal transport. Once in the piazza, the obelisk was moved down an inclined plane and reerected using the same hoists and capstans employed to lower it. The whole operation was carefully planned and supervised by Fontana, who was empowered by the pope to appropriate men, materials, and horses as necessary for the completion of the work. As the obelisk was raised in front of St. Peter's on April 29, 1586, the entire College of Cardinals along with the citizenry of Rome turned out to watch the spectacle. Barricades kept the curious at a safe distance, and absolute silence was enforced during the critical lifting stages so that the workmen could hear and respond correctly to Fontana's signals, given by a trumpet and a bell.

Following his successful removal of the Vatican Obelisk, Fontana was commissioned to relocate three smaller obelisks in Rome. Those standing today in the Piazza del Popolo, at S. Giovanni in Laterano, and at the apse of S. Maria Maggiore were all positioned by Fontana. The pyramidal points of these great shafts are prominent landmarks indicating the important surrounding monuments in the city. Sixtus V's work in Rome doubtless had a major influence on Pierre L'Enfant's late eighteenth-century plan for Washington, D.C., Baron Eugène Georges Haussmann's cutting-through of boulevards in Paris in the mid-nineteenth, and even on the twentieth-century city planner Edmund Bacon, who was responsible for major

redevelopment work in Philadelphia in the 1950s and '60s. Bacon's use of axial avenues to link major areas of the city and not obelisks but high-rise buildings to mark different areas shows the continuing impact of city planning in Baroque Rome.

GIANLORENZO BERNINI
The Completion of St. Peter's

After the death of Sixtus V, work continued on St. Peter's; this project, so long in preparation by a series of architects whose abilities, styles, and philosophies varied considerably, was at last brought to completion during the Baroque period. The dome was finished in 1612 under the direction of architect Giacomo della Porta and engineer Domenico Fontana, and the nave addition, not envisioned by Michelangelo, was made by Carlo Maderno, who also designed the main façade (Figs. 12.4–12.6). The nave shifts orientation imperceptibly to align with the Vatican Obelisk, which Fontana had accidentally set off-center; Maderno considered it easier to turn the nave than to move the Egyptian needle. The largest church in Christendom was finally consecrated in 1626.

Urban VIII's favorite artist was Gianlorenzo Bernini (1598–1680), a man who might easily be compared with Michelangelo. Both were recognized as prodigies at an early age; both had long and productive lives; and both were immensely inventive sculptors who also did important work in architecture and city planning. Bernini was the son of a sculptor, and his artistic education had been directed in part by Urban VIII, a noted patron of the arts even before he was elected to papal office. The vigorous building programs of the Catholic Church in the seventeenth century were responsible for the development of the Baroque style, and for over fifty years Baroque work in Rome was dominated by Bernini.

Nowhere is his presence felt more strongly than at St. Peter's, where he served as official architect from 1629 until his death. Much of the present interior's character is the result of Bernini's genius. Either directly or through workshops under his supervision, Bernini was responsible for the flooring in the nave and narthex, for the decoration of the nave piers, and for the design of four sculptural groupings for altars and tombs. His designs for the crossing and main apse of the church, however, are the most substantial contributions he made to the interior. To reduce the scale of the vast space under Michelangelo's dome, Bernini designed the bronze Baldacchino (1624–33), a symbolic protective canopy over the high altar above the tomb of St. Peter. To match the scale of the rotunda, the Baldacchino is nearly ninety feet high; its twisted columns are not a Baroque invention, but a greatly enlarged version of marble columns from the Constantinian basilica, some of which are preserved as part of the reliquaries at the second-floor level of the crossing piers. It was believed

12.4 (above) St. Peter's, Rome, 1546–64, 1606–12.
Maderno's façade stretches the full width of the church. The small cupolas were the work of Vignola. The dome was planned by Michelangelo and refined by Giacomo della Porta. Bernini added the colonnade that creates the trapezoidal and oval piazzas.

that the original twisted columns were brought by Constantine from the Temple of Solomon in Jerusalem, so their continued use here links St. Peter's with the Holy Land. Material for the Baldacchino was obtained by melting down the Roman bronze supports of the Pantheon's portico, a reuse of historic material sanctioned by the pope over popular opposition; there was even enough metal left over to cast eighty cannons for defense of the city. In the

12.5 (left) Michelangelo Buonarroti and Carlo Maderno, Plan of the completed St. Peter's, Rome, 1546–64, 1606–12.
The extension of the nave after Michelangelo's death documents the clergy's determination to replace the architect-preferred central plan with a Latin-cross conducive to the processional and handling large crowds.

12.6 (above) Longitudinal section through St. Peter's, 1546–64, 1606–12.
Viewing this section, one would hardly suspect that Bramante and Michelangelo intended this church to be the greatest of the Renaissance central plans. However, the architects did succeed in recreating the scale and grandeur of ancient Rome.

12.7 Gianlorenzo Bernini, Site plan of St. Peter's complex and part of the Vatican, Rome, 1748.
In this site plan the southern extremity of Bramante's Belvedere Court is visible to the right. The final plan for the church still carries the imprint of its central-plan origins. The quarter east of the piazza (bottom of the site plan) is shown densely populated, as it was before Mussolini cleared it to provide open space all the way to the Tiber.

Labels on plan: St. Peter's · Scala Regia · Sistine Chapel · Belvedere Court · Piazza Retta · Obelisk · Piazza Obliqua

Holy Spirit. The church of St. Peter's, unlike some Early Christian buildings, is not aligned with its apse to the east but rather to the west, so the rays of the afternoon sun pass through the window and merge with the golden radiance of the sculpture surrounding the chair. By incorporating a window behind the work to provide brilliance for the ensemble, Bernini's design admirably illustrates the theatricality of the Baroque.

As the greatest church in Western Christendom, St. Peter's required an appropriate approach and exterior setting, and Bernini was also commissioned to undertake this work. In 1637 he proposed that two belltowers be constructed at the ends of the narthex in order to counter the horizontal emphasis of Maderno's façade. Only the southernmost tower had been partially built when soil subsidence and subsequent cracking of the structure necessitated removal of the campanile in 1645, almost ending Bernini's architectural appointment in disgrace. In 1657, however, Bernini designed the Piazza of St. Peter's, one of the most famous urban spaces in the world (Fig. 12.7). Composed of two parts, the piazza has an oval section, the Piazza Obliqua, which focuses on the Vatican Obelisk, followed by a trapezoidal section, the Piazza Retta, directly in front of the church entrance. Both sections work together to provide a symbolic embrace for Christians who come to visit the tomb of St. Peter. The Piazza Retta attempts in two ways to ameliorate the proportions of the façade by increasing the apparent height of the church. Its trapezoidal shape, which is perceived as a rectangle, "squeezes" the façade to emphasize verticality, and the flanking colonnade diminishes in height as it extends toward the church, thereby providing a smaller unit to which the engaged Corinthian columns of the façade are compared. Although the converging sides of the Piazza Retta may suggest influence from Michelangelo's Piazza del Campidoglio, the form was probably generated by the oblique placement of the Vatican Palace relative to the narthex of the church.

The Piazza Obliqua is more characteristically Baroque, with curving arms that do not form a true oval but are actually two semicircles connected to a square. Two symmetrically placed fountains and the obelisk establish a cross-axis to the approach to St. Peter's, thus introducing an element of tension into the design. The piazza's sides are formed by freestanding Tuscan-order colonnades, thirty-nine feet high and four columns deep, arranged in radial lines to provide a constantly shifting pattern of light and shadow as one moves around the edge. The colonnades generate a sense of enclosure without confinement; the space is defined without being cut off from the fabric of the city. Over 250,000 people can gather in the Piazza of St. Peter's to be blessed from the Benediction Loggia above the central entrance to the church or from a window in the papal apartments, at the right of the piazza. Through its dignified and all-encompassing design, the Piazza of St. Peter's extends the Church's welcome beyond the boundaries of the basilica itself.

enormous space of the basilica, the Baldacchino distinctly marks the spiritual center of the church, which would otherwise appear insignificant. So large is the interior that the Baldacchino's height, equivalent to a nine-story building, is not overpowering from a distance.

In the angles of the crossing piers Bernini's design placed four dramatic statues of saints associated with the Passion of Christ, all more than twice lifesize. Of these, Bernini himself carved the statue of St. Longinus (1629–38), the Roman centurion who pierced Christ's side at the Crucifixion; Longinus is shown at the moment he realizes Christ's divinity. Beyond the Baldacchino, and framed on axis by its columns, is Bernini's culminating work in the basilica, the Cathedra Petri, or Chair of Peter (1657–66), an elaborate reliquary in bronze constructed around the reputed wooden seat of the first apostle. Lightly supported by four figures representing Doctors of the Church, those men who established the doctrine of the faith, the chair floats above the visitor's head against a glorious backdrop where golden rays emanate from a brightly illuminated stained-glass center on which rises the dove of the

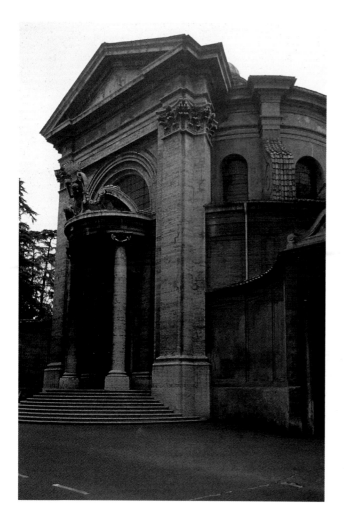

S. Andrea al Quirinale, Rome

Bernini also designed the small oval-plan church of S. Andrea al Quirinale (1658–70) as a quiet retreat for Jesuit novices (Figs. 12.8–12.9). The shape of the interior space is clearly expressed by the convex body of the church. To each side, countercurves turn into concave enveloping arms that connect the building to the street. Entry is made between giant-order Corinthian pilasters supporting a pediment; within this frame a thermal window allows light into the interior and, as though folded down from it, a convex curving portico is supported by Ionic columns. Around the exterior walls at the upper level, scroll-like buttresses stabilize the dome.

The entrance and altar lie opposite one another across the short axis of the oval plan. To maintain emphasis on the altar and establish the short axis as the dominant one, Bernini placed pilasters, not chapels, on the cross-axis, forcing the visitor's attention back to the origin point of the dramatic action. The architectural space around and above provides the setting for what would today be called a multimedia experience, as Bernini combined painting, sculpture, stuccowork, and lighting effects to dramatize the martyrdom and apotheosis of St. Andrew. First, a painted image of the future saint hangs above the altar, lit by a hidden, secondary dome with lantern. Around the painting, sculpted angels and putti, or figures of unclothed, chubby infants, levitate among gilded light rays. Above, a sculpted figure of St. Andrew rises through the broken pediment that defines the altar, accompanied around the base of the dome by more sculpted putti and fishermen representing the profession from which the saint was drawn. The coffered dome includes ten ribs, diminishing in width as they rise to visually support the base of the lantern. Here, an audience of still more putti awaits St. Andrew's admittance into heaven, represented by the glow from the principal lantern. All in all, it is a tour de force of Counter-Reformation theatricality.

FRANCESCO BORROMINI

While the completion of the interiors of the basilica and construction of the Piazza of St. Peter's were to occupy a substantial portion of Bernini's time, these were not by any means the only projects undertaken by this enormously gifted and energetic artist. Nor did he accomplish the work on St. Peter's singlehandedly. He had assistants, some of whom became prominent designers in their

12.8 (above) Gianlorenzo Bernini, S. Andrea al Quirinale, Rome, 1658–70.
A reflection of Counter-Reformation policies, S. Andrea has flanking walls that reach out as if to embrace passers-by. Its huge frontispiece is an essay in semicircular geometries: thermal window, portico roof, and entry stairs.

12.9 Gianlorenzo Bernini, Plan of S. Andrea al Quirinale, Rome, 1658–70.
Bernini chose to place the altar along the short axis of the oval. He also chose to terminate the cross-axis with pilasters rather than chapels. Both were unorthodox, tension-creating choices in the mid-seventeenth century.

12.10 Francesco Borromini, S. Carlo alle Quattro Fontane, Rome, begun 1634.
The theme of the façade is set by the figure of St. Charles Borromeo above the doorway, his eyes uplifted and his hands positioned as if in prayer. This vertical motion extends to the attenuated, superimposed columns and even the oval plaque at the scalloped pediment.

12.11 Francesco Borromini, Plan of S. Carlo alle Quattro Fontane, Rome, begun 1634.
The intensity of Borromini's organizational skills can be read in the dual ordering of the church and the cloister. In each, the theme is sets of paired columns. In the cloister, six sets are freestanding; in the church eight sets are pressed into the undulating surrounding wall.

own right. This was the case with Francesco Borromini (1599–1667), who began his career as a stonecutter in his uncle Carlo Maderno's shop and rose quickly to become a master mason and Bernini's collaborator on the St. Peter's Baldacchino. After a time these two men of strong personalities clashed; before 1630 Borromini had emerged as Bernini's rival. Of his many commissions around Rome, two are of particular interest as demonstrations of Borromini's strikingly original approach to design.

S. Carlo alle Quattro Fontane, Rome

Projects for the monastery and church of S. Carlo alle Quattro Fontane (dedicated to St. Charles Borromeo and also called S. Carlino or Little S. Carlo) involved Borromini on and off from 1634 until his death. He began with renovations to the monks' living quarters, including a

new refectory and cloister (1634–38), a courtyard in which bulging panels above pairs of columns replaced the customary corners.

In 1638 he designed the diminutive but highly innovative church (Fig. 12.10) at the corner of the Strada Felice and the Strada Pia (today known as the Via Quattro Fontane), one of Sixtus V's grand routes linking districts of the city. He embellished the intersection with four fountains set diagonally across from each corner, hence the descriptive words "Quattro Fontane" appended to the name of the church. The church plan consists of an undulating oval, its long axis leading to the main altar (Fig. 12.11). The curving side walls swell outward on the short axis to form shallow side chapels in a counterpoint evoking the spirit of a stretched Greek-cross plan. Borromini's own drawings show that he conceived his complex plan by interlocking a series of geometric figures from circles to

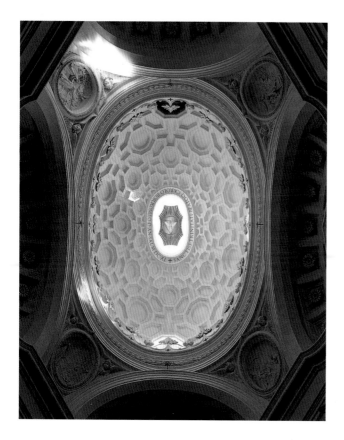

12.12 Francesco Borromini, S. Carlo alle Quattro Fontane, Rome, begun 1634.
At the inside surface, or intrados, of the dome, Borromini introduced a pattern of octagons, hexagons, and trinitarian crosses. These figures diminish in size as they move upward, creating an exaggerated perspective.

12.13 Francesco Borromini, S. Ivo della Sapienza, Rome, begun 1642.
The first two levels of the courtyard were planned by Pirro Ligorio and Giacomo della Porta. Borromini accepted the extant structure as the base for his unorthodox drum with its exotic cupola crowned by a spiral.

equilateral triangles, and he based his proportions in section on more equilateral triangles. This reliance on geometry rather than Renaissance arithmetical ratios reflects Borromini's immersion in the more strongly Gothic design and construction practices around Milan where his father had been a builder. Columns at S. Carlo's lower level appear to have been pressed into the surrounding walls. Pendentives above the entablature reduce the undulating plan to an oval drum supporting an oval dome, elaborately coffered with octagons, hexagons, and Trinitarian crosses, diminishing to an oval oculus (Fig. 12.12).

The principal façade, constructed in 1665–67, mirrors the internal play of concave and convex, swinging in and out over its three-bay width with its two stories separated by an intermediate oscillating entablature. A figure of St. Charles Borromeo with praying hands and eyes uplifted sets the façade's vertical theme, and angels, their wings contorted to form a pediment, shelter the saint and anticipate the almost bizarre character of the interior. This verticality is terminated by a crowning balustrade broken by a large oval **medallion**. With consummate skill Borromini incorporated one fountain and its mitered corner into the façade design, so that all parts project the dynamism of the Baroque.

S. Ivo della Sapienza

At S. Ivo della Sapienza (Fig. 12.13) Borromini created an archetypal masterpiece of the Baroque. The building consists of a chapel inserted behind the curved end of an existing two-story courtyard at the Archiginnasio, a college popularly known as La Sapienza and now part of the University of Rome. Giacomo della Porta had designed the façade inside the curve, which necessarily became the visual base for Borromini's dome when viewed from the entry to the courtyard. Borromini proposed alterations to della Porta's façade, but none of them was carried out.

Pope Leo X donated the site, but the chapel was not begun until 1642 under the patronage of Urban VIII. Urban's coat of arms incorporates bees symbolic of his own family, the Barberini, and Urban was affectionately known as the "King of Bees." Therefore, it is not surprising that Borromini, who had waited ten years for the commission, flattered his patron by incorporating the shape of a flying bee into the form of the plan, which is geometrized as a hexagon (Fig. 12.14a) by the intersection of two

12.14a (left) Francesco Borromini, Plan with reflected ceiling plan of S. Ivo della Sapienza, Rome, 1642–50.
Borromini made use of two interlocking equilateral triangles as a conceptual structure for his complex plan. The reflected ceiling plan reveals the facets of his "pumpkin" vault, similar in spirit to those apparently used by the emperor Hadrian at his villa in Tivoli near Rome.

12.14b (below left) Francesco Borromini, Transverse section through S. Ivo della Sapienza, Rome, 1642–50.
This section reveals Borromini's unconventional layering. Atop the pilasters sits the faceted entablature. Springing from this entablature are the ribs, folded against one another and diminishing in width as they rise.

12.15 (below) Francesco Borromini, S. Ivo della Sapienza dome, Rome, 1642–50.
With obvious similarity to Gothic ribbed vaults, the dome contains symbols of the Barberini family, the building's patrons.

equilateral triangles that also create a six-pointed star. The internal entablature between the lower level of the church and the dome does not separate the two areas in a conventional fashion. Rather, the concave–convex rhythms of the plan rise in planes through the bent and folded entablature into the ribs of the six-lobed dome (Figs. 12.14b, 12.15). Externally, the bulging walls and stepped cap of Borromini's dome support an exotic lantern tower that spirals upward in a form that allows multiple associations: that of the papal tiara, which contains bands of a triple crown, merged into a continuous spiral, symbolizing the pope's authority in priestly, royal, and imperial affairs; that of a conch shell, one species of which was generally known as the *corona papale* because of its resemblance to the papal tiara; and that of Divine Wisdom, which complemented the symbolism of an upwardly rising spiral. In fact, the iconography of the whole chapel expresses the idea that "all wisdom is from the Lord God" and that "fear of the Lord is the beginning of wisdom" (Ecclesiasticus 1:1).

URBAN OPEN SPACES IN BAROQUE ROME

With a few notable exceptions, urban design is a shared undertaking, occurring across several generations. The bold strokes of Sixtus V's plan for Rome created opportunities for later architects to complete his grand scheme with designs for churches, fountains, and piazzas to enrich civic life. For example, Fontana's placement of the Vatican Obelisk preceded and was therefore not part of Bernini's overall design for the piazza, but its position in front of St. Peter's identified the area as one of major importance within the city and contributed to Bernini's specific spatial conception of it as realized in 1657. The collaboration of talented designers in Rome on various urban projects has endowed the city with many handsome public spaces; three particularly fine Baroque ones will be discussed here.

The Piazza Navona

Bernini and Borromini jointly created the urban design of the Piazza Navona, an unusually proportioned space (177 by 906 feet) that was once the Stadium of Domitian (Fig. 12.16). In the medieval period houses were built on the ruins of the grandstands, while the open center was used for informal games and a market. Pope Innocent X's palace faced the square, and on his election in 1644 he undertook the refurbishing of the piazza and its church, S. Agnese in Agone (Fig. 12.17). The church commission was first given to Girolamo and Carlo Rainaldi, but their designs displeased Innocent, and in 1653, with the foundations already in place, Borromini assumed control of the building process. He retained their Greek-cross plan but pulled back the flight of steps protruding into the narrow square and provided a new concave façade, above which rose a

12.16 Gianlorenzo Bernini and Francesco Borromini, Piazza Navona, Rome, begun 1644.
Piazza Navona's outline results from its origins as an ancient Roman circus or racetrack. Around it are the narrow irregular streets of Rome's medieval core. S. Agnese in Agone is #608; S. Maria della Pace is #599; and S. Ivo della Sapienza is #800.

high drum, elongated dome, and slender cupola. After 1657 and the death of Innocent X, Carlo Rainaldi returned to complete the work, adding the twin towers positioned on either side of the curved façade. In its massing S. Agnese represents the silhouette that St. Peter's might have had without the nave addition.

Bernini, temporarily out of favor for political reasons and because of the failure of the towers at St. Peter's, was not considered as a possible architect for S. Agnese, yet his proposal for the central fountain in Piazza Navona so pleased Innocent that the pope set aside personal animosities and awarded Bernini the fountain commission. The Fountain of the Four Rivers (1648–51), located in the center of the piazza but off the main axis of S. Agnese so as not to compete with it, has symbolic figures set amid splashing water and representing the major rivers of the continents to which Catholicism had spread. The Ganges figure holds an oar because of that river's great navigable length; the Danube looks toward emblems of Innocent X; the Nile's face is obscured because its origin was then unknown; and the Rio della Plata figure is a highly imaginative evocation of a native South American, bald, bearded, and surrounded

12.17 Carlo Rainaldi and Francesco Borromini, S. Agnese in Agone, Rome, begun 1644.
Borromini chose to place the dome close to the façade so it could be seen between flanking towers. It is the same scheme intended by Bernini at St. Peter's before his towers became unstable.

by coins to reflect the wealth of the New World. The figures support a central obelisk, crowned with a representation of the dove of the influential Pamphili family symbolizing the triumph of Christianity over paganism, and, by extension, Catholicism over Protestantism. Thus, in Baroque hands, even so secular an item as a public fountain became an allegory for the Roman Catholic Church. At either end of the piazza are additional fountains; all three provide visual delight while refreshing the air with cooling moisture.

Just behind Piazza Navona is one of Rome's smallest squares, in front of the church of S. Maria della Pace, which is the work of Pietro da Cortona (1596–1669). The main church building dates to the fifteenth century; Cortona gave it a new convex façade in 1656–58 (Fig. 12.18), its

12.18 Pietro da Cortona, S. Maria della Pace, Rome, 1656–58.
Cortona's façade appears to have been bent and expanded from within. The flanking walls are analogous to stage wings and connect the church to existing buildings.

plasticity restrained by flanking Corinthian pilasters supporting a pediment. That pediment frames yet another pediment with a curved top cornice and a dropped lower one. Cortona improved access to the church by demolishing parts of surrounding buildings to create the tiny piazza. A semicircular portico with paired Tuscan columns protrudes into the square, and the portico's curve is answered by countercurving wing walls. The concave–convex interplay is subtle but effective in this diminutive Baroque stage setting.

The Piazza del Popolo and the Spanish Steps

The next Baroque square to be considered is the Piazza del Popolo. Fontana's placement of an obelisk at the point where its three radial streets converge (see Fig. 12.3) gave the space a monumental focus. In the mid-seventeenth century, Roman planners wanted to regularize this important gateway to Rome by placing identical domed churches on the trapezoidal sites created by the three streets. This posed a geometric dilemma, however, for the sites were of unequal width. Carlo Rainaldi, assisted by Bernini, solved the problem by giving one church, S. Maria dei Miracoli

12.19 Carlo Rainaldi and Gianlorenzo Bernini, S. Maria dei Miracoli and S. Maria in Montesanto, 1662–79.
As at St. Peter's, Pope Sixtus V had anticipated the development of a great piazza here by placing an Egyptian obelisk in the then formless terrain first seen by pilgrims arriving in the Eternal City from the north. The so-called twin churches were designed by Carlo Rainaldi.

(1675–79), a circular plan, and the other, S. Maria in Montesanto (1662–75), an oval plan to accommodate its narrower site. Viewed from the obelisk, the churches look identical because of their domes and porticoed façades, and their profiles enhance the dignity of the piazza (Fig. 12.19). In 1816–20, the architect Giuseppe Valadier carved out an oval volume for the piazza in imitation of Bernini's plan for the Piazza of St. Peter's and added a set of viewing terraces to the east leading up to the Borghese Gardens (Fig. 12.20). The terraces offer viewers the opportunity to appreciate the geometry of the oval plan from above.

Halfway down the Via del Babuino from the Piazza del Popolo is the point where the route to S. Maria Maggiore envisioned by Sixtus V sidesteps to connect with the Via Sistina at the top of the Pincio Hill (see Fig. 12.3). Topographic difficulties here required the route to make a steep ascent, which was imaginatively resolved by the Spanish Steps (1723–26), built by Francesco de Sanctis following designs made a decade earlier by Alessandro Specchi (Fig. 12.21). The project was underwritten by a wealthy Frenchman and constructed on land owned by the French church of the Trinità dei Monte; the steps were so named because the Spanish Embassy was nearby. From the fountain at its base, gentle curves and countercurves form a dramatic cascading stair that narrows and then divides before reaching an intermediate platform, beyond which the stairs again unite, only to split once more into opposing curves that ultimately ascend to the platform in front of the Trinità dei Monti, at the end of the Strada Felice. It is a popular and effective stage setting, inviting promenaders to

12.20 Giuseppe Valadier, Piazza del Popolo from the Pincio Hill, Rome, 1816–20.
While the former trapezoidal piazza can still be identified, it has been subsumed in Valadier's new oval, its long axis directed up the slope of the Pincio Hill. The steep hillside is made accessible by ramps and has been terraced into platforms serving as overlooks. The twin churches stand to the left in this view.

12.21 (below) Francesco de Sanctis and Alessandro Specchi, Spanish Steps, Rome, 1723–26.
If architecture can be "frozen music," as suggested in the Introduction to this text, then the Spanish Steps are an excellent example of the phenomenon. The principal elements are the steps with their landings, the obelisk, and the church of the Trinità dei Monte, built at separate times but deftly pulled together by Francesco de Sanctis and Alessandro Specchi in the eighteenth century.

Piazza Navona—A Space for Spectacle

by Julia M. Smyth-Pinney

12.22 Giovanni Paolo Pannini, *Piazza Navona Flooded*, 1756. Oil on canvas, 37 1/2 x 54 in (95.5 x 137 cm). Landesgalerie, Hanover.

T he year is 1756, and this is Piazza Navona, in the heart of Rome (Fig. 12.22). Already, the Baroque age is ending and the wonderful monuments of the piazza, created for the glorification of the Pamphili family's pope, Innocent X, are a hundred years old. Yet the setting designed by the greatest Roman Baroque architects at the height of their powers, reflected in the waters of the flooded square, recreates the spirit of Innocent's High Baroque papacy.

Innocent's renovated family palace is in the foreground on the left-hand side of the piazza; from the balconies he and his retinue could participate in the dramatic pageantry occurring in the "royal front yard." Among the pope's guests would have been visitors from many countries, diplomats representing the absolutist monarchs of expanding European nations, still competing for the Catholic pope's favor despite his declining power.

Life in Piazza Navona thus offered itself as a permanent theatrical event, managed by increasingly stringent rules of etiquette, supported by New World wealth, and dominated by open enjoyment of artifice and unusual entertainments. Whether it was a festive secular event planned to honor a visiting dignitary, or a sacred ceremonial occasion, sights and sounds, smells and tastes were organized to delight the senses and to sway hearts and minds. This silent and static painting captures the emotional excitement of the parade, and strives to suggest the shouts and splashes, the rich perfumes wafting along with the carriages, all continuously moving, animated by the bright sunlight striking silk and gilt and silver lamé, light refracting from the active surfaces of spouting, rippling water.

At nightfall, from the interiors of the palaces and churches, more solemn processions lit by tapers and torches flowed out into a Piazza Navona illuminated by bonfires and colored waxed paper lanterns. For ceremonies celebrating the election of Innocent to the papacy, the sober surface of the Renaissance church in the foreground on the right was the background for an enormous wooden, plaster, and canvas construction—Noah's ark on its mount—which later erupted with dazzling firework displays that delighted an audience of rich courtiers, pilgrims and paupers, shopkeepers and soldiers.

Events such as these proceeded with occasional hiatuses for the harsher realities of the years around 1650: debt-ridden papal finances, serious famines, plague outbreaks, and the terrible battles, both physical and intellectual, among Protestants and Catholics, Christian forces and "non-believers." Statues could sometimes still spout wine, not water. Does all this recall the excesses of ancient Rome? Certainly one of the aims of Baroque rulers was to impress their rivals and subjects, and the underlying classicism evident in the Baroque age arises from explicitly revivalist dreams of an idyllic classical "Golden Age." It is not surprising, then, that Rome was the site of the style's initiation.

Yet fierce inner devotion often animated individual Baroque lives, activating the outward drama of the exuberant public events. Innocent himself, for example, was pious and moderate in his personal habits, and the great sculptor and architect Bernini regularly practiced St. Ignatius Loyola's prescribed spiritual exercises. Combining private piety and public devotion, secular power united itself with religious organizations to demand excesses of scale and emotional effect. Innocent and his architects created the lasting grandeur of Rome's Piazza Navona, and the space has served the city's inhabitants and visitors magnificently ever since.

be both actors and audience, and the design brings enjoyment to the mundane task of climbing or descending by encouraging the pedestrian to linger and look.

THE SPREAD OF BAROQUE ARCHITECTURE TO NORTHERN ITALY

Guarino Guarini

Borromini's work, especially his design for S. Ivo della Sapienza, became the starting point for the work of Guarino Guarini (1624–83), an architect whose buildings in Turin represent the northern extension of Baroque Rome. Guarini was a member of the Theatine monastic order, and he served an eight-year novitiate in Rome from 1639 to 1647. His early work in Modena for the Theatines does not survive; political difficulties led to his expulsion from the city in 1655, and he was to spend the following decade in various places, including France and possibly Spain. On his return to Turin in 1666, he worked on two central-plan churches.

The Cappella della SS. Sindone, or Chapel of the Holy Shroud (Figs. 12.23a,b), was added to the east end of the cathedral of Turin to house the important relic of the Holy Shroud. Guarini received the commission in 1667, after another architect had begun construction on a circular plan, which Guarini was obliged to retain. By inscribing an equilateral triangle in the circle and redesigning the access

stairs and landing vestibules, Guarini brought mystery and dynamism to the unimaginative original scheme. The domed chapel pulsates with the countercurves introduced by the vestibules and an axial niche, and three pendentives touch tangentially the circle of the dome above, which is not really a dome at all but an ascending hexagonal network of arches diminishing to an interlaced-arch oculus topped by a spiraling lantern. Light filters into the upper zone through small windows set within the arch network and pours in from six large windows at the base of the dome.

For his own order Guarini designed S. Lorenzo (1668–80), based on an octagon defined by convex Serliana surfaces bulging into the main space, all set within a square and completed by an elliptical choir (Figs. 12.24a,b). The geometric complexity here is astonishing. Squares, octagons, a Greek cross, ovals, and circles are involved. Again the dome is not a solid vault but an openwork structure with eight interlacing elliptical ribs. The church is illuminated by oval, pentagonal, and circular openings set between the ribs and by scattered chambers that capture and modulate the light. Over the choir is a lower, six-pointed ribbed-star vault, which, like the main vault, is reminiscent of Islamic ribbed domes at the Great Mosque of Córdoba (see Figs. 7.10–7.11); possibly the mosque was known to Guarini from his travels. S. Lorenzo's dome, drum, and cupola mirror the play of concave and convex forms seen on the interior (Fig. 12.25). Further examples

12.23a Guarino Guarini, Plan and partial reflected ceiling plan of the Sindone Chapel, Turin, begun 1667. Guarini inherited the plan, but the reflected ceiling plan reveals his innovations: a telescoping, layered vault of rotated polygons.

12.23b Guarino Guarini, Section through the Sindone Chapel, Turin, begun 1667. The drawing reveals the extraordinary organic quality of Guarini's dome construction. It is a dramatic change from the hemispherical domes of Brunelleschi.

12.24a (far left) Guarino Guarini, Transverse section through S. Lorenzo, Turin, 1668–80.
Guarini used a cantilevered vault at the first level and interlocking elliptical ribs at the dome. Most interesting perhaps are the many light modulators that form the transition from the exterior to the interior space.

12.24b (left) Guarino Guarini, Plan of S. Lorenzo, Turin, 1668–80.
This plan, with reflected ceiling plan, reveals the complex patterns of Guarini's vaults. The four pairs of rotunda columns provide a richness through the layering of architectural elements. However, their small diameters indicate that they are false structures, with the loads above being carried by the cantilever.

of ribbed domes on unbuilt projects appear in Guarini's *Architettura civile*, published posthumously in 1737.

THE BAROQUE IN CENTRAL EUROPE

While Guarini's influence continued in and around Turin, the artistic ideals of Baroque Italy were being spread to the north and east through Switzerland, Austria, southern Germany, and Bohemia. There Italian influences merged with local tastes and surviving craft-guild traditions to create a version of the Baroque distinctive to central Europe. As in Italy, the driving force was the Catholic Counter-Reformation, yet the style received support not only from Church officials, but also from princes and monarchs, who hoped to project a progressive image, and from the common people, for whom it reflected deeply held religious beliefs. In many respects Baroque churches in central Europe continued medieval themes, and architecture, sculpture, and painting advanced a single idea: the evocation of a heavenly realm. Number symbolism is prominent, as are the images of saints serving as intercessors between earth and heaven. Twin-towered west fronts are commonly found capped by bulbous domes rather than Gothic spires. The impression of lofty volume that is conveyed in the Gothic by soaring vaults is created in the central European Baroque by much lower plaster vaults on which paint and stucco have been expertly applied to create the illusion of an open sky filled with heavenly hosts. These Baroque churches are bright and airy; the windows are glazed with clear glass, and daylight is directed onto white interior surfaces embellished with gold and pastel hues.

The Baroque monuments of Italy were important sources for central Europe. Il Gesù in Rome was particularly influential because its design led to the development of the **Wandpfeiler** or **wall-pillar** that characterizes many central European Baroque churches. At Il Gesù the barrel-vaulted lateral chapels are separated from one another by cross walls faced at the nave with pilasters. North of the Alps, these cross walls became wall-pillars, which Baroque architects exploited for both structural stability and the shaping of internal space. Although the churches may retain side aisles, some even with galleries overhead, the wall-pillars were used as space-shaping elements to establish the concept of centrality within what were generally longitudinal plans. Thus, the interaction of axial and centralized plans, already seen in the oval designs of Borromini and Bernini, was continued in the Baroque of central Europe.

12.25 (opposite) Guarino Guarini, Intrados of the dome, S. Lorenzo, Turin, 1668–80.
The ribbed vaults of the Great Mosque at Córdoba, which Guarini may have seen during his travels, are often mentioned as his inspiration. The lantern appears to float above the ribs.

The life and work of Johann Bernhard Fischer von Erlach (1656–1723) exemplify one of the ways in which Italian ideas were transferred to central Europe. Fischer von Erlach came from an Austrian family of masons, and he was sent to Rome for training in the studio of Carlo Fontana. During the sixteen years he spent in Rome he became familiar with both ancient and contemporary works there, and these influences, combined with knowledge from travels across Europe, were later reflected in his own designs and in the illustrated *Entwurf einer historichen Architektur* (*Historic Architecture*), a precocious history of architecture that he published in 1721. Fischer von Erlach's architectural fortunes were tied to those of the Hapsburgs. He joined the imperial court at Vienna as architectural tutor to Joseph I in 1689, was raised to the nobility in 1696, and served as chief inspector of court buildings from 1705 until his death. During his lifetime, Austria experienced a surge of nationalistic pride after decisively repelling the Turkish attack on Vienna in 1683. Seeking to create an impressive international city that would rival Rome or Versailles, Viennese princes built Baroque palaces and raised new churches.

Fischer von Erlach's major contribution to Vienna was the Karlskirche (1716–25), a building that reflects his view that every work should be unique (Fig. 12.26). By borrowing from a wide range of historical sources, he created a highly original design that referred to many major buildings of the past. The church was dedicated to St. Charles Borromeo, the emperor's patron saint, and was built in fulfillment of a vow Charles VI made in 1713 during an outbreak of the plague. Its broad façade is dominated by a dome on a drum rising above a pedimented portico, flanked by columns in a manner recalling the front of S. Agnese in Agone, where the central dome is flanked by twin campaniles. Elements from historical buildings incorporated here include the columned portico from Roman temples such as the Pantheon; Trajan's Column from imperial Rome, repeated on both sides of the rotunda and adorned with scenes from the life of St. Charles Borromeo rather than reliefs of the Dacian Wars; the drum and dome from papal Rome; and an overall composition suggesting the dome and minarets of Hagia Sophia in Constantinople. The interior is impressive for its elongated oval nave (Figs. 12.27a,b), the ceiling of which is embellished with illusionistic frescoes depicting St. Charles Borromeo appealing to the Virgin Mary as intercessor for relief from the plague. Fischer von Erlach had seen the ceiling frescoes being installed at Il Gesù during his residence in Rome, so he used painting, rather than coffering or ribs as Bernini or Borromini would have done, to complete the dome's interior.

The rather severe and classical approach of Fischer von Erlach contrasts with the work of his contemporary, the Tyrolese architect Jacob Prandtauer (1660–1726), who was trained in Munich as a mason and practiced as an architect-sculptor. The works of Borromini and Guarini

12.26 Johann Bernhard Fischer von Erlach, Karlskirche, Vienna, 1716–25.
Fischer von Erlach possessed an early knowledge of classical architectural history, which he put to use here. The triumphal columns symbolically connect the Hapsburg Empire to Roman antiquity and the dome alludes to papal Rome.

12.27a Johann Bernhard Fischer von Erlach, Section through the Karlskirche, Vienna, 1716–25.
Compared to the plan and elevation, the section is tame. Cut along the central axis, however, it gives no hint of the cowboy-storefront quality of the façade.

12.27b Johann Bernhard Fischer von Erlach, Plan of the Karlskirche, Vienna, 1716–25.
It is hard to imagine a more unusual plan than this one. The attitude of its designer, who borrowed from numerous sources, anticipates the tide of eclecticism that would reach a high point in the late nineteenth century.

12.28 Jacob Prandtauer, Abbey church interior, Melk, 1702–14.
The oscillating walls and pillars create a dynamism in sharp contrast to the serene, modular interiors of a Renaissance building such as Brunelleschi's S. Lorenzo, Florence (see Fig. 11.6).

12.29 Christoph Dientzenhofer, St. Nicholas on the Lesser Side interior, Prague, 1703–11.
One of five architect brothers, Christoph Dientzenhofer designed this church using wall-pillars. Setting these pillars on the diagonal, he was able to support syncopated, three-dimensionally curving transverse arches that meet tangentially at the centers of the bays, producing dual spatial readings.

are reflected in his designs, but he was also influenced by Fischer von Erlach. A member of a religious brotherhood, Prandtauer was closely involved with his designs while they were under construction, and he is known primarily for monastic projects, including rebuilding the great abbey of Melk (1702–14), set dramatically atop a rocky ridge rising 200 feet above the Danube. The monastery's buildings are arranged in an elongated U-shape, with the church placed inside the U, its compressed cloister interrupting one long range of rooms. From the river below and the small courtyard that precedes the west front, the twin towers of the main façade dominate, while the drum and dome over the crossing are best seen from the major courtyard at the east end of the church. This is a wall-pillar church with galleries above the oval chapels instead of aisles; a longitudinal emphasis was unavoidable because of site restrictions, and Prandtauer emphasized verticality through fluted pilasters and a dome on pendentives that soars above the clouds and the swirling drapery of the figures in the ceiling frescoes (Fig. 12.28). The undulating cornice of the nave supports recessed arches around clerestory windows, causing the whole ceiling to appear as a floating world. The painted illusion of heavenly figures spilling out from the vaults above provides a dramatic link between earthly matters and the spiritual world.

In Switzerland, Bavaria, and Bohemia (now the Czech Republic), Baroque design was generally the province of families of architects, sculptors, and painters, in which fathers, sons, uncles, and nephews collaborated on building projects. For example, five Dientzenhofer brothers—Georg, Christoph, Leonhard, Johann, and Wolfgang—were active in Bohemia and southern Germany just before and after 1700, where they combined the free-swinging curves found in the works of Borromini and Guarini with Slavic and Gothic motifs; Christoph's son, Kilian Ignaz, also became an established designer. These families of master builders should not be thought of as rustics: a number of them were trained in major centers such as Turin, Vienna, and Prague, and they knew both the built and the unbuilt designs of leading Italian architects, even though they practiced architecture as guild members. Christoph Dientzenhofer (1655–1722) designed the church of St. Nicholas on the Lesser Side in Prague (1703–11) (Fig. 12.29) to have a longitudinal plan with deep wall-pillars set between chapels below and galleries above. The wall-pillars near the nave are splayed to support doubly curving arches. This configuration creates what has been called syncopation: a double reading of the spatial units as either a traditional bay system or a series of overlapping ovals.

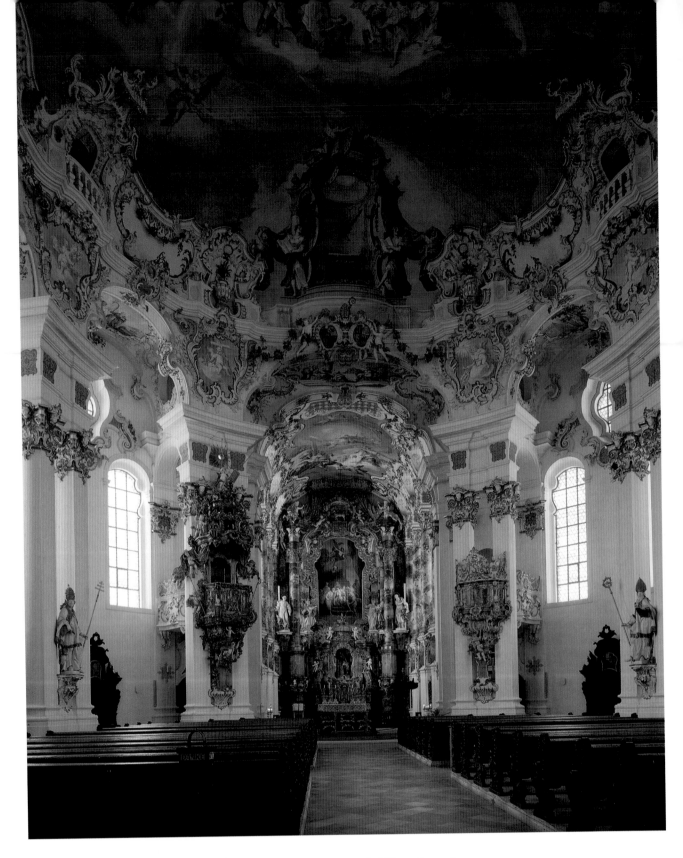

12.30 Dominikus Zimmerman, Die Wies interior, near Munich, 1746–54.
The fairly plain exterior walls and steep draping roof of this small church give little indication of the dramatic, illusory effects waiting on the interior. Die Wies attracted pilgrims who came to see an image of the Scourged Christ said to weep real tears.

Die Wies, Bavaria

An alternative strategy of spatial dematerialization was employed by Dominikus Zimmerman (1685–1766) at the church of Die Wies, or The Fields (1746–54) (Fig. 12.30), located in a meadow beneath the Bavarian Alps. Fusing hall church and oval schemes and creating an outer bearing-wall layer and an inner trabeated layer of coupled columns, Zimmerman supported a nearly flat wood-and-plaster vault on which his brother, Johann Baptist Zimmerman

(1680–1758), could create an expansive illusionistic fresco of Christ at the Last Judgment. Applied to a background of white plaster dematerialized by brilliant light from large, surrounding windows, paintings, areas of pastel and gold colors, organic stucco ornament, and cut-outs in the vault supports produce an apparently weightless visual unity from this abundance of elements and effects.

The collaboration of two other brothers can be seen in the abbey church of Einsiedeln (1719–35), where the design was begun by a lay brother of the monastery, Caspar Moosbrugger (1656–1723), and was finished after his death by his brother Johann Moosbrugger and others. Einsiedeln is still a major center of religious activity in Switzerland, and the monastery has an appropriately grand façade fronting a sloping plaza at the end of the town. In the center of the composition is the church, its great bowed front with twin towers projecting from the straight line of the flanking monastic buildings. This curved element directly reflects the principal feature of the interior, the shrine constructed on the site of the cell of St. Meinrad, who is venerated here. A great octagon completed by a dome surrounds the shrine, which thus occupies the first and largest bay of the nave. Wall-pillars pierced by aisles and galleries help define this space and form the transition to the smaller, circular domed bays of the nave.

The Asam brothers, painter Cosmas Damian (1686–1739) and sculptor Egid Quirin (1692–1750), were responsible

12.31 Johann Balthasar Neumann, Würzburg Residenz, begun 1720.
Here is the garden front of the palace, or Imperial Hall, reached by one of the great stairs of the period (see page 340).

for the wonderfully coordinated fresco- and stuccowork that graces the interior of the abbey church of Einsiedeln (1719–35). The narrower choir, built to the designs of Egid Quirin, is completed by an enormous altar and embellished with floating stucco figures that complement the ceiling frescoes above. The Asams tended to create pictorial rather than architectural space. With paint and stucco they transformed what appear to be rather commonplace plans and sections into an extraordinary confection of light, color, and illusionistic space. The nave ceilings combine paint and plaster to create a joyous expression of the Nativity, with angels perched on high cornices and putti floating down to earth bearing the good news.

Not all central European Baroque buildings were churches. As in Italy and France, the nobility wanted to display their importance by building great palaces, and the theatricality of the Baroque was well suited to providing them with an appropriate setting. Of these princely abodes, the grandest was the Würzburg Residenz (Fig. 12.31), begun in 1720 for the prince-bishops of the Schönborn family. Its architect was Johann Balthasar Neumann (1687–1753),

12.32 Johann Balthasar Neumann, Plan of Vierzehnheiligen, near Bamberg, begun 1744. This drawing shows the vaults above reflected onto the floor plan. Together, they illustrate how, within the cruciform plan, Neumann interlocked highly ornamental oval and circular bays by inserting spherical triangles at their intersections.

12.33 Johann Balthasar Neumann, Vault detail Vierzehnheiligen, near Bamberg, begun 1744. A spherical triangle is created by tracing a triangle onto a spherical surface. Here, craftsmen overlaid these curving surfaces with organic plaster ornamentation.

generally regarded as the greatest master of the German Baroque. Neumann was trained in mathematics, engineering, and architecture. He served the Schönborns as an artilleryman, civil engineer, and military engineer, before being encouraged to devote his designing talents and engineering dexterity to the creation of architectural spaces. The enormous Residenz was symmetrically disposed around a deep entrance court, with four interior courts providing light and air to the side wings. Neumann's plans for the palace were scrutinized by leading architects in Paris and Vienna before construction began and as the work proceeded; such oversight and changes in the prince-bishops resulted in a twenty-three-year construction period, with an additional five years required to complete the interior decorations. Neumann's masterpiece within this complex was the sequence of major reception rooms, beginning with the low vestibule, made large enough for a coach to turn

around in the column-free space, and extending through the majestic Stair Hall to the White and Imperial Halls on the second floor.

It is the lofty Stair Hall that most clearly exhibits the architect's technical skill (page 340). At nearly 100 by 60 feet, the hall is the largest single room in the palace, and it is roofed by a clear-span stone vault. The centrally placed stair rises in a single flight to a landing, where it reverses direction and divides before extending to the upper floor— a so-called **imperial stair**. A balcony placed around the staircase allows onlookers a view of the processional space. The ceiling is enriched by the world's largest fresco, executed by Giovanni Battista Tiepolo and celebrating the sun god Apollo and the prince-bishops as patrons of the arts. Representations of the seasons, the zodiac, Europe, Asia, Africa, and America are assembled at the perimeter, the figures gazing into the clouds opening up in the heavens or staring down at those ascending the stair. Among the individuals depicted on the parapet are Tiepolo, the stucco artist Antonio Bossi, and Neumann himself, seated with his dog among items of artillery and taking a well-earned rest. Statues on the balustrades and stucco **cartouches**, swags, and putti above the door and window surrounds harmonize with the allegorical host overhead. Further delights of stucco and fresco await in the subtle shades of the White Hall, which serves as a foil for the Imperial Hall, the most important room in the palace. Its elongated-octagon plan rises to a high oval, vaulted ceiling filled with Tiepolo's allegorical frescoes, alluding to historical scenes of the Holy Roman Empire and peopled with contemporary members of the Würzburg court.

Neumann was also a designer of churches, the most celebrated of which was the pilgrimage church of Vierzehnheiligen (begun 1744), outside Bamberg. Vierzehnheiligen commemorates the hilltop on which a shepherd boy in 1445 had an apparition of the Fourteen *Nothelfer* (a sort of heavenly witness, or guardian angel) for whom the church was named. A previous chapel on the site had become inadequate, and jurisdictional conflicts between the prince-bishop of Bamberg and the Cistercian abbot whose monastery was financing the work led to confusion over Neumann's appointment as architect. Construction was finally begun in 1744, but the foundations were laid too far to the east by the supervising architect, who also made design changes of which Neumann did not approve. Neumann redesigned the church, producing a scheme that is remarkable for the way its basically basilican ground plan is transformed into a composition of Baroque circles and ovals (Fig. 12.32). The freestanding altar of the fourteen saints occupies a central position in the nave, while the transepts become circles and the apse is defined as an oval. Neumann manipulated the interior space by arranging the aisle piers freely, both to support the oval vaults overhead and to form screens obscuring direct vision of windows in the side wall, thus combining the drama of light from unseen sources with swirling, curving forms (Fig. 12.33). He used delicate pastel colors, accented with gold, on marble piers and ceiling frescoes to emphasize the airy volumes of the interior. The warm sandstone exterior is grand but restrained, and the twin towers of the entrance front respond to the axis established by the Baroque abbey of Banz on a hill across the valley.

This discussion of major Baroque monuments should not obscure the fact that the Baroque became an almost vernacular style for churches in the countryside of southern Germany, Switzerland, Austria, the Czech Republic, and Poland, much as medieval styles characterize the French and English landscape. Existing churches were remodeled and new ones were built in the Baroque style; their distinctive reverse-curve domed towers still dot the rural districts. The Baroque even had an impact in Russia, where St. Petersburg was laid out early in the eighteenth century by French and Italian architects.

THE BAROQUE IN FRANCE

The ideas of the Italian Baroque were transferred, although not without modifications, to France. By the mid-seventeenth century, as Louis XIV was coming into his majority, Renaissance-inspired classicism was sufficiently well established in France to mute the most elaborate excesses of the Roman Baroque. French official patronage of the period was more than ever centered on the royal court, and the propaganda of the Catholic Counter-Reformation was not an important issue. The official court style glorified the monarch, and the primary function of the state-run artistic establishment was to provide splendid settings, furnishings, and objects for the display of royal power. In pursuit of this objective, French architects built impressively elaborate works on a scale seldom seen, and the manners, costumes, and style of the French court became the model for other European capitals.

The Louvre, Paris

Several building projects exemplify this process. In Paris the rebuilding of the Louvre, begun over a century earlier with the interior court wing by Lescot, was still not complete. First Lemercier and then Louis Le Vau (1612–70) worked on the interior elevations of the square court. During the 1660s a number of architects, including four Italians, were invited to submit designs for the east façade. Bernini, the leading European architect, sent a design proposing a central oval pavilion terminated by end pavilions, the whole composed of giant engaged columns and colonnades better suited to the bright sun of Italy than to the overcast skies of northern Europe. After hearing French objections to the scheme, Bernini sent a second proposal, this time with a concave plan, but Louis XIV and his ministers were still not satisfied. At the insistence of the king, Bernini came to Paris for six months in 1665 to consult directly on the Louvre design, in spite of opposition from French architects who hoped to receive the commission themselves. While in Paris, Bernini prepared a third proposal, not just for the east wing but for the entire palace. In this plan, the original square court was completely shielded by open loggias with blocky staircases protruding at the corners. The exterior façades were no longer curved but articulated by giant engaged columns on the central pavilion and pilasters on the end pavilions; the ground floor was treated as a rusticated base for the giant orders above.

Perhaps because Bernini failed to reflect French taste in his designs, Louis decided not to adopt any of these schemes. Instead he gave the commission to a trio consisting of the architect Le Vau, the painter Charles Lebrun (1619–90), and a doctor of medicine, Claude Perrault (1613–88). While the exact contributions of each remain unclear, these three men were responsible for the present-day east façade (1667–70), composed of a colonnade of paired Corinthian columns with central and end pavilions,

12.34 Louis Le Vau, Charles Lebrun, and Claude Perrault, East façade of the Louvre, Paris, 1667–70.
The paired columns symbolize the monarchy. The façade composition is distinctly French: end pavilions, central pedimented unit, and connecting stoalike wings.

all set atop a rusticated ground story (Fig. 12.34). This use of paired columns links the work to Baroque precedent, although the design is far more restrained than contemporary architecture in Italy. In contrast to earlier French Renaissance works, the roof of the east façade is hidden by a balustraded parapet, reinforcing the horizontal emphasis of the whole elevation.

The austerity of the east façade, with its central pediment, end pavilions, and paired columns carrying a continuous architrave, is often associated with Perrault's ideas about architecture. He edited a well-received French edition of Vitruvius in 1673, in which he illustrated the grave monumentality of the trabeated Roman work of the republic. In 1683, he produced a controversial treatise on the orders in which he argued that their proportions were not absolute but were best determined by a discerning eye. This attitude of relativism had profound implications for the development of subsequent architectural theory, including twentieth-century Modernism.

François Mansart

François Mansart (1598–1666) is as well known for his difficult disposition as for his design genius. Trained by his master-carpenter father, Mansart was "arrogant, touchy, and unpopular," and perhaps corrupt. His inclination to work and rework projects almost endlessly caused him to lose control over many of them before completion. While owing much to the continuing importation of both High Renaissance and Mannerist forms from Italy, he produced work that was chauvinistic in its emphasis on openwork structure, a continuation of French Gothic traditions, and on stereotomy—the art of precise stone masonry. Regarding the latter, his buildings exhibit a precision of detail and conviction of composition that give them a "severe richness" achieved by few others.

Mansart's Ste. Marie de la Visitation in Paris (1632), built for a group of nuns who served the sick and needy outside their convent, demonstrates his interpretation of the central-church scheme, a radical innovation in France at the time. He took his plan (Fig. 12.35) through a number of iterations before settling on a rotunda ringed by column screens and apsidal and kidney-shaped chapels cut into the thick, surrounding wall, with one chapel leading to a nuns' choir. His section studies reveal a fascination with telescoping vertical spaces generated by a series of truncated low-slung domes, which were to become his trademark. The entrance façade (Fig. 12.36), with its huge Serliana-like composition capped by a convex pavilion roof, recalls the work of Salomon de Brosse, designer of the Luxembourg Palace.

12.35 François Mansart, Plan of Ste. Marie de la Visitation, Paris, 1632.
Mansart's central-rotunda plan was unique at the time in France. The column screens were motivated by the need to shield the nuns' choir from the public space of the church.

Nuns' choir

12.37 (right) François Mansart,
**Early section drawing for the church
of Val-de-Grâce, Paris, 1644–46.**
Low-slung vaults in the stunted
nave and steep, telescoping domes
at the crossing connect Mansart's
work to spatial investigations in the
work of Guarini and Vittone.

12.36 François Mansart, Ste. Marie de la Visitation, Paris, 1632.
Here Mansart combined an entry pavilion, based upon the
gateway pavilions of earlier French châteaux, with a tall rotunda.
While relatively small, the entry pavilion is impressive, illustrating
the French preference and aptitude for monumentality.

12.38 (right) François Mansart,
**Plan of the church of Val-de-Grâce,
Paris, 1644–46.**
Mansart simplified his early
schemes for this church in order
to make it economically viable. The
hatched-in portions were added by
Jacques Lemercier, who replaced
Mansart during construction.

Mansart began the Parisian church of the Val-de-Grâce
in 1644; it was completed by Lemercier after 1646. Built
with funds granted by Anne of Austria after she conceived
Louis XIV, it gave Mansart an opportunity to explore the
longitudinal church plan in a scheme not unlike Il Gesù
in Rome. Several projects preceded the design as built.
One early scheme included a great baldachin like that at
St. Peter's, a truncated double dome at the crossing, and a
distinctive combination of intersecting barrel vaults, semidomes, and domes in the short nave (Fig. 12.37). As built
(Fig. 12.38), the structure became much simpler, with a
hemispherical dome at the crossing capped by a second,
larger dome scaled to be seen above the façade, and a barrel-vaulted nave.

At Maisons-sur-Seine near Paris, Mansart built a château
(1642–51) that has few equals in its confident composition

and masonry treatment. His grand site plan, some of which
has been lost, included an elaborate entry sequence with
monumental gateways and tree-lined boulevards leading to
a forecourt defined by stables and an intended **orangery**.
Next comes a moat, an entry court, then the body of the
house, the **corps-de-logis**, surrounded by garden parterres. Mansart arranged the building to have a U-shaped
plan (Fig. 12.39) with end pavilions capped by truncated
pyramidal roofs and a larger central pavilion with a three-
story centerpiece of attached columns and a pediment.
The masonry façades (Fig. 12.40), articulated using crisp
pilasters, have the appearance of a skin stretched tightly
over a structural skeleton beneath. The same sober, assured

12.39 François Mansart, Plan of the château, Maisons-sur-Seine, near Paris, 1642–51.
Of particular interest here is the central entry. Its cruciform plan is defined by massive walls inside which stand four pairs of columns. The plan also illustrates the French preference for dominant end pavilions.

12.40 François Mansart, Château, Maisons-sur-Seine, near Paris, 1642–51.
Mansart's façade appears as a thin, taut skin stretched over a sharp-edged skeleton. It reveals the French reverence for stereotomy: the combined results of projective-geometry knowledge and skill in stonecarving.

classicism can be seen on the interior, where the main vestibule appears as a thick-walled masonry box inside which Mansart inserted a set of eight columns, producing what appears to be a trabeated building inside an arcuated one. Space in the adjacent stair tower extends upward through low, truncated domes like those at Ste. Marie de la Visitation and his additions to the château at Blois (begun ca. 1635).

The Château of Versailles

The designers of other French country estates also enthusiastically adopted aspects of the Baroque style. In 1624

Louis XIII had built a hunting lodge with a C-shaped plan on swampy land at Versailles, some twenty miles southwest of Paris. When the future Louis XIV was a child, he spent relatively happy times in this twenty-room château, and on becoming monarch he decided to make modifications to it. Being sentimental about the original lodge, he would allow none of it to be removed. So, in 1661 Louis Le Vau first added two freestanding service wings projecting to the east and extending the enclosure of the château's east-facing forecourt. Then, in 1669, Le Vau enveloped the north and south flanks of the original château with **enfilades** of rooms in front of courtyards and stairs.

From the first, Louis intended Versailles to be the permanent residence of the royal court, dismissing medieval Paris as an unfit setting for the Sun King. A site less suitable for major construction than Versailles would have been difficult to find. The marshy ground was fine for game, but it was incapable of supporting elaborate plant life, and there was no adequate water supply readily available to run fountains. Under the direction of André Le Nôtre

(1617–1700), the army drained 37,000 acres of land and diverted an entire river thirty miles to supply water for the fountains, which eventually numbered 1400. Then Le Nôtre planned vast gardens, with axial vistas, terraces, sculpture, formal flowerbeds, fountains, water basins, and paths integrated into a grand plan that focused on the king's bedroom in the center of the palace (Figs. 12.41–12.42).

In 1678, when the entire court took up residence at Versailles, the palace was again enlarged, this time

12.41 (left) André Le Nôtre, Plan of the palace and gardens, Versailles, begun 1661.
The vast axial plan at Versailles is a fulfillment of the proposal put forward in the sixteenth century by Sixtus V in his replanning of Rome. The young Pierre L'Enfant lived at the palace and remembered his experience when he laid out the axes-over-grid plan for Washington, D.C.

12.42 (below) Pierre Patel, Bird's-eye view of Versailles from the east, 1668.
This view shows the old C-shaped château, or hunting lodge, at the center, with the addition of Le Vau's projecting service wings of 1661 and the surrounding gardens by Le Nôtre. Le Vau's 1669 north and south enveloping of the old château's flanks and J.-H. Mansart's vast north- and south-wing extensions were yet to come but can be seen in Fig. 12.41.

0   25 m
0   75 ft

12.43 Jules-Hardouin Mansart, St.-Louis-des-Invalides, Paris, 1670–1708.
J.-H. Mansart made use of drawings inherited from his uncle, François, in preparing his design of this church. His central plan can also be compared to Bramante's scheme for St. Peter's.

12.44 Jules-Hardouin Mansart, Section through St.-Louis-des-Invalides, Paris, 1670–1708.
Mansart's triple-shell dome not only creates two scales, interior and exterior, but also pursues his uncle François Mansart's experiments with spatial layers resulting from dome truncations.

under the direction of François Mansart's nephew, Jules-Hardouin Mansart (1646–1708), who continued to work there until his death thirty years later. At one point, in 1685, 36,000 men and 6000 horses were involved in construction of the buildings and grounds. A town of about 20,000 people grew up adjacent to the palace to house the aristocracy, their soldiers and servants, and other minor courtiers. Like the gardens, the town was organized around radiating boulevards extending from the center of the palace—a device first seen in Rome, with the three streets extending south from the Piazza del Popolo. Mansart extended the palace symmetrically to the north and south by building long wings, continuing the 1669 elevation scheme established by Le Vau. Mansart also added the Galerie des Glaces, or Hall of Mirrors, and two adjacent salons of War and Peace behind the west façade of the central block, finally completing the envelopment of the original château. Le Vau's Staircase of the Ambassadors (begun 1671) divided to lead to both salons, so that any ambassador would know of Louis's intentions before these were actually announced to him in the appropriate setting. A large circular panel in the Salon of War

depicted Louis as Mars triumphant over his enemies. The king's own suite of rooms included salons where paintings depicted monarchs of antiquity with the attributes of the gods representing the seven known planets, including Mercury and wisdom; Venus and love; Mars and war. His throne room was the Salon of Apollo. The only vertical feature at Versailles is the chapel added by Mansart in 1698–1710 on the right side of the forecourt, a building of Gothic proportions and a spatial conception expressed using the classical language.

All of the interior decoration at Versailles was carried out under the direction of Lebrun, and his ornamental work, furniture, tapestries, reliefs, and paintings were as elaborate as anything to be found in Baroque palaces of the period. However, while Versailles has much of the grandeur, it has little of the dynamism of seventeenth-century architecture in Italy.

Jules-Hardouin Mansart

Jules-Hardouin Mansart also designed structures in Paris. He added the church of St.-Louis-des-Invalides (Fig. 12.43) to the hospital for disabled soldiers. Although the interior of Les Invalides, as it is known, was still incomplete at Mansart's death in 1708, it was essentially finished by 1691. Its plan is based on Bramante's design for St. Peter's, and the drum and dome are derived from Michelangelo's design for the same church, though Mansart gave his interpretation a strong vertical accent. The dome of Les Invalides is buttressed by pairs of Ionic columns protruding from the fenestrated surface of the drum. The dignity of the exterior is achieved by a system of three dome shells (Fig. 12.44). The innermost, truncated masonry dome relates to the scale of the interior space; the intermediate masonry dome caps the truncated one and supports the external timber-framed dome, which is covered with lead sheets and is scaled to the building's exterior silhouette, mass, and composition.

CHRISTOPHER WREN AND THE BAROQUE IN ENGLAND

Mansart's design for Les Invalides was to have a direct impact on the most outstanding architect of the English Baroque, Christopher Wren (1632–1723). Wren came to national prominence as a result of the Great Fire, which began on September 2, 1666 and destroyed 373 of the 448 acres comprising the walled area of the City of London, including 13,200 houses, forty-four city companies, eighty-seven churches, the Royal Exchange, the Custom House, and St. Paul's Cathedral. Numerous prominent men made plans for rebuilding the burnt area. Wren produced a plan dated September 11; the diarist Sir John Evelyn, September 13; and Robert Hooke, Curator of Experiments at the Royal Society, September 19. Wren proposed a grid superimposed with axial routes connecting commercial, religious, and governmental centers within the city. Precedent for this plan organization can be found in the Baroque designs for Rome and Versailles. None of the plans submitted for the rebuilding of London was used in the actual work. Merchants wanted to reestablish their homes and businesses as rapidly as possible, in the same location within the city, without having to wait for radical planning changes to be approved and implemented.

Christopher Wren has been acclaimed as Britain's greatest architect. Trained as a mathematician, he was also well connected in the Church, his father having been Dean of Windsor. In 1661 Wren became Professor of Astronomy at Oxford University. While there, he designed the Sheldonian Theatre (1662–63) for an alumnus, Archbishop Sheldon, basing it on the semicircular Theater of Marcellus in Rome (see Fig. 5.30). Huge wooden roof trusses above the theater space support a canvas ceiling, which Wren had painted to resemble the open sky, complete with simulated ropes to hold the shading device taut. The entrance front is a pedimented pavilion with a raking cornice carried down to the perimeter walls. Arcades,

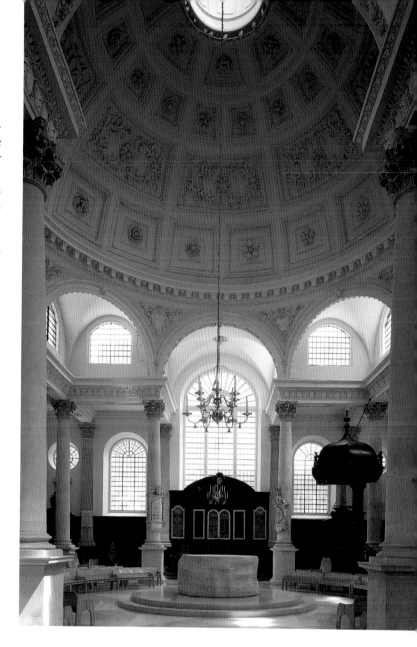

12.45 Christopher Wren, St. Stephen Walbrook interior, London, 1672–87.
Striking in this view is the slenderness and wide spacing of the columns that support the entablature and, in turn, the dome. These proportions are possible because the vaults are not stone, but wood and plaster.

12.46 Christopher Wren, Plan of St. Stephen Walbrook, London, 1672–87.
Wren organized St. Stephen Walbrook by means of a modulated grid—an orthogonal grid with the bay spacing varied. He removed four columns to produce the rotunda defined by an octagon of dome-supporting arches.

half-columns, pilasters, oval dormers, and a cupola complete the design. It was based on a plate in Serlio's *Five Books of Architecture*, as was the pilastered and pedimented design of the street façade of Wren's Pembroke College Chapel, Cambridge (1663–65), created for his uncle, Matthew Wren, Bishop of Ely. The chapel's ceiling is elaborate, and its woodwork was richly carved by the master woodcarver Grinling Gibbons.

Wren visited Paris from July 1665 through March 1666, probably to escape the plague that was sweeping Britain at the time. There he met Bernini and wrote, "I would have given my skin for . . . a few minutes' view" of Bernini's design for the Louvre.

The City Churches

After the fire of 1666 Wren became one of the six commissioners who prepared the Act for Rebuilding the City of London (1667), specifying, among other things, the use of brick walls and slate roofs to reduce the spread of any future fires. Fifty-one (just over half) of the burnt parish churches of the city were rebuilt to designs done by Wren from 1670 to 1686, although much of the detail was probably left to the master carpenter or mason in charge of each individual church since Wren was preoccupied with his major lifework, the rebuilding of St. Paul's Cathedral. The towers and spires of his churches, perhaps influenced by what he had seen in Gothic France, created a distinctive silhouette on the skyline, rising above the lower brick buildings and contrasting with the domed profile being developed in the design of St. Paul's. Wren's parish church designs vary considerably as he had to accommodate many different site conditions; he sometimes provided a reinterpretation of the earlier church destroyed in the Great Fire, so not all the designs are classically derived. Several of the steeples are particularly memorable. The spire of St. Mary-le-Bow rises on a circular plan above a square-plan tower, while St. Bride's, Fleet Street has four diminishing octagons of arched openings in its upper stories. In contrast, the steeple of St. Dunstan-in-the-East was built in a simplified Gothic form that reflected the previous church.

Like many others of Wren's city churches, the church of St. Stephen Walbrook (1672–87) served him as a rapidly built experimental model during his ongoing effort to design St. Paul's Cathedral. Except for its rather medieval tower capped by a Renaissance crown, the exterior of St. Stephen Walbrook is insignificant, but the interior is an extraordinary centrally planned space developed on a modulated grid, with a stubby nave and a coffered Pantheon-like dome (Figs. 12.45–12.46) that rests on eight arches supported by an octagonal arrangement of Corinthian columns atop high pedestals. Since the dome was a wooden construction, the supports could be slender and refined; for this reason it did not present any of the structural problems involved in the triple-shelled masonry dome of St. Paul's.

St. Paul's

Wren's design for St. Paul's Cathedral went through a number of changes. The so-called "Great Model" (Fig. 12.47), dating from 1673, consisted of a major dome on eight piers ringed with secondary domes forming a continuous ambulatory similar to Bramante's 1506 design for St. Peter's; but this design was too strongly linked with Roman Catholicism to be found acceptable by the cathedral's dean and chapter. A Latin-cross plan, similar to the previous Gothic building on the site, was requested, and that was what Wren provided in the "Warrant Design" of 1675. Even its silhouette was Gothic, consisting as it did of a minuscule drum and dome capped by a six-tiered cupola. Construction began on the basis of this design, which Wren modified slowly over the thirty-year building period. The structure completed in 1709 was refined and academic, incorporating elements from a wide variety of sources (Figs. 12.48–12.49). In plan the cathedral is a basilica, a form that Wren admired in the basilica at Fano as published by Vitruvius. Most of Wren's nave-and-aisle churches were based on the Roman basilica. At St. Paul's, the basilican structure is comprised of saucer domes in the nave and aisles, with buttresses above the aisle roofs (Fig. 12.50). To hide these buttresses and impart a classical character to the exterior, Wren raised the aisle walls to create screens articulated in a manner similar to those in Inigo Jones's Banqueting House (see Fig. 11.75), while the north and south transept porticoes were a restatement of Cortona's façade of S. Maria della Pace (see Fig. 12.18) in Rome. The west front is based on Perrault's façade for the Louvre (see Fig. 12.34), with towers like S. Agnese in Agone in the Piazza Navona in Rome (see Fig. 12.17). Wren greatly changed the dome, not begun until 1697, from that proposed in the "Warrant Design" of 1675, synthesizing Michelangelo's buttressing system for St. Peter's in Rome with Bramante's original design for the drum. Such a large dome required substantial supporting piers, necessitating the infill of the sides of the four diagonal arches of the central crossing to create segmental rather than hemispherical arches. The external massing of the dome had to be tall and dignified to dominate the London skyline, but this would have created an excessively vertical internal space. Thus Wren resorted to the triple-domed strategy employed by J.-H. Mansart at his church of St.-Louis-des-Invalides (see Fig. 12.44). The innermost dome is of masonry. Above this, a brick cone supports both the cupola and the wooden superstructure of the lead-covered exterior dome. Despite Wren's background as a mathematician, there is no evidence that he used his academic knowledge to make calculations predicting structural behavior.

The richness of St. Paul's relies equally on the architecture and the internal decoration, which includes work by woodcarver Grinling Gibbons (1648–1721) and master ironworker Jean Tijou. Gibbons was born in Rotterdam and discovered there by John Evelyn. He carved numerous Wren interiors, including Trinity College Library in Cambridge

12.47 Christopher Wren, "Great Model" plan for St. Paul's Cathedral, London, 1673. Wren's so-called "Great Model" was unacceptable in England because it had strong Catholic overtones, derived from the churches of the Italian Baroque style in Rome.

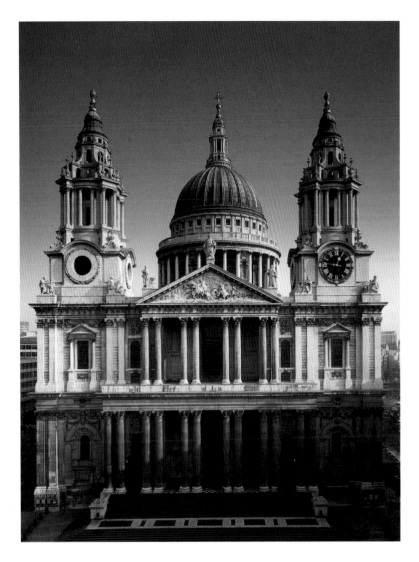

12.48 Christopher Wren, St. Paul's, London, 1675–1709. Wren's façade composition looks back to such models as S. Agnese in Piazza Navona (see Fig. 12.17). His triple-shell dome includes the unique feature of a conical intermediate shell that supports both the lantern and the timber superstructure of the outer shell.

12.48 ▷

12.50

12.49 Christopher Wren, Plan of and section through St. Paul's, London, 1675–1709. Remnants of the "Great Model" can be found in the many domed units covering both nave and aisles. It is Wren's interpretation of an ancient Roman basilica.

CHRISTOPHER WREN AND THE BAROQUE IN ENGLAND **373**

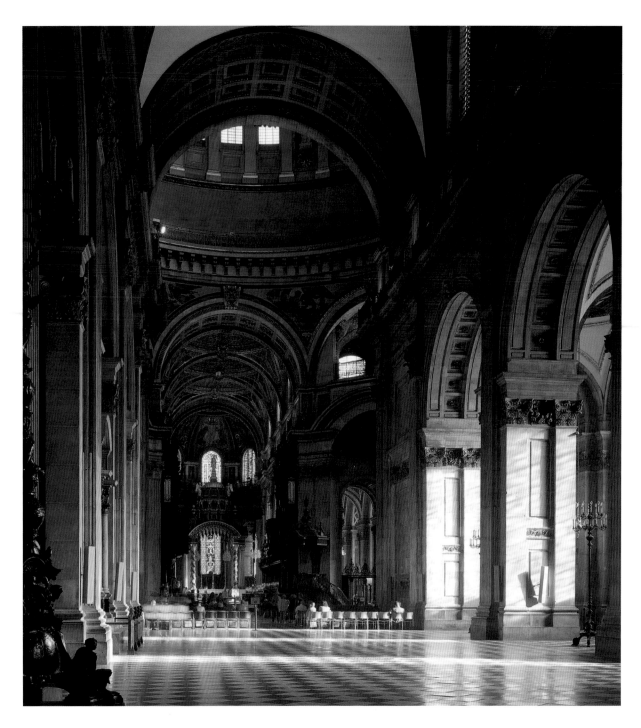

12.50 Christopher Wren, St. Paul's interior, London, 1675–1709.
In this view looking east, the saucer-domed bays of the nave lead to the octagonal rotunda. About it rises the triple-shell dome, comparable to the one J.-H. Mansart designed for Les Invalides (see Fig. 12.44).

and St. James's Piccadilly in London, but he excelled himself in the choir stalls and organ case of St. Paul's. Tijou, a French Huguenot, was patronized by the monarchs William and Mary. He worked mainly at Hampton Court and St. Paul's, where rosettes and embossed leaves distinguish his elaborate creations in wrought iron.

Housing in the Manner of Wren

Wren was much too busy with royal commissions to design private houses. Often presented as a residential building in the manner of Wren is Coleshill, Berkshire (ca. 1650) by Roger Pratt (1620–84) (Fig. 12.51). The two-room-deep or double-pile plan included a transverse service corridor. Such a house can claim ancestry to many Georgian mansions that would appear in eighteenth-century America, although the later buildings would have longitudinal central halls. Uppark, Sussex (1695) (Fig. 12.52) by William Talman (1650–1719) has a façade anticipating many later American works. This house is blocky, with a central, projecting pedimented bay and an elaborate **frontispiece** but no use of the orders except astride the doorway. Similar houses can be seen in such places as the cathedral close in Salisbury; the related American examples are often more refined and possessed of finer proportions because they were drawn from publications in which English experience had been codified.

12.51 (above) Roger Pratt, Coleshill, Berkshire, ca. 1650.
While Wren designed no houses as modest as this one, Coleshill seems to exhibit his form preferences. Its water table, belt course, entry frontispiece, heavy cornice, dormers, and rooftop balustrade all became standard features of the English and American Georgian styles. The house was destroyed by fire in the 1950s.

12.52 (below) William Talman, Uppark, Sussex, 1695.
Ironically, Georgian houses in America were more successful than their English models such as this one. In America, designs were often based upon drawings in English and American books, which represented refinements of the built originals.

NICHOLAS HAWKSMOOR, SIR JOHN VANBRUGH, AND JAMES GIBBS

While working on St. Paul's, Wren employed a domestic clerk who eventually became his assistant. This man was Nicholas Hawksmoor (1661–1736), who added to St. Paul's the west-front towers that emphasize massing, in contrast to the linear façades and accurate detailing of Wren's design. Hawksmoor also collaborated with an equally famous contemporary, Sir John Vanbrugh (1664–1726), a gentleman-soldier and colorful character who at one time was imprisoned by the French on suspicion of spying and who on his return to England became a successful comic playwright. In 1699 the Earl of Carlisle chose him over William Talman to design a palace in Yorkshire called Castle Howard (Fig. 12.53). Work on this elaborate and extensive complex began in 1701, with the assistance of Hawksmoor, who contributed architectural know-how to Vanbrugh's theatrical daring. They proposed a symmetrical design anchored by a domed great hall from which the principal apartments would extend laterally. Curved colonnades flanking the great court maintain strict axiality while connecting the main block with subsidiary courts for kitchens and stables that were never built.

The most celebrated house of the Vanbrugh–Hawksmoor partnership is Blenheim Palace (Fig. 12.54), built by a grateful England for the Duke and Duchess of Marlborough in commemoration of the duke's success at the battle of Blenheim in 1704. A large and pompous

building following the themes established at Castle Howard, Blenheim is representative of this period of grandiose design and is one of the most monumental pieces of domestic architecture of any period in Britain. The exterior is dominated by giant Corinthian columns and massive corner pavilions. Entrance is made through the north portico, which leads on axis from the great court into the hall and salon. Symmetrically disposed on either side of this central group are smaller rooms arranged around two internal courts; on the west front is a long gallery. Colonnades link the main block to the kitchen and stable courts, which balance each other on either side of the great court. Sarah, Duchess of Marlborough, objected to its impracticality as a home, because kitchen and dining room were a quarter-mile apart. The poet Alexander Pope observed, "'Tis very fine, But where d'ye sleep, or where d'ye dine?"

While Vanbrugh designed some ten grand country houses, Hawksmoor's major architectural works were the six churches he built in London; two were paid for under the Act for Building Fifty New Churches of 1711, for which he was appointed commissioner. Most of his basilican planning is derived from Wren, but the exuberance is all Hawksmoor's. At Christ Church, Spitalfields, London (1723–29), Hawksmoor's interest in the late Roman temples at Baalbek is reflected in his overscaled and unusually detailed scheme. The nave is illuminated by clerestories above elliptical barrel vaults running parallel to the nave. Below these vaults, the nave arcade is composed of cylindrical columns with complete entablatures surmounting

12.53 Sir John Vanbrugh, Plan of Castle Howard, Yorkshire, begun 1701.
While Palladian in conception, Castle Howard is vast in scale, with a width of almost 600 feet.

12.54 Sir John Vanbrugh and Nicholas Hawksmoor, Blenheim Palace, Woodstock, Oxfordshire, 1705–24, engraving.
This sprawling residence was financed by the British Crown as a means of rewarding the Duke of Marlborough for his military exploits at the battle of Blenheim.

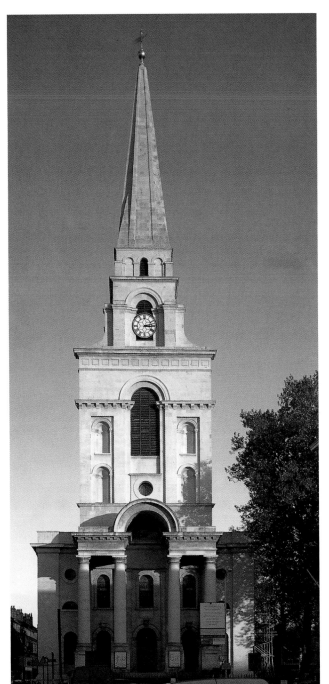

12.55 Nicholas Hawksmoor, Christ Church, Spitalfields, London, 1723–29.
For this façade, Hawksmoor fully exploited the well-worn Serliana or Palladian motif. A giant version appears as the entry porch, a smaller one as the base of the tower, and a third, still smaller one as the frame for the clock.

each one. The nave is not vaulted but is covered with a flat coffered ceiling, and the whole of the interior is bold. On the exterior, the porch is composed of a large Serliana, above which the tower rises, buttressed at front and back by screen walls containing windows arranged in another Serliana composition (Fig. 12.55). The styles of Vanbrugh and Hawksmoor are very personal and individualistic, forming a rich extension of the more academic work of Wren and thus presenting a distinctive part of the English tradition.

The church of St. Martin-in-the-Fields, London (1721–26) by James Gibbs (1682–1754), who was unusual in England for having studied in Rome, is an essay on the Corinthian order, employing giant columns and pilasters both inside and out (Fig. 12.56). A Wren-derived tower and steeple lie on the main axis; the entrance to the church is through their base and is protected by a dominating Corinthian portico. This church set a precedent for countless religious buildings, most notably in the American colonies both before and after the Revolution, mainly as a result of Gibbs's *A Book of Architecture*, published in 1729, which illustrates his numerous designs. For instance, Joseph Brown's Baptist church at Providence, Rhode Island (1774–75), is based on St. Martin, as are St. Michael's in Charleston, South Carolina (begun 1752, possibly by Peter Harrison), and churches in Vermont and Connecticut by Lavius Fillmore.

12.56 James Gibbs, Plan, section, and elevation of St. Martin-in-the-Fields, London, 1721–26.
Gibbs successfully united the temple front, Wren-like tower, and basilican nave to produce a prototype for churches in England and America. He tried out several variants before settling on this tower composition, which begins as a square in plan, moves through sets of octagons, and terminates with a faceted spire.

Gibbs is an architect whose works establish a bridge between the most elaborate examples of the English Baroque and more restrained designs based on the serenity of Andrea Palladio. The designs in his publication illustrate both inspirations. By the middle of the eighteenth century, the return to purer interpretations of classical antiquity emerged as Neo-Classicism, an important movement to which Gibbs gave an impetus and which is discussed in the next chapter.

CONCLUSIONS ABOUT ARCHITECTURAL IDEAS

During the Baroque period, architects retained the classical language, but often permitted themselves considerable license in its interpretation and made it only one part of a larger "multimedia" experience. At the Council of Trent in 1545, the Catholic hierarchy, while setting in motion the Counter-Reformation, concluded that art was to be exploited as an instrument of Church policy, captivating the currently faithful and enticing back the wayward. A decade earlier Ignatius Loyola had founded the evangelical Society of Jesus (the Jesuits), and its missionary educators

eventually took Catholic teachings worldwide. The order's mother church in Rome, Il Gesù, established a new direction for façade design and for interior spatial organization, being a modestly scaled, acoustically coherent preaching environment.

Il Gesù became one among many monuments made urbanistically prominent by the replanning of Rome continued under Pope Sixtus V. By cutting through long, straight streets that minimized travel distances, papal engineer Domenico Fontana connected the city's seven major churches, including St. Peter's, with S. Maria Maggiore at the center of the nexus. Architects responded by creating grand civic spaces within the dense antique-medieval fabric, including the Piazza del Popolo at the northern gate, the Spanish Steps beneath the church of the Trinità dei Monti, and the Piazza Navona within the boundaries of an ancient Roman circus. Streets and piazzas acted in concert, producing a dynamic new urbanism that would affect city planning for the next three hundred years.

The churches of S. Andrea al Quirinale and S. Carlo alle Quattro Fontane present two applications of Counter-Reformation theory. Bernini's S. Andrea is stagelike, a container for the reenactment of the martyrdom and ascension of Saint Andrew. In the service of this dramatic action, Bernini brought together painting, sculpture, and stuccowork within a dynamic oval-plan space. At S. Carlo alle Quattro Fontane, Borromini employed almost exclusively architectonic means to produce drama through the manipulation of form, as for instance the elongated columns and sinuous curves of the façade and the internal paired columns "pressed" into the oscillating walls that define an elongated-Greek-cross plan.

Both structures had important progeny. Following Bernini's line of investigation, Johann Bernhard Fischer von Erlach, author of *Historic Architecture*, the first book on architectural history, designed the Karlskirche in Vienna as a carrier of Hapsburg symbolism to have a broad, billboardlike façade and oval, illusionistically painted, worship space. The Zimmerman brothers' Bavarian church of Die Wies, with its wood-and-plaster vaults, took illusory experience to an extreme of artistic fusion where stuccowork, sculpture, painting, and architecture bathed in brilliant light became a unified vision.

Borromini, on the other hand, inspired the architect and engineer Guarino Guarini to experiment with new vaulting types, concealed structure, and dramatic light manipulation in such projects as S. Lorenzo, Turin. In Prague, in what was then called Bohemia, Christoph Dientzenhofer exploited the wall-pillar as a means for creating dual spatial readings and, as a result, a sense of spatial ambiguity and syncopated rhythms. Near Würzburg, at the pilgrimage church of Vierzehnheiligen, court architect Johann Balthasar Neumann designed complex masonry vaults with double curvatures that required his engineer's knowledge of mathematics and the strength of materials, then a legion of craftsmen applied stucco, paint, and gilding—without detailed direction from the architect—in pursuit of a homogeneous spatial and dramatic experience appropriate for a church dedicated to the mystical vision of a local shepherd. Neumann enlisted the same strategies in producing the Würzburg Residenz, where a monumental stairway (see page 340), inside a room painted illusionistically by Tiepolo, became a stage-set for the ascent and descent of men and women in exquisite court dress.

In France, surface effects never subsumed the techniques of building. Here François Mansart pursued spatial investigations like those of Borromini, but also remained loyal to the local Gothic vision of lofty interior space and to the French medieval emphasis on stereotomy. Working at the east façade of the Louvre, physician Claude Perrault, architect Louis Le Vau, and painter Charles Lebrun collaborated on a building expansion with Mansartian precision that was dominated by columns (in this case paired), a condition repeated throughout the remainder of the palace as constructed both before and after the mid-seventeenth century.

The English scientist Sir Christopher Wren traveled to France where he studied the Gothic cathedrals, becoming especially impressed by their towers, and met Bernini, who was there consulting on the Louvre extension. Wren returned in 1666 to a post-fire London that desperately needed dozens of neighborhood churches rebuilt to include easily seen and identified towers, as well as a new St. Paul's Cathedral. The production of Wren and his contemporaries Vanbrugh and Hawksmoor swung as far toward the Baroque as English work ever would, before taste moved back to a more gentle classicism. Designed by others than Wren, but following his lead, houses such as Coleshill and Uppark set the direction for the kind of English domestic design that would be imported to the American colonies as the Georgian style. James Gibbs, trained in Rome to appreciate the late Baroque, returned to London to build St. Martin-in-the-Fields in a form that would become the model for innumerable churches in America (through Gibbs's illustration of it in his 1729 *A Book of Architecture*) and that was compatible with the emerging Neo-Palladian taste discussed in the next chapter.

Chapter 13
Neo-Classicism, Romanticism, and the Rococo

Eighteenth-century architectural developments were complex, with divergent elements and themes, some old, some new. Especially in central Europe, Late Baroque work lingered, particularly in major commissions for the nobility and the Catholic Church. Vierzehnheiligen and the Würzburg Residenz in Germany as well as Blenheim Palace in England and the later stages of French construction at Versailles all date from the eighteenth century. One strain of the Late Baroque became the ultra-decorative Rococo style, so extreme in its playful ornamentalism that by mid-century it encouraged, in countering response, the return to a more proper classicism, this time called Neo-Classicism. Renewed interest in the classical past then required restudying the ruins of antiquity and stimulated English, French, and German architects and architectural students to make the pilgrimage to Italy, Greece, and anywhere else where classical remains could be found. This focused study was part of a much larger historical event—the Enlightenment (discussed below in this chapter's first essay)—begun in France and exported elsewhere, including to the nascent United States. The force of Enlightenment rationalism and accompanying scientific thinking, along with the early stirrings of the Industrial Revolution, provoked, in turn, another response in some people: an anti-rational and emotional reaction in the form of Romanticism and its esthetic ideal, the Picturesque.

THE ROCOCO

During the beginning decades of the eighteenth century, some architects produced confections such as François Cuvilliés's Amalienburg Pavilion at Nymphenburg Castle near Munich (1734–39) (Fig. 13.1). Within this diminutive garden structure, which includes kennels almost as elaborate as the principal salon, Johann Baptist Zimmerman's stucco ornamentation breaks out in a riot of color and texture to accompany the **boiserie** or ornate woodwork. This late flowering of the Baroque during the first half of the eighteenth century is known as the Rococo.

Horace Walpole, Strawberry Hill Long Gallery, Twickenham, begun 1748.
Antiquarian Horace Walpole was fascinated by the English Gothic. Rather than being academically correct, this interior is a highly personal architectural statement that expresses the emotion of Romanticism.

The name combines the words **rocaille**, describing the organic shapes of water-worn rocks, plants, and shells, and **coquille**, meaning "seashell." In France, the Rococo was primarily a style for interiors, typified by those of J.A. Meissonier (1695–1750) (Fig. 13.2).

In the work of others there were already harbingers of things to come. Though Germain Boffrand (1667–1754) worked during the Rococo period, his manner looked back to the conservative classicism of Louis Le Vau, and so anticipated the Neo-Classicism that would dominate French architecture in the second half of the eighteenth century. Boffrand designed the Parisian Hôtel d'Amelot (1712) around an elliptical court with loggias (Fig. 13.3). Its varied room shapes, modest room sizes, and attention to service functions make it a model of convenience and comfort.

THE ENGLISH NEO-PALLADIANS

Even as construction was being completed on the grandiose Blenheim Palace, discussed in the previous chapter, some English architects were turning away from the style of Wren, Vanbrugh, and Hawksmoor in favor of the simpler approach that they found in the works of Andrea Palladio. The leaders of this Neo-Palladian movement included Colen Campbell (1676–1729), a Scottish architect and

Chronology

Jean-Baptiste Colbert founds the Académie Royale d'Architecture	1671
Colen Campbell publishes *Vitruvius Britannicus*	1715–25
Louis XV begins his regency	1715
Regular design competitions are offered by the French academy	1720
J.B. Fischer von Erlach publishes *Historischen Architecture*	1721
Beginning of the European Enlightenment	ca. 1750
Beginning of the Industrial Revolution	ca. 1750
French pensionnaires begin to study in Rome	ca. 1750
Piranesi publishes *Vedute di Roma* 1750s and after	
Abbé Marc-Antoine Laugier publishes *Essai sur l'architecture*	1753
Edmund Burke publishes *A Philosophical Inquiry into the Origins of Our Ideas on the Sublime and the Beautiful*	1756
J.-F. Blondel publishes *Cours d'architecture*	1771–77
Sir John Soane at work on the Bank of England	1788–1833
Benjamin Henry Latrobe becomes Thomas Jefferson's surveyor of public buildings in Washington, D.C.	1803
Karl Friedrich Schinkel becomes state architect in Prussia	1810

13.1 (above) François Cuvilliés, Amalienburg Pavilion at Nymphenburg Castle near Munich, 1734–39.
Rococo ornament covers the exterior walls of this small hunting pavilion and reaches an even higher level of profusion on the interior, where gilded woodwork and abundant mirrors make for an immersive ornamental environment.

13.2 (below) J.A. Meissonier, Engraved section drawing for the Maison du Sieur Brethous, Bayonne, 1733.
The classical ordering of a room using pilasters has evolved here to become one of decorative panels dripping with Rococo ornament. Note the consistency of the architectural motifs with the designs of the Louis XV chairs.

13.3 Germain Boffrand, Plan of the Hôtel d'Amelot, Paris, 1712.
The challenge in planning an urban house such as this one, which is arranged around an oval court, was to give all of the family's rooms quite regular shapes while absorbing the inevitable irregularities into service spaces and stairs, all of which Boffrand did. The result was an elegant and comfortable residence.

editor of the influential book *Vitruvius Britannicus*, which appeared in three volumes from 1715 to 1725; Richard Boyle, third earl of Burlington (1694–1753), a wealthy nobleman who pursued his study of architecture while fulfilling governmental duties; and William Kent (1685–1748), an Englishman who originally trained in Rome as a

painter and branched out into architecture and landscape design under the patronage of Lord Burlington. All three men were political Whigs and staunch supporters of the House of Hanover, which had replaced the Stuart line on the English throne. Both the first volumes of *Vitruvius Britannicus* (1715) and Giacomo Leoni's English translation of Palladio's *I quattro libri dell'architettura* (1716) were dedicated to King George I. Central to the movement they spawned was a great respect for Vitruvius, enthusiasm for the buildings of Palladio, and admiration for the works of Inigo Jones.

Colen Campbell's illustrations of classical English buildings in *Vitruvius Britannicus*, including country houses influenced by Inigo Jones as well as his own designs, brought him to the attention of Lord Burlington, who commissioned him to undertake renovations to Burlington House in London (since further modified and enlarged into the Royal Academy). At Mereworth Castle (1723) in Kent, Campbell designed a near-replica of the Villa Rotonda (as Palladio illustrated it) at a slightly larger scale (Fig. 13.4).

Like many aristocrats of the period, Lord Burlington made the Grand Tour of Europe, traveling from 1714 to 1715; in 1719 he returned to Italy specifically to study the buildings of Palladio. There he met William Kent, whose work so impressed him that they began a lifetime of friendly collaboration. With Kent's assistance in landscape design and interior detailing, Lord Burlington designed his own variation of the Villa Rotonda at Chiswick House (1725–29) on the outskirts of London (Figs. 13.5–13.6). Chiswick is a smaller version of the Palladian original, enlivened by a certain amount of creative borrowing from other sources. It has one portico instead of four, and its octagonal drum and dome perhaps owe more to Vincenzo Scamozzi than to Palladio. Obelisks placed at the edge

13.4 Colen Campbell, Section through Mereworth Castle, Kent, 1723.
Colen Campbell was among the circle of Neo-Palladians assembled around Lord Burlington. This is Campbell's English interpretation of the Villa Rotonda.

13.5 Lord Burlington (Richard Boyle), Chiswick House, London, 1725–29.
Lord Burlington was certainly thinking about the Villa Rotonda when he added this pavilion for entertaining to this estate. However, there are features not used by Palladio: the dominant twin stairs, the thermal windows placed in the octagonal drum, and the Pantheon-like dome.

13.6 Lord Burlington (Richard Boyle), Plan of Chiswick House, London, 1725–29.
The plan is even more unlike Palladio's work than the elevation. It is a nine-part grid of squares, rectangles, circles, and polygons.

of the roof contain the chimney flues in an antique disguise, derived perhaps from similar features on villas in the neighborhood of Vicenza, while the garden elevation is distinguished by three windows of original design, composed of Serliana inside recessed arches. The interior spaces follow Palladian proportions and incorporate elements from designs by Inigo Jones in their details.

In addition to his work with Lord Burlington at Chiswick, Kent edited a two-volume collection published in 1727 as *Designs of Inigo Jones*. After about 1730 he began

to practice architecture on his own, designing Holkham Hall in Norfolk in 1734 (Fig. 13.7). This is a grand country seat in the tradition of Vanbrugh and thus much larger than the villas of Palladio. Pavilions, pediments, Serliana, and a certain simplicity in the composition of multiple elements recapture the spirit of the sixteenth-century master in what could be termed a cluster of five Italian residences, consisting of a central reception block and four wings containing the kitchen, a chapel, a music gallery, and private rooms with associated accommodation spaces.

13.7 William Kent, Holkham Hall, Norfolk, 1734.
This sprawling complex continues the vast scale of country houses established by Vanbrugh and Hawksmoor during the period of the Stuart Restoration in the late seventeenth century. Each of its dependencies is the size of a large eighteenth-century Georgian house in America.

The Enlightenment and the Abbé Laugier's Primitive Hut

by Michael Fazio

The eighteenth century witnessed the birth of the Enlightenment, the movement in which scientists and mathematicians laid the foundations for modern achievements in their fields; philosophers pondered political legitimacy; archaeologists and explorers probed past and distant civilizations for an understanding of other cultures; and first traditional mechanics, then modern engineers invented devices and machines that were to transform industry, commerce, and transportation. Enlightenment historians also began the first accurate chronology of world events, with which came an understanding of the architectural accomplishments of the various Western civilizations. France was the center of this extraordinary phenomenon and the place where Enlightenment thinking about the world was assembled in Denis Diderot's thirty-five-volume *Encyclopédie* (1751–72), which included entries by the likes of Voltaire and Jean-Jacques Rousseau. The Enlightenment stimulated the ongoing development of the modern age by calling for a separation of church and state and so encouraging secularization, by challenging the authority of hereditary monarchies in favor of egalitarianism and political democracy, and, as a corollary, by advancing economic capitalism. Both the French and American revolutions were creatures of the Enlightenment, and Thomas Jefferson,

13.8 Abbé Marc-Antoine Laugier, Primitive Hut, Frontispiece from his *Essai sur l'architecture*, 2nd edition, 1755, engraving by Charles Eisen (1720–88). Here a female figure representing the Genius of Architecture and sitting atop classical fragments points at the "primitive hut" as a model for rational building design.

whose architectural work is discussed at the end of this chapter, drew on the writings of Enlightenment philosophers

like John Locke and David Hume when composing the Declaration of Independence.

If one were to choose a single voice to represent Enlightenment thinking as it applied to architecture, it might be that of the Abbé Marc-Antoine Laugier (1713–69). Born in Provence, Laugier had Jesuit training before becoming a Benedictine monk and wrote on a wide variety of subjects, including architecture. He saw Renaissance, Baroque, and even ancient Roman buildings as impure, praising only what he perceived to be the skeletal logic of ancient Greek and French Gothic structures. Like other Enlightenment thinkers, he looked to the natural world for guidance and concluded that architecture's "principles are founded on simple nature, and nature's process clearly indicates its rules." In his widely read *Essai sur l'architecture* (*Essay on Architecture*, 1753), from which this quoted phrase is drawn, he argued that all proper architecture could be derived from a single prototype in prehistory, the so-called "primitive hut" (Fig. 13.8), which was entirely rational, being composed only of freestanding columns (meaning no attached columns or pilasters), lintels or entablatures, and a sloping roof or pediment. His conception is not to be taken literally, however, but must be interpreted as an allegory promoting absolute architectural beauty independent of custom and convention. Laugier's French contemporary Jacques-Germain Soufflot, whose Panthéon in Paris is discussed later in this chapter (see Figs. 13.23–24), came closest to fulfilling the Abbé's vision.

THE RETURN TO ANTIQUITY

The Neo-Palladians in England were among the first, but far from the last, to undertake a thorough study and revival of architecture from the classical past. By the middle of the eighteenth century the artistic elite of Europe had developed a renewed interest in the buildings of antiquity. This had happened before. Carolingian architects had looked to Roman, Early Christian, and Byzantine buildings for inspiration, and the architects of the Italian Renaissance had made extensive studies of the ruins of Rome and the writings of Vitruvius. This eighteenth-century interest in antiquity, however, differed in both its focus and its breadth of impact. Artists and architects of the Neo-Classical period sought an accurate understanding of ancient buildings and artworks, and historians placed these creative achievements in a proper context through their comprehensive studies of ancient civilizations. Popular curiosity about remote places and exotic cultures encouraged travel by English *dilettanti*, or gentleman amateurs, as well as artists and architects.

During the eighteenth century, publications of measured drawings from ancient sites greatly expanded the available information relating to architectural history. Remains of the Greek colonial town of Paestum were closely examined, and the Roman cities of Pompeii and Herculaneum were discovered in the course of road construction in the Kingdom of Naples. Excavations, begun at Herculaneum in 1735 and at Pompeii in 1748, eventually freed a wealth of buildings from the volcanic ash and mud that had buried both sites during the eruption of Mount Vesuvius in 79 CE. For the first time scholars and architects had abundant detailed evidence of imperial Roman architecture, decoration, and daily life. Thomas Major published *The Ruins of Paestum* in 1768, contributing measured examples of Archaic Greek temples to the growing knowledge of Greek architecture; in 1762 James Stuart and Nicholas Revett began publishing *Antiquities of Athens*, a series of four volumes completed by others in 1816. Roman settlements around the Mediterranean were also investigated. Robert Wood's *Ruins of Palmyra* (1753) and *Ruins of Baalbec* (1757) documented these important sites in the Middle East.

This interest in antiquity was not confined to the classical civilizations of Greece and Rome. Napoleon's military expedition to Egypt in 1798 included a large group of archaeologists and engineers whose published reports, notably the *Voyage dans la basse et la haute Egypte pendant les campagnes du Général Bonaparte* (1807) and the twenty-volume *Descriptions de l'Egypte* (1809–22) by Baron Dominique Vivant Denon, encouraged popular enthusiasm for things Egyptian. Public interest in non-Western civilizations had already been sparked by trading contacts and by Jesuit translations of the writings of Confucius and the Qur'an; soon architectural knowledge was extended still further by Thomas Daniell's *The Antiquities of India*

(1800). Historical information documented through drawings of ancient buildings provided designers with a greater repertoire of artistic forms than ever before, and eighteenth-century publications made possible the freedom in design that subsequently led to nineteenth-century eclecticism.

The leading exponent of Neo-Classicism in Italy and an unabashed promoter of ancient Roman architecture was Giovanni Battista Piranesi (1720–78) (discussed in the essay on page 404). From the mid-1750s until the end of his life, he issued a series of engravings titled *Vedute di Roma*, or *Views of Rome*. These views of ancient ruins rising enigmatically and provocatively from the accumulated detritus and among Renaissance and Baroque buildings designed by the masters of those ages sparked the imaginations of artists and architects throughout Europe.

THE STYLE CREATED BY ROBERT ADAM

An Englishman who went south to Rome and became friends with Piranesi was the Scottish-born Robert Adam (1728–92). At the age of twenty-six he met and accompanied Charles-Louis Clérisseau to Nîmes. Together they traveled on to Split, Croatia, where they made measured drawings, which Adam published in 1764 as *Ruins of the Palace of the Emperor Diocletian at Spalato, in Dalmatia*. Adam was initially as interested in Vitruvius as the Palladians, but during a trip to Italy, which lasted from 1754 to 1758, he became aware that, while the greatest archaeological interest had followed Vitruvius in focusing on the religious architecture of antiquity, little thought was being given to the houses. Adam devoted his attention to what little was known about ancient residential design and interior detailing, in part because he realized that his architectural practice, like that of his father and brothers, would rely on clients who required homes, not temples or churches.

Adam's Williams-Wynn House at 20 St. James's Square in London (1772) demonstrates both his dexterous planning and extraordinary system of interior design (Figs. 13.9, 13.10). On a narrow site he ingeniously arranged a variety of room shapes in a fashion akin to the French designers of Parisian residences like the Hôtel d'Amelot (see Fig. 13.3). He employed a distinctive graphic method for representing interior elevations, arranging them orthographically around a room's plan as if they were walls folded down. Thus he could study five related interior surfaces simultaneously. The unified results are evident in the Williams-Wynn House where Adam spread a thin "net" of stucco ornament, inspired by Raphael's and Giulio Romano's inventive grotesques, themselves based on the sixteenth-century excavations at Nero's Golden House, and introduced colors taken from the excavations at Pompeii and Herculaneum. Adam claimed, and probably rightly, that his elegant, attenuated decorations brought about a revolution in English architectural taste, and the results became known as the "Adam Style" or simply the Adamesque.

Court —

Stable

Coach house

Powder room

Dressing room

Library

Music room

Service stairs

Principal stair

Dining room

Porter's hall

Wash house

Hay loft

Laundry

Powder room

Bedroom

Dressing room

13.10

Drawing room

Drawing room

0   20 m
0   60 ft

Adam's work on country houses often consisted of remodeling or adding to late Elizabethan and Jacobean structures. An exception is his Luton Hoo, Bedfordshire, built in 1767–69 but damaged by fires and rebuilt twice in the nineteenth century. Adam conceived the broad front façade as a five-part scheme dominated by a central pavilion with a bulging entablature supported by attenuated Corinthian columns, altogether a composition akin to those imaginary architectural depictions Adam had seen as wall paintings at Pompeii and Herculaneum (Figs. 13.11–13.12). On the interior, Luton Hoo's planning is

13.9 Robert Adam, Plans of the Williams-Wynn House, 20 St. James Square, London, 1772.
On a long, narrow site, Adam disposed a variety of spatial types, including apsidal and double-apsidal rooms, rectangles, and polygons, without a trace of awkwardness. Not unrelated to developments in French hôtels, such residential designs provided a context for Adam's interior-ornamentation inventions.

13.10 Robert Adam, Rear drawing room of the Williams-Wynn House, 20 St. James's Square, London, 1772.
Adam had been inspired by the wall paintings he had seen in Pompeii and Herculaneum, and he translated motifs from this ancient Roman work into his own distinctive system of interior architecture. The resulting so-called "Adam Style" was not only extremely popular in England but also in the United States during the early years of the republic.

13.11 Robert Adam, Exterior view of Luton Hoo, Bedfordshire, 1767–69.
Tall, graceful proportions are a hallmark of the Adam Style, and they are on display in this engraved view. With its central unit, flanking masses, and projecting end pavilions, the building's overall form looks back to Palladio.

ingenious. Primary circulation occurs along cross-axes, with the longitudinal axis passing through an elongated oval expanded by niches, a rotunda with a ring of interior columns, and a rectangle with apse and lateral tripartite column screens—an overall arrangement reminiscent of Roman baths. To either side, Adam arranged rectangular and double-apsidal rooms until he reached the end pavilions, where he returned to the rotunda and column-screen motifs. The spatial experience for someone moving along the axes or through the enfilade arrangement of rooms must have been extraordinary before the many subsequent modifications.

WILLIAM CHAMBERS, AN ENGLISH NEO-CLASSICIST TRAINED IN FRANCE

A contemporary and countryman of Adam, Sir William Chambers (1723–96) spent four years in Rome as an extension of his studies in Paris with Jacques-François Blondel, whose teaching and theories are discussed in the next section. He produced an influential *Treatise on Civil Architecture* (1759) and even published *Designs of Chinese Buildings* (1757) as a result of his travels in China while a young merchant seaman. Chambers's great work is Somerset House

13.12 Robert Adam, First-floor plan of Luton Hoo, Bedfordshire, 1767–69.
One might compare the spatial effects that Adam created in the core of this house to those found in the ancient Roman Hadrian's Villa. Along the central entry axis, intermingled perforated walls and column screens make for a many-layered three-dimensional experience.

(Fig. 13.13) on the north bank of the Thames in London, done while he served jointly with Robert Adam as architect to the king. Here Chambers was called upon to centralize the British government offices. After proposing a number of complex schemes, he settled on a rigorous C-shaped plan (Fig. 13.14), some 500 feet square, with a freestanding entry block to the north along the Strand, the road running parallel to the river. It is comparable in formal conception to the many green residential squares developed throughout London. One can only imagine the cleverness and diplomacy required of Chambers in satisfying the myriad political fiefdoms, each determined to have the most prominent and desirable locations within the complex. Along the Thames the façade rises from a great rusticated, Piranesian arcade to linked pavilions reflecting Chambers's French training but marred by an undersized dome that reflects the English difficulty with monumentality. Sculpted figures and groups arrayed throughout the complex celebrated British maritime prowess.

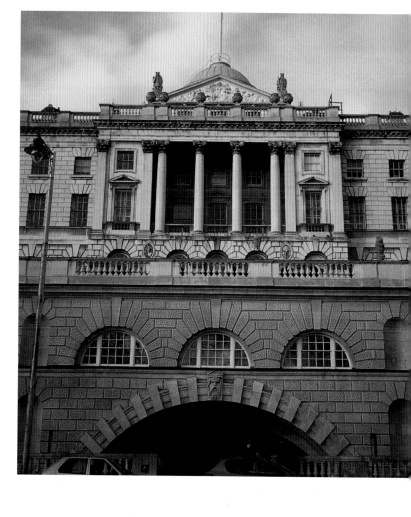

13.13 William Chambers, Somerset House river-front façade, London, 1776–86.
Along the Thames, Chambers created a façade organized in the French manner, with pavilions punctuating highly textured expanses of masonry walls. At the highly rusticated base, he inserted thermal windows and below them huge arches with prominent voussoirs, like something from Piranesi's etchings of grand remains in ancient Rome or Ledoux's gatehouses.

13.14 William Chambers, Plan of Somerset House, London, 1776–86.
Unlike most Englishmen, William Chambers went to Paris for his architectural education. The scale and rigor of his plan reflect the French tradition of J. -F. Blondel and the Ecole des Beaux-Arts.

ARCHITECTURAL EDUCATION AND ARCHITECTURAL THEORY IN FRANCE

Jean-Baptiste Colbert, minister to Louis XIV, founded the Académie Royale d'Architecture in 1671. Its purpose was to direct the arts toward the glorification of the king and, in turn, the state. The academy brought practicing architects together to discuss architectural problems and theories, and it presented public lectures. From 1720 onward, it offered regular design competitions for students, but the task fell to William Chambers's teacher Jacques-François Blondel to form the first actual architectural school in 1743. His success encouraged the academy to do the same, and by 1762 Blondel was one of its professors in what would eventually become the famous Ecole des Beaux-Arts. As early as the 1750s French architectural students were spending extended periods in Rome as **pensionnaires**. While in the Eternal City, they made careful drawings of ancient buildings and made new designs of their own.

During the eighteenth century, most French architects still worked for the government. Consequently, their buildings were most often intended to serve public functions. In 1771–77 Blondel set forth his ideas about architecture in his *Cours d'architecture* (*Lectures on Architecture*), really the notes from his own classes. Blondel discussed *l'art de la distribution*, which involved arranging the plan, and *l'art de la décoration*, which involved composing a façade. Both were governed by **ordonnance**, **convenance**, and **bienséance**. Ordonnance referred to the correct relationship of parts to one another and to the whole. Convenance and bienséance concerned appropriateness and the correct form of a building relative to its purpose and social rank. Thus, Blondel's writings explain in detail the essential elements of good architecture and the appropriate hierarchy and related treatments of buildings, from individuals' residences up to those royal buildings associated with the king.

THE INVENTIVE NEO-CLASSICISM OF ETIENNE-LOUIS BOULLEE AND CLAUDE-NICOLAS LEDOUX

Two men who studied with Blondel, Etienne-Louis Boullée (1728–99) and Claude-Nicolas Ledoux (1736–1806), became the most inventive French Neo-Classicists and both designed many hypothetical as well as real projects. Boullée's imaginary schemes give prominence to spheres, cylinders, hemispherical domes, pyramids, and cones, most often at a gigantic scale. His design for a **cenotaph** for Sir Isaac Newton, the discoverer of the laws of classical mechanics, is a hollow sphere 500 feet in diameter, the top half of which represents the dome of heaven, perforated with holes to give the impression of stars and the moon when viewed from the interior (Fig. 13.15). Suspended inside the sphere is a giant lamp representing the sun. Boullée explained his concept of the design in a tribute to Newton contained in his *Treatise on Architecture*: "Sublime mind! Vast and profound genius! Divine Being! Newton! Accept the homage of my weak talents. . . . I conceive the idea of surrounding thee with thy discovery, and thus, somehow, surrounding thee with thyself." Another project by Boullée, this one for a national library, houses books inside an enormous semicylinder lit by an equally enormous skylight cut into the coffered vaulting. The vault is supported by stoalike files of columns, and the columns are in turn supported by terraces of book stacks working their way down to the main floor so that the books can be lowered from level to level by attendants, rationally obviating the need for hazardous stepladders.

Ledoux's designs for Chaux (1775–79) reveal his vision for an ideal town to include a saltworks (Fig. 13.16). Significantly, while completely Neo-Classical in their architectural language, these designs explore the phenomenon of eighteenth-century industrialization. In plan the community is organized in a great oval of workers' houses, with the buildings for saltmaking placed across the lesser diameter. Outside the oval are gardens, recreational facilities, and various communal buildings. Through its integration of planned open space with residential and industrial development, the design for Chaux anticipated the Garden City movement of the late nineteenth century, which was similarly concerned with providing a healthy environment for city-dwellers. In architectural terms the linkage of man and nature at Chaux is expressed in basic geometries. The cemetery building is a sphere, symbolizing the eternal cosmos, and the wheelwright's house is identified by large circles incorporated into its façade. Ledoux's design for the "Inspector's House at the Source of the River Loüe" is shaped like a hollow cylinder set horizontally on a podium, with the stream flowing through the lower half of the cylinder and the rooms of the building arranged in buttresslike rectangular blocks along its tunnel sides. None of these highly symbolic projects was actually constructed, although portions of the plan of Chaux were built between the towns of Arc and Senans. Ledoux's executed designs make use of simplified versions of the classical orders realized in heavily rusticated masonry. The authority of the director of the saltworks is stated emphatically by the heavy banded columns of his house. Under the portico of the main entry gatehouse, with its baseless Tuscan columns, a heavily rusticated apse beneath huge rusticated voussoirs becomes a grotto, and the windows of this building take the form of urns spilled over on their sides to disgorge petrified water. The severity of the composition reflects the state's jealous monopoly of salt production.

In the eighteenth century, it became fashionable for French nobles to build urban dwellings called **hôtels particuliers**. These were often freestanding, with entry

13.15 Etienne-Louis Boullée, Cenotaph for Sir Isaac Newton, 1784.
The most striking feature of Boullée's design is certainly its intended vast scale, with the width of the sphere some 500 feet in diameter. The selection of Newton as the figure to be honored expresses Enlightenment admiration for reason through a celebration of the discoverer of the clocklike universe.

courts and rear gardens, and, though relatively large, they were designed for convenience and comfort and so stood in sharp contrast to the vast, drafty palace at Versailles. Ledoux's Hôtel de Thelluson in Paris (1778–83, destroyed 1826) was a remarkable exercise in the manipulation of three-dimensional space, both externally and internally. His composition for a newly developing residential section of Paris began with a massive triumphal-arch gateway sunken into the ground as if it were a half-buried monument in ancient Rome (Fig. 13.17). Entry was made through this arch, then along a two-part elevated carriageway over landscaped gardens, then through the corps-de-logis, or detached house; a service court stood to the rear (Fig. 13.18). A full appreciation of Ledoux's achievement can only be had by examining a longitudinal building section cut along the central axis, where his skill in modulating the ceiling plane and creating various lighting conditions is apparent (Fig. 13.19). On the second or piano-nobile floor, one moved along the principal axis through the curving colonnade—treated like part of an embedded circular temple—into a grand oval salon lit from high windows by

13.16 Claude-Nicolas Ledoux, Plan of Chaux, 1775–79, engraving.
In the center of the plan is the Director's House, with buildings for salt production flanking it and workers' housing in the surrounding oval.

13.17 (above) Claude-Nicolas Ledoux, Hôtel de Thelluson,
Paris, 1778–83, engraving.
In the foreground, Ledoux placed a gateway like an ancient
Roman, half-buried triumphal arch. A walkway at the second
level then leads back to the corps-de-logis, or main block of
the house, with its central motif appearing as an embedded
trabeated circular temple.

13.18 (above right) Claude-Nicolas Ledoux, Ground-level
plan of the Hôtel de Thelluson, Paris, 1778–83, engraving.
Built in a developing Parisian suburb, this hôtel was placed
on an open site. Consequently, Ledoux had room to combine
house, courts, gardens, and systems of pedestrian and
vehicular circulation.

13.19 Claude-Nicolas Ledoux, Longitudinal section through
the Hôtel de Thelluson, Paris, 1778–83, engraving.
Perhaps this section gives the most informative view of Ledoux's
hôtel. It reveals the bi-level organization, the situation of
the building components in the landscape, and the extreme
manipulation of the ceiling plane in the corps-de-logis.

means of a truncated dome, then into an octagonal antechamber lit by a roof lantern, then into a square antechamber with enfilade connections along the rear wall.

Ledoux also built a series of tollgates for the city of
Paris, most of which have since been demolished. While
they were despised by the Parisian people as symbols of
tyrannical taxation and criticized at the time of their construction by other architects as inappropriate interpretations of the classical language, they have come to be seen
as remarkably successful variations on a common theme:
the urban gateway inserted at intervals in a circumferential
city wall. Ledoux first argued for a set of triumphal arches
based upon those of ancient Rome or the Propylaea leading into the ancient Athenian Acropolis. However, because

his tollgates had to include rooms on one or more floors, Ledoux was forced to conceive of new types, drawing upon both ancient and Renaissance precedents. His forms included gable-roofed temples, circular temples akin to Bramante's Tempietto, several variations on Palladio's Villa Rotonda, pavilions with banded columns like the Director's House at Chaux, and even some compositions that appear, like images from Piranesi, to be half-buried. The still-extant Barrière de la Villette (1784–89) (Fig. 13.20) is composed of a cylinder, without a dome but ringed with Serlianas, rising out of a low square block. The massing and the masonry, including baseless, square Tuscan columns, are handled to convey a sense of ponderousness befitting the structure's tollgate function.

OTHER NEO-CLASSICAL ARCHITECTS IN FRANCE

Ange-Jacques Gabriel (1698–1782) designed the Petit Trianon (1761–64) in the grounds at Versailles as a convenient and comfortable alternative residence to the sprawling palace. It exhibits a cool, chaste classicism and again illustrates the cleverness of French domestic planning in the eighteenth century. The tripartite north, or entry, façade has a rusticated basement, Corinthian pilasters, and a prominent balustrade; it is comparable to some English Palladian villas but is at once more grand and more restrained (Fig. 13.21). To the south, the basement level disappears and the piano nobile opens out only a few steps above grade. On the west, freestanding Corinthian columns rise above garden parterres. The east façade offers yet another unique arrangement, having neither columns nor pilasters. These varied façade compositions, all symmetrical, in no way compromise the interior planning, where only the larger garden-front rooms are symmetrically placed (Fig. 13.22). Gabriel slid walls about, distributing

13.20 (above left) Claude-Nicholas Ledoux, Barrière de la Villette, Paris, 1784–89.
In the late eighteenth century Paris was ringed by Ledoux's tollgates, many of them not so grand as this one, which achieves its architectural effect by contrasting the almost primitive portico, with its baseless columns and elemental capitals, against the drum rising above and behind it, with its repetitive Serliana producing a rich column screen.

13.21 (above) Ange-Jacques Gabriel, Petit Trianon, Versailles, 1761–64.
Gabriel's cool classicism represents the end of seventeenth-century French Renaissance developments begun by such men as François Mansart. This rigorous design attitude was never completely lost, even during the period of Rococo extravagances.

13.22 (above) Ange-Jacques Gabriel, Plan of the Petit Trianon, Versailles, 1761–64.
Each façade of this building is symmetrical. However, only one set of rooms, that on the west front, is symmetrically distributed. Otherwise the partitions are cleverly arranged to achieve internal convenience without sacrificing external formality.

13.23 Jacques-Gabriel Soufflot, Plan of the Panthéon, Paris, 1757–90.
Like the exterior, the interior of Soufflot's building, designed as a church, has been altered: the piers of the crossing have been modified, as the original columns began to fail. The many other columns remain intact, demonstrating Soufflot's interest in lofty Gothic openness.

13.24 Jacques-Gabriel Soufflot, Panthéon interior, Paris, 1757–90.
As a young man, Soufflot had traveled to Rome and had been much impressed by the scale and monumentality of the ancient ruins. At the Panthéon he recreated this grandeur in a manner that also reflects his admiration for the great seventeenth-century French architect François Mansart.

them around a central service and vertical-circulation core while maintaining spatial order through enfilade connections among the various clusters of rooms. The restrained interior decoration, dominated by rectilinear paneling and mirrors, matches the character of the exterior and looks back to the Versailles interiors created for Louis XIV.

The architect Jacques-Gabriel Soufflot (1713–80) set out to build a structure according to the rationalist dictates of the Abbé Laugier (discussed on page 385) and within the rich tradition of French openwork structures revered since the emergence of the Gothic. This would turn out to be the church of Ste.-Geneviève, first dedicated to the patron saint of Paris but since secularized and renamed the Panthéon (1757–90). Soufflot traveled to Rome and farther south to the dramatic ruins at Paestum in the company of the Marquis de Marigny, and it was the

13.25 Marie-Joseph Peyre and Charles de Wailly, Elevation of the Comédie-Française, Paris, 1770.
Large theaters were a new phenomenon in eighteenth-century Paris. They were more than venues for entertainment, also being settings for social spectacle and something akin to temples of French drama.

marquis who secured for him the Panthéon commission. Its central plan (Fig. 13.23), deftly lengthened at the choir and portico, follows in the tradition of Bramante and Michelangelo at St. Peter's and of Wren's "Great Model" for St. Paul's (discussed on page 372). However, Soufflot based his design on Laugier-inspired freestanding columns and lintels rather than the traditional piers with pilasters and arches, and he experimented with concealed flying buttresses to stabilize the dome (Fig. 13.24). Openwork structures had been preferred by such highly regarded French architects as François Mansart and his nephew J.-H. Mansart, who were inspired by the spaciousness of local Gothic cathedrals. Like François Mansart at the central pavilion of his château at Maisons-sur-Seine (see Fig. 12.40), Soufflot placed what amounted to a columnar building inside a bearing-wall building. However, his skeletal system eventually proved to be too open, and the piers of the crossing had to be modified. In addition, some of his windows have been infilled to make the building serve as a tomb for French notables, and the original sculptural program has been destroyed. Consequently, the Panthéon does not express the radical views of Laugier to the degree that Soufflot intended.

Soufflot was, of course, far from alone in traveling south for study, and many academic exercises by the French pensionnaires, who spent extended periods in Rome absorbing the reality and the atmosphere of the Eternal City, exhibit a megalomania and almost obsessive fascination with antiquity, which, applied to the realities of site, client, and budget, yielded imposing monumental buildings when they returned home. Such monumentality was essential in Paris, where both the range and scale of public buildings were increasing, with larger buildings often covering their sites completely. Compositions were required that successfully included large expanses of unadorned wall surface,

13.26 Jacques-Denis Antoine, Ground-floor plan of the Hôtel des Monnaies, Paris, 1768–75.
The public front of this mint faces the Seine, with the principal court behind the center façade. The rooms of the main foundry and minting shops now house a coinage museum.

13.27 Jacques-Denis Antoine, Hôtel des Monnaies, Paris, 1768–75.
This building has an unusual French façade composition. Its central columns carry no pediment; the wings have no orders; and there are no end pavilions.

that provided adequate light and ventilation, and that were prominently displayed in the cityscape.

This attitude was given an opportunity for expression in the commission for a royal theater, at a time when the theater as a building type was a particular fascination of French culture. Marie-Joseph Peyre and Charles de Wailly, both back from years in Rome, designed the Comédie-Française with a Piranesian vision of the ancient city firmly in mind. Influenced perhaps by the ancient Roman insula, the theater once had shops on the ground floor at its flanks. The main façade of relentlessly rusticated masonry features a temple front without pediment, the first such form used for a theater (Fig. 13.25). The order is Tuscan, a connection, the architects said, to Apollo, protector of the arts. Peyre and de Wailly presented theatergoers with a social spectacle. From the street, the audience entered into a square vestibule with monumental stairs to either side; de Wailly left a moody drawing of one of the stairs amid a forest of columns that competes favorably with Piranesi's dramatic perspective scenes. The stairs led up to a domed vestibule and, in turn, to the theater boxes. The circular arrangement of the theater seating, while controversial at the time, was thought by the architects to be the most intimate arrangement.

Another pensionnaire, Jacques-Denis Antoine (1733–1801), designed the Hôtel des Monnaies, or Royal Mint (1768–75). His challenge was to house what amounted to a foundry within appropriately dignified quarters. On a triangular site, he cleverly arranged the minting shops

and their many support spaces around a main court (Fig. 13.26). At the side wall along the Rue Guénégaud, he employed heavy rustication (as did Sansovino at his Venetian mint; see Fig. 11.58), to indicate the security that he had provided for the activities inside. For the main façade facing the river Seine and the city, he chose to cap a central pavilion with a deep attic story but, as at the Comédie-Française, no pediment, and to stretch the wings laterally. In so doing, he produced a strongly horizontal, subdued, and elegant composition appropriate for a building that symbolized the strength of the nation's finances (Fig. 13.27). Spaces on the interior, such as the salon for the School of Mines located on the second floor of the central pavilion, are ornamented with a sumptuous inventiveness traceable to the architect's Roman experiences and his admiration for the work of Ange-Jacques Gabriel.

Roman traveler Jacques Gondouin (1737–1818) built the Ecole de Chirurgie, or School of Medicine and Surgery, between 1769 and 1774. It is characteristic of French Neo-Classicism in its use of art to express and even influence societal values. The entrance façade is decidedly un-French, having no end pavilions or central focus, with access provided through a triumphal-archlike opening behind a colonnade capped by a deep frieze and balustrade (Fig. 13.28). A sculptural panel shows the king and Minerva, both surrounded by the sick, ordering the construction of the building; the Genius of Architecture presenting the plan; and the figures of Surgery, Vigilance, and Providence guiding the actions of the king. Together, these images

13.28 Jacques Gondouin, Ecole de Chirurgie, Paris, 1769–74.
The idea of professional surgeons and a school for them was a new one in eighteenth-century France. At this entry façade, which combines a stoa and a central triumphal-arch-like motif, a sculpted panel includes the goddess of learning, Minerva, the king, and the genius of architecture.

13.29 Jacques Gondouin, Plan of the Ecole de Chirurgie, Paris, 1769–74.
In this plan, the entrance façade is at the bottom. Behind it, the court leads to a temple front, then the semicircular anatomical theater.

13.30 John Soane, Bank of England rotunda, London, begun 1788. Drawing by J.M. Gandy.

Gandy was an architect in his own right, but is more celebrated for his many atmospheric renderings of Soane's buildings, some shown complete, some shown during the process of construction, some even shown as ruins. In this drawing, Gandy illustrates Soane's preference for top-lighting, made necessary in the Bank of England by its many densely packed spaces with little if any exposure along the unpierced perimeter walls.

announce the ongoing elevation of French surgeons to the position of medical professionals, a change sanctioned by the French monarchy. Once through the entry, visitors pass into a court, with a public hall to the left and chemistry laboratory and hospital ward to the right. Opposite the entry, a temple front announces the semicircular anatomical theater behind, its plan based upon the theaters of antiquity and its coffered semidome with oculus comparable to the dome of the Pantheon in Rome (Fig. 13.29).

THE DISTINCTIVE STYLE OF SIR JOHN SOANE IN ENGLAND

A leading but idiosyncratic exponent of Neo-Classicism in England was Sir John Soane (1753–1837), whose career extended well into the nineteenth century. In his London building complex for the Bank of England (1788 and later; now destroyed except for its perimeter walls) he had to use daylight in imaginative ways because bank security required absolutely blank exterior walls (Fig. 13.30). Soane met the challenge with courtyards, clerestories, and skylights that, when coupled with the pure forms of the rotundas and vaulted spaces of the interior, seem inspired by Piranesi engravings, and indeed Soane may have met Piranesi when traveling in Italy. The bank's ornamentation was incised into the stone rather than sculpted out of it and was generally linear, simple, and minimal. Soane's own London house (now a museum) at 13 Lincoln's Inn

13.31 John Soane, The Colonnade, 13 Lincoln's Inn Fields (Sir John Soane's Museum), London, 1812–37. Drawing by J.M. Gandy.
Soane made the rear portion of his own house into a museum. Here he collected paintings by Hogarth, etchings by Piranesi, and shards from classical and medieval sites visited by him or his friends.

13.32 John Soane, Breakfast Room, 13 Lincoln's Inn Fields, London 1812–37.
The vault in this small room is the type preferred by Soane: low-slung arches springing directly from elegant columns or piers and supporting a billowing, ribbed dome. His ornament was most often incised, or cut into the surface, in order to emphasize spatial volumes.

Fields contains a diverse array of spaces and levels, which are lit by clerestories and top lights and articulated by layered wall planes and include both flat and convex mirrors for their reflections (Fig. 13.31). Such a design does not fit easily into any one stylistic category, though it includes many Neo-Classical features such as those in the shallow saucer-domed breakfast room (Fig. 13.32), where daylighting is brilliantly handled by means of a central lantern and lateral light monitors.

THE GERMAN NEO-CLASSICISM OF KARL FRIEDRICH SCHINKEL

Neo-Classicism in the area equivalent to modern-day Germany is closely identified with the work of Karl Friedrich Schinkel (1781–1841), most of which was done in the initial decades of the nineteenth century. Schinkel shared some of the formal concerns of the Frenchmen Boullée and Ledoux, but relied much more on the elements of Greek architecture. Akin to Alberti, Schinkel saw

architecture as a means to foster civic consciousness and saw polis-driven Greek classicism as its ideal symbolic language. He joined the Prussian public works office at the conclusion of the Napoleonic Wars, at a time when Prussia was seeking to raise its stature to that of a major European state, with Berlin as its capital.

The Neue Wache, or Royal Guard House (1817–18) (Fig. 13.33), located on the Unter den Linden, Berlin's most important ceremonial street, celebrated the emerging power of Prussia under King Friedrich Wilhelm III. Schinkel's final proposal placed a Doric portico between heavy pylons, both detailed with such austerity that the building achieves monumentality despite its modest size. Here, he succeeded in uniting the architectural forms of fortification and civic splendor.

In the summer of 1817, the Prussian national theater in Berlin, designed by Carl Gotthard Langhans (1732–1808) in 1800–02, burned to the ground. By early 1818 Schinkel had produced a new design for the Schauspielhaus (Fig. 13.34) to sit atop the old foundations between existing French and German churches. He treated the space

13.33 (above) Karl Friedrich Schinkel, Neue Wache, Berlin, 1817–18.
Here Schinkel projected a classical temple front forward from a pylonlike block. While modest in size, it is made monumental by Schinkel's skillful handling of proportions.

13.34 Karl Friedrich Schinkel, Schauspielhaus, Berlin, 1818–21.
For this theater, Schinkel chose a wall treatment of superimposed pilaster strips that anticipates the gridlike façades of twentieth-century skyscrapers. He illustrated it and his other work in his book *Sammlung Architektonischer Entwürfe (Collection of Architectural Designs)*.

13.35 (above) Karl Friedrich Schinkel, Altesmuseum, Berlin, 1823–28.
Schinkel carefully planned for his museum along the banks of the River Spree. He also designed a loggia on the second level at the central entry to act as a viewing platform to the urban landscape outside.

13.36 (below) Karl Friedrich Schinkel, Plans of the Altesmuseum, Berlin, 1823–28.
At the first- and second-floor levels, Schinkel combined a stoa along the front façade with a central rotunda, or pantheon of art, beyond, flanked by twin temples, their cellas' courtyards, and their prostyle columns part of the stoa front.

captured by them and by his new structure as a great vestibule and placed the monumental entry stair on the outside, unlike the practice in Neo-Classical France where the stair became part of the initial, dazzling interior space. Schinkel's stair leads to a building at once monumental, taut, and planar. The entire structure is raised on a high base and is dominated by an Ionic portico with receding masses to either side articulated by plain pilasters and precise, shallow moldings that appear to have been stretched tightly over an internal skeleton. The plan is equally clever and precise, effortlessly uniting multiple room sizes within a symmetrical distribution.

Easily Schinkel's most famous building is Berlin's Altesmuseum, or Old Museum (1823–28) (Fig. 13.35), the first public art museum in Europe. He sited it opposite the existing palace and arsenal to the south, creating a great civic court with a wall of trees along its east side. The museum's façade is a giant Ionic colonnade raised on a high base and stretching the full width of the building. Its orthogonal simplicity both creates a sense of urban dignity and prepares the visitor for the clever rigor of the plan behind (Fig. 13.36). Here, Schinkel placed a central rotunda flanked by open courts that are surrounded by flexible gallery spaces. Read as an interlocking set of classical prototypes, the museum is like the Pantheon caught between two temples, both fronted by a stoa. From the second-floor stair landing, a viewer can look back through the double file of columns for a framed view of Schinkel's Berlin.

Second foor

13.35

Galleries

Court   Rotunda   Court

Second-floor landing

First floor

Basement

THOMAS JEFFERSON, BENJAMIN HENRY LATROBE, AND NEO-CLASSICISM IN THE UNITED STATES

One of the most prominent Neo-Classical architects in the United States had no formal training, but learned to design from books and from personal observations of buildings made while he was abroad. This was the Roman Revivalist, founding father, and the country's third president, Thomas Jefferson (1743–1826). The son of a land surveyor and a graduate of William and Mary College, Jefferson trained to be a lawyer but made contributions in many fields. He was a statesman, philosopher, scientist, educator, economist, inventor, and gentleman architect—in short, a personification of the Renaissance ideal of an educated man. While serving as minister to France in 1785, Jefferson was asked to propose a design for the State Capitol of Virginia (Fig. 13.37). The model he prepared in response was based on the Maison Carrée in Nîmes (see page 104), a building he knew then only through the architectural treatise of Colen Campbell. Jefferson converted the relatively small Roman temple into a two-story legislative building, with a circular, domed assembly room that is not expressed on the exterior. He changed the Corinthian order of the Maison Carrée to the Ionic for Richmond because he feared American stonecarvers would lack the skill to handle the more complex Corinthian capitals.

Jefferson began his own home, Monticello (Figs. 13.38–13.39), in 1770 and used it as an architectural laboratory, continuing to evolve it until his death more than fifty years later. At first he envisioned a Palladian villa with two-story portico, but the final realization documents Jefferson's French architectural experiences, specifically his admiration for the new Parisian hôtels. More than any single influence, however, Monticello reveals Jefferson's extraordinary

13.37 Thomas Jefferson, Virginia State Capitol, Richmond, Virginia, 1785–89.
Jefferson based this temple design on the ancient Roman Maison Carrée in Nîmes, which he had seen and much admired while minister to France. Initially designed to stand on open ground, it is now surrounded by additions and high-rise government and office buildings. The flanking wings are not Jefferson's.

13.38 (below left) Thomas Jefferson, Plan of Monticello, Charlottesville, Virginia, begun 1770.
This plan shows the ground floor of the central block and the basement level of the wings.

13.39 (below) Thomas Jefferson, Monticello, Charlottesville, Virginia, begun 1770.
For his own house Jefferson turned the familiar Palladian five-part organization backward in order to focus the complex on spectacular mountain scenery. This view from the front shows that Jefferson disguised the two-story elevation to appear as only one story.

13.40 Thomas Jefferson, University of Virginia lawn, Charlottesville, Virginia, 1817–26.
Still the most admired example of campus planning in America, the University of Virginia was called an "academical village" by Jefferson. He intended for the view from the library down across the lawn to be open, but against the recommendations of architects McKim, Mead, and White, university officials chose to locate Cabell Hall at the south end in 1899.

13.41 Thomas Jefferson, Plan of the University of Virginia campus, Charlottesville, Virginia, 1817–26.
Extending from the library at the top of the scheme are the two files of five pavilions each connected by the walkways fronting dormitory rooms or what Jefferson called "ranges." Behind the pavilions are gardens and behind them more ranges as well as dining halls.

powers of synthesis. In its final form, the house's central block is two stories tall above the basement, but through clever placement of fenestration appears to be a single story. The house is crowned by an octagonal dome, not apparent on the interior except as an isolated attic room, and is connected to the landscape by two walkways atop basement spaces that extend to enclose the rear lawn. Here Jefferson placed the service functions—kitchens, storage, ice house, stables, and so on—below the grade of the lawn, so that they remained close at hand yet out of sight. The walkways, which capture rainwater and channel it to a cistern, terminate at the Honeymoon Cottage (above the "Brewins room" as it was called), where Jefferson and his wife first lived, and Jefferson's law office (above "Fodder storage"). The house's interior contrivances testify to the inventiveness of its owner. A clock in the entrance hall operates on a mechanism driven by cannonball weights that disappear through a hole in the floorboards. Wind direction can be determined indoors from a weather vane set on a tripod atop the east portico. Double doors between the hall and the drawing room open together even if only one is pushed because of a pulley mechanism under the floor. Jefferson's bed separates his study and sleeping quarters, and its narrowing of space between the two rooms gives greater velocity to summer breezes.

In his later years Jefferson turned his architectural talents to the design of a campus for the University of Virginia at Charlottesville (1817–26), an institution that he had done much to establish and for which he served as rector after its opening in 1825 (Fig. 13.40). His early site plan consisted of a U-shaped distribution of student rooms, linked by colonnades and punctuated by larger pavilions serving as lecture halls and faculty residences. Jefferson planned for the design of each pavilion to serve a didactic purpose, informing students about the best of architecture from antiquity. He called this extraordinary complex an "academical village," and he solicited comments on the site plan and pavilion designs through correspondence with William Thornton and Benjamin Henry Latrobe. Thornton contributed a suggested design for Pavilion VII; Latrobe contributed at least two and also recommended that the layout have a dominant focal element, an idea that Jefferson had originally rejected because of his opposition to centrality in government. The compositional improvement inherent in such a focus became obvious, however, and Jefferson designed a library based on the Pantheon (at half-scale) to serve as the head of the scheme (Fig. 13.41).

Latrobe (1766–1820) became Jefferson's architect of choice. He was born in England, educated there and in Europe, and practiced as an architect and engineer in and around London, before immigrating to America to become the country's first professional architect. In 1803 Jefferson commissioned him to work on the U.S. Capitol, which had been begun by William Thornton and continued, sometimes haphazardly, by Stephen Hallet and George Hadfield. Latrobe completed both the north and

13.42 Benjamin Henry Latrobe, Roman Catholic cathedral, Baltimore, 1805–18.
Latrobe presented both Gothic and Neo-Classical designs of this church to his client. The classical proposal was selected but did not include the towers seen here; they were added by the architect's son, John H.B. Latrobe, who also saw to the construction of the portico in 1863 according to his father's designs. Notice the skylights at the top of the dome.

13.43 Benjamin Henry Latrobe, Roman Catholic cathedral interior, Baltimore, 1805–18.
The choir was lengthened in 1890. The building reopened in 2006 after a radical restoration. The interior now has its original paint colors, white marble floor, and largely white pews.

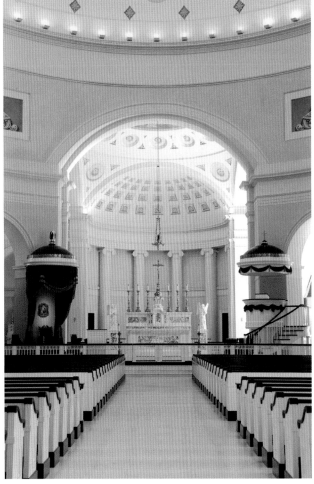

south wings, introducing into the work his own designs for American orders: tobacco-leaf capitals in the rotunda of the Senate chamber and corncob capitals in the north basement vestibule. He also used capitals based on those of the Archaic Greek temples at Paestum in the Supreme Court chamber.

In Philadelphia, Latrobe designed the Bank of Pennsylvania (1799), combining in it Greek Ionic porticoes front and back and a central dome with oculus that covered the monumental banking space. Late in his life, he was commissioned to design the Roman Catholic cathedral in Baltimore (Figs. 13.42–13.43). For this project he supplied two alternative schemes for the same plan, one based on Gothic precedent and one on Roman. The latter version was selected by the client, resulting in a building of remarkable Neo-Classical clarity, with a dome sixty-five feet in diameter at the crossing.

Piranesi's View of Rome
by Michael Fazio

13.44 Giovanni Battista Piranesi, *The Forum, or Campo Vaccino,* from *Vedute di Roma* (1745).

Walking through Michelangelo's Campidoglio (see Figs. 11.38–11.39) and continuing south beyond the crest of the Capitoline Hill, an eighteenth-century visitor to Rome would have found a panoramic view over the ancient Roman Forum Romanum (Fig. 13.44), with the triumphal arch of the emperor Septimius Severus in the foreground and the Colosseum in the background. Since Giovanni Battista Piranesi made this engraved view, the scene has changed considerably as archaeologists and modernity have done their work. The valley between the Palatine and Esquiline hills has been cleared (of vegetation) and earth that had half-buried the monuments has been excavated. Fallen stones have been reassembled and inferior constructions removed.

In Piranesi's day, the panorama was incomplete, even mysterious, and the artist reveled in it. Raised in densely built-up Venice, surrounded by its tradition of dramatic urban-scene painting by artists such as Canaletto, and trained as an artist-engraver, Piranesi had come to Rome in 1740, where he supported himself by producing *vedute*, or views, of the city to be sold as souvenirs. Operating from his showroom on the Via Sistina atop the Spanish Steps (see Fig. 12.21), he became very successful, even a sought-after celebrity. But Piranesi was much more than a local entrepreneur. Fascinated by the grandeur that had once been ancient Rome, he participated in the radical examination of the past that grew out of the Enlightenment.

In this engraved view of the Forum Romanum, Piranesi ponders the effects of time and invites the viewer to imagine the scene centuries earlier when the Roman Empire was at its zenith. His moody, atmospheric depiction is enhanced by the eruption of erratic

vegetation and an array of actorlike figures, all dwarfed by the ruins around them. This engraving and others like it appealed not only to the casual tourist but also to the waves of pensionnaires (see page 390) who drank here from one of the fountainheads of classicism.

Piranesi's influence did not end with his reproductions of existing conditions or his imaginative illustrations of the past. As his career evolved, he became more and more interested in architectural reconstructions and speculative archaeology. Experimenting with provocative evidence from the past, he sought to give architects a glimpse of architecture's inherent possibilities. Gradually his work became more and more eclectic, more and more fantastic, distasteful to some but ever more inspiring to others.

Perhaps most provocative are his *Carceri*, or *Prisons*, a series of fourteen plates made in 1745, and reissued in around 1760, depicting vast spaces teeming with unidentified toilers whose labors are illuminated by obscure light sources. The scale is gigantic, of the magnitude of the great Roman baths, while the spatial organization is even more complex. Arches, vaults, and staircases rise in the gloom and are revealed by shafts of light that perhaps mimic the spotlighting of partially excavated rooms in Pompeii and Herculaneum, where archaeologists tunneled into them from above.

Because they were inexpensive, produced in large quantities, and easily transported, Piranesi's engravings were widely distributed across Europe in his own time, and they continue to impress architects and artists today. While his work certainly stimulated the minds of Neo-Classicists, it also inspired those pursuing a contrary way of thinking and feeling, and their ideas and work are discussed in the subsequent sections.

ROMANTICISM AND THE PICTURESQUE

Even as Neo-Classical architects and antiquarians were using reason and intellect to reassess the past through archaeological work and scholarly inquiry, a parallel and often overlapping orientation in art and architecture called Romanticism was developing. Its design beginnings can be seen in the English landscape movement that accompanied the Neo-Palladians during the first half of the eighteenth century and its literary beginnings in the *Sturm und Drang* (Storm and Stress) movement, which started in Germany in the 1760s with the writings of such luminaries as Johann Wolfgang von Goethe and that stressed the power of emotion and the importance of individual subjectivity. Romantics delighted in the asymmetrical and irregular because of the highly scenic qualities they could produce, which partially explains the popularity of Piranesi's engraved scenes of fallen vaults and moldering, half-buried monuments populated by enigmatic, tattered beggars, images that expressed the Romantic longing for a perfect place and a perfect time that would remain always remote and unreachable. Ruins in general became a Romantic obsession, as their ruggedness, wildness, and fragmentation illustrated the powerlessness of men and women in the face of irresistible natural forces and the melancholy, relentless erosion of their works over time.

The esthetic doctrine of Romanticism was the Picturesque. Edmund Burke wrote about it in his *A Philosophical Inquiry into the Origins of Our Ideas on the Sublime and the Beautiful* (1756). Here he differentiated between picturesque conditions that were beautiful—possessed of such qualities as delicacy and smoothness—and those that were sublime—possessed of such alternative qualities as power, vastness, and obscurity. So one can see, for instance, that Etienne-Louis Boullée's interest in enormous structures aligns him with the sublime.

THE ROMANTIC LANDSCAPE

William Kent's Neo-Palladian landscape creations, including the grounds of Chiswick and Holkham Hall, are probably more important than his architectural contributions. He is regarded as one of the founders of the English landscape-garden tradition, in which the landscape architect exaggerated and "improved" on natural conditions. Instead of the rigid geometric plantings favored by the French, English garden designers cultivated a certain irregular wildness. They exploited the natural contours of the land, formed trees into apparently natural patterns, and developed seemingly fortuitous, but actually carefully contrived, views of carefully sited buildings. Likewise, equally carefully planned views from the windows of buildings extended beyond nearby clumps of trees into the more distant landscape, where cows grazed as in a landscape painting. A ditch with a fence or hedge at its bottom prevented the cows from encroaching upon the lawns in the immediate vicinity of the house; discovery of this concealed barrier was a surprise, causing one to laugh or exclaim, "Aha!"—thus providing the name ha-ha for this landscape device. To the Neo-Palladians, who saw "natural" qualities in the architecture of Palladio and Inigo Jones, there was nothing contradictory in having a symmetrical classical house set in a landscape with naturalistic elements that reflected a painter's vision of the Roman countryside.

Lancelot Brown (1716–83) was the leading promoter of this Picturesque attitude toward landscape architecture. When asked his opinion of a piece of ground, he would say that it had "capabilities," and thus he became known as Capability Brown. He practiced as an architect in the Palladian tradition, but in that field he was a minor figure compared to Kent, for whom he worked as a gardener at Stowe from 1740. However, he knew much more than Kent about horticulture, expressed his ideas with clarity, and followed up his plans with informed supervision if the client requested it. Among his most celebrated works are the relandscaped gardens and park at Blenheim Palace (Fig. 13.45), laid out after 1764 and still extant. This plan included the creation of a serpentine lake and an encircling drive, the planting of tree clusters that still make for a pleasing dappled pattern in the sunlit landscape, and intermittent views of the building. Brown's impact on the English landscape can hardly be overstated. Working throughout the length and breadth of the nation, he transformed large areas of unkempt countryside into the kind of lush parkland for which England has become renowned.

13.45 Lancelot Brown, Blenheim Palace grounds, after 1764.
The English Romantic landscape garden drew some of its inspiration from the garden traditions of China. The English sought to imitate the irregularity of nature rather than artificially ordering natural elements in geometric patterns as in the Italian and French garden traditions.

PICTURESQUE BUILDINGS

Picturesque architecture in England began with follies, the use of small and sometimes fanciful structures or ruins of structures as focal points in the layout of gardens. At Hagley Park, Worcestershire, Sanderson Miller built a sham ruin in the Gothic style in 1747, and other landscape designers soon took to the idea. Horace Walpole had his house at Strawberry Hill, Twickenham, near London, put up in a medieval manner by a committee of architects and literary friends. Work began in 1748, and the structure soon emerged as an eclectic assortment of Gothic details. The Holbein Room has a chimneypiece adapted from the tomb of Archbishop Wareham at Westminster Abbey; the Long Gallery (page 380) features **pendant vaulting** based on that in the Henry VII Chapel at Westminster Abbey; and the Round Room has ceiling plasterwork inspired by the rose window of old St. Paul's Cathedral. The Rococo chandeliers and purple wallpapers used throughout contribute to a sense of playfulness in this passionate, picturesque amusement. This early phase of Romanticism in England is often termed "Gothick" (the spelling deliberately medievalized) to reflect the rather lighthearted character of the work.

While the interior treatments at Strawberry Hill are interesting for their naïve antiquarian enthusiasm, the exterior form is important for the attitude that it displays toward picturesque massing. To understand this condition, it is first necessary to consider the plan (Fig. 13.46),

which has virtually no traditional formal order. Certainly there is a clear functional division between Walpole's rooms and those for his servants, and there are various other such practical concessions to the activities of daily life. However, to appreciate the house's design fully, one must view it externally (Fig. 13.47). Here, it becomes clear that Walpole, amateur though he was, intended for Strawberry Hill to present a rich silhouette against the sky, intended that its character should change as one moved around the perimeter, and intended for the ensemble to appear as though it had been built not all at once, but had grown up randomly over time, as had its medieval inspirations. This was a new way of thinking about building composition and one that would be explored by both eighteenth- and nineteenth-century designers. Likewise, nineteenth-century scholars would make an intense study of Gothic buildings, establish a chronology of Gothic stylistic development, and master the recomposition of accurately reproduced Gothic elements. And the return of the Gothic would be only one among many such revivals in that rampant borrowing from the past called **eclecticism**.

Among the trained Neo-Classical architects, Robert Adam also designed Romantic garden follies and Gothic-inspired buildings such as the Scottish Culzean Castle, a turreted and crenelated rebuilding of an existing country house. Sir John Soane included mock ruins at his own Pitzhanger Manor, now surrounded by part of West London, and had the visionary architect and delineator Joseph Gandy produce paintings for him showing his buildings, such as the Bank of England, as ruins, as well as more conventional but still evocative renderings of his various projects. Karl Friedrich Schinkel, who began his career as an artist and set designer, created many such painted images, including a "Gothic Cathedral on a River"

13.46 Plan of Strawberry Hill, Twickenham, begun 1748.
No one could call this plan conventionally orderly. However, antiquarian Horace Walpole was little concerned with two-dimensional geometries. Rather, he so arranged a variety of three-dimensional forms that their resulting massing would be varied and irregular and even surprising—in a word: picturesque.

13.47 Horace Walpole, Strawberry Hill, begun 1748.
Antiquarian Horace Walpole wanted his rambling house to look like the medieval buildings that he had seen and admired, buildings that had been built in stages and by accretion and so had picturesque charm. Precocious as his house was at the time, its outward effect is quite convincing.

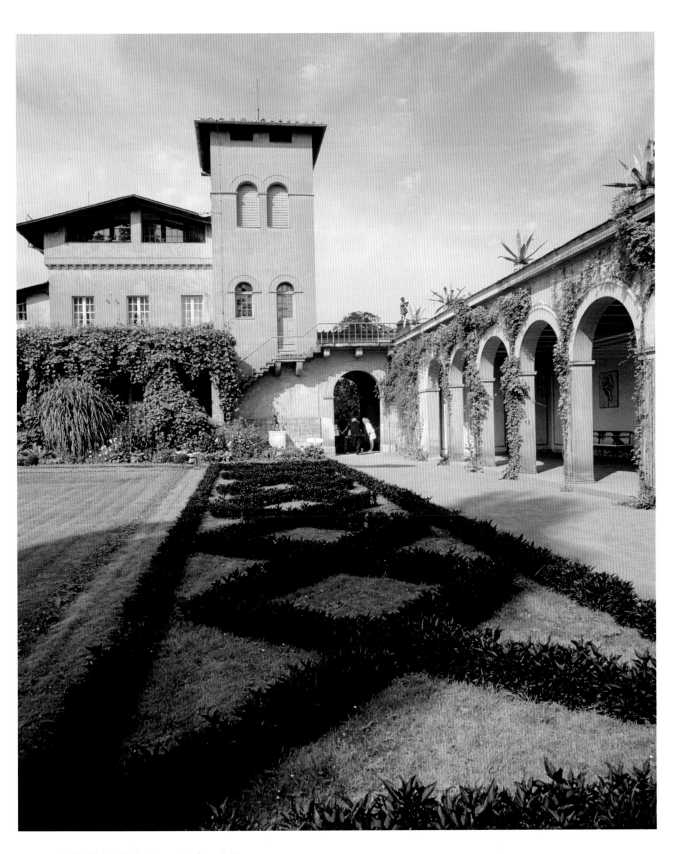

13.48 Karl Friedrich Schinkel, Court Gardener's House,
Charlottenhof, 1826–33.
Schinkel wanted this building to resemble the vaguely classical, vernacular
farmsteads that he had seen while traveling in Italy as a student. The
tower, the low-sloping, gabled masses, and the many arched openings
and pergolas are all united in a singular picturesque composition.

13.49 Karl Friedrich Schinkel, Site and building plan of the Court Gardener's House, Charlottenhof, 1826–33. In this layout, formal geometric parterres spread out adjacent to the curving shorelines and winding paths of a romantic landscape. Likewise, while the individual components of the building's plan are frequently symmetrical, the overall configuration is artfully asymmetrical.

(1813), with the church seen in silhouette on a promontory and looming portentously over the surrounding town. He was equally deft in creating picturesque designs, including those for a number of Gothic Revival structures. At the Charlottenhof (1826–33), a sprawling estate near Potsdam, Schinkel based his asymmetrical composition for the Court Gardener's House (Fig. 13.48) on rural Italian buildings he had seen during his student travels and situated it in a carefully conceived landscape setting that includes picturesque water features and winding paths as well as geometric parterres (Fig. 13.49).

CONCLUSIONS ABOUT ARCHITECTURAL IDEAS

Historians commonly divide the history of the Western world into three periods: antiquity, the Middle Ages, and the modern age, meaning, in this nomenclature, that the Renaissance represents the beginning of "Modernism." While this subdivision is true in the broadest sense, it was the eighteenth-century Enlightenment, with its emphasis on scientific empiricism, evolving secularism, and nascent democratic thinking, and the incipient Industrial Revolution that more specifically ushered in the modern era.

Following the final flowering of the Baroque as the Rococo, Neo-Classicism arose during the heady years of the Enlightenment's emergence, becoming to some extent synonymous with it. Neo-Palladianism, an early eighteenth-century English brand of Neo-Classicism, preceded both the Enlightenment and the Industrial Revolution and looked for its inspiration not directly back to ancient Greece or Rome but rather indirectly, through Andrea Palladio's and, in turn, Inigo Jones's interpretation of classicism.

Inigo Jones, on the move at the beginning of the seventeenth century, was precocious in journeying south to Italy to make direct contact with classical architecture, but he was eventually only one among many to do so from England, where it became fashionable to make the Grand Tour. Robert Adam took such a tour in the mid-eighteenth century and was galvanized by what he saw at Pompeii and Herculaneum, where extraordinary evidence of ancient life and art was gradually being brought to light through archaeological excavations. Based on his study of ancient Roman wall paintings, Adam developed a style of interior architecture that pushed aside the heavy Palladian taste of the first half of the eighteenth century in England. Adam was also among those who, after closely studying antique sites in Italy, Greece, and elsewhere, published their findings in an illustrated form and so made knowledge of them widely available. Adam's principal competitor, Sir William Chambers, followed the lead of James Gibbs and actually took up residence in Rome for a period of extended study. In the process, he encountered the engraver Piranesi, a contact reflected in his choice of huge, rusticated, Piranesian arches to support Somerset House on its Thames-side elevation. Chambers also fell into the company of the French pensionnaires, architectural students who had come south as part of their formal architectural training.

France became the first country in Europe to develop architectural schools, meaning that design training became highly organized and was based on a codified body of architectural theory. J.-F. Blondel ranked among the most influential of the French theorist-teachers, and his *Cours d'architecture* laid out the principles for an architecture that reflected the hierarchical ordering of French society. Among the many pensionnaires who returned from Italy to work for the French government and so produced buildings at the top of this hierarchy were Marie-Joseph Peyre and Charles de Wailly, designers of the Comédie-Française; Jacques-Denis Antoine, designer of the Hôtel des Monnaies; and Jacques Gondouin, architect of the Ecole de Chirurgie.

More polemical in his writing than Blondel, the Abbé Laugier set forth an ideology for an Enlightenment architecture based on the fundamental elements of construction as represented by the supposed rationality of the primitive hut. Jacques-Gabriel Soufflot, subsequent to his time spent in Rome, acted upon Laugier's *Essai sur l'architecture* in producing an extravagantly trabeated design for Ste.-Geneviève in Paris, now known as the Panthéon. While Soufflot necessarily made some compromises in adapting theory to practice, Etienne-Louis Boullée did not, choosing instead to present his architectural ideas in the form of imaginary, often unbuildable projects. Vast in scale and sweeping in vision, they fired the imaginations of many who saw them. Claude-Nicolas Ledoux produced rhetorical projects of his own but also built both for the Crown and private clients. His "Inspector's House at the Source of the River Loüe" illustrates an *architecture parlante* by overtly expressing function through ideal, abstract forms. In this case, the house sits astride the river, so that the rushing waters flow dramatically through it. Of his *barrières*, or tollgates, that once ringed Paris, some reflective of the half-buried Roman ruins seen and admired by French architectural students, a few remain to attest to his inventiveness and unique interpretation of the classical language. His Parisian hôtels particuliers verify both the extreme cleverness and efficiency of eighteenth-century French domestic planning and the concomitant French skill in manipulating space in three dimensions along the principal path of movement.

Neo-Classicism continued well into the nineteenth century. In England, Sir John Soane was perhaps the most adept practitioner, but was also one who developed his own distinctive style. No Neo-Classicist was more gifted than the German Karl Friedrich Schinkel, who populated the center of Berlin with monumental buildings for the Prussian State. And in America, the gentleman amateur Thomas Jefferson took time away from his political pursuits to design his own house called Monticello and a capitol and a university for the State of Virginia, and, while president, hired the country's most talented Neo-Classicist, English immigrant Benjamin Henry Latrobe, to work on the new nation's public buildings.

Eventually, Enlightenment rationalism and rigid classicism as well as the beginnings of the Industrial Revolution stimulated the counterdevelopment of Romanticism and the Picturesque. Englishman Edmund Burke wrote about both fragile beauty and overwhelming sublimity. Romantic garden designers like William Kent and Lancelot Brown went nature one better by amplifying existing landscape conditions. Amateur building designer Horace Walpole gave his house called Strawberry Hill "Gothick" detailing and picturesque massing. Robert Adam worked in a Gothic mode when the commission demanded it, and a Picturesque sensibility can be found in much of Sir John Soane's work. Likewise, Karl Friedrich Schinkel complemented his formal Neo-Classical compositions with informal but carefully composed picturesque ones like the Court Gardener's House at Charlottenhof.

In the nineteenth century, Romanticism would find new fertile ground as a reaction against the excesses of the Industrial Revolution, which brought about the exploitation of new energy sources, the proliferation of machines, and the dramatically expanded production of manufactured goods. These matters will be discussed in the next chapter.

Chapter 14

Eclecticism, Industrialization, and Newness

Architecture in the nineteenth century was perhaps more varied than ever. The freedoms introduced by Neo-Classicism and Romanticism encouraged the revival of other historical styles, such as Gothic, Greek, Islamic, Egyptian, Byzantine, and Early Christian, along with inventive new creations, such as the Chinoiserie, Japonais, Moorish, and Hindoo styles. For example, colonial officials returning from India with their fortunes to retire in England built pleasure palaces such as Sezincote in Gloucestershire, its skin designed in the Indian manner in 1805 by Samuel Pepys Cockerell (1754–1827) for his brother Charles. Likewise, between 1818 and 1821, John Nash (1752–1835) built the Royal Pavilion at Brighton (Fig. 14.1) for the prince regent in a combination of Indian, Islamic, and Chinese styles. Significantly, however, this building, which one author has called an "orgy of refinement and bad taste," was built all of cast iron, and it is this material, along with steel, concrete, and large expanses of glass, that are an emphasis of this chapter.

Dramatic progress in materials science, which began in the eighteenth century, eventually enabled architects and engineers to address construction problems in fundamentally new ways, contributing further to the diversity observable in nineteenth-century work. Buildings in Britain and the United States now termed "Victorian" often have little in common with one another, save that they were built during the exceptionally long reign (1837–1901) of Queen Victoria. Amid the stylistic revivals and engineering accomplishments also came new design ideas that were to provide the foundation for Modernism in the twentieth century. This chapter addresses all these developments.

THE CHALLENGE OF THE INDUSTRIAL REVOLUTION

Industrial technology advanced in the eighteenth century as inventors and technicians sought more efficient means for accomplishing various tasks: the spinning of yarn, the weaving and finishing of cloth, the mining and processing of metallic ores, and so on. Machine work began to replace the handwork of men and women, and steam engines supplanted the motive power of men and horses. The changes

these new innovations brought to society were many and far-reaching, including an increase in population, the rise of a new urban working class, the substantial growth of factory towns, some redistribution of wealth, and improved living conditions for many.

Structural calculations were first applied to the design of the Panthéon in Paris, a building discussed in the previous chapter. By the middle of the nineteenth century, it was possible to predict the behavior of most structural materials under specified loading conditions, freeing builders from reliance on a process of trial and error. One unfortunate result of such developments was the increasing separation between architecture and engineering. Since the Middle Ages, the architect—described by Vitruvius as a man skilled in the design of everything from cities to buildings, mechanical devices, astronomical instruments,

---

Chronology

Abraham Darby begins iron production in Coalbrookedale, Shropshire, England	1696
Iron bridge over the river Severn, Shropshire	1779–81
Invention of the balloon frame	1830s
A.W.N. Pugin publishes *Contrasts* and *True Principles of Christian Architecture*	1836 and 1841
Karl Marx publishes the *Communist Manifesto*	1848
John Ruskin publishes *The Seven Lamps of Architecture*	1849
Joseph Paxton builds the Crystal Palace	1851
Sir Henry Bessemer patents his steelmaking process	1855
Charles Darwin publishes *On the Origin of Species*	1859
Beginning of the Arts and Crafts Movement	ca. 1859
First architectural school in the U.S. established at MIT	1861
Eugène-Emmanuel Viollet-le-Duc publishes *Entretiens sur l'architecture*	1863–72
Great Fire in Chicago	1871
H.H. Richardson builds Trinity Church	1872–77
Beginning of the Art Nouveau	ca. 1880
Invention of the fireproof metal frame for tall buildings	1880s
Gustave Eiffel builds the Eiffel Tower	1889
Frank Lloyd Wright develops the Prairie house	1890s
Sigmund Freud formulates his first major theory and method of psychoanalysis	1892–95
World's Columbian Exposition in Chicago	1893
Louis Sullivan publishes "The Tall Building Artistically Considered"	1896
Formation of the Viennese Secession	1898

Gustave Eiffel, Eiffel Tower, Paris, 1889.
The Eiffel Tower was seen as a blight on the Parisian skyline when it was built; it was maintained initially in part because of its use as a radio tower. Today it has become a symbol of Paris itself.

and machines of war—had been gradually released from responsibility for mechanical contraptions and items for defense, which passed instead to the newly recognized fields of mechanical and military engineering. Now a growing body of scientific data on materials provided the basis for civil engineering, which was taught at schools organized apart from architectural academies. Civil engineers were charged with the increasing body of utilitarian construction—roads, bridges, mines, factories, warehouses, lighthouses, and canals—while architects were employed on buildings where esthetics and symbolism outweighed pragmatism. Thus it was engineers, not architects, who first experimented with the building materials made possible by industrial technology, and it was in utilitarian structures that they were first used.

Of all the construction materials improved or developed during the Industrial Revolution, none was more important than iron. People had been smelting iron from ore since the prehistoric Iron Age, but the quantity of metal produced was small and its quality was highly variable. Therefore, the use of this material in buildings was limited to occasional ornamental work, fasteners, and hardware. Improved means of producing iron were sought by refiners, including Abraham Darby, whose furnace at Coalbrookdale, Shropshire, in England, began production as early as 1696. In an attempt to advance his work, Darby imported Dutch ironworkers in 1704 and soon succeeded

in smelting cast iron for commercial use. Cast iron has a relatively high carbon content and is brittle, though very strong in compression. By 1713 Darby had pioneered a method for producing cast iron using coal instead of expensive charcoal in his furnace. The structural properties of his cast iron made it a suitable material for columns, where its high compressive strength could be exploited. When used for beams, which must resist both tension and compression forces, iron is not so suitable because of its relatively modest tensile strength. If refined iron with a lower carbon content is hammered into shape instead of being cast, it is known as wrought iron, a material with considerably higher compressive and tensile strength and so much better than cast iron for beams.

Builders soon found applications for these two types of iron. Darby's furnaces produced wrought-iron railroad ties as early as 1750 and supplied cast iron for the world's first all-metal bridge in 1779–81. Abraham Darby III, grandson of the pioneering industrialist, collaborated with the architect Thomas Pritchard to design this bridge using five parallel semicircular arches to span 100 feet over the river Severn (Fig. 14.2). The bridge cost £6000, a large sum but only about one-third the price of an equivalent masonry span. Its design was conservative but it nonetheless represents the first essay in metal construction for bridges.

The incombustible properties of iron, together with its strength, were exploited in the construction of "fireproof"

14.1 John Nash, The Royal Pavilion, Brighton, 1818–21.
Built as a getaway for royals in the fashionable seaside town of Brighton, this exotic cast-iron building combines Indian and Islamic motifs on the outside and has more of the same on the inside, along with extravagant Chinoiserie—decorative elements in a fanciful Chinese style created by Frederick Crace. It is actually an enlargement of a modest rural structure dating from the eighteenth century.

14.2 Abraham Darby III and Thomas Pritchard, Bridge over the river Severn, 1779–81.
With its multiple supporting arches, this bridge uses relatively brittle iron in a condition of compression. Subsequent bridges would take advantage of the iron alloy steel's considerable tensile, as well as compressive, strength.

14.3 William Strutt, Plan of and sections through West Mill, Belper, 1793–95.
With masonry exterior walls and a grid of interior columns, this mill has an open, flexible plan. A challenge for architects during the late nineteenth century would be expressing this internal skeleton on the exterior while covering it with fireproof materials.

multi-story textile mills. As early as 1793 the Englishman William Strutt designed and built a six-story calico mill at Derby with cast-iron columns; his West Mill at Belper, constructed the following year, is similar (Fig. 14.3). The dust-laden air of textile mills, combined with coagulated oil and lint on the floors under the machinery and illumination from open flames, created ideal conditions for mill fires in which equipment, raw materials, and workers' lives were lost. To protect the structure, improve sanitation and ventilation, and reduce the opportunities for fire, Strutt and others designed mills with external walls of masonry, cast-iron internal columns, and protected wood beams. An early version of "fireproof" construction had the large wooden floor beams socketed into cast-iron shoes attached to the cast-iron columns. Segmental brick arches spanned from beam to beam, supporting level floors made of sand, screed, and clay tiles, with wrought-iron rods tying the structure together. Undersides of the wooden members were coated with plaster; with sand on top and plaster below, the wood was protected from fire. Later improvements to this system substituted wrought-iron rails (forerunners of **rolled steel sections**) for the wooden beams. A surviving example of such a structure is the former Benyon, Benyon, and Bage Flax Mill at Shrewsbury in England (1796). Eventually the segmental brick arches at Belper were discarded in favor of other materials, but even with these changes, the metal-frame structure of today remains essentially the same as that built by Strutt in 1793–95.

DEVELOPMENTS IN STEEL

In seeking to expand the market for iron and improve the desirable qualities of the material, nineteenth-century ironmakers experimented with new methods for manufacturing steel, which is an alloy of low-carbon iron and

trace amounts of other metals. Small quantities of steel had been manufactured in India as early as 1500 BCE, and Celtic peoples in Austria, Spain, and Britain had made and worked the material at sites where iron ore containing manganese occurred in natural deposits. Blacksmiths, knifesmiths, and swordmakers could work the extracted iron and make steel, which was prized for its ability to hold a superior cutting edge. Industrialization of this process required reducing the carbon content of the molten iron and using less charcoal in the furnace because that fuel was becoming scarce and expensive.

An American ironmaker, William Kelly (1811–88), was the first to develop a converter that burnt off excess carbon with a blast of air. He constructed seven of them at his works in Eddyville, Kentucky. When he was ready to apply for a patent on his process in 1856, however, he found that the Englishman Henry Bessemer (1813–98) had just been granted one for the same idea. Although Kelly's prior claim to this invention was subsequently demonstrated, he received neither the recognition nor the financial rewards that should have been his. Bessemer became known as the inventor of the converter that made reliable quantities of steel efficiently and affordably. From 1875 onward, steel began to replace both cast and wrought iron in construction because its compressive and tensile strengths exceeded those of iron and it was cheaper to produce.

Steel was first used for railroad ties and in engineering works. The first steel bridge built in the United States was the Eads Bridge (1869–74) over the Mississippi river at St. Louis. Its designer, Captain James B. Eads (1820–87), had been a riverboat captain and salvage operator on the river, and despite his complete lack of engineering training (as he was assisted by capable engineers and mathematicians who provided the technical abilities he lacked), he was able to gain the confidence of local businessmen who backed the construction of the bridge. Eads understood the behavior of the river and insisted that the bridge foundations extend to bedrock, which lay under fourteen feet of water and eighty-one feet of sand. The bridge required four stone piers to support three segmental-arched steel spans of 502, 520, and 502 feet; the arches were fabricated of eighteen-inch-diameter cast-steel tubes, interconnected by triangulated bracing to form an integrated unit. Construction was accomplished by sinking pneumatic caissons for pier foundations and then cantilevering the arch sections out from each pier until the arch could be closed, as centering to support the arch in construction would have interfered with navigation on the river.

Steel was also employed for the major suspension bridge of the nineteenth century, the Brooklyn Bridge, connecting Manhattan and Brooklyn over the East river with a 1600-foot clear span (Fig.14.4). The bridge was designed by John Augustus Roebling (1806–69) and constructed under the supervision of his son, Washington Augustus Roebling (1837–1926). They sank two gigantic caisson foundations for the bridge towers, and spun galvanized

14.4 J.A. and W.A. Roebling, Brooklyn Bridge, New York City, 1869–83. No suspension bridge has been more celebrated than this one connecting Manhattan to Brooklyn across the East river. Its steel cables were not raised intact but were woven by a spider-like machine that passed repeatedly from bank to bank.

steel wire for the two main cables that supported the roadway. Each cable contains over 5000 strands of wire, compacted and wrapped with a continuous spiral of softer steel. Diagonal stays radiating from the towers provide wind bracing and are probably strong enough to carry the bridge's loads by themselves should the main cables break, while a stiffened deck checks any tendency the bridge might have to develop destructive vibrations resulting from wind loads. One of the most enjoyable experiences in New York City is to walk the pedestrian level of the bridge from Brooklyn Heights back toward Manhattan and its skyline.

IRON AND GLASS GREENHOUSE DESIGNS

Iron and steel were not generally admired for their architectural qualities throughout much of the nineteenth century, as architects could produce the eclectic buildings that they and their clients preferred using traditional materials and methods. Consequently and ironically, it was greenhouse designers who first made an outwardly expressive, dramatically open iron and glass architecture.

Prosperous from the wealth of their empire, the Victorian English had a fascination with the tropical plants that were brought back from India, Africa, and the Far East. Keeping these specimens alive in the cool, overcast climate of Britain required structures that could reproduce the humid heat of their native countries, so gardeners set about erecting greenhouses large enough to contain palm or banana trees. Unfettered by ancient precedent, the builders turned to lightweight iron framing systems with glass infill panes. The Palm House at Kew Gardens, London (1845–47) (Fig. 14.5) by architect and garden designer Decimus Burton and ironmaker Richard Turner is an example of this kind of work.

Joseph Paxton and the Crystal Palace

Among the greenhouse builders, horticulturalist Joseph Paxton (1801–65) is the most celebrated as a result of his unsolicited design for a structure built in Hyde Park, London to house the first modern world's fair in 1851. Fairs like this one provided manufacturers with mass exposure for their products, introduced the public to new technologies and scientific discoveries, and presented designers with the opportunity for architectural innovation. The building committee for the London exhibition had received 245 designs of all sorts, none of which was entirely suitable, so

14.5 Decimus Burton and Richard Turner, Palm House, Kew Gardens, London, 1845–47. Greenhouses provided an impetus for the design of lightweight, quickly constructed, transparent structures. Between the iron arches, the glass frames were folded in alternate ridges and furrows, which provided rigidity.

GROUND PLAN

END ELEVATION

AN AUTHENTIC VIEW OF THE GREAT INDUSTRIAL EXHIBITION PALACE OF 1851.
DESIGNED BY JOSEPH PAXTON, ESQ., F.R.S.

Length, 1848 feet; width, 456 feet in the broadest part, exclusive of the Machinery Room, on the North side, which will be 936 feet long, and 48 feet wide; height of centre roof, 64 feet; adjacent side portions, 44 feet; outer sides, 24 feet; and the transept, which will enclose large timber trees, 108 feet in height, and 72 feet wide. The ground floor occupies 752,832 superficial feet, and the space provided in galleries, 102,528 feet; exhibition surface, 21 acres. Total cubic contents being 33,000,000 feet. The quantity of glass about 900,000 superficial feet, weighing upwards of 400 tons. 3,300 cast and wrought iron columns, varying from 14 feet 6 inches, to 20 feet in length; 2,224 cast iron girders, and 1,128 intermediate bearers for supporting the floors of galleries; 34 miles of gutter to carry off water. Length of sash bar, 205 miles.—*From Mr. Paxton's own Report.*
The great central walk, 72 feet wide; gallery, 24 feet wide; length of table space for exhibiting, 8 miles.   Contract for use of building, £79,800; or, if the building be permanently retained, £150,000.

it had decided to produce its own, a great domed structure with a brick drum and heavy walls. Even this traditional structure could probably not have been built rapidly enough and within the £300,000 budget. These circumstances made Paxton's tardy submission in July 1850 all the more attractive (Fig. 14.6). His design proposed a 1851-foot-long structure of glass and iron at an estimated price of £150,000; and, through negotiations with the suppliers of the materials, Paxton could guarantee completion on time. His scheme was accepted. In constructing the building, the contractors Fox and Henderson made one of the first large-scale demonstrations of prefabrication. The repeated iron-and-glass sections required a limited number of different components, which meant that supplying factories could easily mass-produce the tremendous quantity of material required for the eighteen-acre building: 3800 tons of cast iron, 700 tons of wrought iron, twenty-four miles of rainwater guttering, 900,000 square feet of glass, and 600,000 cubic feet of wood (Fig. 14.7). Materials arrived at the site preassembled into subsections, and final assembly proceeded at an unprecedented rate. Once the exhibition opened, the building was visited by about one-quarter of the population of England and, though called a "glass monster" by one critic and a "magnified" conservatory by another, it was widely acclaimed for its vast, airy interior space. Journalists dubbed it "the Crystal Palace," a name it has retained. The construction success and public praise for the Crystal Palace had much to do with the increasing acceptance of a larger amount of glass and iron in buildings designed by architects. After the exhibition ended, the building was dismantled and reerected in a park at Sydenham, outside London, where it remained until it was destroyed by fire in 1936.

14.6 Joseph Paxton, Crystal Palace, London, 1851, lithograph.
Joseph Paxton designed a building with prefabricated parts that could be mass-produced and erected rapidly. It stood in stark contrast to traditional, massive stone constructions.

14.7 Joseph Paxton, Crystal Palace interior, London, lithograph.
Such a structure as this one was not considered to be "architecture" by theorist and critic John Ruskin because it lacked permanence. However, its lightweight, skeletal, transparent construction pointed toward the future.

ESSAY
The Coming of the Railroad
by Mark Reinberger

14.8 W.P. Frith, *The Railway Station*, 1866, engraving.

No single development had a greater impact on life in the nineteenth century than the railroad. After the first line opened from Stockton to Darlington in England in 1825, this new means of transportation spread with astonishing rapidity. By the 1840s railroads reached all parts of England. In the 1830s lines were begun in France, Germany, Ireland, Russia, and Italy. The first American line was the Baltimore and Ohio, which began operations in 1830. Ten years later the country had 3000 miles of track, and, by the outbreak of the Civil War, 30,000 miles had been laid. In 1869, the first American transcontinental line linked the east and west coasts.

More than any other invention, the railroad linked all regions of countries together, creating unified nations and leading to more integrated economies and the century's stronger sense of nationalism. Regional differences in consumption, fashion, and architecture lessened in the wake of the railroads, which made possible fast, long-distance mail delivery, the rapid spread of news,

and the easier distribution of products including building materials.

The growth of the railroads spurred, and in turn was dependent upon, nineteenth-century industrialization. A large-scale railroad network was unthinkable without such elements of a modern industrial economy as a large and mobile labor force, the creation of steel for rails capable of withstanding heavy loads, the standardization of tools and machinery, finer tolerances in manufacturing, new structural capabilities for bridges and tunneling, and a prodigious amount of mining for coal. All of these industries, in turn, provided jobs for millions of workers. Railroads also made possible the modern extended city, and allowed more than just the upper and upper-middle classes (who could afford a carriage) to live in suburbs. Subways and streetcars also made possible denser concentrations of businesses in city centers, necessitating the development of the tall office building late in the century. In America, railroads also helped open up remote areas to mining and settlement

and were responsible for much town-founding. They also tied together colonialized countries abroad, allowing international powers such as Britain to extract resources more economically and exercise closer control over places such as India.

The accompanying engraving (Fig. 14.8), painstakingly composed by W.P. Frith, depicts Paddington Station in London in 1866. The artist's acknowledged goal was the portrayal of modern urban life with its crowds, its mixture of social classes, and its great bustle. He aimed to create a kind of literary tableau in the spirit of Charles Dickens, then England's most popular author. He also lovingly portrayed the iron-and-glass architecture of a new building type—the railroad station—and the details of the train. The many tender family scenes in the image remind us that the train allowed for greater communication between friends and family, and diminished the isolation of rural areas. In both city and country, the railroad station to some degree replaced the town square as the center of social intercourse.

EUGENE-EMMANUEL VIOLLET-LE-DUC AND RATIONAL DESIGN

Across the English Channel in France, medievalist, theoretician, and architect Eugène-Emmanuel Viollet-le-Duc (1814–79) saw the Gothic system of rib vault, pointed arch, and flying buttress as highly rational and analogous to nineteenth-century iron framing, and he imagined a modern architecture based on engineering accomplishments that would have the integrity of form and detail found in medieval works (Fig. 14.9). His theoretical writings—especially the two volumes of *Entretiens sur l'architecture* (*Discourses on Architecture*), published between 1863 and 1872—stress the importance of rationality in design.

Much of Viollet-le-Duc's time was spent opposing the French architectural establishment's attitude toward medieval styles. The government-sponsored Ecole des Beaux-Arts, which is discussed later in this chapter, was dominated by architects working in classical styles, and efforts by Viollet-le-Duc and others to have its courses include

14.9 Eugène-Emmanuel Viollet-le-Duc, Iron-frame assembly hall from the *Entretiens*, 1863–72, drawing.
Viollet-le-Duc was more successful as a theorist than as a practitioner. Interpreting Gothic structure as a highly rational response to the problem of load and support, he proposed the substitution of iron members as a logical use of the products of the Industrial Revolution.

the study of Romanesque and Gothic buildings met with little success. However, the extended controversy identified Viollet-le-Duc as an architect knowledgeable about medieval architecture, and from 1840 onward he was involved in scores of restoration projects for the major historical monuments of France, including Notre-Dame Cathedral and the Sainte-Chapelle in Paris; the abbey church of St. Denis; St. Sernin at Toulouse; Ste. Madeleine at Vézelay; the ramparts of Carcassonne; and the cathedrals of Reims, Amiens, and Beauvais. Out of this rich experience in dealing first-hand with medieval projects came the ten-volume *Dictionnaire raisonné de l'architecture française du XIe au XVIe siècle* (*Encyclopedia of French Architecture from the Eleventh to the Sixteenth Century*) (1858–65), which remains an important scholarly resource for medievalists. Contemporary architectural preservationists shudder at Viollet-le-Duc's philosophy of restoration—"to restore a building is not only to preserve it, to repair it, or to rebuild, but to bring it back to a state of completion such as may never have existed at any given moment"—which is quite the opposite of current attitudes toward this sort of work, whereby only original work is restored. Nevertheless, one must acknowledge that many of the buildings restored by Viollet-le-Duc might not have survived into the present without his intervention. While the architectural projects he designed as original undertakings are not particularly distinguished, his theories had a major impact on the development of nineteenth-century rationalism and twentieth-century Modernism.

HENRI LABROUSTE AND HIS LIBRARY DESIGNS

While the French Ecole des Beaux-Arts remained largely uninterested in emerging technologies, Ecole-trained architect Henri Labrouste (1801–75) took the road less traveled when he used exposed cast iron in the Bibliothèque Ste.-Geneviève (1842–50) in Paris, with its façades based on the lateral walls of Alberti's S. Francesco in Rimini (see Fig. 11.14), a church that drew inspiration from both the nearby Arch of Augustus and the Tomb of Theodoric in Ravenna. On the exterior (Fig. 14.10) the stonework presents a **Neo-Grec** countenance, meaning a bold, linear, abstracted form of Neo-Classical detailing then stylistically fashionable; but on the interior at the second-floor level one finds an unprecedentedly large reading room (Fig. 14.11), which extends the length and breadth of the building and is spanned by light semicircular cast-iron arches comparable to those illustrated in the essay on railway stations (see Fig. 14.8). Sixteen slender cast-iron columns, with proportions previously found only in Pompeiian wall paintings, divide the long space into two barrel-vaulted halves. The ceiling vaults, consisting of interlaced wires covered with plaster, rest on the delicately scrolled cast-iron arches.

14.10 Henri Labrouste, Bibliothèque Ste.-Geneviève, Paris, 1842–50.
Labrouste's design would later inspire Charles McKim in his façade composition for the Boston Public Library. The panels between the piers of the arcade contain the names of celebrated members of the French intelligentsia.

14.11 Henri Labrouste, Bibliothèque Ste.-Geneviève reading room, Paris, 1842–50.
Labrouste spanned his great reading room with two sets of cast-iron arches supported down the centerline by slender cast-iron columns set atop masonry piers. The round-arched windows to the right are those of the front façade.

In 1854 Labrouste was named architect of the Bibliothèque Nationale (the French National Library), an institution with a rapidly growing collection of books and inadequate quarters in which to house them. He worked on the library's buildings for the next twenty-one years, designing around existing structures to create a central reading room (Fig. 14.12) and a separate book stack, the first to be provided in a library. As in the Bibliothèque Ste.-Geneviève, Labrouste used masonry for the Neo-Classical exterior walls and iron for the interior. The most spectacular use of iron is again in the reading room, where nine domes, each nearly thirty-five feet in diameter, rest on a grid of sixteen slender iron columns. Illumination for the space comes from clerestories and glazed oculus openings in each dome. Equally important, but less celebrated, is the iron framing of the book stacks. Here there are six floors of shelving and aisle space, toplit by skylights and light-wells. The grillwork of the floors and the columns supporting the shelf units form a structural framework independent of the enclosing masonry walls.

GUSTAVE EIFFEL AND HIS TOWER

The most famous French designer using iron in the second half of the nineteenth century was the engineer Gustave

14.12 Henri Labrouste, Bibliothèque Nationale central reading room, Paris, 1858–68.
Labrouste's reading room for this library lies in the center of the plan. While the attenuated proportions of the cast-iron columns were new, the domical vaults were based on traditional masonry forms.

and during construction, but Parisians of all classes were thrilled by the magnificent views from its top, and they soon adjusted to its gigantic silhouette being cast against the skyline. The opening of the tower in 1889 also provided the first large-scale demonstration of the passenger safety elevator, a device designed by the American Elisha Graves Otis.

SKELETAL CONSTRUCTION IN CONCRETE AND WOOD

The ancient Romans had, of course, built using concrete. But this material had fallen into disuse for some 1400 years before Englishman Joseph Aspdin developed Portland cement in 1824. As early as 1774, the English engineer John Smeaton had experimented with a mixture of quick-lime and clay that hardened under water for his famous Eddystone Lighthouse. By the late nineteenth century, designers in America and Europe were using concrete reinforced with steel—**ferroconcrete**—for tensile strength, most notably Frenchmen Ernest Ransome (1844–1917) and François Hennebique (1842–1921). Ransome, whose father had patented a "concrete stone," made innovations in both reinforcing steel and formwork that enabled him to produce a true concrete frame by 1900. Hennebique developed a system that he licensed to others, resulting in the construction of some 40,000 reinforced concrete

Eiffel (1832–1923), who gained fame for his graceful bridge designs, such as the Garabit Viaduct over the river Truyère (1880–84) in southern France (Fig. 14.13), and then used his experience with iron construction to build what was then the world's tallest structure, the 1010-foot-high Eiffel Tower, erected for the Paris International Exposition of 1889 (see page 410). Not until the completion of the Chrysler Building in New York was Eiffel's tower exceeded in height, and it remains the largest iron construction in the world, for steel was rapidly becoming the preferred material for metal framing. Eiffel's tower design was derided by the artistic elite of France before

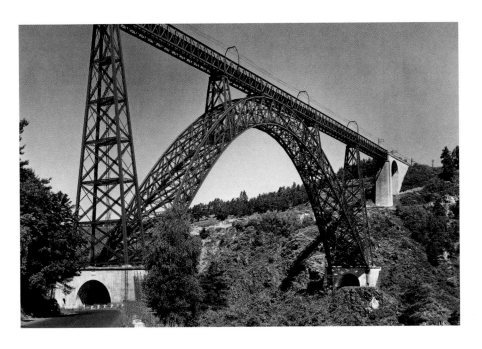

14.13 Gustave Eiffel, Garabit Viaduct over the river Truyère, Garabit, France, 1880–84.
Eiffel made the steel-frame bridge into an art form. Striking even today in its grace and lightness, this structure was considered absolutely shocking in the late nineteenth century.

14.14 Balloon-frame construction, 19th century.
The origin of the term "balloon" for wood framing remains unverified. This new method of building using mass-produced materials transformed building in wood from a craft practiced by highly skilled labor to an industry.

structures by 1921. By 1894 Anatole de Baudot, a student of Henri Labrouste, had constructed the Parisian church of St.-Jean de Montmartre with a ferroconcrete skeleton, which expresses the theories of Viollet-le-Duc with whom Baudot was associated.

Another innovative system of skeletal construction developed in the nineteenth century, this time in wood, was the American **balloon frame** (Fig. 14.14). Traditional wood-frame construction had involved heavy timbers shaped by hand and assembled using mortise-and-tenon joints held together by wooden pegs. While it inspired a high level of craftsmanship, it was an inefficient method of construction and one that had only a minimum of lateral bracing in the form of diagonal members. In the nineteenth century, the appearance of dimensioned lumber—that is, lumber produced in standard sizes in water- or steam-driven sawmills—and the development of machines for mass-producing nails made possible a radical change. The balloon frame consists of a sill plate from which rise long studs, placed at fairly close intervals, which are received by a top plate. These wooden members are nailed in place and braced laterally with diagonal studs. It only remained for plywood to appear in the twentieth century, which provided a lateral-bracing diaphragm as a result of

diagonal nailing. Balloon framing eventually evolved into platform framing, where the first floor rises to a platform and the skeletal construction is repeated, eliminating the need for two-story-tall studs.

A.W.N. PUGIN, THE GOTHIC REVIVAL, AND OPPOSITION TO INDUSTRIALIZATION

Eighteenth-century Romanticism had begun primarily as an esthetic movement resistant to Enlightenment rationalism, but when the Industrial Revolution and related capitalism began to radically change society and dramatically alter the environment, often for the worse, Romanticists found themselves with what they believed to be a demonic adversary. And many of them chose as an antidote a return to the past, particularly to the perceived harmony of the Middle Ages and to Gothic architecture.

In England, Augustus Welby Northmore Pugin (1812–52), a convert to Catholicism, regarded the Gothic as an embodiment of proper moral and religious values from the past that he felt were all but absent in his own time, and he was well versed in the realities of medieval buildings, having worked with his father as a draftsman in preparing a four-volume study of Gothic ornament. It was another book by Pugin that brought him into the public eye, however. In 1836 he published (second edition, 1841) *Contrasts; or, A Parallel Between the Noble Edifices of the Fourteenth and Fifteenth Centuries, and Similar Buildings of the Present Day; Shewing the Present-Day Decay of Taste*, a brief volume whose long title sums up the author's message. Pugin compared his view of medieval and modern conditions by means of drawings (Fig. 14.15). The "Catholic

14.15 A.W.N. Pugin, Ancient and modern towns compared, from *Contrasts*, second edition, 1841.
In the lower view, the benign medieval town appears in urban harmony, announcing its values through the silhouettes of its church towers. In the upper view, the malignant nineteenth-century city is a deplorable cacophony of prison, factories, and almost-obscured churches.

Law Courts

Victoria Tower   House of Lords   Central Hall   Westminster Hall   House of Commons

14.16 (above) Charles Barry and A.W.N. Pugin, Plan of the Houses of Parliament, London, 1836–68. The long façade faces the Thames. Behind it, the dominant spaces are the House of Commons and the House of Lords. At the rear of the site is Westminster Hall, saved from the fire of 1834.

14.17 (left) Charles Barry and A.W.N. Pugin, Houses of Parliament, London, 1836–68. Barry and Pugin produced a picturesque composition as seen across the river Thames, particularly through their use of many towers and pinnacles, which yield a rich silhouette seen against the sky. This picturesque quality is belied, however, by the rigor of their plan, which is broken into five parts and symmetrically disposed along its east side.

Town in 1440" had fifteen church spires and a guildhall tower marking its skyline, while "The Same Town in 1840" had factory smokestacks as the dominant element in an industrial townscape; Protestant chapels of a vaguely classical form had replaced Catholic churches, and many spires had had their tops lopped off.

Pugin's comparison of public charity past and present was even more damning. The medieval "residence of the poor" was shown as a monastery where the almoner received the needy with kindness; fed them a hearty diet of beef, mutton, ale, cider, milk, porridge, bread, and cheese; robed them in clean garments; preached a sermon to enforce discipline; and provided them with a decent Christian burial. By contrast, the "modern poor house" was a prisonlike walled building with a temple-front portico. The poor here were kept shackled in cells; fed a diet of small amounts of oatmeal, potatoes, gruel, and bread; cruelly beaten to enforce discipline; and loaded in a box labeled "for dissection" after death. Pugin was of course overstating the virtues of medieval institutions while detailing all the evils of his own time, but to him

the medieval town was a total visual and religious environment, while the industrial town, with its vested interests and greedy capitalists, was a detestable degradation of human existence.

In 1841 Pugin published *The True Principles of Pointed or Christian Architecture*, in which he enumerated his ideals: "First, that there should be no features about a building which are not necessary for convenience, construction, and propriety, and second, that all ornament should consist of the enrichment of the essential construction of the building." He regarded the Gothic as the "only correct expression of the faith, wants, and climate" of England and advocated its use for all buildings, including modern secular ones such as railroad stations.

While writing treatises and giving lectures, Pugin was also busy as a designer. He collaborated with Sir Charles Barry on a competition-winning design for rebuilding the Houses of Parliament, which had been destroyed by fire in 1834. The overall conception of the building was Barry's (Fig. 14.16), while the profusion of lively and historically correct detail, inside and out, was Pugin's contribution (Fig. 14.17).

JOHN RUSKIN AND THE ARTS AND CRAFTS MOVEMENT

While Pugin was reacting to the decline of moral and spiritual values that he associated with the Middle Ages, others were becoming concerned about the decline of artistic standards in manufactured goods because trained designers were not involved in creating such wares for industrial production. These two issues—social values and the artistic quality of manufactured products—were at the heart of the Arts and Crafts Movement, which flourished from about 1850 to 1900 in Britain and later in the United States. Originating in Victorian England, its ideas spread to Europe and finally found a "modern" resolution in postwar Weimar Germany, which is discussed in the next chapter. John Ruskin (1819–1900), a prolific critic of art and society, may be regarded as the originator of Arts and Crafts ideals. In his view, the Industrial Revolution was a grievous error exerting a corrupting influence on society. He avoided technological progress whenever possible, insisting, for example, on traveling by coach rather than rail and vigorously advocating a return to the handicrafts, where the work produced reflected the shape of the tool and the passage of the worker's hand. Like Pugin before him, Ruskin associated high moral values with certain historical styles in which he believed truth and beauty in building were to be found. Ruskin had only contempt for those who hoped to teach industrial design to students. He wrote:

The tap-root of all this mischief is in the endeavor to produce some ability in the student to make money by designing for manufacture. No student who makes this his primary object will be able to design at all; and the very words "School of Design" involve the profoundest of art fallacies. Drawing may be taught by tutors, but design only by Heaven; and to every scholar who thinks to sell his inspiration, Heaven refuses his help.

In *The Stones of Venice* (1851–53), Ruskin wrote about an architecture reflective of craftsmen's devotion to building. In *The Seven Lamps of Architecture* (1849), he laid out seven "lamps" or principles of great architecture. The Lamp of Sacrifice is dedicated to the craft of building and asks "Was it done with enjoyment. . .?" The Lamp of Truth expresses the moral quality necessary for exemplary building. The Lamp of Power explores the esthetic force of the sublime, the Lamp of Beauty extolls nature as the source of architectural order, and the Lamp of Life demands outward expression of the human mind, while the Lamp of Memory argues for an architecture of permanence. Finally, the Lamp of Obedience urges that no new styles should be created, but that Ruskin's favored Italian Romanesque of Pisa and the Gothic of northwestern Italy should serve as the only proper models.

William Morris

Ruskin's speeches and writings had a tremendous influence on a younger generation of sensitive men, who put many of his ideals into practice. The leader of this activist group in England was William Morris (1834–96), an Oxford divinity student who abandoned theology and studied both architecture and painting after encountering Ruskin's teachings. After his marriage Morris could find no house that met his standards of design, so he commissioned his architect friend Philip Webb (1831–1915) to design what became known as the Red House at Bexleyheath (1859–60), a redbrick structure that harkened back to the medieval domestic vernacular (Figs. 14.18–14.19). Its straightforward approach to structure and its undisguised use of materials surprised contemporary visitors, as did its elaborate use of decorative detail on the interior. Partly as a result of collaborating with his artist friends in the work on the Red House, Morris founded the firm of Morris, Marshall, Faulkner and Company in 1862, establishing workshops where artist-craftsmen created wallpaper, textiles, stained glass, utensils, furniture, and carpets using handicraft techniques. Morris's firm reflected his philosophy of dignity and joy through honest craftsmanship.

It was intended to be an alternative to the factory system, where mass-produced elements were assembled by workers who had become little more than cogs in a machine and had no interest in, control over, or love for the goods produced. Morris believed that the provision of well-designed, handcrafted products in the homes of ordinary working-class people would raise them above the level of disinterested bread-winning employment. His concern for the welfare of the working class extended to his

14.18 Philip Webb, First-floor (*left*) and second-floor (*right*) plans of Red House, Bexleyheath, Kent, 1859–60.
The plan seems even less exceptional than the exterior appearance. However, its direct response to light and ventilation and to everyday needs anticipates the functionalism of twentieth-century Modernists.

14.19 Philip Webb, Red House, Bexleyheath, Kent, 1859–60.
This house near London appears to be no more than a comfortable composition using forms familiar in the mid-nineteenth-century English countryside. What sets it apart is Webb's attempt to produce a design true to its materials and means of construction and expressive of the site and local culture.

enthusiastic and active espousal of Socialism, and architectural historian Nikolaus Pevsner has argued that Morris's social consciousness represents one of the origin points for the development of European Modernism, with its casting of the architect as a molder of society. Unfortunately the output of Morris's workshops was insufficient to meet the needs of a broad market, and the prices of his well-made objects tended to be higher than comparable factory-made goods, so his vision of supplying quality furnishings to ordinary people was never realized. The establishment of his firm, however, marks the first attempt to address the inferior quality of manufactured goods and the dehumanizing aspects of industrial production.

Richard Norman Shaw, C.F.A. Voysey, and Herman Muthesius

While in no way a social revolutionary, Richard Norman Shaw (1831–1912) made significant contributions to the development of Arts and Crafts architecture in England. Pugin's Gothic Revivalism impressed him as a youth. After traveling in Europe, he worked for Gothicist George Edmund Street, whom he considered his mentor. Shaw's early buildings are rationally conceived, as are Street's, but picturesque. Leyswood (1870) (Fig. 14.20) in Sussex has been much published in the form of Shaw's dramatic bird's-eye-view perspective. Its façades of "Old English" character, based upon Shaw's sketchbook studies of

14.20 Richard Norman Shaw, Leyswood, Sussex, 1870, drawing.
Richard Norman Shaw trimmed away the excesses of the Victorian Gothic to produce a rural vernacular known as "Old English." Picturesque Leyswood looks as if it grew over time in response to functional needs and the exigencies of its site.

medieval buildings in Sussex, are carefully wrapped around a central court, have a rich silhouette of clustered chimney stacks and multiple steeply sloping gable roofs, and reflect a straightforward use of natural building materials. Much more ornamental, but equally rigorous and attuned to English precedents, is his New Zealand Chambers (1871–73) (Fig. 14.21), which looks back to the red brick and stone trim of the Queen Anne buildings of the early eighteenth century. Shaw designed it to be extremely efficient, including some eighty small offices

14.21 Richard Norman Shaw, New Zealand Chambers, London, 1871–73.
Shaw looked back to both the seventeenth and eighteenth centuries in creating his "Queen Anne" style for urban buildings. Characteristics include red brick, white window sash, and carefully controlled ornament.

and a suite for the owners, and composed the façade using tall **oriel windows** and lush wood, plaster, and stone ornament. Shaw's work influenced the development of the Queen Anne, Shingle, and Craftsman styles in the United States.

Of the English architects influenced by the Arts and Crafts Movement, the most notable was Charles Francis Annesley Voysey (1857–1941), whose early commissions included wallpaper designs that owe much to Morris. He seldom used wallpaper or ornament in the houses he

14.22 C.F.A. Voysey, The Orchard, Chorleywood, Hertfordshire, 1899.
Houses like this one and related furniture designs by C.F.A. Voysey prepared the way for an early twentieth-century Craftsman style in both England and the United States. Based on Voysey's study of the residences of yeoman farmers, The Orchard has no applied ornamentation and so emphasizes utilitarian building components, including chimney flues and even rainwater downspouts.

14.23 C.F.A. Voysey, Broadleys, Lake Windermere, Cumbria, 1898.
Early chroniclers of the Modern Movement saw C.F.A. Voysey as one of its pioneers. However, he eschewed such an attribution, considering his work to be instead in the tradition of yeoman buildings in the southern English countryside.

designed, however, preferring instead the purity of white plaster walls or unfinished oak paneling. Because of this omission, he was considered by others (although he did not accept the label) as a Modernist pioneer. Voysey's houses, such as The Orchard in Chorleywood (1899) (Fig. 14.22) and Greyfriars near Guildford, Surrey (1896), are informal and reminiscent of the medieval vernacular. They feature wide, overhanging eaves; steeply pitched roofs; broad and bold chimneys; leaded casement windows; and either whitewashed masonry or stone walls. Their interiors feature natural-finish materials, such as slate flooring and untreated oak paneling; Arts and Crafts furniture, some of it designed by Voysey himself; and evidence of handcrafting in both ornamental and functional fittings, including carpets, pottery, clocks, candlesticks, hinges, and latches. Voysey created a bold but simple scheme in his design for Broadleys (1898), a vacation house on Lake Windermere

for A. Currer Briggs (Figs. 14.23–14.24). Three bowfront windows extend through the two stories of the house, interrupting the roofline, to provide views over the lake to the west. The house is constructed of local stone, laid two feet thick in the walls, and is capped by a slate roof with a series of iron brackets supporting the overhanging eaves. The overall composition is asymmetrical yet dignified.

The spirit of Arts and Crafts design was carried to Germany by Herman Muthesius, a representative of the Board of Trade attached to the German embassy in London from 1896 to 1903. Germany was experiencing the same

14.24 C.F.A. Voysey, Plan of Broadleys, Lake Windermere, Cumbria, 1898.
Broadleys was planned to take advantage of views out over the lake. The great bowfront windows light each of the principal rooms, while bedrooms and service spaces stretch out to the rear.

absence of good design in industrial products that had been noted earlier in Britain, and Muthesius was assigned the task of reporting on the state of English architecture and design, by then very highly regarded on the continent. The result was a three-volume report, *Das Englische Haus* (*The English House*), which documented all aspects of late Arts and Crafts work, from architecture to plumbing fixtures. On his return to Germany in 1903, Muthesius was appointed head of the Board of Trade, where he was responsible for selecting notable designers to teach in schools of arts and crafts. The impetus for the formation of the German design school called the Bauhaus can be traced to the work of the men he chose, including Peter Behrens, Hans Poelzig, and Bruno Paul, and a more complete discussion of that development appears in the next chapter.

THE ART NOUVEAU

In considerable contrast to Voysey's unornamented designs, a new and highly decorative style arose during the latter two decades of the twentieth century, a period known as "La Belle Epoque." Nurtured by a variety of sources as diverse as the Gothic Revival, William Morris, and the arts of China and Japan, it was a widely practiced style that was given different names in different countries. It was known as the Art Nouveau in France, England, and the Low Countries, "Stile Liberty" or "Stile Floreale" in Italy, and "Jugendstil" in Germany and Austria. Whatever its name, its designers set out to produce something excitingly new. In their hands, linear, sinuous lines like those found in Late Baroque and Rococo work became free-flowing compositions based loosely on plant and animal forms. In fact, a parallel can be drawn with Celtic art or the Animal Style of the early Middle Ages, although Art Nouveau curves have a freedom to change width and direction that exceeds medieval practice.

One finds the earliest examples of florid ornament in England, although the fullest expression of the style was to come elsewhere. As early as 1876–77, James Abbott McNeill Whistler (1834–1903), an American painter with strong English ties, created the Peacock Room for Frederick Leyland's London mansion, a design marked both by Japanese delicacy and by exotic peacocks, which represented the designer and his client feuding over the fee! (The Peacock Room is now installed at the Freer Gallery in Washington, D.C.) Arthur Mackmurdo's (1851–1942) swirling linear design for the title-page of *Wren's City Churches* (1883) is commonly cited as the first true Art Nouveau piece (Fig. 14.25), but its influence was limited. Wallpapers and carpets designed by William Morris at about the same time share its linearity, as do the illustrations and decorative flourishes included in the Kelmscott Press editions of books published by Morris after 1890. Other illustrators, especially Aubrey Beardsley, made woodcuts that exhibit the lively, curving Art Nouveau line.

14.25 Arthur Mackmurdo, Title page of *Wren's City Churches*, 1883. The Art Nouveau style is characterized by the long, sinuous curve seen here. Mackmurdo was sympathetic to the writings and work of William Morris, John Ruskin, and Richard Norman Shaw.

If one looks beneath the florid surface of Art Nouveau work, however, there are more substantive forces at work. On the one hand, Art Nouveau architecture manifested through its slender iron construction the kind of direct, expressive, skeletal structure advocated by the rationalist Viollet-le-Duc. On the other, there are moments in Art Nouveau interiors when space itself seems to flow and openness dominates, anticipating the more radical spatial experiments of such early twentieth-century architects as Adolf Loos, who is discussed at the beginning of the next chapter.

Victor Horta and Hector Guimard

Art Nouveau architects turned structural necessity into a language of organically derived curves. The earliest architectural innovator was Victor Horta, a Belgian architect and the designer of the Tassel House in Brussels, built in 1892–93 (Fig. 14.26). Horta incorporated swirling tendril designs not only in surface patterning on floors, walls, and ceilings, but also in structural elements such as the staircase, balustrades, and balcony railings. Historian Sigfried Giedion celebrated Horta's "flexible" ground plan with its levels and half-levels and interior light-wells, seeing it as the forerunner of the subsequent spatial investigations

14.26 Victor Horta, Tassel House, Brussels, 1892–93.
At the end of the century, designers throughout Europe
were looking for new ideas. In urban houses such as this
one, Horta explored the tensile and ductile potential of iron.

14.27 Victor Horta, Hotel Van Eetvelde interior, Brussels, 1897.
On his interiors, Horta used iron for columns, ceilings, windows,
and handrails. Here he made the stairwell a brilliantly lighted
core in the constrained urban environment.

by Modernists. The interior of Horta's Hotel Van Eetvelde
(1897) in Brussels exhibits these same qualities (Fig.
14.27). His later Maison du Peuple (1896–99) exploited
its structural relationship to plant forms, particularly in
the upper-floor auditorium, where undulating iron ceiling trusses merged with upright supports in the manner
of branches leaving a tree trunk. Even the balcony was
sculpted into a curvilinear form, its delicate supports terminating as protective railings. While the expressive linearity of iron construction was masterfully handled in this,
the first iron-and-glass façade building in Belgium, the
plan was quite traditional, with a central axis and cross-
axis on the ground floor.

Hector Guimard (1867–1942) was the French architect
most celebrated for his Art Nouveau designs. The most
famous of his works were made from 1899 to 1904 for the
entrances to the Métropolitain, or Métro, the Paris subway
system (Fig. 14.28). These are canopies over staircases that
descend from the sidewalk, and Guimard provided several
designs that employ wrought-iron swirls and curves, some
of which support glass roofs. The unity of these little projects is remarkable, for all the elements are deftly integrated

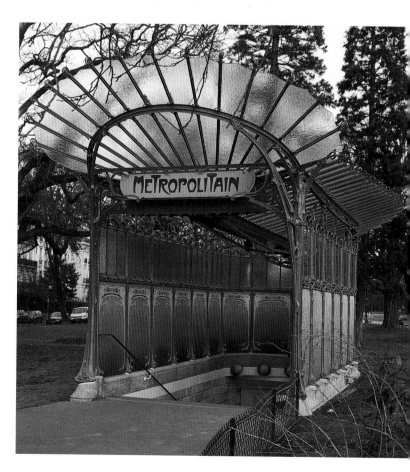

14.28 Hector Guimard, Métro entrance, Paris, 1899–1904.
Guimard's Métro stations still cover the entries into several
of Paris's subway stations. In this example, plantlike iron
members support a fanlike canopy.

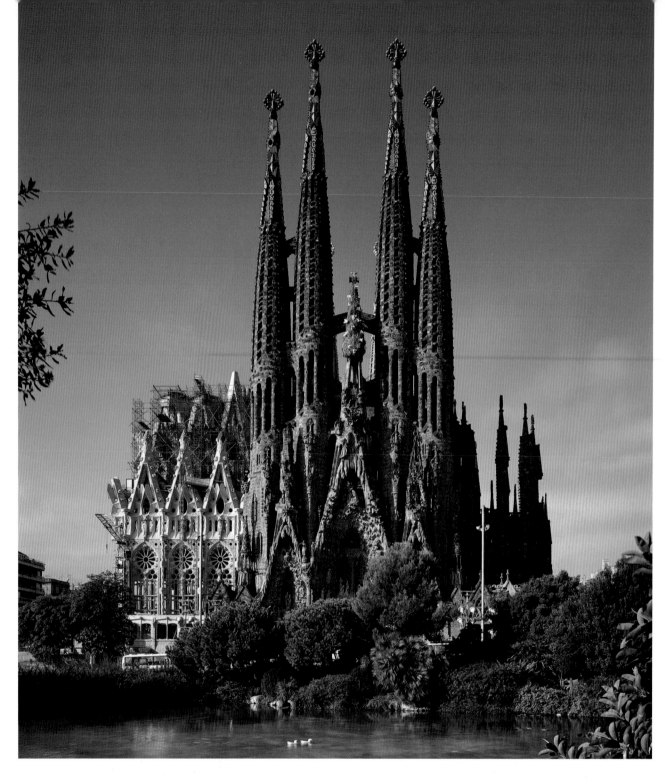

14.29 Antonio Gaudí, Façade of the Nativity, Church of the Sagrada Família, Barcelona, begun 1882.
14.29 Antonio Gaudí, Façade of the Nativity, Church of the Sagrada Família, Barcelona, begun 1882.
Partly inspired by the Catalan Gothic, showing traces of Cubism, and commonly associated with the Art Nouveau, the Sagrada Família fits into no single stylistic category. Like many before him, Gaudí drew upon nature and exploited local methods of workmanship.

in the plantlike forms. Lighting standards (upright supports) are terminated by bud-shaped electric bulbs, while patterns derived from vegetable leaves are used as infill on the railings. Guimard's other architectural projects reflect his ability to blend the decorative with the functional, as can be seen at the Castel Béranger (1894–98), an apartment building in Paris, where latent medievalism is nicely balanced by free-flowing asymmetrical decoration in iron and ceramic to form a unified whole.

Antonio Gaudí

In Spain, the Art Nouveau reached its most idiosyncratic expression in the work of Antonio Gaudí (1852–1926), a Catalan influenced by the writings of Ruskin and who

began as a Gothic Revivalist. Because of his interest in medieval styles, he was asked in 1884 to take charge of construction of the Sagrada Família (the Expiatory Temple of the Holy Family) in Barcelona, begun two years earlier by another Gothic Revivalist and still incomplete to this day. In the course of work on the Sagrada Família and on the Colònia Güell Chapel, where he hung sandbags on ropes and covered them with canvas to determine ideal vault cross-sections, Gaudí moved away from the Gothic Revival style to an intensely personal one that he used for apartment buildings, houses, and landscape designs as well as ecclesiastical works. While his three-dimensional curvilinear forms, floral decoration, and plastic, flowing plans link it more closely with the Art Nouveau than any other stylistic movement, Gaudí's work ultimately resists categorization. The Sagrada Família, for example, retains Gothic structural overtones, yet has such a heavy, towering, sculptural presence, enriched with lovingly crafted details, that it is clearly not Gothic. Its Façade of the Nativity is an array of grotto-eroded elements flowing together, with four great spires towering above (Fig. 14.29).

Gaudí's design for Casa Milá (1905–07), a large apartment house in Barcelona (Fig. 14.30), has an undulating plasticity in its façade and a curvilinear plan that is made possible by its expressive exterior load-bearing wall. There are no bearing walls inside, giving the designer the freedom to sculpt individual, non-orthogonal spaces, no two alike. His designs for the Parc Güell (1900–14), a real-estate development situated on a hillside west of Barcelona, allowed an extensive merging of naturalistic forms into walkways, stairways, and seating. Vaulting leans at oblique angles in a grotto walkway; stairs flow downward like lava; and benches, conforming to the irregular curves of the seated human form, wind along the upper-level plaza edge. Ceramic-tile finishes and details contribute durable surfaces and an appropriate touch of whimsy. The informal, amorphous, and rambling park is a skillfully inventive total design.

Charles Rennie Mackintosh

Gaudí's highly individualistic interpretations of the Art Nouveau have a Scottish parallel in the work of Charles Rennie Mackintosh (1868–1928), a gifted designer whose architectural career was brief. Mackintosh and a small circle of friends worked primarily in Glasgow, developing a unique style that is related to the Art Nouveau in its use

14.30 Antonio Gaudí, Casa Milá, Barcelona, 1905–07.
This apartment block is so massive and so apparently natural in its use of stone that it is referred to locally as the "stone quarry." The iron railings were made from salvaged material, and at one spot, the roof sculpture creates a framed view of the Sagrada Família.

of curves derived from natural forms. Other influences are detectable in Mackintosh's work as well, from the massive forms of Scottish baronial architecture to the delicate interlacing decoration of Celtic art. His buildings tend to have bold massing deftly composed, with light and airy interiors accented by subtle attenuated curves or linear patterns that are usually symmetrical. Like Art Nouveau architects, Mackintosh was greatly concerned with furniture, light fixtures, and details such as window hardware.

The Glasgow School of Art (1897–1909) was Mackintosh's first and largest commission (Fig. 14.31). Located on the north side of a sloping site, the building presents three elevations to the perimeter streets. The main entrance façade on Renfrew Street is a tight monolithic mass dominated by two rows of large, north-facing studio windows and a heavily sculpted central-entry composition, while the later west façade along Scott Street rises austerely as the hill drops, in the manner of medieval fortifications. This elevation, expressing the library, is a bold design broken by the three twenty-five-foot-high windows along the upper section of wall. The library interior is the most celebrated space (Fig. 14.32). Mackintosh designed its furniture and light fixtures to harmonize with the dominant pattern of horizontals and verticals in the windows and mezzanine balcony. A more fluid linearity is found in other rooms, and the southern rear attic level has simple arched openings that are reminiscent of Romanesque work. To the rear or south and facing the railroad yard, the façade (Fig. 14.33) is seemingly perfunctory, with windows punched wherever interior spaces required them. However, Mackintosh

14.31 Charles Rennie Mackintosh, Glasgow School of Art, Glasgow, 1897–1909.
This is the main façade on Renfrew Street. The huge windows gather northern light for painting and design studios. The central entry includes motifs drawn from Glasgow's medieval vernacular.

14.32 Charles Rennie Mackintosh, Library interior, Glasgow School of Art, Glasgow, 1897–1909.
The supporting columns are heavy timber with a dark finish typical of late nineteenth- and early twentieth-century interiors. Mackintosh designed the reading tables and light fixtures as well.

14.33 Charles Rennie Mackintosh, rear elevation of the Glasgow School of Art, Glasgow, 1897–1909.
While the north elevation provides the proper public face, this rear elevation is no less powerful a composition. Its reliance on the simple but deft application of windows as figures on the plain field of the masonry walls is comparable to Mackintosh's concern for figure–ground relationships in his watercolor drawings from nature.

14.34 Charles Rennie Mackintosh, Hill House, Helensburgh, 1902–04.
The picturesque silhouette and massing of Hill House are very expressive of nineteenth-century sensibilities. The stark, unornamented wall surfaces, however, have received much attention from those tracing the origins of twentieth-century Modernism.

14.35 Charles Rennie Mackintosh, first floor (*below*) and second floor (*above*) plans of Hill House, Helensburgh, 1902–04.
These plans could not be more straightforward in their functional organization, but the building's perimeter was obviously determined with three-dimensional expression in mind. Notable are the circular stairs that notch into a reentrant (internal, or inside) corner, and the stair that projects outward in the form of a semicircular landing.

Bedrooms

Nursery and servants' bedroom

Cloakroom

Entrance

Hall
14.36

Servants' wing

Library   Drawing room   Dining room

N

0   20 m

0   60 ft

manipulated these simple openings in an otherwise plain, clifflike wall so as to produce a composition of power, variety, and conviction that has few equals.

Other Mackintosh commissions include Windyhill (1900–01), a residence located outside Glasgow at Kilmacolm; Hill House (1902–04) at Helensburgh; and the Scotland Street School (1904–06) in Glasgow. Hill House (Fig. 14.34), designed for a Glasgow publisher, stands like a castle on rising ground, reflecting the influence of the Scottish vernacular in its turrets, expressive chimneys, and dominant roof. The monolithic character of the exterior is achieved by **pebble-dash** stucco. Its plan (Fig. 14.35) is logically compartmentalized into functional areas: the library and cloakroom near the entrance, for the easy conducting of business, followed by the drawing and dining rooms and a servants' wing at the end. Upstairs are the bedrooms, with the nursery and servants' bedrooms over the service wing. All interiors are handcrafted in the

14.36 Charles Rennie Mackintosh, Hill House interior, Helensburgh, 1902–04.
On the interior, Mackintosh designed Hill House to have both regimented orthogonals and Art Nouveau curves.

14.37 Otto Wagner, Postal Savings Bank, Vienna, 1904–12.
Marble veneer attached by means of aluminum-capped bolts creates the pattern of Wagner's façade. Aluminum also appears at the columns and the roof supports of the entry canopy.

Arts and Crafts tradition, with custom-designed carpets, light fixtures, stencil decorations, and furniture (Fig. 14.36). Dark woodwork contrasts with pastel colors on floor and wall surfaces. A barrel-vaulted ceiling in one bedroom becomes a canopy over the bed.

Art Nouveau designers in various parts of Europe were aware of one another's work through international publications. Mackintosh's entry in the 1901 German competition to design the "House of an Art Lover" brought him second prize, and his project drawings became known through inclusion in a publication edited in the Austrian city of Darmstadt. Darmstadt had become a center of the Jugendstil in 1899, when Ernst Ludwig, grand duke of Hesse, established an artists' colony in the suburb of Mathildenhöhe, attracting artists from Munich and Vienna. While the colony's life as an art center was brief, the houses built in the Mathildenhöhe district remain today as a Jugendstil preserve and include a house for Ernst Ludwig designed by Joseph Maria Olbrich (1867–1908), who came from the Viennese Secessionists (discussed in the next section), and an elaborate and expensive residence (1899) built for his own family by the young German painter Peter Behrens—Behrens quickly outgrew

the Jugendstil and went on to figure prominently in the development of modern architecture in Germany and so is discussed in the next chapter.

THE VIENNESE SECESSION

Jugendstil architects in Austria were members of the Viennese Secession, an association primarily of artists formed in 1898. The oldest member of the group, although not one of its founders, was Otto Wagner (1841–1918), a Neo-Classical architect who was promoted to the post of professor of architecture at the Vienna Academy of Fine Arts in 1894. Upon his appointment to an academic post, Wagner seems to have undergone a philosophical shift away from archaeologically correct architecture to a more rational, modern expression suited to current-day requirements. The Secession movement was formed by some of his most outstanding students, and Wagner soon joined them in espousing Jugendstil ornament.

Wagner's most notable designs in this mode were thirty-six stations for the Vienna subway system, the Stadtbahn (1894–1901). While not as exuberant as Guimard's work for the Paris Métro, Wagner's designs do employ the characteristic stylized ornament in cast and wrought iron. After 1900, Wagner's enthusiasm for the Jugendstil waned, and he abandoned the style completely for his masterpiece, the Postal Savings Bank (1904–06 and 1910–12) in Vienna (Figs. 14.37–14.38). Within an

14.38 Otto Wagner, Postal Savings Bank interior, Vienna, 1904–12.
Wagner originally intended for the glazed vault of the banking room
to be suspended from masts and cables above it. Today, a rain-
shedding, two-level gable roof protects the glazing. Against the rear
and right-side walls are cylindrical aluminum air-supply standards.

irregularly shaped block, he placed a grand staircase leading up to a wide vestibule, then into the central banking
room, which he surrounded with offices. He faced the
front façade with white Sterzing marble in shinglelike panels, which he attached to the superstructure by means of
bolts covered with aluminum caps that create a distinctive
grid. Using more aluminum, a radical choice at the time,
he created an elegant entry canopy supported by thin aluminum columns with cantilevered arms. Passing through
this canopy to the banking room, one enters a space filled
with light brought in through a glass-vaulted ceiling that
Wagner originally intended to support with cables hung
from aluminum masts. Some of the light passes through
glass-brick floor panels to illuminate the rooms below.
Within the banking room, two files of columns create a

basilican plan, with the tellers' counters in the "aisles" and
with cylindrical aluminum air-supply standards around
the perimeter. As at the façade, connections are everywhere
made prominent, from the bases of the aluminum-clad
columns to the newel posts of the handrails.

Wagner's talented pupil Joseph Maria Olbrich became
the leading architect of the Viennese Secession, influenced
in part by the work of Mackintosh. Like Mackintosh,
Olbrich found an essentially orthogonal basis for his
architectural forms, embellishing them with the controlled
vegetation of the Jugendstil. His first major commission
was from the Secessionists themselves, a small building
for meetings and art exhibitions. The Secession Building
(1898–99) is a Neo-Classically inspired mass, crowned
by a pierced metal dome (Fig. 14.39). Along the exterior
walls between high windows Olbrich set low-relief ornament based on plants and flowers. Compared to French
or Belgian work, Olbrich's designs seem rather heavy and
symmetrical, but publication of this building brought
widespread acclaim to its architect, and the grand duke
of Hesse, Ernst Ludwig, invited Olbrich to join his artists'

14.39 Joseph Maria Olbrich, Secession Building, Vienna, 1898–99.
Olbrich covered his dome with a laurel motif symbolic of Apollo, god of poetry, music, and learning. The building served as a meeting and exhibition space for the Secession.

colony at Darmstadt. From 1899 until his death from leukemia in 1908, Olbrich worked at Darmstadt, erecting numerous houses, studio buildings, entrance gates, and a Wedding Tower or Hochzeitsturm (1907–08) to commemorate the duke's marriage.

THE ECOLE DES BEAUX-ARTS, RICHARD MORRIS HUNT, AND FRANK FURNESS

To this point, the only mention of nineteenth-century architecture in the United States has involved bridge design and the balloon frame, meaning work done in the domains of engineers and technologists. In the first half of the nineteenth century there was no institutional teaching of architecture in the United States, as the first architectural program at the Massachusetts Institute of Technology (MIT) did not have classes until 1868. So to learn the profession, American architects either worked in an architectural office (as did, say, Robert Mills and

William Strickland for Benjamin Henry Latrobe early in the century) or studied abroad. The careers of two men, Richard Morris Hunt and Frank Furness, illustrate the forces at work at mid-century in a country that was only beginning to come of age as a world power and as a producer of national art; their story begins in France.

French architectural teaching was reorganized during the French Revolution and again under Napoleon Bonaparte. By 1819 the Section d'Architecture of the Ecole des Beaux-Arts was well established, with its own faculty and with quarters in a building adapted for its use by Félix Duban (1797–1870). The name "Ecole des Beaux-Arts" became synonymous with architectural education in France, to some extent in England, and eventually in America, and the Ecole continued to operate in this location until 1968.

While details of the educational system changed over time, the general philosophy did not. Would-be students had to pass a challenging qualifying examination that included diverse subjects from drawing to history. Once accepted, a student, or *élève*, entered a studio, or atelier, where he worked under the supervision of a *patron*, who was a practicing architect or a member of the Ecole faculty. Simultaneously, he attended a variety of Ecole lectures and was examined on those involving technical knowledge. In addition, he had to enter design competitions, or *concours d'emulation*, in the form of either an *esquisse* (a sketch problem) or a *projet rendu* (a fully rendered project), with these two types being held in alternate months. For both, the student received a *précis*, or program describing the essential elements. He then entered *en loge*, that is, into a cubicle, and worked alone for twelve hours to produce a proposal. For the *esquisse*, his project was then finished. For the *projet rendu*, he would then return to his atelier to develop his schematic idea, assisted by comments from his *patron*, until the time of final submission, which involved elaborate rendered drawings. At the appointed time, projects were picked up throughout Paris by a cart or *charrette*; students sometimes jumped on board to apply finishing touches, hence the term charrette used today by architectural students to describe a period of intense work at the end of a project. Comparing the initial sketch to the final solution, a jury would first determine whether the two represented the same idea, in order to ensure the originality of the scheme; then they would award points relative to the project's merits. It was through the accumulation of these points that a student could progress through the Ecole. The highest award given was the *prix*, which eventually became the *"Grand Prix de Rome"* and which paid for a winner to live and study in Rome for an extended period.

In 1846 Richard Morris Hunt (1827–1895) became the first American to attend the Ecole des Beaux-Arts and so absorb its system of education. He had lived in Paris since 1832, when his family had moved there after the death of his father. In the French capital, he would have seen buildings like Labrouste's Bibliothèque Ste.-Geneviève, and he worked for the French government on the construction of the column-laden Second Empire-style New Louvre,

which had been partially designed by his teacher Hector Lafuel. Returning to New York in 1855, Hunt established a thriving practice and briefly ran an Ecole-modeled atelier, where American students could come for architectural training. His buildings ran the gamut from the neo-Grec and Second Empire styles to the Romanesque and a fairly tame interpretation of the Victorian Gothic. He was particularly successful in catering to newly rich industrial magnates who wanted houses that imitated the ancestral mansions of European nobility. For the Vanderbilt family alone, he designed a town house on Fifth Avenue, a "cottage" called The Breakers at Newport, Rhode Island (Fig. 14.40), and Biltmore, their châteauesque country mansion at Asheville, North Carolina, all well known; but he also designed the base for the Statue of Liberty (1880) and the central portion of the Fifth Avenue façade of the Metropolitan Museum of Art in New York (1895), a consummate work of Beaux-Arts classicism.

Frank Furness (1839–1912), whose designs eventually reflected the writings of John Ruskin and Eugène-Emmanuel Viollet-le-Duc, was the son of a Unitarian minister and abolitionist who was expected to attend Harvard like his brother. However, he spurned higher education and at age seventeen went to work as a draftsman for

14.40 Richard Morris Hunt, The Breakers, Newport, Rhode Island, 1892–95.
Richard Morris Hunt was the first American to attend the Ecole des Beaux-Arts in Paris. The knowledge he gained there of academic planning and monumental design made him the architect of choice among the late nineteenth-century American elite.

14.41 Furness and Hewitt, Pennsylvania Academy of the Fine Arts, Philadelphia, 1871–72. Later in his career and without George Hewitt as a partner, Frank Furness abandoned the bold color palette used here both inside and out. He obtained this commission in a design competition, and his winning scheme exhibits a bold eclecticism that connected viscerally with Victorian-age Americans.

Philadelphia architect John Fraser (1825–1906). In 1856 he met Richard Morris Hunt and the next year moved to New York and entered Hunt's atelier. While there, he had as fellow students Henry Van Brunt and William Ware, who would later become partners and two of New England's most able Victorian Gothicists. When the Civil War broke out, Furness joined a Pennsylvania cavalry unit, rose to the rank of captain, and by the end of the war was a steely-eyed veteran ready to produce robust, aggressive, muscular buildings, which were extreme even in a Victorian era of headlong western expansion, buccaneering capitalism, and perceived manifest destiny. Furness eventually took

on more than 600 commissions, and though a high percentage of his buildings have been lost, two that remain demonstrate his talents. In partnership with Victorian Gothicist George Hewitt (1840–1916), he produced an Anglo-French design for the Pennsylvania Academy of the Fine Arts (1871–72) in Philadelphia. Its front façade (Fig. 14.41) has stone elements seemingly slid and slotted like the moving parts of a huge nineteenth-century machine, flamboyant textures, neo-Grec moldings, Venetian Gothic coloring, and Victorian Gothic and Islamic arches beneath Second Empire mansard roofs. When it opened, there was nothing else like it in the country. (In 1873, while this building was being constructed, a young Louis Sullivan worked for Furness, whom he considered to be the finest architect in the country, but was then laid off due to an economic downturn.) In 1876 Furness produced an equally bold design for the Centennial Bank (Fig. 14.42) in Philadelphia. On a canted façade at a corner site, he incorporated forms that he used repeatedly, including a formidable "porch" with a layered, granite gable roof (which some wags have compared to Furness's similarly triangular spreading mustache) and a tall, locked-on aedicula, or attenuated temple-frame, with pistonlike compressed columns and a steep gable capped by spiky crockets.

14.42 Frank Furness, Centennial Bank, Philadelphia, 1876.
The three main components of this building—chamfered rear mass, lower front porch, and tall entry pavilion—appear to interlock like the pieces of a giant puzzle. Built in the year of the country's centennial, the bank was Furness's take on what an American building should be in an era of headlong national expansion and industrialization.

14.43 Henry Hobson Richardson, Trinity Church, Boston, Massachusetts, 1872–77.
It was Stanford White, then working in H.H. Richardson's office, who designed the church's tower, basing it on the Romanesque Salamanca Cathedral. With its three arched openings, the base is quite similar to the Romanesque church of St. Gilles-du-Gard in Provence.

Parish house

Church

N

| 0 | | | 20 m |
| 0 | | | 60 ft |

14.43

14.44 Henry Hobson Richardson, Plan of Trinity Church, Boston, Massachusetts, 1872–77.
Richardson's plan is remarkably simple. Its vaults are ornamented with murals by John LaFarge. Connected to the chancel end of the church is the parish house, laid up in the same polychromatic stone.

HENRY HOBSON RICHARDSON AND THE SEARCH FOR AN AMERICAN STYLE

H.H. Richardson (1838–86) followed Richard Morris Hunt as the second American to attend the Ecole des Beaux-Arts. Born to a wealthy Louisiana family, Richardson completed the course at the Lawrence Scientific School of Harvard University before enrolling at the Ecole in 1860. The onset of the Civil War cut off his financial support from home, forcing him out of school and into the Paris office of Théodore Labrouste (brother of Henri), where he worked until 1865, when he returned to New York. After a few years, he moved his office to the Boston area and gained national acclaim for his competition-winning design for Trinity Church (1872–77) in Copley Square.

Trinity Church (Fig. 14.43) was to become the most celebrated building of its age; a national poll of architects in 1885 identified it as the best building in the United States. What was it that designers (and the general public) admired about it so much? In many respects the design is a pastiche, very much in the tradition of nineteenth-century eclecticism. The plan (Fig. 14.44) is based on a stubby Latin-cross basilica, and the polychrome stonework and general massing come from French Romanesque churches of the French Auvergne region; the triple-arched portal is derived from St. Gilles-du-Gard in Provence (see Fig. 8.48); and the great crossing tower reflects the tower of the Old Cathedral in Salamanca, Spain. Despite these borrowings, an abundance of original thinking gives Trinity Church its distinctive character. Richardson conceived of the building as polychromatic, both inside and out, and his design shows a true flair for scale and texture. Ashlar stonework in warm gray contrasts with the red-brown sandstone trim, and slate roofs on the parish house set off the red clay tiles prominent on the tower roof. Murals painted by John LaFarge (1835–1910) and his pupil Augustus Saint-Gaudens (1848–1907) enrich the plaster walls inside, and William Morris and Edward Burne-Jones (1833–98) made the stained-glass windows, an artistic collaboration that was entirely in accordance with Arts and Crafts ideals.

The success of Trinity Church assured the prosperity of Richardson's career, and it established what was to become his characteristic architectural style: an intelligent and personal interpretation of the Romanesque. This was far from a slavish imitation, however, so his work is usually designated "Richardsonian" to indicate its personal nature. His adoption of the Romanesque was in fact the starting

14.45 Henry Hobson Richardson, Marshall Field Wholesale Store, Chicago, Illinois, 1885.
There has been no more satisfying composition in American architecture than this one. Notice the vertical unity of each window bay, which begins with a rectangular opening lighting the basement, and terminates with four vertical rectangles over two round-headed windows. Unfortunately, the building has long since been destroyed.

point in his search for an appropriate American building tradition, for, while he had seen and been impressed by medieval buildings in Europe, he had not been instructed in any medieval modes at the Ecole des Beaux-Arts—the omission about which Viollet-le-Duc had complained.

Richardson was a romantic who was inspired by the abundant stone of New England, and he worked to evolve a style worthy of its rugged massiveness and load-bearing capacities, while technical advances in glass and metal construction had little impact on him. A chronicle of his major commissions illustrates the progressive development of his thinking about the proper expression of masonry. In 1878 he designed Sever Hall for his alma mater, Harvard University. It is a classroom building, executed in brick to harmonize with existing structures in the Harvard Yard, but the expression that Richardson gave to the material, built into a low arch at the entrance and modeled into bowfronts that resemble turrets, conveys a feeling of solidity, quite a contrast to the rather delicate Georgian buildings that are its neighbors. Two years later Richardson designed nearby Austin Hall to house the law

school, an almost symmetrical stone structure that was a free and romantic reinterpretation of Romanesque forms.

Richardson's Marshall Field Wholesale Store in Chicago (1885) (Fig. 14.45) has long since been demolished, but it was a revelation when it was constructed, and none was more impressed with it than Louis Sullivan, who would be a leader in the development of that most quintessential of American buildings: the skyscraper. At the Marshall Field store, Richardson chose not to express its internal steel skeleton, but he eschewed ornamentation and historical trappings, leaving the unadorned rusticated masonry and the great arched openings of the six-story block to convey

14.46 Henry Hobson
Richardson, Glessner House,
Chicago, Illinois, 1885.
This was Richardson's smaller
commission in Chicago. The
most impressive feature of
the front (south) façade is the
huge semicircular arch made
of rock-faced voussoirs. The
large opening to the left is the
carriage portal.

power and monumentality. It has been proposed that his model for the broad arches of the central stage of the store may have been the Roman aqueduct at Segovia, Spain, a construction included in Richardson's collection of photographs. Whatever his inspiration, he succeeded in creating a design as bold and monumental as the architecture seen in the Roman engravings of Piranesi.

In 1885 Richardson designed the Glessner House in Chicago (Figs. 14.46–14.47) for a wealthy industrialist. It is restrained and austere on the front and sides, where rooms open outward carefully onto the public streets, and more generous and irregular to the rear, where rooms look out on an interior courtyard sheltered from street noise and dirt by the building's U-shaped plan. While the courtyard walls are laid up in brick, the street-front façades are constructed in varied courses of rock-faced stone interspersed with

orthogonal windows, grills, and a massive semicircular arch.

In his residential commissions Richardson also did much to create what became known as the "Shingle style." Built with wooden frames, these houses were covered with wooden shingles on both the wall and roof planes, providing a sense of both volumetric continuity and simplicity. His design for the Watts Sherman House (1874) in Newport, Rhode Island has rusticated stone on the ground-floor walls and shingles on the upper-floor walls and roof, which are stretched like a membrane over the dormers and bay windows (Fig. 14.48). Great overhanging eaves at the steeply pitched roof and substantial chimneys present a picturesque profile against the sky. Its textural variety and massing irregularity anticipate the residential Queen Anne style of the 1880s and 1890s. Richardson's subsequent design for the Stoughton House (Fig. 14.49)

14.47 Henry Hobson Richardson,
Plan of the Glessner House,
Chicago, Illinois, 1885.
This plan occurs at the level of
the paired windows and semicircular arch. The outside walls of
this U-shaped plan are laid up in
rock-faced stone, while the walls of
the inner court are brick. The scale
change is striking, but appropriate.
Compare the projecting stairs and
bays in the court to the work of
Charles Rennie Mackintosh.

14.48 (above) Henry Hobson Richardson, Watts Sherman House, Newport, Rhode Island, 1874.
Richardson also worked in wood, in this case assisted by Stanford White. Close observation of the textures created by the mock-heavy timber and the shingles of the roofs and gables reveals the similarity in feeling to Richardson's compositions in stone. The treatment of the wood members is also comparable to the Queen Anne style of Richard Norman Shaw in England.

14.49 (below) Henry Hobson Richardson, Stoughton House, Cambridge, Massachusetts, 1882–83.
Here Richardson drew partly upon the New England Colonial vernacular to produce a building completely clad in shingles. Particularly effective is the curving shingle-covered wall of the projecting stair.

in Cambridge, Massachusetts (1882–83) shows how far he had gone toward simplifying the rather complex forms of the Sherman House. Here, the shingle skin covers a bold composition of geometric solids atop an L-shaped plan. Although the design owes something to the forms of early Colonial-era houses in New England in its absence of ornament, it transcends any one period or style. The interior of the Stoughton House features a two-story living hall, an element originated in Pugin's design for his own house at Ramsgate in England.

MCKIM, MEAD, AND WHITE

H.H. Richardson's most prominent employees were Charles Follen McKim (1849–1909) and Stanford White (1856–1906), who became two principals in the firm of McKim, Mead, and White. One author has metaphorically described the careful Mead as the keel, the esthete McKim as the hull, and the flamboyant White as the sail of an imaginary ship in this, the first large-scale architectural office in America, which eventually had more than 100 employees and produced almost 1000 commissions. William Rutherford Mead (1848–1928) was born into a family of painters and sculptors and began his professional life working in New York for German-trained architect and critic Russell Sturgis, whose Victorian Gothic buildings reflected the influence of John Ruskin. Subsequent to travel and study in Europe, Mead returned to America and met McKim, then working for Richardson. Always interested in construction, Mead provided the technical and business

14.50 McKim, Mead, and White, Villard Houses, New York City, 1882–85.
The firm of McKim, Mead, and White established the model for the large-scale American architectural practice. They based this residential structure on Roman palazzi such as the Palazzo Farnese.

acumen needed in a large, complex architectural firm.

McKim's parents were Quaker abolitionists, and their spirit of idealism remained with him throughout his life. Growing up in a hotbed of mid-century avant-garde culture, Llewellyn Park near New York City, McKim had contact with such luminaries as William Cullen Bryant, Horace Greeley, Henry David Thoreau, and the country's first great landscape architect, Frederick Law Olmsted (1822–1903). McKim attended Harvard's Lawrence Scientific School, worked briefly for family friend Russell Sturgis, then set out for Paris and the Ecole des Beaux-Arts. In 1870 he entered Richardson's office. In mid-1872 Mead and McKim set up a practice of their own.

Stanford White's father was an art and music critic for literary magazines. Among his contacts were the architect Calvert Vaux (1824–95), the painter John LaFarge, and Olmsted. Through the latter, White became a precocious apprentice to H.H. Richardson without the benefit of any formal architectural training. In 1878 White left to travel in Europe, and in 1879 returned to enter into partnership with Mead and McKim. He became legendary for his prodigious output of work and indeed for his appetites in general.

McKim, Mead, and White designed the Villard Houses (Fig. 14.50) in New York City in 1882–85. Consisting of

14.51 McKim, Mead, and White, Boston Public Library, Boston, Massachusetts, 1887–95.
Charles McKim looked back to Henri Labrouste's Bibliothèque Ste.-Geneviève for his façade composition. He made numerous studies, including full-scale mock-ups of the cornice, before settling on his final design.

six separate houses arranged around a central courtyard, the building takes on the appearance of a single Italian Renaissance palazzo. The results are large, grand, chaste, and refined, and at once presented a face of civic decorum in a city then taking its place among world capitals and provided their owner, shipping tycoon Henry Villard, with instant credibility among his nouveau-riche associates.

Charles McKim was largely responsible for the Boston Public Library (1887–95) (Fig. 14.51), which faces H.H. Richardson's Trinity Church across Copley Square. Then housing the largest public collection of books in the United States, it symbolized Boston's cultural heritage. Its form has layers of precedent, the most recent being Henri Labrouste's Bibliothèque Ste.-Geneviève in Paris (see Figs. 14.10–14.11). McKim organized the library around a central court, placing the public reading room and elaborate entry sequence to the front of the plan. The structure is faced with Milford granite but includes advanced technology such as thin-shell vaults. Sculpted panels above the main entry were designed by Augustus St. Gaudens and the bronze entry doors by Daniel Chester French (1850–1931).

Back in New York City, the firm produced the vast Pennsylvania Station (1902–11) (Figs. 14.52–14.53),

which covered some eight acres on three levels but was tragically demolished in the 1960s. Based upon the model of Roman baths, the terminal provided a grand portal to the city as it brought in passengers some forty-five feet below the ground level and covered them with monumental vaulted spaces lit by great thermal windows; it brilliantly directed the hordes of people passing through each day.

THE FIRST SKYSCRAPERS

Over the course of their careers, McKim, Mead, and White showed little interest in the design of tall buildings, but American designers were to become the primary innovators in high-rise metal-frame construction. From about 1865 onward, architects in New York and then Chicago developed an original building type, the skyscraper, on a scale and at a level of sophistication unmatched by Europeans. Tall buildings were a response to rising urban real-estate values and the desire of businesses to remain close to established centers of commerce. A whole range of technical improvements—including mass-produced structural components, the safety elevator, and fireproofing techniques—made them feasible, and their structural systems were most logically executed in steel frames, laterally braced to withstand wind loads.

Pre-Civil War building technology included the first structural use of iron for buildings in the cast-iron fronts and building frames that were mass-produced by men such as James Bogardus (1800–74) and Daniel Badger (1806–84) in New York and shipped as far as steamships

14.53 (above) McKim, Mead, and White, Section and elevation of Pennsylvania Station, New York City, 1902–11.
Like the plan, McKim, Mead, and White's elevation and section were inspired by the Roman baths. The dominant features were the great thermal windows that lit the groin-vaulted waiting area. The destruction of this terminal must be considered a tragedy for American architecture.

14.52 (above) McKim, Mead, and White, Plan of Pennsylvania Station, New York City, 1902–11.
Of all of McKim, Mead, and White's planning accomplishments, none is more impressive than this train station. Here they looked to the Roman baths for inspiration in managing the huge crowds that passed through these vast spaces each day.

traveled (Fig. 14.54). Cast iron was favored for its strength, fire-resistance, and plastic qualities. The classical detail desired for commercial structures could be economically cast from molds and repeated for as many bays and stories as desired, and the finished façade could be painted to resemble stone or other materials. The simplicity of construction appealed to many businessmen, who built increasing numbers of cast-iron structures from 1849 onward. Whole districts of them, such as SoHo in New York City, sprouted when extensive fires destroyed the previous timber-framed buildings.

In most instances cast-iron buildings lacked the wind bracing essential to high-rise construction, so they cannot be considered the first skyscrapers. However, James Bogardus introduced the European iron **I-section**, now universally employed in the form of wide-flange sections, for steel framing, and his concept of an all-iron building

14.54 Cast-iron façade, Richmond, Virginia, ca. 1870.
Such cast-iron store fronts were attached to buildings with perimeter bearing walls of brick and internal, heavy-timber columns and beams. The cast-iron designs were often based on palazzo façades from Renaissance Venice.

14.55 William Le Baron Jenney, Home Insurance Company Building, Chicago, Illinois, 1883–85.
William Le Baron Jenney was only one of the many architects searching for effective ways to fireproof steel-frame construction for late nineteenth-century buildings. His Home Insurance Company Building was among the first successful solutions.

14.56 Daniel H. Burnham and John Welborn Root, Monadnock Building, Chicago, Illinois, 1890–91.
The front portion of this building—back to the projecting cornice—is original. Built using traditional masonry bearing walls, rather than the new steel frame, it is highly expressive in its use of materials. The need for economy precluded external ornament. As handsome as it is, the Monadnock Building signaled the end of the bearing-wall skyscraper because its thick walls were not economical.

must have encouraged others to think more seriously about the alternatives to masonry bearing-wall construction. In the process of rebuilding the business district of Chicago, largely destroyed by fire in 1871, a number of inventive men perfected fireproofed metal-frame construction for high-rise buildings and thus created the skyscraper. William Le Baron Jenney (1832–1907), the designer of the Home Insurance Company Building (1883–85), is generally credited with the early development of the skyscraper, although the building is not entirely metal-framed, as the first floor contains sections of masonry bearing wall (Fig. 14.55). Above the ground floor the masonry exterior was carried on shelf-angle supports attached to the frame, and steel rather than iron was employed for the structure above the sixth-floor level. The second Rand McNally Building (1889–90) by Daniel H. Burnham (1846–1912) and John Welborn Root (1850–91) of the firm of Burnham and Root had all the elements of the modern skyscraper, including a completely steel frame designed by the structural engineering firm of Wade and Purdy, even though its external appearance looked backward rather than forward. Even where masonry bearing walls were retained, as in Burnham and Root's Monadnock Building (1890–91), an internal iron frame provided lateral bracing through riveted girder-column connections (Fig. 14.56).

Architects who produced the high-rise buildings of Chicago dating from 1875 to 1925 are collectively termed the Chicago School, indicating their common design attitudes and construction technologies. Innovative as the structural systems of these buildings are, they do not necessarily express their metal frames on the outside; most

14.57 Daniel H. Burnham and John Welborn Root, Reliance Building, Chicago, Illinois, 1894–95.
The Reliance Building's external skin of terracotta and glass clips onto an internal steel skeleton. This construction method anticipated the curtain walls of the 1950s and '60s.

are clad in masonry, which gives the impression that this is the structural material. Their façades are derived from classical precedents, which, however, offered very few buildings in which the vertical elements dominated the horizontal, and nothing that even approximated their scale of multi-floor construction. Designers solved the problem in a variety of ways. For instance, the decorative terracotta cladding on the Reliance Building (1894–95) repeats the same exterior elevation from the third floor to the attic story, expressing in the process the slenderness of its metal-frame columns and the depth of the beams supporting the floors (Fig. 14.57). Other Chicago School buildings were composed by grouping floors in three or four horizontal layers, which could then conform to the proportioning of columns and entablatures and the whole idea of streetscape established by Renaissance architects.

14.58 Dankmar Adler and Louis Sullivan, Auditorium Building, Chicago, Illinois, 1886–90. Obviously Sullivan was influenced by Richardson's Marshall Fields Wholesale Store. The projecting block above the triple arches is the hotel lobby.

14.59 Dankmar Adler and Louis Sullivan, Plan of and longitudinal section through the Auditorium Building, Chicago, Illinois, 1886–90. The so-called Auditorium Building is actually a hotel and an office building that surrounded an auditorium. It was certainly the cleverest plan composition that Sullivan (together with Adler) ever produced.

LOUIS SULLIVAN AND THE TALL BUILDING "ARTISTICALLY CONSIDERED"

While the Marshall Field Wholesale Store was being completed, Louis Sullivan (1856–1924), then in practice with Dankmar Adler (1844–1900), was designing the Chicago Auditorium Building (1886–90) (Fig. 14.58). After seeing Richardson's masterpiece, he immediately modified the design, giving greater emphasis to the arches above entrance doors and to those used for wall articulation.

Sullivan was as original an architect as Richardson. While traces of Neo-Classicism and Romanticism appear in his work, he directly engaged the rapidly emerging building technologies of Chicago and expressed them architecturally. Born in Boston, the young Sullivan spent much of his childhood on his grandfather's farm north of the city, where he became acquainted with the natural plant forms that would later be incorporated in his architectural ornament. Determined to become an architect, Sullivan spent a year in the newly created architectural program at MIT and then worked briefly in the offices of Frank Furness in Philadelphia and William Le Baron Jenney in Chicago. He went to Paris in 1874 to study at the Ecole des Beaux-Arts, where he found the teaching uninspiring. After a year there, he traveled in Italy before returning to Chicago and joining the office of Dankmar Adler and Company in 1879. Adler's engineering and managerial expertise complemented Sullivan's artistic inclinations, and in 1881 the firm name changed to Adler and Sullivan.

Adler's understanding of acoustics gained the firm the commission to design the Chicago Auditorium Building, one of the most complex multi-use buildings constructed

Office tower

Hotel lobby

14.60 Dankmar Adler and Louis Sullivan, Wainwright Building, St. Louis, Missouri, 1890.
In his essay "The Tall Building Artistically Considered," Sullivan called for two walk-in, walk-up stories, repetitive office floors, and a cap containing mechanical equipment. Here are his theories at work, with terracotta ornament in the spandrel panels and at the deep cornice. The steel frame is obscured because of fireproofing requirements, but its presence is expressed on the exterior.

floor (where easy access could be made from the street into banks, shops, and the like) and mezzanine or second floor (still conveniently reached on foot) as a unit; he placed stacked offices on the third-through-top floors, where repetitive windows illuminated floor areas that could be subdivided to suit the requirements of various tenants; and he located the mechanical systems, from tanks and pumps to elevator machinery, behind a deep cornice. Sullivan liked nothing better than to discover a general principle, what he characterized as "a rule so broad as to admit no exceptions." His most famous dictum was "form follows function," which was not actually original to him. Sullivan's buildings, however, are generally poor examples of this principle in operation. The Wainwright Building, for instance, has a steel frame with riveted columns behind its red granite, brick, and terracotta exterior cladding. The form of the exterior only partially reflects the structural function of the steelwork, for every second vertical pier is a dummy, covering no steel but necessary for flexible internal planning arrangements and for the visual effect Sullivan desired, and the elaborate, flowing frieze adorns nothing more important than the mechanical floor.

It is better to think of Sullivan's work not in terms of any one maxim, but in terms of the original contributions he made to design. In addition to finding an unashamedly vertical expression for tall buildings, Sullivan evolved a characteristic ornamental style derived from natural plant forms. In fact, this aspect of his work can be considered part of the Art Nouveau, although Sullivan seems neither to have been directly influenced by, nor to have had a direct influence on, contemporary developments in Europe. Ornament for him was an integral part of the building's design, and his swirling patterns were generally designed for ease of production from a master mold or cast in terracotta, iron, or plaster. The Wainwright Building has ornate terracotta **spandrels** under each window and repetitive patterns on the frieze and roof **fascia**. Sullivan used essentially the same formula in the design of the Guaranty Building (1894) in Buffalo, New York (Fig. 14.61).

With allowance for changing architectural fashions, Sullivan's conception of the skyscraper's composition

in the country up until that time. Its name derives from the huge 4237-seat concert hall located at its center, but the building also contained a ten-story hotel and a seventeen-story office tower, with additional offices at the rear (Fig. 14.59). Erecting such a structure on the muddy subsoil of Chicago challenged the engineering talents of Adler, who also made sure that the sightlines were excellent for every seat in the auditorium. Sullivan's task was to give architectural harmony to the diverse elements of the building.

Romantic that he was, Sullivan turned to classical precedent for inspiration when he tackled the problem of artistic expression appropriate to a tall building. In 1890 a commission from a St. Louis brewer, Ellis Wainwright, gave Adler and Sullivan their first opportunity to design a skyscraper, and Sullivan's treatment of the exterior became the exemplar for much of later high-rise construction (Fig. 14.60). Rather than a layering of horizontal elements drawn from one or more historical periods, the Wainwright Building has a base, a middle section, and a top, like a classical column. Sullivan, in his essay "The Tall Building Artistically Considered" (1896), explained his reasons for this organization. He expressed the ground

14.61 (opposite) Dankmar Adler and Louis Sullivan, Guaranty Building, Buffalo, New York, 1894.
This office structure exhibits the same tall-building composition as the Wainwright Building. Even more dramatically displayed here is Sullivan's cast ornament, which illustrates his principle of organic growth.

14.62 Louis Sullivan, Carson Pirie Scott Department Store, Chicago, Illinois, 1899–1904.
At the Wainwright and Guaranty buildings, Sullivan chose to emphasize the vertical. Here he balanced horizontals and verticals and inserted "Chicago windows"—windows that have large fixed panes between operable sashes.

remains valid today. In place of the brick and terracotta infill panels that Sullivan used, subsequent high-rise construction makes extensive use of glass **curtain walls**, where the lightweight frames holding the glass are brought forward of the structural members, a technique first employed by W.J. Polk in the Halladie Building (1918) in San Francisco.

Sullivan used more florid and three-dimensional ornament for the main entrance of the Schlesinger and Mayer Store, now the Carson Pirie Scott Department Store (1899–1904), in Chicago, a building that represents the maturity of Sullivan's design ideas for tall buildings (Fig. 14.62). Here, the large windows are set in wide bays, articulated by white terracotta cladding on the steel columns and spandrel panels. The overall effect of the building is more horizontal than vertical. Display windows on the ground floor are terminated by cast-iron ornamental panels that can be readily viewed from the street level. The ornament becomes far more exuberant around the heads of the doorways, thereby giving emphasis to the entrance, which is further defined by its location at a slightly projecting radiused (i.e. ninety degrees of curvature) corner. Upper-level windows have slender ornamental frames. Thus, the building provides visual rewards from several vantage points. From a distance, its austere white skin reads as a cleanly subdivided rectangular grid resting on a dark base; from a medium distance, the articulated entrance can be easily distinguished; and from a close view, one can appreciate the abundant detail around windows and doorways. With the Carson Pirie Scott Department Store, Sullivan achieved an integration of uninterrupted line and decorative detail that has seldom been equaled.

Having reached its apogee, Sullivan's architectural practice declined precipitously. The Carson Pirie Scott Department Store was to be his last major commission. He and Adler dissolved their partnership in 1895, and neither prospered separately. Within a year Adler proposed rejoining forces, but Sullivan turned him down. Sullivan's misanthropy and growing alcoholism estranged him from his family, his professional colleagues, and most prospective clients. Between 1907 and 1924 he had only thirteen minor commissions, the most impressive being the National Farmers' Bank (1907–08) in Owatonna, Minnesota.

THE WORLD'S COLUMBIAN EXPOSITION

Richard Morris Hunt, Charles McKim, and Louis Sullivan all played prominent roles in the planning of the 1893 World's Columbian Exposition in Chicago, an event that some view as a crossroads in the development of American architecture. Landscape architect Frederick Law Olmsted produced the site plan and a committee of the country's most important architects was formed under the leadership of Daniel H. Burnham to design the mostly temporary buildings for the fair. Hunt used his influence as the profession's leading practitioner to direct the entire plan along Beaux-Arts lines. The principal buildings, their designs assigned to different architectural firms, were disposed around a large Court of Honor and Grand Basin, with the domed Administration Building (Fig. 14.63) by Hunt at its head and McKim's huge Agriculture Building adjacent to it. To ensure unity around the court, it was agreed that all designs would be based on the precedent of the Italian Renaissance; would use a common material—stucco (plaster), painted white; and would maintain a uniform sixty-foot-high cornice line. The effect was stunning to visitors, who named it the "White City" and went away greatly impressed by the dramatic spectacle. The 1893 fair did much to advance the ornate and monumental Beaux-Arts style as the appropriate one for important American buildings and civic designs. As part of a movement that became known as the City Beautiful, train stations, art museums, city halls, post offices, churches, and whole civic centers were built across the country in emulation of the White City.

In their enthusiasm for Beaux-Arts architecture, fair visitors largely overlooked the most innovative buildings in Chicago, the tall metal-framed ones downtown. Louis Sullivan, who designed the fair's Transportation Building, later remarked that the event set the cause of American architecture back by fifty years. His observation is arguably a biased one, however, made late in his life when his career had gone into decline, so scholars continue to debate the fair's impact. However, big changes were afoot at the time, as something called Modernism would soon take hold. It would begin in Europe, with its roots extending back to the mid-nineteenth century, then be exported to the United States. The development of the twentieth century's modern architecture will be discussed in the next chapter.

CONCLUSIONS ABOUT ARCHITECTURAL IDEAS

Materials-science and engineering advances accompanying the ongoing Industrial Revolution have been central to the preceding discussion of the nineteenth century, beginning with utilitarian structures such as bridges and textile mills. Even by mid-century, few architects had taken to the newly available materials, abdicating their role as innovators in favor of technicians and even greenhouse designers—for instance, it was the landscape gardener Joseph Paxton who created the Crystal Palace. Its rapidly mass-produced and assembled skeletal construction represented a sea change

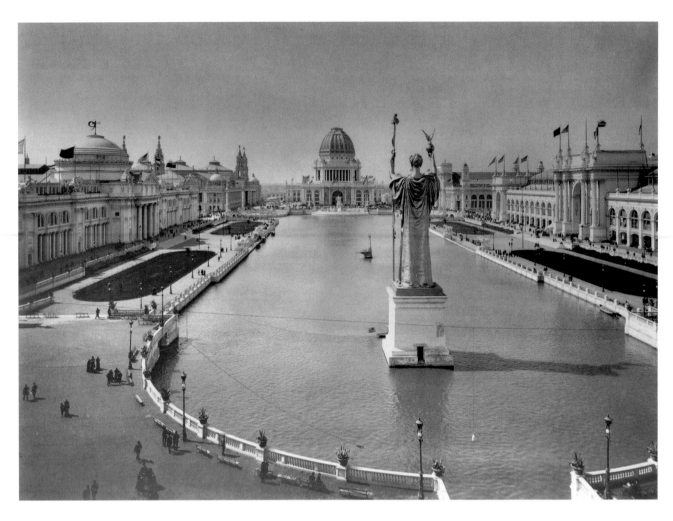

14.63 World's Columbian Exposition, Chicago, Illinois, 1893.
Richard Morris Hunt's Administration Building stands at the head of
the Court of Honor and its lagoon, and Charles McKim's Agriculture
Building appears at the left. The "White City" captivated the American
public. Using widespread exterior electric lighting for the first time,
it started a movement that produced proposals for new civic cores
in cities nationwide.

not only in how buildings were to be built but also how
they were to be perceived.

Architectural theoretician Eugène-Emmanuel Viollet-
le-Duc encouraged the substitution of iron for stone in
his writings, and at mid-century architect Henri Labrouste
inserted spindly iron reading-room columns and lacy
iron domes inside a traditional masonry armature at his
Bibliothèque Nationale and used "transparent" iron
construction for the stack area of his Bibliothèque Ste.-
Geneviève. Soon thereafter Gustave Eiffel honed the skeletal metal esthetic in his bridges and famous Eiffel Tower.
Across the Atlantic, American builders were perfecting
skeletal construction in wood in the form of the balloon
frame, and by the end of the century Frenchmen had taken
the lead in developing the steel-reinforced concrete frame.

Not everyone agreed, however, with this headlong
technological rush toward newness. In mid-century
England, Gothic Revivalist A.W.N. Pugin made a scathing

indictment of industrialization's effect on nineteenth-century architecture and urban life through the publication
of his vividly illustrated *Contrasts*. Accompanying his con-
demnations was an interest in picturesque composition,
given particularly dramatic form as the ever-changing,
irregular silhouette of the Houses of Parliament on which
Pugin worked both early and late in his career.

At the same time, cultural critic John Ruskin set down a
philosophy in his *Seven Lamps of Architecture* that deplored
what he considered to be amoral industrial production and
demanded a rebirth of what he saw as the morally healthy
craft tradition. Responding to Ruskin's call, designers like
William Morris offered as an alternative the Arts and Crafts
Movement, so forward-looking in its honest appreciation
of materials that Arts and Crafts architect C.F.A. Voysey,
actually inspired by English yeoman cottages, became
a proto-Modernist in the minds of those later searching
for the sources of twentieth-century Modernism. Others
working within the Arts and Crafts tradition, like Richard
Norman Shaw, produced compositions that had more to
do with suave eclecticism than ideology or reform. German
cultural attaché Herman Muthesius so admired the houses
of Voysey and his contemporaries that he assembled their
domestic work in *Das Englische Haus*, a book that would
have implications for the rise of Modernism in Germany.

Fueled by a desire for "newness" at the end of the nineteenth century, designers sought to exploit the plastic capabilities of iron in a movement that became known as the Art Nouveau. Victor Horta in Belgium, Hector Guimard in France, and Antonio Gaudí in Spain (his work being by far the most exotic and multifarious of the three) produced buildings with flowing, organic lines as a principal characteristic. Charles Rennie Mackintosh in Scotland has been associated by some with the Art Nouveau, but his work has perhaps more in common with the Arts and Crafts, and it was also admired by members of the Viennese Secession. An elder statesman among these Secessionists, Otto Wagner dabbled in the Jugendstil but settled on a tectonic architecture exploitative of new materials, including aluminum, while maintaining classical ordering principles. Wagner's pupil Joseph Maria Olbrich designed everything from garments to automobiles to buildings, with overt linearity being a formal constant in his work.

In the United States, not yet a century old as a country but already moving toward world-power status, the search was on for a national style. Finding his way to the French Ecole des Beaux-Arts, Richard Morris Hunt learned within the French system and studied modern French buildings, bringing back his worldly view to the United States, where it found an eager client base among the wealth-making captains of industry. His student and employee Frank Furness pushed the limits of Victorian Gothic, neo-Grec, and French Second Empire-style eclecticism and produced buildings that were admired by his short-term employee Louis Sullivan.

Ecole attendee H.H. Richardson created the distinctly American Richardsonian Romanesque style. At his Marshall Fields Store in Chicago, he explored the expressive qualities of massive stone masonry, appropriate in its aggressiveness for a young country on the make, and influenced emerging Chicago School architects, most notably Louis Sullivan. Richardson's Glessner House displays a tectonic grammar in stone, while his proto-Queen Anne-style Watts Sherman House, as much a product of the mind and pencil of employee Stanford White as Richardson, and the Shingle-style Stoughton House near the Harvard campus, owe something to the Arts and Crafts Movement but also to the New England Colonial architecture then being chauvinistically reinterpreted by American architects for the first time.

Richardson employees Charles McKim and Stanford White, along with William Rutherford Mead, formed the first large American architectural firm. In their residential commissions, they continued Richardson's Shingle-style and developed a Colonial Revival style appropriate to the spirit of the times. For their larger commissions, they turned to more suave and urbane inspirations to produce a Renaissance Revival style and even mimicked ancient Roman works, as in their design for New York City's Pennsylvania Station.

At the largest scale, that of the tall office building, it was Chicago architects who would be the innovators in the wake of their city's great fire in 1871. Burnham and Root's Monadnock Building illustrates the economic limitations of bearing-wall construction, while experiments from William LeBaron Jenney's Home Insurance Company Building to Burnham and Root's Reliance Building took functionality and structural rationalism to the level of art in the form of the steel-frame skyscraper. It was the skyscraper that best expressed the energy and ingenuity of a United States celebrating its centennial. And it was Louis Sullivan who elegantly summarized this new building type's proper organization in his essay "The Tall Building Artistically Considered." Along with his partner, Dankmar Adler, he gave form to his ideas in the Auditorium Building in Chicago, and ever more dramatically in the Wainwright Building in St. Louis and the Guaranty Building in Buffalo, New York, before beginning a downward spiral personally and professionally that saw him reduced to designing small but exquisite Midwestern banks by the early twentieth century. It was Sullivan's protégé Frank Lloyd Wright who would become the most famous American architect of the twentieth century, and his work, along with that of other Modernists, is covered in this book's final two chapters.

Despite all of Chicago's forward-looking designers, the architecture of the city's 1893 World's Columbian Exposition became an extension of the Ecole des Beaux-Arts design principles of New Yorker Richard Morris Hunt, who succeeded in enforcing a confectionary Neo-Classicism. Louis Sullivan's proto-modern Transportation Building did not make it into the elite circle of structures surrounding the Court of Honor and Great Basin, and his employee, the young Frank Lloyd Wright, was not yet an architectural force here along the shore of Lake Michigan.

Chapter 15
The Twentieth Century and Modernism

T he development of "modern" architecture was complex, an inescapable condition in the twentieth century. Evaluating this complexity has been made more difficult by the polemical nature of much writing by those advocating or disparaging the Modern Movement, or European Modernism. While a superficial look at Modernist buildings may suggest that this work is reductivistic, or stripped of all but its essential parts, and, some would say, left with little or no meaning, such is not the case. The founders of Modernism intended that their buildings should be didactic; they intended for them to instruct. But benefiting from this instruction often requires an awareness not only of what can be seen, but also of what cannot, that is, of what has been eliminated from the architecture that preceded Modernism and to which the Modernists were reacting.

THE IDEA OF A MODERN ARCHITECTURE

In the wake of the horrors of World War I, many young architects shared a general disillusionment, indeed, a sense that European culture had failed and would have to be replaced by a transformed society; they believed that architecture could and should become an instrument of this transformation. They also believed in the power of rational thought, and ultimately in its handmaidens, economy and functionality, and they believed that rational designs could best be produced through mechanization, yielding efficient, somehow machine-made buildings. As a corollary, and following nineteenth-century social and architectural critics like John Ruskin, they revered the direct expression of building materials and their processes of assembly.

Adding to the difficulty in understanding individual buildings from the formative period of Modernism has been the subsequent general absorption of Modernist buildings into the broader architectural culture and their construction outside the geographical and social contexts in which they originated. Frequently Modernist utopianism has given way to mass culture, economy to parsimony, and honesty to banality. Ironically, this modern architecture,

with its often Socialist roots, was appropriated by corporate America, most dramatically for the glass-and-steel towers that became companies' headquarters and projected their capitalist images. In order to make our way through these potentially confusing circumstances, let us begin by considering the publications and authors of the Modernist press and cast a critical eye on what has been written.

The War of Words

The advocates of Modernism saw writing as a principal means for advancing their agenda. In 1927 Gustav Platz published *Die Baukunst der neuesten Zeit* or *The Architecture of the New Age*. The German word *Zeit* is an important one, as the notion of Zeitgeist, or the Spirit of the Age, had

Chronology

Albert Einstein publishes *Special* and *General Theories of Relativity*	1905 and 1916
Pablo Picasso and Georges Braque create Cubism	1908–12
Filippo Marinetti publishes the *Futurist Manifesto*	1909
Beginning of federal income tax in the United States	1913 and 1916
Henry Ford fully mechanizes mass production of the automobile	1914
World War I	1914–18
Dada art movement	ca. 1915
Bolshevik Revolution in Russia	1917
Theo van Doesburg begins the journal *De Stijl*	1917
Mussolini founds the Fascist Party in Italy	1919
Walter Gropius founds the Weimar Bauhaus	1919
Women granted the right to vote in the United States	1920
Le Corbusier articulates his "five points of architecture"	1926
Joseph Stalin assumes power in the Soviet Union	1926
Werner Heisenberg formulates his Uncertainty Principle	1927
New York Stock Market crashes, signaling the Great Depression	1929
Adolf Loos develops the *Raumplan*	1930
Invention of air-conditioning	1932
"The International Style: Architecture Since 1922" exhibition opens at New York City's Museum of Modern Art	1932
World War II	1939–45
Atomic bomb dropped at Hiroshima	1945
First computer assembled	1945
Francis Crick and James Watson discover DNA	1953
Brown v. Board of Education determines that racial segregation is illegal in United States schools	1954

←······

Walter Gropius, Bauhaus, Dessau, 1926.
At the Bauhaus Gropius radically altered the traditional relationship between structure and enclosure. Gone is the heavy, load-bearing exterior wall of earlier times, replaced by a largely transparent outer layer through which a separate structural system is visible.

been assembled from it by nineteenth-century German art historians. Zeitgeist combines the notions of newness, inherited from the Art Nouveau, and style that somehow together encapsulate the aspirations and accomplishments of an era as did, some have argued, the Gothic in France or the High Renaissance in Italy. The publication of Platz's book was sandwiched between Le Corbusier's *Vers une architecture* (1923), usually translated as *Toward a New Architecture*, Frank Lloyd Wright's *Modern Architecture* (1931), and Walter Gropius's *Die neue Architektur und das Bauhaus*, translated as *The New Architecture and the Bauhaus* (1935). In each of these publications, the author sought to promote his own design philosophy; this had been done before, but, encouraged by the escalating power of the media, it would be done with a vengeance in the twentieth century. In fact, by the 1970s, many architects would begin publishing monographs about their work before they had built anything of consequence.

In 1932 architectural historian Henry-Russell Hitchcock and his protégé Philip Johnson, in support of the recently held exhibition at the Museum of Modern Art (MoMA) in New York City that they had organized with the museum's director, Alfred Barr, Jr., produced a thin volume entitled *The International Style: Architecture Since 1922*. Here, they announced that European Modernism was a new style and dubbed it "international" since it had already been transplanted from Europe to America (and would be exported elsewhere). Historians immediately went to work searching for the origins of the newly announced phenomenon, showing the same zeal and promoting the same confusion that had accompanied Baker and Speke's nineteenth-century search for the source of the Nile. None was more persuasive at the beginning than Nikolaus Pevsner. In his *Pioneers of the Modern Movement: From William Morris to Walter Gropius* (1936), Pevsner identified William Morris, as the title suggests, and his circle of Arts and Crafts designers in England, with Herman Muthesius as a connection to Germany, as the forerunners of the *Neue Sachlichkeit* or, as it is often translated, the "New Objectivity," and he saw the various late nineteenth-century art movements as having established a new set of ideals. He discussed developments in iron, steel, and concrete, spent considerable time on the Art Nouveau, and concluded with an examination of work in Vienna, including that of Adolf Loos, and of Peter Behrens and his Werkbund associates in Germany. While Pevsner mentioned Futurism, he completely ignored Constructivism, De Stijl, and Expressionism, movements that did not fit neatly into his narrative.

Sigfried Giedion took a not dissimilar view in *Space, Time, and Architecture* (1941), a work so persuasive that many Modernist schools of architecture adopted it as a textbook in architectural history classes in the 1940s, '50s, and '60s. Delivered originally as a series of lectures, the text has serious disjunctures, but Giedion wrote with such authority and conviction that, if anything, these lacunae served to intensify his narrative. His principal themes are truth and honesty, the force of technology, and the so-called space–time conception in art and architecture, all presented in a Zeitgeistian context. It is at once a spectacular and insidious book thanks to Giedion's professed method of selecting pertinent materials. In explaining this method, he spoke of "constituent" and "transitory" facts, the former being "tendencies which, when they are suppressed, inevitably reappear" and the latter being trends which "lack the stuff of permanence and fail to attach themselves to a tradition." Giedion's critics have seen this differentiation as a facile way for him to include those historical events that supported his arguments while ignoring those that did not.

The Pevsner–Giedion Modernist vision held sway almost completely until 1960, when Reyner Banham, in *Theory and Design in the First Machine Age*, argued that the two scholars had got it wrong. He quickly dispensed with the German and Austrian developments in the first section of his book; he spent the entire second section on Futurism, and the entire third section on the De Stijl movement and Expressionism in Holland and Germany, then concluded in part four with Le Corbusier, Gropius, and Mies van der Rohe. Six years later Dennis Sharp published *Modern Architecture and Expressionism* (1966), an entire book devoted to buildings that Pevsner and Giedion had seen as inconsequential only thirty years before. The year 1966 also saw the publication of Robert Venturi's iconoclastic *Complexity and Contradiction in Architecture*, a thin volume that both thrilled and shocked students of the time and announced the end of Modernist dominance in education and practice.

What does this series of publishing events tell us? For young students, perhaps, it presents something destabilizing and even frightening: historical truth does not seem to be a constant; and, indeed, it is not. Things change, human perspectives change, ideals change, and so our view of history, and therefore history itself, changes. Students should not be discouraged, however; in fact, quite the opposite is true. History is not dead; it is like a living organism.

Early Modernists were also militant; they sought to annihilate by any means available their revivalist enemies, including the entire Ecole des Beaux-Arts. They assumed ultimate power in the role of designers and design teachers for better than thirty years. In some cases they behaved badly, arrogantly, even ignorantly, and their architecture sometimes showed it, but many of the so-called Post-Modernists (some of whom will be dealt with in the next chapter) who sought to replace them or wrote about those who replaced them in the 1960s and afterward would have us believe that these Modernists were reprobates. How can this be? Can so many, so committed for so long, have been completely wrong? The answer is this: it is just not that simple!

Modern architecture was conceived during a time of tremendous upheaval in Western culture, including a world war and a revolution in Russia and developments in art and science that transformed our fundamental views about, among other things, both time and space. Designers in the first decade and a half of the twentieth century sought to come to terms with new ways of seeing, analyzing, and understanding, with tremendous advances in technology, and with the perceived necessity to create a modern art. Subsequent to World War I, the dominant issue in war-ravaged countries became the desperate need for housing. As Modernists competed with traditionalists, the most extreme among them moved toward the New Objectivity, arguing that modern work was more efficient and cost-effective, which in some cases it was. However, their efforts to make modern architecture appear, if not in fact be, machine-producible and to render it functional and expressive of that functionality led, in the eyes of many, to a reductivistic architecture, one short on character, symbolism, and even "livability." Still, whatever the final assessment, one can only admire the zeal and conviction with which Modernists took to the task at hand, and none of them was more zealous or wrote more polemically than the Viennese architect Adolf Loos.

ADOLF LOOS

Early in his career Adolf Loos (1870–1933) was affiliated with the Secession, but he soon became estranged from it. After completing his architectural education, he worked and traveled in the United States in 1893–96, where he saw the buildings of the Chicago School, visited the World's Columbian Exposition, and encountered the writings of Louis Sullivan, such as his essay "Ornament in Architecture" (1892). Sullivan had written: "I shall say that it would be greatly for our esthetic good if we should refrain entirely from the use of ornament for a period of years, in order that our thought might concentrate acutely upon the production of buildings well formed and comely in the nude." Apparently the young Loos strongly agreed, for when he returned to Vienna, he soon began to speak out against the inclusion of ornament on buildings. This was a difficult position to maintain within the Viennese Secession, for the Jugendstil had nothing if not a highly refined sense of ornament. Some historians have theorized that Loos's turning against the prevailing Viennese school was a response to his losing the commission to decorate and furnish the Secession council chamber. In any case, he set out on an exploration that would lead him not only to advocate the elimination of ornament but also to posit a new method of spatial composition: the *Raumplan*.

Influence of Loos's Lectures and Publications

Loos's first published attack on ornament came as early as 1898, well ahead of a debate that took place in the German press beginning in 1907 and that was stimulated to some extent by the perceived excesses of the Jugendstil. A decade later, Loos spoke to a sparse crowd in Berlin, using the lecture title "Critique of Applied Art," and a newspaper reviewer quoted him as saying that "the evolution of culture is synonymous with the removal of ornament from objects of daily use." In a Vienna lecture, at the beginning of 1910, he first adopted the title "Ornament and Crime" and argued that ornament would naturally disappear with the evolution of modern culture. In October of that year, he used the same lecture title in Berlin, but still attracted only a modest crowd. Then, when his designs for the Goldman and Salatsch Store in Vienna became public and met with fierce criticism because its upper floors were to be unornamented, Loos responded in kind in the German press, so that when he brought "Ornament and Crime" to Munich in December, he attracted a large and outspoken crowd. Still, though he had finally assumed a certain local celebrity, "Ornament and Crime" was not published until 1913, and not in German but in the French *Les cahiers d'aujourd'hui* (*The Notebooks of Today*). Only in 1929 did his by then canonical piece finally appear in German, and this only two years before he included it in his collection of essays titled *Trotzdem* (meaning "nevertheless" or "all the same").

In "Ornament and Crime," Loos took Sullivan's suggestion to abandon ornament in architecture a step further, proposing that the tendency to decorate surfaces was a sign of primitive culture or infancy. In advanced societies or in adults, he said, the urge toward ornamental design was a sign of dependency or criminality. He wrote polemically:

> *Children are amoral, and so, by our standards, are Papuans. If a Papuan slaughters an enemy and eats him, that doesn't make him a criminal. But if a modern man kills someone and eats him, he must be either a criminal or degenerate. The Papuans tattoo themselves, decorate their boats, their oars, everything they can get their hands on. But a modern man who tattoos himself is either a criminal or a degenerate. Why, there are prisons where eighty per cent of the convicts are tattooed, and tattooed men who are not in prison are either latent criminals or degenerate aristocrats. When a tattooed man dies at liberty, it simply means that he hasn't had time to commit his crime.*

Though the Viennese press had made ethnologist Rudolf Pöch's 1901–06 investigations of the Papuan tribe in New Guinea well known, Loos's was a radical message in relation to architecture. When "Ornament and Crime" became known to avant-garde artists in Paris, Loos became a minor Parisian celebrity and he moved there in the early 1920s. By extolling the virtues of architecture without ornament, he addressed an issue that had been of general concern to designers in various places around the turn of the century. His writings led to admiration of the simple vernacular forms of undecorated peasant architecture and the rather plain, functional works of engineers, both types of constructions previously considered to have no particular esthetic merit. Furthermore, Loos's admonition to

15.1 Adolf Loos, Rear elevation of the Steiner House, Vienna, 1910.
Orthogonal massing, punched-out windows, a pipe-rail balustrade, and an absolute lack of ornament announce the nature of Loos's radical architectural proposals. At the front elevation, he made concessions to the surrounding residential context that he would not make again.

15.2 Adolf Loos, Longitudinal section through the Steiner House, Vienna, 1910.
Neither Loos's plan nor section yet suggests the investigations of spatial interpenetrations that will appear in his mature houses.

15.3 Adolf Loos, Rear elevation of the Moller House, Vienna, 1930.
Gone is the symmetry of the Steiner House. Even more dramatically used are the simple window frames and the linear railings. The space on the inside has become the dominant element of the composition.

15.5 Adolf Loos, Longitudinal section through the Moller House, Vienna, 1930.
In this section, Loos has begun to manipulate the floor heights and to cantilever floor plates. Rather than being stacked, the floors are spatial units displaced horizontally across one another.

15.4 Adolf Loos, Second-floor (*right*) and third-floor (*left*) plans of the Moller House, Vienna, 1930.
Above the ground floor Loos inserted few full-height walls. However, his plans never had the horizontal spatial interactions of Frank Lloyd Wright's residential designs of the turn of the century.

build without ornament suggested a way to build in a style appropriate to a mechanized age.

The *Raumplan* and Loos's Buildings

Loos's architectural designs are largely absent of ornament, befitting his theories. Moreover, unlike many revolutionaries, who only identify what to eliminate, Loos had proposals for what should be added too. A sequence of his house designs will illustrate his contributions. His Steiner House of 1910 (Fig. 15.1) in Vienna is an unadorned white cubical mass with plain, modest window openings and a streetfront façade that pays at least lip service to the more traditional surrounding residences. Its plan is straightforward and largely symmetrical, and its section (Fig. 15.2) shows layered floor slabs of equal height. Its interior offers a slightly richer set of experiences, with considerable use of wood for wainscots, door and window casings, and ceiling grids; but this interior is not unlike the work of many others during this period. His Moller House of 1930 (also in Vienna) shows several dramatic advances. The exterior mass (Fig. 15.3) is still without conventional ornament, but each element—doors, windows, handrails, parapets, cantilevered slabs—becomes a distinctive and carefully disposed part within an asymmetrical but balanced whole. The plan (Fig. 15.4) is also asymmetrical, with some rooms interconnected spatially by large door openings or low-walled apertures. The section (Fig. 15.5) is more dramatic than that of the Steiner House in its spatial explorations, as the floor levels vary in height and some become mezzanines. On the interior, the materials are plain but rich by virtue of their natural character, the conspicuously grained wood in particular. Of the Müller House in Prague (1930) the same can be said of its exterior massing and plans, but the section is even more adventurous, with multiple ceiling heights and an overt use of stairs to unify space vertically. Likewise, the interior materials are richer, particularly the use of marble without moldings such that its grain alone is left to provide scale and detail. Finally, in his earlier but more experimental (and unbuilt) villa on the Lido in Venice (1923), Loos demonstrated the full potential of his style of spatial composition, his *Raumplan*. The section (Fig. 15.6) is the most revealing drawing, with multiple ceiling heights, mezzanine levels, and bold openings among spaces. Here Loos accomplished spatially what Giedion could only claim for Victor Horta, and he prepared the way for Le Corbusier's Modernist spatial compositions based upon his five points and Mies van der Rohe's meticulous compositions using stainless steel, onyx, marble, glass, and water, which are discussed later in this chapter.

FRANK LLOYD WRIGHT

No American architect's name is more widely known than that of Frank Lloyd Wright (1867–1959), who considered Louis Sullivan to be his mentor, and in the late nineteenth and early twentieth centuries he made spatial investigations at least as advanced as those of Adolf Loos. Wright was born in Wisconsin, the son of a domineering Welsh mother and an itinerant preacher-musician father, and he grew up in a variety of locations until his mother moved back near her family in Wisconsin when Wright was eleven. There he worked on his uncle's farm and attended school sporadically, all the while involving himself in drawing, crafts, painting, and printmaking. Wright's mother had decided before his birth that her son would become an architect, so she encouraged his interest in artistic and spatial investigations. After his parents divorced in 1885, Wright dropped out of high school and worked as an office boy for a professor of civil engineering at the University of Wisconsin. He later entered the university's evening school as a special student, taking one semester of descriptive geometry and failing to complete a class in French. At the age of nineteen, he went to Chicago and found employment in the architectural office of Joseph Lyman Silsbee, a friend of his uncle's. Wright's ambition, however, was to work for Adler and Sullivan, and he practiced drawing Sullivanesque ornament so that he could make a favorable impression at the job interview.

In 1888 he landed a job there, demonstrating his graphic skill to Sullivan's satisfaction and gaining a five-year contract as draftsman. With an advance on his salary Wright started construction of his own house (1889) in the Chicago suburb of Oak Park. The house began as a modest two-story building, with a Serliana in the shingle-covered gable end turned to the street. Over the years, Wright greatly enlarged and reworked it to provide space for his six children and his mother. In the office of Adler and Sullivan, Wright was sometimes given a free hand

15.6 Adolf Loos, Section through the Lido villa, Venice, 1923. Ceiling heights vary, and the two adjacent shafts of space have been displaced vertically producing multiple floor levels.

0   10 m
0   30 ft

15.7 (above) Dankmar Adler and Louis Sullivan, James Charnley House, Chicago, Illinois, 1891.
For this composition Frank Lloyd Wright, then working in the Adler and Sullivan office, obviously drew upon the Auditorium Building (see Figs. 14.58–59). The projection of the lobby there became a loggia off the central stair hall in the Charnley House.

15.8 (left) Dankmar Adler and Louis Sullivan, Plans of the James Charnley House, Chicago, Illinois, 1891.
These carefully balanced plans only hint at Wright's subsequent interior-space designs. The cross-axes on both floors intersect at the two-story space of the stair opening.

with residential commissions, such as that for the James Charnley House (1891), a two-story structure on a narrow city lot in Chicago (Figs. 15.7–15.8) His symmetrical design has a central doorway with carved Sullivanesque ornament below a second-level loggia with Doric columns.

Developing the Prairie House

Wright soon began designing other houses outside of office time, a practice Sullivan denounced as a violation of his employee's contract with the firm. As a result, Wright was fired and established his own practice, which he based

in a studio built onto his Oak Park house. It was the newly developing Chicago suburbs for the rising middle class, like Oak Park, that Wright would use as his first architectural laboratory. While his clients wanted value for their money, they were frequently willing to allow Wright to experiment. His early years of independent practice were characterized by explorations of many styles of domestic architecture—Colonial, Tudor, Georgian, Shingle, and Queen Anne—although Wright later edited down his body of work to include only those designs that obviously contributed to the development of his Prairie style. Among these was his first independent commission, a house for

15.9 (above) Frank Lloyd Wright, Winslow House, River Forest, Illinois, 1893.
This is another case where Wright looked to Sullivan for inspiration. The ornamental frontispiece echoed such compositions as Sullivan's Getty Tomb.

15.10 (left) Frank Lloyd Wright, Plan of the Winslow House, River Forest, Illinois, 1893.
Wright often spoke of "breaking the box." That process had begun here: the front rooms are self-contained and axially connected, while the side and rear rooms project as a porte-cochère and as semicircular and semipolygonal bays, and the terraces are defined by platforms and projecting walls.

William H. Winslow (1893) in River Forest, Illinois (Figs. 15.9–15.10). Like the Charnley House, the Winslow House is symmetrical, and it displays Sullivanesque ornament. In common with the later Prairie houses, the Winslow House is organized around a central fireplace and dominated by horizontal lines. The hipped roof overhangs the second floor at the level of the window heads, and the apparent height of the ground floor extends to the second-floor window sills, effectively reducing the perceived volume of the upper level and creating the impression that the building hugs the ground. Wright even broadened the chimney mass to emphasize the horizontal aspect rather than the vertical.

With the design of the Ward Willits House (1901) in Highland Park, Illinois, Wright abandoned the compact composition of the Winslow House for a cruciform plan (a commonly used organization in many houses of the period 1900–10) with four arms extending out into the

15.11 Frank Lloyd Wright, Plans and perspective of the Ward Willits House, Highland Park, Illinois, 1901, drawing.
Ten years after the Charnley House, Wright had devised a new kind of residence. In it, the center is solidly anchored by a great hearth, and the rooms project out aggressively into space, covered by long, low, hovering roofs. His distinctive perspective-drawing technique was influenced by an interest in Japanese prints and by his employee, the architect-delineator Marion Mahoney.

landscape from the central chimney mass (Fig. 15.11). Again the horizontal line dominates the exterior, accentuated by the overhanging eaves of the roofline and the extension of the transverse axis of the house to form a porte-cochère (a covered drive-through for vehicles) at one end and a covered porch at the other. The exterior stucco is banded by continuous horizontal strips of dark wood marking the first-floor level and the window-sill line. By lowering the eaves to the level of the window heads and diminishing the chimney's height, Wright again minimized the vertical component of this two-story house.

Wright developed the Prairie house out of his search for an appropriate regional expression for American homes, especially in the Midwest. Taking his cue from the gently rolling land of the prairie, he designed houses that sat close to the ground and seemed to be tied organically to the landscape. The prevailing eclectic Victorian styles, which he had tried and discarded, Wright now dismissed as "pimples" on the land. He also responded to the prevailing materials of construction, including brick and wood cut in standard sizes by sawmills, by trying to devise uses that were sympathetic to them and their modes of fabrication.

Environmental factors also affected his designs. The broad overhanging eaves shielded the windows from the

hot Chicago sun while permitting the lower winter rays to enter and warm the interior. The central fireplace mass gave warmth to the heart of the home, both functionally and symbolically. All major rooms were oriented to provide cross-ventilation. Some of the most remarkable aspects of the Prairie houses are evident on the interiors, where living spaces flow smoothly from one area to another, creating an integrated spatial experience that was to have a profound influence on early Modernist architects in Europe. Wright's Prairie houses are said to "break the box" because neither the external form nor the internal spaces are contained in tight rectangular units. Even the windows wrap around corners as if to deny the traditional structural corner post. Wright extended the spatial freedom of the two-story living hall used by Richardson and Pugin to the entire interior and gave corresponding freedom to the exterior as it embraced the landscape.

Wright incorporated all these features on even the most difficult of sites, such as the narrow suburban lot of Elizabeth Gale, an Oak Park neighbor for whom he designed a house in 1909. Hemmed in by Victorian hulks on either side, the Gale House had little opportunity to spread out to the landscape, so Wright provided the visual link between interior and exterior through a series of balconies cantilevered off the major living spaces. He would return to this idea later when faced with the far more dramatic hillside site of the Kaufmann House (1935–36) called Fallingwater (see Figs. 15.79–15.80). The last and by far the most celebrated of the early Prairie houses was built for Frederick Robie on two small corner lots in south Chicago in 1909 (Figs. 15.12–15.13). Robie was a self-made man, a manufacturer who had an interest in engineering, and he and Wright got along exceedingly well.

15.12 Frank Lloyd Wright, Robie House, Chicago, Illinois, 1909.
This is the most celebrated house from the first phase of Wright's career. It is a "Prairie house" that acknowledges the horizontality of the Midwestern landscape.

Ground floor

Second floor

15.13 Frank Lloyd Wright, Plans of the Robie House, Chicago, Illinois, 1909.
The client owned a small lot on a busy street and had young children. Wright responded with a very compact plan. The front section is very open, while the rear service section consists of more conventional, self-contained rooms, principally for servants and children.

Robie requested a house where he could have privacy from the street and separation from the noise of his small children at play. Wright's response was a three-story design, with the garage, playroom, and service functions on the ground floor, the living and dining areas on the second floor, and the bedrooms on the third. A low wall in front of the house shields the ground floor from passers-by, and the elevated windows of the second floor, protected by a balcony, give the privacy Robie desired. Horizontality was created by the long lines of the walls and balconies, but especially by the great roof of the second floor, which cantilevers daringly at either end of the house. Welded steel beams made this structural bravura possible, and their employment in the Robie House marked the first use of welded steel in residential construction. Bricks for the house, as for other Prairie houses, were custom-made in St. Louis. Shaped like long, thin Roman bricks, they were laid with wide horizontal mortar joints that were sharply raked to cast a horizontal shadow.

In plan the house is organized around the chimney mass. The entrance is off the short side-street frontage into the rear of the house, and the staircase that leads to the second floor is integrated into the masonry of the chimney. The living room and dining room are in effect one continuous volume, interrupted only partially by the fireplace, so that the great linear space, illuminated by long bands of windows on either side of the living space, is airy and unified. Wright designed all the interior fittings to complement the architecture—the light fixtures, furniture, carpets, and even clothes for Mrs. Robie to wear when entertaining. All this was very much in the Arts and Crafts tradition, except for the fact that the designs, especially for the furniture, were based on primary geometric forms and crisp, uncompromising right angles. This made the chairs and tables fit the space well, but all too often Wright's furniture was not sympathetic to the non-orthogonal human body.

One of the architects working in Frank Lloyd Wright's circle was Marion Mahoney (1871–1962), the second woman to receive an architectural degree from MIT. Ironically, Mahoney's design career may have suffered as a result of her brilliance as a delineator, which meant that she spent much of her time producing presentation-quality renderings. A close comparison of Wright's drawings made before 1895 with those made after Mahoney began working in the office (frequently initialing her work) suggests that she had at least as much influence on the celebrated style of Wright's pages in the Wasmuth portfolios (discussed below) as did Wright himself. No one has successfully isolated her other contributions as a designer of furnishings, mosaics, stained glass, and murals for Wright's Prairie houses, but they are likely manifold. After she and her husband, the architect Walter Burley Griffith, struck out on their own, Mahoney continued her production of superb renderings, most notably for their entry in the international design competition for Canberra, Australia.

More collaborative work followed after the couple relocated "down under," but again attribution of specific work to Mahoney has proved difficult.

Wright's Early Public Buildings

Wright's early years as an architect were not entirely devoted to residential commissions. Two notable designs, the Larkin Building in Buffalo, New York and Unity Temple in Oak Park, illustrate his approach to public buildings. The Larkin Building (1904) (Figs. 15.14–15.15) contained offices for a company that sold packaged soap with coupons printed on the labels. Consumers could save these coupons and redeem them for small gifts, a novel practice at the turn of the century. The Larkin Building was populated by rows of young women carrying out clerical tasks and even more rows of filing cabinets holding paperwork. For them Wright designed a frankly vertical six-story building with a full-height sky-lit atrium at the center (Fig.

15.14, 15.15 Frank Lloyd Wright, Plan (far left, below) and perspective view (far left, above) from the street of the Larkin Building, Buffalo, New York, 1904. Unfortunately, the Larkin Building has long since been destroyed. Its innovations were many, including central air-conditioning and built-in filing cabinets, which are visible in Fig. 15.16.

15.16 (left) Frank Lloyd Wright, Interior atrium of the Larkin Building, Buffalo, New York, 1904. A comparison of this perspective with the view from the street shows the continuity. Notice as well the Wright-styled furniture and light fixtures in this top-lit space surrounded by galleries.

15.17 Frank Lloyd Wright, Unity Temple, Oak Park, Illinois, 1906.
It is remarkable to consider that this landmark work is more than 100 years old. Built for a congregation of modest means, its early use of poured-in-place concrete was an economy-driven innovation.

15.18 Frank Lloyd Wright, Plan of Unity Temple, Oak Park, Illinois, 1906.
To the left is the sanctuary; to the right is the Sunday-school wing. Entry occurs between the two. Notice the way that Wright breaks away the corners from each volume.

15.16). He placed banks of filing cabinets in partitions or against the exterior walls with windows above them; light from the atrium balanced the illumination on each floor. Massed plantings at either end of the atrium introduced the natural environment into the workspace, and uplifting moralizing inscriptions, such as "Honest labor needs no master. Simple justice needs no slaves," were cast in the spandrels and placed around the exterior fountains to inspire the workforce. The custom-designed metal furniture used throughout included chairs connected to the desks, so that, after office hours, the back would fold down on the seat and the entire chair would swing out of the way of the cleaning crew's mops. The exterior of the building was rather austere, rising as an uninterrupted vertical brick mass to the height of a thin string course carefully placed to mark the parapet wall around the rooftop

recreation space. The stairs, located in all four corners, rose as towers distinct from the building mass, leaving the walls in between to be articulated by repetitive bands of windows. As an office building design, the Larkin Building was forward-looking. Entirely ventilation-controlled, with filtered air intake and extract ducts in the stair towers, it was planned for modular furnishings and flexibility, while provisions made for employee recreation anticipated the corporate health clubs of the present day. It became one of Wright's most widely published designs, especially in Europe, where it was emulated by various designers, making it all the more unfortunate that the City of Buffalo demolished the building in 1949 to create a parking lot.

A happier fate has been visited upon Unity Temple (Figs. 15.17–15.18), built in 1906 for the Unitarian-Universalist congregation of Oak Park. The site is on the corner of two particularly busy thoroughfares, so Wright turned the building inward to reduce the impact of street noise. The two major elements of the church, the worship space, called an auditorium in Wright's drawings, and the unity house, containing classrooms and a kitchen, are connected by a common vestibule, neatly solving at once the problems of entrance and separation of the noise of Sunday-school classes from adult worship. The worship space is an articulated cube with two levels of balconies on three walls facing the pulpit on the fourth. It is a rich and glowing interior. Light from leaded-glass windows high in the walls balances that from the deeply coffered, amber-colored skylights over the major congregational seating in the center of the main floor. Insofar as possible, the interior trim consists of orthogonal geometries composed of thin strips of wood. The lights, also designed by Wright, are either spheres or cubes of glass suspended from wooden frames.

Equally remarkable is the exterior, which is constructed entirely of poured-in-place concrete. Unity Temple was Wright's first essay in concrete, and it was also one of the first attempts anywhere to design straightforwardly with that material, instead of covering it or disguising the surface to resemble stone. For the worship space Wright designed discrete geometric ornament in the formwork of the piers between the high windows, and he gave the same treatment to the smaller and lower unity house. The church stands today, carefully restored, and still serves its original functions.

The Flight from America

By 1908 Wright was well established as an architect, and his reputation had spread abroad. Public and professional acceptance did not bring happiness, however, and he felt increasingly hemmed in by family responsibilities and office routine. When an offer came from Ernst Wasmuth, a prestigious Berlin publisher, to prepare a portfolio of his work for publication, Wright saw the chance to escape. Abandoning his wife and six children, he took with him instead the wife of a client and neighbor, Mamah Borthwick Cheney, who left her husband and three children, and together they traveled to Europe in September 1909. For the next twenty-five years, Wright's turbulent personal life seriously interfered with his professional work, and he built very little. The publication of the Wasmuth portfolios, *Frank Lloyd Wright: Ausgeführte Bauten* (*Executed Buildings*) (1910–11) and *Ausgeführte Bauten und Entwürfe von Frank Lloyd Wright* (*Executed Buildings and Projects*) (1911), gave European architects access to his work, but the press in the United States was principally interested in Wright's private-life scandals.

In this difficult period the only major commission Wright received was for the Imperial Hotel in Tokyo (1916–22), remembered now chiefly for its ingenious foundations and cantilevered structural system. The very

muddy subsoil conditions of the hotel site prompted Wright to float the foundations instead of digging further for bedrock. The whole of Japan is, of course, prone to earthquake hazard, so Wright sought to balance the building in sections on central concrete pile clusters with a cantilevered concrete slab on top, much as a waiter balances a tray on raised fingertips. The hotel was designed around courtyards with a pool of water in front of the entrance, both for beauty and for firefighting in case of temblors. Its form was complex and its decorative program equally so. Looking to create a language of modern Japanese ornament, Wright began with the elementary geometries of circles and squares, but eventually softened them in favor of a personal adaptation of traditional Japanese forms. Beyond decoration, the structural system worked as intended in the severe earthquake of 1923, one of the few triumphs Wright could record in that unfortunate year. Over subsequent decades, differential settlement, exacerbated by a lowering of the water table under the area, caused large cracks in the building, and the demand for more spacious, air-conditioned hotel accommodation made Wright's structure increasingly obsolete. It was demolished in the late 1960s to make room for a high-rise.

The architectural career of Frank Lloyd Wright was not over, however, for he would enter another phase of great productivity in the mid-1930s. Those works will be discussed later in this chapter.

H.P. BERLAGE AND WENDINGEN

In 1911 and with knowledge of Wright's work obtained from the Wasmuth publications, the Dutch architect Hendrik Petrus Berlage (1856–1934) came to America to see Wright's buildings for himself. What he found directly influenced his own subsequent work, and through lectures and publication he introduced Wright's ideas to architects throughout the Netherlands.

Berlage is best known for a building that preceded his trip to the United States, the Amsterdam Stock Exchange (1897–1903) (Fig. 15.19), a brick and stone bearing-wall structure of medieval inspiration, but one with a sky-lit iron-truss roof over the trading floor (Fig. 15.20). While the Stock Exchange was conceived quite rationally by Berlage, following the precepts of German architect and esthetic theorist Gottfried Semper—about whom Berlage had learned while a student in Zurich—and P.J.H. Cuipers—a designer in the brick tradition of Amsterdam with connections to the thinking of Viollet-le-Duc—its Ruskinian expression of building materials, particularly through the colors and textures of its carefully composed wall surfaces, provided a starting point for the Wendingen group of Amsterdam architects also known as Dutch Expressionists. In their magazine called *Wendingen*, this group lauded Wright's work, culminating in a seven-issue series devoted to him in 1925–26. In their buildings, they

15.19 H.P. Berlage, Amsterdam Stock Exchange, Amsterdam, 1897–1903.
Berlage drew upon the longstanding brick building tradition in Holland. The brickwork of the Stock Exchange is enriched by the use of polychromatic stone both inside and out.

15.20 H.P. Berlage, Amsterdam Stock Exchange interior, Amsterdam, 1897–1903.
On the interior, not only is there brick and stone, but also iron in the form of arched trusses. The material that had once been considered appropriate only for such structures as greenhouses and train sheds had by now become acceptable in institutional buildings.

stressed the handicraft process of making, the revelation of structure, and the resulting high level of sometimes fantastic, construction process-related detail.

In 1901 the City of Amsterdam commissioned Berlage to lay out residential neighborhoods in the area called Amsterdam South. His proposals for two-story walk-ups of brick, with the street as the primary organizing element, provided the environment for buildings by such Wendingen designers as Piet Kramer (1881–1961) and Michel de Klerk (1884–1923). Kramer, an outgoing personality with an interest in the occult as well as Communist sympathies, designed his units for the De Dageraad housing association in 1918–23 (Fig. 15.21). He used brick to make taut planar and bulging curvilinear walls, inserted

15.21 Piet Kramer, De Dageraad housing project, Amsterdam, 1918–23.
The Dutch Expressionist movement, called Wendigen, included such highly imaginative works as this one by Piet Kramer. Inspired by the brick masonry investigations of Berlage, its members sought to be expressive through the natural use of materials in the handicraft tradition.

15.22 Michel de Klerk, Eigen Haard housing project, Amsterdam, 1913–21.
The exotic quality of projects such as this one should not obscure their designers' concerns for making them good places to live. These two-story walk-ups include common areas and landscaped courts.

15.23 Michel de Klerk, Housing on the Henriette Ronnerplein, Amsterdam, Netherlands, 1921.
An obvious apperception for these buildings would be human faces. De Klerk used common elements—walls, roofs, windows, chimneys—and though he modified each of them only slightly from the norm, the cumulative results border on the fantastic. But as apartments they are utilitarian and extremely livable.

gridlike windows with avian overtones, and applied roof tiles and copings to produce aggressive, prickly silhouettes. De Klerk was perhaps the most talented and original of the Dutch Expressionists. His project for the Eigen Haard housing association (1913–21) (Fig. 15.22) is more plastic than Kramer's work, its silhouette more irregular, and its detailing more highly textured. De Klerk's abilities went well beyond the treatment of surfaces, however, as his housing on the Henriette Ronnerplein (1921) (Fig. 15.23) demonstrates. Here, he manipulated battered walls, linking chimneys, and composite windows to produce a three-dimensional architecture that is among the most original and provocative of the early twentieth century.

GERMAN EXPRESSIONISM

Wendingen had a more diverse counterpart in Germany called German Expressionism, which fixated on both form and societal change and so stood in considerable contrast to the state-run and businesslike Deutsche Werkbund, which is introduced below and discussed in the next section. Between 1900 and 1914, painters of the German Brücke (Bridge) and Blaue Reiter (Blue Rider) groups revolted against academic naturalism and sought to express emotions, thoughts, and feelings directly in their paintings. Subsequent to World War I, Expressionist artists and architects reacted passionately to the grinding horrors of trench warfare, as society attempted to come to terms with the guilt, angst, and estrangement of the postwar period.

Central to much German Expressionist architectural thinking was the writing of Paul Scheerbart and his vision for a glass or crystalline architecture that would somehow ameliorate the repressive opacity of modern culture. In part a reaction against attitudes then dominant in the Werkbund, the counterproposals of German Expressionism were illustrated dramatically at the 1914 Werkbund exhibition in Cologne, where Henri van de Velde's Werkbund Theater explored the theme of *Kunstwollen*, or the will to form, in contrast to the mechanistic type-form precepts of mainstream Werkbund thinking. Bruno Taut's Glass Pavilion (Fig. 15.24) gave physical reality to Scheerbart's proclamations. This duality of approaches illustrates the internal stresses at work within the Werkbund: rationality attuned to industrial mass production versus self-expression made possible by the handicrafts, and, as corollaries to the latter, utopian

15.24 (above) Bruno Taut, Glass Pavilion, Werkbund Exhibition, Cologne, 1914.
This pavilion was on display at an exhibition organized by the German Werkbund, an organization dedicated to the improvement of German manufactured products. Taut sought to dramatize the potential uses of glass as a building material.

15.25 (below) Bruno Taut, Glass Pavilion interior, Werkbund Exhibition, Cologne, 1914.
Taut's obsession with glass began with his so-called "glass chain" writings in which, following the lead of philosopher Paul Scheerbart, he celebrated a vision of culture made less repressive through the use of the transparent material.

collectivism and individual romanticism. Taut's Glass Pavilion was quite formal in its organization: a circular concrete base with central, axial stair; a circular rotunda; and a dome. However, Taut so thoroughly exploited the possibilities of glass that the building became a kind of walk-in prism (Fig. 15.25). Glass walls, glass treads and risers, glass panels in the dome, all filtered and reflected light and color to produce a space intended at once to display glass as a product of industrial production and to nourish the human spirit.

Perhaps the most idiosyncratic of all built German Expressionist work was the Goetheanum designed by an amateur, Rudolf Steiner (1861–1925). A philosopher, scholar, and student of the occult, Steiner founded the Anthroposophical Society in 1912 and set out to build a "free high school for spiritual science," which he called the Goetheanum and so connected his thinking to the writings of German literary giant and Romanticist Johann Wolfgang von Goethe. There were, in fact, two Goetheanums, both in Dornach, just across the German border in Switzerland, the first built of wood in 1913 and destroyed by fire at the end of 1922, and the second of concrete, which opened in 1928 (Fig. 15.26). Goetheanum I can be compared to Van de Velde's Werkbund Theater; it was dominated by curvilinear shapes, many that seemed melted and deformed. Underlying this deformity, however, was a symmetrical plan composed of interlocking circles, and some of the roofs were not unlike many traditional German profiles intended to shed snow. Goetheanum II, which is also systematic in plan, is at once more sculptural and faceted, with the most fantastic part of the complex being the boilerhouse with its vegetal chimney stack.

The Einstein Tower in Potsdam (1920–21) (Fig. 15.27) and the design for a hat factory in Luckenwalde (1921–23), both by Erich Mendelsohn (1887–1953), offer yet another Expressionistic approach to architecture. The dynamic qualities of the Einstein Tower, built of brick covered with stucco, demonstrate Mendelsohn's interest in streamlined forms, which share a kinship with Van de Velde's Werkbund Theater and with the Secessionist productions of Joseph Maria Olbrich. The bold graphic technique of Mendelsohn's sketches for it (Fig. 15.28) and related works displays the powerful and often poetic hand of someone forcefully influenced by the act of drawing itself. The appropriateness of dynamism to the activities of a scientist exploring space and time is obvious. Mendelsohn also exploited metaphorical qualities in his Hat Factory and Dyeworks design of 1921–23 (Fig. 15.29). Here he produced, upon a foundation of rational decisions, a scheme appropriate both to the realities of

15.26 Rudolf Steiner, Goetheanum II, Dornach, 1928.
Rudolf Steiner developed a curriculum for what he called a "spiritual high school." Though not a trained architect, he designed a building in which he could put his educational philosophy into practice. Unfortunately, the first wooden Goetheanum was destroyed by fire. Steiner then produced this second, concrete version as a fireproof replacement.

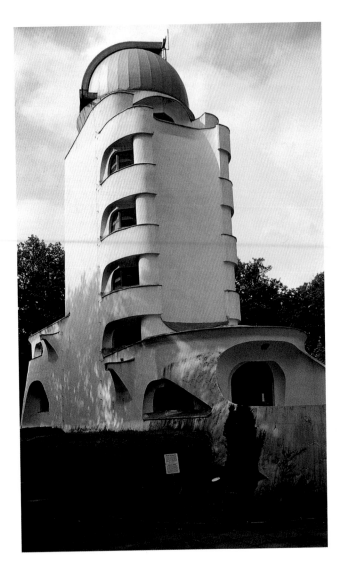

15.27 Erich Mendelsohn, Einstein Tower, Potsdam, 1920–21.
Actually quite modest in size, the Einstein Tower possesses a monumentality befitting its function as a laboratory named for one of the twentieth century's foremost scientists. Intended to be made of concrete, it was constructed of stucco over brick for reasons of economy.

15.28 Erich Mendelsohn, Einstein Tower, Potsdam, Drawings.
Here is evidence of Mendelsohn's extraordinary conceptual thinking. Rapidly executed and energetic, these sketches capture not only the form but also the spirit of the Einstein Tower.

industrial manufacturing and the spirit of German economic aspirations. The administration building has an asymmetrical composition of orthogonal shapes, and in the production facilities Mendelsohn used structural and mechanical systems to produce logical but highly provocative forms. The rigid frame supporting the workshop inspired a rhythmic composition of triangles on the exterior, and the ventilating hood over the dye vats is both purposeful and evocative.

Another much-published German Expressionist monument is Hans Poelzig's (1869–1936) water tower at Posen (now Poznań, Poland) (1911) (Fig. 15.30). Here Poelzig, a stalwart member of the Werkbund, orchestrated a collision of seemingly heterogeneous functions and an almost hallucinogenic industrial esthetic. The skin of the tower is faceted and highly textured, with disparate masonry and glazing patterns. On the inside, set in a skeletal structure comparable to that seen in Fritz Lang's famous Expressionist film *Metropolis* and beneath the water reservoir, Poelzig designed an exhibit space that he planned to be converted into a market hall. The tower is a remarkable amalgamation of purpose and fantasy.

THE DEUTSCHER WERKBUND AND PETER BEHRENS

Discussion of the English Arts and Crafts movement in the previous chapter included reference to the German Herman Muthesius, who was sent to England in 1896 to

15.29 Erich Mendelsohn, Hat Factory and Dyeworks, Luckenwalde, Germany, 1921–23. There is quite a contrast among the rectilinear office block seen in the background to the right and the angular manufacturing buildings seen in the foreground to the right and the dyeworks, with its dramatic ventilation hood, seen to the left. The foreground buildings show that Mendelsohn was not satisfied to work exclusively with the boxy, flat-roofed geometry of what would become known as the International Style.

15.30 Hans Poelzig, Water tower, Posen, 1911. Hans Poelzig was a highly respected member of the Werkbund; today he would be called a corporate man. Even so, he was comfortable producing this evocative design based upon faceted polychromatic panels. Some of the exterior panels carry over to the interior amid a skeleton of trussed columns.

15.31 Peter Behrens, Poster design for AEG, 1908.
As artistic consultant to AEG, Behrens sought to create a graphic image for a large corporate client. He produced letterheads and advertising graphics as well as trade images such as this one.

report on all aspects of English architecture, design, and manufacture, with the intention that his research should prove useful in raising the design standards of German products. Muthesius's subsequent appointment of eminent designers to leadership positions at German arts and crafts schools was one result of the reform process begun after his return to Germany. In 1907 another significant step came when Muthesius, together with sympathetic manufacturers and designers, formed the Deutscher Werkbund. (This German title does not translate easily. Perhaps "German Products Association" would be an appropriate English equivalent.) The Werkbund encouraged fine design in industrially manufactured goods. The motive was primarily economic: Muthesius and others were very much concerned that German products would not be competitive in domestic or international markets unless they could equal the standards set by other countries, especially England. Just what artistic direction the Werkbund would take was the subject of considerable debate in the early years, but the word "quality" was used with great frequency. The Werkbund increasingly promoted abstract forms for manufactured products and standardized parts for production ease, and demanded that esthetic quality should be evaluated separately from manufacturing quality. All these ideas were to be of great importance to designers following World War I.

Another important event of 1907 was the hiring of Peter Behrens (1868–1940), a member of the Werkbund, by the Allgemeine Elektricitäts-Gesellschaft (AEG), or General Electric Company. Behrens was responsible for all aspects of design for the firm—including its letterhead, electric-light fixtures, and production facilities—a brief embracing the modern fields of graphic design, product design, and architecture (Fig. 15.31). The man entrusted with this work was originally trained as a painter, but he was also influenced by the arts and crafts teachings of William Morris.

The buildings Behrens designed for AEG have a quality of transformed classicism. While they were forceful, bold statements, representing nascent architectural attempts to deal with industrial facilities, they were also symbols of the new industrial order then rising in Germany. The most famous is the Turbine Factory in Berlin (1909), where multi-sloped roof trusses make room for a gantry crane and are part of a rigid frame enclosing the large manufacturing assembly hall (Fig. 15.32). Below this roof, a glazed screen at the front façade projects between huge, battered, non-structural corner piers made of concrete but banded with steel and so mimicking traditional stone quoining. At the side wall, the external vertical faces of steel uprights define the building's edge, while the internal canted faces accept wide expanses of glazing. A lower two-story factory block to the left of the assembly hall has horizontal bands of glass and steel at its exposed side wall and so anticipates the innovative exterior walls of such buildings as the Fagus Factory (see Fig. 15.48).

Perhaps because of his AEG work, Behrens's office became known as one of the most progressive in Europe, and three young designers who chose to work for him

15.32 Peter Behrens, AEG Turbine Factory, Berlin, 1909.
Many have commented on the barnlike aspect of this structure's massing and roof profile, suggesting vernacular inspirations. However, the more relevant features for twentieth-century Modernism are the exposed steel supports and the huge, screenlike end-wall glazing set between massive corner piers.

became leaders of the architectural profession after World War I; all are discussed later in this chapter. The German Walter Gropius worked for Behrens in 1907–10 (and met his first collaborator, Adolf Meyer, there). During 1908–11, when Behrens employed the German Mies van der Rohe, he gave him guided tours of Karl Friedrich Schinkel's Berlin work. And in 1910 the young Charles-Edouard Jeanneret-Gris, known as Le Corbusier, made Behrens's office one stop in his architectural-education pilgrimage, this after a year spent in Paris with Auguste Perret, a pioneer in the use of steel-reinforced (or ferro-) concrete.

EXPLOITING THE POTENTIAL OF CONCRETE

In France, Auguste Perret (1874–1954) built numerous apartment buildings, commercial buildings, and churches, such as Notre Dame, Le Raincy (1922–23) (Fig. 15.33), in reinforced concrete. His earliest notable work was the Paris apartment house at 25 bis Rue Franklin (1902), in which the concrete frame allows an irregular disposition of rooms to reflect the non-load-bearing nature of the interior walls (Fig. 15.34). This same freedom is reflected in

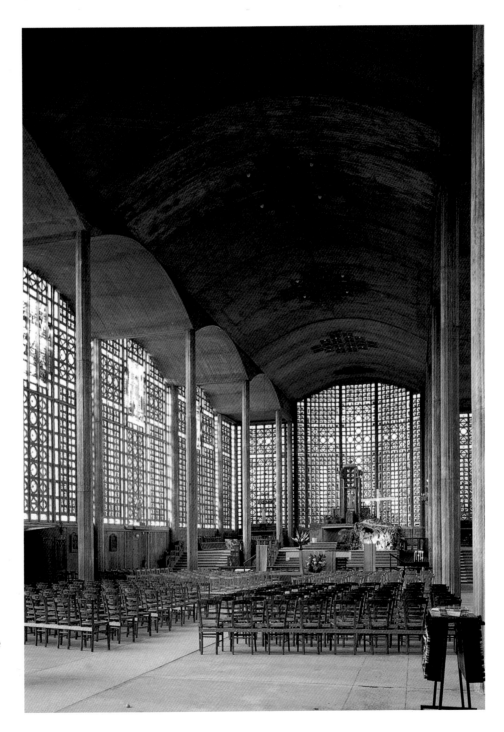

15.33 Auguste Perret, Notre Dame interior, Le Raincy, 1922–23.
Auguste Perret was a pioneer in the architectural use of ferroconcrete. Here thin columns support a low-slung longitudinal vault and short transverse ones, all surrounded by a latticelike enclosing skin.

15.34 Auguste Perret, 25 bis Rue Franklin, Paris, 1902.
Perret's clever design replaced the conventional Parisian
interior light-well with a U-shaped plan that increased the
percentage of daylight-lit exterior walls. He cast ornament
into the building's concrete skin.

15.35 Le Corbusier, Dom-ino House, 1914, drawing.
With this system, Le Corbusier separated structure from
enclosure. The results were the free plan, with its flexible
distribution of walls, and the free façade, which could take
on any desired configuration.

the disposition of the windows, which are closer together
than would be possible in a structure with load-bearing
walls. At Notre Dame, Le Raincy, Perret retained the traditional organization of nave and aisles but substituted
slender columns for massive piers and thin, concrete vaults
for heavy stone ones, and made the surrounding wall into
a perforated, light-modulating screen. The openness and
flexibility of planning that he achieved and his attention
to natural light provided a starting point for the young Le
Corbusier, who became a much more radical innovator.

LE CORBUSIER

Le Corbusier (1887–1965) was born in the Swiss watch-
making town of La Chaux-de-Fonds and received his
formal art instruction in the local arts and crafts school,
which trained its students to do fancy engraving for
watchcases. Recognizing his artistic talents, his teacher,
Charles L'Eplattenier, encouraged him to consider more
ambitious goals than a job in the watch industry. Le
Corbusier then interwove his experiences in the offices of
Perret and Behrens with knowledge gained on sketching
trips throughout the Mediterranean, including the Greek
islands, until returning to La Chaux-de-Fonds in 1912,
teaching in the art school, and designing a variety of housing types.

The Dom-ino and Citrohan Houses

From Auguste Perret, Le Corbusier acquired a firm understanding of reinforced concrete, and from Behrens he
learned about designing for industry. He combined these
two strains in his first innovative project, the Dom-ino
House (1914), made in response to the outbreak of World
War I. Anticipating that destruction caused by the fighting
would increase the demand for rebuilding when hostili-
ties ended, Le Corbusier proposed a mass-produced housing type that reduced components to a minimum: floor
slabs, regularly spaced piers for vertical support, and stairs
to connect the floors (Fig. 15.35). Inherent in the design
was the possibility of factory fabrication of these parts near
the construction site and rapid erection of the frame by
crane. The subdivision of the interior and precise weatherproof enclosure (the walls) of the exterior would be left to
the discretion of the builders so that local preferences
could be observed.

  In 1916 he moved to Paris. It was at this time that he
adopted the pseudonym of Le Corbusier, a name taken
from his mother's family, for his architectural projects.
(He continued to paint under his given name.) With the
war still raging, there was not much work for an unknown
young Swiss architect, and Le Corbusier occupied his time
with painting, writing, and drawing projects. In 1920 he
and the poet Paul Dermée began a small journal, *L'Esprit
nouveau* (*The New Spirit*), which covered all the visual arts,

15.36 Le Corbusier, Citrohan House, 1922, drawing.
This house's name was a play on words taken from the Citroën automobile and connecting it to Le Corbusier's conception of a "machine for living." The largely blank lateral bearing walls show that it was really envisioned as one unit within a multi-unit block.

music, and the esthetics of modern life in its three years of publication. A collection of Le Corbusier's essays on architecture that first appeared in its pages was reprinted as the book *Vers une architecture* in 1923. Here Le Corbusier's tendency for poetic overstatement is indulged in the best traditions of Romanticism, and the book is still illuminating today for the flavor it gives of the arts in Paris during the early 1920s. "Architecture is the masterly, correct, and magnificent play of masses brought together in light," Le Corbusier proclaimed, as he endorsed the design of buildings based on the esthetics of the machine. In anticipation of eventual mass production on a modular basis, he also advocated the use of dimensions derived from both a Golden Section-based system of proportions and the size of an average man for all elements in a building.

Among the projects illustrated in *Vers une architecture* was the Citrohan House (1922), Le Corbusier's attempt to design a modest dwelling that would be as affordable as the Citroën automobiles then being manufactured in France (Fig. 15.36). The house is built of reinforced concrete and raised off the ground on piers or **pilotis**, with a garage and service-storage rooms on the lowest level. The second floor, in the tradition of the piano nobile, has the

living and dining rooms, maid's room, and kitchen; the third floor has the master bedroom overlooking the two-story living room; and children's rooms and a roof garden fill the fourth level. (Many of Le Corbusier's later houses would incorporate a two-story living room with overlooking balcony.) Fenestration consists of simple punched openings filled with industrial windows that divide the exterior into horizontal bands extending continuously with little regard for the location of interior partitions.

The Villa Stein and the Villa Savoye

Later in the decade, Le Corbusier was given the opportunity to build a number of modest and not-so-modest houses, putting his design theories into practice. At Garches he designed the Villa Stein (1927) (Fig. 15.37). As with the Citrohan House, the main living floor is at the piano-nobile level, and the roof becomes an elegant terrace. The regularly spaced structural piers permit freely curving interior partitions, while continuous bands of horizontal windows extend across both the north and south façades. (The end elevations are largely blank, for Le Corbusier was considering this design as a prototype for rather narrow

15.37 Le Corbusier, Plans of the Villa Stein, Garches, 1927.
Here are the results of the dom-ino system in a suburban villa. The walls do not necessarily align with the column bays, and the perimeter wall can be penetrated at any point. The ground floor is at the far right.

15.38 (above) Le Corbusier, Plans of and section through the Villa Savoye, Poissy, 1929–31.
The three free-plan floor layouts (ground floor at the right) have almost no correspondence to one another. Continuity is provided by the columnar structural system and by the ramp—an extension of the accomplishments of Adolf Loos.

15.39 (right) Le Corbusier, Villa Savoye, Poissy, 1929–31.
This view reveals the thin enclosing planes made possible by Le Corbusier's dom-ino system of columns and floor slabs.

15.40 (right) Le Corbusier, Villa Savoye interior, Poissy, 1929–31.
The dining area (right) and the living area (left) form a single long, narrow space lit by almost continuous ribbon windows.

suburban lots, where the neighboring houses would create party walls.) The major building proportions were based on Palladio and determined by the Golden Section, the "regulating traces" being included in the published elevation drawings.

Most expressive of Le Corbusier's vision is the Villa Savoye (1929–31) at Poissy, outside Paris (Figs. 15.38–15.40), designed as a weekend house for an art-loving family. The curving ground-floor wall was determined by the turning radius of the motorcar that would convey the family here from Paris. The driveway extends under the house, between the pilotis, and continues past the main entrance to a three-car garage and the maid's quarters. From the ground-level entrance hall the visitor can choose to climb the sculptural stair or ascend the ramp (which links all three levels) to the second floor. Here, from the main living floor, one obtains an unobstructed view of the clearing in which the house sits and onto the forested hills surrounding the site. The large living room is separated by an enormous sliding glass door from the exterior patio and the ramp that continues to the upper-level terrace with its sculptural windscreen walls. The appearance of regularity is carefully maintained on the exterior. All four elevations are essentially identical, consisting of a horizontal ribbon of windows at the second-floor level in a wall plane supported by regularly spaced, recessed pilotis. In fact, the house is a good deal more complex than this simple exterior skin implies, for a close study of the plan reveals that the structural system is not a regular grid, as both Le Corbusier's theoretical writings and the façade would lead one to believe. Regular spacing would have made it next to impossible to park cars in the garage, and it would have inconvenienced interior spaces on the second floor as well. Nevertheless, Le Corbusier scrupulously avoided having interior partitions coincide with columns.

Le Corbusier's choice of interior finishes and fittings reflects his enthusiasm for industrial products and his admiration for the functional aspects of ocean liners. The entrance hall alone has unglazed ceramic tile flooring; simple pipe rails, painted black; a pedestal washbasin, freestanding in the hallway; and industrial light fixtures, directed upward to provide reflected light. Skylights, painted an intense blue, provide softly colored light reflecting off the white wall surfaces on the second floor, where the master bath has a particularly famous lounging recliner and tub in ceramic tiling. The artful incorporation of varied spatial experiences and lighting conditions within a simple geometric container testifies to the mastery of form Le Corbusier had achieved by 1930.

15.41 Eileen Gray's home at Roquebrune, France, 1926–29.
Few women broke into the ranks of male-dominated European Modernism. Lilly Reich worked with Ludwig Mies van der Rohe on his interiors, but only Eileen Gray produced International Style houses on her own. Interestingly, this house's plain, white walls are quite consistent with the traditional architecture of the Mediterranean coast and islands.

Le Corbusier's "Five Points"

As early as 1926 Le Corbusier had articulated his "Five Points Toward a New Architecture":

1 The supports (pilotis) are precisely calculated, spaced regularly, and used to elevate the first floor off the damp ground.

2 The flat roof or roof garden is used for domestic purposes such as gardening, play, and relaxation—thereby recovering all the built-upon ground for outdoor activities.

3 The interior walls, independent of the support system, can be arranged in a free plan.

4 The horizontal windows, made possible by the support system, assure even illumination from wall to wall and admit eight times as much light as a vertically placed window of equal area.

5 The façade, also independent of the structural supports, can be freely designed.

Some of these points are not logical. Concerning point 4, for example, the amount of light coming through a given area of glass is the same regardless of window orientation, but other conditions in the room, such as color and reflective surfaces, do have a great deal to do with the spatial effect of light in a room. It is also unlikely that the rooftop recreations advocated in point 2 would be equivalent to what was possible on the ground. All the points taken together, however, defined a new esthetic for building design, which Le Corbusier followed in most projects until the mid-1950s. His later works will be treated with contemporaneous developments later in this chapter.

There were women within the circle of Parisian Modernists that included Le Corbusier. Eileen Gray (1878–1976), for example, began as an artist making lacquer-finish objects from ceramics to furniture, then moved on to interior design, then to architecture. In the early 1920s

ESSAY
Futurism and Constructivism
by Michael Fazio

Two fairly short-lived movements that influenced the development of European Modernism were Futurism in Italy and Constructivism in Russia. Filippo Marinetti (1876–1944), who published a foundation manifesto in 1909, believed passionately that Italian culture, including Italian architecture, was in a state of decrepitude. He called for a radical transformation of the Italian landscape—his plans included paving the canals of Venice! He praised speed, danger, audacity, and even war as a cleanser of society, and he announced the end of traditional space and time. Around this fiery rhetoric coalesced both artists and sculptors, but they had no appropriate graphic means for expressing themselves. By 1912 they had visited Paris and met with the artists Braque and Picasso. The Cubism they saw there suggested ways in which they could represent episodic experiences, energy, and motion in paintings and sculpture, which they did. The most celebrated Futurist architect was Antonio Sant'Elia (1888–1916), but with his early death Futurist architecture lost its momentum. Sant'Elia is best known for his "Città Nuova" ("New City") exhibition of 1914 and its accompanying *Messaggio*, which appeared in the foreword of the exhibition catalog and which was rewritten by Marinetti as a "Manifesto of Futurist Architecture." Using a dramatic perspective technique, Sant'Elia proposed designs for airship hangars, apartment blocks, transportation centers, hydroelectric plants, and power stations (Figs. 15.42–15.43). All were characterized by bold massing without ornamentation, verticality and battered or stepped-back walls, multiple levels of horizontal circulation, external elevators, and exposed power-production facilities.

15.42 (above) Antonio Sant'Elia, Project for a Milan power station, 1913.
Antonio Sant'Elia died young as a result of trauma suffered in World War I. His extraordinary perspective drawings made him the best-known exponent of Futurism.

15.43 (right) Antonio Sant'Elia, La Città Nuova detail, 1914.
Sant'Elia explored the possibilities of a dynamic city dominated by multiple means of transportation. Particularly dramatic here are the tall elevator towers connected to building flanks by leaping bridges.

In revolutionary Russia, the Constructivists were in an equally heady mood, but their radical ideas exceeded technological realities and eventually succumbed to stultified Stalinist classicism. In a vast land where many in the countryside still lived in medieval conditions, Constructivists envisioned a new architecture driven forward by the forces of industrialization and its new building materials: steel, concrete, and expanses of glass. Like the Futurists, they proposed the dramatic use of external transportation systems, and they added monumental external graphics, prefiguring today's huge displays.

Vladimir Tatlin (1885–1953) designed the *Monument to the Third International* (Communist Congress) in 1919 (Fig. 15.44). This tower was to be a fantastic double spiral some 1300 feet tall, with a revolving cone and

15.44 (right) Vladimir Tatlin, *Model of the Monument to the Third International*, **1919.** This tower project, with its dramatic proposal for the use of new materials and construction methods, strongly influenced young Russian designers. Gone are solid walls in favor of a technologically efficient, open frame.

cylinders housing governmental and propaganda offices. It was unbuildable, but the vision caught the attention of the world. In 1924 the Vesnin brothers, Viktor (1882–1950) and Alexandr (1883–1959), produced a Pravda Newspaper Building design (Fig. 15.45), complete with a loudspeaker system, which was to house the primary instrument of Soviet propaganda. To its exposed, skeletal frame of steel, including X-bracing, they attached external elevators and a clock with digital readouts, and atop it all they placed a searchlight as a metaphor for the Communist experiment. Konstantin Melnikov (1890–1974) designed the Soviet Pavilion (Fig. 15.46) for the 1925 Exposition Internationale des Arts Décoratifs et Industriels Modernes in Paris. Its rhomboidal volumes and cantilevered structure emphasized dynamism, and its interconnected spaces expressed the still-open agenda of Soviet Communism. Melnikov's Rusakov Workers' Club in Moscow (1927–28) (Fig. 15.47) shows the same fascination with dramatic structure, in this case through boldly cantilevered reinforced concrete.

15.45 (far right top) Viktor and Aleksandr Vesnin, Pravda Newspaper Building, Moscow, 1924, drawing.
Features such as exterior elevators and huge changeable graphics did not become common on modern buildings until the second half of the twentieth century. Equally portentous are the diagonal braces that were to give rigidity to the slender structural frame.

15.46 (below left) Konstantin Melnikov, Soviet Pavilion, Exposition Internationale des Arts Décoratifs et Industriels Modernes, Paris, 1925.
Melnikov achieved this dynamic form through the use of a deformed planning grid intersected by a diagonal stair-concourse. His structure appeared in the same Paris exhibition that included the display of Friedrich Kiesler's Cité dans l'Espace (see Fig. 15.53) and Le Corbusier's Pavillon de l'Esprit Nouveau.

15.47 (below) Konstantin Melnikov, Rusakov Workers' Club, Moscow, 1927–28.
Melnikov's club not only demonstrates the kind of dramatic use of structure aspired to by the Constructivists; it also housed the kind of collective activity made desirable by the Russian Revolution. However, within a few years, the progressive Constructivist mentality was replaced by the crushing control of Stalin.

she opened a gallery called Jean Désert and had a complete issue of *Wendingen* dedicated to her work. In 1926–29 she built a house for herself in Roquebrune on the rugged south coast of France (Fig. 15.41). Displaying a complete Modernist vocabulary, it is distinguished by the specificity of its response to site, intelligent use of sunscreens, private settings within an open plan, original furniture designs, and varied systems of built-in storage. Gray built another nearby residence for herself in the 1930s and a final, small summer house in the 1950s, and left a number of other projects unbuilt.

WALTER GROPIUS

The son of an architect, Walter Gropius (1883–1969) received an academic architectural education at universities in Berlin and Munich before entering Peter Behrens's office. When he left, he set up an independent practice with his fellow employee Adolf Meyer (1881–1929). Their first major project, the Fagus Factory at Alfeld-an-der-Leine (1911), is still considered a landmark in the history of modern architecture, though Gropius and Meyer received the commission only after a previous designer had already laid out and begun construction of the complex and so were hired primarily to design the exteriors of the buildings. Its most celebrated portion (Fig. 15.48) is the embedded, three-story block running along the south side of the main building and housing the packaging and shipping departments. A subtle and apparently simple structure, but actually a complex and critical rethinking of Behrens's Turbine Factory, it includes battered piers, projecting and seemingly suspended walls of glass, and dramatically cantilevered concrete stairs visible from the outside. In the 1920s Gropius and Meyer made unexecuted drawings

for remodeling and expanding the production building, and these prefigured Gropius's canonical design for the Bauhaus building in Dessau, which is discussed below.

Like Behrens, Gropius was a member of the Werkbund. For its exhibition in Cologne in 1914, Gropius and Meyer designed a model factory (Fig. 15.49) to demonstrate the possible architectural expression of a hypothetical manufacturing plant with an attached office block. In consultation with local industry, Gropius devised the building's program to answer the needs of a medium-sized business. The rear of the office block was a glass curtain wall, which extended dramatically around the sides and around the circular stair towers on the front corners, while the front façade was windowless and clad with limestone made to look like brick. Symmetry governed the entire ensemble; the central entrance was placed on axis; and the stair cylinders were overshadowed by tower elements (with hovering roofs comparable to those used by Frank Lloyd Wright) containing roof-level dance floors connected by a covered restaurant. Separating the office block from the manufacturing plant was a large open courtyard, which led axially to the industrial area, a large basilican hall, itself divided into thirds by the supports for its double-pitched sky-lit roof. It was far more daring and complex than anything that had yet been constructed for German industry. Impressed by this design, the grand duke of Sachsen-Weimar-Eisenach asked Gropius to assume direction of the ducal arts and crafts school.

The Bauhaus in Weimar and Dessau

World War I delayed implementation of the grand duke's invitation, as Gropius served from 1914 to 1918 in the German army on the western front. At the conclusion of the war the German nobility lost their domains, but

15.48 Walter Gropius and Adolf Meyer, Fagus Factory, Alfeld-an-der-Leine, 1911. Gropius and Meyer did not intend to create a new style with their rigorously functional esthetic. However, the strips of steel-frame windows and related spandrels and flat roofs created a type used in the United States not only for factories but also for schools and even gas stations.

15.49 Walter Gropius and Adolf Meyer, Model Factory, Werkbund Exhibition, Cologne, Germany, 1914.
The factory's office building stands to the right. Many have noted the similarity of its hovering roofs to the Prairie-house roofs of Frank Lloyd Wright. Its most exceptional features, however, are the glass-enclosed, cantilevered, spiraling, concrete stairs.

the grand duke's offer was reextended by the new civil authorities, and in 1919 Gropius combined the former Grossherzoglich Sachsen Weimarische Hochschule für Angewandte Kunst (Ducal School of the Applied Arts) and the Grossherzoglich Kunstakademie (Ducal Art Academy) in Weimar into the Staatliches (State or Public) Bauhaus Weimar. (The German word *Bauhaus* can be literally translated as "House of Building.")

"The ultimate aim of all visual art is the complete building!" Thus began the 1919 prospectus advertising the Bauhaus to students, and in joining the former ducal arts and crafts school with the fine-arts academy, Gropius created a new type of institution dedicated to training students in all aspects of design and to enabling them to work collaboratively. In the early years most of the faculty were painters from Berlin and Vienna whom Gropius or his wife had known before the war. Dominant at the beginning was the Viennese painter and educator Johannes Itten, who created the *Vorkurs*, or introductory course. Itten's radical, anti-authoritarian philosophy, austere lifestyle, and eccentric mode of dress spread to the students and eventually created friction with the community. The model used for organizing the curriculum was the medieval guild, and students were called apprentices and graduated with journeymen's certificates (see page 239). Gropius was firmly convinced that fine art came through mastery of craft, and he arranged the teaching program so that students were given manual instruction in one of the many craft workshops (such as wood, metal, weaving, pottery, and mural painting) and were introduced to principles of form by separate instructors, most often painters such as Paul Klee and Wassily Kandinsky. As Gropius wrote in an essay in 1923:

By depriving handicrafts and industry of the informing services of the artist, the academies drained them of their vitality, and brought about the artist's complete isolation from the community. Art is not one of those things that may be imparted. Whether a design be the outcome of knack or creative impulse depends on individual propensity. But if what we call art cannot be taught or learnt, a thorough knowledge of its principles and of sureness of hand can be. Both are as necessary for the artist of genius as for the ordinary artisan.

And Gropius envisioned that workshop projects would attract outside support, in the form of commissions or production licenses, and that the Bauhaus might soon become self-supporting.

He saw the curriculum of the Bauhaus as a sharp break with Beaux-Arts training, and he had harsh words for the older methods:

The besetting vice of the academy schools was that they were obsessed by that rare "biological" sport, the commanding genius; and forgot that their business was to teach drawing and painting to hundreds and hundreds of minor talents, barely one in a thousand of whom could be expected to have the makings of a real architect or painter. In the vast majority of cases, this hopelessly one-sided instruction condemned its pupils to the lifelong practice of a purely sterile art. Had these hapless drones been given a proper practical training, they could have become useful members of society.

As the Bauhaus matured, the thrust of its program, which began with the idea of handicraft as a means to art, shifted to handicraft as a means of making prototypes for industrial production. Adjustments were made by 1923, in response to three main influences: outside pressure created by growing scandal about flamboyant faculty members and the bohemian lifestyles of the students; the visit of the Dutchman Theo van Doesburg (discussed in the next section) and his haranguing of these students; and Gropius's

15.50 **Walter Gropius, Bauhaus, Dessau, 1926.** The plan of this building is a pinwheel and reaches out into space like a Mondrian painting. The workshop wing, which projects to the lower left, is a concrete column-and-slab frame enclosed by a glass curtain wall. The tallest block to the lower right is a dormitory, which is connected to a dining hall and auditorium. Elsewhere, there are offices and classrooms. Considered decadent and expressive of Communist values, the building was shut down by the Nazis in 1932 but today once again houses a design school.

own interests in mass production. Moreover, the antici-pated support from trade groups or industrial concerns had not materialized, which left the Bauhaus in bad finan-cial straits. If designs could be sold to manufacturers, the income would help alleviate the financial situation. More importantly, in placing emphasis on design for industrial production the Bauhaus had found an appropriate resolu-tion of the relationship of art to the machine. Rather than seeing the two as adversaries, as had Ruskin and those in the Arts and Crafts Movement, the *Bauhauslers* saw the integration of art with mechanized production as the great challenge for the twentieth-century designer and organized their teaching to address this issue.

Despite these changes, the position of the school in Weimar became increasingly difficult. Gropius removed the most eccentric members of faculty and requested that the students wear ordinary clothes, but the radio and newspaper attacks on the Bauhaus continued. At Easter in 1925 the progressive mayor of Dessau offered assistance, and the Bauhaus moved to temporary quarters there. By December 1926 the school was established in a new building designed by Gropius that ranks among the fin-est expressions of the emerging Modern Movement (Fig. 15.50). It consists of four connected reinforced-concrete-frame elements, arranged freely on the flat site so that there is no "front" in the customary sense. The workshop wing, four stories tall, is the largest mass, containing behind its glass curtain wall the studio spaces for preliminary instruc-tion and workshops for printing, carpentry, dyeing, sculp-ture, weaving, and wall painting, in addition to exhibition and lecture spaces. A road runs through the site beside this workshop building, requiring an enclosed bridge to con-nect it to the separately administered trade school. In the bridge were administrative offices for the Bauhaus and Gropius's private architectural office. Parallel to the road and extending behind the workshop wing is the low din-ing hall and auditorium building, equipped with a stage between the two spaces and provided with movable walls for maximum flexibility. Beyond this is a five-story student dormitory with twenty-eight rooms and related facilities.

What made the Bauhaus building so remarkable? Several characteristics can be identified. The asymmetrical, pinwheeling composition represented a break with the typical monumental disposition employed for educational facilities. Separate articulation was given to each element of the program, resulting in an abstract, sculptural treatment for the whole, and the introduction of a road and bridge reinforced the sense of plastic or flowing space. Bauhaus workshops designed and executed all the interiors, with the metal workshop responsible for lighting fixtures and tubular steel furniture (designed by Bauhaus student-become-teacher Marcel Breuer), the printing workshop for graphics, and so on. Thus, the building was a total work of art, a unity of architecture and related crafts. Its industrial construction materials, concrete and glass, were employed without ornament, and circulation was clearly expressed.

Gropius also designed a series of seven dwelling units—one detached house and three duplex houses—for Bauhaus faculty. The duplex units are identical, yet by changing their orientations and making one the mirror image of another Gropius obtained the effect of three dif-ferent designs. Thus, standardization was combined with variety. Like the Bauhaus buildings, these houses are flat-roofed and were originally painted white with industrial-looking pipe railings on the balconies.

The Bauhaus in Dessau continued to emphasize design for industrial production and licensed a number of prod-ucts to German manufacturers. Bauhaus designs, whether for architecture, graphic design, or manufactured prod-ucts, tended to favor primary geometric shapes and solids, coupled with linear elements, to achieve an appearance of simplicity. The forms of finished goods reflected both the nature of the materials and the manufacturing processes required for fabrication. Although Gropius always denied that there was a Bauhaus "style," there is a strong visual affinity among many of the student projects and faculty designs created there.

These designs became widely known through exhi-bitions and publications, gaining general acclaim for the school throughout Europe. The facilities in Dessau provided workspace superior to anything the Bauhaus had had in Weimar, and it seemed that the turmoil of the school's early years was past. This was not to be, however. Financial problems, while greatly reduced, were not entirely solved, and the reactionary political forces accompanying the rise of Nazism were gaining strength in the area around Dessau. In hopes of diminishing criticism of the Bauhaus, criticism he interpreted as being directed at him personally, Gropius resigned as head of the school in April 1928 and returned to his private architectural practice.

A young left-leaning architect and faculty member, Hannes Meyer, was appointed to succeed Gropius. Meyer initiated a formal architectural program, added courses in mathematics and engineering, and emphasized through lectures and studio projects the social responsibilities of architects. He enabled the workshops to increase production so that more designs were licensed to industry and more royalties came to the school. But Meyer also encouraged students to become active in politics, a courageous, if imprudent counsel in the deteriorating political climate of the time, and in the summer of 1930 the authorities asked him to resign. His replacement was former Behrens employee Mies van der Rohe, an architect long active in the Deutscher Werkbund, whose reputation was by then international and whose career is discussed below.

Mies moved to stabilize the school by flatly prohibiting any political activity and insisting on the highest possible standards of work. More powerful political forces were gathering, however, and in 1932 the Nazis gained control of Dessau. One of their first acts was to move against the Bauhaus, which to them symbolized Communism, decadence, and subversion, and in October 1932 they closed the school. Shortly afterward Mies managed to reopen the Bauhaus as a private institution in Berlin, but in April 1933 the facilities were raided by the Gestapo, and the school closed its doors in July 1933.

DE STIJL

As we shall see in the next section, Mies van der Rohe's work was informed by the Dutch De Stijl movement, which was the creation of Bauhaus interloper Theo van Doesburg (1883–1931). De Stijl, meaning literally "The Style," had two phases, both of them guided by this Dutch painter, designer, typographer, critic, writer, and general rabble-rouser. The origins of the movement can be traced to the work of the painter Piet Mondrian (1872–1944) and the architect H.P. Berlage (discussed earlier in this chapter in the context of Dutch Expressionism), whose writings espoused what he considered to be elementary truths: the primacy of space, the wall as the creator of form, and the need for systematic proportions. Both men sought a modern expression in their work, Berlage through a moralistic search for truth in building and Mondrian through a reductivism that, he believed, would reveal and subject to criticism the essence of early twentieth-century culture. As Dutch Expressionists tended to be extremely figurative and attuned to handicraft means of building production, so De Stijl designers sought in equal and opposite measure to be ultra-rational, abstract, and mechanistic.

An art student in Amsterdam from age twenty, Mondrian moved to Paris in 1911 and was immediately influenced by Cubism. Back in Holland during World War I, he met Theo van Doesburg, and they founded the journal *De Stijl*. Here, Mondrian set out his doctrine of Neo-Plasticism, influenced by the writings of esoteric mathematician-mystic M.H.J. Schoenmaekers, who believed that the world functioned with absolute regularity and that this regularity could be expressed through "plastic" mathematics. Mondrian later returned to Paris and, following his published philosophy, began a gradual process of abstraction that led him to produce frameless panels laid out in grids, with squares and rectangles painted in the three primary colors.

15.51 J.J.P. Oud, Hook of Holland housing project, Rotterdam, 1924. The contrast between Oud's housing and that of the Dutch Wendigen designers is almost shocking. Oud had made contact with members of the Dutch De Stijl movement and at the Hook of Holland housing displayed the latter's reductivist desire to deemphasize applied ornament.

In 1917 van Doesburg brought together the first group of De Stijl participants, which included Mondrian, several other Dutch painters, and the architects Rob van t'Hoff (1887–1979) and J.J.P. Oud (1890–1963). The group advocated the creation of forms that were universal, spatially unbounded, and attuned to modern technology. Van t'Hoff, who had been to Oak Park, produced a house in Huis ter Heide (1916) that is a convincing adaptation of Frank Lloyd Wright's work, with strong horizontals, including clusters of windows, and cantilevered roof and floor slabs. Oud, though never fully committed to De Stijl principles, produced a significant body of related work before he returned to a more staid traditionalism later in his career; the early buildings eventually earned him stature as a first-generation European Modernist. His Hook of Holland housing project (1924) (Fig. 15.51), while not very experimental spatially, is highly reductivist, with its long, seemingly extruded white stucco walls on a base of red and yellow brick, large expanses of glass with plain metal window frames, and details painted in primary colors—a remarkable contrast to the work of fellow countrymen Kramer and de Klerk of about the same period.

In 1921–22 the roster of De Stijl participants changed significantly, becoming much more international in profile. Mondrian departed, but van Doesburg remained as the catalyst. New on the scene were the Russian Constructivist El Lissitzky (1890–1941), who, in his *Proun* (or "Object") paintings, applied an axonometric drawing technique to the problem of elementary geometric composition; the unclassifiable Austrian Friedrich Kiesler (1890–1965) from the Berlin G Group (which had included the young Mies van der Rohe); the planner Cornelis van Eesteren (1897–1988), whom van Doesburg had met in Weimar while both were taking in the Bauhaus; and the Dutch architect and furnituremaker Gerrit Rietveld (1888–1964).

Van Doesburg and van Eesteren soon began a close collaboration, which culminated in a highly successful Parisian exhibition at the Galerie de l'Effort Moderne. Their work included a "Maison Particulière" and a "Maison d'Artiste," both hypothetical and designed by van Eesteren. Both were displayed in model form and by means of axonometric drawings, and consisted of interlocking rectangular blocks arranged asymmetrically in three dimensions. Van Doesburg the painter developed their color schemes and in so doing produced separate analytical, axonometric views with planes selectively removed, which yielded some apparently levitating walls (Fig. 15.52).

The most dramatic piece of De Stijl construction was Friedrich Kiesler's Cité dans l'Espace (Fig. 15.53), an exhibition framework for the Austrian display at the 1925 Exposition Internationale des Arts Décoratifs et Industriels Modernes in Paris. Relieved of the responsibility to serve as a conventional building, this "Cité" was a three-dimensional grid of linear elements suspended in and organizing infinite space.

15.52 Theo van Doesburg, Axonometric analysis of the Maison Particulière (lithograph hand-colored with gouache), 1923.
Van Doesburg's provocative drawings of Cornelis van Eesteren's design made space the primary stuff of a new architecture, but his images were impossible to translate into earthbound building construction. Still, they offered a goal to which space-obsessed Modernist architects could aspire.

15.53 Friedrich Kiesler, Cité dans l'Espace, Exposition Internationale des Arts Décoratifs et Industriels Modernes, Paris, 1925.
While only an exhibit piece and not a building, Kiesler's composition succeeds in translating Mondrian's two-dimensional ideas into three dimensions. Kiesler was a member of De Stijl in its later stages, when it had reached out to German and Russian designers.

15.54 (left) Gerrit Rietveld, Red-Blue Chair, 1917–18.
This chair is still produced. Its apparent construction from discrete elements explains Rietveld's description of his work as "Elementarism."

15.55 (above) Gerrit Rietveld, Schroeder House, Utrecht, 1924.
It is not hard to imagine the degree of shock felt by neighbors in their traditional brick houses when this unfamiliar composition appeared on their street. It had been some twenty years since Adolf Loos first stripped a house of its applied ornamentation.

15.56 (left) Gerrit Rietveld, Schroeder House interior, Utrecht, 1924.
Such an interior shows that it was not easy to translate Mondrian's paintings or van Doesburg's planar compositions into livable spaces. There is, however, a rigor and a palette of primary colors like those preferred by Mondrian.

Gerrit Rietveld developed his own idiom, called Elementarism, in which he so assembled multiple elements that each maintained its individual integrity, and the completed assembly made clear the entire process of construction. His much-celebrated Red-Blue Chair (1917–18) (Fig. 15.54) is still in production today. Rietveld's Schroeder House in Utrecht (1924) (Fig. 15.55) is most often cited as the quintessential De Stijl building, but it is limited by the realities of habitation. From the exterior, it looks like one of van Eesteren and van Doesburg's house compositions: planes in various orthogonal orientations intersecting and interconnected by linear steel sections. The interior (Fig. 15.56) is very open, dominated by linear, Elementarist components and primary colors, but is hardly an investigation of infinite space as defined by Mondrian or expressed graphically by van Doesburg or exploited by Kiesler.

LUDWIG MIES VAN DER ROHE

The third of Peter Behrens's employees to become an architectural luminary was Ludwig Mies van der Rohe (1886–1969). He was the son of a stonemason and gained practical experience in construction from his father, and he later worked as an apprentice in the office of furniture designer Bruno Paul. Behrens, of course, introduced him to the work of Karl Friedrich Schinkel, and Mies's early designs as an independent architect show the influence of Germany's greatest Neo-Classicist, as in the projected house for Mrs. Kroller-Müller (1912), which was to be a symmetrical rectangular solid with a stripped classical colonnade across the front.

After World War I, Mies worked on a series of projects that were to have an enormous impact on later modern architecture even though they were never constructed. The first was a competition entry for an office building above the Berlin Friedrichstrasse station (1919), a twenty-story skyscraper completely sheathed in glass. In 1920–21 Mies carried the concept of a transparent skyscraper a step further in a project for a thirty-story tower, again wrapped entirely in glass, with a highly irregular perimeter and two circular elevator-stair cores. Mies's idea was to capitalize on the varying reflections. The irregular curves of the walls were actually composed of short line segments representing the width dimension of the curtain-wall panels, so the entire building was to be a highly faceted, shimmering shaft. Its internal structure was provided by reinforced-concrete slabs, cantilevered to a thin edge at the outside wall. However, because materials science and construction techniques in 1920 were inadequate to construct these designs, the first completely glazed office building was not built until 1950–52: Lever House on Park Avenue in New York City, designed by Gordon Bunshaft of Skidmore, Owings, and Merrill. Its curtain-wall construction includes horizontal strips of plate glass with dark-green spandrel glass covering the floor construction, both set in stainless-steel frames.

Two other projects from the early 1920s show that Mies was thinking about materials other than glass. His project for a concrete office block (1922) has seven floors, each a great horizontal tray with cantilevers. The height of the tray edge was determined by the vertical dimension of filing cabinets; windows above ran in a continuous horizontal strip in a plane recessed from the outer edge of the concrete. If one recalls Wright's Larkin Building, which had incorporated the same idea on its office floors, one can perhaps detect the influences of the Wasmuth publications on Mies. The idea of free-flowing space as explored by those in the De Stijl movement also strongly affected Mies's designs. His 1923 project for a brick country house, with its walls extending as vertical planes out into the landscape, seldom intersecting one another but effectively defining space, is an early example. Some of this freedom would reappear in his 1929 masterpiece, the Pavilion of the Deutscher Werkbund for the International Exposition in Barcelona.

The Barcelona Pavilion and the Tugendhat House

The Barcelona Pavilion (Figs. 15.57–15.58) has become one of the most celebrated architectural designs of the twentieth century, even though until recently it was known to most people only through photographs, since after the exposition was over, the building was dismantled and its materials were sold at auction; a replica has now been built on the original site. It is a small structure; unlike most exhibition buildings, it contained no displays. Aside from the stainless-steel-and-leather tables, stools, and chairs designed by Mies specifically for the building, the only object on view was a sculpture of a dancing girl by Georg Kolbe, carefully placed in a reflecting pool at one end of the building.

The influence of the Barcelona Pavilion derived not from what it contained but from the building itself. Mies intended that it should stand for quality design, materials, and craftsmanship. The design is at once simple and sophisticated. Raised on a low podium, as if to elevate it above the frenzy of the fair, most of its ground plane was occupied by an exterior courtyard, dominated by the large reflecting pool lined with black glass. Eight cruciform columns supported a horizontal roof slab that appeared to hover, independent of the vertical walls (Fig. 15.59). The walls were not incorporated in or aligned with the column grid; in this way, Mies deliberately expressed a separation between structure and enclosure while conforming both to the same orthogonal geometry. The columns were shiny chromium-plated steel; the walls were onyx and polished book-matched marble in deep shades of green and red; the floors were Roman travertine; and the gray-tinted glass contributed to the feeling of sophisticated taste and luxury. The Mies-designed Barcelona chairs and stools were chrome-plated steel with white kid upholstery. Mies's collaborator, Lilly Reich, shares credit with him for the interior design.

15.57 (above) Ludwig Mies van der Rohe, Barcelona Pavilion, Barcelona, [1929] 1986.
Mies's building was dismantled at the end of the Barcelona exhibition. However, it has recently been rebuilt, using stone from the original quarries, so that Mies's ideas can be personally experienced once again. The image seen here is of the reconstruction of 1986.

15.58 (right) Ludwig Mies van der Rohe, Plan of the Barcelona Pavilion, Barcelona.
Compare this plan to the early work of Frank Lloyd Wright or the dom-ino houses of Le Corbusier. All sought a new means of spatial expression, which was the most significant area of study among twentieth-century Modernists.

Line of the roof above

Sculpted figure of dancing girl   Edge of podium

Pool

Pool

15.57

15.59

0   20 m
0   60 ft

N

15.59 (left) Ludwig Mies van der Rohe, Barcelona Pavilion interior, Barcelona, 1929.
While Mies was not a member of De Stijl, his spatial conceptions certainly corresponded to those of the movement. The materials he used were travertine for the floors, marble and onyx for the partitions, and stainless steel for the columns. The stools and chairs are also his designs.

15.61 Ludwig Mies van der Rohe, Tugendhat House rear view, Brno, 1930.
The private terrace to the rear is surrounded by a retaining wall of rock-faced masonry. The glass walls offer unobstructed views out into the natural landscape.

15.60 Ludwig Mies van der Rohe, Plan of the Tugendhat House, Brno, 1930.
Mies's spatial experiments could be applied to day-to-day living conditions. The family space lies to the top in the plan and is only minimally subdivided. The service spaces are much more enclosed.

Influences on the pavilion's architecture can be identified: Schinkel for the podium and formality of the composition; Wright perhaps for the great horizontal sweep of the roof; and De Stijl for the spatial fluidity and almost abstract composition of solid, void, and line. The masterful integration of these diverse influences into a new architectural synthesis remains the great accomplishment of Mies van der Rohe.

Mies used his concepts from the Barcelona Pavilion in a residential commission of 1930, the Tugendhat House (Fig. 15.60) in Brno, Czech Republic. The same regular grid of chromium-steel cruciform columns supports the roof, and polished slabs of marble serve as walls to define interior spaces in an open plan. Because of the hilly site, the Tugendhat House has two stories, set firmly within a series of terraces cut into the slope; but thanks to its largely glass walls, the predominant view is out to the surrounding landscape (Fig. 15.61). Color on the interior is subdued,

confined to the natural hues of the finish materials and a white linoleum floor, so that the changing light and colors of the outside world determine much of the color inside the house.

Mies, the Weissenhof Siedlung, and the International Style

In 1925 the Deutscher Werkbund proposed that an exhibition be held in 1927 to demonstrate the latest thinking about housing design, interior fittings, and construction technology. The City of Stuttgart and various materials suppliers contributed land and money for the construction of thirty-three permanent buildings on a hillside on the outskirts of the city. Mies van der Rohe, as vice-president of the Werkbund, was placed in charge of the enterprise; he developed the master plan and contributed the design for a block of flats. He invited participation by sixteen leading architects from across Europe, assigning them sites for detached houses, duplexes, or row houses. The permanent buildings became known as the Weissenhof Siedlung (or model housing estate at Weissenhof).

The concept behind the exhibition was to design modestly scaled, modern dwelling units suitable as prototypes for mass production. A variety of approaches were adopted by the individual designers, but it was the elements their designs had in common that were crucial in the development of Modernism. All the buildings were white; they had "functional" windows that emphasized the horizontal; and almost all had flat roofs, some with garden terraces. Industrial character was expressed in the cylindrical pipe railings on balconies, the major "decorative" element on the exterior. Window trim was minimal, and there were no cornices. Mies had originally planned to keep cars on the perimeter, with only pedestrian access to the housing area; but the city authorities, who wanted to resell the units as individual dwellings after the exhibition, requested that the land be divided into plots with separate access. Mies was able to retain his basically sculptural conception of the overall form of the site, with the tallest and largest building, his own four-story block, set on the highest portion of the hill (Fig. 15.62).

Mies's building included standard elements—a kitchen-bathroom core, prefabricated partitions, and storage walls—that allowed each of the twenty-four units to be arranged differently in plan. Standardization and rational planning, together with a steel frame, made this flexibility possible. The roof terrace provided recreational facilities, and each apartment has a small balcony. Horizontal strip windows facilitated cross-ventilation for each dwelling unit.

Walter Gropius built two detached houses, but neither remains. Continuing the approach being studied at the Bauhaus, he designed in close collaboration with several manufacturers, and both houses were constructed entirely of prefabricated panels. The module of the panels could readily be seen inside and out, and the interior was furnished with the products designed by Marcel Breuer and produced in the Bauhaus workshops. It is interesting to note that, after coming to the United States in 1937, Gropius continued his interest in prefabricated housing but failed to interest American manufacturers in the idea. When he built his own home at Lincoln, Massachusetts (1938), in collaboration with Breuer, Gropius turned instead to the building components already available in light-industrial construction and artfully incorporated them as the major elements of the house.

Le Corbusier also contributed two designs, one a single-family dwelling in reinforced concrete and the other a duplex with a steel frame (Fig. 15.63), a realization of the Citrohan concept. The latter was one of the most controversial structures at the exhibition, in part because of its unorthodox interior proportions. The main circulation spine is a corridor that runs the length of the house,

15.62 Ludwig Mies van der Rohe, Weissenhof Siedlung blocks of flats, Stuttgart, 1927.
Mies developed the site plan for this exposition and built his apartment block on the highest ground. Notice the mass-produced windows and pipe-rail balconies like those used twenty years earlier by Adolf Loos.

15.63 Le Corbusier, Weissenhof Siedlung housing unit, Stuttgart, 1927.
Le Corbusier composed this housing unit using by-now-familiar elements: supporting columns or pilotis, an unornamented façade, horizontal ribbon windows, and a roof garden.

with dimensions and windows that suggest a train more than a residence, particularly as some bedrooms are narrow, like the sleeping compartments of European trains. Le Corbusier was fascinated by the functional designs of ocean liners and airplanes, and it is possible that railway cars also inspired his architecture.

The common thread of rational or functional design could be detected in all buildings at the Weissenhof Siedlung, and the projects of German architects were not dissimilar in appearance to those produced by designers from other countries. This esthetic affinity and a book, *Internationale Architektur* (1925) by Walter Gropius, led Alfred H. Barr of MoMA in New York to call such modern architecture of the late 1920s the International Style.

European architectural developments were a major focus of the MoMA show (mentioned at the beginning of this chapter) organized by Barr, Henry-Russell Hitchcock, and Philip Johnson in 1932. It increased awareness in the United States of postwar advances in Germany, France, Holland, and Belgium, as works like Gerrit Rietveld's Schroeder House were displayed alongside early Wright designs such as the Winslow House, and the abstract rationalism of De Stijl appeared alongside the work of Mies, Gropius, and Le Corbusier.

According to Barr's definition, the International Style was characterized by an "emphasis upon volume—space enclosed by thin planes or surfaces as opposed to the suggestion of mass and solidity; regularity as opposed to symmetry or other kinds of obvious balance; and dependence on the intrinsic elegance of materials, perfection, and fine proportions, as opposed to applied ornament." Hitchcock later revised this statement to include the articulation of structure in place of the point about ornament.

As an indication of the strength of Beaux-Arts classicism and the Moderne style (discussed below) in the United States in the 1920s, only a handful of American buildings were included in Hitchcock and Johnson's book, *The International Style,* and the associated MoMA exhibition, and most of these had some connection to Philadelphia architect George Howe (1886–1955). The largest American International Style building exhibited was the Philadelphia Savings Fund Society Building (1929–32, remodeled in 2000 as a hotel) (Fig. 15.64) by Howe and Swiss-born William Lescaze (1896–1969), whom Howe had taken on as a partner to bring his office up to date. The entire Market Street façade is cantilevered beyond the column line, allowing the windows to wrap in a horizontal band around the corner and so glorify the freedom from structural constraint. No towers quite so bold as this would be built in the United States for the next decade, in part because of the Great Depression and World War II. Smaller structures that were built according to the dictates of the International Style, or at least in imitation of it, were often seen as cheap because they lacked presumably expensive ornament or because they were simply bad imitations of the European originals.

15.64 George Howe and William Lescaze, Philadelphia Savings Fund Society Building, Philadelphia, Pennsylvania, 1929–32.
George Howe brought in William Lescaze to inform his office about European Modernism. The vertical articulation masks stacked horizontal ribbon windows and spandrels.

THE CONTINUATION OF TRADITIONAL DESIGN

Despite the best efforts of Modernists, modern architecture never came close to eradicating eclecticism, particularly for residences, but the level of originality among traditional designers varied considerably. The Englishman Edwin Lutyens was born in 1869 (died 1944), the same year as Frank Lloyd Wright. While his work was consistently eclectic, his interpretations were inventive, clever, even ambiguous and idiosyncratic. Lutyens organized his plans by means of a profusion of interlaced axes that often extend out into gardens designed by his longtime collaborator Gertrude Jekyll, and it is safe to say that he would not have risen to the level of achievement that he did without her contributions. Typically working for the newly monied classes, Lutyens manipulated his houses within their settings to make them appear larger than they were. Internally, he delighted in denying selected axes, turning enfilades in one room into a central axis in another (and vice versa), and creating layers of space by manipulating the apparent thickness of walls and inserting bands of carefully placed columns (Fig. 15.65). Externally, he subscribed to the honest expression of materials advocated by those in the Arts and Crafts Movement and developed his ability to create picturesque compositions by closely studying vernacular structures in the English countryside. While his reputation had declined by the mid-twentieth century, it rose again abruptly in the 1970s, when he was celebrated in print for his "mannerist" tendencies, to the point that a retrospective of his work was mounted at MoMA in 1978.

Erik Gunnar Asplund (1885–1940) and his like-minded colleagues brought Modernism to the fore in Sweden at the Stockholm Exhibition of 1930. Asplund had apparently rejected classicism two decades earlier when he, Sigurd Lewerentz, and four other students abandoned education at the Royal Academy of Art in favor of attending the short-lived, atelier-driven Klara School. These events give a slightly misleading impressionism, however, for while a few of Asplund's commissions, notably the Bredenberg Department Store in Stockholm (1933–35), display overtly Modernist features, most do not. Intent on producing an architecture that spoke of its time yet had both the graceful authority of classicism and the authenticity of the regional vernacular favored by the contemporary National Romanticists, or Realists, Asplund, like Edwin Lutyens, produced original work. Two of his commissions, the Stockholm Public Library (1918–27) (Fig. 15.66) and the Woodland Cemetery, illustrate his personal vision.

The library's plan is one of extreme clarity: a circle within a square that is open on one side. In three dimensions, the circle rises as a cylinder containing the book stacks, and the sides of the square hold support spaces. While an early scheme had a dome, Asplund eliminated it and everything else that seemed superfluous, achieving a kind of distillation to essence that can be compared to

15.65 Edwin Lutyens, Heathcote House interior, Ilkley, Yorkshire, 1906.
This view of a typically intricate, even tricky, Lutyens interior includes two Serliana, their arches defining the hall's principal cross-axis (with a parallel enfilade). The varied spacing of double, paired, green-marble columns to each side amplifies the room's complex spatial ordering.

15.66 Erik Gunnar Asplund, Stockholm Public Library, 1918–27.
Asplund produced a somewhat abstracted and cool but extremely approachable form of classicism. Here he juxtaposed an oversized, shouldered doorway with a planar façade and a rising cylinder that announces the location of the book stacks inside.

15.67 Erik Gunnar Asplund, Woodland Cemetery, Stockholm, 1915 and after.
To the left, alongside the flagstone path, is a stone wall that accompanies visitors to the top of the hill and the crematorium, columbarium, and chapel. Asplund and Lewerentz reclaimed this serene, noble landscape from the ravages of a gravel quarry, something of a metaphor for the cycle of birth, death, and rebirth.

Ledoux's Barrière de la Villette in Paris (see Fig. 13.20). In a manner suggesting entry into the tomb of some mythical Nordic king, access to the circular, central lending hall is made through tall shouldered doorways; beyond, a cloud of light inside the rising drum illuminates the three levels of stacks. The effect is as crisp and clear as a cloudless, wintry Swedish day.

In 1915 Asplund collaborated with his former classmate Sigurd Lewerentz to win the competition for the design of the Woodland Cemetery, which took twenty-five years to complete. Part of a broad burial-reform effort in Sweden, it takes on meaning through the long-standing Nordic affinity for nature. The site plan does little to explain the architects' efforts to express the connection of the dead to the living and to acknowledge the necessity for mourning. Understanding the extraordinary landscape resurrected from abandoned gravel pits must come from ground-level experience. A canted semicircle at street-side announces the cemetery's shielded existence. Upon entering, a visitor experiences not a formal axis but a serene panoramic view up to a stone cross and a hillock with a grove of weeping elms, then proceeds up along a sloping stone path (Fig. 15.67), compared by some to Rome's Appian Way. To the left and parallel to this approach runs a rock-faced stone wall that glistens with a constant film of water, then beyond it noble structures: a columbarium, a crematorium, and a chapel called Mount Hall—a building

of classical essences with a square-columned, projecting portico. In front of the chapel, hidden from view from below, lies a flat sheet of blueness in the form of a lily pond. Within the surrounding forest the burial plots are informally distributed among the tall trees. Axes cutting through them lead to additional structures, including Asplund's Woodland Chapel, a Laugieresque columnar pavilion with a hemispherical dome covered by a pyramidal roof. Asplund treated the children's cemetery like a sunken garden, with ranks of delicate crosses surrounded by vertical pines. The entire setting speaks of humility, humanity, and spirituality.

ART DECO OR STYLE MODERNE

Slid in between Modernism and traditionalism was an architectural phenomenon called the Art Deco or Style Moderne. Moderne is a slippery term describing a diverse design idiom that encompassed everything from graphics to ceramics, furniture, and architecture, that has been associated with modern movements like the Viennese Secession and Expressionism and with individual modern architects from Auguste Perret to Frank Lloyd Wright, and that meets up on its margins with the International Style. Like the Art Nouveau, it is a style whose designers were in search of newness, though at its heart it was yet another reinterpretation of classicism.

Art Deco decorative arts, then known as *l'art moderne*, thrived in France from 1910 or so. Much in evidence at the 1925 Exposition Internationale des Arts Décoratifs et Industriels Modernes in Paris, Art Deco then waned in popularity in Europe, but took hold in England and America. Art Deco architecture continued to be popular in the United States until World War II, but the style has only been formally recognized since the mid-1960s and is now seen to have had three major subsets: the Zig Zag Moderne of the flamboyant 1920s, which was used mostly for commercial buildings and was characterized by highly decorative, extremely assertive geometric motifs; the PWA Moderne of the sober 1930s and beyond, which was largely unornamented and more monumental, was often used for government projects, and was frequently made possible by funds from the Public Works Administration— hence the PWA prefix; and the Streamline Moderne of the late 1930s and beyond, which was unornamented and was dominated by horizontal lines (comparable to those of the International Style) and curvilinear elements and so was indeed "streamlined." Common to all this work was a "thin-skinned" look, produced by minimizing the surface projections of both architectural and ornamental features.

Art Deco designers used sumptuous materials to produce objects of supple elegance, and their inspirations were eclectic in the extreme. From Cubism, they drew overlapping and faceted patterns, from Russian Constructivism the language of mechanization, and from Futurism a fascination with motion. Added to these sources were historical motifs drawn from ancient Egypt, Africa, the Orient, and elsewhere, such as stylized flowers, coiled tendrils, faceted geometries including chevron patterns, and stylized, idealized, heroic human figures.

Ironically, there were abundant French examples of Art Deco architecture at the 1925 exposition, but they were razed at the end of the event. In England, Art Deco designers sought modernity through the expression of function and economy, so the style became particularly popular for power stations, airports, and theaters. In the 1920s in the United States, architects searching for a decorative vocabulary applicable to skyscrapers (which had previously been modeled on everything from campaniles to ziggurats) adapted the Zig Zag Moderne to create the American Vertical style as something up-to-date, stylish, and expressive of a machine age.

The most famous Art Deco skyscraper is the Chrysler Building in New York City (1928) (Fig. 15.68), designed by William Van Alen (1883–1954). Its crownlike dome of stainless steel, with tiered arches filled with sunbursts and capped by a spire, remains a classic for skyline-makers. Its other notable ornamental features include eagle gargoyles and the famous radiator-cap acroteria and adjacent frieze of abstracted car wheels.

The tallest structure of the period was, of course, the Empire State Building (1931) (Fig. 15.69) by Richmond Shreve (1877–1946), William Lamb (1883–1952), and Arthur Harmon (1878–1958). Its Art Deco ornamentation includes a vast number of sandblasted aluminum spandrel

15.68 William Van Alen, Chrysler Building, New York City, 1928.
There is still no more distinctive silhouette on the New York skyline than the stainless-steel crown of the Chrysler Building. Long ignored by Modernists, this aspect of tall-building design reemerged as almost a fetish in the 1970s and '80s.

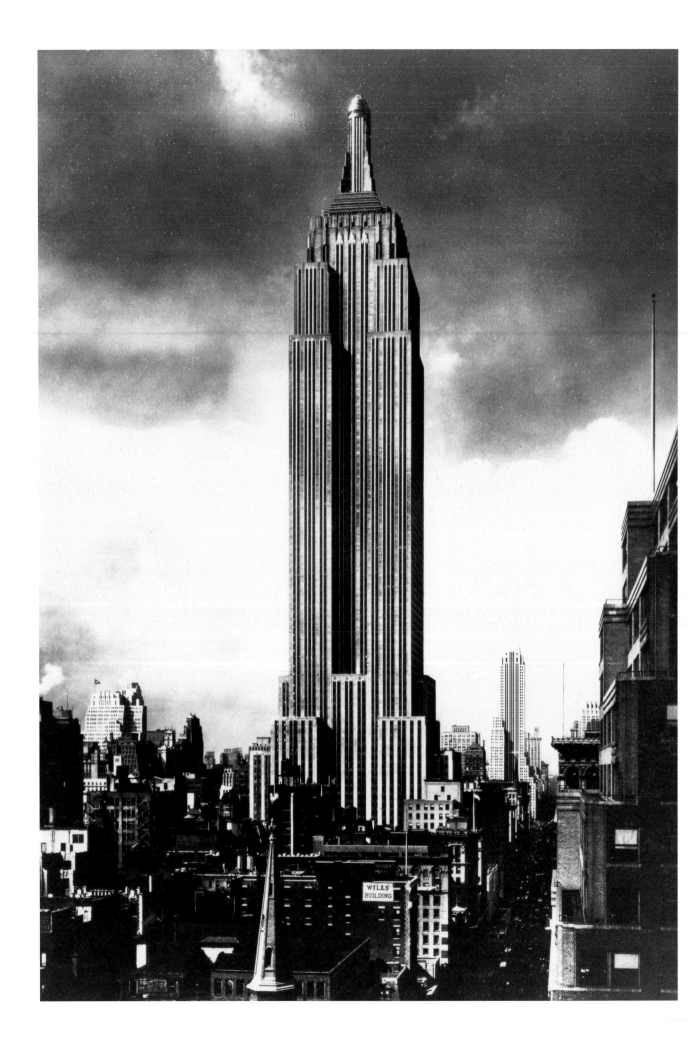

This building would be famous even if the only popular image
of it were King Kong batting at airplanes from its summit.

15.70 (below) Ely Jacques Kahn, Number Two Park
Avenue, New York City, 1927.
Ely Jacques Kahn was probably the most prominent
practitioner of Art Deco in New York City. While ignored
in all accounts of the development of twentieth-century
Modernism, he had an extraordinarily productive career
that stretched over fifty years.

panels with zigzag patterning. New York's most prolific Art
Deco designer was Ely Jacques Kahn (1884–1972), whose
career spanned some fifty years. Representative of his output is the building found at Number Two Park Avenue
(1927) (Fig. 15.70), with its wealth of faceted and geometric detail both inside and out.

In 1929–30 Raymond Hood (1881–1934) designed
the New York Daily News Building (Fig. 15.71), which
in some ways approaches the minimalism of the
International Style but also displays incised decorative
panels of Art Deco inspiration (Fig. 15.72) and includes
a subtle color palette of greens and terracottas—colors
outside the range of European Modernist dicta. Hood and

15.71 (above) Raymond Hood, New York Daily
News Building, New York City, 1929–30.
Contemporary with the Chrysler and Empire
State buildings, the New York Daily News
Building approaches International Style
minimalism but displays incised decorative
panels of Art Deco inspiration, as seen on the
next page. The tall structure behind and to
the left of Hood's tower is the United Nations
Headquarters, designed by a consortium that
included the Modernist Le Corbusier.

15.72 Raymond Hood, New York Daily News Building incised ornament, New York City, 1929–30.
The Art Deco style made its appearance at the base of the tower. The sources for Art Deco ornament were many, from Pre-Columbian imagery to forms responding to the period's penchant for speed.

15.73 Reinhard and Hofmeister, Corbett, Hood, Fouilhoux, and others, Rockefeller Center, New York City, begun 1929.
While the individual buildings are distinctive, it is the urban ensemble they create and the space they define that has caused the Rockefeller Center to be so celebrated. For many, it is the very heart of Manhattan. At the center of the complex, the tallest tower, with its distinctive setbacks, is the RCA Building.

Fouilhoux, along with other firms, designed the complex of buildings in Manhattan comprising the Rockefeller Center (begun 1929) (Fig. 15.73), and located within it a significant body of public art, including Art Deco sculpture by a variety of artists and the famous Diego Rivera fresco that was destroyed soon after completion because of its sympathetic treatment of Communism. An artwork in itself is the center's Radio City Music Hall (Fig. 15.74), with its plush furniture and lush materials and lighting, much of which was the work of the young Edward Durrell Stone, who would become a Modernist then abandon the movement for an eclectic variant all his own.

Representative of the Streamline Moderne is the Coca-Cola Bottling Plant (1936) in Los Angeles (Fig. 15.75) by Robert Derrah (1895–1946). Actually a remodeling, it includes nautical motifs such as porthole windows, hatch-like doorways, and offices reached by way of a "promenade deck." Among the most common Streamline Moderne buildings were the many Greyhound bus terminals, which brought big-city sophistication to smaller communities. Their sleek outlines suggest speed; their hovering entrance canopies welcome riders; and their large expanses of glass project interior bustle out to the sidewalk.

Expressive of PWA Moderne sensibilities, though erected

15.74 Wallace K. Harrison, Radio City Music Hall foyer, New York City, 1933.
Within Rockefeller Center, no single interior space is better known than this one. Its plush furniture, opulent materials, and dramatic lighting capture the spirit of New York City in the 1920s and '30s.

15.75 Robert Derrah, Coca-Cola Bottling Plant, Los Angeles, California, 1936.
A variation on the already diverse Art Deco was the "Streamline Moderne" style. This production facility, with its sleek curves and porthole windows, was actually a remodeling of an existing building.

15.76 Charles McCauley, Birmingham, Alabama City Hall (foreground, 1950) and Holabird and Roche, Jefferson County (Alabama) Courthouse (background, 1929–32).
These buildings stand to either side of Linn Park. The Neo-Classical Linn-Henley Library is the lower building to the right and offers a reminder that Moderne buildings can be interpreted as yet another recasting of classicism.

15.77 Anton Skislewicz, The Breakwater, Miami Beach, Florida, 1939.
The most popular massing compositions for Art Deco buildings in Miami combine several horizontal floors with a tall, central feature, here a hotel sign and stair tower.

years apart, are Alabama's Jefferson County Courthouse (1929–32) and Birmingham City Hall (1950) (Fig. 15.76), which face one another across a park and were designed respectively by the Chicago firm of Holabird and Roche and local architect Charles McCauley. During the Depression years, such buildings were routinely outfitted with sculpture and wall paintings in order both to embellish the civic realm and to give unemployed artists commissions.

A particularly rich body of Art Deco work can be found at Miami Beach, Florida, where the national idiom was fused with a local color palette and adapted to the subtropical climate (Fig. 15.77). These modestly scaled buildings are painted in vivid pinks, greens, peaches, and lavenders that would be garish inland but are appropriate here. They are often outfitted with strongly horizontal sunscreens and balconies and punctuated with dramatically vertical entry bays and stair towers. Decoration includes stock Art Deco motifs such as sunbursts, but extends to local flora and fauna, including the ubiquitous Miami palms and flamingos.

THE ONGOING MODERNIST PROGRAM

While the public embraced Art Deco buildings, doctrinaire Modernists found them to be eclectic, ornamental, and even trivial, and derided them as "modernistic." By and large, these Modernists stayed their course, exploiting modern materials and technologies, often treating architecture as a means for social reform, and, most of all, constantly exploring the possibilities of plastic, or free-flowing, space. This path of continuing development can be traced through the later twentieth century in the work of Frank Lloyd Wright, Le Corbusier, and Ludwig Mies van der Rohe, each of whom pursued a distinctive Modernist course. Wright remained something of an island unto himself and in some instances made overt counterproposals to the work of other Modernists, Le Corbusier in particular.

LATER WORK OF FRANK LLOYD WRIGHT

The initial discussion of Wright concluded with the end of his first marriage and his design of the Imperial Hotel. While his architectural practice in the 1920s suffered because of his personal difficulties, he did manage to do some work, notably in California. There he built a series of houses with their walls laid up stacked-bond fashion in patterned concrete blocks made to his own designs and held together by internal steel reinforcing bars. One such house, built in Pasadena for Alice Millard (1923), illustrates the group. The use of concrete blocks imposed an orthogonal geometry on the design, although Wright, as usual, created

15.78 Frank Lloyd Wright, Alice Millard House, Pasadena, California, 1923.
Wright's so-called textile-block houses like this one illustrate how ornamental his buildings could sometimes be. His mentor, Louis Sullivan, had, of course, developed elaborate systems of ornamentation but had written warily about what he perceived to be the dangers of ornamentalism.

an open and flowing plan, with balconies and terraces linking the house to its hillside site (Fig. 15.78).

Toward the end of the decade, Wright's chaotic private life became more orderly. He was still hounded by the press and pursued by creditors (his home at Spring Green, Wisconsin—Taliesin East—almost being forcibly sold for non-payment of taxes), but in his third wife, Olgivanna Lazovich, he found a steadying influence. To rescue him from financial pressures, a group of loyal friends incorporated Wright and paid off the mortgages on Taliesin, counting on his future earnings to repay their investment. Wright formed the Taliesin Fellowship in 1932 for young men and women who wished to work under his tutelage, charging them a fee for the experience. It became a highly personal educational setting, reflecting Wright's disdain for the formal trappings of academic enterprises. Students, called apprentices, participated in all aspects of life and work at Taliesin, from helping with farm and kitchen chores, to constructing the ever-expanding physical plant, performing in musicals and theatrical events, and assisting Wright in the drafting room. With Olgivanna's encouragement, Wright also began to write, and the first edition of his *Autobiography* dates from 1932.

Broadacre City

Just as Wright was again becoming a productive architect, the national economy sank into the Great Depression. There was little work for anyone, so he turned his attention to a utopian scheme that he christened Broadacre City and that was his critique of Le Corbusier's Radiant City plans, which are discussed below. It illustrated many of Wright's ideas about the proper manner of living in America. The single-family house, set in about one acre of land, was the basic dwelling unit. The urban center was rather small

and dispersed, for Wright anticipated that efficient communications and high-speed transportation would largely eliminate the need for the congestion associated with city life and business. (He seems to have conveniently overlooked heavy industry.) In some respects Broadacre City looked backward to the nineteenth century and to the small, largely agrarian towns that characterized much of the United States then. Small, self-sufficient communities clustered around cultural and recreational facilities conjure up romantic visions of a past that probably never existed. In other respects Wright's scheme was farsighted, for it seemed to incorporate enduring American attitudes: a mistrust of bigness, a love of the land and open air, and the opportunity for individual expression. The phenomenal suburban growth around American cities after 1945 reflects in part the popular interpretation of concepts embedded in Broadacre City.

Many of Wright's later buildings were designed to fit into a setting like Broadacre City. For residences, he developed his Usonian house, to some extent a response to Le Corbusier's Citrohan houses, and he constructed many variations across the country from the mid-1930s until the late 1950s. Usonian houses differed from Prairie houses in several respects. They were generally smaller, reflecting the reduced size of the American family and middle-class budgets, and they were designed for families without household servants. Their designs provided easy access by automobile, and interior activities could be easily supervised from the kitchen, identified as the principal workstation of the housewife. The interior opens up to outdoor spaces away from the street, either to the side or the rear.

Buildings by Wright were, of course, included in the 1932 MoMA show on modern architecture, although not in the book illustrating the International Style. To Wright's chagrin, Hitchcock and Johnson considered him to have been a "proto-Modernist," not a fully fledged Modernist like the luminaries from Europe. Wright, in turn, had scathing comments to make about the leading Internationalists and their designs, remarking with a characteristic lack of humility to Henry-Russell Hitchcock, "Not only do I fully intend to be the greatest architect who has yet lived, but the greatest who will ever live. Yes, I intend to be the greatest architect of all time." But by International Style standards, Wright's work in the 1920s was loaded down with fussy detail and excessive ornament. Seeing the 1932 exhibition in New York must have influenced him to a certain degree, for afterward he began to design in a much less ornate way and produced several masterpieces in the 1930s.

Fallingwater

One of the young men who came to Taliesin as an apprentice was Edgar Kaufmann, Jr., son of a wealthy Pittsburgh department-store owner. Hearing that his father was contemplating the construction of a vacation house in the mountains of western Pennsylvania, young Edgar persuaded Edgar Kaufmann, Sr., to employ Wright as architect. The result was Fallingwater (1935–37), perhaps the most famous house not built for royalty or the U.S. president anywhere in the world (Figs. 15.79–15.80). (Fallingwater is now open to the public under the trusteeship of the Western Pennsylvania Conservancy.) Wright took the major natural feature of the site, a rocky outcropping where a small stream falls over a series of ledges, and planted the house beside the stream, letting the reinforced-concrete balconies cantilever dramatically out over the water. In order to see the waterfall, one must go outside, below the house, where the falls and the house can be seen together in the classic view that Wright planned, and he did a rendering from just that point to convince Kaufmann of the efficacy of his design.

Stone quarried on the site was laid in irregular horizontal courses to form the four great piers supporting the living room, the fireplace mass, and the remaining bearing walls. The balconies, which form dominant and dramatic elements, cantilever in two directions and are stiffened at their edges by upturned parapet walls. Large expanses of glass float between slate floors and stuccoed ceilings, minimizing the distinction between interior and exterior. Fallingwater's planar treatment of surfaces and abstract fragmentation of volumes suggest a debt to the European Modernists. It was cultural historian Lewis Mumford's assessment that, in Fallingwater, Wright "created a dynamic multidimensional composition that made Le Corbusier's buildings seem flat cardboard compositions." At age sixty-eight, Wright was just beginning his second great period of creativity.

15.79 Frank Lloyd Wright, Edgar Kaufmann House, "Fallingwater," Ohiopyle, Pennsylvania, 1935–37.
A stream runs under the house and the stratified stone walls appear to grow from the landscape as they support cantilevered balconies. Part of Wright's genius was to cantilever the house out over the waterfall.

15.80 Frank Lloyd Wright, Plan of Fallingwater, Ohiopyle, Pennsylvania, 1935–37.
Wright had set out to "break the box" while at work in Oak Park forty years earlier. In this plan, the service spaces are more enclosed to the rear, while the living spaces in front break out dramatically onto the landscape. Compare it to Mies's Tugendhat House plan (Fig. 15.60).

The Guggenheim Museum and Taliesin West

Wright was interested in the possibilities of circular forms, especially those involving continuous ramps. A project for an observatory atop Sugar Loaf Mountain in Maryland (1925) may have first set his mind to the idea, and the concept reappeared in the V.C. Morris Gift Shop (1949) in San Francisco and in a car park proposed for Pittsburgh. The notion was brought to full realization in the Guggenheim Museum (1957–59) in New York City (Figs. 15.81–15.82), where a quarter-mile-long ramp spirals around a six-story interior sculpture court. The Guggenheim has extensive holdings of twentieth-century art, and it has been suggested that, by designing a museum with a continuously sloping floor and outward-leaning, curving walls, Wright was expressing his scorn for modern art. Display possibilities are certainly restricted by the design, and no artist can single-handedly compete with the strong three-dimensional spatial experience Wright created on the interior.

As he grew older, Wright preferred the warm weather of the desert southwest to the blustery Wisconsin winters, so the Fellowship moved south to avoid the cold, returning to Wisconsin only in the spring. Near Phoenix, Arizona, Wright began construction of Taliesin West (1938 onward), a sprawling, angular encampment set in the rugged spareness of the desert and replacing the wood-and-canvas Ocotillo desert camp dating from 1927. Using materials taken from the locale, he combined adobe and local boulders with redwood beams and canvas to create a shaded interior that moderated the sun's heat and glare and fit in perfectly in its harsh context.

Wrightian Connections

Austrians Richard Schindler (1887–1953) and Richard Neutra (1892–1970) both knew Adolf Loos, and they both immigrated to America, where they met in Frank Lloyd Wright's studio before moving on to Los Angeles. Long on spatial intuition and short on concern for detailing and craftsmanship, Schindler produced the much-publicized Lovell Beach House at Newport Beach (1926) for Richard and Leah Lovell. A more instructive example of Schindler's

15.81 (opposite top) Frank Lloyd Wright, Guggenheim Museum, New York City, 1957–59.
The Guggenheim is considered to be one of the great buildings of the twentieth century even though art lovers have a limited viewing distance and must negotiate the constant slope of the spiraling ramp.

15.82 (opposite bottom) Frank Lloyd Wright, Guggenheim Museum interior, New York City, 1957–59.
This view shows clearly Wright's fascination with geometric ordering. To him the art housed within the building was perhaps incidental to his architectural genius. Such circular (as well as triangular, and polygonal) geometries dominated Wright's work in what was the third phase of his long career.

work, however, is his own Kings Road House (1921–22), which he claimed to be the first modern residence in the United States. Crudely built using tapered, tilt-up concrete slabs with glass seams between them and trimmed out in wood, it displays an open plan with extraordinary relationships between interior and exterior spaces and today has a layered landscape of restored native plant material.

Neutra, a fine technician as well as a gifted designer, took detailing seriously. None of his projects has been more admired than the steel-stud-construction, so-called "Health House" (1927–29) that he designed for the same

Lovells for whom Schindler built the beachfront home. He also designed an extraordinary desert house (1946) in Palm Springs for the same Edgar Kaufmann, Sr. for whom Wright had created Fallingwater. Both Neutra designs are rational and strongly connected to the landscape, in the case of the desert house to a level of sublimity. Perhaps most interesting in terms of Modernist intentions transported to America was Neutra's own residence (built in 1932, burned in 1963, and rebuilt by his son Dion). This so-called V.D.L. Research House (Fig. 15.83) was relatively cheaply constructed, exquisitely proportioned, and open to views from front-facing rooms, balconies, and a rooftop solarium out across a sweeping reservoir and to the rear into an atrium. Though modest in size, it was replete with innovations, from a variety of materials obtained from local building suppliers to mirrors positioned so as to extend apparent space, as in the eighteenth-century Rococo.

15.83 Richard Neutra, V.D.L. Research House, Los Angeles, 1932 (burned and rebuilt in 1963).
This is not the building that Neutra constructed, but a more-or-less exact replica that his son Dion rebuilt after fire destroyed the original. Its site is part of a subdivision that includes other Neutra designs and looks out onto a panoramic water reservoir.

15.84 (above) Le Corbusier, Unité d'Habitation, Marseille, 1946–52.
Not visible here are the pilotis that support this ferroconcrete structure. The exterior walls are faced with brises-soleil (sunscreens) that modulate light entering the apartments. The continuous vertical baffles about halfway up and toward the rear shield the ill-fated "shopping street" that was to provide for tenants' every need.

15.85 (left) Le Corbusier, Section through and plans of the Unité d'Habitation, Marseille, 1946–52.
The apartments are obviously very narrow, particularly when they are divided into hall-like bedrooms. The section shows that each unit has a two-story living space with an overlooking balcony.

LATER WORK OF LE CORBUSIER

Just as Wright designed his later works to fit into Broadacre City, Le Corbusier conceived many of his later works as elements of an ideal metropolis that he called La Ville Radieuse (The Radiant City). His first opportunity to build a related apartment block came after World War II, when the mayor of Marseille invited him to construct the first Unité d'Habitation, or Unified Dwelling House (1946–52) (Figs. 15.84–15.85). Some critics consider the Unité a masterpiece, both for its bold sculptural forms and its novel approach to the problems of apartment living. The Unité block is set in a landscaped park and raised on pilotis. The apartments are ingeniously arranged to have frontage on both the east and west sides of the building, making possible cross-ventilation, a desirable trade-off for their long, narrow plans. Balconies, integrated into brises-soleil or sunscreens, give each side exterior living space. The building originally featured a two-story shopping floor (grocery store, beauty shop, repair services, etc.) halfway up, and the roof levels were devoted to extensive recreational and health facilities: a gymnasium, running track, movie theater, health club, nursery school, sun terraces, and the like. The concrete work throughout is forceful. Patterns resulting from the carpentry formwork can be regarded as surface ornament disciplined by the fabrication process. Le Corbusier created the building's proportions using a system that he called "Le Modular," based upon the height of an average person repeatedly subdivided using the Golden Section ratio (approximately 5:8). Ship imagery characterizes the rooftop ventilation stacks, elevator housing, and recreational facilities, for here Le Corbusier could exercise his formal repertoire quite freely. Above all, the desire for abundant sunlight, air, and green open space for all 1600 residents guided the design.

Le Corbusier's critics have pointed out that the scheme is essentially anti-urban, turning its back on the architectural and street patterns of Marseille. Even the provision of shops (which were a financial failure) was attacked, because it meant the residents would have little need to associate with the commercial life of the town. Rather than an affront to Marseille, however, the Unité must be seen as a design in harmony with Le Corbusier's idealized city, a world that was quite different from any existing urban setting.

Ronchamp and Ste. Marie-de-la-Tourette

In the east of France, not far from the Swiss border, Le Corbusier designed the pilgrimage chapel of Notre-Dame-du-Haut at Ronchamp near Belfort (1951–55) (Figs. 15.86–15.87) to replace a previous church destroyed by artillery fire during World War II. This small building allowed him to give maximum expression to the sculptural possibilities of architectural form. The rationalism of earlier works was laid aside—no proportioning system, no five points, no pilotis!—and a dramatic, highly symbolic

15.86 Le Corbusier, Axonometric view of Notre-Dame-du-Haut, Ronchamp, 1951–55.
Built as a pilgrimage site for worshipers, Ronchamp (near Belfort, France) has become as much a pilgrimage site for architects and architectural students. The tower lights an altar below. Services can be held inside or held outside on the concrete apron and adjacent lawn to the left.

15.87 Le Corbusier, Notre-Dame-du-Haut, Ronchamp, 1951–55.
The chapel is built of brick covered with stucco. The random window openings in the south wall to the left contain glass decorated with Le Corbusier's painted images. The principal entry lies between this wall and the tower, with a secondary entry in the rear between the two smaller towers.

design emerged. Even the structural system appears to be non-rational as a metal frame is made to look like massive masonry. The walls are rough-textured stucco painted white, and the roof is a sail-like cap of board-formed concrete that rolls over the east wall to provide protection for the exterior pulpit. Large crowds attend services out of doors, sitting on the lawn; the interior provides seats for only fifty people, although there is standing room for more. The spectacular south wall has exaggerated thickness and an array of splayed windows inset with handpainted colored glass. From the outside, they look like an irregular series of small apertures, but on the interior, the wall turns into a glowing light sculpture, as moving in its own way as the windows of Chartres Cathedral. A very thin strip of clear glass intervenes between the walls and roof, which makes the roof seem to float. Meditation chapels underneath the towers have top illumination from high clerestories in the walls behind the worshipers.

Southwest of Lyon is the small town of Eveux-sur-l'Arbresle, outside of which Le Corbusier was commissioned to design a Dominican monastery, Ste. Marie-de-la-Tourette (1956–60) (Figs. 15.88–15.89). Here he accomplished a modern reworking of the medieval monastic program. The church, a simple rectangular solid with sculptural subsidiary chapels in the crypt, is located on the northeast side of an open courtyard, which is crisscrossed by enclosed passageways connecting the church to other

15.88 Le Corbusier, Plan of Ste. Marie-de-la-Tourette, Eveux-sur-l'Arbresle, 1956–60.
Here, Le Corbusier transformed the traditional monastic plan. Ramps and a small chapel inhabit the traditional interior cloister, with the latter's functions moved to the roof. This arrangement was never found acceptable by the monks, who chose to meditate in the wooded areas nearby.

15.89 Le Corbusier, Ste. Marie-de-la-Tourette, Eveux-sur-l'Arbresle, 1956–60.
Monks' cells rise about the pilotis on the south façade. The rooms have sunscreens like those used in the Unité (Fig. 15.84).

Palace of the Governor   Monument of Martyrs   Open Hand   Palace of Justice

Parliament
Building

Tower of
Shadows

Secretariat
Building

0   50 m
0   150 ft

15.90 Le Corbusier, plan of Chandigarh, Punjab, 1951–59.
This master plan illustrates Le Corbusier's preference for large buildings set wide apart within a gardenlike landscape.

15.91 Le Corbusier, Parliament Building, Chandigarh, Punjab, 1951–59.
Here Le Corbusier continued to explore ways to manipulate sunlight. The poured-in-place concrete structure is sculpted along one side and cut away sunscreen-fashion along the other. His goals were certainly in part environmental, but he also sought to celebrate the state by associating it with the sun.

parts of the monastery. The remaining monastic quarters are arranged in three wings: the refectory on the level of the church; the library, study rooms, and an oratory on the second level; and two floors of monks' cells around the upper levels.

All the construction is in concrete. Le Corbusier returned to the use of pilotis and the "regulating traces" of his proportioning system, although the sculptural freedom found at Ronchamp is present here, too, and he manipulated light in dozens of ways to enrich the experience of the building's elemental forms. Window mullions vary according to a harmonic rhythm; scoops catch the light and direct it through colored conical sections to focus on altars in the crypt; long horizontal ribbons provide even illumination for the corridors on the dormitory floor; each monk's room has a virtual wall of glass looking out over

the balcony brise-soleil to the distant horizon; and a truncated pyramidal roof with a skylight provides an ethereal glow for the oratory.

Chandigarh

Despite his numerous city-planning projects on paper, Le Corbusier was invited only once to design an actual town. In 1951 the government of India asked him to work on the design of Chandigarh, the new capital of the northern state of Punjab (Figs. 15.90–15.91). Le Corbusier made a master plan, while the designs of individual sectors and most buildings were left to others. However, he did design the symbolic governmental buildings, which he located on the highest ground at the head of the scheme, with the majestic foothills of the Himalayas beyond, in a manner that recalls the Acropolis in Athens. He grouped four major buildings around a great ceremonial plaza: the palace of the governor (not built), the Secretariat Building (1951–57), the Parliament Building (1956–59), and the Palace of Justice (1951–56). All these buildings blend the rational discipline so evident in his early works with the sculptural freedom of his later projects. The Parliament Building, for example, is almost square in plan, with stacked rows of offices arranged around two sides. The legislative chamber is circular, located at the base of a truncated hyperbolic surface of revolution (a hyperbolic curve rotated about a central axis) equipped with monitors at the top to filter the intense Indian sun. Control of light was of great importance, for with shade comes coolness. The brises-soleil were designed to introduce indirect sunlight and to provide views. Concrete, Le Corbusier's favorite material, was well suited to the Indian context. It is labor-intensive to form up and pour, but in India, with its cheap labor, inexpensive to produce, and its mass also buffers climatic extremes.

DIASPORA AND THE LATER WORK OF MIES VAN DER ROHE

We last saw Ludwig Mies van der Rohe failing in his attempt to keep the Bauhaus going in the face of rising Nazism, and the Nazi regime soon made Germany untenable for modern architects. Walter Gropius was the first to leave and, after a period of professional practice in England, he came to the United States in 1937 to direct the Department of Architecture in the Graduate School of Design at Harvard University. Marcel Breuer, a pupil and teacher at the Bauhaus, also immigrated and taught under Gropius at Harvard and collaborated with him in his architectural work. Mies came to Chicago in 1938 to head the architecture school at the Armour Institute of Technology, which soon merged with the Lewis Institute to become the Illinois Institute of Technology, or IIT.

Planning and Building at IIT

In his twenty years at IIT, Mies had the opportunity to plan the new campus, design many of its buildings, and influence the architectural education of a whole generation of students. The curriculum he laid down stressed clarity, rationality, intellectual order, and discipline, and progressed from the study of wood to stone, brick, concrete, and finally steel. Once students understood the materials, they considered problems of design. The highest standards of draftsmanship and precision were expected at all levels, and the essence of architecture was reduced to skin and bones—the glass spandrel panels or brickwork (skin) set in the structural frame (the bones).

The master plan Mies made for IIT reflects the order and rationality of the curriculum. A square grid subdivides the rectangular site, and the buildings are all conceived as rectangular masses conforming to the grid, creating a continuous series of interlocking courtyards and exterior walks. Mies saw that steel was the major American industrial building material (as labor costs for formwork often made concrete less economical), so he set about designing the purest, most elegant steel expressions achieved up until that time. For the IIT campus he designed Crown Hall (1956) (Fig. 15.92) to house the School of Architecture. It is a one-story building raised above a high basement. Four deep panel girders straddle the building, supporting the roof and leaving the entire interior free of columns. Except for the stairs and toilet rooms, which are fixed, the possible locations of subdividing walls are not hindered by the architectural container. As in his other projects, Mies was designing for flexibility and change, so that unforeseeable uses might easily be accommodated within the building at a later time.

In his office Mies designed a range of other projects. On a beautiful site in downtown Chicago overlooking Lake Michigan, he built a pair of apartment towers known by their address, 860 Lake Shore Drive (1949–51), the first

15.92 Ludwig Mies van der Rohe, Crown Hall, IIT, Chicago, Illinois, 1956.
"God is in the details," said Mies. At IIT he demonstrated his mastery of detailing in steel, glass, and brick. The steel skeleton of Crown Hall is completely exposed, including the plate girders that rise above the roof.

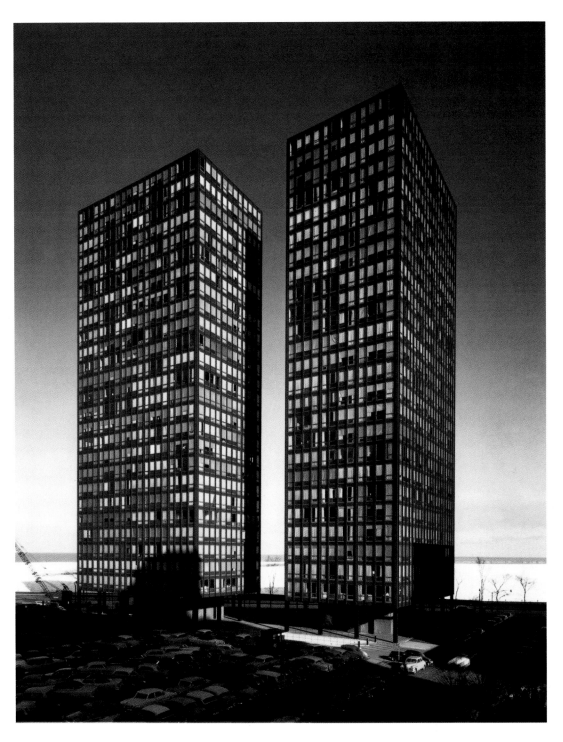

15.93 Ludwig Mies van der Rohe, 860 Lake Shore Drive, Chicago, Illinois, 1949–51.
Notice that Mies designed the blinds to be positioned up, down, or halfway between, and in no other positions. His reductivist mentality made accommodation of individual tastes impossible.

glass-and-steel high-rise residential construction in the United States (Fig. 15.93). Twenty-six stories tall, they are the realization of the concept he first proposed in the glass-tower schemes of 1919–21. The 860 Lake Shore Drive buildings are framed in steel, made fireproof by a masonry

casing. Mies was able to express the actual structural material only by attaching additional non-structural steel to the exterior of the frames. To increase the vertical appearance of the buildings, thinner I-beams run continuously up the building as window mullions. This exterior steel serves no structural purpose, of course, but Mies judged it necessary to make the building "look right."

As early as 1946 Mies was at work on a glass-enclosed house for Dr. Edith Farnsworth, to be located on land near the Fox River in Plano, Illinois. Design and construction took six years, during which time Mies disciple Philip

15.94 Ludwig Mies van der Rohe, Farnsworth House, Plano, Illinois, 1950–52.
Whatever the complaints about Mies's reductivism, the formal results are elegant, almost timeless. In fact, the Farnsworth House can be interpreted as a classical temple, its stylobate or base slid forward to create an arrival sequence.

Johnson built a glass house for himself (1949) in New Canaan, Connecticut. The Farnsworth House (1950–52), raised off the ground because the river occasionally flooded the site, sits as a simple white frame in the landscape, as elegant an expression of skin-and-bones architecture as could be imagined (Fig. 15.94).

None of Mies's works became more celebrated than his Seagram Building (Fig. 15.95) in New York City, designed (with Philip Johnson) for the Canadian whiskey distillers. Like the Lakeshore Drive apartments, it has an external non-structural grid, in this case of bronze-tinted steel holding bronze-tinted glass, which represents outwardly its fireproofed, and so concealed, internal steel frame. When the tower was erected in 1958, the granite-paved plaza next to it offered a level of civic generosity then uncommon in midtown Manhattan.

CONCLUSIONS ABOUT ARCHITECTURAL IDEAS

Anyone looking for the apparent safety of a conveniently single-minded and inevitable historical path will probably have welcomed this chapter's presentation of European Modernism as the product of energetic, frantic,

even desperate investigations, with the outcome being a directed architectural juggernaut of prescriptive design sensibilities. However, the triumph was to be relatively brief, and in the next chapter the tenets of Modernism will be questioned.

Modernist motivations were often noble, frequently heroic, sometimes arrogant, and even utopian. After the cataclysm that was World War I, many European architects saw building design as a potential instrument of societal transformation. In chaotic economies desperately in need of housing, they chose as their principal concerns utility and efficiency and a related mechanization of the building process, but leavened their pragmatism with advanced spatial conceptions then current in the visual arts. These emerging Modernists saw themselves in a winner-take-all conflict with the obstructionist forces of bourgeois traditionalism. Armed with arguments of rationality and prepared to speak and write polemically, they set out to win the battle among the avant-garde and in the architectural media, where they were successful, and, they hoped, in the hearts and minds of the larger population, where they were not.

There was no scarcity of new ideas: Adolf Loos and his attack on "decadent" ornamentation and his development of the *Raumplan*; Frank Lloyd Wright and his determination to invent a unique American domestic type, which he did with his Prairie houses, and his technical innovations like central air-conditioning at the Larkin Building and economical poured-in-place concrete at Unity Temple; and the German experience wherein Peter Behrens and others like him founded the Deutscher Werkbund in an effort to raise the general quality of manufactured goods and Walter Gropius developed a new system of design education at

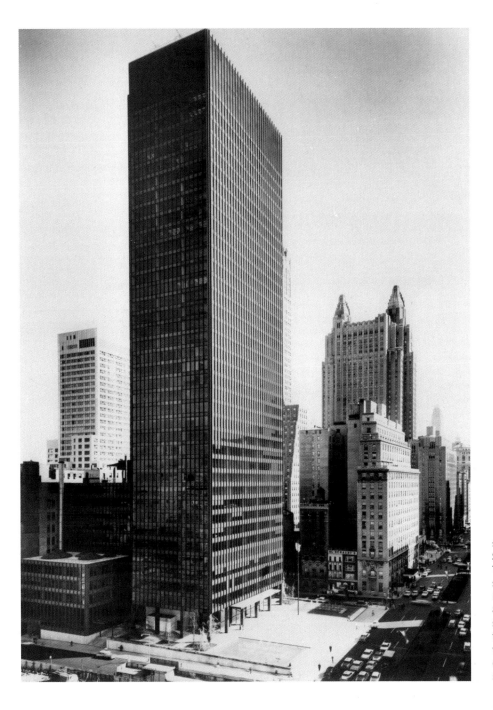

15.95 Ludwig Mies van der Rohe, Seagram Building, New York City, 1958. There is no more celebrated Miesian skyscraper than this one. Unlike Crown Hall and the Farnsworth House, but like 860 Lake Shore Drive, this high-rise structure was required by building codes to have all of its steel structure covered with fireproofing. The steel frame expressed on the outside is therefore structurally redundant.

the Bauhaus, first in Weimar, then in Dessau, before its dissolution by the Nazis. Add to this yeasty mix the radical proposals, frequently drawn but less frequently built, for dynamism by the Italian Futurists, for infinite-space modulations by the De Stijl designers, and for extreme material assemblies by the Russian Constructivists. In the end, space was the stuff of Modernism. This can be seen consistently, if in differing interpretations, in the works of the triumvirate of Le Corbusier, Walter Gropius, and Ludwig Mies van der Rohe (with Frank Lloyd Wright as a constant American competitor and even antagonist).

In addition to all these happenings, there were concurrent advances in building technology, especially the use of steel and steel-reinforced concrete, and new visions of the city as a place of modern industry and modern systems of transportation and as a place of physical and emotional health, even a place of utopian ideals. As if this were not enough, remember that most built architecture of the period did not fit the Modernist prescriptions, from the alternative forms of the Dutch and German Expressionists to the hybrid forms of the Art Deco to the latent forms of continuing traditionalism, which in terms of sheer numbers of built works still held the field. And as if this were *still* not enough, the situation in the late twentieth century and beyond would only become more complex, as will be seen in the final chapter.

Chapter 16

Modernisms in the Mid- and Late Twentieth Century and Beyond

T his final chapter still concerns Modernism, but also addresses reactions to it and against it, and takes architecture into the twenty-first century. Inevitably lacking in historical distance, it is more a report on current events than a history, as the canon—or list by consensus of the most significant buildings—has not yet been firmly established.

Beginning in 1928, an organization with the acronym CIAM (Congrès Internationaux d'Architecture Moderne) promoted modern architecture and addressed pressing building-design and city-planning issues. Le Corbusier was a principal figure, but most of the Modernist luminaries participated. After World War II, the organization attempted to reformulate its goals, but it soon became clear that a new generation of designers found the old doctrine constraining. In 1953, at a meeting in southern France, a loosely organized group calling itself Team-X ("X" being the Roman numeral ten) was given responsibility for planning the next conference, which it did, only to see CIAM dissolved.

Team-X included husband and wife Peter (1923–2003) and Alison (1928–93) Smithson and Ralph Erskine (1914–2005), all three from England, and Aldo van Eyck (1918–99) from Holland. Their thinking differed from that of mainline Modernists, particularly in being more attuned to the problems of the postwar era and to the stated wishes of end-users, and they were more interested in matters of regional and local context and less obsessed with an overtly rational design process.

The Smithsons' work, dubbed Brutalism, certainly owes a debt to Le Corbusier and is best illustrated by their elongated, multi-story, concrete housing units. Constructed as late as 1972, Robin Hood Gardens in London is tough and gritty (or brutal) in its outward appearance, but was intended as a sympathetic response to modern English working-class urbanism (Fig. 16.1).

Ralph Erskine produced his own solution to urban living for workers by developing an inclusive design process for the long Byker Wall Housing (1969–75) (Fig. 16.2) in Newcastle upon Tyne that involved a close dialogue with future occupants. One high face of his oscillating housing

slab looks north onto a highway, and so is fortresslike, while the opposite and more private face is a riot of picturesque, multicolored heavy-timber and wood-lattice balconies and brickwork. Aldo van Eyck moved even further toward the intuitive and even the spiritual, as in his Orphanage in Amsterdam (1957–60), where he organized space to stimulate imagination and play and sought to imbue his timeless, not Zeitgeistian, forms with deep meanings and values.

The work of these designers suggests some of the diversity arising in the postwar era. In the discussion that follows, this diversity has been directed into categories, which must be viewed as conveniences of the moment. In each category the discussion begins with a designer active at least by the mid-twentieth century.

MODERN REGIONALISM

Some modern architects have followed the path defined by some members of Team-X and have sought to develop

---

Chronology

Development of "Post-Modern" architecture	1960s
Rachel Carson publishes *Silent Spring*, beginning the environmental movement	1962
Vietnam War	1965–73
Robert Venturi publishes *Complexity and Contradiction in Architecture*	1966
Assassination of Martin Luther King	1968
Apollo astronauts land on the moon	1969
First Earth Day celebration	1970
Creation of the Internet	ca. 1981
Introduction of the personal computer	1982
Fall of the Berlin Wall	1989
Dissolution of the Soviet Union	1991
Al Qaeda terrorist attacks destroy World Trade Center	2001
Beginning of the war in Iraq	2003
Completion of the Human Genome Project	2003
Hurricane Katrina	2004
Tsunami in Southeast Asia	2004
World financial crisis	2007–10 and beyond
Election of Barack Obama, the first black president of the United States	2008
China becomes the world's second-largest economy	2010
Uprisings in the Middle East	2011
Tsunami and nuclear-plant disaster in Japan	2011

⬅----

Frank Gehry, Guggenheim Museum Bilbao atrium, Bilbao, 1997. With its walls, glass, railings, and steel frame all twisting as they rise, the atrium offers an exhilarating sense of dynamic space. Inhabiting the structure makes manifest the previously impossible: entering and moving through a building-size piece of free-form sculpture.

16.1 (above) Alison and Peter Smithson, Robin Hood Gardens, London, 1972.
Inspired by the housing-unit designs of Le Corbusier but with a greater empathy for occupants, the Smithsons used raw concrete to create large apartment blocks like this one. Notice the "skybridges" that appear frequently in their work.

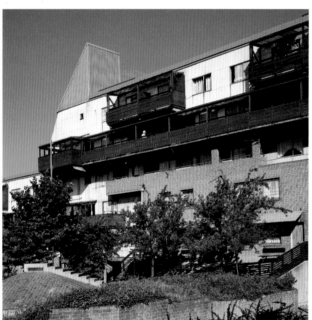

16.2 (left) Ralph Erskine, Byker Wall Housing, Newcastle-upon-Tyne, 1969–75.
Among the concerns of Team-X members ("X" being the Roman numeral ten) in the post-World War II period was the sensitive response to context, or localized site conditions. In designing this housing project, Ralph Erskine sought to take contextualism one step further by responding directly to the suggestions of multiple end-users.

16.3 (below) Alvar Aalto, Ground-story plan of the Municipal Library, Viipuri, 1930–35.
This configuration, with one rectangle slid against another, was used frequently in the twentieth century. Two other notable examples are Frank Lloyd Wright's Robie House (see Figs. 15.12–15.13) and Mies van der Rohe's Farnsworth House (see Fig. 15.94).

Reading room

Children's library

Entry lobby

Auditorium

a contemporary idiom by responding to more localized conditions. In part, this effort can be interpreted as a reaction against the cultural homogenization produced by enhanced communications, increased and more rapid travel, and the pervasiveness of mass media. The most gifted regional designers have grounded themselves in local values, building traditions, and form languages and have remained sensitive to local site conditions, while leavening their design proposals with the yeast of modern compositional principles, new technologies, and a lingering social conscience.

Alvar Aalto

Early in his career, Alvar Aalto (1898–1976) embraced the International Style, but then moved on to become a regionalist in his native Finland. During his formative years, Finnish architects were searching for a regional architectural identity and so were experimenting with

16.4 Alvar Aalto, Municipal Library interior, Viipuri, 1930–35.
Aalto consistently manipulated the ceiling plane in inventive ways. Here a field of skylights illuminates the main reading room. The ceiling of the theater in the adjacent rectangle is an undulating plane of matched boards that is both sculptural and acoustically beneficial.

a Nordic version of Neo-Classicism and a nationalistic Romanticism associated with chauvinistic myths and local building traditions. Aalto developed, apparently independently, a functional approach that closely paralleled the Deutscher Werkbund architects of the same period, but with overtones of both classicism and Romanticism. In 1924, after graduating from the Helsinki University of Technology, he traveled to Italy, and after returning north never lost his enthusiasm for traditional Italian architecture, particularly from its hilltowns.

In 1927 he won the competition to create a municipal library for Viipuri (now Vyborg, Russia) (Fig. 16.3) with a design of such a thoroughly modern cast that conservative local forces delayed its construction until 1930–35. Its carefully proportioned form might be described as stripped classicism, but this apparent reductivism is tempered by a poetic sensitivity to both materials and occupancy (Fig. 16.4).

Aalto's design for the Tuberculosis Sanatorium (1929–33) at Paimio brought him international acclaim. Located on a hilltop surrounded by evergreens, the ensemble rises dramatically in the landscape (Figs. 16.5–16.6). The block of south-facing patients' rooms, a long, thin, six-story wing, dominates the grouping, connecting via an entrance and bent corridor to dining and service blocks. In order to have it conform to the topography and the sun's path,

16.5 Alvar Aalto, Tuberculosis Sanatorium, Paimio, 1929–33.
None of Aalto's commissions has been more celebrated as
an International Style icon than this one. Notable features
are the long strip windows and related spandrels and the
extensive balconies for convalescing patients.

**16.6 Alvar Aalto, Plan of the Tuberculosis
Sanatorium, Paimio, 1929–33.**
The plan appears at first glance to be randomly
organized. However, its splayed distribution of
components is a response to orientation toward the
sun. As pure form, the composition can be compared
to Russian Constructivist work of the 1910s and '20s.

Service wing

Dining wing

Doctors' wing

Entrance canopy

Patients' wing

16.5

N

0   50 m
0   150 ft

Council chamber

Library with shops below

Offices

Courtyard

N

0   20 m
0   60 ft

16.7 Alvar Aalto, Roof-and-courtyard-level plans of the Town Hall, Säynätsalo, 1951–52.
Aalto's plan *parti* suggests the kind of spontaneous design found in Italian hill towns. The roughly square courtyard has one of its sides slid away just far enough to allow a slightly deflected path through the complex. One stair is orthogonal, while the other cascades out of the plaza over grass-covered treads as seen in Fig. 16.8.

Aalto rotated these units in a manner suggestive of Russian Constructivist work.

Finland's greatest natural resource is wood, and Aalto used this material in innovative ways. He developed a technique for bending and laminating thin layers to form plywood sheets of any desired curvature. In 1932 he designed his first chair with a one-piece plywood seat and back supported by a tubular metal frame. Subsequent designs were fabricated entirely in wood, and many of these are still available on the commercial market.

After World War II, Aalto's mature style moved away from the white rectangular masses and linear pipe railings of the International Style. During a teaching appointment at MIT in the late 1940s, he designed Baker House (1947–49), a campus dormitory. Located on a site parallel to the Charles river, the seven-story brick building has its riverfront plan arranged in a sinusoidal curve, permitting oblique views from the dormitory rooms up or down the river.

A more ambitious program was involved in the commission for a Town Hall for Säynätsalo (1951–52), designed as a group of buildings around a grassy courtyard (Figs. 16.7–16.8). In fact, it provides the entire civic center for this small community, housing the municipal offices, council chamber, public library, and retail shops. Within a basically orthogonal layout, the brick volume of the council chamber dominates the ensemble, its sloped-roof profile reflecting a graceful wooden fan truss inside. The Town Hall is entered by sets of either brick or turf stairs. The building's scale, which seems appropriately monumental from without, becomes almost diminutive within the courtyard.

16.8 Alvar Aalto, Town Hall, Säynätsalo, 1951–52.
Aalto's complex exhibits multiple scales. It rises two stories on the outside, but only one story in the courtyard over which the tower of the council chamber stands. This view suggests that Aalto was still being influenced by his travels in Italy almost thirty years before.

Luis Barragán

Luis Barragán (1902–88), from Guadalajara, Mexico, was self-trained and pursued a poetic vision of place-intensive design that incorporates traditional Mexican building materials and uses water so advantageously that it can stand comparison to Moorish work at the Alhambra in Spain (see Fig. 7.38). The many lava-wall houses that he designed for his own planned residential development called El Pedregal (1945–50) are composed using both white and intensely colored planes that provide privacy, often frame the sky, and unite interior space with the landscape. Modern in its results, Barragán's work is ultimately timeless and intensely personal. The focused simplicity of his El Bebedero (1959–62) in Las Arboledas (Fig. 16.9) yields a level of quietude rarely equaled.

Alvaro Siza

Portuguese architect Alvaro Siza (born 1933) graduated from the University of Porto with a degree in architecture. Among his buildings is the Galician Center of Contemporary Art (1985–92) in Santiago de Compostela, Spain, which incorporates the Modernist fusion of space, prevalent since architecture's early twentieth-century instruction by Cubist, Futurist, and Constructivist artists, and Adolf Loos's invention of the *Raumplan*. However, as a tangible object, the center speaks to its particular situation in a town whose rich pilgrimage tradition goes back to the Middle Ages. It stands on a down-slope below a seventeenth-century Baroque monastery (Fig. 16.10), of which Siza allowed glimpses from selected points within his building. While he abstractly composed his masses by paring them down into simple volumes, intersecting them, celebrating their connections, and leaving a seam of circulation in their midst, he also made them tangible, using

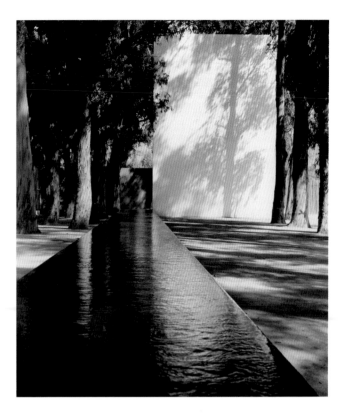

16.9 Luis Barragán, El Bebedero (drinking trough and fountain), Las Arboledas, Mexico City, 1959–62.
Water is a precious commodity in arid places like much of Mexico, and water has associations with life, rebirth, and renewal, meaning that though designated a "drinking trough," this mirror-like pool and its garden surroundings become an introspective landscape of reflection and contemplation. Compare this scene to Islamic or Moorish work such as the Patio of Myrtle Trees at the Alhambra in Spain (see Fig. 7.38).

local granite applied in a brindled pattern that speaks sympathetically to adjacent, lichen-covered, masonry walls. This affinity for site is amplified by the great care that Siza took in preserving, restoring, and supplementing the remains of the monastic gardens.

16.10 Alvaro Siza, Galician Center of Contemporary Art, Santiago de Compostela, Spain, 1985–92.
First, Siza related his building to the road, then he united the adjacent older convent, cloister, and church with his new museum by means of their shared landscapes, including monastic gardens. Just as there is a carefully shaped seam of space between the two structures, there is a corridor and interior court inside the museum and between the galleries.

Siza has also designed a number of structures for the Portuguese port town of Leça da Palmiera. On a coastline where grassy slopes erupt at the water's edge into craggy rock formations, he has built in concrete, stucco, wood planking, and heavy timber and with terracotta for roof tiles. The contrast of cool, white planar surfaces and warm interior finishes can be compared to Alvar Aalto's houses of the 1930s and Siza's organic site placements to those of Frank Lloyd Wright or of Charles Moore at Sea Ranch, which is discussed later in this chapter.

Samuel Mockbee and the Rural Studio

Samuel Mockbee (1944–2001) took his architecture conceptually and geographically to a place not chosen—or even considered—by anyone else. Imagining buildings through revelatory drawings and paintings, he transferred his architectural practice from Jackson, Mississippi to the middle of nowhere: Hale County in West Central Alabama. Here he conjured up from his collective teaching experiences the "Rural Studio," gave it a social conscience, gathered students from his alma mater, Auburn University, around him, and led them in the production of a small universe of authentic and even noble buildings, often using unorthodox, even salvaged, building materials, and, unlikely as it seems, became famous doing it.

Hale County was discovered by the outside world decades ago, when Walker Evans took pathos-evoking Great Depression-era photographs of it and James Agee wrote sympathetic but censorious prose about the conditions among its sharecropper poor, both black and white. Since that time, local grinding poverty has been mitigated only marginally, so it is hard to imagine a less likely place for an architect to seek out clients. But cobbling together university funding, state social-services assistance, and private and foundation contributions, and teaching and inspiring his students and making use of his own gift for turning life into art, Mockbee somehow did the undoable.

The Rural Studio's building types and construction methods include a hay-bale-wall residence; student housing constructed of compressed corrugated cardboard and partially clad in old license plates; a baseball field, a playground, a children's center, a boys-and-girls club; the list goes on, all the construction somehow both anonymous and intensely personal, all of it designed and built by the privileged without being patronizing or condescending. The question of individual authorship, that is, Mockbee's contributions versus those of his students, has been little talked about and appropriately so, as he seems to have accepted and encouraged the creative sensibilities of all those who were drawn to him.

Both the Mason's Bend Community Center (2000) in New Bern and the Yancey Chapel (1995) in Sawyerville illustrate these conditions. Like those of Mockbee's other buildings, the plans of these two are of little consequence, with the result that they are rarely shown in publications

16.11 Samuel Mockbee, Mason's Bend Community Center, New Bern, Alabama, 2000.
When Samuel Mockbee died in 2001 at the age of fifty-seven, the world lost one of its most original artist–architects. As modest evidence of this fact, the walls of this building are made of automobile windshields overlapped like shingles.

of Rural Studio work. The community center (Fig. 16.11), built by four thesis students, has walls made of rammed earth and a faceted roof of tin and Chevrolet Caprice windshields. It looks like an excavated archaeological site given a new protective canopy. The chapel, built by three students, is situated on a bluff, has a sway-back roof inspired by those on local collapsing barns and, as its principal wall material, donated tires packed with earth and reinforcing rods, wrapped in wire mesh, laid up like masonry, and covered with stucco. After passing by an existing cattle trough transformed by its altered context into an art installation, visitors proceed through a dimpled tire-canyon before entering the longitudinal chapel that is covered by a skeletal wooden roof, not without similarity to the chapel frames of Arkansas architect Faye Jones (1921–2004). Above the floor of scavenged slate, with a narrow channel of water running along one side, light enters at the ridge through a continuous skylight, and at the far end, beyond an altar assembled from scrap steel, the space extends out into the landscape, like a vacant pier into a calm sea. The whole building cost $15,000.

16.12 Kenzo Tange, Olympic Sports Complex, Tokyo, 1964.
The dragonlike apperception of this building is created by
steel-reinforced-concrete walls and a roof supported by steel
cables. The plan is a spiral, with arriving viewers drawn in
along the perimeter of the unwinding, dynamic geometry.

**16.13 (below) Fumihiko Maki, Kaze-no-Oka Crematorium near
Nakatsu, Japan, 1997.**
The octagonal crematorium rises up to the left, with other buildings
arranged so as to create a central courtyard. Like the best work of
Frank Lloyd Wright, this grouping appears to grow out of the land.

A REGIONAL MODERNISM
IN JAPAN

Traditional Japanese architecture was discussed in Chapter 4. A survey of the images reproduced there makes clear two of its limitations: a reliance on wooden construction and a scarcity of large buildings. While these conditions had changed to some extent by the end of World War II, it became clear to Japanese architects that they were faced with a challenge: how to synthesize traditional Japanese values and principles with modern political, economic, and technological realities; how to build in a country with limited natural resources; and how, living near a subduction plate off the country's Pacific coast, to prepare for earthquakes and tsunamis such as the devastating example that occurred in 2011.

Kenzo Tange

In 1949 Kenzo Tange (1913–2005) achieved notice early on with his competition-winning design for the Hiroshima Peace Center (1949–55), built in a city destroyed by an atomic bomb in World War II. Working most often with reinforced concrete and in a manner with obvious early affinities to the work of Le Corbusier, he had evolved a personal style by the time of his Kurashiki City Hall (1957–60) that expressed both continuity and newness and addressed the communal reconstruction of his country along democratic lines. His St. Mary's Cathedral (1961) and Olympic Sports Complex (Fig. 16.12) in Tokyo, the latter built for the 1964 games, are suspension structures in which Tange was able to define entry and movement sequences and create soaring spaces through logical responses to the laws of physics, while still acknowledging Japan's traditional, formal architectural language. Later in his career, he explored a kind of mechanistic architecture capable of growth and change. A group of younger Japanese architects, calling themselves the "Metabolists," further pursued this line of enquiry and proposed vast utopian schemes dependent on transcendent technologies such as large-scale standardized components plugged into enormous organizing infrastructures.

Fumihiko Maki

To some extent a rationalist and a student of Tange, Fumihiko Maki (born 1928) has embraced the scale of the individual, Japan's history-laden modern condition, and the fractured, noble incompleteness of the contemporary worldview. In a country where cremation is preferred over burial and in a manner that must be compared to the Woodland Cemetery in Stockholm (see Fig. 15.67), his Kaze-no-Oka (Hill of the Winds) Crematorium (1997) (Fig. 16.13) rises gently out of the ground on its site near the small southern Japan city of Nakatsu. Already extant there was a cemetery and some ancient burial mounds.

In their midst, Maki added his building, which contains a reception area with offices, the crematorium, and a hall for vigils and funeral services. The hall is a tilted brick octagon situated at the front of the overall structure and adjacent to a porte-cochère and forecourt, while the entrance vestibule behind it has a triangular plan created by conceptually swinging out the front wall of the crematorium. A placid courtyard with a reflecting pool and tall, surrounding concrete walls provides a serene core for the crematorium and its adjacent spaces.

Arata Isozaki

Arata Isozaki (born 1931) worked for Kenzo Tange from 1963 to 1973, encountered Metabolism, but did not embrace radical new technologies; over the course of his career he has pursued his own, sometimes idiosyncratic, sometimes ironic, interpretation of Modernism. His Kamioka Town Hall (1976–78) looks like an alien spacecraft that has improbably landed in this remote town in north-central Japan. His Fujima Country Club in Oita to the south (1974) has a porte-cochère elevation that alludes to Palladio's Villa Poiana and an enveloping copper roof with a form that would become almost his signature: the barrel vault (Fig. 16.14). For the Museum of Contemporary Art in Los Angeles (1981–86), he chose to repeat the barrel vault, add pyramids, and employ the Golden Section as a means, he said, for expressing the integration of

16.14 Arata Isozaki, Fujima Country Club, Oita, Japan, 1974.
While vaulted roofs like these became something of a fashion in the 1980s, they were quite original, even exotic, in Japan in the 1970s. That Isozaki insinuated Andrea Palladio into his design sources says something about today's "global village."

Eastern and Western cultures on the U.S. West Coast. Still present are references to Palladio, and the detailing is highly refined.

Tadao Ando

Tadao Ando (born 1941) is self-taught, never having studied architecture in a school or served an apprenticeship. Through a long process of external investigation and personal introspection, he has become one of the most successful form-makers of his generation. Consider, for instance, his Museum of Wood (1994) in the Mikata-gun forest northwest of Osaka. Here, a long, spinelike wooden path through a pristine forest connects a hollow, truncated cone, containing an exhibition hall and having

its inner and outer faces covered with horizontal, lapped boards, with a rotated concrete cube attached to a gatelike baffle-plane (Fig. 16.15). The heavy-timber construction inside the hall acknowledges traditional Japanese carpentry practices.

Ando's Modern Art Museum of Fort Worth, which opened in 2002, stands 100 yards northeast of Louis Kahn's Kimbell Art Museum, and a short ride from Renzo Piano's Nasher Sculpture Gallery in Dallas, both of which buildings are discussed later in this chapter. While it hardly seems obvious from the finished structure, Ando's conceptual sketches suggest that he used the Kimbell's building section as a starting point for his own design. He did finally produce a series of side-by-side pavilions, but their parallel arrangement seems unimportant when viewed on-site, and the area between his and Kahn's building is sympathetic to neither structure. Ando's museum works best where it addresses a large, L-shaped pool of water on its northeast side.

COUNTERPROPOSALS TO MODERNISM

We have already seen in this chapter's introduction that the monolith of Modernism began to show some hairline cracks immediately after World War II, and eventually heretics began to challenge the Modernist establishment openly. The most overt of these challenges came to be called Post-Modernism, whose first emissary was a young architect from Philadelphia.

Robert Venturi

Robert Venturi (born 1925) received his architectural education at Princeton and worked for Louis Kahn and Eero Saarinen, another architect discussed later in this chapter. In 1966 Venturi published what amounted to a Post-Modern architectural manifesto under the title *Complexity and Contradiction in Architecture*, which was hailed by architectural historian and commentator Vincent Scully, perhaps hyperbolically, as "the most important writing on the making of architecture since Le Corbusier's *Vers une Architecture* of 1923." In it, Venturi made the case for a non-straightforward, multivalued architecture. Roots for this shift in architectural thinking can be found in the cultural diversity manifested in political and social movements of the period; increased attention to vernacular architecture, stemming in part from Bernard Rudofsky's

16.15 Tadao Ando, Museum of Wood, Mikata-gun, Hyogo, Japan, 1994.
Seen from the air, this striking composition of circle, line, and square nested in a forest seems more like a monastery than a museum. The Japanese have a long history of expert woodworking, as can be seen in Chapter 4.

"Architecture without Architects" exhibition at MoMA in 1964; British Brutalism; and the unique work of Louis Kahn. Using a style that echoed the phraseology of earlier manifestos, he observed:

Architects can no longer afford to be intimidated by the puritanically moral language of orthodox Modern architecture. I like elements which are hybrid rather than "pure," compromising rather than "clean," distorted rather than "straightforward," ambiguous rather than "articulated," perverse as well as impersonal, boring as well as "interesting," conventional rather than "designed," accommodating rather than excluding, redundant rather than simple, vestigial as well as innovating, inconsistent and equivocal rather than direct and clear. I am for messy vitality over obvious unity. I include the non sequitur and proclaim the duality.

His book extolls the ambiguities, inconsistencies, and idiosyncrasies of Palladio, Michelangelo, Nicholas Hawksmoor, Sir John Soane, Edwin Lutyens, Alvar Aalto, and Le Corbusier, and glorifies Mannerist and Baroque architecture generally. Venturi equated the atmosphere, lighting effects, and theatrics of Las Vegas casinos with Counter-Reformation art. By celebrating the "ugly and ordinary" aspects of twentieth-century buildings, as exhibited in roadside strip developments, neon advertising signs, and billboards, he discarded the orderly purity and pristine character of Modernism in favor of pluralistic, often anonymously designed, and eminently practical populist work, dubbed by some detractors as the "New Banality." Venturi wittily restated the Miesian dictum "Less is more" as "Less is a bore."

When *Complexity and Contradiction in Architecture* was published, Venturi had actually built very little, although he had placed well in architectural competitions. His largest completed commission was the ninety-one-unit Guild House (1960–63) (Fig. 16.16), an apartment block for the elderly in Philadelphia, in which common building elements were used in pragmatic yet unconventional ways. Double-hung windows are overscaled, a gold-anodized, roof-mounted, non-functioning television antenna demarcates the central axis of the symmetrical façade, and a single polished granite column denotes the entranceway and contrasts with the white glazed brick around the door.

More famous, perhaps, is Venturi's 1962 house for his mother in Chestnut Hill, Pennsylvania. In this modest dwelling, he combined simplicity of external form with complexity of interior layout, and conventional symbols and elements with contradictory arrangements. For instance, while the building presents a bold gable end to the street, in the manner of a Shingle-style house, its landlord-green color and stucco finish speak a completely different architectural language.

16.16 Robert Venturi and John K. Rauch, Guild House, Philadelphia, Pennsylvania, 1960–63.
The architects celebrated the ordinary in this housing unit for the elderly. From the mundane signage to the false, gold-anodized television antenna and aluminum window frames, the building presents itself as an unapologetic product of mass culture.

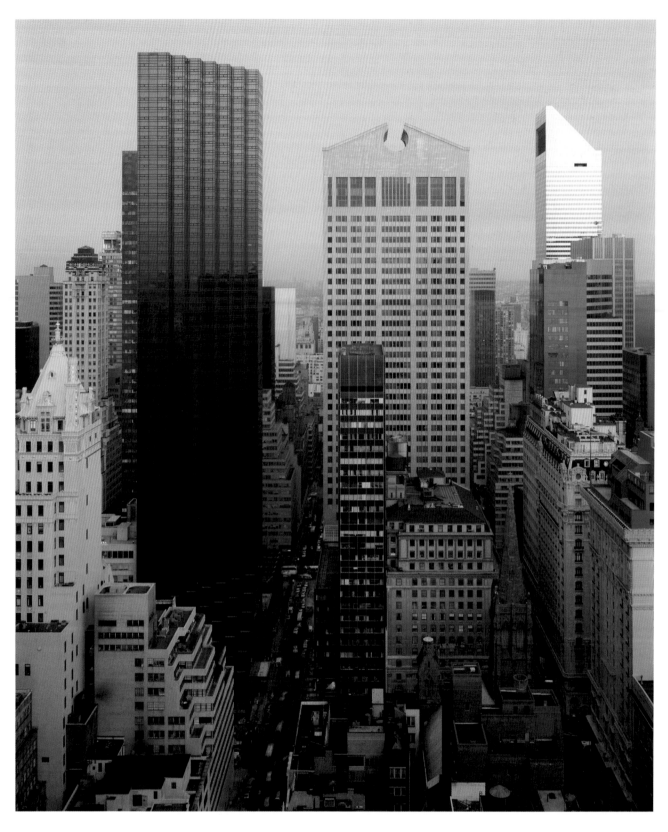

16.17 Manhattan looking east along 56th Street, 1984.
Left to right, one sees Trump Tower by Der Scutt, Swanke, Hayden, and Connell; the AT&T Building (now Sony Plaza) by Johnson/Burgee; and Citicorp by Hugh Stubbins Associates. With the AT&T Building and its references to architectural styles of the past, Philip Johnson broke completely with the Miesian tradition. In fact, his client said emphatically that the company did not want another Miesian box.

Venturi, working with his wife, Denise Scott Brown (born 1931), has continued to make controversial proposals. In 1986–91 their firm placed an addition, known as the Sainsbury Wing, on the National Gallery in London. They erected this building on a difficult site in Trafalgar Square near James Gibbs's St. Martin-in-the-Fields (see Fig. 12.56). It is highly erudite and somewhat self-effacing and much more complex internally than its principal façade would lead one to believe. It projects east from William

Wilkins's (1778–1839) museum, a competent building at best, erected in 1830, and faces Pall Mall East. Venturi and Scott Brown "adapted" it to its context by means of an accordionlike series of Corinthian reentrant pilasters; then other pilasters and an attached column more widely spaced; a related entablature and balustrade/parapet; various openings, some blind, some with surrounds; a discontinuous molding; and a grid of more modern windows, looking all in all to detractors like a bad remodeling of an existing building. In the end, the façade presents the same dilemma as much modern art: self-consciously contrived and unashamedly hermetic, it requires an almost painful effort from the public to understand it.

Philip Johnson

If Robert Venturi was the father of Post-Modernism, then Philip Johnson (1906–2000) was its godfather, though Johnson was discussed in the previous chapter for his actions on the behalf of Modernism. No twentieth-century architect has received more attention for historicism than has he, nor did any twentieth-century, brand-name architect practice or live longer, nor did any modern architect have a more varied or controversial career. (Johnson was dogged, for instance, by allegations that he had been a Nazi sympathizer.) We have seen in the previous chapter that, when a twenty-six-year-old graduate of Harvard with a degree in philosophy, he co-authored *The International Style: Architecture Since 1922* to accompany the 1932 MoMA exhibition on the International Style. While the exhibition was only modestly successful at the time, it eventually became the stuff of myth within the modern-architecture community, and Johnson's successful efforts to promote the new building style foreshadowed the persona of detached tastemaker that he would create for himself later in the century. In 1938 he entered the Harvard Graduate School of Design, then headed by Walter Gropius, and, once graduated, opened his own office, with the most prominent result being his own Mies-inspired glass house in New Canaan, Connecticut. By the late 1950s, however, he moved away from his strongly Miesian, International Style tendencies and produced a series of projects traceable to various sources, such as his Boissonas House in New Canaan (1956), which owes much to the domestic work of Louis Kahn. But it was twenty-one years later, in 1984, that Johnson took the center of the Post-Modernist stage with his AT&T Building (now Sony Plaza) in New York City (Fig. 16.17), designed in partnership with John Burgee. At its base is a giant Serliana, which has been compared by some to the façade of Brunelleschi's Pazzi Chapel (see page 286), and at its crown a broken pediment, which has been compared by some to a grandfather clock or a tall, eighteenth-century chest-of-drawers, meaning that Johnson has received less than consistent critical acclaim. Rather than his ability as a designer, it seems to have been his cleverness in garnering

media attention and his role as a power broker in the awarding of commissions and the selection of participants in exhibitions that made for his fame.

Charles Moore

While Philip Johnson was ironic, Charles Moore (1925–93) brought to Post-Modernism a gentle but studied playfulness that made his buildings immediately accessible to the public and professionals alike, and while Moore also took pleasure in historical allusions, he leavened them with more than a little whimsy. His critics have called his work superficial and ephemeral, while his supporters have called it refreshing. In 1963–65, at a time when he was practicing as a partner in Moore, Lyndon, Turnbull, and Whitaker (MLTW), he was a principal designer for Sea Ranch I, a set of ten contiguous condominium units on the coast north of San Francisco. On the exterior, the rough-hewn, redwood wall surfacing, long part of the Bay Area vernacular, produces a serene comment on regionalism and a statement about building in visual harmony with the environment. On the interior, each cubic unit is organized around an **aedicula**—four columns supporting a roof—that yields lighthearted and convivial, yet complex, spaces. Moore's Piazza d'Italia in New Orleans (1975–79) (Fig. 16.18), designed in collaboration with Perez Associates, consists of a flamboyant, sometimes irreverent, neon-outlined, wildly Neo-Classical, scenographic

16.18 Charles Moore, Piazza d'Italia, New Orleans, Louisiana, 1975–79.
Moore's work took on an almost carnival aspect with projects like this one, a fountain with backdrop for a developing New Orleans public space. Here, the classical language has become a medium for wit and glibness, as in the Mannerist compositions of sixteenth-century Italy.

backdrop for a contour map of Italy set in a pool of water that is demarcated by concentric rings of marble paving. It is as much spectacle as architecture, and its many details, such as the portrait of Moore's face in stainless steel spouting water like the fountain masks at the Villa d'Este near Rome, exhibit the kind of wit that became his personal and professional trademark.

Michael Graves

Michael Graves (born 1934) has described his work as "figurative," with the figural elements traceable to "classical and anthropomorphic sources." His earliest projects, particularly house additions in Princeton, New Jersey done while he was teaching at Princeton University, were

16.19 **Michael Graves, Elevation of the central portion of the Fargo-Moorhead Cultural Center Bridge, 1977.**
Graves's projects and drawing style were influential long before he had constructed many buildings. Here he created his version of Claude-Nicolas Ledoux's eighteenth-century river-keeper's house.

neo-Corbusian, but he soon began to explore new ground. Graves's unbuilt Fargo-Moorhead Cultural Center Bridge (1977) (Fig. 16.19) proposes broadcasting facilities and a concert hall on one bank of the Red river and a history museum on the other, all linked by an art museum spanning from Fargo, North Dakota, to Moorhead, Minnesota. At the conceptual level, imagery for the bridge is traceable principally to Ledoux's design for the Inspector's House at the Source of the River Loüe, but Graves transformed details such as keystones into windows and roof drains through a clever manipulation of the classical language. Graves's beautiful colored-pencil rendering of the bridge exhibits a lyricism that has become a constant in his work. The constructed Portland Building in Portland, Oregon (1980) (Fig. 16.20) is equally famous as a rendered elevation. It is replete with quotations from the classical language: the temples on the roof (never built), the giant keystone beneath them, the pair of fluted pilasters of indeterminate order, and the tiered stylobate at street level. Graves was also a force in reintroducing color into twentieth-century architecture, as here with the green base, terracotta-colored columns, and tan flanking walls punctured

MODERN CLASSICISM AND ONGOING TRADITIONALISM

While Michael Graves's mannered classical references were Post-Modern amusements, others in the late modern era have treated the classical language more reverently. The discussion of classical architecture—be it that of ancient Greece and Rome or any of its later reinventions from fifteenth-century Italy to eighteenth-century Enlightenment Europe and North America—has consumed much of this book. The popularity of classical elements among both the most knowing and innovative designers and the broader public speaks of the expressiveness, flexibility, and nuance of the classical language. But can or should Neo-Classicism or any other form of revivalism be a major part of the contemporary architectural scene? Some architects, like those discussed below, argue yes.

Aldo Rossi

Aldo Rossi (1931–97) graduated from the Politecnico di Milano and became a contributor to, then editor of, the journal *Casabella*. His buildings forgo any sense of their construction in favor of a Platonic universality of form. Modern in his elimination of ornament, Neo-Classical in his concern for architectural continuity, and urbanistic in his search for "collective memory," Rossi approached architecture through distinctive drawings that evoke a sense of mystery and timelessness as well as fantasy. His competition-winning scheme for the Cemetery of San Cataldo in Modena (Fig. 16.21), on which he worked from 1971 to 1984, consists of a large rectangular plot surrounded by a gable-roofed arcade, with repetitive, square openings in its friezelike upper reaches. Along the cemetery's central axis running the short dimension of the rectangle lies first a shrine in the form of a cube with an unbroken grid of windows in all four façades, all atop a subterranean columbarium (depository for ashes of cremated bodies), then a series of planar ossuaries (depositories for the bones of the dead) that form a triangle in both plan and section, and, finally, a truncated cone above the common grave for the homeless and abandoned. Rossi's 1972–76 elementary school in Fagnano Olona near Varese shares some of the cemetery's enigmatic sense of solitude yet somehow seems to be an appropriate setting for teaching the young. Rossi also received much attention for his analysis of urbanism in *L'Architettura della città* (*The Architecture of the City*, 1966).

Quinlan Terry

English architect Quinlan Terry (born 1937) has delved widely and deeply into his country's architectural past and to great popular acclaim, but his work has been decried by English Modernists and even compared unfavorably to that of his mentor and former partner Raymond

16.20 Michael Graves, Portland Building, Portland, Oregon, 1980.
It becomes almost a game with compositions such as this one to count all of the quasi-classical elements. Some of the appurtenances in Graves's published designs for the building, such as a flying figure and a rooftop village, were never realized.

by square windows. His Swan and Dolphin hotel projects (1987) at Disney World in Orlando, Florida demonstrate his ability to design at all scales from building to flatware. He first developed a master plan for the area, then designed the buildings to be placed around a crescent-shaped lake. The Dolphin Hotel has a diverse set of appurtenances in addition to its central Boullée-having-fun triangular façade and Napoleonic-Empire-one-better tented rotunda lobby. While only a pedant or an unreconstructed Modernist could fail to enjoy the place, one can question whether it has the staying power of the grand resort hotels of the late nineteenth and early twentieth centuries such as the Belleview-Biltmore in Belleair, Florida (1897), or the Grand Hotel on Mackinac Island, Michigan (1887). Much the same has been said about Post-Modernism in general by those looking on it disapprovingly.

16.21 Aldo Rossi, graphic rendering of Cemetery of San Cataldo, Modena, 1971–84.
Working in a country where the remains of the ancient Roman and Renaissance pasts lie around in abundance, it is not surprising that Italian architects continue to respect and reinterpret classicism. In Aldo Rossi's case, he sought not architectural fashion but a world of archetypal forms that aspire to display larger truths.

16.22 Quinlan Terry, Richmond Riverside Development, Surrey, England, 1984–87.
Seen here is a period landscape that never was. The buildings are either new or older ones given new fronts. While generally reflecting the manner of the eighteenth century, their styles and sources are varied.

Erith (1904–73), who taught him at the Architectural Association in London. His largest project is the Richmond Riverside Development (1984–87) (Fig. 16.22) on the river Thames in Surrey. Here, his designs for new shops, flats, restaurants, and car parks are indebted to Andrea Palladio (a Terry favorite), Bernini, Nicholas Hawksmoor, William Chambers, and various nineteenth-century English Gothic Revivalists. Depending on a visitor's point of view, the place is either a triumph of historical panache or a shallow historical pastiche.

In 2000 Colonial Williamsburg, Virginia brought Terry in to design façades for new buildings in its Merchants

Square, the principal downtown shopping area at the western end of Duke of Gloucester Street. Evaluations again vary, from laudable lesson in historical continuity to eighteenth-century Disney World.

Outspoken historian and critic David Watkin has praised Terry as the most able classicist in the Western World and one who "has attempted more completely than any other architect in Britain to pull the rug from beneath the false certainties of Modernism." What can be said without question is that the debate over the merits of historicism in a modern world is far from over.

Allan Greenberg

No one has embraced classicism in the modern era more completely and less apologetically than the American Allan Greenberg (born 1938 in South Africa), who graduated from Yale and worked for Jørn Utzon, whose work is discussed later in this chapter. He argues that classicism is modern because it expresses "eternal human values" and is "rooted in the physiology and psychology of the individual human being." Even those who disagree with his philosophy must admit that his detailing and appointments are exquisite and his compositions, if not original, are supple and confident. His Treaty Room for the U.S. Department of State (1986) (Fig. 16.23) was inserted into the State Department Building (1941, 1958) in Washington, D.C. T-shaped in plan, it consists of an elevator lobby with paired Doric columns and a coffered ceiling in the form of a shallow vault, leading to the elliptical treaty room with anterooms to each end. The ellipse contains paired Corinthian columns supporting a full entablature above a floor pattern inspired by the paving of Michelangelo's Campidoglio in Rome (see Fig. 11.39).

Robert A.M. Stern

Architect and architectural historian Robert A.M. Stern (born 1939) received his architectural education at Columbia and Yale and began his career as a Post-Modernist embracing the triad of **contextualism**, **allusionism**, and, in defiance of all Modernist standards, ornamentalism. Contextualism here refers to connections between buildings and their setting, as Post-Modern architects sought to link their work to established patterns, geometries, and possibilities for future growth, rather than conceiving of each design as an isolated object in the landscape, as they felt Modernists had done. Allusionism refers to buildings that are culturally accessible to their users. Early on, Stern quarried New England sources, producing, for instance, many convincing neo-Shingle-style houses. Less convincing but much published at the time of its construction is his Lang House (1973–74) (Fig. 16.24) in Connecticut with its pencil-thin, classically motivated label moldings applied almost like piping on the sleeve of a garment. Stern has moved on from such Post-Modernism

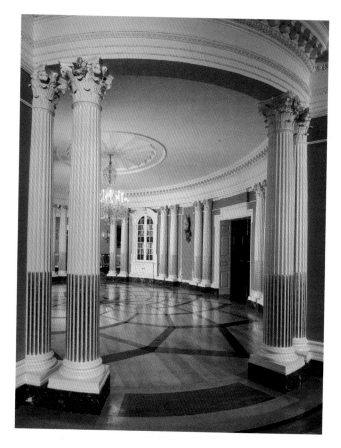

16.23 Allan Greenberg, Treaty Room, U.S. Department of State, Washington, D.C., 1986.
One can only describe this elliptical room as exquisite. It provides evidence of Greenberg's refined skill and taste and is a testament to the longevity of the classical language. The room shape can be compared to the oval room on the south side of the White House, which George Washington used for formal receptions.

16.24 Robert A.M. Stern, Lang House, Washington, Connecticut, 1973–74.
This house in the country has a cowboy-storefront-like façade, over which extended label moldings have been added like piped-on cake icing. This is Stern's early brand of classical allusionism.

16.25 (above) Robert A.M. Stern, George W. Bush Center, Dallas, Texas, 2012.
It is telling that a Republican—meaning politically conservative—former president chose to use Neo-Classical architecture as an expression of his legacy. Here, an abstracted classical portico supports a roof monitor in the form of an abstracted classical temple.

16.26 Léon Krier, Town of Poundbury, Dorset, England, 1988.
While such an aerial view does not allow for a ground-level appreciation of the humane scale sought by client and architect, it does make clear the close interaction of buildings and streets and the use of buildings to shape the kind of irregular spaces developed over time in traditional English villages.

to becoming perhaps the best-known American practitioner of a twenty-first-century traditionalism. For instance, his Newport Bay Club Hotel at Disneyland Resort Paris (1988–92) was successfully derived from classic resorts such as the Michigan Grand Hotel mentioned above. His more recent George W. Bush Center (2012) at Southern Methodist University in Dallas is a serene, quasi-classical composition at home to one side of a largely Neo-Classical campus (Fig. 16.25).

Léon Krier

Léon Krier was born in Luxembourg in 1946, received some architectural education in Germany, then moved to England, where he worked for, among others, James Stirling, whose career is discussed later in this chapter. He has championed the abandonment of consumer-driven, automobile-dominated sprawl, savaged the "disposable, adaptable, plug-in" city advocated by the Metabolists (described above), and disparaged the zoned Modernist city, promoted by the likes of Le Corbusier, in favor of the city as a "document of intelligence, memory, and pleasure." In 1988, on 400 acres of land owned by the Duchy of Cornwall, Prince Charles (an architectural dilettante or a savior of the built environment, depending on which critic you ask) chose Krier to design the model new town of Poundbury (Fig. 16.26) in the southern English county

of Dorset. It was to be a socially inclusive and sustainable village of 5000 residents, with its architecture following traditional Dorset models and its scale conducive to walking. Opened to occupancy in 2000, it has roads that gently curve and meander, as well as courts and squares that invite community interaction. A Poundbury Building Code ensures the continuity of traditional materials and forms and an appropriately humane scale.

Andres Duany and Elizabeth Plater-Zyberk

In 1981 Yale and Princeton graduates Andres Duany (born 1944) and Elizabeth Plater-Zyberk (born 1950) produced Seaside (Fig. 16.27), a coastal residential community in the Panhandle of Florida. Their instrument of control was the design standard they called a "Traditional Neighborhood Development Ordinance," with an emphasis on the "Traditional." With this project, they established a design

16.27 Andres Duany and Elizabeth Plater-Zyberk, Seaside coastal residential community, Florida, 1981.
Following the wishes of developer Robert Davis, Andres Duany and Elizabeth Plater-Zyberk sought an architecture based on local building traditions for their planned town called Seaside. To this end, they created detailed design guidelines but did not impose a specific architectural style. Some critics, however, have seen this unity as artificial and divorced from reality.

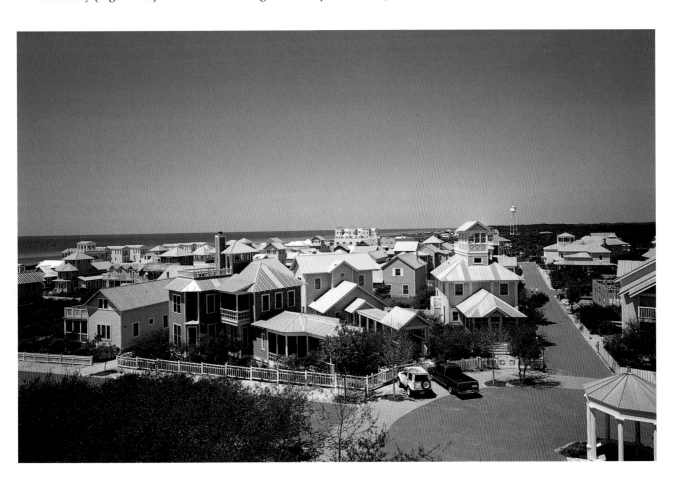

philosophy that has become known as the New Urbanism, meaning somewhat contradictorily an urbanism drawn from historical patterns. Duany and Plater-Zyberk have been lightning rods for urbanistic controversy, with opinions on their design proposals diverging wildly. Some have accused them of social engineering because of the prescriptive nature of their ordinances. Others dismiss their architectural ensembles as artificial, nostalgic villages for the well-to-do. While both views contain elements of truth, few would argue that Modernism has produced more than its share of ugly, failed urban environments, and since Jane Jacobs's *Death and Life of Great American Cities*, with its stinging criticism of Modernism and its handmaiden, urban renewal, appeared in 1961, few have pretended there was not a problem. Duany and Plater-Zyberk press on with their solution to this dilemma and have now designed more than 200 communities.

DECONSTRUCTION

Post-Modernism has also included within its boundaries work described as Deconstructivist. In 1988 the wily and perceptive Philip Johnson assembled a Deconstructivist exhibition at MoMA, but it was fraught with controversy even before it opened and was showered with constant criticism afterward because of the vagaries of Deconstruction's meaning and relevance. Included in the exhibition was the work of Frank Gehry and Zaha Hadid, both discussed elsewhere in this chapter, and Peter Eisenman (born 1932) and Bernard Tschumi (born 1944), who has said of his Parc de la Villette in Paris (1982–85) (Fig. 16.28) that it explores the disjunctures in culture, emphasizing fragmentation and dissociation rather than traditional unity and synthesis. Post-Modern analyst Charles Jencks sums up his view of Deconstruction this way, describing it as principally iconoclastic:

> Deconstruction . . . always depends for its meaning on that which is previously constructed. It always posits an orthodoxy which it "subverts," a norm which it breaks, an assumption and ideology which it undermines. And the minute it loses this critical role, or becomes a dominant power itself (as in so many academies), it becomes a tyrannical bore. The same is true of Deconstructionist architecture: it works best as an exception within a strongly defined norm.

The work of Peter Eisenman certainly fits Jencks's description. He is an architect who has reinvented himself more times than Philip Johnson, and like Johnson has exhibited a genius for self-promotion. In a career driven by an almost maniacal extraction of ideas from the then-current cultural milieu in areas as diverse as linguistics and the potential geometries created by fractals, Eisenman has honed his image as a provocateur and man of intellect among lesser

16.28 Bernard Tschumi, *Folie*, Parc de la Villette, Paris, 1982–85.
The Parc de la Villette is intended to be an open-air cultural center with space for workshops, gymnasium and bath facilities, playgrounds, exhibitions, concerts, and more. Each *folie* is an undifferentiated, neutral object in the landscape where designated activities can take place.

minds. Some criticize his work as contrived and opportunistic, while others see it as endlessly investigative and serious to the point of tragedy. He first became known for the series of houses, most of them unbuilt, that he designed in the late 1960s and early 1970s (Fig. 16.29). While they respond to complex programs based upon both individual and societal issues, they are outwardly formalistic experiments using colliding and interlocking geometries that seem only self-referential; Eisenman touted them as linguistic-architectural inquiries into the basic grammar and syntax of space.

With artist Richard Serra, Eisenman won a design competition for the Holocaust Memorial in Berlin, completed in 2004. Located a block south of the Brandenburg Gate on a site that once accommodated offices for Nazi propagandist Joseph Goebbels and later became part of the no-man's-land adjacent to the Berlin Wall, it consists of 2711 stone pillars of varying heights set on a grid plan. The result is a mute city of stelae, a cogent abstraction simultaneously claustrophobic and expansive.

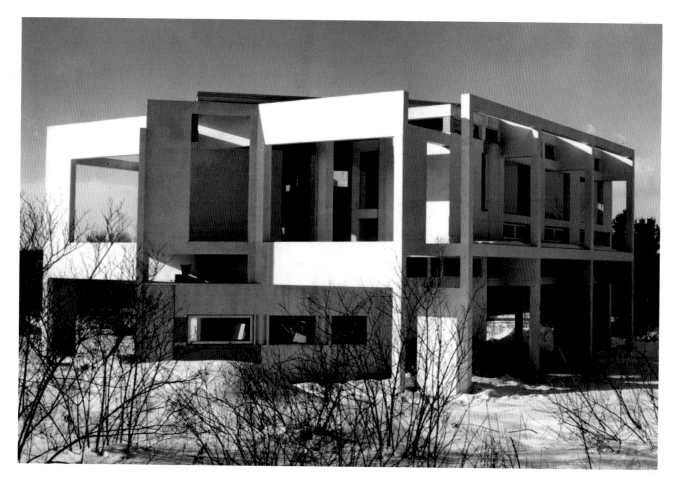

16.29 Peter Eisenman, House III, Lakeville, Connecticut, 1969–71. In the 1960s, Peter Eisenman explored the abstract possibilities of rotated grids. Spaces became an effect caused by the manipulation of selected elements according to a set of rules.

MODERN FORM-MAKERS

As quoted in the previous chapter, Le Corbusier wrote that "Architecture is the masterly, correct, and magnificent play of masses brought together in light." While the work in this next section certainly resulted from a broad range of conditions, and the buildings are commensurately diverse, all of them display an abiding interest in "masses brought together in light," or, put more simply, form. Some of their designers have even been described as "formalists," meaning that they have been concerned with form for its own sake.

Louis I. Kahn

The work of Louis I. Kahn (1901–74) represents the fusion of seemingly contradictory sources. In 1905 his family immigrated to the United States from the small Russian island of Saarama in the Baltic Sea. He received a Beaux-Arts-influenced architectural education at the University of Pennsylvania, where he learned to create symmetrical, hierarchically arranged compositions and to produce monumentality, even in everyday circumstances. In so doing, he somehow became able to render the common uncommon, and the uncommon transcendent.

The medieval vernacular forms of Italian hilltowns inspired Kahn in his design for the Richards Medical Research Building (1957–61) at the University of Pennsylvania (Fig. 16.30). The medical laboratories are square, open-plan, glass-walled spaces stacked into towers. Pairs of columns set to each side support the structural grid of each floor, while ducts, mechanical services, elevators, and stairs are set in attenuated brick shafts. By wedding this straightforward functional planning with a picturesque massing, Kahn created one of the most influential architectural compositions of the 1960s.

Kahn also absorbed some Modernist principles, and he traveled in Europe, where Greek temples, ancient Roman construction systems, and the works of Brunelleschi created lasting impressions on him. He admired the simple geometries of Boullée and Ledoux, and considered these men to have been as important to architecture as Johann Sebastian Bach was to music. Among Kahn's often poetic writings, one finds the following: "Spirit in will to express/ Can make the great sun seem small/ The sun is/ Thus the Universe/ Did we need Bach/ Bach is/ Thus music is/ Did we need Boullée/ Did we need Ledoux/ Boullée is/ Ledoux is/ Thus Architecture is." Inspired by such poetic visions

Fresh air intake stacks

Laboratory animals

Laboratory animals

Medical laboratory

Plenum

Plenum

Medical laboratory

Lobby

Medical laboratory

Exhaust stacks

0   20 m

0   60 ft

N

16.30 Louis Kahn, Plan of the Richards Medical Research Building, University of Pennsylvania, Philadelphia, 1957–61. This plan illustrates Kahn's conception of servant and served spaces. The medical laboratories are served by the stairtowers and fume exhaust stacks, or plenums. The functional towers and stacks all become elements in a picturesque composition.

as well as by a high regard for rational construction, Kahn imbued structural forms such as the arch and vault with a mystical, even sublime quality and made them metaphors for the human condition.

Probably no twentieth-century building has become more of a pilgrimage site for admiring architects than Kahn's Salk Institute for Biological Sciences (1959–65) in La Jolla, California. A unique situation for him where his client, Dr. Jonas Salk, had as profound a vision as did the architect, the project began with a **parti**, or design sketch, indicating a split between laboratories at one end and a place for community at the other. It evolved to have a configuration not unlike Thomas Jefferson's University of Virginia campus (see Fig. 13.40), with the lawn becoming a paved plaza between canted, concrete faces of laboratory towers, all ennobled by a narrow, linear seam of water leading to the ocean and the horizon (Fig. 16.31).

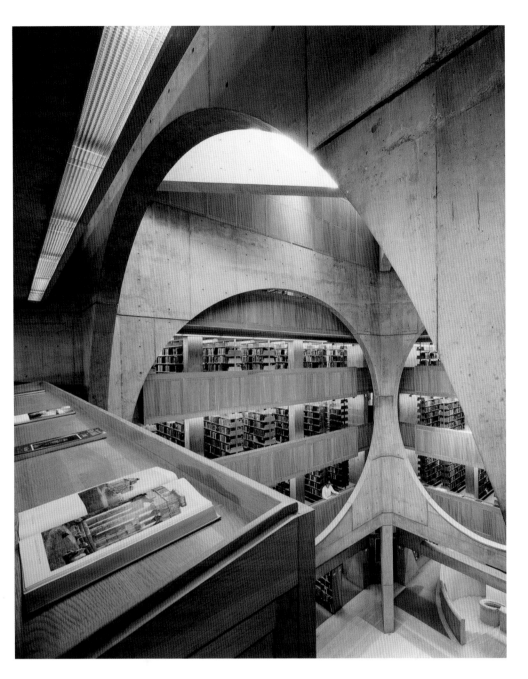

16.31 (opposite bottom) Louis Kahn, Salk Institute for
Biological Sciences plaza, La Jolla, California, 1959–65.
As much a poet—or even a mystic—as an architect, Louis Kahn
was interested in expressing the eternal rather than the transitory.
Here in La Jolla, California, he did so by framing the plane of the
earth, an axial water channel, and an expanse of sky between
rhythmically receding concrete towers.

16.32 (above) Louis Kahn, Library interior, Phillips Exeter
Academy, Exeter, New Hampshire, 1967–72.
Kahn admired imperial Roman architecture and here sought
to capture both the period's monumentality and the rich
layering seen in such complexes as Hadrian's Villa.

The influence of French rational Neo-Classicism is
manifest in Kahn's designs for the National Assembly of
Bangladesh in Dhaka (1962–74). The building is composed of ideal geometric forms, circles and squares,
expressed volumetrically as prisms, and its layering of
spaces recalls buildings at Hadrian's Villa. A similar treatment is found inside the library of Phillips Exeter Academy
(1967–72) in Exeter, New Hampshire, where the essentially square building is dominated by a cubical volume
at the center (Fig. 16.32). Huge circular cutouts provide
vistas into the library stacks on the surrounding floors in a

manner reminiscent of Giovanni Battista Piranesi's *Carceri*
engravings, discussed in Chapter 13.

Kahn was never more successful than in his design for
the Kimbell Art Museum in Fort Worth, Texas (1966–72).
In his site plan, one enters into a court through a grove of
trees, with reflecting pools to each side. He chose as his
spatial and structural unit an apparently barrel-vaulted bay,
which is actually covered by a pair of cantilevers meeting at
a continuous skylight (Figs. 16.33–16.34). Kahn placed sixteen of these units side by side in three ranks (Fig. 16.35),
combining many spatially by replacing the load-bearing

walls with longitudinal beams. As materials he chose poured-in-place concrete, travertine, oak, and stainless steel, all bathed in natural light, with much of it reflected by baffles beneath the skylights. The spaces are ancient Roman in their monumentality, gravity, and exquisite finishes, yet humane in their combined effect. A half-underground addition by Renzo Piano is now underway.

Kahn was a late bloomer, emerging as an original voice in American architecture only in his late fifties. Looking at his body of work, one can make the argument that he was the most original architect of the twentieth century. Kahn's son has produced and directed a film about his father titled *My Architect* (2003), which sheds much light on Kahn's life and serves as a kind of parallel universe to his work.

Jørn Utzon

Jørn Utzon (1918–2008) studied at the Royal Danish Academy of Fine Arts and worked for Erik Gunnar Asplund, who is discussed in Chapter 15, among others. When he won the competition for the Sydney (Australia) Opera House (Fig. 16.36) in 1957, he immediately became one of the world's most well-known architects. However, immense problems with its construction and associated cost overruns stigmatized him on the international scene, even though the completed building, with its "billowing," sail-like, parabolic, post-tensioned, concrete shells set atop

16.33 Louis Kahn, Kimbell Art Museum, Fort Worth, Texas, 1966–72.
Almost sepulchral in character, the apparently barrel-vaulted units house the museum galleries. Where necessary, Kahn opened them up, as in the external passage or porch in the foreground.

16.34 (opposite top) Louis Kahn, Kimbell Art Museum interior, Fort Worth, Texas, 1966–72.
Kahn's modular units are not really barrel-vaulted, as the summit of each intrados is a void into which a baffled skylight has been inserted. The structural system is actually repetitive double-cantilevered butterfly canopies.

16.35 (opposite) Louis Kahn, Plan of the Kimbell Art Museum, Fort Worth, Texas, 1966–72.
One would hardly anticipate the spatial richness of Kahn's interiors from the simple geometry of his plan. This richness is amplified by the elegance of the building materials: silver-gray concrete, travertine, natural-finish wood, and stainless steel.

Gallery

Entrance court

Sculpture Garden

Gallery

Gallery

16.34

Entrance gallery

Bookshop

Library

Gallery

Gallery

Service

Cafeteria

Theater

Parking

0   50 m
0   150 ft

N

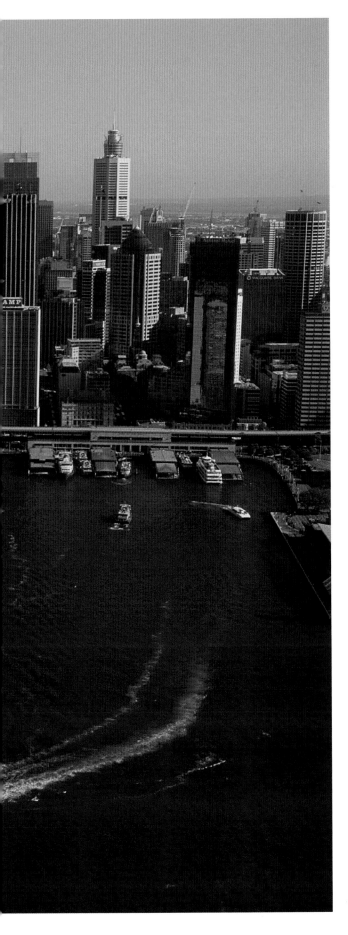

platforms of Pre-Columbian inspiration, has become virtually the symbol for Australia. Utzon should not be known, however, only as the originator of one profound building idea. Particularly successful is his Bagsvaerg Church (1976), with its disciplined orthogonal plan, oscillating, thin-shell-concrete ceiling, exquisite masonry detailing, and Nordic luminosity. With his design for the Dunker Cultural Center (2002) in Helsingborg, Sweden, Utzon, by then eighty-four years old, received renewed media attention for a lifetime of architectural accomplishments.

Ove Arup

Solving the complex engineering problems presented by the Sydney Opera House in 1957–63 brought international acclaim to the firm now known as Arup Associates, which operates around the world and is cited multiple times throughout the remainder of this chapter. Arup Associates now has some 8000 employees and many principals, but its trajectory was set by its founder, Ove Arup (1895–1988). Arup was the child of a Danish father and Norwegian mother. He was born in England in Newcastle upon Tyne and trained first in philosophy and mathematics, then in engineering: from this breadth of inclination and education proceeded his determined effort to avoid hermetic specialization in favor of multidisciplinary cooperation. In the 1930s he joined CIAM, of which he was the only engineer member, and established friendships with such Modernists as Le Corbusier and Walter Gropius. While working for others, Arup participated in the design of such celebrated Modernist projects as the Penguin Pool at the London Zoo (1933–34) and the Highpoint I apartments (1933–35), both designed by Berthold Lubetkin (1901–90). He founded Ove Arup, Consulting Engineers in London in 1946 and did work for, among others, Alison and Peter Smithson. In 1963, and then including architect Peter Dawson, the firm became Arup Associates. In the current era, when the lion's share of a project's costs pays only for electrical, mechanical, and structural systems, the need for technical designers determined to produce "delight" as well as "firmness" and to do so innovatively is undeniable. Arup Associates is arguably the best in the world at this, because of its highly creative, open-minded work environment and emphasis on breadth as well as depth of knowledge.

16.36 Jørn Utzon, Sydney Opera House, Sydney, 1957–73.
With downtown Sydney in the background, the sail-like roofs of the Opera House rise above tiered platforms on a paved peninsula. No modern building has become a more visible architectural symbol for a country than this one.

The Boston City Hall

In the late 1960s no building made a greater impact on the American architectural scene than the Boston City Hall (Fig. 16.37), its 1962 competition-winning design submitted by Gerhard Michael Kallmann (born 1915) and Noel Michael McKinnell (born 1935) together with Edward F. Knowles (born 1929), the former two then faculty members and the latter a student at Columbia University. Somewhat shocking today in its aggressive posture facing the figuratively cowering eighteenth-century Faneuil Hall, it presents an immediately legible façade composition. Three-part, like a classical column or a sonata, it absorbs pedestrians at a largely transparent lower level, ensconces government officials and bodies in a middle range of sculptural protrusions, and fixes workers in repetitive bays of offices defined by vertical fins and collectively producing a terminating cornice. Its compositional similarity to Le Corbusier's Ste. Marie-de-la-Tourette monastery (see Figs. 15.88–15.89) is obvious. Some have talked recently of demolishing the Boston City Hall, which dramatizes the low esteem in which such Modernist icons are often held by the public.

Justus Dahinden

If architects in Japan have been challenged by the need to maintain continuity with historical traditions while addressing modern issues, architects working in Africa have been even more so. A particularly successful result of such an effort is the Mityana Pilgrims Shrine (1983) in Uganda, north of Lake Victoria, designed by the Swiss architect Justus Dahinden (born 1925). His use of tinted, poured-in-place concrete recognizes the long-established African adobe building tradition, as do the relatively unarticulated

16.37 (above) Gerhard Michael Kallmann, Noel Michael McKinnell, and Edward F. Knowles, Boston City Hall, Boston, built 1968. This building is now almost old enough to be eligible for listing on the National Register of Historic Places. It may need such a designation of significance, as much of the public has remained skeptical about modern architecture to the point that some now advocate the city hall's demolition.

16.38 (left) Justus Dahinden, Mityana Pilgrims Shrine, Uganda, 1983. Conceptually, this building could once have been a hemisphere, its sections now disengaged to reveal its inner workings. Built of concrete, it can nonetheless be interpreted within Africa's long tradition of adobe construction (see for instance Figs. 10.56 and 10.57).

but dramatic building volumes (Fig. 16.38). The complex building program included a parish hall, presbytery, and Carmelite convent as well as a school and social center. Because the church is dedicated to three African martyrs, Dahinden raised up three, tall segments of spheres, each based on a quadrant-of-a-circle plan, housing a chapel, a confessional, and a baptistery. The central worship space is covered by a horizontal volume with a ribbon window and a skylight above the altar. It would be hard to imagine this precise and rational but slightly mysterious building existing anywhere other than Africa. While firmly planted there, it reflects Dahinden's eclectic influences, from the Japanese Metabolists to the German Expressionist Rudolf Steiner to African Bantu religious structures.

Frank Gehry

Frank Gehry (born 1929) has succeeded in having a host of designs that would have once seemed destined to remain as models or conceptual drawings actually built. He has been strongly influenced by artists, many of whom are his close friends. Early in his career he realized, as have many other architects, that he often preferred buildings in an incomplete state of construction to the finished products because of their openness and incompleteness. While most would have left it at that, Gehry began to design new buildings, with an obvious kinship to Russian Constructivist work, that seem frozen in a state of becoming. His own,

much-published house in Santa Monica, California (1977–78) is a case in point. Its ribbed metal siding, chain-link fencing, and unpainted wood, all pouring forth from a seemingly bewildered early twentieth-century bungalow behind, make the composition look as much like an active construction site as an occupied structure. Then Gehry began to explode buildings, breaking them up into discrete volumes in a way that, to some, reflects the fragmentation in modern society, which placed him temporarily in the Deconstructionist camp. His Winton Guest House, built in Wayzata, Minnesota (1983–86) and now relocated to the grounds of the University of St. Thomas's Daniel C. Gainey Conference Center in Owatonna, Minnesota (where Louis Sullivan built one of his celebrated small-town banks), originally stood adjacent to and so could be advantageously viewed from a main house designed in 1952 by Philip Johnson. Gehry somewhat awkwardly but powerfully arranged a set of very sculptural forms—one vaultlike, one a shed-roofed box, the others boxes with flat roofs—around a central truncated pyramid. His objective, he said, was to create a building with a "certain amount of humor and mystery and fantasy."

Gehry's Nationale Nederlander office building in Prague, in the Czech Republic, is known locally as the "Dancing House" (1997) (Fig. 16.39). Here, within a historic context, he took movement as his theme for a corner-sited building that twists and projects in space with an energy expressive of the opening up of eastern Europe since

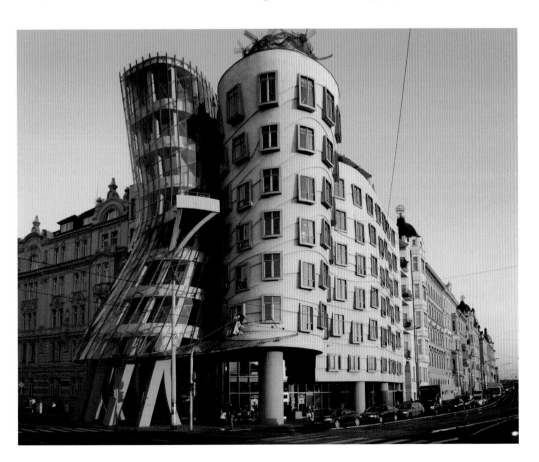

16.39 Frank Gehry, Nationale Nederlander ("Dancing House"), Prague, 1997.
Taken out of context, this building perhaps appears shocking. However, it actually fits quite well among its neighbors. The nearby curving gables, spiky towers, and richly textured façades convey the same energy and urban liveliness as Gehry's intervention.

16.40 Frank Gehry, Guggenheim Museum Bilbao, Bilbao, 1997.
No recent building has garnered more attention in the popular press or been a more popular site for architectural pilgrimages. Visitors love to touch its shiny skin of titanium.

the dissolution of the Soviet Union. Economic constraints called for one more floor than in neighboring buildings, but accommodated within the same cornice height. In order to resolve the conflict, Gehry lowered and camouflaged the floor levels by means of fishscalelike undulating layers of cement plaster and displaced windows.

Gehry's Guggenheim Museum Bilbao in Spain (opened 1997) (Fig. 16.40) has aroused a kind of popular and critical interest equaled by few other twentieth-century constructions. His exhilarating structure replaced dock facilities on a site adjacent to the Nervión river in a gritty manufacturing city. Out of a four-story mass blossom "pleated petals" of titanium attached to a steel frame. The museum acts as a mirror, reflecting and absorbing the city, reflecting and absorbing itself. Giving off a metallic luminescence, it hovers and shimmers at the end of hard-edged

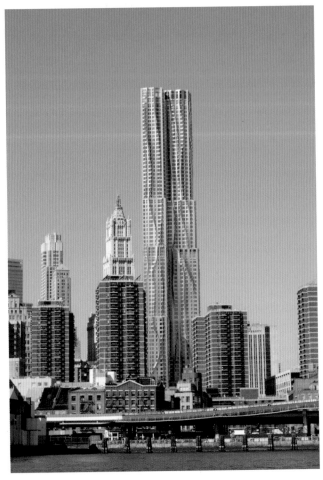

16.41 Frank Gehry, 8 Spruce Street, New York City, 2011.
The rippling skin of this tower gives it distinctiveness even in tower-rich Manhattan. The shorter structure behind and immediately to the left of it is Cass Gilbert's Woolworth Building of 1913, which has much-admired Gothic detailing.

urban vistas. Visitors have come to Bilbao in droves, more to see the building than its contents. They want to be in it and around it, and they want to touch it. In the complex first-floor plan, where the only orthogonal spaces house mechanical systems, the loading dock, and storage and exhibition-preparation rooms, a towering central atrium connects to an auditorium and galleries, one of them a trapezoid, one L-shaped, and the largest one a long and narrow boatlike giant that passes beneath the Puente de la Salve, the major road through Bilbao, as it reaches out to the east beside a free-form water garden. On the second and third floors, the plan becomes more regular, including a series of square galleries placed in an enfilade arrangement. The space inside the atrium (see page 514) is enormous, half as tall again as Wright's Guggenheim rotunda, with bowing steel, angular stone-faced walls, and undulating masses cut away to admit light; it is the fulfillment of a Baroque spatial dream made possible by modern building and computer technology.

With Bilbao, Gehry became a so-called "starchitect," meaning one whose buildings bring status to his clients and their communities, and his production thereafter was considerable, if slightly predictable. This changed, however, with his first New York City skyscraper, the luxury residential tower at 8 Spruce Street (2011) (Fig. 16.41), which has been described by some as the city's best tall building of the last fifty years. It rises up seventy-six stories in lower Manhattan, where it holds its own with Cass Gilbert's (1859–1934) iconic 1913 Woolworth Building. At its base there is a grammar school, which is clad in orange brick. The tower above is covered with more than 10,000 stainless-steel panels, many of them strategically bulging and so giving the impression that a conventional building has been draped with a giant folded and gathered cloth.

Richard Meier

Cornell University graduate Richard Meier (born 1934) has continued the early directions of Modernism. While his architecture owes an obvious debt to Le Corbusier's houses of the 1920s, as in his use of cubical massing relieved by gentle curves, he also claims to have been influenced by the spatial layering and light quality of Baroque interiors and by such works as Wright's Guggenheim Museum (see Figs. 15.81–15.82). Qualities abstracted from these and other sources include columnar planning grids with clearly expressed building skins enclosing volumetric space; planar elements that slice through masses and penetrate one another; and impeccable white-panel exteriors comparable to the late works of the Austrian Secessionists Josef Hoffmann and Otto Wagner.

The results of this approach can be seen in Meier's design for the Museum für Kunsthandwerk (Museum of Decorative Arts) in Frankfurt, Germany, which won a limited competition in 1980 and was completed in 1983 (Fig. 16.42). Although nominally an addition to an old

16.42 Richard Meier, Axonometric drawing of the Museum für Kunsthandwerk, Frankfurt, 1980–83. Meier graduated from Cornell University at a time when its design studios were dominated by the compositional manipulations celebrated in Colin Rowe and Fred Koetter's *Collage City*. This building seems to be ideally viewed in a bird's-eye axonometric drawing such as this one.

villa containing the existing museum, Meier's building is nearly ten times larger than the Neo-Classical original and, except for a second-floor glass-enclosed connector, it stands free of it in an L-shape. The position of the villa and the angle of the frontage road paralleling the Main river prompted Meier to indulge in two overlapping grid systems set at an angle of 3.5 degrees to one another. While such a minor shift is imperceptible in reality (unless the museumgoer commonly notes slight misalignments in normally orthogonal building materials), the two grids are distinctly seen in the plan drawings, and their interaction obviously inspired Meier to employ room shapes that would otherwise have seemed arbitrary. Le Corbusier-style regulating traces were overlaid on elevation studies to show that both the villa and the new building have similar proportions; a module derived from the older building relates to basic quadrants in the addition. Panels cover the exterior and align with square mullions in the generously sized windows.

Meier employed a similar vocabulary in the High Museum (1981–84) (Fig. 16.43) in Atlanta, Georgia. He disengaged the continuous ramp of the Guggenheim Museum and made it the dominant circulation path around the circumference of a quarter-cylinder glass-enclosed atrium, off which he arranged more conventional orthogonal galleries, which have artificial illumination.

16.43 Richard Meier, High Museum, Atlanta, Georgia, 1981–84.
This art museum stands along Peachtree Street. The ramp in the foreground takes visitors to the bulging entry vestibule, then into the three-story, switchback-ramped rotunda that gives access to the gallery floors.

Whereas the ramp in the Frankfurt museum is immediately adjacent to gallery displays, in the Atlanta museum their separation isolates the art from the building's most interesting architectural feature. The conditions most curators demand for the display of paintings are in part responsible for this decision. Strong sunlight quickly deteriorates pigments, so works of art need to be kept in controlled lighting conditions.

Meier's billion-dollar Getty Museum (1984–97) in West Los Angeles spreads out in the form and at the scale of a Modernist hilltown. For the outside walls, he combined his signature modular porcelain-enameled panels with equally modular but textured stone. A circular garden by landscape architect Robert Irwin (born 1928) suggests the island enclosure at Hadrian's Villa.

Antoine Predock

Antoine Predock (born 1936) has created a body of work with a decidedly spiritual-become-extraterrestrial quality, none of it more arresting than his American Heritage Center and Art Museum in Laramie, Wyoming (Fig. 16.44), a place where winds have been known to topple semi-trailers and temperatures casually plunge to negative

16.44 Antoine Predock, American Heritage Center and Art Museum, University of Wyoming, Laramie, Wyoming, 1993.
Designing a building for the stern and frequently hostile landscape of Wyoming offers a special set of challenges. Everything about this building's form, from the canted cone to the low, windowless wing, speaks of protection from the elements.

While this would seem to be a conventional view from the
narthex, entry into this church is actually made at the far altar
end and to the right of the visible frame. Tapestries hang on
the side walls.

numbers. Only with this context in mind does the appropriateness of Predock's building become clear. As seen from the parking lot, a truncated cone rises up, evoking multiple associations: a Native American hogan or tipi, the surrounding mountain peaks, a spaceship. It is egg-shaped in plan, contains a reception area and myriad other small spaces, and is connected to a long, orthogonal wing that houses galleries, a library, and offices. When experienced from within and at its base, with mountains seen through broad windows in panorama, the building evokes a sense of geological time, and the skin of the cone, made of black-patinated copper, is penetrated by apertures that align with the cardinal points and certain astronomical phenomena, evoking even a sense of cosmic time.

Rafael Moneo

Rafael Moneo (born 1937) worked at one time for Jørn Utzon, before returning to his native Spain. In 1986 he completed the National Museum of Roman Art in Mérida, which merges antique and modern forms as well as construction methods. Built using load-bearing brick walls and arches that support reinforced-concrete floors, it stands directly atop archaeological remains in a city founded by the emperor Augustus. On the exterior, Moneo employed large expanses of Roman-brick relieving arches, more as wall articulation than as a method for transferring loads. On the interior, an axial series of arched openings is braced by the floor plates, their huge scale broken down only by linear steel handrails. The effect is comparable to that in the Baths of Diocletian in Rome, where vast, vaulted interior spaces house Roman antiquities (and a church; see Fig. 5.27) in a setting that is spare yet rich in visual experiences.

Moneo's Roman Catholic Cathedral of Our Lady of the Angels opened in Los Angeles in 2002. It has been met with more than a little criticism, which demonstrates yet again how skeptical the public remains about the ongoing Modernist program. Even some in the architectural press have found it to have awkward moments and to be inconsistently successful in making the traditional cathedral a modern monument—a tall order. As for successes, its tawny shingle-patterned exterior walls of carefully formed, poured, and cured concrete welcome the brilliant Southern California sunlight and more than hold their own adjacent to a depressed but roaring freeway and near to Frank Gehry's highly aggressive and reflective Disney Concert Hall (1999–2003). The plan of the nave looks like a much larger and more symmetrical Ronchamp pilgrimage chapel (see Figs. 15.86–15.87) but is wrapped in a U-shaped, reverse-oriented ambulatory. This configuration is made necessary by Moneo's unorthodox but highly successful decision to have the faithful enter at the eastern end, adjacent to but obscured from the chancel, then move down a wide, limestone-floored corridor, alongside chapels on the right and a tall concrete exterior wall on the left, until they reach an imported Baroque retable, or decorative altar screen, then turn right to enter the nave or move beyond and down the opposite corridor. Within the nave (Fig. 16.45), the wooden ceiling suggests the suspended hull of a ship, with clerestory lighting to each side beneath it, and still lower, depicting "everyday parishioners," hang photorealistic tapestries that possess an undeniable gravity even if some have criticized them as near-kitsch. Built in a well-known earthquake zone with engineering by the Arup firm, the whole building sits atop rubber and steel isolators introduced, along with other measures, to dampen the effects of a major seismic event.

Rem Koolhaas and the Office for Metropolitan Architecture

When the Dutch architect Rem Koolhaas (born 1944) published *Delirious New York* in 1978, he established himself as a thinker about urbanism with a highly original, intellectualized, and edgy view of the architectural scene. For those interested in Rockefeller Center, the influential delineator Hugh Ferris, or Le Corbusier's view of the Big Apple, as well

16.46 Rem Koolhaas, graphic rendering of Hotel Sphinx, as published in *Delirious New York* (1978).
Koolhaas brought a cerebral European perspective to the study of that most reinvented of places: New York City. It has taken him more than a quarter of a century to transform his published urban visions into radical, built realities.

as case studies of New York City buildings infrequently included in standard architectural histories, such as the Waldorf-Astoria Hotel, the New York Athletic Club, and all of Coney Island, this book will prove both insightful and amusing. Koolhaas's own imaginary designs for the city, such as his Hotel Sphinx (Fig. 16.46), show him to have been little concerned then with construction but fascinated by the richness and diversity of modern culture.

In Rotterdam, he was among those who founded the Office for Metropolitan Architecture (OMA) in 1975, wherein he operates more as a philosopher and visionary than as a traditional designer. Called Modernist works by some, Deconstructivist by others, many of his early projects exist only on paper.

In 1992 OMA completed the Kunsthal, or Art Hall, in Rotterdam, taking advantage of a sloping site located between a basalt dike and the new Museum Park. The south elevation has a relatively low, horizontal profile, not without connections to Rotterdam's De Stijl movement of the period during and after World War I, while the east elevation boldly displays an auditorium behind extensive glazing. The building's interiors owe something to the spatial investigations of Le Corbusier, with a penetrating north–south street that runs tangent to the auditorium. Materials most often avoid elegance in favor of tough-minded translucencies in the form of metal-grid floors and corrugated plastic sheeting.

Opened to the public in 2004, OMA's Seattle Central Library covers an entire city block (Fig. 16.47). On the outside, it is a reflective prism with glazing set in a diamond-grid exoskeleton that is ideally viewed in the Seattle mist. The huge interior volume, part hotel atrium, part space station, with cantilevered floor levels connected by a giant ramp or "Books Spiral," aspires to be the city's living room, a true public domain and a techno-sphere where hard-copy volumes and the digital world can be good neighbors.

OMA's most recognizable, but star-crossed, project is the competition-winning China Central Television (CCTV) Headquarters (2012) (Fig. 16.48) in Beijing executed together with the East China Architectural Design and Research Institute. Remembering that Koolhaas had been imagining high-rise castles in the air when he wrote *Delirious New York*, it is not surprising to find him still infatuated with buildings that seem to defy gravity and that are large enough (in this case 768 feet tall and enclosing 5.1 million square feet of floor space) to become cities unto themselves. In a sprawling urban setting where new conventional towers are constantly competing for recognition, the CCTV structure rises as two slightly canted shafts that bend to join as great intersecting cantilevers; and it has become an instant landmark. With structural engineering done by the Arup firm, the glass-enclosed monolith has an irregular-diagonal-exoskeleton frame. Unfortunately, in 2009 an unsanctioned fireworks display ignited the north wing of the building; following repairs the building was finally completed in May 2012.

16.47 (left) Office for Metropolitan Architecture, Seattle Central Library, Seattle, Washington, 2004. It is not difficult to connect the inventor of the Hotel Sphinx with the creator of the Seattle Central Library, but it is hard to imagine a building with more dramatic cantilevers, unless it is Koolhaas's CCTV Headquarters (below). Some have questioned whether his concern for materials assemblages and detailing matches his penchant for conceptualization.

16.48 (below) Office for Metropolitan Architecture, CCTV Headquarters, Beijing, 2012. This 768-foot-tall convoluted structure needs all of the X-bracing that it can get, given the outlandish cantilever. The Dutch author of *Delirious New York* (written as part of his architectural studies at the Architectural Association School in London) built this tower-object as the largest structure in China.

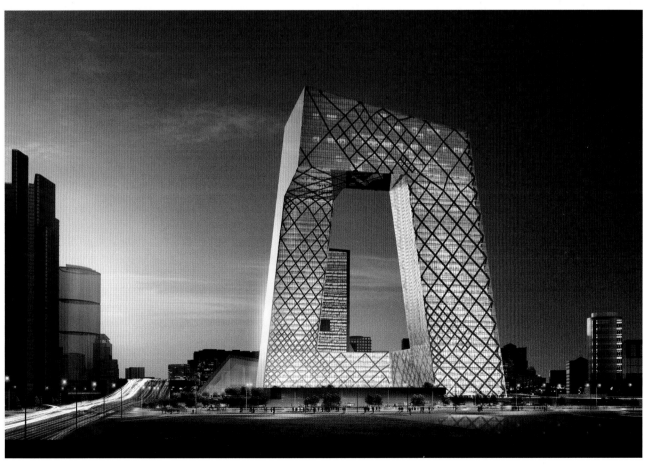

Zaha Hadid

At the Architectural Association in London, Zaha Hadid (born 1950) was taught by the only slightly older Rem Koolhaas. Iraqi, female, and at one time apparently destined to create fantastic, unbuilt, and perhaps unbuildable projects that could be experienced only as translucent layers of computer graphics and that seemed disassembled (and so, to some, Deconstructivist), she has now become an international architectural star laden with real commissions and arguably the most famous female architect of all time. Her first built project, the Vitra Fire Station (1993) in Weil am Rhein, Germany, is a projectilelike construction of concrete and metal that figuratively slashes through space. Due to changes in local fire districts, it became a display area for the Vitra furniture company's chairs. Her Austrian Bergisel Ski-jump (2002) (Fig. 16.49) has a square, concrete shaft capped by a cantilevered, helmet-like, metal-and-glass summit that accommodates a café as well as waiting athletes and looks out from its mountaintop site over the Tyrolean Alps and down on Innsbruck. Evolving in space like a piece of Futurist sculpture, from tight turn to a straight run, the metal ski-ramp figuratively uncoils before reaching down into the sloping landscape.

Hadid's Rosenthal Center for Contemporary Arts (Fig. 16.50) in downtown Cincinnati (2003) has been criticized by some for being too tame relative to her previous work and lionized by others for the way it raises the urbanistic standards in this often-ignored Midwestern city. This is not to say that Hadid's preferred angular geometries and dramatic means of vertical circulation are entirely absent. In an exhibition space designed to accommodate only temporary shows, walls soar, light penetrates dramatically, stair ramps figuratively leap, and floors bend. If space can be considered the stuff of modern architecture, then this museum is an undeniably modern building.

Her long-in-development MAXXI National Museum of XXI Century Arts (1998–2010) (Fig. 16.51) in the Flaminio neighborhood of Rome is a mélange of piloti-porticoes, concrete volumes, and glass, with flowing building masses responding to two adjacent and different city grids. Inside, leaping and "floating" steel stairs and concrete ramps lead to enveloping galleries in a spectacle that is part the Rome of the Caesars, part giant Baroque church, and part early Hadid unbuildable-ness, now become buildable. Her competition-winning BMW Central Building (2005) (Fig. 16.52) in Leipzig, Germany has the look of an interstellar craft just landed. Inserted among three existing production sheds that house some 5000 workers, it comingles offices with elevated conveyors carrying in-progress vehicles from one location to another. Hadid's Guangzhou (the city formerly known as Canton) Opera House (2010) must be compared to the Sydney Opera House and Guggenheim Bilbao as a construction intended to put a huge but largely ignored city on the world map. The triangulated steel frame of its main building appears to erupt from the earth. On the inside, angular concourses carry operagoers into the cavernlike performance hall, its swirling, bulging surfaces seemingly frozen during a morphing process.

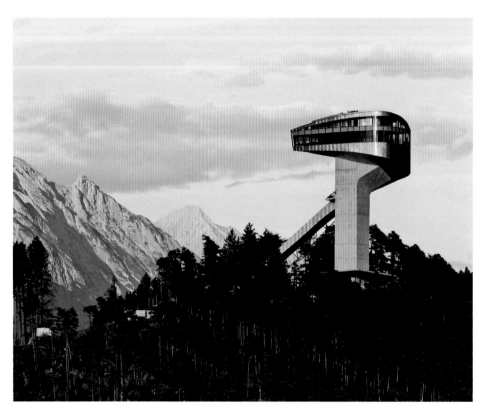

16.49 Zaha Hadid, Bergisel Ski-jump, Innsbruck, Austria, 2002. At a time when women are assuming greater prominence on the international architectural scene, none is more celebrated than Iraq-born Zaha Hadid. Designing a ski-jump afforded her the opportunity to explore her interests in speed, change, and related angularities of form.

16.50 (opposite) Zaha Hadid, Rosenthal Center for Contemporary Arts, Cincinnati, 2003. On the interior of this downtown Cincinnati building, Hadid made a bold but relatively conventional gesture to the urban street edge. On the interior, however, she continued her intense enquiry into the nature of dynamic space.

16.51 (above) Zaha Hahid, MAXXI National Museum of XXI Century Arts, Rome, Italy, 1998–2010.
Hadid's museum appears as a coiled snake preparing to strike. A structure considered equally exciting in its own time, Pier Luigi Nervi's concrete Sports Palace built for the 1960 Summer Olympics, occupies a site off the bottom of the image.

16.52 Zaha Hadid, BMW Central Building, Leipzig, Germany, 2005.
This office building, which has automobile conveyors passing through it, is relatively modest in plan size relative to the assembly buildings with which it connects, one of them visible behind and under the new structure. Hadid's challenge was to transform the dull image of a factory complex into an exciting symbol of BMW.

Maya Lin and the Vietnam Veterans Memorial

It can be said with certitude that no built object in the twentieth century has received greater initial condemnation or greater ultimate acclaim than Maya Lin's Vietnam Veterans Memorial (1982) in Washington, D.C. (Fig. 16.53). Now, more than two decades since its construction and more than three since the end of the Vietnam War, it has become a symbol, indeed an instrument, of national reconciliation. Lin (born 1959), a landscape-architecture student at Yale at the time of the competition for the memorial, made the names of those Americans who died or went missing in Vietnam between 1959 and 1975 not simply visible, as required in the competition brief, but the essence of her winning submission. Carving a walkway down into the earth and raising a folded, black granite-veneered retaining wall inscribed with the names above it, she simultaneously created a sepulcher and a safe harbor and proved that an abstract Modernist setting can be nationally cathartic.

Anyone who has ever arrived on the west end of the Mall, been drawn down the sloping ramp, and passed by, fixated upon, reached out and touched, or even knelt at this disarmingly simple, planar construction will attest to its nobility and poignancy. As a corollary, so many objects, offerings really, are left here by visitors, be they flowers inserted into the seams between the stone panels, a relinquished purple heart, or entire nurses' uniforms left pressed and folded, that they have to be collected every night by the National Park Service. Some of them are displayed in the nearby National Museum of American History.

16.53 Maya Lin, Vietnam Veterans Memorial, Washington, D.C., 1982.
No photograph can capture the emotional experience of arriving at the west end of the Mall in the shadow of the Lincoln Memorial, walking down the ramp carved into the earth, and being confronted by this extraordinary construction. The wall material is highly polished black granite.

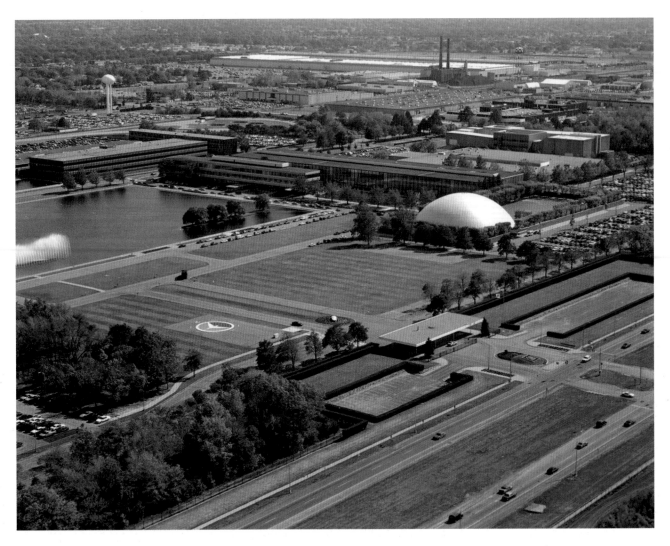

MODERN MATERIALS AND TECHNOLOGIES

Advances in technology have affected buildings everywhere, most dramatically perhaps in Europe. Work runs the gamut from the craftsman-level processes demanded by the work of Carlo Scarpa to the dazzling technological eloquence of Renzo Piano and the high-tech engineering-become-art of Santiago Calatrava. Common to it all, however, is a transcendent expressiveness and an overt celebration of the process of making. Among the first to take this path was a Finnish American who died in mid-career: Eero Saarinen.

Eero Saarinen and his Office

Eero Saarinen (1910–61) is perhaps most famous among the larger public for his design of the Gateway Arch in St. Louis (1947–65). His works are remarkably varied, but all resulted from a relentless, exploratory, inventive attitude toward new materials and technologies. Like Alvar Aalto, Saarinen was born in Finland; his architect father, Eliel (1873–1950), created the exquisite campus at Cranbrook Academy outside Detroit, Michigan after relocating the

16.54 Eero Saarinen, General Motors Technical Center, Warren, Michigan, 1948–56.
The American automobile industry in Michigan was flying high when this complex was built. Saarinen quite consciously added the domed auditorium, seen to the right, as a geometric foil for the unrelieved rectangular geometries of the office buildings behind and to the left of it. These office buildings are early examples of curtain-wall construction.

family to the United States in the 1920s. Eero studied sculpture in Paris, completed his architectural education at Yale in 1934, and practiced with his father until 1950.

In the General Motors Technical Center (1948–56) (Fig. 16.54) at Warren, Michigan, Eero Saarinen took an apparently Miesian approach, setting modular steel-and-glass-walled rectangular volumes in a campuslike park. The orthogonal theme is broken only by a circular, domed auditorium and a metallic-sphere water tower that give verticality and sensuality to a composition of otherwise horizontal, seemingly mass-produced objects.

For the Trans World Airlines (TWA) Terminal (1956–62) at Kennedy Airport in New York City, Saarinen abandoned the orthogonal General Motors esthetic in favor of a fluid, sculptural form expressive of flight (Fig. 16.55).

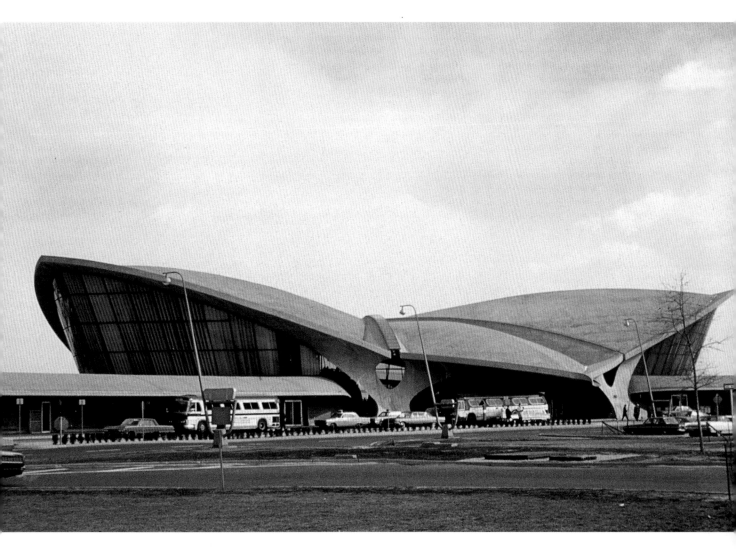

16.55 Eero Saarinen, TWA Terminal, Kennedy International Airport, New York City, 1956–62.
Saarinen died while still in his early fifties. He had not yet established a single direction for his architectural development. Here, he explored the potential of poured-in-place concrete to create expressive shapes and dynamic spaces.

He created thin-shelled concrete vaults supported by free-form, poured-in-place concrete piers, so that the terminal's "billowing" roof resembles a great bird alighting. Inside, the flowing space is equally dramatic but intimate. Most fittings were custom-designed to match the spirit of the building: ordinary furniture looks out of place in a space where curves dominate the walls and ceilings and ramps generate motion in the floor plane. A later design for Dulles Airport (1958–62), outside Washington, D.C., drew its inspiration from early sketches done by German Expressionist architect Erich Mendelsohn. Outward-leaning concrete pylons rise on the exterior to support the concrete-panel-covered cable-hung roof, which provides a clear span inside. (In 1997 the firm of Skidmore, Owings, and Merrill doubled the length of the terminal by replicating Saarinen's profile of pylons and catenary cables.)

Architect Charles Eames (1907–78) and his wife, sculptor and painter Ray Eames (1912–88), created the prototype for all those fiberglass-reinforced plastic airport chairs familiar to travelers throughout the world. The two designers met at Cranbrook Academy at a time when Eero Saarinen was its director, and Charles subsequently entered Saarinen's office. As part of a competition promoting Modernism and industrialization in architecture, the Eameses, initially working with Saarinen, produced a Case Study House, in which they used lightweight structural steel and off-the-shelf, prefabricated parts. As built in 1945–49, this project became their residence in Pacific Palisades, California.

Carlo Scarpa

Venetian architect Carlo Scarpa (1902–78) embraced European Modernism in general and Italian Rationalism in particular in the 1940s. However, his idiosyncratic search for expression through attention to materials and their assemblage set him apart from those ideologies with which he initially identified. His unfinished Brion Cemetery (begun 1969) (Fig. 16.56) in the village of San

16.56 Carlo Scarpa, Brion Cemetery, San Vito, Italy, begun 1969.

This project enabled Scarpa to make an extremely personal architectural statement. Working on it over a long period of time, he treated the place like a laboratory for architectural experimentation.

16.57 (below) James Stirling, History Faculty Building, Cambridge University, Cambridge, England, 1968.

Stirling's use of dramatic, exposed structural elements can be compared to Russian Constructivist explorations of the early twentieth century. Offices occupy the tower, with a library in the cascade of glass.

Vito near Venice includes a pavilion, sacristy, chapel, Brion family tombs, and pools of water. It sits adjacent to the village cemetery and is surrounded by the flat ground of the Veneto that extends to distant mountains. Scarpa's construction is executed largely in concrete and prominently displays somewhat enigmatic geometric motifs, such as interlocking circles and repeatedly set-back planes that present themselves both as highly personal statements and expressions of the mystery inherent in the human condition. Scarpa oversaw construction on the site as he sought to translate hundreds of his delicate colored-pencil drawings into a physical yet poetic reality.

James Stirling

In the 1960s the British architect James Stirling (1926–92) used the theme of industrial assemblage in his commissions for the Engineering Building at Leicester University (1964) and the History Faculty Building at Cambridge University (1968), both of which were startling for their sculptural forms and unconcealed use of standard building materials. Aluminum-framed commercial greenhouse windows were set in the industrial brick walls of the Engineering Building's office tower and were also employed to wrap completely the walls and ceiling of its attached laboratory wing, where sawtooth skylights are treated as prismatic solids. In the History Faculty Building (Fig. 16.57), which contains a library on the lowest levels and faculty offices in the L-shaped block that rises on two sides, industrial glazing systems were used to cover the library and enclose the long exterior walls of the offices. A giant cascade of glass brings abundant light (and solar greenhouse-effect heat build-up in summer) to scholars working in the fan-shaped library. Stirling's Staatsgalerie

(1977–83) (Figs. 16.58–16.59) in Stuttgart, Germany shows that he moved toward Post-Modernism and beyond in his mid-career. It owes much to Schinkel's Altesmuseum in Berlin (see Fig. 13.35), contains a host of historical allusions, and responds to its site in a fashion somewhere between the search for a *genius loci*, or peculiar character of a place, and literal deconstruction. The building contains galleries in a U-shape around a central, open rotunda, hence the Schinkel connection. Stirling made the rotunda a sculpture garden and part of a public walkway designed in homage to an established pedestrian path through the site. As for the allusions, which range from Greek or Roman pediments to Egyptian **cavetto** cornices to displaced stonework like that used by the Mannerist Giulio

Galleries   Public walkway

Rotunda

Gallery level

Exhibition
Hall

Theater

Workshop

Entrance level

N   0   50 m
0   150 ft

16.58 James Stirling, Plans of the Staatsgalerie, Stuttgart, 1977–83.
By this stage of his career, Stirling had forsaken dramatic technology for an almost archaeological-dig historicism combined with spatial manipulations derived from the European Modernists.

16.59 James Stirling, Staatsgalerie rotunda, Stuttgart, 1977–83.
Stirling presents this space almost as a ruin. Elsewhere, he left stone blocks strewn on the ground as though dislodged over time.

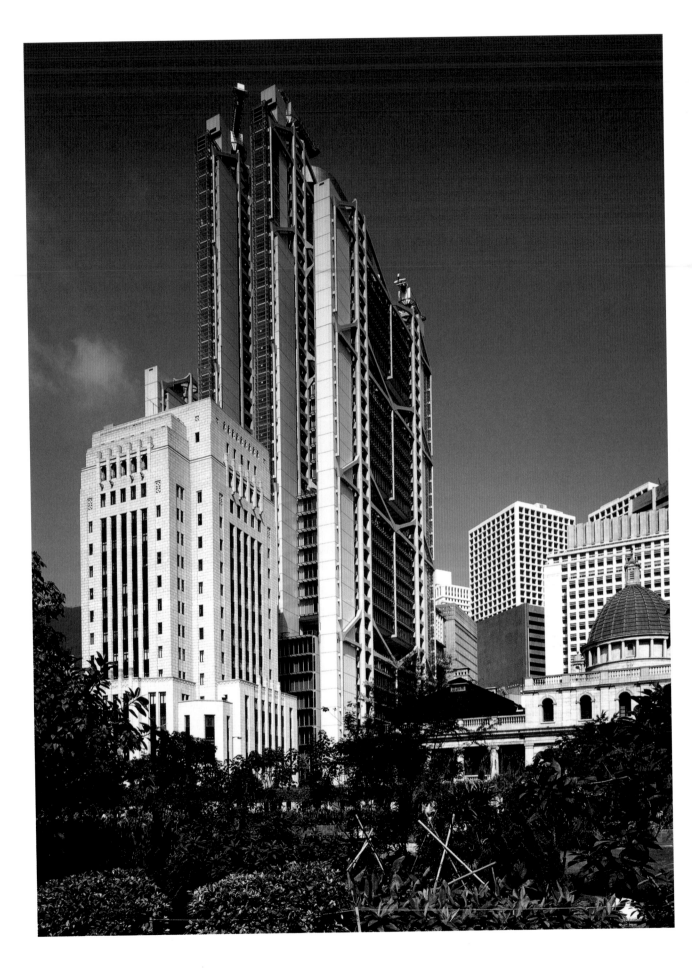

Romano, Stirling said that he was "sick and tired of the boring, meaningless, non-committed, faceless flexibility and open-endedness of the present architecture," meaning that he had moved on from his high-tech phase. At the interrupted side of the U in his plan, he set out a sculpturelike display of ramps, platforms, and a sinusoidal-curve lobby. The walls are laid up throughout in a striated coursing of variegated stone that gives the impression of an excavated classical site.

Norman Foster

The Englishman Norman Foster (born 1935) met Richard Rogers at Yale, subsequently partnered with him, before forming Foster Associates with his wife, Wendy Cheesman Foster (1938–89). An admirer of R. Buckminster Fuller (discussed at the end of this chapter), whom Foster credits with giving him early direction both in construction innovation and what has become known as sustainable design, he has explored the potentialities of twentieth- and now twenty-first-century technologies, but with a consistent concern for the environment.

In designing the international headquarters for the Hong Kong Bank (1986) (Fig. 16.60), Foster responded to a site which has splendid views of Hong Kong harbor (to the north) and Victoria Peak (to the south) by creating a forty-seven-story rectangular prism with its long sides oriented to the views while mechanical and service functions close off the short east and west elevations. The most public banking areas are housed in the third through twelfth floors, which are grouped around a central atrium lit by mirrors attached to a south-facing, adjustable "sunscoop."

In 1993 Foster won a competition for the redevelopment of the century-old German Reichstag, left in ruins after a suspicious fire in 1933 amid the Nazi Party's grab for power and further mutilated when Allied and Russian armies entered Berlin in 1945. In close proximity to the Berlin Wall, it was largely ignored until the reunification of East and West Germany in 1989. Intervening within the remains of the nineteenth-century structure, Foster added a transparent dome and spiral exterior ramp above the legislative chamber and an internal faceted cone that reflects light downward and works like a chimney to channel heated air upward (Fig. 16.61).

16.60 (opposite) Norman Foster, Hong Kong Bank, Hong Kong, 1986. Like an insect, this high-rise bank has an exoskeleton. Its long sides orient to views, while mechanical and service functions close off the short east and west elevations.

16.61 (below) Norman Foster, Reichstag interior, Berlin, 1993. Around the perimeter of this rotunda, figures ascend and descend on the circumferential ramp. Below is the legislative chamber and rising within is the inverted cone that reflects light downward and channels heat upward.

The symbolism of a phoenix rising from the literal ashes is obvious.

Standing near the vertically expressive Tower Bridge and with engineering by the Arup firm, Foster's incongruously leaning London City Hall (2002) (Fig. 16.62) bows toward the south as if to announce that paradigms once considered unchallengeable are no longer so. Arrived at as a simultaneous solution to problems of form and environmental performance, this deformed-egg-shaped yet elegant building has a minimum surface area (for its enclosed volume) exposed to direct sun; includes horizontal sunscreens at its overhanging orientation; and incorporates triple glazing and operable sash. On the north side, wedding-cake layers of glazed triangles open up the Assembly Chamber to public view from the outside. Vertical circulation occurs within a spiral stair that provides a dynamic rotunda for this chamber and can only be compared in its combined functionality and beauty to the structure of a chambered nautilus.

Foster's London office tower at 30 St. Mary Axe (2003) is made of steel and glass in a shape that has been compared to a gherkin (pickle) but could as easily be the shoot of a giant spring bulb emerging from the ground, and cannot but be compared to Jean Nouvel's Torre Agbar (see Fig. 16.75). It stands on the site once intended to hold the Millennium Tower, also designed by Foster, but that was found to be too tall and too expensive to construct. The

16.62 Norman Foster, London City Hall, 2002.
London's Tower Bridge can be seen in the background, and it offers a striking contrast to Foster's hall, which can be viewed as a descendant of the iron-and-glass Crystal Palace of the mid-nineteenth century. Just as the Crystal Palace shocked visitors with its openness, City Hall shocks with its unconventional sloping form.

triangulated exoskeleton of 30 St. Mary Axe means that there are no interior columns, and its spiraling bands of lighter and darker glazing make it appear to be in motion. Once more working with the Arup firm, Foster again made sustainability a primary concern. His John Spoor Broome Library (2008) at the California State University, Channel Islands consists of a great canopy with perimeter cantilevers that takes in a 1930s Mission and Spanish Colonial-style building and looks to combine dramatically the traditional library of books and the emerging library of digital media.

Renzo Piano

It is hard to say what is more impressive about Italian architect Renzo Piano (born 1937): the geographic coverage of his practice or the consistently exceptional quality of his work. While technological innovation seems, at least superficially, to be a primary interest, it is really technology's benefits, paid out in the currency of free-flowing space, a sense of shelter, quality of craftsmanship, and environmental appropriateness, that invigorate his process of design enquiry. The same can be said for his contextualism, as environmental benefits also accrue naturally from his concern for quality of light and his placing of inhabitants in an immediate relationship with the natural world. In his 1998 Pritzker Prize acceptance speech, he compared himself to Robinson Crusoe, "an explorer capable of surviving in foreign lands," and described himself as someone "ignoring boundaries between disciplines" and "taking risks and making mistakes." Born into a family of builder-contractors, Piano earned an architectural degree from the Politecnico di Milano in 1964, then apprenticed, among other places, in the office of Louis Kahn.

Along with Richard Rogers, Piano achieved international recognition in 1976 with the competition-winning design for the Pompidou Center in the Beaubourg section of Paris (Fig. 16.63), not far from the former site of Les Halles, the great wholesale marketplace with iron-and-glass buildings designed by Victor Baltard (1805–74). The principal architectural features of the Pompidou Center hang on the outside of the building, where the white web of diagonally braced steel framing, bright blue air-handling ducts, red exhaust stacks, and exterior escalator snaking up the front façade surround a transparent, multistory, rectangular volume. The galleries contained inside are unremarkable when compared with the exterior, and the building's bristling mechanics are conspicuously out of place in its nineteenth-century neighborhood.

In 1982 Piano designed the Menil Collection Museum in Houston, Texas as a low-slung, light-articulated box. He wrapped a series of reinforced-concrete, light-modulating baffles, with apostrophe-shaped cross-sections, around a cellalike core of galleries. On the interior, he suspended extended versions of the baffles from a series of steel-lattice girders and distributed a grid of square steel columns between them and a black wooden floor. Anticipating the ceiling conditions at Piano's Nasher Sculpture Center discussed below, the light modulators create a rhythmic wave effect.

Piano was one among an international group of architects who contributed to rebuilding around Berlin's Potsdamer Platz, an area laid to waste at the end of World War II. On what had been a no-man's-land for half a century, Piano brought a triangular pool of water in from the Landwehrkanal to the south and responded to Hans Scharoun's (1893–1972) expressionistic State Library (1967–72; completed 1978) to the west. Between the library and his new "B1" and "Debis" office towers and the new Marlene Dietrich Platz, Piano located a casino and theater, clad with anodized aluminum that harmonizes with Scharoun's work and capped by a series of suspended metallic roofs. It is an altogether inclusive design in a long-fragmented city.

Renzo Piano is the only architect in this book to have done nautical design, resulting in the superstructures of the sister ships Crown Princess (1989) and Regal Princess

16.63 Renzo Piano and Richard Rogers, Pompidou Center, Paris, 1976.
The innards of a building (structural skeleton, mechanical systems and piping, etc.) that had long been concealed or downplayed are allowed here to become the principal architectural expression. The site quickly became one of the most visited in Paris.

16.64 (above) Renzo Piano, Jean-Marie Tjibaou Cultural Center, Nouméa, New Caledonia, 1991.
More like wispy sculpture or part of the local flora than buildings, these tall, unconventional constructions announce the conventional galleries below them. The fingerlike vertical members are made of laminated wood.

16.65 (left) Renzo Piano, Nashe Sculpture Center interior, Dallas, Texas, 2003.
At the beginning of this chapter, Eero Saarinen was identified as an architect still searching for his "style" when he died in 1961 at the age of fifty-one. Renzo Piano's buildings are as diverse as Saarinen's but are in no way immature. Piano also shares Saarinen's intense concern for innovative building materials. This view looks through one of th galleries and into the rear court.

(1991). Streamlined in a form that updates the 1930s Moderne style of industrial designer Raymond Loewy (1893–1986), their hull profiles evolved from the form of a dolphin. As with his buildings, Piano sought to make the ships modest and humane, in this case by connecting the passengers as much as possible with the sights, sounds, smells, and feelings of the sea.

No work of any living architect is more lyrical than Piano's 1991 design for the Jean-Marie Tjibaou Cultural Center in Nouméa, New Caledonia (Fig. 16.64). He placed a series of tall, perforated, sail-like structures along a forested ridge between a lagoon and the ocean, their forms based on local huts but reaching dramatically skyward like attenuated fingers. The "huts" are constructed of double layers of laminated wooden uprights atop hinge-connection bases, are stabilized by cable-and-strut wind bracing, and are partially covered with wooden staves. Adjacent to them lie more conventional galleries and support spaces, some below grade, that share a high level of detailing and craftsmanship with Piano's other work. At once technologically innovative and grounded in local building traditions, the ensemble is stunning when seen from a distance and engaging when entered to view the artifacts.

In 2003 Piano completed the Nasher Sculpture Center on a site in downtown Dallas, Texas. The collection of twentieth-century artworks is housed indoors and in a quiet rear court, which includes a sky-viewing installation by artist James Turrell (born 1943). Acknowledging Louis Kahn's Kimbell Art Museum in nearby Fort Worth (see Figs. 16.33–16.35), Piano created five long, narrow, parallel pavilions; but there the similarity ends. The lateral walls of his pavilions have unctuous travertine on their interior faces, while shorter end walls are completely glazed (Fig. 16.65). Above, stainless-steel rods support slightly arching steel ribs that, in turn, support low-iron-content (and therefore extremely clear) glass atop an aluminum mesh, its complex pattern of oblique holes developed by the Arup firm to allow in abundant but only indirect sunlight. In the basement, Piano placed light-sensitive works, research and conservation facilities, an auditorium, and offices.

Recently, Piano has completed a number of projects in the United States, including a series of museums. These projects include an expansion of Richard Meier's High Museum of Art in Atlanta (2005), an expansion of Charles McKim's Morgan Library in New York City (2006), the construction there of the New York Times Building (2007), the rebuilding of the California Academy of Sciences in San Francisco (2008), and the construction of the Art Institute of Chicago's Modern Wing and connecting

16.66 Renzo Piano, Modern Wing, Art Institute of Chicago, 2009.
This view under the footbridge shows Piano's museum to be pavilionlike, with its carefully engineered roof supported by tall, thin columns.

Nichols Bridgeway (2009) (Fig. 16.66). The Modern Wing is pavilionlike, delicate and refined, and made of steel and limestone blocks; so it is something of an homage to the work of Mies van der Rohe, who made Chicago his post-immigration home. Its roof, like that of the Nasher Gallery, is a carefully engineered diaphragm for modulating sunlight. The museum's refinement carries over to the 620-foot-long bridge, which all but levitates as it extends to a nearby park and so connects the museum to the heart of the city. The Arup firm again supplied engineering services, which, unfortunately, have resulted in an ongoing lawsuit.

Eric Owen Moss

Los Angeles architect Eric Owen Moss (born 1943) has taken the architectural road less traveled. Educated at UCLA and the University of California at Berkeley, he was hired in the late 1980s by client-patrons and real-estate developers Frederick and Laurie Samitaur-Smith and has done the lion's share of his work in a single, unlikely locale: the eastern edge of gritty Culver City, a forgotten place halfway between downtown LA and Santa Monica and once well known for its movie studios. The area had long been mostly industrial and so was replete with warehouses, and was cut through by the abandoned tracks of the Southern Pacific Railroad. Embracing what his friend and former teaching colleague Thom Mayne, whose work

is discussed at the end of this chapter, calls "disruption, dislocation, and instability," and with a mind to making architecture a means for change, Moss has favored the toughest industrial materials and has sometimes built afresh but has more often transformed existing warehouses by ripping them open and inserting new construction distinguished by aggressive geometries. Many critics who saw his initial efforts as self-conscious and strident have changed their minds and now view his collective accomplishments as their own validation.

What he has assembled might best be described as an architectural menagerie, with each building being unique and given its own name. In 1992 Moss conceived the long, low office building called Samitaur. Raised on steel columns and girders, it bridges an access road and connects to three reclaimed warehouses. Its hand-troweled plaster surfaces ripple slightly and become dramatically sculptural at the front-entry stair. Once built, it became a locus for additional development. The construction named Slash and Backslash (2000) (Fig. 16.67) began with existing sawtooth-profile warehouses. Moss removed most of the wooden structural members, added new plaster to side

16.67 Eric Owen Moss, Slash and Backslash, Culver City, California, 2000.
In an extreme landscape, Eric Owen Moss gutted this warehouse, then transformed it into a faceted building-sculpture.

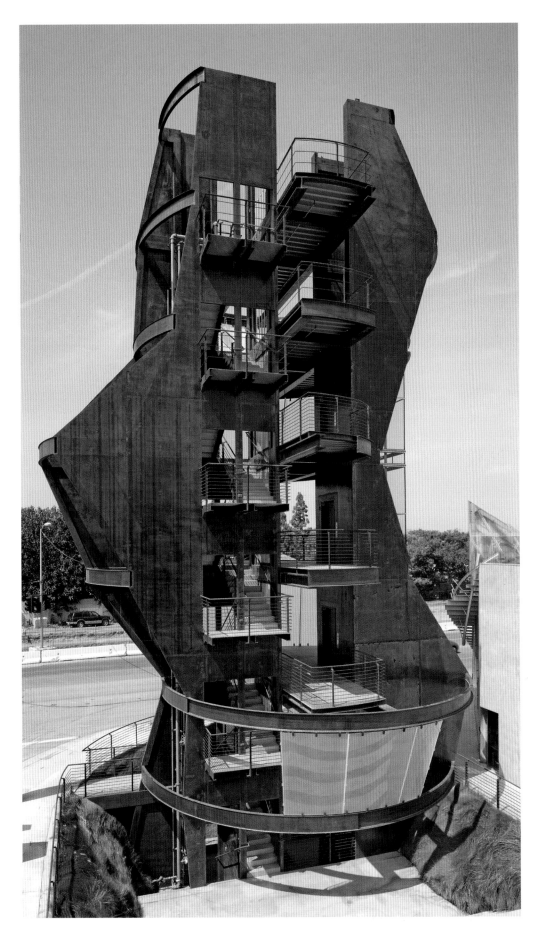

16.68 Eric Owen Moss, Samitaur Tower, Culver City, California, 2011. Seen here is the back side of the tower, where its cantilevered balconies are reminiscent of Russian Constructivist work from the early twentieth century. The structure serves as an observation platform for surveying the building accomplishments of Moss and his clients.

walls, and exploded the front section toward a courtyard using counter-sloping walls of steel and glass, hence the slash/backslash label. At the Beehive, Moss transformed another warehouse block and attached to it a circular module covered with overlapping steel panels that have the appearance of armor plate. The ensemble functions as an office and conference center. In 2011 he added the Samitaur Tower (Fig. 16.68), a constructivistic symbol for the entire redeveloped district and an orientation point with displays for visitors, including those arriving at a nearby light-rail stop. From the front, it appears as a stack of inverted tilted-cone slices, with steel rings binding translucent panels that are used for rear-screen projection. The back side is a vertical plane of steel through which stacked, cantilevered balconies project. There are more buildings in the area with unlikely names, like Umbrella and Pterodactyl; the list and the work go on.

Tod Williams and Billie Tsien

There is an almost unnerving intensity in the work of Tod Williams (born 1943) and Billie Tsien (born 1949). Because the site for their Neurosciences Institute in La Jolla, California (1995) is located less than a mile from Louis Kahn's Salk Institute (see Fig. 16.31), the architects felt obliged to "confront" but certainly not mimic this iconic building. A "monastery for science," their facility houses a small number of visiting fellows in an environment designed to promote constant interaction and exchange of ideas (Fig. 16.69).

Williams and Tsien set out to make every experience, even the smallest moments, potentially meaningful. They had the hilltop site graded in order to provide space for a modern cloister defined by a U-shaped building that houses a Theory Center and laboratories. At the open end of the U, they largely denied a distant view to the mountains by inserting an auditorium that rises from a low berm, but located a switchback ramp in such a way that it becomes a viewing promontory. Their chosen building materials contribute to a sense of timelessness: fossil-implanted limestone, sandblasted glass and concrete, redwood, and stainless steel. Given that their client, Dr. Gerald Edelman, has argued for a nuanced, Darwinian-evolutionary, environmentally interactive development of the individual human brain, it seems most appropriate that Williams and Tsien sought to acknowledge this theory architecturally by creating an environment of random

16.69 Tod Williams and Billie Tsien, Neurosciences Institute, La Jolla, California, 1995.
Being so understated and contemplative in its site development, this monasterylike building ensemble comes close to being unphotographable. In this vignette, looking from the Theory Center to the auditorium, the reference to Louis Kahn's nearby Salk Institute (see Fig. 16.31) is unmistakable. However, Williams and Tsien have downplayed views to the mountains (not the ocean) and have set their pool (not channel) of water at an angle (not on the principal axis), emphasizing the skydome as the enframed feature and creating a metaphor for the complex, nuanced activities of the human brain and its creative powers that are studied here.

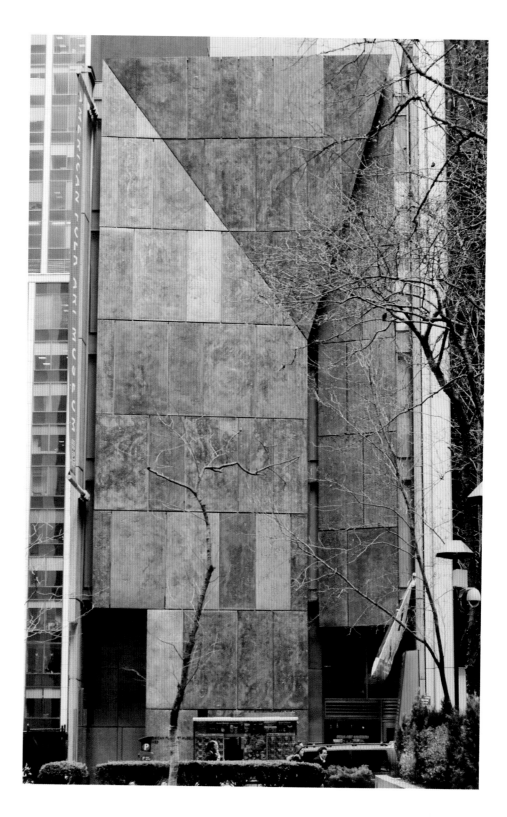

16.70 Tod Williams and Billie Tsien, Museum of American Folk Art, New York City, 2001.
The heavy, white-bronze panels of the façade offer quite a contrast to the elegant International Style front face of MoMA, which is located a short distance to the east.

episodic incidents and encounters that can be experienced in myriad sequences and combinations and that results in a unique, cumulative awareness for each participant.

Their Museum of American Folk Art (2001) (Fig. 16.70) stands just west of the entrance to MoMA on 53rd Street in New York City. Almost menacing, with white-bronze panels hanging like giant shields on the outside, its eight stories rise as a narrow canyon on the interior. It is difficult to imagine what the construction documents looked like, as the compressed complexity of detailing is as dizzying as the internal spatial manipulation. The materials used suggest the same kind of indestructibility as seen on the exterior, and include ironlike wood from long-submerged Douglas-fir logs, bush-hammered concrete, cold-rolled steel, and aged Italian limestone. The architects have compared the rich and varied experience of moving through their building to that at Sir John Soane's 13 Lincoln's Inn Fields (see Figs. 13.31–13.32). The comparison is valid, as both contain tall, top-lit spaces and make virtues of their designers' obsessions.

Mack Scogin and Merrill Elam

Difficult to characterize—part 1950s drive-in restaurant, part Russian Constructivism, part art installation, part (by economic necessity) local hardware store—the early work of Atlanta architects Mack Scogin (born 1943) and Merrill Elam (born 1943) speaks with the voice of authenticity in the language of originality. Their eclectic inspirations seem to know no bounds, be they the Mannerist Villa Giulia in Rome or a thrown-together barbecue stand in some forgotten corner of the South; in the potentially spirit-numbing architectural marketplace, they have somehow retained their sense of wonder about the process of building.

Long before the computer made it possible to more easily define irregular geometries and so to emphasize complex building-enclosure systems, Scogin and Elam moved the selection of external cladding materials outside the realm of the familiar and into that of admirable strangeness. The Branch Library in Clayton County (1989) outside Atlanta looks like a miniature airplane hangar wrapped in the mottled cover of an outlandishly oversized

composition book (actually made by camouflage-painting corrugated sheet metal). When the facility opened, patron numbers soared.

In 2000 they completed their design for Knowlton Hall, which houses the architectural school at Ohio State University; the building opened in 2004. The earliest plans looked like collages of overlapping trapezoidal planes, with their lines responding to the campus's pedestrian-traffic patterns (a more site-specific take on Daniel Libeskind's Jewish Museum, which is discussed below). Because of budgetary constraints and concerns for internal orientation, a second scheme became completely orthogonal, with studio spaces and faculty offices to each side of a "system of inclined [circulation] planes" (not unlike Álvaro Siza's museum in Santiago de Compostela—see Fig. 16.10). Eventually, the architects gave their gridded plan dynamism, by exposing it to the original set of pedestrian-traffic patterns, and nuance, by expanding it to the limits of the irregularly shaped site. Commensurately, the building's cladding became as aggressive as the site-generated lines of force. Highly textured expanses of marble shingles (their patterning inspired by quarrying practices but, given the architects' lexicon of Southern inspirations, perhaps comparable to a masonry armadillo) present a hovering curtain in front of set-back glazing. Canyonlike, transparent, landscaped courts and a huge, almost intimidating, carved-out corner entry and interior spaces where architectural intentions never seem to end make for a building that demands engagement.

16.71 Mack Scogin and Merrill Elam, Wang Campus Center, Wellesley College, Wellesley, Massachusetts, 2006.
As something of a metaphor for the freewheeling and varied student organizations at Wellesley College, this building moves up, in, out, cants, and torques. An appreciation of the diversity of the interior spaces will require a visit.

At Wellesley College, southwest of Boston, Scogin and Elam got to take the architectural gloves off, so to speak, with their design for the Wang Campus Center (2006) (Fig. 16.71). The Wellesley buildings are strewn across an almost wild landscape that works its way down to a lake. The jaggedly massed Wang Campus Center looks like something uplifted, forcefully carved, and then deposited here during the last period of glaciation. Wellesley has long prided itself on diversity, before the word became politicized jargon, and on educating students to think for themselves, which means that the right institution and the right architects have met.

The center stands at the heart of the campus and has a plan outline that looks like a New England decapod crustacean (think crab or lobster), claws extended and making its way knowingly across the landscape. The program called for spaces to support Wellesley's multifarious student organizations as well as a bookstore, pub, café, and big room for varied events. Consequently, the wildly angular plan contains only a limited number of identifiable rooms, largely being made up instead of "unowned spaces" and banks of lockers that invite student groups to gather up what they need and appropriate a place of their liking.

These non-rooms become lived-in sculpture, not of the Frank Gehry type, where flamboyant exterior form sometimes gives way to conventional interior planning, but rather a spatial plurality that befits the program and the institution. As for comparable thinking, the work of Hans Scharoun comes to mind, but also Herbert Greene's (1871–1932) birdlike prairie houses and the unlikely, fluid-space investigations of Friedrich Kiesler for his "endless house." But comparison could just as easily be made to grown-up-over-time buildings in back-alley Boston or in rural Georgia. All this contextual and historical energy notwithstanding, the Wang Campus Center is artfully composed without being overwrought and, with its "geological" layers of copper-shingle cladding, could even speak coherently to a 1970s Roman-brick subdivision house. It is another building from the minds of Mack Scogin and Merrill Elam that could not have been conceived without modern art, the computer, and steel erectors who appreciate a challenge.

Scoggin and Elam's accessible but dignified U.S. Courthouse in Austin, Texas (2012) sits on a high plinth in order to ward off potential vehicular attacks in an era when this kind of eventuality cannot be ignored. This design move enabled them to enclose their building with apparently thin, planar walls of cut-face Texas limestone and translucent glass (with this glass often extended right to the building's edges), which together give the impression that all the trappings of a traditional courthouse have been sheared off, make many of the inner workings visible, provide most occupants with a visual connection to the outside, and acknowledge the city's Moderne-style courthouse built in 1935, a building with the same thin-skinned quality, but one that is much more introverted. On the inside of the new building, a pinwheeling plan is raised up as seemingly thin, frequently punctured, and once again light, planar walls, with the result being abstract and almost ethereal, as though a Theo van Doesburg De Stijl house-drawing of levitating planes (see Fig. 15.52) had been brought into the twenty-first century and somehow built.

Daniel Libeskind

Daniel Libeskind was born in Poland in 1946 but studied architecture in England and in the United States at Cooper Union in New York City. At one time labeled a Deconstructivist, he is perhaps better described as someone intent upon expressing ideas and happening to use architecture as his means of communication. His working method has involved typography and collage. In urban circumstances, he has explored the palimpsestic, or overlaid, nature of the city, as in his winning design for the City Edge competition in Berlin (1987). He created the plan for his competition-winning Jewish Museum design in Berlin (1989–99) by means of determinants ranging from the geographical plotting and connecting of addresses for notable Jewish Berliners to a close reading of the texts for Arnold Schoenberg's unfinished opera *Moses and Aaron* and literary and art critic Walter Benjamin's collection of essays titled *One-Way Street* (1928). Needless to say, connecting the physical reality of the building with such myriad and, some would say, arcane inspirations

16.72 Daniel Libeskind, Jewish Museum, Berlin, 1989–99. Libeskind's building snakes its angular way through the cityscape and proposes that the extreme events of the Holocaust require an unorthodox architecture. This lack of orthodoxy is made particularly obvious by the presence of the quite traditional, orthogonal, U-plan building to its right.

requires perseverance, if not clairvoyance, on the part of an observer. Supporters say that only through such rarefied means can such an extreme circumstance as the Holocaust even be approached, never mind understood, and that Libeskind has accomplished exactly that. His building is an extended, zigzagging, concrete box covered with a metallic skin in which angular openings have been left in a variety of shapes and patterns (Fig. 16.72). The poured-concrete interior has the quality of a three-dimensional maze, more akin to a house of illusions or the inner space of a building described in one of Franz Kafka's stories than a conventional museum.

Libeskind won the international competition for the World Trade Center after Minoru Yamasaki's (1912–86) towers, which opened in 1973, were tragically destroyed by terrorist-piloted airliners in 2001. The intensely political and emotional circumstances surrounding this commission and the many overlapping jurisdictions and economic interests on a site at the base of Manhattan have led to co-authorship with David C. Childs and significant revisions in his proposal, which included an angular, faceted, spiky, 1776-foot-tall "Freedom Tower."

In 2008 Libeskind, with GBBN Architects, completed the Ascent at Roebling's Bridge, a condominium complex in Covington, Kentucky, which curves elegantly and so promotes views out over the Ohio River. The building takes its name from the adjacent suspension bridge built by John A. Roebling in 1866, just before he began work on the Brooklyn Bridge, which was discussed in Chapter 14.

Steven Holl

Steven Holl (born 1947) has established himself as a skilled watercolorist and a contemporary master of natural- and artificial-light manipulation in his architecture. Nowhere is this more apparent than in his Chapel of St. Ignatius (1997) in Seattle, what he calls (based on an early conceptual drawing) a "stone box, containing seven bottles of light." The stone box is a puzzlelike assemblage of monochromatic concrete panels, and the bottles are rooftop, tubular-steel-frame monitors (their effects mimicked by artificial light at night) that direct sunlight down through multihued glass lenses, where it bathes the worship spaces in a highly specific atmosphere of glowing color. The resultant environment has been found by visitors, even the unchurched, to be one of enveloping spirituality.

On an MIT campus where Alvar Aalto built his celebrated dormitory in 1947–49, exemplary architecture has generally been in short supply. Here Holl has chosen to repeat Aalto's theme of the wall, but with different emphases and building at an unapologetically huge size. The variable-height cliff-face (Fig. 16.73) that is his Simmons

16.73 Steven Holl, Simmons Hall dormitory, MIT, Cambridge, Massachusetts, 2002.
This massive block with huge cut-outs and a seemingly endless grid of windows looks like a dormitory for the digital age. On the inside, in the free-form lobbies, Holl took the opportunity to display his skill in introducing natural light.

16.74 Steven Holl, Linked Hybrid, Beijing, China, 2009.
The outer faces of these tall buildings are not unlike Holl's
Simmons Hall dormitory. What sets them apart are the "links"
that span high up from building to building, not unlike the
bridges used by Alison and Peter Smithson in their English
housing complexes built some fifty years earlier.

Hall dormitory (2002) has a gridded, screenlike façade of
anodized aluminum cladding behind which lighting conditions, volume cutouts, and splashes of color make for a
level of energy consistent with modern student life.

The "Linked" in Holl's Linked Hybrid (2009) (Fig.
16.74), a mixed-use development in Beijing, China near
the old Forbidden City, refers to a cluster of eight apartment towers with concrete exoskeletons "linked" by high-
up skybridges, some of them sloping, which are intended
to house art galleries, shops, cafés, and a fitness center.
While the concrete structural components of the towers
are designed for appropriate rigidity, the Vierendeel steel-
truss bridges were designed for maximum transparency and
require "friction pendulum isolators," which allow for the
swaying of the towers in winds and during earthquakes.
Five of the towers have thirty-three-foot-tall cantilevers at
their summits, and the various façade grids are broken by

diagonal bracing. At the ground level, there are shops, restaurants, a preschool, a cinema with a green roof, a hotel,
and even a tea house. In a signature Steven Holl fashion,
the entire complex, including fountains in the central retention basin, glows at night from artificial lighting. And in a
city with enormous environmental problems, the project is
built on a reclaimed brownfield site, and heating and cooling energy comes from geothermal wells.

Jean Nouvel

The Arab World Institute in Paris (1987) displays varied
aspects of Arab culture. Designed by Jean Nouvel (born
1949), it is located on the left bank of the Seine upriver from
the Ile de la Cité and is built around a central light-well, but
offers framed views of nearby Notre-Dame Cathedral. Its use
of water was inspired by the Alhambra in Toledo, and the
south façade is a huge screen of geometric ornamentation,
but one controlled by photovoltaic cells so that it constantly
changes in response to light levels. To the south and inside,
the building becomes a modern steel skeleton.

In ancient Roman times Nemausus was the name for
modern-day Nimes in France. Here, in 1987, Nouvel completed his Nemausus, two parallel, bull-nosed housing

blocks made from the kind of relatively inexpensive materials usually associated with industrial construction. Rejecting historicism but also Le Corbusier's specific brand of Modernism, Nouvel has sought through technology and a close reading of contemporary culture to produce buildings decidedly of their time. In Nîmes he chose to build with raw concrete, corrugated aluminum sheeting, commercial glazed partitions, and perforated aluminum for continuous, projecting balcony shields that represent a metallic version of Le Corbusier's brise-soleil. Adjacent parking, landscaped with plane trees, is sunken, leaving the ground level free as a conceptual sea, through which the shiplike Nemausus volumes appear to ply. Despite this Romantic sensibility, Nouvel's forms more than hold their own among the surrounding industrial construction and warehouses.

Nouvel's Torre Agbar (2005) (Fig. 16.75) in Barcelona, Spain is an office tower for the local water company and is meant to be something of a critique of the American skyscraper. Rising thirty-four floors in a generally low-rise city and in the shape of a bullet, it became an immediate local icon and cannot but be compared to the nearby towers of Antonio Gaudí's Sagrada Família (see Fig. 14.29). Nouvel's high-rise is built as a double shell, the inner one being concrete pierced by window openings and covered with metal panels tinted in a spectrum of colors from orange to red to blue, with some green at the base and random splashes of yellow, and with clear glass between steel ribs at the tower's summit. The outer shell is a fixed-glass louver system, with panels in varied densities and illuminated by LEDs at night.

In 1963 local architect Ralph Rapson designed Minneapolis's Guthrie Theater, which is celebrated for its thrust stage. In 2006 Nouvel built a replacement for it (Fig. 16.76) and included a virtual replica of the original stage and its surroundings. For his system of enclosure, he drew inspiration from his site's adjacency to the Mississippi River and from nearby flour-mill silos, which have been adapted for use as condominiums and which he mimicked with a ten-story tower. Blue aluminum panels curve to wrap Nouvel's building and have ghostly images screen-printed on them, and LED signage on the mastlike tower is constantly changing. A bold, bridgelike, two-story lobby and viewing platform cantilevers toward the river and offers framed views of it. More such calculated views await those who go inside.

16.75 Jean Nouvel, Torre Agbar, Barcelona, Spain, 2005.
This structure is partly a response to the towers of Antonio Gaudí's nearby Sagrada Família, seen on the right side of the image, and partly a suggestion by a European architect that the American skyscraper form has not yet been fully explored.

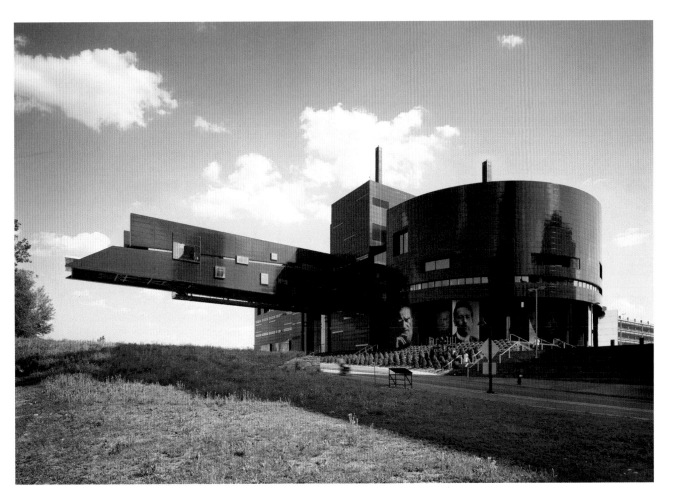

16.76 Jean Nouvel, Guthrie Theater, Minneapolis, Minnesota, 2006.
The cantilevered bridge reaches out toward the nearby Mississippi
River. The curving wall suggests the theaters inside. The tower
to the rear acknowledges the former flour-mill silos now become
condominiums in the vicinity.

Nouvel has designed two high-rise buildings for
Manhattan, one 1250 feet tall and situated next door to
MoMA but as yet unbuilt, and the other erected in Chelsea
across the street from Frank Gehry's IAC Building in 2010.
This Chelsea Building has two personalities. Seen from the
west, it is a quilt of variously sized glass panes set in metal
frames and canted at various angles. Seen from the east, it
offers sporadic windows cut into matte-black brick walls,
meaning that the building acknowledges both the area's
history as a working-class meatpacking district and the current process of gentrification.

Santiago Calatrava

Born in Spain in 1951, Santiago Calatrava is an architect
and an engineer and, arguably, a sculptor too. Exploiting
new technologies, particularly those capable of producing long spans and dramatic cantilevers, he has pursued a course like his countryman Antonio Gaudí's a
century before, using structural logic and metaphorical

references to forms found in nature to produce his buildings. His Stadelhofen Railroad Station (1990) in Zürich,
Switzerland makes dramatic use of bridges and roof extensions above a vaulted, underground arcade. Like Gaudí's
Güell Chapel and Güell Park viaduct, the station walls and
roof become an organic whole, reaching upward like the
trunk and branches of trees.

In 2001 Calatrava completed an addition, largely in concrete, to the Milwaukee Art Museum. It appears as an avian
creature about to take flight, its most prominent element
being a soaring, kinetic sun-control device that tempers the
environment in the museum's glazed reception area (Fig.
16.77). Beneath this fantastic contrivance, the low-slung
galleries run north–south, seemingly extruded from the
base of the brise-soleil, until they reach the War Memorial
Art Gallery built in the 1960s by Eero Saarinen. Finally, a
pedestrian bridge supported by a leaning mast and cables
reaches back to the east and downtown Milwaukee.

In recent years Calatrava has made bridges something
of a specialty, many of them involving masts for suspension cables. These include the Sundial Bridge at Turtle Bay
(2004) in Redding, California, the Chords Bridge (2008)
in Jerusalem, and the Samuel Beckett Bridge (2009) in
Dublin. His arched-truss footbridge over the Grand Canal
(2008) is a rare modern insertion into the historic fabric of
Venice, Italy.

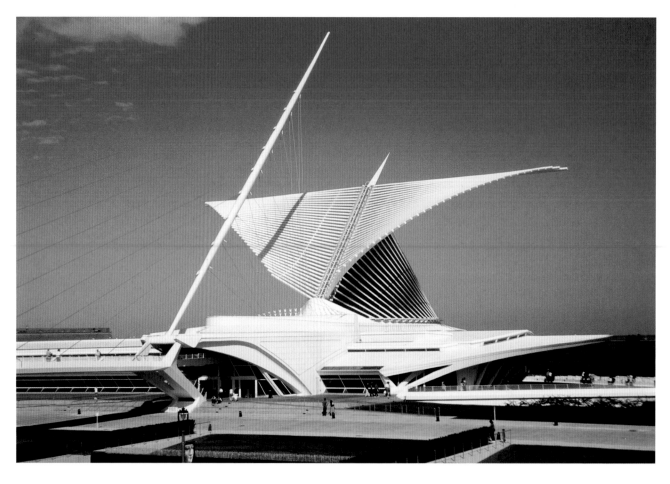

16.77 (above) Santiago Calatrava, Milwaukee Art Museum addition, Milwaukee, Wisconsin, 2001.
While this roof could easily be a large piece of sculpture, it is actually a kinetic sunscreen. Eero Saarinen designed the original museum to which Calatrava made this distinctive addition.

16.78 (below) Santiago Calatrava, Liège Guillemins TGV Railway Station, Liège, Belgium, 2009.
Looking as much like a fabric canopy as a steel construction, this station's giant roof hovers over the travel functions below it. The forms demonstrate that a logical response to the laws of physics can produce art.

Calatrava's Liège Guillemins TGV Railroad Station in Liège, Belgium (2009) (Fig. 16.78), which is surrounded by traditional, low-rise brick buildings, is a giant, white, vault-like steel construction composed of ribs that span over 500 feet, with cantilevered canopies reaching out from it into surrounding space. Station functions spread out sedately on a universal platform raised fifteen feet above ground level.

Herzog and de Meuron

Avoiding any form of representation, the Swiss architects Jacques Herzog and Pierre de Meuron (both born 1950) aspire to an "immediate, visceral impact" with their buildings, meaning that they have paid particular attention to enclosure systems and have become famous for the results. Their Rue des Suisses Housing in Paris (2000) is a long concrete box fixed on three sides with outriggers supporting a diagonal grid of rope that, in turn, serves as a trellis. On the fourth side, rippling expanses of roll-down wooden shutters protect balconies.

Herzog and de Meuron designed their Laban Centre for Movement and Dance (2002) for a site in Deptford, a London naval center from the early sixteenth century but a place from which former glories have largely vanished. Their building stands adjacent to an unimpressive stream that flows into the Thames and is surrounded by mediocre urban development (Fig. 16.79). Into this largely characterless scene the architects inserted a kind of warehouse of their own, a glowing one sheathed in durable plastic panels, some of them painted on their inner faces in pastel shades of lime, magenta, and turquoise. The building's plan is trapezoidal, with its shorter base deformed in a gentle concave arc that responds in kind to the area's most notable building, Thomas Archer's Church of St.

Paul (1712–30) on Deptford High Street, with its circular tower rising from a semicircular portico. At the center's core sits a windowless auditorium, and around it and lit by skylights run corridors of constantly changing widths, with reflecting pools below on the ground floor. Interior spatial character varies from corporate mechanistic to New Age ethereal. Dancers' forms appear as moving apparitions to those in Deptford viewing the building at night, and carefully selected window placements provide users with intermittent connections to their surroundings.

As an object in the city, Herzog and de Meuron's Prada Tokyo store (2003) is Mies van der Rohe's glass skyscraper project of 1922 become a pleated crystal of diamond-shaped, concave, convex, and flat glass panels. At night, as seen from the street, vertical steel elevator shafts and plenums rise like tree trunks, their limbs being horizontal tubes used as dressing rooms, all made homogeneous through the application of creamy hues of acrylic paint. Adjacent to the angular tower lies a plaza, an anomaly within Tokyo's dense urbanism.

In the United States, Herzog and de Meuron's 2005 addition to the Walker Art Center in Minneapolis (Fig. 16.80) doubled the size of the careful and hermetic 1970s building designed by Edward Larrabee Barnes (1915–2004). The principal feature, rising from a base of one-story, skewed masses, is a sculpted tower sheathed in quilted aluminum mesh and pierced with irregular openings. It contains a

16.79 Jacques Herzog and Pierre de Meuron, Laban Centre for Movement and Dance, Deptford, England, 2002.
Seen in daylight, this building is reflective and is reflected in the foreground water. Seen at night, it is translucent and delicately polychromatic. The steeple to the left belongs to the early eighteenth-century Church of St. Paul.

restaurant, theater, and event spaces, and is cantilevered out over the sidewalk, where it appears to hover.

None of Herzog and de Meuron's buildings has achieved a higher profile than the National Stadium in Beijing (2007), built for the 2008 Summer Olympics (Fig. 16.81). The design was derived from an initial concept presented by the China Architecture Design and Research Group and developed in consultation with controversial Chinese artist Ai Weiwei and with engineering done by the Arup firm. Inspired by traditional Chinese ceramics and made of steel tube sections, the outer skeleton of bent trussed columns and crisscrossed trusses behaves as a space frame but looks to have been woven, to the point that locals dubbed it the "bird's nest," a name that in China carries with it a sense of extraordinariness. The "visually porous" outer layer conceals the conventional concrete seating and allows for the building to be extremely dramatic when illuminated at night.

Elizabeth Diller and Ricardo Scofidio

The development of modern architecture has been intertwined with modern painting since the beginning of the twentieth century. While painting has given way to various other media in the art world, the connections between art and architecture are still strong, and nowhere more so than in the work of Elizabeth Diller and Ricardo Scofidio (both born 1954), the former an art and architecture student at

16.80 Herzog and de Meuron, Walker Art Center, Minneapolis, Minnesota, 2005.
This image illustrates the skill with which Herzog and de Meuron have come to manipulate building envelopes. The material is quilted aluminum with panels arranged in a grid and with sections strategically folded.

16.81 Herzog and de Meuron, National Stadium, Beijing, China, 2007.
The three-dimensionality of this structure makes it different from most of Herzog and de Meuron's work. The stadium became the most prominent symbol of the 2008 Summer Olympics.

Cooper Union when the latter was a teacher there. Anyone examining the exhibition of their various installations at the Whitney Museum of American Art in 2003 would have been impressed by their use of moving images, robotic systems, translucent materials, sophisticated assemblies, and transferred technologies, as well as their pursuit of a host of artistic themes.

The application of their art thinking to architecture can be seen to advantage in their Brasserie restaurant (2000) located within the base of Mies van der Rohe's Seagram Building in New York City. Necessarily hermetic because it lies below grade, it demanded the creation of an artificial environment. Diller and Scofidio introduced a backlit wall of apparently floating bottles behind the bar, above which a strip of video screens displays images of entering patrons. A perforated metal ceiling becomes a wall, then becomes the seating inside a space that seems to glow from within. The artist-architects' Blur Building (really a large installation) in Lake Neuchâtel in Yverdon-les-Bains, Switzerland (2002) took transparency and luminosity a step further and to a much larger scale, being a lightweight metal frame from which a fine mist of water was sprayed, creating a localized environment like a cloud descended to earth.

Diller and Scofidio's Slither Housing (2000) in Kitagata, Japan applies translucency to the problem of low-income urban living. Here, fifteen modular towers are set at slight angles to one another, creating a gentle arc in plan and allowing the perforated metal façade panels to overlap at their edges. As in the Brasserie, the detailing of handrails, cantilevered sunscreens, and internal, sliding, durable-plastic panels seems to be a logical extension of assembly investigations in their art installations.

Now practicing as Diller, Scofidio, and Renfro (with Charles Renfro (born 1964) added in 2004), the firm produced the High Line on the West Side of Manhattan (2004–09; second phase opened in 2011) (Fig. 16.82). Working along with James Corner Field Operations, their problem was to make an abandoned one-and-one-half-mile-long elevated railroad into a public garden and promenade. Atop steel columns and girders, which raise the High Line thirty feet above street level, they removed the rail surface and replaced it with concrete planks interwoven with plots of hardy plantings more suggestive of the wild growth that had volunteered here after the trains disappeared than a traditional well-maintained park. Intermittent developed spaces, benches and heavy chaise longues, and pieces of the old rails provide a varied rhythm for those walking, and the location of the High Line at the third-floor level of adjacent buildings makes for a unique perspective on the cityscape.

16.82 Diller, Scofidio, and Renfro, High Line, New York City, 2004–09, 2011.
Abandoned elevated tracks in Lower Manhattan had long been an obstruction and an eyesore. Now reborn as the High Line, they provide New Yorkers with a linear park and a platform for viewing the surrounding city.

SUSTAINABLE DESIGN

The subject of sustainable design, or green architecture, meaning architecture that has the least possible negative impact on the environment, ideally none at all, is a difficult and often paradoxical one. It involves not only a building's effects on its site during and after construction, but the repercussions of gathering and processing the building materials, providing the required energy for ongoing use, and much more. Architects, some more than others, have always been concerned with environmental issues, but the breadth and depth of concerns, including such matters as dwindling energy supplies, global warming, widespread destruction of habitat and extinction of species, and overpopulation have pushed sustainability to the fore. General cultural and governmental responses have as yet been sporadic and incomplete (more aggressive in Europe than the United States), and architectural responses can only be described as immature. It seems obvious, however, that environmental degradation will become one of the most important issues, if not the single most important one, facing coming generations.

One of the most visible instruments of green-architecture advocacy is the U.S. Building Council's Leadership in Energy and Environmental Design (LEED) certification program, which rates everything from air quality to noise levels. Some critics have argued that the program is useless unless building performance is tested after construction, and this has indeed now become a requirement. Others

16.83 R. Buckminster Fuller, Geodesic dome, U.S. Pavilion, Montreal International Exposition 1967.
In the 1960s, Buckminster Fuller traveled far and wide, wearing watches from three time zones (one each for where he was, where he had been, and where he was going) and lecturing to every student who would listen. Within his multi-hour presentations were detailed discussions of his geodesic domes illustrated by his hand drawings.

have warned that by cherry-picking LEED requirements, project developers can use LEED certification as a sales pitch rather than a defining philosophy. Within extremely complex circumstances, efforts to refine this and other means for advocating, mandating, and measuring good environmental stewardship go on.

Many of the architects already discussed have made sustainability a significant component of their designs, like Norman Foster at his London City Hall and Steven Holl at his Linked Hybrid. Renzo Piano has done so consistently with his roofs engineered by the Arup firm to carefully modulate the rays of the sun. His reconstruction of the California Academy of Sciences in San Francisco (2008) retained ninety percent of the existing building, has conditioned space only in animal-and-plant display and storage areas, uses photovoltaic cells to control a giant glass canopy over the central plaza, and has an undulating green roof, all done in consultation with the Arup firm.

Three designers have been singled out below only to suggest varied approaches: R. Buckminster Fuller for what might be termed a "world vision"; Glenn Murcutt for his reliance on passive (meaning non-energy-driven) systems for temperature modulation; and Thom Mayne for his efforts to combine active (or energy-driven) and passive systems, and to do so in a way that still allows for radical form-making.

R. Buckminster Fuller

R. Buckminster Fuller (1895–1983) can only be categorized as uncategorizable, but he was certainly a pioneer in the efficient use of materials. With wildly divergent influences, such as family connections back to New England transcendentalists and navy experience in applied engineering, he became to some a visionary savant of advanced technologies and an early proponent of global-resource conservation; to others, he was more of a showman and gadfly. In any case, he streaked like a meteor through the architectural sky on a trajectory of cosmic-scale predictions and universal design strategies. At least conceptually, his Dymaxion House (1927–29), a low-cost living unit suspended from

a central mast and intended for placement on sites by sky-cranes, was certainly a more mass-producible, efficient "machine for living" than anything offered up by a European Modernist architect. Most of his built projects were geodesic domes, or domes made of light, straight structural members held largely in tension. The best known of these was constructed in 1967 for the Montreal International Exposition, or Expo '67 (Fig. 16.83).

Glenn Murcutt

Working in a one-man practice, the Australian architect Glenn Murcutt (born 1936) has pursued a personal line of inquiry that emphasizes both form-making and adaptation to environment in a way that is quiet, effective, and genuine. Among the early influences on him were Mies van der Rohe, particularly through his Farnsworth House, and Richard Neutra and Craig Ellwood (1922–92) in California, both of whom produced elegant post-and-beam frames like Mies. Murcutt was also imbued with a reverence for site by the so-called Sydney School of designers at work in Australia in the late 1950s and early 1960s. He became interested in lightweight, permeable structures, building upon his experiences with a father who exposed him to the Australian agricultural buildings of wood and

16.84 Glenn Murcutt, Local History Museum and Tourist Office, Kempsey, New South Wales, 1976, 1979–82, 1986–88.
Murcutt has drawn upon the local vernacular for many of his forms, but has reinterpreted them in terms of modern materials and methods of construction. The exhaust turbines on the roof become important formal elements.

corrugated metal and who sensitized him to the act of making. Murcutt tends to design units that are long and narrow, with their long sides facing north and south in order to assure proper ventilation and respond to the path of the sun. He extrudes their cross-sections, but gives them complex profiles, again responding to sun and wind as well as to human habitation. He then details these skins to accept louvers and screens that both modulate climatic forces and articulate their surfaces. Subsequent to contact with the Mexican architect Luis Barragán (see Fig. 16.9), Murcutt has made pools of water a significant feature in many of his projects.

The Douglas Murcutt House in Sydney (1969–72) is Farnsworth House-like in form but lowered to the ground and merged with nature by means of a courtyard planted with native vegetation. The Ball-Eastaway House (1980–83), located northwest of Sydney, consists of a tubular-steel-frame pavilion, minimalist in its structure and minimal in its environmental impact. Sited in a forest of acacias, eucalyptuses, and banksias, it has a vaulted cross-section with walls largely covered by louvers and a down-spout system that is akin to sculpture. In Kempsey, New South Wales, Murcutt designed a Local History Museum and Tourist Office (1976, 1979–82, and 1986–88) (Fig. 16.84) that is equally subtle and overt in its responses to

environmental forces. He placed non-bearing brick walls atop a brick base, insulated them, then covered them with zinc alloy panels; the corrugated metal roof is supported by a separate tubular-steel frame. Ventilation occurs in the seam between the systems and is enhanced and dramatized by roof monitors. The rich textures of the walls and ceiling, and the light qualities they allow, belie their straightforward construction origins. The Magney House at Bingi Point, New South Wales (1982–84) (Fig. 16.85) is a Miesian box no more. Its asymmetrical butterfly roof, metal cladding, louvers, and downspout system leading to subterranean cisterns come together in a metallic organism fine-tuned to its windswept environment and its purpose as a vacation house for clients who had long visited and admired the site.

As a metaphor for Australian mining structures, Murcutt's unbuilt Minerals and Mining Museum in Broken Hill, New South Wales (1987–89) (Fig. 16.86) exaggerates both the frame and the skin, yielding something

16.85 (right) Glenn Murcutt, Magney House, Bingi Point, New South Wales, 1982–84.
Beneath the slab of this house, Murcutt placed cisterns to collect rainwater. The apparently eccentric roof form actually responds both to the path of the sun and to prevailing winds.

16.86 (below) Glenn Murcutt, Plan of the Minerals and Mining Museum, Broken Hill, New South Wales, 1987–89.
Many of Murcutt's plans are long and narrow, like this one, in order to take advantage of orientation and cross-ventilation. The skin, separate from the structural grid, seems alive in its sensitivity to its context.

the studio, and alongside the pool and the living quarters is calculated to give the occupants a sense of gradual withdrawal into a private realm with almost monastic qualities.

Thom Mayne and Morphosis

The Los Angeles firm called Morphosis (meaning here "manner of formation") began with Thom Mayne (born 1944) and, until 1991, Michael Rotondi (born 1949) as partners and had strong connections to the Southern California Institute of Architecture, of which they were both founders. The body of their early work, much of it unbuilt, is striking for its adventurous use of computer modeling; dramatic expression of structural elements; transparencies and translucencies; and the related disintegration of traditional enclosure systems—a kind of Futurism–De Stijl–Constructivist collision conceived for the nowhere urbanism of Southern California in which a building often has to fight for its life.

For the Diamond Ranch High School in Los Angeles (1999), Mayne did not allow a modest budget to deter him from the kind of spatial experimentation for which he has become well known. Using corrugated metal as a wall material, he created a central, linear student mall flanked by angular, leaning, sometimes cantilevered building masses. One mass with a secondary circulation spine alternates classrooms and courtyards and culminates with an outdoor theater and gymnasium. Opposite this aggressive assemblage, more classrooms sit atop parking and alternate with dramatic ramps adjacent to bulging courtyards. The project has been celebrated for both its internal civic nature and its external integration into the freeway sprawl around its steeply sloping site.

As Mayne's work has evolved, he has become more concerned with environmental issues, particularly energy efficiency, and in so doing he has become a favorite of the Federal Government's General Services Administration, which chose him to design the un-air-conditioned San Francisco Federal Building (2005) (Fig. 16.87). This facility, which has a wide and shallow plan to facilitate ventilation and sun control, uses half the power of a conventional building its size, though it must be said that many occupants have complained that it is uncomfortable to work in. It has a concrete structural frame and a perforated, partially operable skin of stainless steel on its southeast side, along with a north-facing green-glass wall that has the appearance of iconic Modernist buildings. Ironically, the Federal Building does not satisfy LEED requirements.

In 2009 Mayne completed the building at 41 Cooper Square for the Cooper Union for the Advancement of Science and Art in Manhattan's East Village (Fig. 16.88). It has a poured-in-place-concrete skeleton, a sculpted skin of perforated, semi-transparent, sometimes-operable stainless steel, and a scooped-out atrium with stairs intended to serve as a "vertical piazza" for seeing, meeting, and interacting in a place that houses multiple disciplines. Mayne

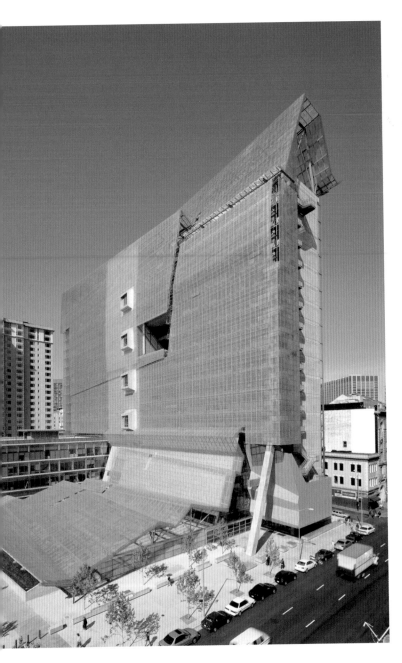

16.87 Thom Mayne, San Francisco Federal Building, 2005. Instead of aspiring to be primarily a dignified civic monument, this federal building sets an example for a culture in need of decreasing its energy consumption—hence the wide, shallow plan and the absence of such trappings as a dome.

akin to—but more explicable perhaps than—the work of the Deconstructivists. Rammed-earth walls outfitted with wind traps of Egyptian inspiration keep the interior space ten degrees centigrade cooler than the outside air without the benefit of mechanical air-conditioning. Finally, the Simpson-Lee House in Mount Wilson, New South Wales (1989–94) possesses an equipoise that results from the placement of each piece—frame-constructed pavilions, linear walkway, and pool of water—in a kind of environmental equilibrium. Movement along the walkway, past insists that the building was designed outward from this socio-spatial core. Like the San Francisco Federal Building, it aspires to green-ness through ample daylighting, heat recovery, and a green roof.

CONCLUSIONS ABOUT ARCHITECTURAL IDEAS

The lion's share of buildings discussed in this final chapter have interiors that are accessible, at least in part, to the public; this emphasis is deliberate. Reading about architecture while studying drawings and photographs is one good way to get some architectural education, but as a vicarious activity it has its limits. Architecture needs to be walked through, touched, and used; it needs to be experienced; and the authors hope that this is what will happen.

The principal conclusion to be drawn from this chapter must be that there is no main line of development in building design at the beginning of the twenty-first century. Post-Modernism has come and gone, and Deconstruction has proved to be more of a label than a direction. Like culture in general, and for better or for worse, pluralism best describes the current situation. There are some new forces at work, perhaps the most obvious being the computer. Electronic drafting programs and the Internet have made it much easier for architects and architectural offices to cooperate. Numerous individuals, including engineers, can now have access to drawings simultaneously, and changes in them can be made easily and universally with little concern for geography. In addition, the ability of the computer to rapidly draw polygons and curvatures and represent the three-dimensional results in a form that is now approaching photorealism has made complex shapes more conceivable and buildable and so more fashionable and, in tandem with new construction technologies, has encouraged wide-ranging investigations of new building-enclosure systems, meaning exterior walls or skins.

Finally, it is also impossible to imagine that the twin issues of environmental degradation and dwindling energy supplies are not going to radically alter daily life worldwide, sooner rather than later. That well-known view from space of the third planet from the Sun—our beautiful but finite and fragile blue orb, or, as R. Buckminster Fuller enjoyed saying, "spaceship Earth"—is being despoiled at an alarming rate. This book is replete with cultures that variously degraded their environments, some, like the Pre-Columbian Maya, to a point where they became unlivable; but this was only a regional catastrophe. The issue is now global and will demand global solutions of which architecture must be a part.

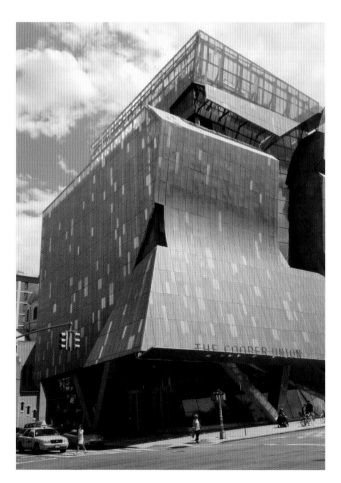

16.88 Thom Mayne, 41 Cooper Square, New York City, 2009.
This extravagant but introverted building has a dramatic central atrium. Beneath the sculpted exterior covering of stainless steel some angular elements of the concrete structural system are visible. The Cooper Union for the Advancement of Art and Science owns the land on which the Chrysler Building stands and so receives ground rent from the owners, who have changed over time.

Glossary

Abacus On a classical column, the stone set directly over the capital.

Abbey A monastery governed by an abbot.

Acanthus A plant used as a model for decoration on Corinthian and Composite capitals.

Acropolis Literally "high city". In Greek city-states, the acropolis was the location of the most important temples and religious shrines.

Acroterion An upright ornament placed at the apex and eaves of gabled roofs in Greek architecture.

Adobe A wall-building material made from sun-dried clay or clay-like earth.

Agora In Greek cities, the term applied to the area of markets and city government.

Aisle In a basilican church, the portion set parallel to the nave, generally separated from it by columns or piers.

Allée A linear garden walk defined by trees on both sides.

Ambulatory The curving passageway behind the choir of a church, often used to connect the radiating chapels.

Amphitheater An arena with raked seating arranged around a circular or oval floor.

Aniconic Ornamentation that is symbolically suggestive rather than literally representational.

Anta A pilaster-like thickening of the wall edge or jamb of a wall opening that responds to an adjacent column.

Apadana An audience hall in Persian palace architecture.

Appartements A suite of rooms (French).

Apse The termination of the nave of a basilica or the choir in a basilican church.

Aqueduct A pipe for conducting water under gravity flow. The term is often applied to the arched structure built to support the pipe across valleys.

Arcade A series of arches carried on columns or piers.

Arch A curved element that spans an opening and supports the structural loads above it. Most often, arches are made of small, wedge-shaped masonry elements called voussoirs. The profile of an arch may vary from semicircular to pointed to almost flat.

Architrave In classical architecture, the bottom portion of an entablature.

Arris The intersection of two curved surfaces, most commonly applied to the line formed when the flutes of a Doric column join.

Ashlar Smooth stone masonry laid so that the joints are visible.

Atelier An architect's studio or workplace.

Atrium The central space of a Roman house, open to the sky and serving as a source of light and fresh air. In Early Christian churches, the atrium was a large open courtyard, surrounded by covered galleries, which preceded the entrance to the church.

Attic The story built above the cornice of a building, sometimes used to conceal the roof.

Axis A line at the end of which movement terminates at a significant feature and thereby divides a composition into two equal parts.

Balcony A platform cantilevered from a wall, generally surrounded by a railing or balustrade.

Baldachin or **Baldacchino** An elaborate canopy erected over an altar.

Balloon framing A wooden framing system composed of vertical studs extended unbroken from bottom sill to top plate even in multistory construction.

Baptistery A building, generally octagonal, used for the Christian rite of baptism.

Barrel vault A semicircular vault over a rectangular space.

Base The lowest part of a column or pier, often broader than the sections above to spread the load to the foundation.

Basilica Literally, "king's hall". In Roman architecture, a hall used for public administration. The term generally refers to a rectangular building that has a central section with a higher roof (the nave if a double) flanked by lower aisles on both long sides. A semicircular projection, the apse, was often set at one or both of the shorter ends. Early Christians adapted the form as a basis for church design, replacing one apse with the main entrance and establishing a processional axis the length of the building. The altar was placed in the apse at the end.

Bastide A medieval new town founded both for defense and economic development of an unsettled region.

Bay A building module defined by the repetition of an element such as a column or pier.

Bazaar A covered market in Islamic cities.

Beam A horizontal element that carries structural loads between upright supports.

Bellcote A modest belfry located astride the ridge of a church roof or made as a narrowed extension upward of the principal gabled façade.

Belfry The tower or steeple in which bells are hung.

Beltcourse A projecting horizontal board or projecting course(s) of brick or stone that define a floor level on the inside.

Belvedere An elevated room or structure situated to afford a fine view or capture breezes.

Bienséance Concerned with appropriateness and the correct form of a building relative to its purpose in eighteenth-century French architectural theory.

Blind opening A framed element like a window applied to a wall but lacking an opening to the outside.

Bochki Reverse curve gables seen in Russian architecture.

Boiserie Interior wood paneling enriched by carving, gilding, painting, or inlay.

Book-matched Side-by-side sheets of veneer arranged to have symmetrical graining about their common joint.

Bosco A dense grove of trees.

Bouleterion In classical Greek architecture, a building used for senate or council meetings.

Bracket set Elaborate interlocking supports in Chinese architecture that produce a roof overhang.

Brise-soleil A screen attached to a building to shade windows from the sun.

Buttress Masonry reinforcement applied to a wall to provide additional strength.

Caisson An airtight box or chamber used for work on river bottoms.

Caldarium The hot or sweating bath chamber in Roman baths or thermae.

Campanile In Italy, the name given to a freestanding belltower.

Cantilever A beam firmly anchored on one end and unsupported at the other end.

Capital In classical architecture the termination of a column, generally given decorative carving.

Caravanserai Accommodation for traveling merchants, usually built around a large open court and provided with stables for animals, secure storage for cargo, and an inn for travelers.

Cardo In Etruscan and Roman cities, the principal north-south road.

Carolingian The term applied to buildings constructed under the influence of the emperor Charlemagne, who reigned from 792 to 814.

Cartouche A boldly decorated frame hung above doorways.

Caryatid A pier carved in the form of a standing woman and used in place of a column.

Castrum A Roman military camp or garrison (pl. *castra*).

Cathedral The church that serves as seat of a bishop. (The bishop's chair is called a cathedra.)

Cavetto A concave molding, usually a quadrant of a circle and often used for cornices.

Cella The shrine room in the center of a temple.

Cement The binding component of concrete. Natural cements occur in areas of former volcanic activity, as around Puteoli in Italy, where the Romans exploited deposits they called pozzolana. Artificial cements have been made since 1824, when Joseph Aspdin discovered a process for heating limestone, clay, and sand to a very high temperature and then grinding the results.

Cenotaph A monument erected in memory of someone who is not interred within it.

Centering The wooden scaffold or form required to support a masonry vault or arch while under construction.

Chaitya In India, a traditional village memorial erected over the grave of an honored person. A structure built to enclose such a memorial and permit circulation around it is known as a chaitya hall.

Chancel The east end of a church, in which the main altar is placed.

Chapter house An assembly room in a monastery, generally located off the cloister, where the monks and abbot gathered daily for reading a chapter of the Rule by which monastic life was governed.

Charrette A period of intense work on an architectural project at its conclusion. The term is derived from the cart, or charrette, used to pick up Ecole des Beaux-Arts student projects throughout Paris.

Château The French word for castle. In Renaissance France, the term is generally applied to a large country residence without any military pretentions.

Chatra A triple-tiered umbrella form set atop a stupa, symbolic of the Bodhi tree under which Buddha gained enlightenment.

Chigi In Shinto architecture, upward extensions of bargeboards at gable ends of the shrine, forming an X-shape.

Choir The eastern end of a basilican church, where the divine service was sung.

Classical language of architecture The architectural grammar based on the classical orders of ancient Greece and Rome.

Clerestory Windows placed high in a wall, generally above lower roof elements.

Cloister In a monastery, the covered walk surrounding a quadrangular court that connects the domestic buildings and the church.

Cloister vault A dome with groined surfaces rising from a square or octagonal base. Also known as a domical vault.

Coffers Ceiling recesses set in a geometric pattern.

Colonnade A linear series of columns with entablature.

Column In classical architecture, the upright structural element consisting of a base, shaft, and capital.

Composite A Roman order combining features of the Ionic and Corinthian.

Concrete A plastic building material consisting of sand, water, cement, and aggregate, which hardens to a stone-like consistency.

Console A bracket, generally decoratively curved, that supports a cornice or projecting element.

Convenance Concerned with appropriateness and the correct form of a building relative to its purpose in eighteenth-century French architectural theory.

Coquille A seashell-like organic form.

Corbel Masonry that projects slightly from a wall and serves as a support.

Corbeled vault Construction, without true arching action, made by shifting opposing courses slightly and regularly inward until they meet.

Corinthian The order that features acanthus-leaf capitals atop a fluted shaft.

Cornice The uppermost element of an entablature, which projects beyond the plane of the exterior wall; more generally, the overhanging molding atop any building.

Corps-de-logis The main, freestanding unit in a French building complex.

Cortile In Italian architecture, the term applied to an open courtyard inside a building.

Crockets Decorative bud-like protrusions on the angles of Gothic stonework, especially on spires and towers.

Crossing In a basilican church, the space where transepts, nave, and choir intersect.

Cross-in-square Another name for the quincunx plan.

Cross vault The vault formed by two intersecting barrel vaults. Also known as a groin vault.

Crypt The basement level of a church, originally used for burial.

Cupola A dome. The term is also applied to the lantern on any roof structure, and is generally used to describe the structure over the oculus of a dome.

Curtain wall In medieval castles, a section of defensive walling between projecting towers. In modern construction, a nonstructural exterior surface hung from metal framing.

Cyclopean masonry Walls made of very large stones, only minimally shaped.

Decorated period Phase of the English Gothic following the Early English, sometimes divided into the Geometric and subsequent Curvilinear; its features include elaborated tracery and lierne and tierceron ribs.

Decumanus In Etruscan and Roman cities, the principal east–west road.

Dentil A type of cornice molding composed of rectangular blocks set in a row like teeth; hence the name.

Diagonal rib A rib crossing a bay diagonally from pier impost to pier impost.

Dome A continuously curved roof over a polygonal or circular plan, generally having a semicircular or elliptical section.

Domical vault A dome with groined surfaces rising from a square or octagonal base. Also known as a cloister vault.

Domos The principal space in a megaron.

Doric The Greek order that has a fluted shaft, no base, and an echinus molding supporting the abacus. Roman Doric columns have a base.

Dormer A window that projects above the slope of a roof.

Drum The cylindrical volume supporting a dome.

Early English period First phase of the English Gothic, more or less equivalent to the French High Gothic.

Eave The edge of the roof plane that projects over the exterior wall of a building.

Echinus The curved cushion-like molding that, together with the abacus, forms the capital in the Doric order.

Eclecticism The selection and combination of architectural elements from a variety of styles.

Egg-and-Dart An egg-shaped ornament alternating with a dart-shaped one.

Elève An entering student at the Ecole des Beaux-Arts.

Enfilade The aligning of a series of doors through a series of adjacent rooms.

En suite A series of rooms arranged side by side.

Entablature In classical architecture, the horizontal elements supported by columns, consisting (in ascending sequence) of the architrave, frieze, and cornice.

Entasis The slight outward curve of a column, which then tapers toward the top of the shaft.

Esquisse A preliminary sketch or quickly drawn design solution expressing the germinal idea in the Ecole des Beaux-Arts design process.

Exedra A semicircular niche, often used as a seat of honor or place for a statue.

Façade The exterior elevation of a building.

Faïence A mainly quartz and sand (non-clay), glazed, ceramic material, usually light blue-green in color with subtle surface variations.

Fan vault In English Perpendicular Gothic buildings, vaults with ribs having the same curvature and radiating or fanning out from the springing of the vault.

Fascia Horizontal bands in the architrave of the Ionic and Corinthian orders; more generally, the end board of a roof at the eaves.

Feng shui The Chinese art of adjusting a design to site-specific conditions so as to promote harmony in accordance with Daoist principles.

Ferroconcrete Concrete with embedded steel wire or rods. The combination takes advantage of the compressive strength of the former and the tensile strength of the latter.

Fillet The flat vertical face between the flutings of a column shaft.

Fluting Vertical grooves incised in the shaft of a classical column.

Flying buttress In Gothic architecture, the combination of external buttress pier and slender arch, which attaches to a wall just below the springing of the vaulting in order to resist lateral thrust.

Forum In Roman towns, the open space near the center used for commerce and civic life.

Fresco A painting executed on wall surfaces by working pigments into wet plaster.

Frieze The horizontal element above the architrave and below the cornice in an entablature.

Frigidarium The cold-water baths in a Roman thermae.

Frontispiece An elaborated door surround at the front façade of a building.

Gable The pedimented end of a classical temple; more generally, the triangular space at the end of a double-pitched roof.

Galilee A porch or chapel at the west end of medieval churches.

Gallery The passage over the aisle in medieval churches.

Garbhagriha The "womb chamber" or shrine room at the heart of a Hindu temple.

Gargoyle A decorative rainwater spout, often carved to resemble a fanciful animal.

Geodesic dome A grid-like structure that takes the form of a dome and is composed only of small, linear elements, most of them held in tension.

Gopura In Hindu architecture, a monumental gateway erected on axis with the temple.

Grand salon The major living space in a Venetian palace, usually extending from front to back of the house.

Greek-cross plan A plan in the form of a cross having arms of equal length.

Groin vault The vault formed by two intersecting barrel vaults. Also known as a cross vault.

Ha-ha A ditch used to control the movement of livestock, which is not visible in a planned landscape.

Half-timbering Wall construction with heavy-timber members carrying the structural load and made weather-tight with infill materials.

Hall church A basilican church where the nave and aisles are of similar height.

Hammerbeam A bracketed cantilevered beam used as support for a timber roof truss.

Haram Literally, "private" or "sacred". Used to describe the sanctuary in a mosque and the family living quarters in an Islamic house.

Harmika The square railing at the top of a stupa.

Hemicycle A semicircular room or recess.

Hipped roof A roof built with inclined gables on all four sides.

Hôtel A French urban domestic building.

Huaca An ancient Peruvian sacred artifact, animal, or land form inhabited by a god or spirit.

Hypostyle hall A large hall composed of many columns placed close together to support the roof.

Iconostasis A screen in Byzantine churches that divides the nave from the chancel and that is used as a support for devotional images or icons.

Imperial stair A stair that rises up a central flight to a landing then doubles back on either side to complete its ascent.

Impluvium In Roman houses, the shallow pool that collected rainwater draining from the atrium roof.

In antis columns Columns in the plane of a wall and often between antae.

Insula A Roman apartment house.

Intarsia Mosaic inlay in wood.

Intercolumniation The space between columns.

Ionic The order that features volutes in the capital; the shaft is usually fluted.

I-section A structural member with an I-shaped cross section; its horizontal members are called flanges and its vertical member a web.

Iwan Roofed or vaulted chamber open on one side, often facing the courtyard of a mosque.

Jetty A short wooden cantilever supporting an upper wall section, most commonly found on timber houses of the medieval period.

Jian A module used in Chinese wooden architecture, particularly houses, measuring about twelve by twenty feet.

Katsuogi Short horizontal elements set atop the ridge of Shinto shrines; probably used originally to hold down the thatch roof.

Keep The central enclosed tower of a medieval castle.

Keystone The central voussoir of an arch.

Ki A brush-and mud-covered domical structure built by indigenous tribes in the American southwest.

Kiva A ritual or assembly space in the Ancestral Pueblo culture, often circular, and usually sunken into the ground.

Kodo In Japanese Buddhist architecture, the name given to the lecture hall.

Külliye The Turkish word for a mosque and its related buildings, typically including educational, charitable, medical, and commercial facilities.

Label molding A molding that extends horizontally across an opening, then returns vertically for a short distance down each side.

Labyrinth A building with, or arrangement of, winding or confusing pathways.

Lantern A tower with windows rising above the roofline or above the oculus of a dome.

Lierne A decorative, nonstructural supplementary rib added to Gothic vaulting.

Linga An upright stone in traditional Indian shrines symbolic of the male element.

Lintel Any horizontal member that spans an opening.

Loggia An open porch, generally raised above the ground floor and covered by a roof.

Lombard bands Decorative wall detailing composed of corbeled arches and pilasters.

Long-and-short work Quoin-like masonry corners with units oriented alternately horizontally and vertically.

Long gallery A wide and long passageway in English and French Renaissance houses used for living purposes.

Lunette The semi-circular or crescent-shaped projection of a window opening into a vaulted ceiling.

Lustral basin A pool used for ritual purification.

Machicolation In medieval fortifications, a corbeled stone gallery projecting in front of a defensive wall, open at the bottom to allow materials to be dropped on those below.

Madrasa Islamic college for theological, legal, and literary studies.

Mandala The geometrical diagram based on a subdivided square that is used to generate proportions for Hindu temple designs.

Mandorla An almond-shaped frame surrounding the image of a saint, used to indicate divinity.

Maqsura In early mosques, an area in front of the mihrab reserved for officials and sometimes given extra ornamentation (unusual vaulting or a dome) or special screening for security.

Marché Movement along a defined architectural path.

Martyrium A building associated with a Christian martyr.

Masjid A district or neighborhood mosque.

Mastaba An Egyptian tomb with a flat top and sloping sides, built over a grave shaft.

Mausoleum An elaborate tomb, named after the tomb of King Mausoleus.

Medallion An ornamental plaque, frequently oval or square.

Megalith Large stones or boulders used in prehistoric architecture.

Megaron In Mycenaean architecture, a rectangular room having a central hearth and four columns supporting a roof with an atrium opening. More generally, the term applies to a single-cell house in the Aegean region.

Metope An element of the Doric frieze, set alternately with triglyphs. Metope panels contain low-relief carvings.

Mihrab A niche in the qibla wall indicating the direction of Mecca.

Minaret In Islamic architecture, the tower associated with a mosque from which the faithful are called to prayer.

Minbar In a mosque the pulpit from which the imam leads prayers.

Minka Wooden Japanese folk houses, typical of rural communities.

Moat A broad surrounding ditch, sometimes filled with water, constructed for defense.

Modillion Another word for console, sometimes applied to a series of ornamental brackets supporting a cornice.

Moment connection A connection between two elements, usually beam and column, that is capable of resisting a bending force.

Monastery A religious institution providing living accommodations and worship space for monks.

Mortise A rectangular opening, or socket, prepared to receive a tenon, usually in wooden construction.

Mosaic A floor, wall, or ceiling decoration composed of small pieces of colored glass or stone that form designs.

Mosque An Islamic house of prayer.

Motte-and-bailey Medieval castle with a mound (motte) and yard (bailey) defined by a ditch and wall.

Muqarna Islamic vault treatment that fragments the surface into many concave segments. Muqarnas may be built in masonry or suspended as elements from an overhead structure.

Mutules A block beneath the soffit of a Doric cornice, usually decorated with cylindrical or truncated conical elements.

Naos The sanctuary of a Greek temple.

Narthex The entrance porch or chamber before the nave of a church.

Nave The western arm of a basilican church.

Neo-Grec A mid-nineteenth-century interpretation of Neo-Classicism emphasizing bold, linear, abstracted forms.

Newel The center post around which a circular stair winds or a straight stair turns.

Niche A wall recess.

Nymphaeum A room or building with a fountain or spring and intended for relaxation.

Obelisk A stone monolith, square in plan, with sides tapering toward a pyramidal top.

Oculus The circular opening at the apex of a dome.

Opisthodomos The enclosed room at the back of a Greek temple, often used as a treasury.

Opus incertum Roman walls built of irregularly shaped stones facing a concrete core.

Opus listatum Roman walls constructed of stone and brick in alternate courses.

Opus quadratum A Roman wall built of squared masonry.

Opus reticulatum A Roman wall formed of pyramidal stones, their points set inward and their square heads set to form a diagonal grid.

Opus testaceum Roman walls constructed of brick facing on a concrete core.

Orangery A building used to protect ornamental shrubs and trees in cold weather.

Orchestra In a Greek theater, the circular floor used for dancing.

Orders The trabeated systems of architecture developed by the Greeks and extended by the Romans. The Greek orders—Doric, Ionic, and Corinthian—differ slightly from the Roman orders. The Romans developed the Tuscan and Composite orders.

Ordonnance Correct relationship of parts to one another and to the whole in eighteenth-century French architectural theory.

Oriel window A corbeled bay window in English medieval architecture.

Pagoda A tapering tower with multiple roof levels, built by Buddhists particularly in China and Japan. The word derives from the Sanskrit dagoba, meaning stupa.

Palaestra A Roman building used for exercise; a gymnasium.

Palazzo A palace type; in the Italian Renaissance, a four-square block with central court or cortile and the main floor on the second or piano nobile level.

Palladian motif A central arched opening with lower trabeated openings to each side.

Parapet A low wall at the perimeter of a roof.

Parterre An ornamental, geometrical arrangement of flat, planted beds.

Pavilion A prominent feature in a façade composition, usually at the center or at the ends and typically set forward, raised higher, and capped with a distinctive roof form.

Pebble dash A stucco wall given a pitted texture by throwing pebbles against it.

Pediment The gable end of a temple, framed by cornices.

Pendant vaulting Vaults with suspended, decorative elements hanging from their ribs.

Pendentive A spherical triangle that transforms a square bay into a circle for the springing of a dome.

Pensionnaires French architectural students who spent an extended period studying in Rome.

Peripteral columns Columns placed around all sides of a building.

Peristyle A colonnaded court or garden.

Perpendicular period Final phase of the English Gothic characterized by strongly vertical panel tracery and fan vaults.

Piano nobile The main living floor of a house, generally raised a story above ground level.

Piazza An open space surrounded by buildings; in nineteenth-century American architecture, the term is sometimes applied to a porch on a house.

Pier A structural element, square or rectangular in plan, that supports an arch.

Pietra serena A gray stone used extensively in Renaissance Florence for architectural details.

Pilaster A rectangular column, engaged in a wall, which is sometimes articulated as an order.

Pilotis Freestanding posts or supports for an upper-level structure; the term was most commonly used by Le Corbusier.

Pit house A semi-subterranean structure with its one-room excavated space roofed by an earth-covered wood frame.

Plank house Similar to the shed house, a rectangular, post-and-lintel structure covered on its walls and roof with hand-split wood planks.

Pointed arch A two-centered arch, pointed at its apex.

Polis The ancient Greek city-state.

Polychromy The decorative use of colored stone, seen primarily in medieval architecture.

Pomochi In Russian wooden architecture, a series of stacked cantilevers.

Porte-cochère A projecting canopy or carriage porch.

Portico A colonnaded porch.

Post An upright structural member; a column.

Pozzolana A volcanic ash containing silicon and aluminum, which will harden as a cement when ground fine and mixed with lime and water.

Precis A brief or short, precise building program describing the essential elements to be designed that was issued at the Ecole des Beaux-Arts at the beginning of a design competition.

Prodomos See pronaos.

Projet rendu A fully rendered or highly developed and closely detailed design solution at the Ecole des Beaux-Arts.

Pronaos The vestibule or antechamber to the shrine room (naos) of a Greek temple.

Proskenion The area directly in front of the skene in the ancient Greek theater.

Prostyle A portico of columns on the front of a building.

Pueblo A communal house or group of houses built of adobe or stone.

Purlin A secondary beam, usually supporting roof rafters.

Putti Representations of plump, naked, often winged young children in paintings or sculptures.

Pylon A massive entrance to an Egyptian temple, with sloping walls and a central opening.

Qasr An Arabic word for castle.

Qibla The direction of Mecca, indicated in a mosque by the mihrab; by extension, the wall in which the mihrab is placed.

Quadripartite vault A vault over one bay divided by diagonal ribs into four parts.

Quatrefoil A four-lobed (or foiled) pattern seen frequently in Gothic architecture.

Quincunx Five objects arranged in a square, with one in the center. Byzantine churches with a quincunx plan typically have five domes, the center one being balanced by four domes at the corners.

Quoin A brick or piece of stone used to give strength or visual prominence to an external corner.

Ramada A flat-roofed rectangular post-and-lintel structure roofed with brush.

Ratha A wheeled cart or chariot. In Hindu architecture, the stone building form carved or constructed to resemble such a chariot.

Rayonnant Thirteenth- and fourteenth-century French Gothic tracery that is characterized by radiating lines.

Rib A raised molding applied to the arris of a vault.

Rib vault A vault where ribs ride below and usually support the vault web.

Rocaille Eighteenth-century scroll ornament based upon water-worn elements such as rocks and seashells.

Roundel A small circular panel or opening.

Rustication Rough stonework with exposed joints.

Sahn An open courtyard in a mosque.

Salient A projecting element, particularly an arrowhead-shaped projection from the walls of a fort.

Semidome A surface representing one-fourth of a sphere and often covering an apse.

Serdab In Egyptian tombs, an above-ground chamber where offerings to the deceased were placed.

Serliana A central arched opening with lower trabeated openings to each side. Also sometimes called a Palladian or Serlian motif.

Sexpartite vault A vault over two bays divided by diagonal ribs and a transverse rib into six parts.

Shaft The vertical element above the base and below the capital in an architectural order.

Shatyor Tent-roof forms used on Russian churches.

Shed house Similar to the plank house, a flat- or gable-roofed, post-and-lintel structure covered with wood planks.

Shikhara The tall curving roof, often with a parabolic profile, that rises like an artificial mountain over the garbhagriha in a Hindu temple.

Sipapu A fist-sized depression in Ancestral Pueblo Kivas, perhaps intended as a portal to the spirit world.

Skene The backdrop building in a classical theater.

Spandrel A wall surface, ornamented or unornmented, between major architectural elements such as windows or arches.

Sphinx A mythological creature with the body of a lion and a male human head.

Squinch A corbeled arch used to transform a square bay into an octagon for the springing of a dome.

Stave A tall post, generally a peeled tree-trunk, used in construction.

Stele An upright slab, often carrying images or inscriptions.

Stereotomy The art of carving stone in complex, three-dimensional forms.

Stoa In Greek architecture, a linear building with one or more rows of columns. Stoas could be used for shops, meetings, or exhibitions.

Stupa In Buddhist architecture, the mound of earth and stones erected over relics of the Buddha or, by extension, over the remains of a holy person.

Stylobate The base, usually having steps, on which a colonnaded temple sits.

Superimposed orders Orders placed atop one another.

Suq A street in an Islamic market.

Tablero The vertical, often ornamented, plane in Pre-Columbian pyramid construction, comparable to the frieze in ancient Greek architecture.

Tablinium In Roman atrium houses, a reception area, usually on axis with the entrance.

Talud The inclined plane in Pre-Columbian pyramid construction.

Tatami Mats woven of rice straw, approximately three by six feet, that establish the module for room dimensions in traditional Japanese houses.

Tenon A usually wooden knob or tongue prepared for insertion into a mortise.

Tepidarium The warm-water chamber in Roman baths or thermae.

Terracotta Unglazed fired clay, often used for ornamental purposes.

Thermae Roman baths, usually containing rooms for hot-, warm-, and cold-water bathing.

Tholos A dome over a circular-plan building, or more generally the building itself.

Totem pole The popular name for large cedar posts carved with effigies by Native Americans in the northwest.

Tierceron In Gothic vaulting, a secondary rib extending from the support to the crown of the vault.

Tokonoma In Japanese houses, an alcove in the vestibule of a house where treasured objects are displayed.

Torana An elaborate entrance gate into a Buddhist shrine.

Torii An elaborate post-and-lintel gateway into Buddhist shrines in Japan.

Torus Convex, roughly semi-circular molding often seen at the base of a classical column.

Tracery The stonework divisions in Gothic windows.

Transept The north and south arms of a basilican church.

Transfer beam A heavy beam that distributes (transfers) loads from the structure above to supports that are not directly aligned below.

Transom An opening above a door for light and/or ventilation.

Transverse arch An arch spanning across a long hall or nave.

Trefoil A three-lobed (or foiled) pattern seen frequently in Gothic architecture.

Triclinium A dining room in Roman houses and palaces.

Triforium In Gothic churches, the narrow passage below the clerestory corresponding to the lean-to roof over the aisle.

Triglyph A channeled block set between metopes in a Doric frieze.

Trilithon Two upright stones supporting a lintel stone.

Triumphal arch In Roman architecture, a gateway structure, with one or three arched openings, built to celebrate the return of a conquering army.

True arch A curving, often semi-circular arch composed of voussoirs.

Truss A structural frame composed of relatively short elements, typically configured into triangles, used to form a bridge or span a roof.

Tuscan An order based on Etruscan architecture, employing unfluted columns and simplified capitals.

Tympanum A panel, generally semicircular, over the lintel and under the arch of a doorway. Also, the central triangle of a pediment.

Vault An arched ceiling or roof of brick or stone.

Verdika Fence surrounding a stupa.

Vestibule An antechamber before a major space.

Vihara A Buddhist monastery.

Villa The Roman word for a farm. By extension, the term used during the Renaissance and afterward for a rural house, often of extensive size.

Villa rustica A Roman agricultural establishment that included living quarters for family members and slaves as well as stalls, store rooms, etc.

Volute A decorative spiral found in Ionic, Corinthian, and Composite capitals.

Voussoir A wedge-shaped masonry unit set to form an arch.

Wall pillar Space-shaping, pilaster-faced cross walls providing lateral stability for nave vaults in German Baroque churches.

Wandfeiler See wall pillar.

Westwerk The narthex, chapels, and towers set at the entrance end of churches of the Carolingian and later periods.

Yoni Concentric circles surrounding the linga and representing the female principle in traditional Indian architecture.

Ziggurat A stepped pyramid form used in ancient Mesopotamia as the platform for a religious building.

Bibliography

Chapter 1

Arnold, Dieter. *Building in Egypt: Pharaonic Stone Masonry.* New York: Oxford University Press, 1991. A summary of what is known from archaeology about methods used in Egyptian monumental stonework, from quarrying to transport to erection.

Arnold, Dieter. *The Encyclopedia of Ancient Egyptian Architecture.* Princeton: Princeton University Press, 2003. Use as a reference volume.

Bourdier, Jean-Paul and Trinh T. Minh-Ha. *Drawn From African Dwellings.* Bloomington, IN, 1996. Covers a wide variety of housing types and is amply illustrated.

Burenhult, G. (ed.) *Old World Civilizations: The Rise of Cities and States.* New York: Harper Collins, 1994. An illustrated overview of history and artifacts of the ancient world.

Denyer, Susan. *African Traditional Architecture.* New York: Africana Publishing Company, 1978. General introduction to the vernacular architecture of Africa.

Duly, Colin. *The Houses of Mankind.* London: Thames and Hudson, 1979. Includes a section on Africa.

Fagan, Brian M. *The Seventy Great Mysteries of the Ancient World.* London: Thames and Hudson, 2001. For anyone curious about the unanswered questions surrounding early civilizations and peoples, this is a treat. Summaries of current knowledge are presented straightforwardly by international experts.

Guidoni, Enrico. *Primitive Architecture,* trans. Robert Erich Wolf. *History of World Architecture* series. New York: Harry N. Abrams, 1978. Worldwide survey with substantial discussion of traditional architecture in Africa.

Gurney, Oliver Robert. *The Hittites.* London: Folio Society, 1999.

Hawkes, Jacquetta. *The Atlas of Early Man.* New York: St. Martin's Press, 1993. In measured time frames, developments across the world are presented through text, maps, and drawings.

Hawkins, Gerald. S. *Stonehenge Decoded.* Garden City: Doubleday,

1965. This is the pioneering study that demonstrated how Stonehenge was used.

Isler, Martin. *Sticks, Stones and Shadows: Building the Egyptian Pyramids.* Norman, OK: University of Oklahoma Press, 2001. Isler looks at practical issues associated with cutting, moving, and placing very large stones, advancing the idea that staircases may have been used instead of ramps in constructing the great pyramids. Compare this book with Arnold's study.

Lerner, Mark. *The Complete Pyramids.* New York: Thames and Hudson, 1997. Well-illustrated and concise text on all aspects of the pyramids, from religion to construction.

Lloyd, Seton, Hans Wolfgang Müller, and Roland Martin. *Ancient Architecture: Mesopotamia, Egypt, Crete, Greece.* New York: Abrams, 1973. Dry text but good illustrations, especially for reconstructions of now-ruined buildings.

Mellaart, James. *Catal Hüyük: A Neolithic Town in Anatolia.* New York: McGraw-Hill, 1967. Mellaart led the excavations at Catal Hüyük, and this book presents what he found there.

Nnanmdi, Elleh. *African Architecture: Evolution and Transformation.* New York: McGraw-Hill, 1997. A reasonably comprehensive survey that includes a variety of building types.

Oliver, Paul. *Shelter in Africa.* New York: Praeger Publishers, 1971. Very useful but the coverage is spotty, subject to the interests of the contributor.

Renfrew, Colin. *Before Civilization.* Harmondsworth, England: Penguin, 1973.

Rudofsky, Bernard. *Architecture Without Architects.* New York: Doubleday, 1964. Discussed in the text.

Smith, Earl Baldwin. *Egyptian Architecture as Cultural Expression.* Watkins Glen: American Life Foundation, 1968. Somewhat dated text, but the line illustrations are well done.

Smith, W.S. *The Art and Architecture of Ancient Egypt.* New Haven, CT: Yale University Press, 1998.

Soffer, Olga. *The Upper Paleolithic of the Central Russian Plain.*

Orlando, FL: Academic Press, 1985. One of the few sources in English on the prehistoric settlements in Ukraine.

Wilkinson, Richard H. *The Complete Temples of Ancient Egypt*. New York: Thames and Hudson, 2000. Covers not only the temples themselves, but also places these monuments in context of history, religion, and society. Excellent illustrations.

Chapter 2

Camp, John M. *The Athenian Agora: Excavations in the Heart of Classical Athens*. New York: Thames and Hudson, 1998. Clear documentation of the Agora's development from earliest times through the Roman period, based on work undertaken by the American School of Classical Studies in Athens, with plans and reconstruction views for buildings no longer extant.

Coulton, J.J. *Ancient Greek Architects at Work*. Ithaca, NY: Cornell University Press, 1977.

Hoepfner, Wolfram and Ernst-Ludwig Schwandner. *Haus und Stadt im klassischen Griechland*. Munich: Deutscher Kunstverlag, 1994. Although written in German, this book is still valuable for its extensive illustrations. It is the most recent book to report on field work at sites associated with the Classical city-states.

Lawrence, Arnold Walter. *Greek Architecture*. New Haven, CT: Yale University Press, 1996. Part of what was originally the generally excellent Pelican series on the history of art.

Marinatos, Nanno. *Minoan Religion: Ritual, Image, and Symbol*. Columbia, SC: University of South Carolina Press, 1993. Excellent study of Minoan religious practice, impeccably researched and clearly presented.

Rhodes, Robin Francis. *Architecture and Meaning on the Athenian Acropolis*. Cambridge, England: Cambridge University Press, 1995. A lively examination of the cultural references incorporated in the architecture on the Acropolis.

Robertson, Donald Struan. *Greek and Roman Architecture*. Cambridge, England: Cambridge University Press, 1969. Dry but thorough.

Scully, Vincent. *The Earth, the Temple, and the Gods*. New Haven, CT: Yale University Press, 1979. Studies at a somewhat intuitive level of the specific relationship of individual Greek temples to their settings.

Tzonis, Alexander and Phoebe Giannisi. *Classical Greek Architecture: The Construction of the Modern*. Flammarion, 2004. A comprehensive study in which the authors attempt to shed new light on engrained perceptions of often-studied structures.

Wycherley, Richard Ernest. *How the Greeks Built Cities*. New York: Norton, 1976.

Chapter 3

Deva, Krishna. *Khajuraho*. New Delhi: Archaeological Survey of India, 2002. Well-illustrated account of the temples at Khajuraho, setting the monuments in cultural and historic perspective.

Grover, Satish. *Buddhist and Hindu Architecture in India*. New Delhi: CBS Publishers and Distributors, 2003. A general text, written for Indian architecture students. Good diagrams and clear explanations of culture and terms.

Huntington, Susan L. *The Art of Ancient India: Buddhist, Hindu, Jain*. New York: Weatherhill, 1985. A summary text for art as well as architecture.

Johnson, Gordon, general editor. *The New Cambridge History of India: Architecture and Art of the Deccan Sultanates*. Cambridge: Cambridge University Press, 1999. A huge project intended to eventually include more than thirty volumes. Those already published include Catherine Asher's *Architecture of Mughal India* and George Mitchell's *Architecture and Art of Southern India*. Coverage extends to the present day and includes social and economic issues as well as architecture.

Michell, George. *The Hindu Temple: An Introduction to Its Meaning and Forms*. Chicago, IL: University of Chicago Press, 1988. Clearly written volume that provides religious and cultural background needed to understand Hindu temple design.

Michell, George and Mark Zebrowski. *The New Cambridge History of India: Architecture and Art of the Deccan Sultanates*. Cambridge: Cambridge University Press, 1999.

Miksic, John. *Borobudur: Golden Tales of the Buddhas*. London: Bamboo Publishing, 1990. Handsome illustrations of and extensive narration on the architecture and iconography of the monument.

Rowland, Benjamin. *Art and Architecture of India: Buddhist, Hindu, Jain*. Harmondsworth, England: Penguin, 1953. One of the generally excellent volumes in the Pelican History of Art series.

Stierlin, Henri. *Hindu India: From Khajuraho to the Temple City of Madurai*. Cologne: Taschen, 1998. Part of a projected forty-volume set on world architecture, this book contains many color illustrations to support the text.

Tadgell, Christopher. *The History of Architecture in India: From the Dawn of Civilization to the End of the Raj*. London: Architecture Design and Technology Press, 1990. A more complex text than some, this book has good illustrations.

Chapter 4

Boyd, Andrew. *Chinese Architecture and Town Planning, 1500 BC—AD 1911*. Chicago, IL: University of Chicago Press, 1962. This volume is older than most, but its text is still worth reading closely. As "a very small book on a very large subject," it carries off the presentation exceptionally well.

Bussagli, Mario. *Oriental Architecture. History of World Architecture* series. New York: Harry N. Abrams, 1973. Another volume in the *History of World Architecture* series, this book covers not only China, Japan, and India, but also Sri Lanka, Vietnam, Cambodia, Thailand, Tibet, and Korea, among others.

Chinese Academy of Architecture. *Ancient Chinese Architecture*. Hong Kong: Joint Publishing Company and Beijing: China Building Industry Press, 1982. Remarkable for demonstrating how the writing of history can also be a political statement. Good color photographs are juxtaposed with a collectively written text intended for English-speaking audiences. Among other things, readers are informed that "[t]he Great Wall is a masterpiece of ancient China. It manifests the tough, determined, and unwavering spirit of the Chinese, and the brightness of the wisdom of the working people."

Chinese Academy of Sciences, Institute of the History of Natural Sciences. *History and Development of Ancient Chinese Architecture*. Beijing: Science Press, 1986. A massive book, methodically treating the subject with concise text, clear illustrations, and a minimum of political commentary. It includes separate coverage of buildings by China's ethnic minorities.

Frankfort, Henri, Michael Roaf and Donald Matthews. *The Art and Architecture of the Ancient Orient*. New Haven, CT: Yale University Press, 1996.

Isozaki, Arata. *Katsura Villa: Space and Form*. New York: Rizzoli, 1987. A thoughtful text with extensive and beautiful photography.

Jinghua, Ru and Peng Hualiang. *Palace Architecture. Ancient Chinese Architecture*. Vienna: Springer-Verlag, 1998. A volume in the extensive *Ancient Chinese Architecture* series. Beautifully illustrated.

Kawashima, Chugi. *Minka: Traditional Houses of Rural Japan*. Tokyo: Kodansha International, 1986. Clearly written and handsomely illustrated study of the great variety of minka, with particular attention paid to construction techniques and design features.

Liu, Laurence G. *Chinese Architecture*. New York: Rizzoli, 1989. A well-written account supplemented with clear photographs and plans.

Nishi, Kazuo and Kazuo Hozumi. *What Is Japanese Architecture?* Tokyo: Kodansha International, 1985. A concise text illustrated with line drawings showing the basic characteristics of traditional Japanese buildings.

Qijun, Wang. *Vernacular Dwellings. Ancient Chinese Architecture*. Vienna: Springer-Verlag, 2000. Another volume in the *Ancient Chinese Architecture* series.

Suzuki, Kakichi. *Early Buddhist Architecture in Japan*. New York: Kodansha International, 1980.

Tange, Kenzo and Noboru Kawazoe. *Ise: Prototype of Japanese Architecture*. Cambridge, MA: M.I.T. Press, 1965. Features beautiful photographs by Yoshio Watanabe taken after the 1953 rebuilding of the shrines and offers views not normally available. Separate essays by Tange and Kawazoe cover architecture and cultural context.

Xinian, Fu, Guo Daiheng, Liu Xujie, et al, Nancy S. Steinhardt, ed. *Chinese Architecture. The Culture and Civilization of China* series. New Haven and Beijing: Yale University Press and New World Press, 2002. The best available general survey of architecture in China.

Zhu, Jianfei. *Chinese Spatial Strategies: Imperial Beijing*. London: RoutledgeCurzon, 2004. A specialized study based on a dissertation, this book explains Chinese planning in terms of court life, rituals, authority, etc.

Chapter 5

Grant, Michael. *Cities of Vesuvius*. Harmondsworth, England: Penguin, 1976.

MacDonald, William L. *The Architecture of the Roman Empire*. New Haven, CT: Yale University Press, 1982.

——— *The Pantheon: Design, Meaning, and Progeny*. Cambridge, MA: Harvard University Press, 1976.

——— and John A. Pinto. *Hadrian's Villa and Its Legacy*. New Haven, CT: Yale University Press, 1995. This is a very readable account of the villa and its place in architectural history.

Packer, James E. *The Forum of Trajan in Rome: A Study of the Monuments*. Berkeley, CA: University of California Press, 1997. A monumental, three-volume study of this forum, including new restoration drawings based on excavations.

Richardson, Lawrence. *Pompeii: An Architectural History*. Baltimore, MD: Johns Hopkins University Press, 1988.

Sear, Frank. *Roman Architecture*. Ithaca, NY: Cornell University Press, 1992. A useful text with good illustrations, this book includes substantial coverage of Roman works outside Italy, in Africa, the Middle East, and Europe.

Taylor, Rabun. *Roman Builders: A Study in Architectural Process*. Cambridge: Cambridge University Press, 2003. A detailed study that takes the reader sequentially through the Roman building process using selected structures such as the Colosseum and Pantheon. Considerable speculation about the Roman use of construction cranes.

Vitruvius, M. *The Ten Books on Architecture*. New York: Dover, 1960. English translation of the only complete surviving architectural treatise from antiquity.

Ward-Perkins, John B. *Roman Imperial Architecture*. Harmondsworth, England: Penguin, 1981.

Chapter 6

Brumfield, William Craft. *A History of Russian Architecture*. Cambridge, England: Cambridge University Press, 1993. Text and photographs covering all aspects of Russian architecture, including the churches considered here.

Krautheimer, Richard. *Early Christian and Byzantine Architecture*. Harmondsworth: Penguin, 1986. Part of the generally excellent Pelican History of Art series.

——— *Rome: Profile of a City, 312–1308*. Princeton, NJ: Princeton University Press, 1980. A fascinating account of Rome from the Early Christian period through the medieval period.

Lowden, John. *Early Christian and Byzantine Art*. London: Phaidon Press, 1997. A beautifully illustrated and lucid book that covers selected monuments in detail, placing them firmly in their historical context.

Mainstone, Rowland J. *Hagia Sophia: Architecture, Structure, and Liturgy of Justinian's Great Church*. New York: Thames and Hudson, 2001. A detailed examination of this masterpiece church. Clear text and ample illustrations.

Opolovnikov, Alexander and Yelena Opolovnikova. *The Wooden Architecture of Russia: Houses, Fortifications, Churches*. New York: Abrams, 1989. The best available source in English for information about wooden buildings in Russia, which vastly outnumber structures in masonry.

Chapter 7

Aftullah, Kuran. *Sinan: The Grand Old Master of Ottoman Architecture*. Istanbul and Washington, D.C: Institute of Turkish Studies and ADA Press, 1987. A complete study of the architect who took Hagia Sophia as a point of departure for designing Istanbul's domed mosques.

Armstrong, Karen. *Islam, A Short History*. New York: The Modern Library, 2002. A short, readable account of the history and current status of Islam in the world.

Dazhang, Sun. *Ancient Chinese Architecture: Islamic Buildings*. New York: Springer-Verlag, 2003. A beautiful book that covers Islamic work not addressed in this chapter.

Esposito, John L., ed. *The Oxford History of Islam*. Oxford: Oxford University Press, 1999. A reliable reference source.

Grabar, Oleg. *The Alhambra*. Cambridge, MA: Harvard University Press, 1978. Even though almost 30 years old and without color images, this book places the Alhambra in its broader context.

Hillenbrand, Robert. *Islamic Architecture*. New York: Columbia University Press, 1994. Comprehensive study by categories: mosques, minarets, mausoleums, caravanserai, and palaces.

Hoag, John D. *Islamic Architecture*. New York: Harry N. Abrams, 1977. Thorough and well illustrated coverage of North Africa, Spain, the Middle East, Egypt, Turkey, and India.

Jairazbhoy, R.A. *An Outline of Islamic Architecture*. New York: Asia Publishing House, 1972.

Kostoff, Spiro. *A History of Architecture: Settings and Rituals*. New York: Oxford University Press, 1995. See pages 454–68 on Istanbul.

Mitchell, George, ed. *Architecture of the Islamic World and Its History and Social Meaning*. New York: William Morrow, 1978. This survey of building types includes sections on craftsmen, construction methods, decoration, and traditional housing.

Petersen, Andrew. *Dictionary of Islamic Architecture*. New York: Routledge, 1999. Only lightly illustrated but a very useful companion to narrative histories.

Stierllin, Henri. *Islam*, vol. 1: *Early Architecture From Baghdad to Corboda*, Cologne: Taschen, 1996. A volume in Taschen's *World Architecture* series. It covers Islamic architecture from its inception through the thirteenth century.

Yeomans, Richard. *The Story of Islamic Architecture*. New York: New York University Press, 1999. Large format with plenty of color illustrations.

Chapter 8

Braunfels, Wolfgang. *Monasteries of Western Europe: The Architecture of the Orders*. Princeton, NJ: University Press, 1980. Clear explanation of Western monasticism and its architectural manifestations.

Calkins, Robert. *Medieval Architecture in Western Europe*. New York: Oxford University Press, 1998. A readable and comprehensive guide to architecture from 330 to 1500.

Conant, Kenneth John. *Carolingian and Romanesque Architecture, 800–1200*. New Haven, CT: Yale University Press, 1978. A basic guide to this period, originally part of the excellent Pelican History of Art series.

——— *Cluny: Les églises et la maison du chef d'ordre*. Macon: Imprimerie Protat Freres, 1968. The culmination of a lifetime of scholarly work. Although the text is in French, the extensive illustrations are universally understandable.

Horn, Walter, and Ernest Born. *The Plan of St. Gall*. Berkeley, CA: University of California Press, 1979. A model of research and scholarship, this beautiful three-volume work traces the impact of antique building on Carolingian architecture and the influence of the Plan of St. Gall on later buildings.

Kinder, Terryl N. *Cistercian Europe: Architecture of Contemplation*. Grand Rapids, MI: Cistertian Publications, 2002. Specialized study of one of the principal monastic organization of the Middle Ages. Splendid illustrations.

Kubach, Hans Erich. *Romanesque Architecture*. New York: Abrams, 1975. An extensive review of Romanesque architecture.

Male, Emile. *Religious Art in France: The Twelfth Century*. Princeton, NJ: Princeton University Press, 1978. An excellent guide to understanding the medieval mind and religious symbolism in Romanesque sculpture.

Shaver-Crandell, Annie and Paula Gerson. *The Pilgrim's Guide to Santiago de Compostela: A Gazetteer*. London: Harvey Miller, 1995. Includes a translation of the twelfth-century "Pilgrim's Guide" and an alphabetical guide to the sites as they would have appeared to a contemporary traveler.

Stalley, Roger. *Early Medieval Architecture*. New York: Oxford University Press, 1999. Lucid text, good photographs: highly recommended.

Chapter 9

Beresford, Maurice and John Hurst. *Wharram Percy: Deserted Medieval Village*. New Haven, CT: Yale University Press, 1991. For anyone interested in the ordinary buildings of the medieval period, this book serves as a readable introduction to the complex and tentative nature of our knowledge of non-monumental architectural history.

Bony, Jean. *French Gothic Architecture of the Twelfth and Thirteenth Centuries*. Berkeley, CA: University of California Press, 1983. Notable for its thorough treatment of Gothic churches in France, together with clear photographs and many building plans.

Coldstream, Nicola. *Medieval Craftsmen: Masons and Sculptors*. London: British Museum Press, 1991. A concise summary of the builders and building processes of medieval times.

Erlande-Brandenburg, Alain. *Cathedrals and Castles: Building in the Middle Ages*. New York: Harry N. Abrams, 1995. Well-illustrated account of the entire medieval building process, including translations of selected historic documents related to building sites and construction matters.

James, John. *Chartres: The Masons Who Built a Legend*. London: Routledge and Kegan Paul, 1982. James's detailed studies of the physical fabric of Chartres lead him to conclude that eight teams of master masons worked simultaneously on different parts of the cathedral. His thesis is not universally accepted, but his book provokes thought.

Mark, Robert. *Experiments in Gothic Structure*. Cambridge, MA: M.I.T. Press, 1982. The author considers engineering problems posed by

Gothic buildings through analysis of models using polarized light.

Taylor, Arnold. *The Welsh Castles of Edward I*. London: Hambledon Press, 1986. A concise account from documentary sources of the construction of seventeen castles in Wales, this book demonstrates what surviving records tell us about the process of castle-building.

White, John. *Art and Architecture in Italy, 1250 to 1400*. New Haven, CT: Yale University Press, 1993. Originally part of the excellent Pelican series on the History of Art, this volume is particularly interesting for its extended summary of the debates over the design of Milan Cathedral.

Wilson, Christopher. *The Gothic Cathedral: The Architecture of the Great Church, 1130–1530*. New York: Thames and Hudson, 1992. Discusses cathedrals and large churches across Europe, including lesser-known examples.

Chapter 10

Andrews, G.F. *Maya Cities: Placemaking and Urbanization*. Norman, OK: University of Oklahoma Press, 1975. Contains an introductory section on city components, then a city-by-city survey.

Broda, Johanna, David Carrasco, and Eduardo Matos Moctezuma. *The Great Temple of Tenochtitlán: Center and Periphery in the Aztec World*. Berkeley: University of California Press, 1987. These essays by scholars in different disciplines offer interpretations of the principal Aztec shrine.

Driver, H.E. *Indians of North-America*, 2nd revised edition. Chicago, IL: University of Chicago Press, 1969. Broad discussion of Indian cultures.

Gasparini, G. and L. Margolis. *Inca Architecture*. Bloomington, IN: Indiana University Press, 1980. A good place to begin when doing research on the Incas. Abundant images accompany the text.

Heyden, D. and P. Gendrop. *Pre-Columbian Architecture of Meso-America*. New York: Abrams, 1975. Part of the Abrams series on Western architecture. It covers Mexico and Central America and is filled with black-and-white photographs and drawings.

Kosok, P. *Life, Land and Water in Ancient Peru*. New York: Long Island University Press, 1965. This book emphasizes the Inca manipulation of the land, especially their extraordinary systems of irrigation. It includes material culture as well as architecture.

Miller, Mary E. *Maya Art and Architecture*. New York: Thames and Hudson, 1996. Covers sculpture, mural painting, ceramics and small objects, as well as architecture.

Moctezuma, Eduardo Matos and Felipe Solis Olguin, eds. *Aztecs*. London: Royal Academy Books, 2003. Beautifully illustrated exhibition catalog that concentrates on the art of royalty.

Morgan, W.N. *Ancient Architecture of the Southwest*. Austin, TX: University of Texas Press, 1994. Covers Native American sites in Utah, Colorado, Arizona, and New Mexico. Maps and some drawings, but no photographs.

Moseley, Michael. *The Incas and Their Ancestors: the Archaeology of Peru*. London: Thames and Hudson, 1992. Broad survey that places the architecture in a larger cultural context.

Nabokov, P. and R. Easton. *Native American Architecture*. New York: Oxford, 1989. An excellent survey with plenty of photographs and drawings. This is the first book to look at for an introduction to Native American building in North America.

Robertson, D. *Pre-Columbian Architecture*. New York: Braziller, 1963. A short but very useful look at ancient building practices from Mexico to Peru.

Various editors. *Handbook of North American Indians*. 17 vols. Washington, D.C.: Smithsonian Institution, beginning 1978. Offers in-depth information on Native-American cultures. Volumes 4–11, 15 and 17 have so far appeared.

von Hagen, Adriana and Craig Morris. *The Cities of the Ancient Andes*. London: Thames and Hudson, 1998. Comprehensive, well illustrated survey of Inca and pre-Inca cultures.

Chapter 11

Ackerman, J.S. *Palladio*. New York: Penguin, 1986. A very readable account by the foremost American scholar on Palladio.

——— *The Architecture of Michelangelo*. Baltimore: Penguin, 1971. A thoroughly illustrated account of Michelangelo's building designs.

Alberti, L.B. *On the Art of Building in Ten Books*. Cambridge, MA: M.I.T. Press, 1988. Alberti's fifteenth-century treatise expressing his ideas and theories about architecture.

Bruschi, Arnaldo. *Bramante*. London: Thames and Hudson: 1977. A focused, understandable and well-illustrated study. The line drawings are particularly useful.

Burckhardt, J. *The Architecture of the Italian Renaissance*. London: John Murray, 1985. A classic text first published in 1860. Much of the

information has been superseded, but a comparison with later works provides insights into changing attitudes about the period.

Heydenreich, L.H. and W. Lotz. *Architecture in Italy, 1400 to 1600*. Harmondsworth, England: Penguin, 1974. Another volume in the useful and workmanlike Pelican *History of Art* series.

Howard, Deborah and Sarah Quill. *The Architectural History of Venice*. New Haven, CT: Yale University Press, 2002. A readable account of the broader architectural trends in a city that participated in Eastern as well as Western traditions.

Murray, P. *Renaissance Architecture*. New York: Abrams, 1971. Peter Murray offers the best general survey of Renaissance buildings. The text is accessible to the undergraduate and is supported by ample illustrations.

Norberg-Schulz, C. *Intentions in Architecture*. Cambridge, MA: M.I.T. Press, 1965. Architectural history written from the existential point of view.

Palladio, A. *The Four Books of Architecture*. New York: Dover, 1965. Palladio's highly influential treatise that includes illustrations of his own work.

Saalman, H. *Filippo Brunelleschi: The Buildings*. University Park, PA: Pennsylvania State University Press, 1993. Saalman wrote extensively on Brunelleshi throughout his career, eventually yielding this thorough account.

Serlio, S. *The Five Books of Architecture*. New York: Dover, 1982. The first Renaissance treatise to contain a significant number of illustrations.

Shepherd, J.C. and Geoffrey Alan Jellicoe. *Italian Gardens of the Renaissance*. New York: Princeton Architectural Press, 1993. The beautiful watercolor plans and sections alone make this book worth thumbing through.

Summerson, J. *Inigo Jones*. Harmondsworth, England: Penguin, 1966. The literature on Jones is almost uniformly dull. Much of this can be traced to inadequate knowledge of his life. Summerson's account is the most readable.

Wittkower, R. *Architectural principles in the Age of Humanism*. London: Academy, 1988. Theories of proportion from Alberti to Palladio. A strong influence on twentieth-century archiecture.

Chapter 12

Blunt, A. *Art and Architecture in France, 1500–1700*. New Haven, CT: Yale University Press, 1999. Sir Anthony Blunt is equally known as an architectural historian, as director of the Courtauld Institute of Art, and as a Communist spy. Originally another volume in the Pelican *History of Art* series.

——— *Borromini*. Harmondsworth, England: Penguin, 1979. A good place to begin on Borromini for whom much of the literature has not been translated from the Italian.

Braham, A. *François Mansart*. London: Zwemmer, 1973. While Braham's separating of this work into a volume of text and a volume of illustrations makes using them slightly inconvenient, they are well researched and well written.

Hibbard, H. *Bernini*. Harmondsworth, England: Penguin, 1965. A short but useful text.

Meek, H. A. *Guarino Guarini and His Architecture*. New Haven, CT: Yale University Press, 1988. A relatively brief and to the point study of this architect-engineer.

Norberg-Schulz, C. *Baroque Architecture*. New York: Abrams, 1971.

——— C. *Late Baroque and Rococo Architecture*. New York: Abrams, 1971. These volumes cover all aspects of Baroque architecture throughout Europe. The two offer the best starting point for undergraduate research on the subject.

Pommer, R. *Eighteenth-Century Architecture in Piedmont*. New York: New York University Press, 1967. Pommer treats Guarini, Vittone, and Juvarra in their development of Late Baroque architecture in Italy.

Portoghesi, P. *Rome of Borromini; Architecture as Language*. New York: Braziller, 1967. Portoghesi is not the most readable source on Borromini, but the illustrations, especially Borromini's drawings, are splendid.

Summerson, J. *Architecture in Britain 1530–1830*. New Haven, CT: Yale University Press, 1993. Sir John Summerson wrote particularly well. All of his books, article and essays are worth spending some time with. Originally part of the Pelican *History of Art* series.

Walton, G. *Louis XIV's Versailles*. Chicago, IL: University of Chicago Press, 1986. Just as there are monographs on individual architects, there are works dedicated to individual buildings. Intended for the non-specialist, this book tries to explain why Versailles took the form that it did.

Wittkower, Rudolf, Joseph Connors and Jennifer Montagu. *Art and Architcture in Italy, 1600–1750*. New Haven, CT: Yale University Press, 1999. Originally another volume in the comprehensive Pelican *History of Art* series. Wittkower was one of the most eminent European scholars to emigrate to America as a result of events leading to World War II.

Chapter 13

Bergdoll, Barry. *European Architecture, 1750–1890. Oxford History of Art*. Oxford: Oxford University Press, 2000. A volume in the *Oxford History of Art* series. Clearly written and well illustrated. Perhaps the best current survey of the period.

Braham, A. *The Architecture of the French Enlightenment*. Berkeley, CA: University of California Press, 1980. The most comprehensive and up-to-date source for French Neo-Classicism in the eighteenth century.

Dennis, Michael. *Court and Garden: From the French Hotel to the City of Modern Architecture*. Cambridge, MA: MIT Press, 1986. A well illustrated study of French hôtel design by an architect become architectural historian.

Honour, H. *Neo-Classicism*. Harmondsworth, England: Penguin, 1977. Honour emphasizes painting and sculpture, but includes architecture in what he intended as a study of "all manifestations of the Neoclassical style."

Kalnein, W.G. and M. Levy. *Art and Architecture in Eighteenth-Century France*. Harmondsworth, England: Penguin, 1972. Penguin's effort to deal with the eighteenth century offers significant doses of painting, sculpture, and architecture.

Kaufmann, E. *Architecture in the Age of Reason: Baroque and Post-Baroque in England, Italy, and France*. New York: Dover, 1968. Kaufmann was the first scholar to write comprehensively on the period. Others have superseded him in many areas, but his book is still worth studying.

Kimball, Fiske. *The Creation of the Rococo Decorative Style*. New York: Dover Publications, 1980. An older book but still a good introduction to the Rococo.

Chapter 14

Baker, Paul R. *Richard Morris Hunt*. Cambridge, MA: MIT Press, 1980. Strong on text, adequately illustrated, this book places Hunt within the context of the beginnings of architectural professionalism in the United States.

Benton, Charlotte, Tim Benton, and Ghislaine Wood, eds. *Art Deco, 1910–1939*. London: V&A Publications, 2003. A series of essays collected to accompany an exhibition at the Victoria and Albert Museum in London.

Clark, K. *The Gothic Revival: An Essay in the History of Taste*. London: J. Murray, 1962.

Condit, Carl. *American Building Art—The Nineteenth Century*. New York: Oxford University Press, 1960. A survey of developments in wood framing, iron framing, iron bridge construction, and concrete.

——— *The Chicago School of Architecture: A History of Commercial and Public Building in the Chicago Area, 1875–1925*. Chicago, IL: University of Chicago Press, 1990s. A place to start in understanding the development of the Chicago School skyscraper.

Drexler, A. (ed.). *The Architecutre of the Ecole des Beaux-Arts*. Cambridge, MA: M.I.T. Press, 1977. Published to coincide with an exhibition at the Museum of Modern Art in New York City, this volume includes a series of essays and reproductions of many drawings made by the Ecole's students.

Greenhalgh, Paul, ed. *Art Nouveau, 1890–1914*. London: V&A Publications, 2000. A series of essays collected to accompany an exhibition at the Victoria and Albert Museum in London.

Hitchcock, H.R. *Architecture: Nineteenth and Twentieth Centuries*. New Haven, CT: Yale University Press, 1987. An encyclopedic survey, long on description and short on analysis. Many photographs. Originally a volume in the Pelican *History of Art* series.

Lewis, Michael J. *Frank Furness: Architecture and the Violent Mind*. New York: W. W. Norton and Company, 2001. As this title suggests, the author sees Furness as the product of a violent age, which included the American Civil War (in which the architect was a cavalry officer) and the period of rampant economic development and social upheaval that followed it.

Middleton, R. and D. Watkin. *Neoclassicism and 19th-Century Architecture*. London: Faber, 1987. The best place to begin for a survey of Neo-Classicism throughout Europe.

Scully, V. *The Shingle Style and the Stick Style*. New Haven, CT: Yale University Press, 1971. Written as Scully's doctoral dissertation, this lively volume sheds much light on the complex architectural developments in late nineteenth-century America. It deals primarily with domestic buildings.

Stanton, P. *Pugin*. New York: Viking, 1971. Some have traced the roots of Modernism to the kind of passionate search for truth or at least honesty promoted by Gothic Revivalist Augustus Welby Northmore Pugin.

Twombly, R. *Louis Sullivan: His Life and Work*. New York: Viking, 1986. One of many monographs on the man that Frank Lloyd Wright called his master.

Woods, Mary N. *From Craft to Profession: The Practice of Architecture in Nineteenth-Century America*. Berkeley: University of California Press, 1999. A discussion of the American architectural profession from the time of Benjamin Henry Latrobe at the end of the 18th century to the present.

Chapter 15

Banham, R. *Theory and Design in the First Machine Age*. New York: Praeger, 1967. Early revisionist writing on Modernism, challenging the arguments made by such scholars as Pevsner and Giedion.

Benevolo, L. *History of Modern Architecture*. Cambridge, MA: M.I.T. Press, 1971. Comprehensive history by an author who emphasizes city planning and urban development.

Boesiger, W. (ed.). *Le Corbusier and Pierre Jeanneret: Oeuvre Complète*. Zurich: Girsberger, 1935–65. These volumes provide the opportunity to view a life's work by one of the principal European Modernists.

Collins, P. *Changing Ideals in Modern Architecture, 1750–1950*. Montreal: McGill-Queens University Press, 1998. A book about ideas that have influenced modern architecture, so few illustrations.

Colquhoun, Alan. *Modern Architecture. Oxford History of Art*. Oxford: Oxford University Press, 2002. Another volume in the *Oxford History of Art* series. Covers the period from the Art Nouveau through the 1960s.

Doordan, Dennis P. *Twentieth-Century Architecture*. Upper Saddle River, NJ and New York: Prentice Hall and Harry N. Abrams, 2002. A concise, readable, well-illustrated survey.

Frampton, K. *Modern Architecture: A Critical History*. London: Thames and Hudson, 2003. A thoughtful, comprehensive survey, but a little dense for anyone just beginning a study of the period.

Giedion, S. *Space, Time, and Architecture*. Cambridge, MA: Harvard University Press, 1980. A classic of polemical writing that purports to examine the roots of Modernism. Giedeon hobnobbed with many of the great architectural talents of the mid-twentieth century and was an unabashed proponent of European Modernism.

Gropius, Walter. *The New Architecture and the Bauhaus*. London: Faber and Faber, 1965. In this book first published in 1937, Gropius relates the radical experiment in design education at the Bauhaus to the "new architecture" then being produced in Europe.

Hayden, Delores. *Building Suburbia: Green Fields and Urban Growth 1820–2000*. New York: Pantheon Books, 2003. A critique of the sprawling residential development that has accompanied the disintegration of the modern American city.

Hitchcock, H.R. *In the Nature of Materials: The Buildings of Frank Lloyd Wright, 1887–1941*. New York: Duell, Sloan, and Pierce, 1942. The literature on Wright is almost endless. This book, by a scholar who wrote on a broad variety of architectural-history topics, accompanied an exhibition on Wright at the Museum of Modern Art in 1940.

——— and P. Johnson. *The International Style: Architecture Since 1922*. New York: Norton, 1932. This small book accompanied the exhibition of European and American Modernism mounted at the Museum of Modern Art in New York City. A 1995 edition is now also available.

Jordy, W.H. *American Buildings and Their Architects: The Impact of European Modernism in the Mid-Twentieth Century*. Garden City, NY: Anchor Press/Doubleday, 1976. A readable author's interpretation of Modernism in America through the close study of six seminal buildings.

Le Corbusier. *Towards a New Architecture*. New York: Praeger, 1972. Le Corbusier's ideas about architecture, first published in 1923.

Le Corbusier, Pierre Jeanneret, Willy Boesiger, Oscar Stonorov and Max Bill. *Oeuvre Complète*. Zurich: Editions d'Architecture Erienbach, 1946–1970 (8 vols). Le Corbusier's publication of his work showing his drawing style.

Paperny, Vladimir. *Architecture in the Age of Stalin: Culture Two*, trans.

by John Hill and Roann Barris. Cambridge: Cambridge University Press, 2002. While not ideal for the beginning student, this text does explore architecture in a setting that has long been ignored.

Pevsner, Nicholas. *Pioneers of Modern Design: From William Morris to Walter Gropius*. Harmondsworth, England: Penguin, 1975. When this book was first published in 1936, Pevsner was among the first to look for the sources of European Modernism. While he later admitted that he should have been more inclusive, his small book does illuminate many of the principles that Modernists held dear.

Schulze, F. *Mies van der Rohe: A Critical Biography*. Chicago, IL: University of Chicago Press, 1985. A thorough study but with limited illustrations.

Sharp, D. *Modern Architecture and Expressionism*. New York: Braziller, 1966. The first work to focus on a large part of twentieth-century architectural production that was not intensely "rational" and so at odds with the fundamental tenets of Modernism.

Tafuri, M. and F. Dal Co. *Modern Architecture*. New York: Rizzoli, 1986. Modernism interpreted from the Marxist perspective.

Wingler, Hans Maria and Joseph Stein. *The Bauhaus: Weimar, Dessau, Berlin, Chicago*. Cambridge, MA: MIT Press, 1983. A history of the Bauhaus in its various manifestations. Large format with abundant illustrations.

Wright, F.L. *Modern Architecture*. Princeton, NJ: Princeton University Press, 1931. Some of Wright's ideas about architecture and his answer to the polemics of Le Corbusier.

Note: Also see monographs on individual architects.

Chapter 16

Curtis, William J.R. *Modern Architecture Since 1900*. London: Phaidon, 1996. An excellent, very readable, well-illustrated world-wide survey with many color images.

Drexler, A. (ed.). *Five Architects: Eisenman, Graves, Gwathmey, Hejduk, Meier*. New York: Oxford University Press, 1975. This thin, overtly promotional publication advanced five careers and gave the false impression that their work was alike.

Jencks, C. *Modern Movements in Architecture*. New York: Penguin, 1985. Charles Jencks explores the demise of Modernism and the then-emerging pluralism that he saw as taking its place.

——— *Late-Modern Architecture*. London: Academy Editions, 1991. Jencks's first effort (when first published in 1980) to pull together his ideas about the "end" of Modernism.

——— *The New Paradigm in Architecture: The Language of Post-Modern Architecture*. New Haven, CT: Yale University Press, 2002. One among many volumes by the high priest of Post-Modernism. Like Sigfried Giedion for Modernism, Jencks has been a tireless promotor as well as a reporter and analyst.

Klotz, H. *The History of Post-Modern Architecture*. Cambridge, MA: MIT Press, 1988. The most complete survey of the various architectural directions that have been lumped into the category of Post-Modernism.

The Phaidon Atlas of Contemporary World Architecture. New York: Phaidon Press, 2004. This behemoth includes entries on more than one thousand buildings by over five hundred architects practicing around the world.

Venturi, R. *Complexity and Contradiction in Architecture*. New York: Museum of Modern Art, 1990. Robert Venturi's iconoclastic work (first published in 1966) announced the crumbling of the edifice of Modernism.

Wigley, M. and P. Johnson. *Deconstructivist Architecture*. Boston, MA: Little, Brown, 1988. Published by the Museum of Modern Art in New York City to accompany an exhibition of the same name.

The monographs on individual architects are too numerous to list here, but there are many worthy and well illustrated volumes. Another essential sources is architectural journals such as *Architectural Record* (US) and *The Architectural Review* (UK) and many others published in various countries and languages. Journals are usually the first place where buildings are published after they have been completed, and they are often the only place to find plan, elevation, and section drawings and even site plans.

Picture credits

The authors and Laurence King Publishing Ltd thank the sources of photographs for supplying and granting permission to reproduce them. Every effort has been made to contact all copyright holders, but should there be any errors or omissions Laurence King Publishing Ltd would be pleased to insert the appropriate acknowledgment in any subsequent printing of this publication.

Frontispiece A F Kersting/akg-images; 0.2 Ronald Scott; 0.1 & 0.3, 0.4, 0.7, 0.8, 0.10 & 0.11, 1.4, 1.7 Marian Moffett; 0.6 R Bruce Moffett; 1.0 DeA/C Sappa/The Art Archive; 1.5 Jason Hawkes/Corbis; 1.8 Kimbell Art Museum, Fort Worth; 1.9 Courtesy of the Oriental Institute, University of Chicago; 1.12 Hirmer Fotoarchiv; 1.17 Robert Harding/Robert Harding World Imagery; 1.19 Michael Fazio; 1.20 Paul M R Maeyaert; 1.23 Spectrum/Heritage Images/Photo Scala, Florence; 1.25 Raiford Scott; 1.28 J Stevens/Ancient Art & Architecture Collection; 1.32 Charles & Josette Lenars/Corbis; 1.33 C Murray Smart, Jr; 2.0 Kathy Collins/Robert Harding World Imagery; 2.2 Rachel McCann; 2.3 Herbert Kraft/akg-images; 2.4 C M Dixon/Ancient Art & Architecture Collection; 2.5 Marian Moffett; 2.8 Craig & Marie Mauzy; 2.10 Dagli Orti/The Art Archive; 2.11 Hirmer Fotoarchiv; 2.13 Marian Moffett; 2.19 J William Rudd; 2.20 Kenneth Moffett; 2.22 Michael Fazio; 2.23 Sonia Halliday Photographs; 2.24b Universal Images Group/SuperStock; 2.25 British Museum, London; 2.28 Hirmer Fotoarchiv; 2.31 C M Dixon/Ancient Art & Architecture Collection; 2.32 Craig & Marie Mauzy; 2.34 Allan Cash Picture Library; 2.37 Michael Fazio; 2.39 BPK, Berlin/Photo Scala, Florence; 3.0, 3.4, 3.6 A F Kersting/akg-images; 3.2 Richard Ashworth/Robert Harding World Imagery; 3.9 Paul Almasy/akg-images; 3.11 Dinodia/age fotostock; 3.12 Dinodia; 3.13 Lawrence Wodehouse; 3.15 & 3.16 Norman/Ancient Art & Architecture Collection; 3.17 Jean-Louis Nou/akg-images; 3.18 A F Kersting/akg-images; 3.20 David Beatty/Robert Harding World Imagery; 3.22 Bob Krist/Corbis; 4.0 Liu Liqun/Corbis; 4.2 Gerald Anderson; 4.3 Orientphoto; 4.7, 4.8, 4.10 Chinapix; 4.15 Robert Harding World Imagery; 4.16, 4.19 Robert Craig; 4.20 Kin Cheung/Corbis; 4.22, 4.25, 4.36 Japan Information and Cultural Center, Embassy of Japan; 4.23 M Williams/Ancient Art & Architecture Collection; 4.24, 4.26, 4.30, 4.37 Gerald Anderson; 4.28 Courtesy Jingu Information Office; 4.31 akg-images; 4.33 Lawrence Wodehouse; 4.34 Robert Holmes/Corbis; 5.0, 5.4 Paul M R Maeyaert; 5.3 Alinari Archives; 5.6 B Norman/Ancient Art & Architecture Collection; 5.10, 5.12, 5.18, 5.20, 5.21 Vincenzo Pirozzi; 5.17, 5.19 Fototeca Unione, American Academy in Rome; 5.15 Photo Scala, Florence: 5.22 National Gallery of Art, Washington DC, Samuel H. Kress Collection; 5.25 akg-images; 5.31 Lawrence Wodehouse; 5.32 Guido Alberto Rossi/Tips Italia srl/Alamy; 5.35 Alinari Archives; 5.36 Robert Harding/Robert Harding World Imagery; 5.37 Michael Newton/Robert Harding; 5.38, 6.8 Vincenzo Pirozzi; 5.42 DeA/Pubbli Aer Foto/Getty Images; 6.0 Erich Lessing/akg-images; 6.2 & 6.3, 6.5 & 6.6, 6.10, 6.11 Marian Moffett; 6.9 Mary Evans Picture Library; 6.12 Turkish Tourist Office; 6.14 Kenneth Moffett; 6.16 Dagli Orti/The Art Archive; 6.17 A F Kersting/Conway Library, The Courtauld Institute of Art, London; 6.18 Alinari Archives; 6.20, 7.2 A F Kersting/akg-images; 6.23 Vanni Archive/Corbis; 6.24, 6.29 Erich Lessing/akg-images; 6.27, 6.30, 6.31 Marian Moffett; 7.0 Richard Ashworth/Robert Harding World Imagery; 7.1 Kazuyoshi Nomachi/Corbis; 7.4 Gyori Antoine/Sygma/Crobis; 7.5 Zainal Abd Halim/Reuters/Corbis; 7.8 Charles & Josette Lenars/Corbis; 7.9 A F Kersting; 7.11, 7.12 & 7.13 Lawrence Wodehouse; 7.16, 7.18 R Bruce Moffett; 7.17 Chris Rennie/Robert Harding World Imagery; 7.20 G Richardson/Robert Harding World Imagery; 7.21, 7.32 A F Kersting/akg-images; 7.22, 7.25 Sonia Halliday Photographs; 7.24 Vanni/Art Resource/Photo Scala, Florence; 7.27 Bildarchiv Foto Marburg; 7.29 Nevada Wier/Corbis; 7.31 Ludovic Maisant/Corbis; 7.36 Robert Harding/Robert Harding World Imagery; 7.38, 7.39 Paul M R Maeyaert; 7.40 Spectrum Colour Library/Photo Scala, Florence; 7.41 Adam Woolfitt/Corbis; 8.0 Robert Craig; 8.2, 8.17, 8.20 Paul M R Maeyaert; 8.3 Ancient Art & Architecture Collection; 8.4, 8.15 Marian Moffett; 8.5 Michael Fazio; 8.10, 8.12 Erich Lessing/akg-images; 8.13 Allan Cash Picture Library; 8.19 A F Kersting/Conway Library, The Courtauld Institute of Art, London; 8.21 Bildarchiv Foto Marburg; 8.22 Studio Fotografico Quattrone, Florence; 8.24 Massimo Listri/Corbis; 8.25 A F Kersting/Conway Library, The Courtauld Institute of Art, London; 8.26, 8.27 Giancarlo Costa/Leemage; 8.29, 8.46, 8.47 & 8.48, 8.49, 8.51, 8.52 Paul M R Maeyaert; 8.31 & 8.32, 8.33 & 8.34, 8.38 & 8.39, 8.40, 8.44, 8.53, 8.56 Marian Moffett; 8.41 & 8.42 Robert Craig; 8.54 Bildarchiv Foto Marburg; 8.57, 9.2, 9.7 A F Kersting/Conway Library, The Courtauld Institute of Art, London; 9.0, 9.4, 9.18, 9.25 Paul M R Maeyaert; 9.5, 9.12 Angelo Hornak/LKP; 9.6, 9.10 Marian Moffett; 9.9 Art Resource/Photo Scala, Florence; 9.11 Museum of Notre Dame de Paris; 9.16 James Austin/Conway Library, The Courtauld Institute of Art, London; 9.17 Marian Moffett; 9.20 Angelo Hornak; 9.21 Sonia Halliday Photographs; 9.22 A F Kersting/Conway Library, The Courtauld Institute of Art, London; 9.28, 9.34, 9.38 & 9.39 Marian Moffett; 9.27, 9.29, 9.30, 9.32, 9.33, 9.36 A F Kersting/akg-images; 9.31 Angelo Hornak/LKP; 9.41 Alinari Archives;

9.42 Private Collection/Bridgeman Art Library; 9.48, 9.50, 9.58, 9.62 Marian Moffett; 9.52, 9.54 Kenneth Moffett; 9.56 Francesco Venturi/Corbis; 9.61 Cameraphoto Arte; 10.0 A F Kersting/akg-images; 10.2, 10.3, 10.4, 10.11 National Anthropological Archives, Smithsonian Institution; 10.5, 10.9, 10.12 Michael Fazio; 10.6 Wolfgang Kaehler/Corbis; 10.10 Jamen Berk; 10.15 Tony Morrison/South American Pictures; 10.17 & 10.18, 10.19, 10.21 & 10.22, 10.23, 10.24, 10.25, 10.26, 2.30 Michael Fazio; 10.27 & 10.28 Ronald Scott; 10.29 Justin Kerr; 10.32 Robert Fried/Alamy; 10.35 Kathy Jarvis/South American Pictures; 10.36 Tony Morrison/South American Pictures; 10.37 Hulton-Deutsch Collection/Corbis; 10.38 Charles & Josette Lenars/Corbis; 10.39 Michael Fazio; 10.40 Jack Dabaghian/ Reuters/Corbis; 10.41 EP.0.0.820, collection RMCA Tervuren; photo C Zagourski © DACS 2013; 10.42 Scheufler Collection/Corbis; 10.43 Dave G Houser/Corbis; 10.44 Bettmann/Corbis; 10.46 Robert Harding World Imagery/Alamy; 10.48 Musée du Quai Branly/Photo Scala, Florence; 10.49 Frobenius-Institut, Frankfurt am Main; 10.50 Yann Arthus-Bertrand/Corbis; 10.51 David Wall/Alamy; 10.52 Sylvain Grandadam/Robert Harding World Imagery; 10.54 Brian A Vikander/Corbis; 10.55 Julia Bayne/Robert Harding World Imagery; 10.56 Gavin Hellier/JAI/Corbis; 10.57 Michel Gounot/Godong/Corbis; 11.0 Erich Lessing/akg-images; 11.2, 11.9 Studio Fotografico Quattrone, Florence; 11.4, 11.6 A F Kersting/Conway Library, The Courtauld Institute of Art, London; 11.11, 11.14 Alinari Archives; 11.13 Malandrini Collection, Florence/Alinari Museum Collections; 11.15 Lawrence Wodehouse; 11.16 Ralph Lieberman and LKP; 11.19 James Austin/Conway Library, The Courtauld Institute of Art, London; 11.22 Marian Moffett; 11.25, 11.34 A F Kersting/Conway Library, The Courtauld Institute of Art, London; 11.27, 11.40 Vincenzo Pirozzi; 11.32, 11.35, 11.46 Michael Fazio; 11.37 Studio Fotografico Quattrone, Florence; 11.42, 11.47 Alinari Archives; 11.43 James Morris/LKP; 11.48 R Ashworth/Ancient Art & Architecture Collection; 11.50, 11.54 Marian Moffett; 11.51 Michael Fazio; 11.55 CuboImages srl/Alamy; 11.57, 11.69 A F Kersting/Conway Library, The Courtauld Institute of Art, London; 11.58 & 11.59 Cameraphoto Arte; 11.62 Vincenzo Pirozzi; 11.63, 11.64, 11.66, 11.67 Paul M R Maeyaert; 11.65 Photo Scala, Florence; 11.70 Country Life; 11.72 Lawrence Wodehouse; 11.73, 12.8 Michael Fazio; 11.75 Reproduced by permission of English Heritage; 11.77 Michael Jenner/Robert Harding World Imagery; 12.0 Paul M R Maeyaert; 12.4 Photo Spectrum/Heritage Images/Photo Scala, Florence; 12.10 Vladimir Khirman/Alamy; 12.1, 12.12 & 12.13, 12.15, 12.17, 12.19, 12.21 Vincenzo Pirozzi; 12.20 Peter Kent; 12.22 akg-images; 12.25 Erich Lessing/akg-images; 12.26, 12.28 Paul M R Maeyaert; 12.29 Stefan Drechsel/akg-images; 12.30, 12.33 A F Kersting/akg-images; 12.31 Michael Fazio; 12.34 Paul M R Maeyaert; 12.36, 12.40 Pamela Scott; 12.42 Roger-Viollet; 12.43 J William Rudd; 12.45, 12.50, 12.55, 13.0, 13.5 A F Kersting/akg-images; 12.48 Angelo Hornak; 12.51 reproduced by permission of English Heritage; 12.52 A F Kersting/Conway Library, The Courtauld Institute of Art, London; 13.1 Andrew Michael/Alamy; 13.7 Lawrence Wodehouse; 13.10 Country Life; 13.13 Peter Kent; 13.20 The Art Gallery Collection /Alamy; 13.21 Pamela Scott; 13.24 Giraudon/The Bridgeman Art Library; 13.27 Leonard de Selva/Corbis; 13.28 Roger-Viollet; 13.30, 13.3l courtesy Sir John Soane Museum; 13.32 A F Kersting/Conway Library, The Courtauld Institute of Art, London; 13.33 Erich Lessing/akg-images; 13.34 Dieter E Hoppe/akg-images; 13.35 akg-images; 13.37 The Library of Virginia; 13.39 Marian Moffett; 13.40 Robert Llewellyn/Photis/Getty Images; 13.42 & 13.43 courtesy of the Basilica of the Assumption Historic Trust; 13.45 Ronald Scott; 13.47 David Churchill/arcaidimages.com/Alamy; 13.48 Werner Otto/age fotostock/Robert Harding World Imagery; 14.0 Paul M R Maeyaert; 14.1 Dave Porter/Alamy; 14.2 David Cole/Alamy; 14.4 Hulton Deutsch/Getty Images; 14.5 A F Kersting/akg-images; 14.6 & 14.7 SSPL/Getty Images; 14.8 Science Museum/Science & Society Picture Library, all rights reserved; 14.10 Paul M R Maeyaert; 14.11, 14.12 James Austin/Conway Library, The Courtauld Institute of Art, London; 14.13 A F Kersting/Conway Library, The Courtauld Institute of Art, London; 14.17 Peter Ashworth; 14.19 Michael Fazio; 14.21 reproduced by permission of English Heritage; 14.22 G Beech/The Architectural Association; 14.23 courtesy www.visitcumbria.com; 14.26 & 14.27 Bastin & Evrard © DACS 2013; 14.28 Paul M R Maeyaert; 14.29 Inigo Bujedo Aguirre/View; 14.30 Ralph Lieberman and LKP; 14.31 Michael Fazio; 14.32 Glasgow School of Art; 14.34, 14.43 Marian Moffett; 14.36 RCAHMS (Henry Bedford Lemere Collection). Licensor www.rcahms.gov.uk; 14.37 Bildarchiv Foto Marburg; 14.38, 14.39 Paul M R Maeyaert; 14.40, 14.46 J William Rudd; 14.41 NiKreative/Alamy; 14.45 Chicago Historical Society; 14.48 A D White Architectural Photographs, Cornell University Library; 14.49 Historic American Buildings Survey/Library of Congress; 14.50 Collection of The New York Historical Society; 14.51 J. William Rudd; 14.54, 14.55 Marian Moffett; 14.57, 14.63 Chicago Historical Society; 14.56, 14.58, 14.60, 14.62 Historic American Buildings Survey/Library of Congress; 14.61 Ralph Lieberman and LKP; 15.0 View Pictures/akg-images; 15.7 Pamela Scott; 15.9 Michael Fazio ©

ARS, NY and DACS, London 2013; 15.10, 15.11 ©ARS, NY and DACS, London 2013; 15.12 Marian Moffett © ARS, NY and DACS, London 2013; 15.13, 15.14, 15.15, 15.16 & 15.18 ©ARS, NY and DACS, London 2013; 15.17 Hedrich Blessing Collection/Chicago History Museum/Getty Images © ARS NY and DACS, London 2013; 15.19 akg-images; 15.20 Courtesy Beurs van Berlage; 15.21 Jeff Elder; 15.22 Netherlands Architecture Institute; 15.23 photo R H Herwig, courtesy Stadsarcheif Amsterdam; 15.24 & 15.25 Bildarchiv Foto Marburg; 15.26 Michael Fazio; 15.27 J William Rudd; 15.28, 15.29 BPK, Berlin/Photo Scala, Florence; 15.30 Architekturmuseum TU Berlin, Inv. Nr. F 1506; 15.32 Courtesy AEG; 15.33 Paul M R Maeyaert; 15.34 Michael Fazio; 15.35, 15.36, 15.37, 15.38 © FLC/ADAGP, Paris and DACS, London 2013; 15.40 Peter Kent © FLC/ADAGP, Paris and DACS, London 2013; 15.39 Marian Moffett © FLC/ADAGP, Paris and DACS, London 2013; 15.41 National Museum of Ireland; 15.46 Les Arts Décoratifs, Paris © DACS 2013; 15.47 Canadian Center for Architecture © DACS 2013; 15.48, 15.55 Marian Moffett © DACS 2013; 15.49, 15.58 © DACS 2013; 15.50 Wolfgang Thoener © DACS 2013; 15.51 Marian Moffett © DACS 2013; 15.52 Digital image, The Museum of Modern Art, New York/Photo Scala, Florence; 15.54, 15.62 Michael Fazio © DACS 2013; 15.56 Frank den Oudsten © DACS 2013; 15.57 & 15.59 Erich Lessing/akg-images © DACS 2013; 15.61 J William Rudd © DACS 2013; 15.63 Marian Moffett © FLC/ADAGP, Paris and DACS, London 2013; 15.64 G E Kidder Smith; 15.65 Country Life; 15.66 Architectural Association; 15.67 Courtesy of Skogskyrkogarden; 15.68 akg-images; 15.70 Museum of the City of New York; 15.71 Hulton Archive/Getty Images; 15.72 AA World Travel Library/Alamy; 15.73 The Rockefeller Group; 15.74 Peter Aaron/OTTO; 15.75 Robert Landau/Alamy; 15.76 Special Collections, Birmingham Public Library; 15.77 Peter Aaron/OTTO; 15.78 Tim Street-Porter © ARS, NY and DACS, London 2013; 15.79, 15.80, 15.82 © ARS, NY and DACS, London 2013; 15.81 J William Rudd © ARS, NY and DACS, London 2013; 15.83 Michael Fazio; 15.84 Anderson & Low/LKP © FLC/ADAGP, Paris and DACS, London 2013; 15.85, 15.86, 15.88, 15.90 © FLC/ADAGP, Paris, and DACS, London 2013; 15.87 Marian Moffett © FLC/ADAGP, Paris and DACS, London 2013; 15.89 Danielle Tinero /RIBA Library Photographs Collection © FLC/ADAGP, Paris and DACS, London 2013; 15.91 Mark DeKay © FLC/ADAGP, Paris and DACS, London 2013; 15.92 J William Rudd © DACS 2013; 15.93 Hedrich-Blessing Photographic Collection/Chicago Historical Society © DACS 2013; 15.94 Lawrence Wodehouse © DACS 2013; 15.95 Bettmann/Corbis © DACS 2013; 16.0 Photo Erika Barahona Ede © FMGB; 16.1 Jim Dyson/Getty Images; 16.2 Colin Dixon/arcaidimages.com; 16.4, 16.5 Alvar Aalto Museum; 16.3, 16.6, 16.7 © DACS 2013; 16.8 Marian Moffett © DACS 2013; 16.9 Barragan Foundation © 2013 Barragan Foundation, Birsfelden, Switzerland/ProLitteris/DACS; 16.10 Fernando Guerra/View Pictures; 16.11 Timothy Hursley; 16.12 Angelo Hornak/Corbis; 16.13 Toshiharu Kitajima; 16.14 Photo © Yasuhiro Ishimoto; 16.15 courtesy Tadao Ando; 16.16 Robert Craig; 16.17 Timothy Hursley; 16.18 Michael Fazio; 16.19, 16.21 Digital image, The Museum of Modern Art, New York/Photo Scala, Florence; 16.20 J William Rudd; 16.22 Rolf Richardson/ Spectrum/Heritage Images; 16.23 photo Richard Creek, Courtesy of the Diplomatic Reception Rooms, US Department of State, Washington, DC; 16.24 Edmund Stoecklein for Robert A M Stern Architects, LLP; 16.25 courtesy RAMSA; 16.26 Jack Sullivan/Alamy; 16.27 Michael Moran/OTTO; 16.28 Robert Holden; 16.29 Eisenman Architects; 16.31 Jeff Badger/Alamy; 16.32 © 1996 Steve Rosenthal; 16.33 J William Rudd; 16.34 Marian Moffett; 16.36 James Marshall/Corbis; 16.37 Joseph Sohm/Visions of America/Corbis; 16.38 Professor Dr Justus Dahinden; 16.39 Chris Fredriksson/Alamy; 16.40 Guggenheim Museum Bilbao, 1997. Photo David Heald © The Solomon R Guggenheim Foundation, New York; 16.41 Iain Masterton/Alamy; 16.43 J William Rudd; 16.44 Timothy Hursley; 16.45 Art on File/Corbis; 16.46, 16.48 © OMA; 16.47 Nikreates /Alamy; 16.49 ©Gregory Vore/Alamy; 16.50 John Edward Linden/arcaidimages.com; 16.51 Iwan Baan; 16.52 Werner Huthmacher/Artur/View Pictures; 16.53 Keith Collie/akg-images; 16.54 courtesy Richard Earl of www.carofthecentury.com, a leading website on American automotive design history; 16.55 J William Rudd; 16.56 Schütze/Rodemann/akg-images; 16.57 John Donat/RIBA Library Photographs Collection; 16.59 Michael Fazio; 16.60 Ian Lambot; 16.61 Henk Bosman/age fotostock/Robert Harding World Imagery; 16.62 Nathan King/Alamy; 16.63 A F Kersting/akg-images; 16.64 Archenova/arcaidimages.com; 16.65 John Edward Linden/arcaidimages.com; 16.66 LOOK Die Bildagentur der Fotografen GmbH /Alamy; 16.67 Eric Owen Moss Architects; 16.68 Tom Bonner; 16.69 Michael Moran/OTTO; 16.70 Luay Bahoora/Alamy; 16.71 Timothy Hursley; 16.72 Gunter Schneider; 16.73 Andy Ryan; 16.74 Emanuele Ciccomartino/Alamy; 16.75 Oso Media/Alamy; 16.76, 16.82 Roland Halbe; 16.77 Joseph Sohm/Visions of America/Corbis; 16.78 Iain Masterton/Alamy; 16.79 Dennis Gilbert/View; 16.80 Floto + Warner/OTTO; 16.81 Yang Lei/Xinhua Press/Corbis; 16.83 Tibor Bognar/Corbis; 16.84, 16.85 Max Dupain; 16.87 Roland Halbe; 16.88 Patti McConville/Alamy.

Index

tensile construction 2, 3, 4–5
tension (of structural materials) 2, 3
tents 4, 274, **275**
Teotihuacán, Mexico 259, **260**, 261, 284; Palace of Ateltelco 261, **261**; Pyramid of the Sun 259, **260**
Tepe Gawra, Sumer: acropolis 16, **16**
Terry, Quinlan 529–31; Richmond Riverside Development, Surrey, England 530, **530**
Theater of Marcellus, Rome 124, **124**, 125
theaters: Greek/Hellenistic 57–8, 61, 122; Roman 122, 124
Theoderic, king of the Ostrogoths 135
thermae *see* baths, Roman
t'Hoff, Rob van 486; Huis ter Heide house, Utrecht 486
tholoi 41, 41–2, **55**, 55–6, 58
Thomas of Hoo 227
Thornton, William 402
Thutmose I, II, and III, of Egypt 30, 31
Tiepolo, Giovanni Battista: frescoes, Würzburg Residenz 364–5, 379
Tijou, Jean 372
Tikal, Guatemala **263**, 263–4, **264**
Tikar, the 275, **276**
Tillamook, the 256
Timgad, Algeria **113**, 113–14, 131
Timur 160, 163
Tiryns **40**, 43, **44**
Tivoli, Italy: Hadrian's Villa **110**, 129–30, **130**, **131**; Temple of the Sibyl 118; Villa d'Este gardens (Ligorio) **327**, 327–8
Tiwanaku, Bolivia 272, **272**
Todaji Monastery, Nara, Japan 95–6, **96**
Todi, Italy: S. Fortunato 238; S. Maria della Consolazione (Cola da Caprarola and Bramante) 300, **300**
Tokyo: Imperial Hotel (Wright) 466; Olympic Sports Complex (Tange) **522**, 523; Prada store (Herzog and de Meuron) 575; St. Mary's Cathedral (Tange) 523
Tolowa, the 256
Toltecs 262, **267**, 267–8, 284
tombs: Egyptian rock-cut 28, 29–30; Etruscan 106; Islamic 168–70; megalithic **10**, 11, 11–12, 14; *see also* catacombs; mastabas; mausolea; pyramids; tholoi
toranas **67**, 68, **68**
Torre Agbar, Barcelona (Nouvel) 572, **572**
Torrigiani, Pietro 333
totem poles 256
Toulouse, France: St. Sernin 195, **195**, 196, 211, 417
Tournus, France: St. Philibert 194–5
tower houses: African adobe 275, **276**; medieval 242, **242**
Tower of London 243, **243**
town planning *see* city and town planning
trabeated systems 3
Trajan, Emperor 114
Trajan's markets, Rome **115**, 115–16, **116**, 131
transom lights **11**, 12
Treasury of Atreus, Mycenae **41**, 41–2, **42**
Trier, Germany 113
triglyphs 46, 47
trilithons 13
Trissino, Count Giangiorgio 317
Trump Tower. NYC (Scutt *et al.*) **526**
trusses 3, 4, **4**, 5

Tschumi, Bernard 534; Acropolis Museum, Athens 50; Parc de la Villette, Paris 534, **534**
Tsien, Billie *see* Williams, Tod
Tugendhat House, Brno, Czech Republic (Mies van der Rohe) 490, **490**
Tula, Mexico 267–8
tulou houses, China 93, **93**
Tuni, Badi' al-Zaman 162
tupiks 256
Turin, Italy: S. Lorenzo (Guarini) 357, **358**, **359**, 379; Sindone Chapel (Guarini) 357, **357**
Turner, Richard: Palm House, Kew Gardens, London 414, **414**
Tuscan order 106, **338**
TWA Terminal, Kennedy Airport, NY (Saarinen) 554–5, **555**
Twickenham, England: Strawberry Hill (Walpole) **381**, 406, **406**, 409
tympana, Romanesque 196–7, **197**, **201**, 201–2, **202**

Udaigiri, India: rock-cut temples 71
Uffizi, Florence (Vasari) **308**, 308–9
Uganda: Mityana Pilgrims Shrine (Dahinden) **542**, 542–3; palace of the chiefs 282
Uji, Japan: Phoenix Hall 96, **96**
Uji-Yamada, Japan: Ise Shrine **97**, 97–8
Unité d'Habitation, Marseille (Le Corbusier) **506**, 507
United States 435; Art Deco 494–500; balloon-frame construction 420, **420**; early skyscrapers 443–51, 453; Georgian houses 320; Gothic architcture 248; International Style 492; modern form-makers 535–8, 542, 543–8, 553; modern regionalism 531; Native Americans 251–8, 284; Neo-Classicism 401–3, 409; 19th-century styles 435–43, 453; Post-Modernism 524–9; railroads 416; *see also specific cities*
Unity Temple, Oak Park, IL (Wright) 464, **465**, 465–6, 512
University of Virginia, Charlottesville (Jefferson) 120, 402, **402**
Uppark, Sussex (Talman) 374, **375**, 379
Ur, Iraq: ziggurat 17, **17**, **18**
Urban VIII, Pope 345, 351
Urbino, Italy 299; Palazzo Ducale 297, **299**, 299–300
Urnes, Norway: stave church 184–5, **185**, **186**, 187
Uruk, Sumer: White Temple 15, 16, **16**
Utrecht: Huis ter Heide (van t'Hoff) 486; Schroeder House (Rietveld) **487**, 488, 492
Utzon, Jørn 538; Bagsvaerg Church, Denmark 541; Dunker Cultural Center, Helsingborg 541; Sydney Opera House 538, 541, **541**
Uxmal, Mexico: Governor's Palace 266, **266**; Nunnery 266, **266**
Uzbekistan *see* Bukhara; Samarkand

Val-de-Grâce, Paris (F. Mansart) 5, 367, **367**
Valadier, Giuseppe: Piazza del Popolo, Rome 354, **355**

Van Alen, William: Chrysler Building, NYC 495, **495**
Vanbrugh, Sir John 376, 377; Blenheim Palace, Oxfordshire 376, **377**; Castle Howard, Yorkshire 376, **376**
Van Brunt, Henry 437
Vandals 177
Vardhamana (Mahavira) 65–6
Vasari, Giorgio 306, 315; Uffizi, Florence **308**, 308–9
vaults/vaulting 3, 4, 6; barrel **3**, 110, 110, 121, **121**, 124, 125, 131, 190, **190**, 196, 198, 207; Carolingian 178; domical 237, 238, 239; fan 226, 227, 234, 235; groin **3**, 4, 115, **116**, 121, **121**, **122**, 131, 190, **190**, **191**, 213; muqarnas 153, 154, 161, **161**, **162**, 168, 174, **175**; quadripartite 220, 226; rib 208, 209, **209**, 213, 215, 217, 235, 236; Roman 108, 109, 110, 115, 118, 121, 124, 131; sexpartite 220, **232**; tierceron/"crazy" 232, **232**, 249
Vaux, Calvert 442
V.D.L. Research House, LA (Neutra) 505, **505**
Vedas, the 65
Velde, Henri van de: Werkbund Theater, Cologne 469, 471
Venice 248, 249, 323; bridge (Calatrava) 573; Ca' d'Oro 248, **248**; Doge's Palace 248, **248**, 325; Library of S. Marco (Sansovino and Scamozzi) 318, **324**, 325; Lido villa (Loos) 459, **459**; Palazzo Grimani 325, 326; Palazzo Vendramin-Calergi (Coducci) 323; Piazza di S. Marco **324**, 325; S. Giorgio Maggiore (Palladio) 322, **322**; S. Marco **133**, **141**, 144, **145**, 202, **203**, 325; Scuola di S. Marco 325; La Zecca (mint) (Sansovino) 325, **325**, 396 Venturi, Robert 456, 524–7; Chestnut Hill house, PA 525; *Complexity and Contradiction in Architecture* 524, 525; Guild House, Philadelphia 525, **525**; Sainsbury Wing, National Gallery, London 526–7
verdicas 67, **67**, 68, **68**
Veronese, Paolo 319
Versailles, France 368–70, **369**; gardens (Le Nôtre) 368–9, **369**; Petit Trianon (Gabriel) **393**, 393–4
Vertical style, US 495
Vesnin, Viktor and Aleksandr: Pravda Newspaper Building, Moscow 481, **481**
Vézelay, France: Ste. Madeleine **177**, 200, **200**, **201**, 201–2, 417
Vicenza, Italy: Basilica (Palladio) 318, **318**; Palazzo Chiericati (Palladio) 318, **319**, 337; Palazzo Valmarana (Palladio) 318; Teatro Olimpico (Palladio and Scamozzi) 323, **323**; Villa Americo-Capra (Villa Rotonda) (Palladio) 320, **321**
Victoria, Queen 411
Vienna 359; Goldman and Salatsch Store (Loos) 457; Karlskirche (Fischer von Erlach 359, **360**, 379; Moller House (Loos) **458**, 459; Postal Savings Bank (Wagner) **433**, 433–4, **434**; Secession Building (Olbrich) 434, **435**; Stadtbahn (subway) stations (Wagner) 433; Steiner House (Loos) **458**, 459
Viennese Secession 433–5, 453, 494
Vierzehnheiligen church, Germany (Neumann) **364**, 365, 379